With gratitude to God,

without Whom,

naught would be possible

11 + Sample Essays

Written by **Zahra Hamdulay**

Analyses by Dr Parvez & Kausar Hamdulay

elevenplusessays.co.uk

elevenplusessays@hotmail.com

All rights reserved.

Any part of this publication must not be reproduced.

Any part of this publication must not be circulated online, in hard copy, electronic or any other form.

ISBN 978-1-5272-6800-5

Copyright © 2020

Contents

A Guide to the Parent 5

Creative Writing Guide 6

How to use this book 9

The Train Journey 10

My First Day 13

'I didn't know what the noise was' 18

The Lost Key 21

John's Discovery 24

Petra and Sally 27

Power 30

Tightrope-walking 33

Toad's Journey 38

School Days 42

Forest Adventure 45

The Dark House 48

An Encounter with a Villain 51

The Journey 54

A Guide to the Parent

As parents, we found preparing for the essay writing section the most difficult part of the 11+ examinations. Other subjects seemed to have much more material, books and guides, with hundreds of sample papers available free online, or for purchase. We could not get any realistic, gold standard 'sample essays' anywhere so it was immensely difficult to gauge what level was required or expected from a 10-11yr old child.

After speaking to many parents and teachers the benefit of tutoring was mixed. One of the messages from head-teachers and others (especially during open day speeches) were that essays and comprehension work from tutored children were fairly obvious to identify, compared to those that were not tutored. Thus, as we did not go with a tutor, we are unable to compare the quality of work from within this peer group to that of our child. This book is for parents and children to get some idea of how to write good essays, especially to those who do not wish to get a regular tutor. It is not meant to be a substitute to tutoring but should provide a useful adjunct.

But what is the standard expected to get into a top independent or grammar school? This is what we sought to know prior to our preparation, and, this is what we are trying to achieve with this book – these are all genuine essays written between the ages of 9 ½ and 10 ½ years of age during our preparation. They have been written within a 20-30min time limit, depending on the particular paper's requirements. The essays are included in chronological order so there is a marked difference between the earlier and later essays, providing guidance to see if you're on the right track with your child.

The creative writing guide is kept simple, for quick, easy to remember, take away points for both yourselves and your child. They don't all have to be used in one essay, but a few should be used. It has to be relevant to the story (or continuation piece) and have an apt flow. There is no set word limit but the examples give a good guide to appropriate length. It really is 'quality, not quantity'.

Please spend time reading books with your child and going through tricky words and phrases – these are more important than writing essays alone. Practice describing your surroundings, during strolls in the park, or on long drives, wildlife at the zoo etc.– you have to build up your tools, armoury and weapons before battle!

Teachers have provided excellent feedback for this book and believe it highlights the standard required for entry at 11+. Any further feedback from yourselves would be greatly received. Please email accordingly to elevenplusessays@hotmail.com.

A Creative Writing Guide for the student...from the student

Revising for the 11+ used to be my least favourite thing to do, especially writing essays. But after a while, through practise, they became easier. This book will explain and show you how to write essays that will get you through the exams, using models that I have created and a brief summary of the different techniques I have used after each composition. Here are five simple steps that will help you – and helped me – to get through the 11+ exams:

1   Vocabulary

11+ examiners enjoy seeing a range of exotic and unusual vocabulary. It also helps essays seem more professional, original, and makes the writer seem as though they are confident in what they have written. Try and keep a bank of powerful vocabulary and phrases that describe **characters** and **settings**, so that when it comes to the point where you have to describe one of these, you can just take your pick of whichever phrase/word you want. When I was revising for 11+, I dedicated a notebook just for vocabulary, special words and phrases that I didn't know, or ones that were very good for writing essays. Most of my strong vocabulary comes from this book.

2   M.A.P.S

This stands for **m**etaphors, **a**lliteration, **p**ersonification and **s**imiles. This range of literary devices really 'wows' the examiners, and will get you extra marks. (You could also include rhyme as well, although it isn't the most necessary technique that you can use. I was going to fit it into the acronym, but I wasn't sure how to!).

- Metaphor – when you make a comparison usually using the words **is/was** or **are/were**.
  Example: 'the sky was a grey curtain' or 'the sea was a raging bull'.

- Simile – comparing something to another using the words **as** or **like**.

Example: 'the moon was <u>as</u> white <u>as</u> snow' or 'the flowerbed was <u>like</u> a sea of colour'.

- Personification – when you give human characteristics to a non-human thing. Example: 'the flowers danced in the rain' or 'the snowflakes gracefully pirouetted down to the snow-coated street'.

- Alliteration – when two words next to each other (or one word apart) begin with the same letter/letters for emphasis.

Example: 'the **b**eautiful **b**allerina **g**racefully **g**ilded onto the stage'.

And, bear in mind that it isn't always the *letter* specifically. For example, if you have the phrase 'the train raced down the tunnel', '**t**he' and '**t**rain' wouldn't be alliteration, although they start with the same letter. It is the sound of the letter that matters.

3   Sentence Structure

You may look at this and think: 'that sounds complicated', but I can assure you it isn't. All this means is how you use short sentences or long sentences. For example – 'he froze.' This builds up suspense and makes the reader want to know what happens next. Or: 'the wind howled, the thunder rumbled, another streak of lightning flashed across the sky, as the rain lashed out and whipped the lost and drenched figure, stumbling over the rocks'. This also builds suspense as one reads every clause, anticipating what happens in the next.

4   Reading, Reading, and more Reading!

Reading books that use these literary devices will put you at an advantage for several different reasons, especially classics. For one, they will give you inspiration and ideas if you have to continue an extract or create a short story of your own. Another benefit, even if you dislike reading, is it will give you ideas for metaphors, similes and M.A.P.S in general. Your vocabulary book, which I suggested earlier, will also grow. Also, it's fun! If you enjoy reading, this part will be easy.

5   Other strategies

Anything else you can think of? There are loads of other literary techniques, but of course you don't want to read a boring list that will take days to write and days to read (did you notice my use of repetition?) so I'll give *you* the opportunity to encounter other literary skills.

However, I will mention three more: **repetition** – as I hinted before – sets the atmosphere, adds drama and can sometimes create suspense. Additionally, your use of **colours** helps give detail and description to your essay; they contribute a lot to a piece of writing. For example, if you use the colour red, I may think of danger, anger or love. If you mention yellow, I will think of happiness or summer. If you mention green, I will think of jealousy, greed, something sickening or, quite frankly, just grass. And don't forget your **senses** – sight, smell, hearing, taste and touch. When describing objects, food, animals, people, settings, or creating an atmosphere these will be useful.

There are plenty more in the book – what is onomatopoeia? A hyperbole? Read more to find out!

You can create your own guide as you read each essay, writing down other techniques used, interesting vocabulary and other useful points to writing essays, such as how to plan an essay.

I hope these steps will help you to create fabulous pieces of writing, and, as this book's title suggests, essays!

How to use this book

You can use this book in any way that you would like, but I would suggest the following...

For every essay, there is the **actual essay**, followed by a **colour-coded version**, and then its **analysis**. Read the essay through and try and find some of the techniques that I mentioned previously, or any others that you would include if you wrote the essay. Then, turn the page to the colour-coded copy. Check if you noticed the different techniques I used, or if I missed any. Would you add anything else? Following this is the analysis. It explains how the essays are good and how some could improve.

When you begin to come towards the end of the book, you will begin to start brainstorming ideas automatically, since you would have read quite a few examples already. Choose a title from the contents page and write an essay of your own. It can be one that you haven't read, or one that you have, so you can take a few of my ideas and techniques and alter them. You could also repeat an essay title after several months so that you can see how much you've improved from your first attempt! It's always good to continue/write stories of your own from other books you've read, as in the exams they often like you to continue from their comprehension passages.

At first, don't worry too much about a time limit, and just enjoy writing good stories. Then I'd suggest with one year to go before your exam, maybe keep it to 30-40mins. With practice, you can shorten this to 30mins, within a few months before your exam.

In the colour-coded essays, there is a key for the highlighted words and phrases. It is at the bottom of each page, but it is also here in case you forget:

Hopefully, this guide will help you use this book and write SPECTACULAR essays like mine (or even better!) ☺

KEY

RED – similes

GREEN – metaphors

BLUE – personification

ORANGE – alliteration

BOLD – imagery

The Train Journey

I entered the train and hurriedly sat down before it started up again. Beside me was a plump woman in a pinafore dress; I could tell at once that she was a baker, for the smell of fresh bread up out of her basket towards my nose. This was a comfort to me – the lovely warm smell – because it had been windy outside, and I was glad of the warmth that rose from the reed-woven basket. Glancing out of my window, I realised we were riding past a rushing river, which seemed like it was trying to get somewhere. It separated two meadows, each one filled with trees and bushes laden with fruits and berries bursting with juice. Cows lowed in the distance as they munched on the lush grass. In another field that the train passed, horses raced each other, circling the field that they lived on.

As the train rumbled along, I could hear the sweet song of birds in their nests, and other trains flying past us. If I looked out of the window towards the front of the train, I could see the masses of steam puffing out of the engine, like it was running a race and out of breath, but so close to the finish line.

When the train finally stopped, the doors slid open, and for a brief moment I heard another train roaring and rattling on the railway as it sped out of the station. I disembarked, and quickly turned my head to see the last of my train fading into a distant tunnel. Where the train had stopped a moment ago, now was the fiery sun, gradually dipping behind the horizon in a mass of pink and orange colour, the warm glow slowly abating.

The Train Journey

I entered the train and hurriedly sat down before it started up again. Beside me was a plump woman in a pinafore dress; I could tell at once that she was a baker, for the smell of fresh bread up out of her basket wafted towards my nose. This was a comfort to me – the lovely warm smell – because it had been windy outside, and I was glad of the warmth that rose from the reed-woven basket. Glancing out of my window, I realised we were riding past a rushing river, which seemed **like it was trying to get somewhere**. It separated two meadows, each one filled with trees and bushes **laden with ripe fruits and berries bursting with juice**. Cows lowed in the distance as they munched the lush grass. In another field that the train passed, horses raced each other, circling the field that they lived on.

As the train rumbled along, I could hear the sweet song of birds in their nests, and other trains flying past us. If I looked out of the window towards the front of the train, I could see the masses of steam puffing out of the engine, **like it was running a race and out of breath**, but so close to the finish line.

When the train finally stopped, the doors slid open, and for a brief moment I heard another train roaring and rattling on the railway as it sped out of the station. I disembarked, and quickly turned my head to see the last of my train fading into a distant tunnel. Where the train had stopped a moment ago, now was the fiery sun, gradually dipping behind the horizon in a mass of pink and orange colour, the warm glow slowly abating.

KEY

RED – similes

GREEN – metaphors

BLUE – personification

ORANGE – alliteration

BOLD – imagery

Analysis

This topic is one that can be challenging as it can be tricky to create a vivid description of an otherwise mundane event. In this essay, the writer has structured the paragraphs into three – one at the start of the journey, the second during the journey, and a final paragraph describing the end of it.

In the first paragraph, we have stimulation of our senses – we can *smell* the lovely fragrance of freshly baked bread – a comfort after rushing on to the train, from the cold outdoors. We can *see* the stunning landscape by the utilisation of descriptive words and phrases, 'rushing river', 'separating two meadows', 'cows lowed' and 'fruits and berries bursting with juice'. The second paragraph continues this theme and awakens our sense of *sound* - the rumbling of the train; the sweet song of the birds; the sound of other trains.

The writer has used a simile 'like it was running a race' to build an image of the train in terms of an activity that readers can relate to. Describing engines and trains as 'roaring' is fairly typical.

The final passage aptly recognises the usual hustle and bustle at a train station with a description of the activity of the other trains. The essay reaches its terminus with a description of the sun-setting scenery at her destination, at the end of the day, analogous to the end of the train journey.

My First Day

Feeble rays of sunlight glided down to the busy road and bounced off the wet tarmac. Cars hooted angrily to each other as the traffic lights turned from amber to red. Cars which had sped down the lane gleefully in the hope of making a green light skidded to a halt and slammed on the brakes, their wipers beating furiously at the rain.

A short way along the lane, the mood was sombre as Ava sank down on her bed. What a horrid day! She flung her rucksack onto her pile of belongings. She had only just managed to fit in some time for a rest; she had been packing all morning! Out of her window, she could see her best friend, Jessica laughing and joking with her arch enemy, Sabrina. She felt a sharp pang of jealousy. "Welcome, misery," she sighed, gloomily. Ava had already pleaded with her mother repeatedly, but it was blatant that she wasn't changing her mind.

Her mother had said to take the 'most essential belongings'. "We haven't got much luggage space," her mother reminded her. Ava suddenly remembered something. In her foyer, there was a framed photo of her and her friends. "I mustn't forget that," she thought firmly.

Many hours later, Ava and her mother arrived at their stately manor. "It's huge," she gasped. "But wait…where are all the other houses? There's nothing else here apart from trees. Why are we all alone?" she asked in wonder.

"Don't ask questions," her mother replied, vaguely interested. Ava sighed. She had been parted from her friends, gone to live in an isolated home, and no idea where she was. She scanned the inside of her house curiously. Her mother placed her mauve beret on the freshly-painted mantelpiece. "You could have at least tried to dress smartly. I've told you before: first impressions are lasting impressions. Always dress appropriately."

"Yes, mum," Ava replied dully. She staggered up to her new room, and gasped in surprise. The room had a large variety of furniture positioned all around the room. Her bed gave a lively atmosphere to the room; it was painted a vivid shade of magenta. The mirror's frame was a dazzling lustre, and her cupboard was of white gloss. Astonished, Ava heard a muffled shout from downstairs. "Ava! Where are you? Come and prepare supper!" She rushed back down the stairs, and jumped the last few, knowing that her mother would be furious if she didn't turn up within the next moment.

Flopping down on her bed after supper, and staring at the ceiling, she said to herself, "This was My First Day. And like Jessica always says, 'the first day's the hardest. Get used to that, and you're through. In other words: you're an 'Ace'."

She chuckled to herself. "I guess I'm an 'Ace' now," she thought optimistically.

My First Day

Feeble rays of sunlight **glided down** to the busy road and bounced off the wet tarmac. Cars **hooted angrily** to each other as the traffic lights turned from amber to red. Cars which had **sped down the lane gleefully** in the hope of making a green light skidded to a halt and slammed on the brakes, their wipers **beating furiously** at the rain.

A short way along the lane, **the mood was sombre** as Ava sank down on her bed. What a horrid day! She flung her rucksack onto her pile of belongings. She had only just managed to fit in some time for a rest; she had been packing all morning! Out of her window, she could see her best friend, Jessica laughing and joking with her arch enemy. She felt a sharp pang of jealousy. "Welcome, misery," she sighed, gloomily. Ava had already pleaded with her mother repeatedly, but it was blatant that she wasn't changing her mind.

Her mother had said to take the 'most essential belongings'. "We haven't got much luggage space," her mother reminded her. Ava suddenly remembered something. In her foyer, there was a framed photo of her and her friends. "I mustn't forget that," she thought firmly.

Many hours later, Ava and her mother arrived at their stately manor. "It's huge," she gasped. "But wait…where are all the other houses? There's nothing else here apart from trees. Why are we all alone?" she asked in wonder.

"Don't ask questions," her mother replied, vaguely interested. Ava sighed. She had been parted from her friends, gone to live in an isolated home, and no idea where she was. She scanned the inside of her house curiously. Her mother placed her mauve beret on the freshly-painted mantelpiece. "You could have at least tried to dress smartly. I've told you before: first impressions are lasting impressions. Always dress appropriately."

"Yes, mum," Ava replied dully. She staggered up to her new room, and gasped in surprise. She felt as though she had stepped into a **sea of colour**. The room had a large variety of furniture positioned all around the room. Her bed gave a lively atmosphere to the room; it was painted a **vivid shade of magenta**. The mirror's frame was a **dazzling lustre**, and her cupboard was of white gloss. Astonished, Ava heard a muffled shout from downstairs. "Ava! Where are you? Come and prepare supper!" She rushed back down the stairs, and jumped the last few, knowing that her mother would be furious if she didn't turn up within the next moment.

Flopping down on her bed after supper, and staring at the ceiling, she said to herself, "This was My First Day. And like Jessica always says, 'the first day's the hardest. Get used to that, and you're through. In other word: you're an 'Ace'."

She chuckled to herself. "I guess I'm an 'Ace' now," she thought optimistically.

KEY

RED – similes

GREEN – metaphors

BLUE – personification

ORANGE – alliteration

BOLD – imagery

Analysis

This composition starts with a string of personifications: 'sunlight glided down' followed by another, 'bounced off the wet tarmac', 'cars hooted angrily', 'sped down the lane gleefully' and 'wipers beating furiously'. An unsettling tone is set perfectly, creating a state of melancholy for the story ahead.

The main character is then introduced, Ava. Again, an image of gloom is reinforced with the use of relevant words and phrases 'arch enemy' 'pang of jealousy', 'welcome misery' 'gloomily'.

The third paragraph gives us an idea that Ava is attached to her friends, not forgetting her 'framed photo of her friends' which reinforces the previous statement of jealousy when seeing her friend friendly with someone else. This strengthens our perceptions of Ava's character.

There is use of a short sentence, 'Ava sighed', which provides impact and emphasises her resignation to her fate. The dismal mood is continued throughout the story - 'Ava replied dully'.

The penultimate paragraph suddenly jumps into life with the use of vivid adjectives - 'lively atmosphere', 'vivid change of magenta', 'dazzling lustre' and 'white gloss'.

The essay ends with reference to the title of the essay 'My First Day' and making the title significant by using upper case for the first letters of the words. Her attachment to her friend is highlighted once again which is a source of encouragement and comfort for Ava.

The story is a little different from what would be expected, but the writer touches on the title at the end, and displays the use of imagination to come up with something different. A couple of points to add may have been - where were they going? A holiday home? Visiting family? Why were they in such a hurry? It's always good to plan an essay but with the pressure of time, it's not always possible. Nevertheless, after a brilliant opening paragraph and the use of lots of techniques, a good result is achieved.

'I didn't know what the noise was...'

I didn't know what the noise was, but I wasn't going to wait to find out. I bolted through the archway, raced through the front garden, and out into the streets. I could barely see the moon through the rain that lashed against my unprotected face, and my heart beat like a drum as I heard another roll of thunder. I rushed down the street, without the faintest idea of my bearings. Soon, I felt a lot safer.

For now.

But then I saw it. The Dreaded House. And on top of the roof, the famous statue of the magpie. I had heard rumours that once you enter the house, you could never turn back. I had no idea what the time was; all I knew is that I must have been fugitive for at least a few hours – or so it seemed to me – as I stood there, transfixed, frozen in fear and shock combined together. A queer and eerie chill ran down my spine. I thought of home, and the warm fire, and the comfortable bed, and the diabolical reason why I was here. I shuddered. The magpie was silhouetted against the moon, and I suddenly heard it again. Then, more voices. A shadow towered over me, and I fled. A beech tree loomed out of nowhere, and I narrowly missed it. As I sprinted past, I caught a glimpse of it reading: 'Welcome to Oak Tree Forest. Warning: you may get lost.' I didn't care if I got lost anymore. I was already lost. I had had to absquatulate from some creatures or people or whatever that shadow belonged to. Another flash of lightning, another growl of thunder. I was still running, gradually getting faster, then slower, then faster, but never having a pause for breath.

Now I was officially lost. I had to admit I hadn't a clue where I was. Desperately, I scanned my surroundings for an exit from the forest, but it was in vain. I didn't know whether I was still in pursuit, or whether I was running to get further away from home, or whether I was just running for no good reason. I didn't know what the noise was, but I was not going to wait until I found out.

'I didn't know what the noise was...'

I didn't know what the noise was, but I wasn't going to wait to find out. I bolted through the archway, raced through the front garden, and out into the streets. I could barely see the moon through the rain that lashed out against my unprotected face, and my heart **beat like a drum** as I heard another roll of thunder. I rushed down the street, without the faintest idea of my bearings. Soon, I felt a lot safer.

For now.

But then I saw it. The Dreaded House. And on top of the roof, the famous statue of the magpie. I had heard rumours that once you enter the house, you could never turn back. I had no idea what the time was; all I knew is that I must have been fugitive for at least a few hours – or so it seemed to me – as I stood there, transfixed, frozen in fear and shock combined together. A **queer and eerie chill** crept **down my spine**. I thought of home, and the warm fire, and the comfortable bed, and the diabolical reason why I was here. I shuddered. The magpie was silhouetted against the moon, and I suddenly heard it again. Then, more voices. A shadow towered over me, and I fled. A beech tree loomed out of nowhere, and I narrowly avoided it. As I sprinted past, I caught a glimpse of it reading: 'Welcome to Oak Tree Forest. Warning: you may get lost.' I didn't care if I got lost anymore. I was already lost. I had had to absquatulate from some creatures or people or whatever that shadow belonged to. Another flash of lightning, another growl of thunder. I was still running, gradually getting faster, then slower, then faster, but never having a pause for breath.

Now I was officially lost. I had to admit I hadn't a clue where I was. Desperately, I scanned my surroundings for an exit from the forest, but it was in vain. I didn't know whether I was still in pursuit, or whether I was running to get further away from home, or whether I was just running for no good reason. I didn't know what the noise was, but I was not going to wait until I found out.

KEY

RED – similes

GREEN – metaphors

BLUE – personification

ORANGE – alliteration

BOLD – imagery

Analysis

The reader instantly is enthralled and intrigued by this essay as there is a sound, implied to be dangerous, as the character does not want to find out what it really is. The character flees from the noise which also hints that they are in an unsafe area.

The simile 'my heart beat like a drum' implies that the character is afraid, and the use of short sentences in the paragraph of its own creates impact and gives the reader the impression that the safety will be short-lived - 'For now.' It is followed by two further short sentences in the subsequent paragraph that provides the same impression - 'But then I saw it. The Dreaded House.'

Another literary technique used is repetition; '**another flash** of lightning, **another growl** of thunder'. Additionally, personification is used in the – 'growl of thunder' – even the thunder is a threat here, being portrayed like an animal ready to attack.

There is use of some excellent vocabulary – 'absquatulate', 'queer', 'diabolical' and 'silhouetted'. The use of 'absquatulate' is exceptional.

The writer has carefully concluded the essay using the same phrase with which it began, linking the beginning to the end and making it into a circular narrative. This is a different style in which to end, with the writer continuing to keep us guessing as to what the noise is.

The Lost Key

Eloise skipped through her pleasant garden, right to the back, where the Hidden Hideout stood. The breeze whipped against her cheeks as she traversed across the parched grass. Ivy hung over the now discoloured door, which had been locked for almost half a century; the key was missing, and the heavy, iron lock – which was once shiny and new, was now rusting with age.

Despite all this, Eloise, with her optimistic demeanour, felt certain the key was near. Tugging at the metal handle, she scanned and surveyed the area, for something that would slot into the keyhole. A sturdy, stone wall surrounded and acted as a boundary for the Hidden Hideout, which allowed nobody to enter, unless they unlocked the bare, age-old door.

Pulling the overgrown ivy back in place, she watched intently as a song thrush pecked at some wild berries. They fell to the dried floor. Eloise observed the small thrush fluttering down from the narrow branch down to the ground. Underneath the berries, a gold glimmer caught her eye. She gasped, and the young bird, after devouring the crimson-coloured berries, uncovered the golden key.

The song bird hopped aside, and watched keenly as Eloise scooped the key up. Tremulous, she pushed the key through the aged keyhole. It slid in perfectly, like a knife through warm butter.

She thrust open the wooden door, and peered and stared all around her. It was a beautiful sight. There were azalea shrubs and roses and marigolds and every flower you could imagine, spread out as though they were contestants for a 'best flower' competition. There were nests perched on branches, and songbirds singing softly and fluttering around.

Eloise was in a tumult of joy. As though in a trance, she stepped forward, a smile of wonder playing on her face. Birds and insects continued with their duties, as though nothing had changed. She felt as though she had stumbled into paradise.

The Lost Key

Eloise skipped through her pleasant garden, right to the back, where the Hidden Hideout stood. The **breeze whipped against her cheeks** as she traversed across the parched grass. Ivy hung over the now discoloured door, which had been locked for almost half a century; the key was missing, and the heavy, iron lock – which was once shiny and new, was now **rusting with age.**

Despite all this, Eloise, with her optimistic demeanour, felt certain the key was near. Tugging at the metal handle, she scanned and surveyed the area, for something that would slot into the keyhole. A sturdy, stone wall surrounded and acted as a boundary for the Hidden Hideout, which allowed nobody to enter, unless they unlocked the bare, age-old door.

Pulling the overgrown ivy back in place, she watched intently as a song thrush pecked at some wild berries. They fell to the dried floor. Eloise observed the small thrush fluttering down from the narrow branch down to the ground. Underneath the berries, a gold glimmer caught her eye. She gasped, and the young bird, after devouring the crimson-coloured berries, uncovered the golden key.

The song bird hopped aside, and watched keenly as Eloise scooped the key up. Tremulous, she pushed the key through the aged keyhole. It slid in perfectly, **like a knife through warm butter.**

She thrust open the wooden door, and peered and stared all around her. It was a beautiful sight. There were azalea shrubs and roses and marigolds and every flower you could imagine, spread out as though they were contestants for a 'best flower' competition. There were nests perched on branches, and songbirds singing softly and fluttering around.

Eloise was in a tumult of joy. As though in a trance, she stepped forward, a smile of wonder playing on her face. Birds and insects continued with their duties, as though nothing had changed. She felt as though she had stumbled into paradise.

KEY

RED – similes

ORANGE – alliteration

GREEN – metaphors

BOLD – imagery

BLUE – personification

Analysis

This essay dives straight into the story's plot and setting; the reader immediately knows where the story takes place and who the character is. Personification is used when describing the weather – 'the breeze whipped against her cheeks'. The 'parched grass' also informs the reader of the season, weather and setting – it is a hot, dry summer's day, without needing to state it.

The alliteration and imagery highlighted above, with reference to age and antiquity (age-old, wooden door, 'rusting with age') adds suspense as the character approaches the mysterious door. Urgency and enthusiasm is expressed by Eloise's 'tugging' as she searches for the key.

The reader can visualise the scene around Eloise as there are descriptive adjectives used, such as: 'sturdy, stone wall', 'crimson-coloured berries', 'heavy, iron lock', and 'aged key'. This provides imagery, where the detail added to the otherwise mundane nouns enables the reader to get a clear picture of the story. There is good use of vocabulary – 'azalea', 'tumult' and 'tremulous'.

Inclusion of the delightful song thrush creates a pleasant way to find the lost key, and flow into the close of the story, where a very pleasant and peaceful depiction is created.

John's Discovery...

This essay is a continuation from an extract where the character, John, finds a very old violin hidden behind a secret panel at the back of a painting. He cannot believe his eyes and loses track of the time as the Tower Clock ticks away the minutes of the evening and turns into night.

John continued admiring his new discovery, when an echoing gong from the Tower clock awoke him from his stint of wonder. Two o'clock! Two o'clock! The sound seemed to have entered his mind, and he finally shut the once concealed cupboard door. Carefully, he placed the new violin in his case, latched it, and blocked the door with the painting, leaving his ordinary violin leaning against the floating shelves.

Hauling his violin case upstairs, he pushed open his bedroom door, and stowed the instrument inside his mahogany cupboard. He set the alarm clock earlier than usual, so that he could have another glimpse of the violin in the morning. After tossing and turning, John finally drifted off into a restless sleep, his mind whirling with thoughts about his new discovery.

John dreamt of his violin. He dreamed that he opened the varnished cupboard in his bedroom, and the violin was gone. In its place was a bright magenta vase with lurid pink marigolds. He dreamt that he stormed downstairs, yelling that someone had tried to sabotage him, when he heard a sudden raucous noise, which he assumed was the burglary alarm in his dream. His eyes fluttered open.

His room was a mess. His clothes, his books, and all his belongings were strewn all over the floor. He leapt for his cupboard, and thrust the door open aggressively. There it was. The lurid pink flowers from his dream. There, right in front of him. John desperately stared in his cupboard, hoping the extraordinary violin hadn't been stolen. It was gone.

There *had* been a robbery in the night.

John's Discovery...

This essay is a continuation from an extract...

John continued admiring his new discovery, when an echoing gong from the Tower clock awoke him from his stint of wonder. *Two o'clock! Two o'clock!* The sound seemed to have entered his mind, and he finally shut the once concealed cupboard door. Carefully, he placed the new violin in his case, latched it, and blocked the door with the painting, leaving his ordinary violin leaning against the floating shelves.

Hauling his violin case upstairs, he pushed open his bedroom door, and stowed the instrument inside his mahogany cupboard. He set the alarm clock earlier than usual, so that he could have another glimpse of the violin in the morning. After tossing and turning, John finally drifted off into a restless sleep, his mind whirling with thoughts about his new discovery.

John dreamt of his violin. He dreamed that he opened the varnished cupboard in his bedroom, and the violin was gone. In its place was a **bright magenta vase with lurid pink marigolds**. He dreamt that he stormed downstairs, yelling that someone had tried to sabotage him, when he heard a sudden raucous noise, which he assumed was the burglary alarm in his dream. His eyes fluttered open.

His room was a mess. His clothes, his books, and all his belongings were strewn all over the floor. He leapt for his cupboard, and thrust the door open aggressively. There it was. The lurid pink flowers from his dream. There, right in front of him. John desperately stared in his cupboard, hoping the extraordinary violin hadn't been stolen. It was gone.

There *had* been a robbery in the night.

KEY

RED – similes

GREEN – metaphors

BLUE – personification

ORANGE – alliteration

BOLD – imagery

Two o'clock! Two o'clock! - repetition

Analysis

In the absence of the original extract, one has to take this plot at face value. It starts with plenty of drama, with 'echoing gongs' and the use of repetition of the two o'clock chime.

There is good use of varied vocabulary in 'hauling' and 'stowed', rather than 'carried' or 'put away'. Vivid colours are described in 'magenta' and 'lurid pink'. The use of 'raucous' with powerful verbs 'thrust' and 'leapt', together with adverbs 'aggressively' and 'desperately' continue to add drama and excitement to the story.

We are left with a short and abrupt end to the story created by the short sentences – 'It was gone' and 'there it was' adding suspense. One is eager to read on. There is a confusing element in the middle of the story, as the writer tries to create the confusion surrounding the vivid dream.

One could add similes and metaphors to the descriptive parts of the essay for improvement.

Petra and Sally

This essay is a continuation of an extract where Petra, and her younger sister, Sally, get caught in a storm and their closest place of refuge is a ruined cottage. In the text, it mentions how Petra thinks witches aren't real. The task was to continue the story. Sally has just been given shelter by the cottage's manger, but Petra has to search for shelter in another of the cottage's room's, as not much of the manger is left.

The jungle of weeds swished and swayed as Petra darted for a place of shelter. She finally shielded herself from the raging storm with the crumbling roof that lay above her. She peered and stared all around her, then spotted a rusting, iron handle next to a damp door. Approaching the door, Petra gently pushed the door open. It wailed in protest as she trod silently into a dark-lit room.

Tremulous, Petra stared all around her. The rotting furniture was mostly upside-down, or scattered all over the place, as though the inhabitants had left in a hurry. The varnished cupboards had black cloaks folded up neatly inside it, and the drawers had a sparkling wand and a book with ancient letters on the front, each on a purple pincushion. Petra's body stiffened and she stayed stock-still, as she suddenly heard footsteps behind her.

She turned, and saw a tall woman wearing regal black robes watching her. She had a steeple hat, which threw the lady's face into shadow. Petra trembled and stuttered in disbelief as realisation swept over her.

A real witch.

The witch pulled her hat back and smiled a warm, inviting smile. She introduced herself as Witch Martina, and that Petra was welcome in her house. She pulled an invisible lever, and the stone-flagged floor opened into a cellar staircase, and Witch Martina beckoned Petra to follow with a bony finger. Petra followed eagerly, and soon realised that underneath the ruined cottage was a well-lit cellarage.

Petra explained to the witch that Sally was near the manger and excused herself to go. She brought Sally to the cosy and welcoming cellarage, where they ravenously devoured delicious fare.

Petra and Sally

This essay is a continuation of an extract...

The jungle of weeds swished and swayed as Petra darted for a place of shelter. She finally shielded herself from the raging storm with the crumbling roof that lay above her. She peered and stared all around her, then spotted a rusting, iron handle next to a damp door. Approaching the door, Petra gently pushed the door open. It wailed in protest as she trod silently into a dark-lit room.

Tremulous, Petra stared all around her. The rotting furniture was mostly upside-down, or scattered all over the place, as though the inhabitants had left in a hurry. The varnished cupboards had black cloaks folded up neatly inside it, and the drawers had a sparkling wand and a book with ancient letters on the front, each on a purple pincushion. Petra's body stiffened and she stayed stock-still, as she suddenly heard footsteps behind her.

She turned, and saw a tall woman wearing black, regal robes watching her. She had a steeple hat, which threw the lady's face into shadow. Petra trembled and stuttered in disbelief as realisation swept over her.

A real witch.

The witch pulled her hat back and smiled a **warm, inviting smile**. She introduced herself as Witch Martina, and that Petra was welcome in her house. She pulled an invisible lever, and the stone-flagged floor opened up into a cellar staircase, and Witch Martina beckoned Petra to follow with a bony finger. Petra followed eagerly, and soon realised that underneath the ruined cottage was a well-lit cellarage.

Petra explained to the witch that Sally was near the manger and excused herself to go. She brought Sally to the cosy and welcoming cellarage, where they ravenously devoured delicious fare.

KEY

RED – similes

GREEN – metaphors

BLUE – personification

ORANGE – alliteration

BOLD – imagery

Analysis

Several literary techniques have been used. The use of 'jungle' in 'jungle of weeds' gives the reader an image of chaos, or pending danger being in unknown territory. <u>Onomatopoeia</u> (the use of words which sound like their meaning) is conveyed by 'swished and swayed'. Interesting adjectives add to the drama of the situation – 'raging storm', 'crumbling roof' 'iron handle', 'damp door', 'dark-lit room'.

The insertion of adverbs adds to the cautious atmosphere generated by the author – 'Petra gently pushed' and 'she trod silently'. The door is brought to life through personification as it 'wailed in protest'.

A stimulating first paragraph that makes the reader want to read on and find out what happens next.

The second paragraph is also rich in adjectives to spice up the information given about the surroundings, and help the reader visualise the surroundings in his mind's eye - 'rotting furniture', 'varnished cupboards' and 'sparkling wand'.

The writer has chosen two colours; 'black' cloaks and 'purple' pincushions. Black usually denotes darkness; while 'purple' adds a regal touch complemented by the 'sparkling' wands. The 'black' is repeated in the next paragraph, for emphasis, creating danger, darkness and peril.

'A real witch' – this short sentence as a paragraph on its own, is apt in this case as it creates impact and also reflects understanding and continuation of the given text that preceded this part of the story.

The penultimate paragraph continues the story and again, creating plenty of curiosity through adjectives and vivid imagery with an 'inviting smile', 'invisible lever', 'stone-flagged floor' and 'cellar staircase'. The 'bony finger', 'steeple hat' and 'black, regal robes' adds to the witch-effect – as one can denote a familiar image of a witch. Perhaps a 'hooked nose' would have completed this image.

The final paragraph goes back to the original script and mentions the 'manger' and then re-introduces the other character in this story – 'Sally'. It may appear that the story remains incomplete – but that's fine as this is a continuation of a story, just a snapshot, and the tale is not meant to end here. The use of adventurous vocabulary has got the reader engaged, and one would like to know what happens next. What would happen next? The page is your oyster – let your imagination escape, close your eyes, put yourself in Petra's fearless shoes. Look around you – feel the presence of this fascinating witch and compose the next few paragraphs yourself!

Power

The monotonous room needed to be more lively. The carpet was a dull grey, and the room didn't have any furniture in it. The sun had not yet risen, and the sky was still a turquoise blue. Having the power and control over snow and ice, I rolled out a thick, white carpet of snow all along the floor. I sent fluffy swirls of snowflakes dancing and fluttering around the room and created borders of frost for the window. There were plenty of snowmen and snow castles now; it was enough to create my very own snow-city.

I peered outside. Mum and Dad were still asleep. I froze ice all over the house, until it was like a large, icy plain. An ice slide ran throughout my home. I hauled my sledge up the stairs and balanced it on the ice. Clambering in, I grasped the handle tightly.

Waving my hand elegantly in the air, I sent a gust of biting, brittle wind heading in my direction. Clutching the sledge, I braced myself.

Like a cannonball being fired, I shot down the stairs. I raced through the room. I zigzagged through doorways. Everything around me was a blur as I sped throughout the house. In the next second, I flew into the hall, and hurled into soft tufts of snow. The room was commodious now. The sledge stopped. Footsteps were coming down the stairs.

Hastily, but as swiftly as a magician, I thawed all the ice and snow. Like a sweep of an enchanter's wand, the frost and snowflakes vanished instantly. The silent house was back in its normal state.

I turned invisible – by feeling my pulse – and crept upstairs, as silently, stealthily as a supple ninja, to my bedroom. I creaked open the door, and then locked it again once inside. Turning visible again, I took a moment to admire all my frost and snowflake decorations that were brightening up my room. Snow drifts floated around, like pale, white ghosts. Then I realised, I really did own a magical –

POWER.

Power

The monotonous room needed to be more lively. The carpet was a dull grey, and the room didn't have any furniture in it. The sun had not yet risen, and the sky was still a turquoise blue. Having the power and control over snow and ice, I rolled out a **thick, white carpet** of snow all along the floor. I sent fluffy swirls of snowflakes dancing and fluttering around the room and created borders of frost for the window. There were plenty of snowmen and snow castles now; it was enough to create my very own snow-city.

I peered outside. Mum and Dad were still asleep. I froze ice all over the house, until it was like a large, icy plain. An ice slide ran throughout my home. I hauled my sledge up the stairs and balanced it on the ice. Clambering in, I grasped the handle tightly.

Waving my hand elegantly in the air, I sent a gust of biting, brittle wind heading in my direction. Clutching the sledge, I braced myself.

Like a cannonball being fired, I shot down the stairs. I raced through the room. I zigzagged through doorways. Everything around me was a blur as I sped throughout the house. In the next second, I flew into the hall, and hurled into soft tufts of snow. The room was commodious now. The sledge stopped. Footsteps were coming down the stairs.

Hastily, but as swiftly as a magician, I thawed all the ice and snow. Like a sweep of an enchanter's wand, the frost and snowflakes vanished instantly. The silent house was back in its normal state.

I turned invisible – by feeling my pulse – and crept upstairs, as silently, stealthily as a supple ninja, to my bedroom. I unlocked the door, and then locked it again once inside. Turning visible again, I took a moment to admire all my frost and snowflake decorations that were brightening up my room. Snow drifts floated around, like pale, white ghosts. Then I realised, I really did own a magical –

POWER.

KEY

RED – similes   BLUE – personification   **BOLD** – imagery

GREEN – metaphors   ORANGE – alliteration

Analysis

This enthralling essay begins with a description of the initial lacklustre settings. The writer has given us indication of the time of the day without actually stating it - 'sun had not yet risen'. Then the writer has plunged straight into mentioning the title of the essay to emphasise what is about to unleash. The 'power' is at first described with gentle vocabulary that create an image of decorative prettiness 'fluffy swirls' & 'fluttering'. There is use of personification - 'snowflakes dancing' to liven up the gloomy and static atmosphere.

The second paragraph again uses a technique to give the approximate age of the writer without having to specifically state it. 'Mum and dad were still asleep' implies that the writer is a child and gives an air of mischief which again lifts the original lifeless atmosphere.

A good use of adverbs has added to the delightful playfulness of the activities that the writer has then engaged in 'grasped the handle tightly', 'waving my hand elegantly'. 'Like a cannonball being fired' - this simile gives a good indication of the sheer speed the character is moving with – giving the feel of exhilaration one feels when on a wild rollercoaster ride.

The essay concludes with a sudden stop of all movement returning to the original stationary setting. The theme of mischief hinted at earlier in the story is kept in line as the character hastily tries to return the place into its original state after mentioning 'footsteps were coming'.

The insertion of a series of similes, one after another, in the penultimate and final paragraphs 'as swiftly as a magician', 'like a sweep of an enchanter's wand', 'stealthily as a supple ninja' and 'like pale, white ghosts' gives the reader a cascade of vivid images of an enchanted environment far from reality.

The story concludes with a one-word sentence 'POWER'. This refers back to the title and through this short sentence and repetition emphasises the great impact as to what a wondrous place this 'power' can create.

Tightrope – Walking

This essay is a continuation of an extract, where a tightrope walker performs his act at the local circus. His name is Gabrielli, and the main character is called Dominic, who comes with his friend, Holly Stroud, to watch the performance. At the end of the extract, Holly brings out a washing line and decides to practice tightrope-walking. The task of the essay was to write about Dominic when Gabrielli picks him for a demonstration of tightrope-walking.

The audience applauded again. Gabrielli put his hands up for silence, and at once a wave of quiet swept over the crowd. "Now, children, it is your turn. Your turn to walk across the tightrope." Gabrielli scanned the audience, then pointed at Dominic. "You, come up here." Dominic hastily scrambled into the circus ring. "How can I do it?" Dominic thought, "Without any practice?" He approached the tightrope, and, taking a deep breath, gingerly and gently balanced one foot on the tightrope.

Dominic had no doubt that he would fall. Only one foot was on a stable and solid platform, he looked down – which was the one thing you shouldn't do whilst you are on a high platform. He gulped. There were no mattresses or anything of the sort to cushion his fall when he tumbled off the tightrope. "Come on Dominic! You can do it!" Holly's voice shouted from the crowd. He suddenly felt a boost of confidence and determination as he heard Holly's words of encouragement.

"Yes," he murmured softly. "I can do it." He concentrated on the end platform and cautiously steadied himself on the tightrope. And, yes, there was a moment when he stumbled, when the rope swayed, and he wobbled, teetering on the brink of the tightrope. He felt the world spin around him. But he swung his arms out, altered his balance, and he did not fall. He sighed in relief.

Gabrielli was yelling encouragement from below. "Good job, Dominic! You are doing what no one else dares to do! You are-" but Dominic wasn't listening. He only had a few more steps to go. He was about to step onto the platform, however, in his joy, relief and triumph, his foot missed. He had tripped!

He grabbed the surface of the platform, and desperately clung onto it, as though it was worth his life. He made a first attempt to hoist himself back on to the safe platform. Fortunately, he succeeded. "Hang on Dominic! I'll come and get-" Gabrielli gasped and gaped in astonishment. "Why, I couldn't do *that* when I was a kid, could I?" he told his assistant. The assistant nodded in agreement and clapped along enthusiastically with the rest of the crowd.

Dominic had gained his confidence by now, the whole audience had held his breath for him, and, grinning, he bowed with great pleasure and jubilance. "Thank you all!" he shouted at the audience. "I couldn't have done-"

"Me next!" Holly Stroud shouted, interrupting him and running up to Gabrielli.

"Sorry, we only have time for one today, but you could… practise with a washing line, maybe?" Gabrielli replied, rather surprised that another member of the audience wanted to have a turn.

"Good idea!" Dominic and Holly shouted in enthusiastic agreement.

Tightrope – Walking

This essay is a continuation of an extract…

The **a**udience **a**pplauded again. Gabrielli put his hands up for silence, and at once a **wave of quiet swept** over the crowd. "Now, children, it is your turn. Your turn to walk across the tightrope." Gabrielli scanned the audience, then pointed at Dominic. "You, come up here." Dominic hastily scrambled into the circus ring. "How can I do it?" Dominic thought, "Without any practice?" He approached the tightrope, and, taking a deep breath, **g**ingerly and **g**ently balanced one foot on the tightrope.

Dominic had no doubt that he would fall. Only one foot was on a stable and solid platform, he looked down – which was the one thing you shouldn't do whilst you are on a high platform. He gulped. There were no mattresses or anything of the sort to cushion his fall when he tumbled off the tightrope. "Come on Dominic! You can do it!" Holly's voice shouted from the crowd. He suddenly felt a **boost of confidence and determination** as he heard Holly's words of encouragement.

"Yes," he murmured softly. "I can do it." He concentrated on the end platform and cautiously steadied himself on the tightrope. And, yes, there was a moment when he stumbled, when the rope swayed, and he wobbled, teetering on the brink of the tightrope. He felt the world spin around him. But he swung his arms out, altered his balance, and he did not fall. He sighed in relief.

Gabrielli was yelling encouragement from below. "Good job, Dominic! You are doing what no one else dares to do! You are-" but Dominic wasn't listening. He only had a few more steps to go. He was about to step onto the platform, however, in his joy, relief and triumph, his foot missed. He had tripped!

He grabbed the surface of the platform, and desperately clung onto it, as though it was worth his life. He made a first attempt to hoist himself back on to the safe platform. Fortunately, he succeeded. "Hang on Dominic! I'll come and get-" Gabrielli **g**asped and **g**aped in astonishment. "Why, I couldn't do *that* when I was a kid, could I?" he told his assistant. The assistant nodded his agreement, and clapped along enthusiastically with the rest of the crowd.

Dominic had gained his confidence by now, the whole audience had held his breath for him, and, grinning, he bowed with great pleasure and jubilance. "Thank you all!" he shouted at the audience. "I couldn't have done-"

"Me next!" Holly Stroud shouted, interrupting him and running up to Gabrielli.

"Sorry, we only have time for one today, but you could… practise with a washing line, maybe?" Gabrielli replied, rather surprised that another member of the audience wanted to have a turn.

"Good idea!" Dominic and Holly shouted in enthusiastic agreement.

KEY

RED – similes

GREEN – metaphors

BLUE – personification

ORANGE – alliteration

BOLD – imagery

Analysis

This essay is a continuation of an excerpt from a story and the key element is to keep in line with the character's personalities given in the preceding text. That aside, this text focuses on the importance of good/correct punctuation, especially when writing essays with plenty of speech.

The writer has substituted the mundane word 'said' with a variety of other terms when putting conversation into writing – 'Holly shouted', 'Dominic thought', 'he murmured', 'Gabrielli gasped' and 'Gabrielli replied'. This makes the writing more interesting.

The conversations made are kept in line with children's speech and contains an immature element. "Me next!' Holly Stroud shouted' sums up the exuberance of youth as a child would be excited about a dangerous act. Also, when Dominic is asked to come up, he doesn't refuse – despite his fears about his competence regarding the task, again something a child would be more inclined to do than an adult; 'Dominic hastily scrambled'.

The acrobat Gabrielli is given the speech and behaviour of someone who is theatrical and melodramatic – 'putting his hands up for silence', 'yelled encouragement' and 'you are doing what no one dares to do!', not quite grasping the danger aspect of the task he is inviting a child to perform.

Plenty of suspense is created throughout the passage. Encouraged by his friend, a compelling account is subsequently given on his embarking on the perilous tightrope. Gripping adjectives – 'stumbled', 'swayed', 'wobbled', 'teetered', which all convey suspense to the reader. 'He had tripped', 'he gulped' – these short sentences are used to create tension and drama, which impacts the reader as they would want to know what happens next: does Dominic make it?!

The writer has beautifully captured the tense, yet captivating atmosphere of this circus ring through use of vivid vocabulary to give an image of excitement; 'desperately clung', 'audience held their breath', 'great pleasure and jubilance' and 'gasped and gaped in astonishment'.

This essay concludes with the mention of the 'washing line', information that was given at the beginning which shows understanding of the preceding text and continuation of it that helps to connect the passages.

Toad's Journey

This essay is a continuation of an extract where Toad has disguised himself as a washerwoman and has escaped from a prison. He was imprisoned for stealing a motor, and embarked on a train by means of an escape route to Toad Hall, his home. However, they are pursued by another train that know Toad is escaping. The train driver instructs Toad to jump off the train, and into the woods, which will make him harder to find. Toad did this and has just fallen asleep under a tree.

Toad awoke as early sunlight crept into the woods. The golden ball in the sky splashed deep into the blue sea surrounding it, and the sky dawned a sapphire blue. Toad watched as a tawny owl soared down towards a cluster of animals. It carried something in its beak. All the animals threw sniggering, disgusted glances towards Toad as the owl spread out a sheet of paper, which had a large picture of a 'wanted' Toad. Toad pulled his washerwoman clothes tightly around him, and shivered, despite the sun beaming down on him.

Setting off further away from the animals and the railway, Toad felt his stomach growl angrily. Ravenous, he spied some wild berries nearby; he hurried over to them and plucked them from the bush like picking strawberries. He scoffed them down, then screwed up his face as the sour and bitter taste flooded into his mouth.

Wandering aimlessly through the trees, Toad wondered how far away Toad Hall was. How he wished he had thought better of the motor! "If only I hadn't stolen it," he shook his head miserably. "I wouldn't be in this state right now." Toad sighed glumly. The air of melancholy seemed to follow him around like a snake who had finally found some prey. He wished he was in his welcoming manor of Toad Hall. He yearned to have a comfortable bed and warm, hearty meals. He wished he could see his friends again. But here he was, far from home, in a remote wood, with no idea where he was.

Toad's Journey

This essay is a continuation of an extract...

Toad awoke as early sunlight crept into the woods. The golden ball in the sky splashed deep into the blue sea surrounding it, and the sky dawned a sapphire blue. Toad watched as a tawny owl soared down towards a cluster of animals. It carried something in its beak. All the animals threw sniggering, disgusted glances towards Toad as the owl spread out a sheet of paper, which had a large picture of a 'wanted' Toad. Toad pulled his washerwoman clothes tightly around him, and shivered, despite the sun beaming down on him.

Setting off further away from the animals and the railway, Toad felt his stomach growl angrily. Ravenous, he spied some wild berries nearby; he hurried over to them and plucked them from the bush like picking strawberries. He scoffed them down, then screwed up his face as the **sour and bitter taste flooded into his mouth**.

Wandering aimlessly through the trees, Toad wondered how far away Toad Hall was. How he wished he had thought better of the motor! "If only I hadn't stolen it," he shook his head miserably. "I wouldn't be in this state right now." Toad sighed glumly. The air of melancholy seemed to follow him around like a snake who had finally found some prey. He wished he was in his welcoming manor of Toad Hall. He yearned to have a comfortable bed and warm, hearty meals. He wished he could see his friends again. But here he was, far from home, in a remote wood, with no idea where he was.

KEY

RED – similes

GREEN – metaphors

BLUE – personification

ORANGE – alliteration

BOLD – imagery

Analysis

As *'early sunlight crept'* - the adjective *'early'* gives you an indication of the time of day without having to state 'it was morning'. The idea of sunlight creeping into the woods continues a tense atmosphere of a toad that has escaped prison and makes one question if anyone else may be creeping up on the fugitive.

As an area of improvement one could consider adding an adjective to describe the woods – is it a place of safety for the toad? - 'calm woods' or is it a potentially an unsafe place to be – 'dark woods'?

The second sentence beginning with the metaphor, *'The golden ball in the sky'* creates a cheerful atmosphere reinforced with the phrases, *'sky dawned a sapphire blue'* and the *'blue sea'*. The colour blue is sometimes used to reflect calm, and the use of the adjectives *'golden'* and *'sapphire'* add a touch of sparkle to the image created suggesting a bright and sunny day where one has to shield the eyes from the dazzling display of the sun and its reflection onto the sea. The use of the phrase *'golden ball'* is also an interesting way to replace the mundane use of the word 'sun', and personifying the sun to *'splashing'* into the sea is an interesting description of where the sky meets the sea at the horizon, and gives a playful and again, cheery backdrop to the contrasting mood of Toad.

The *'tawny owl'* displays knowledge of the type of breed of owl – important to display knowledge of creatures, if one has it – as it adds character to the creatures in the writing. *'Soaring down to a cluster of animals'* continues to add information about the scenery and thus creates an image of the woods in the eye of the reader.

The story then moves on to Toad. *'Toad shivered'* brings us back to Toad's discomfort despite the somewhat merry surroundings – with the sun once again personified by *'beaming'*, alluding to the otherwise pleasant day and the hope that Toad is holding on to.

The use of personification in the *'stomach growled angrily'* adds to Toad's inner feelings of discontent and desperate hunger of that of a desperate fugitive. The writer uses a simile *'like picking strawberries'* to create an image of a popular pleasant pastime that the reader can relate to – bringing some relief to Toad's distress. The senses of taste are then stimulated – so the reader has an image of how the activity may be appearing, but also now has an idea of how the berries would taste *'sour and bitter taste'*, again adding to the poor Toad's turmoil who seems to be having no luck at all.

The last paragraph uses phrases to emphasise Toad's dejected state of mind - *'wandering aimlessly'* and *'sighed glumly'*. The use of the metaphor *'air of melancholy'*, compounded by the twist of danger of it 'following him *like a snake'* shows that Toad is being pushed further, and further, to the edge.

The writer concludes with Toad's desperate longing to be home with his friends. With the use of clever adjectives, an image has been created of 'home' to be that of *'warmth', 'hearty'* and *'comfort'* – the complete opposite of his existing feelings, which creates sympathy from the reader.

This is not a long essay, but the 3 paragraphs are extremely well written, with the typical, 'introduction, middle and end' essay plan which all flow perfectly well together. Remember, its 'quality, not quantity' that is important, with many literary techniques used, that also capture the essay brief, reflecting the character, and its predicament, in the aforementioned passage that will earn high marks here.

School Days

Some people like school.

Jeremy was one of them. He loved the pleasure of catching up with his friends after school, or even walking with them in the mornings. He loved the relieving sound of the echoing bell, the rush out of the doors, and games on the school field.

Some people hate school.

The drag out of bed. The boring walk to school. Alfie may seem pessimistic, but to him this was reality. No matter how many admirers he had, and no matter how many minds he had manipulated, Alfie felt as though he didn't belong in St Peter's Secondary School. He had no friends, although many people admired and obeyed him because of the fantastic reputation he had set up with almost every person in the school. Except another boy, who was, in his opinion, the worst at everything he did.

Jeremy.

The single name sent a chill of anger and hatred bubbling inside him, blocking every corner, every inch of himself, wiping away the rest of the world around him, leaving only room and feeling for Jeremy. But the strange thing was, he didn't know why. Maybe it was the fact that one of Jeremy's friends had spilt orange juice all over him and Jeremy had laughed heartily. Or maybe it was the fact that Jeremy had beaten him at every race. Alfie had felt a spurt of envy as Jeremy had been rewarded with the Fastest Boy Award for Year 10. St Peter's gave a lot of awards, though Alfie never recalled being given one that he was genuinely proud of.

School Days

Some people like school.

Jeremy was one of them. He loved the pleasure of catching up with his friends after school, or even walking with them in the mornings. He loved the **relieving sound of the echoing bell**, the rush out of the doors, and games on the school field.

Some people hate school.

The drag out of bed. The boring walk to school. Alfie may seem pessimistic, but to him this was reality. No matter how many admirers he had, and no matter how many minds he had manipulated, Alfie felt as though he didn't belong in St Peter's Secondary School. He had no friends, although many people admired and obeyed him because of the fantastic reputation he had set up with almost every person in the school. Except another boy, who was, in his opinion, the worst at everything he did.

Jeremy.

The single name sent a chill of anger and hatred bubbling inside him, blocking every corner, every inch of himself, wiping away the rest of the world around him, leaving only room and feeling for Jeremy. But the strange thing was, he didn't know why. Maybe it was the fact that one of Jeremy's friends had spilt orange juice all over him and Jeremy had laughed heartily. Or maybe it was the fact that Jeremy had beaten him at every race. Alfie had felt a **spurt of envy** as Jeremy had been rewarded with the Fastest Boy Award for Year 10. St Peter's gave a lot of awards, though Alfie never recalled being given one that he was genuinely proud of.

KEY

RED – similes

GREEN – metaphors

BLUE – personification

ORANGE – alliteration

BOLD – imagery

Analysis

This essay starts with a short, snappy sentence as a paragraph on its own which is then later repeated with only a change in one word. This simple change creates a sudden and marked contrast which leads nicely to the two very different characters the writer goes on to introduce. Alfie's jealousy and the adversity between the two characters is described well, which one could recall as a common, relatable experience of school life for many readers.

Exploring the sense of sound also allures the reader into the school day, with 'echoing bells' and 'rushing students' capturing a typical, hectic day at school. The reader could also relate to other examples such as 'the drag out of bed' or losing races repeatedly to a competitor.

Good use of metaphors and personification helps the reader understand the emotions that Alfie is experiencing, creating some sympathy for him.

This is an open essay title allowing an opportunity to write about any aspect of school. One may choose 'their best day at school', focus on their favourite activity, or talk about their best friend or teacher to cite just a few examples.

The writer has chosen something more difficult here, and perhaps has run into a few obstacles. It is not usually recommended to focus on two characters in a short 11+ essay, due to time constraints. Most experts would advise to focus on a single character or plot. There could have been more on Jeremy and why he enjoyed school so much. Alfie is built up to be an envious character but then why do people admire him? A little further development of the characters would have been ideal but a fairly unique approach to the essay deserves some credit.

Forest Adventure

Kate pushed away vines and shrubs as she trekked through the forest. Vines hung from boughs and branches like icicles, and her torch beam illuminated towering trees with muscly arms and small spindly trees with frail limbs. Broken twigs crunched beneath her feet as the forest hung still and silent. Her heart palpitating with nerves, Kate slunk past charcoal trees as the moon sent shadowy shapes flitting across her vision.

Grey clouds obscured the moon at occasional times. Yearning for daylight, Kate was sure she heard creeping footsteps other than her own. The forest was becoming denser, but the brittle wind found gaps to squirm through and bite into her exposed skin on her face and her numb hands.

Quite suddenly, a pair of luminescent eyes loomed out of the darkness. Kate drew in a sharp intake of breath. The eyes were drawing closer now, much closer, and the nebulous body seemed to be advancing too. She froze, as another pair of eyes appeared. Kate fumbled for her torch and shone it on to the amorphous figure in front of her.

A doe was illuminated. Beside it, a young fawn was standing next to its mother on tremulous legs. The doe's eyes twinkled as it walked ahead. It paused. It walked back towards the astonished girl, and nudged her gently. Again, it walked ahead, and the young deer trotted after its mother. Kate followed.

An owl hooted somewhere in the distance. The trio walked for a while, until suddenly the dark was lit up by a sudden burst of colour. A fire was crackling ahead, sounding like myriads of fireworks exploding, bursting for freedom. The fire cast its flickering rays of light over a cluster of men who sat huddled around the fire, conversing in low voices. Kate backed behind the tree, listening intently.

"...Not got much longer...we're going to be caught for it soon..."

"...Have to act now..."

One of the men who were drinking choked and spluttered the drink all over himself.

"What do you think you're doing, making such a racket like that?" one of the men asked, thumping him on the back.

"There's someone there!" he hissed, thrusting a trembling finger in Kate's direction. "You can see his shadow!"

All eyes were riveted on Kate's shadow, as her heart drummed with adrenaline.

Forest Adventure

Kate pushed away vines and shrubs as she trekked through the forest. Vines hung from boughs and branches **like icicles**, and her torch beam illuminated **towering trees with muscly arms** and **small spindly trees with frail limbs**. Broken twigs crunched beneath her feet as the forest hung still and silent. Heart palpitating with nerves, Kate slunk past charcoal trees as the moon sent **shadowy shapes** flitting across her vision.

Grey clouds obscured the moon at occasional times. Yearning for daylight, Kate was sure she heard creeping footsteps other than her own. The forest was becoming denser, but the brittle wind found gaps to squirm through and **bite** into her exposed skin on her face and her numb hands.

Quite suddenly, a pair of **luminescent eyes loomed out of the darkness**. Kate drew in a sharp intake of breath. The eyes were growing closer now, much closer, and the nebulous body seemed to be advancing too. She froze, as another pair of eyes appeared. Kate fumbled for her torch and shone it on to the amorphous figure in front of her.

A doe was illuminated. Beside it, a young fawn was standing next to its mother on tremulous legs. The **doe's eyes twinkled** as it walked ahead. It paused. It walked back towards the astonished girl and nudged her gently. Again, it walked ahead, and the young deer trotted after its mother. Kate followed.

An owl hooted somewhere in the distance. The trio walked for a while, until suddenly the dark was lit up by a sudden **burst of colour**. A fire was crackling ahead, sounding **like myriads of fireworks exploding**, **bursting for freedom**. The fire cast its flickering rays of light over a cluster of men who sat huddled around the fire, conversing in low voices. Kate backed behind the tree, listening intently.

"...Not got much longer...we're going to be caught for it soon..."

"...Have to act now..."

One of the men who were drinking choked and spluttered the drink all over himself.

"What do you think you're doing, making such a racket like that?" one of the men asked, thumping him on the back.

"There's someone there!" he hissed, thrusting a trembling finger in Kate's direction. "You can see his shadow!"

All eyes were riveted on Kate's shadow, as her heart drummed with adrenalin.

KEY

RED – similes

GREEN – metaphors

BLUE – personification

ORANGE – alliteration

BOLD – imagery

Analysis

The reader is immediately immersed into an eerie, creepy and formidable setting, amongst 'towering trees', within the darkness of a shadowy moonlight. The vocabulary used reinforces this atmosphere - with 'muscly' trunks, 'spindly arms', 'shadowy shapes', 'obscuring grey clouds', with 'hanging vines like icicles'. The forest hanging 'still in silence', broken by 'squirming', 'biting winds', adds a sense of anxious anticipation as to what could come next.

This fear is compounded by the 'nebulous', 'amorphous', figure, with eyes that loomed out, whilst getting 'closer and closer', whist Kate 'freezes and fumbles'; again, adding to the panic she is feeling.

Good vocabulary and knowledge is demonstrated by 'doe' (female deer) and 'young fawn' (young/baby deer).

But the writer then brings about a sharp contrast thereon, the creature is but a doe and her fawn, with eyes that 'twinkled', 'gently' moving along. It's a welcome change to the atmosphere bringing comfort to the character who is now accompanying the deer.

But a sudden 'burst of colour' and 'crackling fire' changes the setting again, and returns some fear and trepidation. Some men, causing mischief, not 'wanting to get caught', eventually gaze towards Kate's shadow. She is in trouble. The essay concludes on a cliff-hanger enticing the reader to read on.

The Dark House

The moon, a pale white ball, was being tossed by the tufts of clouds. Clare glanced sideways through the fractured window. How she wished to be roaming under the twilight sky! That would at least be better than wandering through an empty, dilapidated manor in the dark. The once stately mansion was now neglected and abandoned. Clare shuddered as she creaked open yet another moaning door.

The whole reason she was here was to rescue her foolhardy friend, Liz. Why would Liz ever go venturing out at night? "I even warned her," Clare thought, pushing her ivory-like hair out of her eyes. She then realised that she was making the same mistake as her friend. "At least I'm here for a good reason," she convinced herself.

Approaching another staircase, Clare's mind filled with conflict; should she advance any further? Clare knew that she ought to go and fetch help, but her instincts decided against this. Filled with determination once again, Clare pushed all of her pessimistic thoughts out of her mind, and strode confidently up the half-collapsed flight of stairs, amazed at her own temerity. The staircase meandered like a snake further and further, until Clare felt as though she couldn't move a step more, when at last she stumbled onto a landing. Here, the railings on the stairs were manufactured in a vintage style, and were carved out if mahogany wood, though now it had rotted and was infested with a coat of green mould which was spreading as rapidly as wildfire.

Clare continued loitering through the winding corridors. At the end of a passageway she came across a larger, wooden door, of which breadth was triple the size of any ordinary door. Extraordinary engravings were etched onto it, and, much to Clare's surprise, there was a candle on either side of the door, which let off a rich aroma of lilies. She inhaled the welcoming scent. "Makes a change to the stench of rot," Clare thought, pushing open the dark oak door. The candles hissed like snakes and the musty odour of entombed air was left behind in the coiling corridors, and Clare entered the well-lit room, alive with the whistle of candles, which this time reeked of the stench of copper. A fire was crackling sounding like dozens of bullets being fired at once. Clare stared, stunned, in a trance of shock, horror and astonishment all at once, at the dreadful scene that lay before her. Liz was there, bound against the freshly-painted wall, her body limp and lifeless.

The Dark House

The moon, a pale white ball, was being tossed by the tufts of clouds. Clare glanced sideways through the fractured window. How she wished to be roaming under the twilight sky! That would at least be better than wandering through an **empty, dilapidated manor** in the dark. The once stately mansion was now neglected and abandoned. Clare shuddered as she creaked open yet another moaning door.

The whole reason she was here was to rescue her foolhardy friend, Liz. Why would Liz ever go venturing out at night? "I even warned her," Clare thought, pushing her ivory-like hair out of her eyes. She then realised that she was making the same mistake as her friend. "At least I'm here for a good reason," she convinced herself.

Approaching another staircase, Clare's mind filled with conflict; should she advance any further? Clare knew that she ought to go and fetch help, but her instincts decided against this. Filled with determination once again, Clare pushed all of her pessimistic thoughts out of her mind and strode confidently up the half-collapsed flight of stairs, amazed at her own temerity. The staircase meandered **like a snake** further and further, until Clare felt as though she couldn't move a step more, when at last she stumbled onto a landing. Here, the railings on the stairs were **manufactured in a vintage style**, and were carved out if mahogany wood, though now it had rotted and was infested with a coat of green mould which was spreading as rapidly as wildfire.

Clare continued loitering through the winding corridors. At the end of a passageway she came across a larger, wooden door, of which breadth was triple the size of any ordinary door. Extraordinary engravings were etched onto it, and, much to Clare's surprise, there was a candle on either side of the door, which let off a rich aroma of lilies. She inhaled the welcoming scent. "Makes a change to the stench of rot," Clare thought, pushing open the dark oak door. The candles hissed **like snakes** and the musty odour of entombed air was left behind in the coiling corridors, and Clare entered the well-lit room, alive with the whistle of candles, which this time reeked of the stench of copper. A fire was crackling, sounding **like dozens of bullets** being fired at once. Clare stared, stunned, in a trance of shock, horror and astonishment all at once, at the dreadful scene that lay before her. Liz was there, bound against the freshly-painted wall, her body limp and lifeless.

KEY

RED – similes

GREEN – metaphors

BLUE – personification

ORANGE – alliteration

BOLD – imagery

Analysis

The essay starts with a good description of the scene around the character and, once again, tells the reader what time of day it is, without directly stating that it is night-time. There are literal techniques of personification and similes in the first paragraph as well – the moon was a 'pale, white ball' and the clouds 'tossed' the ball around.

The writer introduces the character and the reason for being in the house in the second paragraph, which shows thought to the plot. There is use of speech and grammar, showing another style of writing, adding variety to the prose.

The character battles her indecision and fear with 'temerity', but continues to 'stumble' throughout the passage, implying determination in Clare's personality. This also creates an impression of loyalty in Clare to her friend, which shows that her friendship means a lot to her. This is thoughtful character development.

The third paragraph ends with good detail and description – 'in a vintage style', 'mahogany wood' and the mould 'was spreading as rapidly as wildfire' (this is a hyperbole - an exaggeration that is not meant to be literal) This descriptive language provides imagery, which enables the reader to visualize the scene.

The writer now creates a contrasting atmosphere to that of before. Dark intrigue allures the character to a 'larger, wooden door', and to candles with the aroma of 'scented lilies'. This contrast creates suspense, which heightens further by her exclaimed surprise - 'makes a change to the stench of rot'. Like a crescendo, the atmosphere gets more alarming and dangerous, with candles 'hissing like snakes' and the 'crackling fire' sounding 'like dozens of bullets' which builds up to the finale - a stunned and horrified Clare who stands in 'shock, horror and astonishment' at the image that lays before her.

An Encounter with a Villain

Will creaked open yet another dank door, more cobwebs falling onto him. Brushing his hand off damp walls, he kept thinking that he would never be able to leave the ruined house which he was in. The dust was illuminated by his torch, and he stared at the walls which had been eaten in, and every door had led to another endless passageway – except for this one. His heart surging with hope, he flung open the door and crept inside.

An ill-omened look hung over the room. Taking a few cautious steps inside, Will peered around the room, shining his torch. Discoloured paintings with rotting wooden frames decorated one wall. Broken glass bottles that were tinted to a green colour hung from the ceiling, but that wasn't what mystified Will. It was the fact that preserved insects in amber were in them. Silent footsteps sounded behind him. Sensing someone watching him, Will spun round, and almost at once wished he hadn't. But he continued to gaze into a towering man's evil eye.

Long black robes were draped over him like a curtain, and a grey eye-patch sewn with silken cloth covered one eye. His hair was like black candle-smoke coiling around his head. A staff with a golden viper's head was in one hand, and the other a piece of jade glistened green under Will's torch's streak of light. The cadaverous man's face looked like it had been carved out of stone, and the thin, bony individual grinned, revealing a mouth of blackened teeth.

He waggled a finger at Will, and began to speak, his voice piercing Will's ears, although it only came out as a croak. "Someone dares to enter my home," he whispered, still plastering that fake, toothy smile on his face. Beginning to feel afraid, Will tried to back away. The eerie, thin man followed, still eyeing Will with the one eye. Will became cornered against the wall.

Banging his golden staff on the floor three times, all the lights went out except for Will's torch, its brilliant glare still aimed at the looming man.

He took another step forward. Will was paralysed with fear. With a wave of his hand, Will was lifted with some sort of invisible force. He screamed for help, but all that came out was a muffled moan. He shrank, until he could fit into one of the glass bottles. He was lifted into one, the amber beneath him. Realising what would happen, Will gulped. Terror cascaded onto him.

An Encounter with a Villain

Will creaked open yet another **d**ank **d**oor, more cobwebs falling onto him. Brushing his hand off damp walls, he kept thinking that he would never be able to leave the ruined house which he was in. The dust was illuminated by his torch, and he stared at the walls which had been eaten in, and every door had led to another endless passageway – except for this one. His **heart surging with hope**, he flung open the door and crept inside.

An ill-omened look hung over the room. Taking a few cautious steps inside, Will peered around the room, shining his torch. Discoloured paintings with rotting wooden frames decorated one wall. Broken glass bottles that were tinted to a green colour hung from the ceiling, but that wasn't what mystified Will. It was the fact that preserved insects in amber were in them. Silent footsteps sounded behind him. Sensing someone watching him, Will spun round, and almost at once wished he hadn't. But he continued to gaze into a towering man's **e**vil **e**ye.

Long black robes were draped over him **like a curtain**, and a grey eye-patch sewn with silken cloth covered one eye. His hair was **like black candle-smoke coiling** around his head. A staff with a golden viper's head was in one hand, and in the other a piece of jade **g**listened **g**reen under Will's torch's streak of light. The cadaverous man's face looked **like it had been carved out of stone**, and the thin, bony individual grinned, revealing a mouth of blackened teeth.

He waggled a finger at Will, and began to speak, his voice piercing Will's ears, although it only came out as a croak. "Someone dares to enter my home," he whispered, still plastering that fake, toothy smile on his face. Beginning to feel afraid, Will tried to back away. The eerie, thin man followed, still eyeing Will with that one eye. Will became cornered against the wall.

Banging his golden staff on the floor three times, all the lights went out except for Will's torch, its **brilliant glare** still aimed at the looming man.

He took another step forward. Will was paralysed with fear. With a wave of his hand, Will was lifted with some sort of invisible force. He screamed for help, but all that came out was a **m**uffled **m**oan. He shrank, until he could fit into one of the glass bottles. He was lifted into one, the amber beneath him. Realising what would happen, Will gulped. **Terror cascaded** onto him.

KEY

RED – similes

GREEN – metaphors

BLUE – personification

ORANGE – alliteration

BOLD – imagery

Analysis

The essay starts with the use of alliteration 'dank door', followed by 'damp walls'. Good use of adverbs 'creaked open' to add tension-building detail to the sentence. The first paragraph throws the reader into suspense amidst settings which have been described articulately to create an image of an anxious character lost in this dilapidated home. The phrases 'endless passageway', 'crept inside', and 'heart surging with hope' all contribute to building anticipation of what is going to follow.

The subsequent paragraph is laden with plenty of descriptive words to allow the reader to step into the character's thoughts and feelings and visualise and absorb the surroundings. 'Discoloured paintings', 'rotting wooden frames', 'broken glass bottles'. Again, adverbs have been inserted to build tension – 'cautious steps', 'silent footsteps'. The writer has also used colours to add to the narrative – 'tinted to a green' alluding to the shade of mould, adding to the rotting scene, and 'insects in amber', the amber referring to decaying, dated and neglected items. This item, insects in amber, is a peculiar trait, and implies eccentric behaviour providing a backdrop to the introduction of the subsequent villainous character.

Long black robes, the black representing evil, fear, power. The simile 'like a curtain' makes one wonder what is beyond the curtain, and likewise the 'eye patch' adds mystery. The patch is made of a luxurious 'silken cloth' portraying a sense of power and wealth. The simile 'like candle smoke' denotes danger. Similarly, the staff has the 'head of a viper', a snake renown for its venom and danger. The villain is described as 'stone' signifying being cold, heartless and possibly inhumane. Repetition of black in his 'blackened teeth' brings out further evil, darkness upon darkness, descends.

The Journey

I hurried out of the house towards the field, where I knew my loyal mare was waiting. I was already in my riding gear, but I had packed a spare set of jodhpurs and boots just in case. Clutching the saddle and my bag of belongings, I watched as the golden ball in the sky splashed deep into the blue sea around it, and the sky dawned a sapphire blue.

A whinny awoke me from my reverie. A horse was standing before me, its hair – as black as ebony – rippling in the breeze. "How are you, Luna?" I asked, saddling her. Luna neighed again.

Hoisting myself onto her, I flicked the reins and Luna trotted forward, beginning the long journey south. The wind whistled and swept through the air, and the crystal-blue sky could not have been any clearer. Luna cantered onwards. The steady rhythm of my hooves was the same as my heartbeat, which was pounding with excitement and exhilaration. Inhaling deep breaths of fresh air, I could feel the sun beaming down on us.

Suddenly Luna came to an abrupt halt. I could tell at once what had stopped her. Ahead was a rushing river, which was flowing so rapidly foam was spraying near the bank. I tried to console her. "Come on, Luna," I whispered soothingly. "You can do it." After a moment, she reared on her hind legs, and galloped forward. I braced myself, and as we leapt over the river everything seemed to be in slow-motion; one moment we were in the air, and the water was flowing beneath us, then the next we were on firm ground again, still galloping. "Good girl!" I exclaimed, leaning forward to ruffle Luna's mane. Luna whinnied in response.

We continued our journey, pausing only for short rests or meals. We cantered through the countryside, and some parts of the city, but it was only at sunset did I stop and dismount Luna. The sun was slipping behind the horizon, illuminating the towering fortress before me. It was immensely tall, and every part of it seemed to radiate royalty and authority. Yet something gave it a touch of mischief as well, though I wasn't quite sure why. I led Luna by the reins towards the regal entrance and knocked once on the great marble doors.

The journey was over. We had arrived.

The Journey

I hurried out of the house towards the field, where I knew my loyal mare was waiting. I was already in my riding gear, but I had packed a spare set of jodhpurs and boots just in case. Clutching the saddle and my bag of belongings, I watched as the golden ball in the sky splashed deep into the blue sea around it, and the sky **dawned a sapphire blue**.

A whinny awoke me from my reverie. A horse was standing before me, its hair – **as black as ebony** – rippling in the breeze. "How are you, Luna?" I asked, saddling her. Luna neighed again.

Hoisting myself onto her, I flicked the reins and Luna trotted forward, beginning the long journey south. The wind whistled and swept through the air, and the **crystal-blue sky could not have been any clearer**. Luna cantered onwards. The steady rhythm of my hooves was the same as my heartbeat, which was pounding with excitement and exhilaration. Inhaling deep breaths of fresh air, I could feel the sun beaming down on us.

Suddenly Luna came to an abrupt halt. I could tell at once what had stopped her. Ahead was a rushing river, which was flowing so rapidly foam was spraying near the bank. I tried to console her. "Come on, Luna," I whispered soothingly. "You can do it." After a moment, she reared on her hind legs, and galloped forward. I braced myself, and as we leapt over the river everything seemed to be in slow-motion; one moment we were in the air, and the water was flowing beneath us, then the next we were on firm ground again, still galloping. "Good girl!" I exclaimed, leaning forward to ruffle Luna's mane. Luna whinnied in response.

We continued our journey, pausing only for short rests or meals. We cantered through the countryside, and some parts of the city, but it was only at sunset did I stop and dismount Luna. The sun was slipping behind the horizon, **illuminating the towering fortress** before me. It was immensely tall, and every part of it seemed to radiate royalty and authority. Yet something gave it a touch of mischief as well, though I wasn't quite sure why. I led Luna by the reins towards the regal entrance and knocked once on the great marble doors.

The journey was over. We had arrived.

KEY

RED – similes

GREEN – metaphors

BLUE – personification

ORANGE – alliteration

BOLD – imagery

Analysis

The writer immediately creates a sense of excitement and anticipation after 'hurrying out' of her house and taking extra riding gear 'just in case'. This suspense urges one to keep reading.

In the middle of the passage, alliteration in the 'rushing river', and 'whistling wind', together with the fast-paced cantering 'to her heartbeat' adds drama, pace and urgency. One gets a sense of movement, and rhythm, as if riding the horse yourself.

The scene is set beautifully, with the rider inhaling the 'fresh air', under a 'crystal blue sky', with a 'beaming sun' upon her. This is the perfect set, for the perfect journey, which lifts the mood and raises expectation of a journey that anybody would look forward to.

There is good use of vocabulary and a variety of sentence structure throughout the passage – jodhpurs, mare, mane, reverie, whinny, regal and cantering. Speech breaks up the passage and provides a touch of realism to the subject, adding a personal touch to a rider, familiar with her 'loyal mare', named 'Luna'. Many could relate to one that has a strong, personal connection to their horse, or indeed other pets or animals.

Suspense is created once again, using short sentences in the final paragraph, 'The journey was over. We had arrived.' Again, one is excited to know what happens next.

The choice of a journey by horse is a good choice. It won't be familiar to everybody so should add something new and exciting to the mindset of the examiner. A car, train or plane journey would not necessarily have been a bad choice, but one would have to add something new and unique to entice the reader to keep reading and create an original piece of writing to a common, and sometimes mundane event, that would stand out from other students.

This piece was written during the actual 11+ exam, with a very successful outcome.

DYNAI

FoxBASE+/MAC™

PROGRAMMING

DYNAMICS OF FoxBASE+/MAC™ PROGRAMMING

George F. Goley IV

DOW JONES-IRWIN
Homewood, Illinois 60430

FoxBASE+/MAC™ is a trademark of Fox Software, Inc.

© RICHARD D. IRWIN, INC., 1990

Dow Jones-Irwin is a trademark of Dow Jones & Company, Inc. *All rights reserved.* No part of this publication may be reproduced, stored in a retrieval system, or transmitted, in any form or by any means, electronic, mechanical, photocopying, recording, or otherwise, without the prior written permission of the copyright holder.

This publication is designed to provide accurate and authoritative information in regard to the subject matter covered. It is sold with the understanding that the publisher is not engaged in rendering legal, accounting, or other professional service. If legal advice or other expert assistance is required, the services of a competent professional person should be sought.

From a Declaration of Principles jointly adopted by a Committee of the American Bar Association and a Committee of Publishers.

Sponsoring editor: Susan Glinert Stevens, Ph.D.
Project editor: Karen J. Murphy
Production manager: Ann Cassady
Printer: R.R. Donnelley & Sons Company

Library of Congress Cataloging-in-Publication Data

Goley, George F.
    Dynamics of Foxbase/Mac programming/George F. Goley, IV.
      p.   cm.
    ISBN 1-55623-272-1
    1. Data base management. 2. FoxBASE+ (Computer program)
  I. Title.
QA76.9.D3G653   1990
005.75'65—dc20   89–29682
                                                                    CIP

Printed in the United States of America

1 2 3 4 5 6 7 8 9 0 DO 6 5 4 3 2 1 0 9

DEDICATION

To my wife Patty and my daughter Nessa, whose love and trust make all my work possible. I love you Patty. I love you Nessa.

Table of Contents

1. Introduction 1
    What's required 2

    How to use the book 2

    Manuals are your best friend 3

    Acknowledgements 4

1. Preparing the System 5
    Creating a work place 5

    The first program 12

    Your first dialog box 19

2. Beginning the User Interface 27
    Variables and constants 27

    The user's turn 30

    Full screen editing 34

    A Mac-like exit 37

    Of rows, columns, and pixels 39

    More about pixels 42

    Picture templates 46

    Help for the programmer 49

Effect of pictures on variables 52

3. Taking Control 55

The calculator 55

DO WHILE 57

Priming and endless loops 61

IF...ENDIF 65

Nested IFs 66

The trace window 69

DO CASE...ENDCASE 73

4. Data Types 79

Comparing items 79

Mixing data types 80

The Debug window 84

The STR() function 88

Date math 91

Concatenating strings 92

5. Database Management 95

Definition of terms 95

What is a record pointer? 102

What is an index and why do we need it? 103

Using an index file to make records appear in order 106

Keeping a database in more than one sequence 110

Using the SEEK command to find records quickly 112

Who cares about upper and lower case letters? 115

Using multiple database files simultaneously 116

6. Menus and System Design 121

Event-driven vs. Menu-driven 121

Local vs. activity options 122

Mastering menus 123

Recognizing a menu hit 127

Submenus 128

Arrays vs. Delimited strings in menus 130

Creating and using arrays 132

Fancy menu displays 134

Descriptive menu systems 135

7. System Design 143

More on event-driven applications 143

Creating a main program 145

Modular programs and stubs 148

Watching program execution with trace 149

DOing programs 150

Public and private memory variables 151

Parameter passing 154

The mechanics of lbcenter.prg 158

Notes on creating common subroutines 160

Changing variables with subroutines 161

Looking ahead 167

8. Single File Data Entry 177

The skeleton 178

Generating the data entry items 181

Adding a new item or SEEKing an existing id number 183

Moving forward or back in the file 188

Deleting and recalling records 193

Looking ahead 194

9. FoxForm Automates Screen Creation 195

What took you so long? 195

What does FoxForm do? 195

Using FoxForm 196

Generating a program 200

Using FoxForm-generated programs 202

Pros of using FoxForm 205

Cons of using FoxForm 206

10. Enhanced Data Entry 209

The programs 209

APPENDing records directly 220

The VALID clause 220

Validation loops 226

The pop-up edit 226

Check boxes 228

Radio buttons 228

Scrolling lists 229

Text edit ranges 232

Queries 234

About the BROWSE command 238

Screen layouts 240

Tips for using STYLE 242

Lookups for validation 244

11. Multi-File Data Entry 249

Relationships 249

Correspondence overview 252

Correspondence programs 252

12. Enhanced Multi-file Data Entry 265

13. Reports 277

Preliminaries 277

Every report needs lbrepo.prg 278

The first report 283

Of fonts and layouts 286

The case of SORTing vs. INDEXing 287

The mechanics of SORTing 291

Totals and statistics 292

Processing selected records 293

Let the user choose 294

Subtotals 295

14. Advanced Reporting 299

Using the content of lookup tables 299

All my children (and other relations) 304

Beautiful printouts 307

Single command statistics 310

Subtotals on non-grouped records 312

Multi-column "snaked" reports 315

15. FoxReport 317

Lining up 317

Directly modifying .frx files 317

Table of Contents

Using reports in programs 318

Using memory variables in reports 320

Using IIF() in reports 320

Programs inside reports 322

16. Multiuser 325

General Considerations 325

The easy way out 326

Editing a LOCKed record 329

Editing a record in memory variables 330

Waiting for a lock 332

Multiple record processing 333

Adding records in a multiuser environment 334

Major surgery 336

Temporary work files 337

Table of Figures

Figure 1-01. Installed fox folder. 6

Figure 1-02. New folder in fox folder. 6

Figure 1-03. Book folder in fox folder. 7

Figure 1-04. Initial Command Window. 7

Figure 1-05. Select View Window from Window Menu. 8

Figure 1-06. View Window Miscellaneous Icon. 9

Figure 1-07. SET DEFAULT Dialog Box. 9

Figure 1-08. Result of Set Default Menus. 10

Figure 1-09. Editing config.fx. 11

Figure 1-10. Save config.fx. 12

Figure 1-11. DISPLAY STATUS. 13

Figure 1-12. New program file via menus. 14

Figure 1-13. Save untitled.prg to hello.prg. 15

Figure 1-14. Do hello.prg via menus. 16

Figure 1-15. Results of hello.prg. 16

1. Figure 1-16. Result of flawed hello.prg. 17

1. Figure 1-17. Save hello.prg as.... 20

1. Figure 1-18. Save hello.prg as hello1.prg. 20

1. Figure 1-19. Result of hello1.prg. 22

2. Figure 2-01. Results of hello2.prg. 29

2. Figure 2-02. Start of hello3.prg. 32

2. Figure 2-03. Hello3.prg during entry. 32

2. Figure 2-04. Hello3.prg after entry. 33

2. Figure 2-05. Many gets. 34

2. Figure 2-06. Many gets with continue 39

2. Figure 2-07. Pixel addressing. 41

2. Figure 2-08. Combine overlap scheme. 42

2. Figure 2-09. Better spacing through pixels. 44

2. Figure 2-10. First picture entry. 48

2. Figure 2-11. Help topics. 50

2. Figure 2-12. Selecting help for @...SAY/GET. 51

2. Figure 2-13. Help for picture clauses. 51

Table of Figures

2. Figure 2-14. Pict1.prg variable contents. 53

2. Figure 2-15. Pict2.prg "@R" picture clause. 54

3. Figure 3-01. Dumb calculator. 56

3. Figure 3-02. Continuous calculator. 58

3. Figure 3-03. Count to 100. 61

3. Figure 3-04. Finishable calculator. 63

3. Figure 3-05. Four function calculator. 68

3. Figure 3-06. Edit preference dialog. 70

3. Figure 3-07. Trace from window menu. 71

3. Figure 3-08. Trace window. 71

3. Figure 3-09. Active trace window. 72

3. Figure 3-10. Otherwise command. 76

4. Figure 4-01. Numeric vs. character. 81

4. Figure 4-02. All types of data. 84

4. Figure 4-03. Open trace window. 85

4. Figure 4-04. Open debug window. 85

4. Figure 4-05. Filled debug window. 86

Table of Figures

4. Figure 4-06. Confused data2. 87

4. Figure 4-07. Trace & debug. 87

4. Figure 4-08. Flexible STR() function. 90

4. Figure 4-09. Date math. 93

4. Figure 4-10. Concatenation. 93

5. Figure 5-01. Creating a database. 96

5. Figure 5-02. Client structure. 97

5. Figure 5-03. Simple file entry. 100

5. Figure 5-04. Conceptual presentation of an index. . 103

5. Figure 5-05. Student.dbf. 105

5. Figure 5-06. Student entry. 107

5. Figure 5-07. Indexed student list. 107

5. Figure 5-08. Unindexed student list. 108

5. Figure 5-09. Multiple open files. 119

6. Figure 6-01. First menu selection. 125

6. Figure 6-02. Result of 1st menu selection. 126

6. Figure 6-03. Annotated menu selection. 126

Table of Figures

6. Figure 6-04. Submenus. 130

6. Figure 6-05. Fancy menu options. 136

6. Figure 6-06. Descriptive menu returns. 140

7. Figure 7-01. Menu driven program flow. 143

7. Figure 7-02. Event driven program flow. 144

7. Figure 7-03. Debugging Multiple DO's. 150

7. Figure 7-04. Pubpriv and pubpriv1. 154

7. Figure 7-05. Pubpriv2. 155

7. Figure 7-06. Some centered messages. 158

7. Figure 7-07. Mystery variables. 165

7. Figure 7-08. Mystery variables 2. 166

7. Figure 7-09. Lbq.prg UDF. 169

8. Figure 8-01. Main inventory item screen. 182

8. Figure 8-02. Add inventory item screen. 185

8. Figure 8-03. Second part of add item. 186

8. Figure 8-04. Lookup item by description. 191

9. Figure 9-01. First look at FoxForm. 196

Table of Figures

9. Figure 9-02. Screen setup. 198

9. Figure 9-03. Text entries in FoxForm. 198

9. Figure 9-04. Iv_id in FoxForm. 199

9. Figure 9-05. Lookup field name in FoxForm. 199

9. Figure 9-06. Picture format in FoxForm. 200

9. Figure 9-07. Completed inventr3.scx. 201

9. Figure 9-08. Generate dialog. 201

9. Figure 9-09. File to generate. 202

10. Figure 10-01. Structure for prempl.dbf. 210

10. Figure 10-02. Structure for prproj.dbf. 210

10. Figure 10-03. Data for prproj.dbf. 221

10. Figure 10-04. Standard valid clause. 222

10. Figure 10-05. UDF valid clause message. 224

10. Figure 10-06. Multiple choice valid UDF. 225

10. Figure 10-07. Pop-ups. 227

10. Figure 10-08. GETEXPR at work. 235

10. Figure 10-09. BROWSE expensive employees. 236

10. Figure 10-10. Structure for ivsupp.dbf. 243

11. Figure 11-01. Structures for correspondence. 251

11. Figure 11-02. Sample Correspondence. 263

12. Figure 12-01. Enhanced correspondence screen. .. 266

15. Figure 15-01. Vidrents.frx design on screen. 319

Introduction

Thank you for buying *The Dynamics of FoxBASE+/Mac Programming*. This book is designed to help you write FoxBASE+/Mac programs, thereby harnessing the full power of FoxBASE+/Mac.

FoxBASE+/Mac has been hailed by a variety of trade publications as the fastest, most powerful database management system available for the Macintosh. FoxBASE+/Mac gives the user the ability to write programs that include windows, pull-down menus, text buttons, radio buttons, icons, picture buttons, scrolling lists, pop-up lists, and dialogs in the finest Macintosh tradition.

While the features of FoxBASE+/Mac may be familiar to Macintosh users, the concept of programming may not be so familiar. Indeed, many Mac users bought their Macintosh specifically to avoid programming.

FoxBASE+/Mac is not only powerful, as programming languages go, it's pretty easy to use. So even if you've never written a program, this book can help you start as painlessly as possible.

No matter how well I do my job in this book however, learning to program is going to require a commitment from the reader. This is especially true of those Mac users who avoid typing at all costs.

What can you expect to receive in exchange for this effort? Control of the most powerful database available for the Macintosh. Once in control of this product, there are very few applications beyond the capability of the dedicated FoxBASE+/Mac user.

What's required

If you have enough RAM and disk space to load FoxBASE+/Mac onto your Macintosh, you have enough computer to work with all of the examples in the book. The more RAM you can make available for FoxBASE+/Mac the faster it and the examples in the book will run. Therefore, if you are using Multifinder, provide as much RAM as possible to FoxBASE+/Mac by clicking on the FoxBASE+/MAC icon, and obtaining information from the FILE menu.

Next, make sure that you are using version 2.0 of FoxBASE+/Mac. Also make sure that your version 2.0 is dated after August 22, 1989. To obtain the version number and date of your copy of FoxBASE+/Mac, enter the following command in the command window:

```
? VERS(1)
```

If you don't know what a command window is, or you don't care what version of FoxBASE+/Mac you are using, postpone this investigation until after you have completed Chapter 1.

Throughout most of the book, I will assume that you know how to use the standard Macintosh desktop tools. For example, I will assume that you know how to drag, close, or expand a window on the Macintosh desktop. I will assume that you know how to click and double-click your mouse. Finally, I will assume that you know how to access menus from a pull-down menu system. If you don't have these skills, you have probably not worked with a Macintosh before. Don't worry, the Mac is famous for its ease of use. You will pick up these simple skills quickly.

How to use the book

If you have no programming background, please start with Chapter 1 and work your way through every example in the book. Type in the programs, and experiment with making these sample programs perform a useful task for you. While every chapter in the book will be beneficial to you, you may want to postpone your study of chapters 9, 12, 15, and 16 until you have some experience applying your new-found programming skills to your own applications.

If, like many of us, you would prefer to have all of the programs and databases from the book on diskette, please call Micro Endeavors at (215) 449-4690 to order a program disk. The disk costs $19.95 (Pennsylvania residents add 6% Sales Tax) and includes all of the programs, databases, indexes, forms, and screen files referenced in the book.

If you are a PC-DOS programmer familiar with FoxBASE+ or dBASE, you will want to pay special attention to chapters 6, 7, 10, 12, and 13 as these chapters emphasize FoxBASE+/Mac-specific features including fonts, event-driven programming, printing, PIXEL addressing, and others.

If you are a Macintosh programmer who is familiar with other Macintosh database management systems, you will want to move quickly through chapters 1 through 5, before concentrating on system design and real-world programming in chapters 6 through 15. If you intend to make use of FoxBASE+/Mac's screen and report generators, pay special attention to chapters 9 and 15.

Manuals are your best friend

The manuals that Fox Software includes with FoxBASE+/Mac are invaluable reference aids, and this book does not replace them. Indeed, I strongly suggest that you keep your FoxBASE+/Mac manuals close by while you enter the sample programs, and especially when you begin to experiment with your own versions of the examples. In short, consider your FoxBASE+/Mac manuals as reference tools, and consider this book a tutorial guide to programming FoxBASE+/Mac.

Acknowledgements

Many people helped make this book a success. I am especially grateful to the following people:

Lawrence R. Jones, who spent many painstaking hours assembling, scaling, and placing the 100+ screen shots that populate this work. Without Larry's help, this would be a much less visual book. Thanks Larry.

Edward J. Martini, who found a way to keep Micro Endeavors moving smoothly along while I disappeared into my writer's garret to produce this book. Ed was also responsible for acquiring all of the Macintosh and PC hardware required to write the book. Finally, he took the time to review the rough drafts, an act which in itself takes courage. Thanks Ed.

Susan Glinert Stevens, my editor, who provided patience, typesetting expertise, and a much-appreciated critical eye when I needed a reality check. Thanks Susan.

Janet Walker, Beverly Grafton, James Weiner, and Randy Selhorst, all of Fox Software, who provided invaluable insights into the needs of the typical FoxBASE+/Mac user. In addition, Randy and Bev in particular fielded an inordinate number of support calls from me, without a whimper. Finally, Bev devoted at least one holiday weekend to a review of an early draft of the book, and returned with a wealth of useful ideas, including the inclusion of the chapter on multiuser programming. Thanks folks.

1. Preparing the System

For the duration of our discussions, I will assume that you have followed the instructions in your FoxBASE+/Mac User's Guide to install FoxBASE+/Mac in a folder named "FOX" on your Mac's hard disk. If you have installed FoxBASE+/Mac in a folder other than FOX, you will need to adjust the commands that reference the FOX folder accordingly.

Further, the system on which the examples for this book were written, identifies its hard disk as "HD40:". If your Mac has a different name for its hard disk, and it probably will, remember to substitute your hard disk name for "HD40:" wherever it appears in the text.

Creating a work place

If you have followed the suggestions in the User's Guide, you should have a folder that looks something like Figure 1-1. Now, let's create a folder to hold the examples in the rest of the book. Use the New Folder option shown in Figure 1-2 to create an empty folder. Finally, change the name of the empty folder to "BOOK". The result is shown in Figure 1-3.

To run FoxBASE+/Mac, double-click on the FoxBASE icon. Unless you have already created a config.fx file that supercedes the default settings in FoxBASE+/Mac, you should now be presented with the command window as displayed in Figure 1-4.

Now we need to tell FoxBASE+/Mac to put the results of any programming or database management operations in the "HD40:FOX:BOOK:" folder. The following command will accomplish this goal nicely when we type it into the command window, and press [Return].

```
SET DEFAULT TO "HD40:FOX:BOOK:"
```

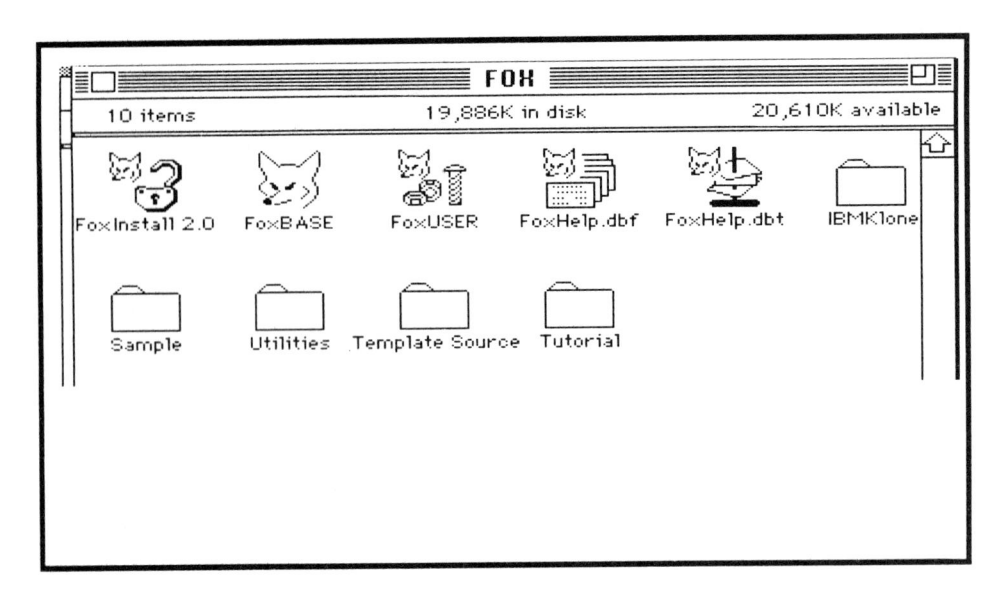

Figure 1-01. Installed fox folder.

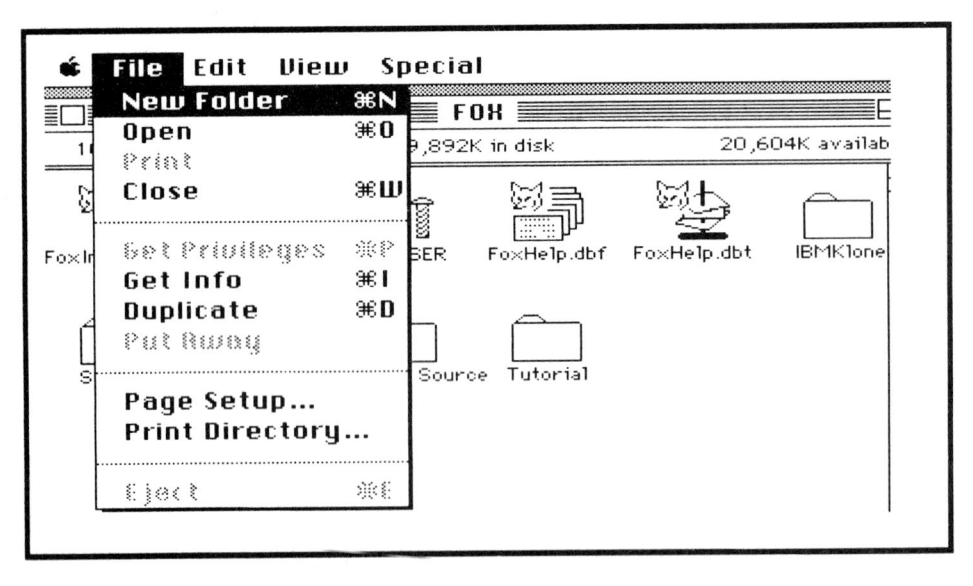

Figure 1-02. New folder in fox folder.

Chapter 1: Preparing the System

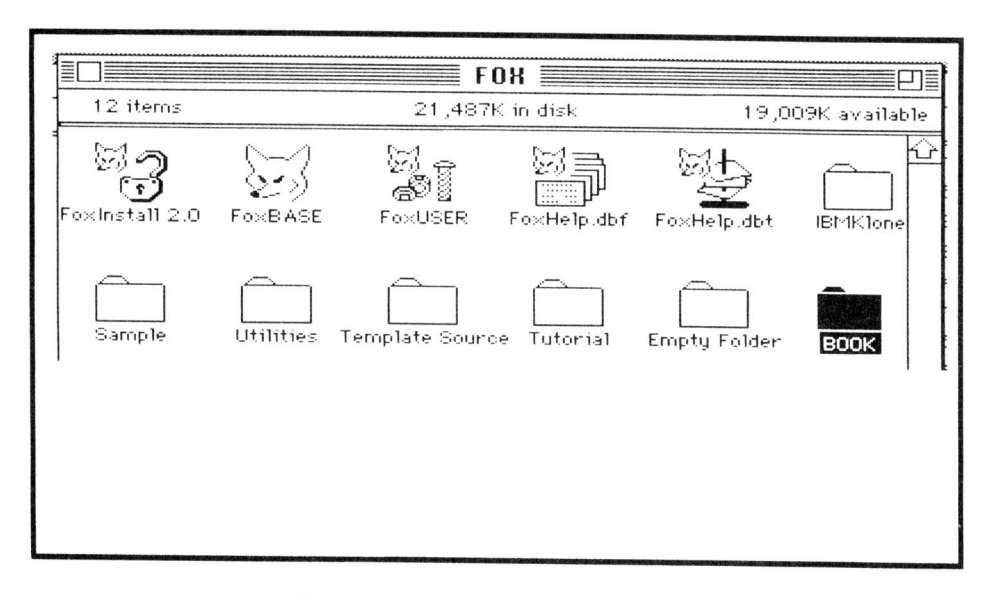

Figure 1-03. Book folder in fox folder.

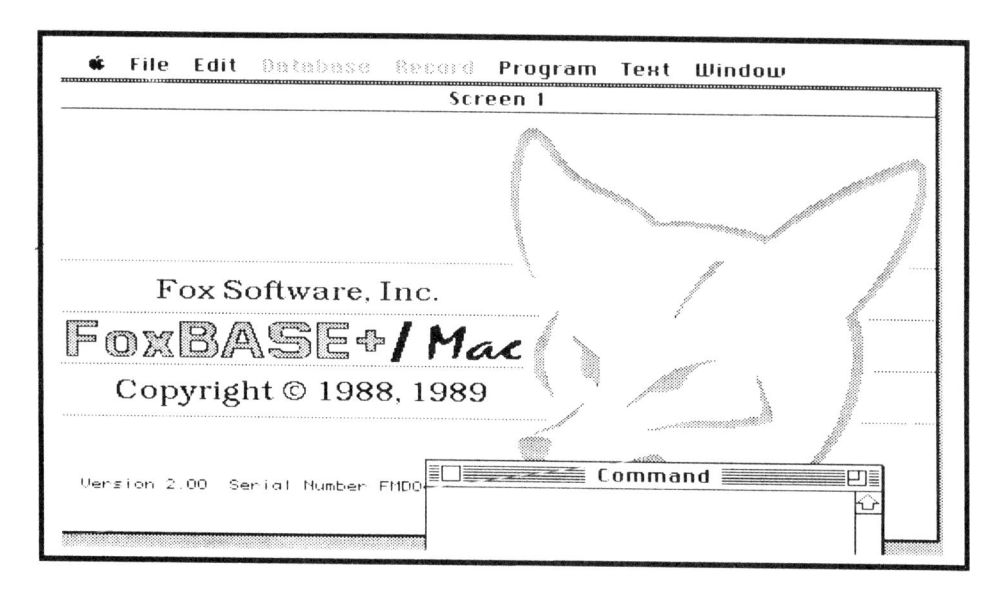

Figure 1-04. Initial Command Window.

Creating a work place

Alternatively, you could select the View window from the Window menu, click on the Misc icon, click on the Default check box, and select the "HD40:FOX:BOOK:" folder in a dialog box. All of this activity is depicted in Figures 1-5 through 1-8. Note that all of this clicking results in the insertion of the aforementioned command into the command window.

Most menu options can be reproduced by typing commands directly into the command window.

The use of the command window or the menu system is a matter of personal preference. As a programmer, I usually find it faster to type the command I need than to mouse through a series of menus. As a result, many of the examples in this book make use of the command window rather than FoxBASE+/Mac's menu system. Since the menu system produces commands, and issues those commands through the command

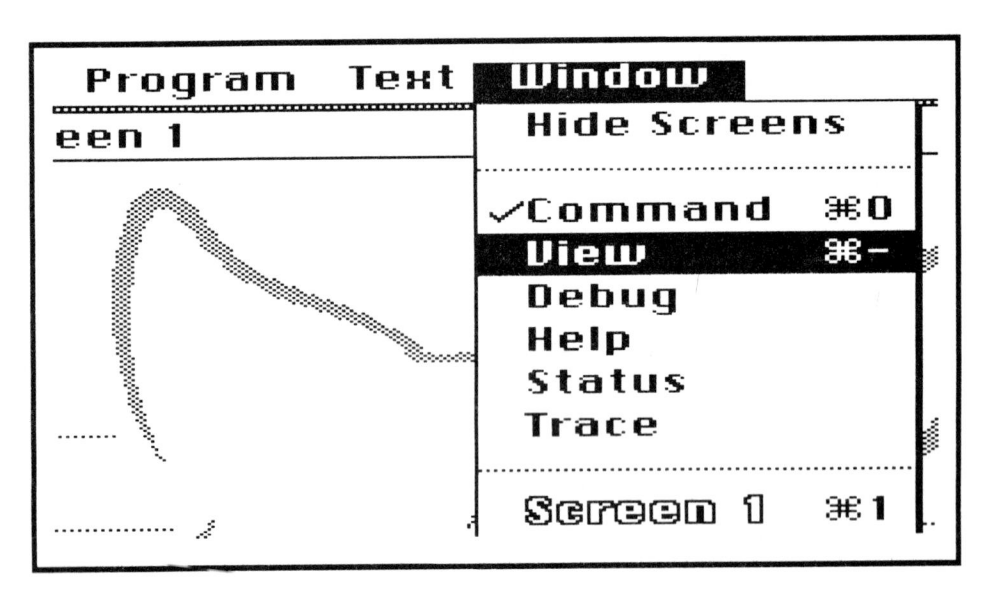

Figure 1-05. Select View Window from Window Menu.

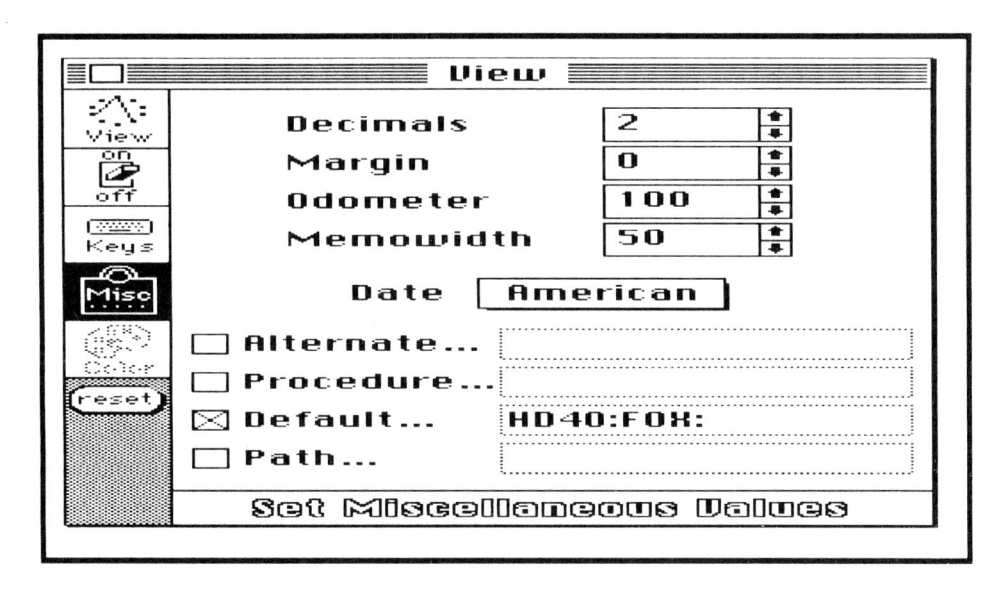

Figure 1-06. View Window Miscellaneous Icon.

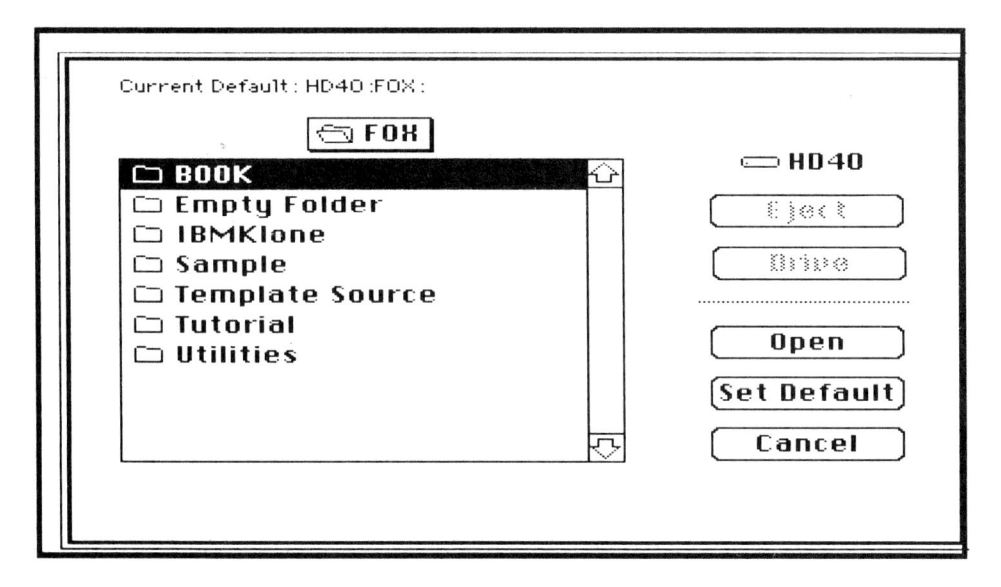

Figure 1-07. SET DEFAULT Dialog Box.

Creating a work place

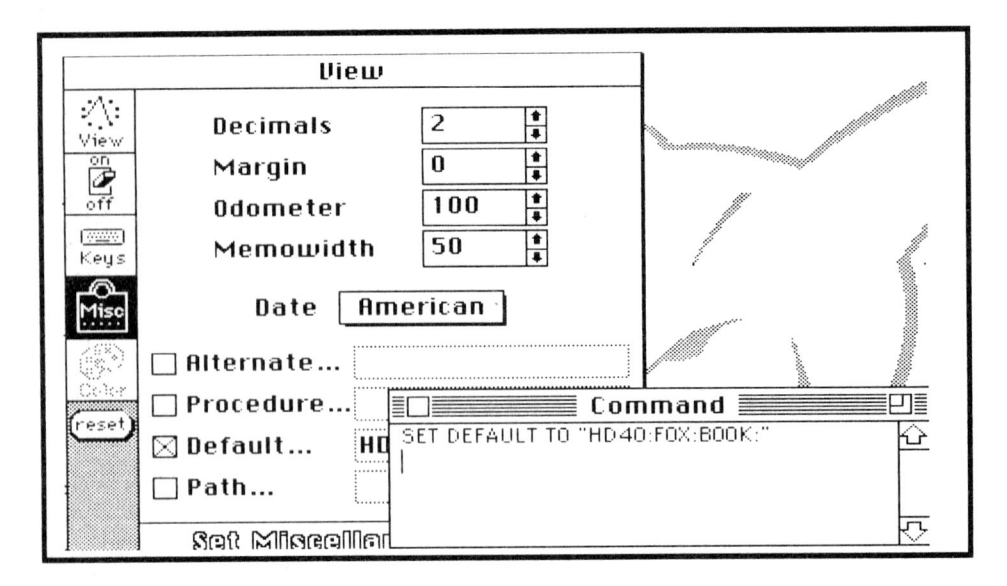

Figure 1-08. Result of Set Default Menus.

window, feel free to use the menu system whenever you like.

The keyboard shortcut for the command window is [Command]+0.

Whatever method you prefer to SET the DEFAULT folder in FoxBASE+/Mac, you can automate this function by the use of the config.fx file. As we investigate the features of the config.fx file, we will also begin the more important job of learning to use the FoxBASE+/Mac editor.

Issue the following command in the command window, and press [Return]:

`MODIFY FILE config.fx`

This will present you with a rather plain screen like the one in Figure 1-9. You can consult your FoxBASE+/Mac manual for full instructions on the use of the editor, but for now, please enter the following text:

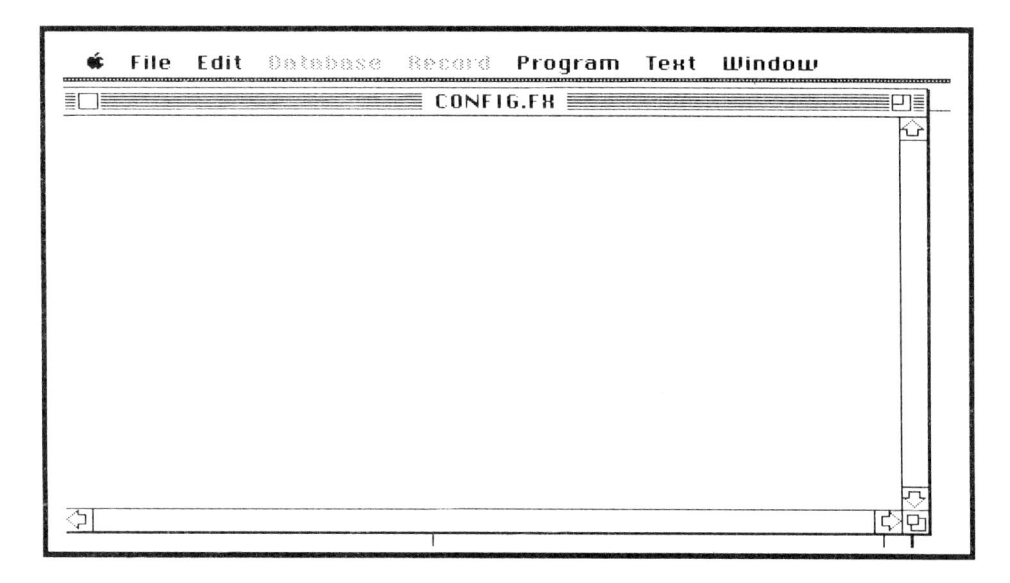

Figure 1-09. Editing config.fx.

```
DEFAULT = HD40:FOX:CONFIG.FX
TALK = OFF
STRICT = ON
```

Now, pull down the FILE menu, and choose the SAVE option, as I have done in Figure 1-10. Next, click the open box in the upper left corner of the window displaying the CONFIG.FX file. This will take you back to the command window. If you are not presented with the command window, press [Command]+0 to access the command window. Finally, issue the following command, and press [Return]:

```
QUIT
```

Make sure that all of your FoxBASE+/Mac sessions end with a QUIT command!

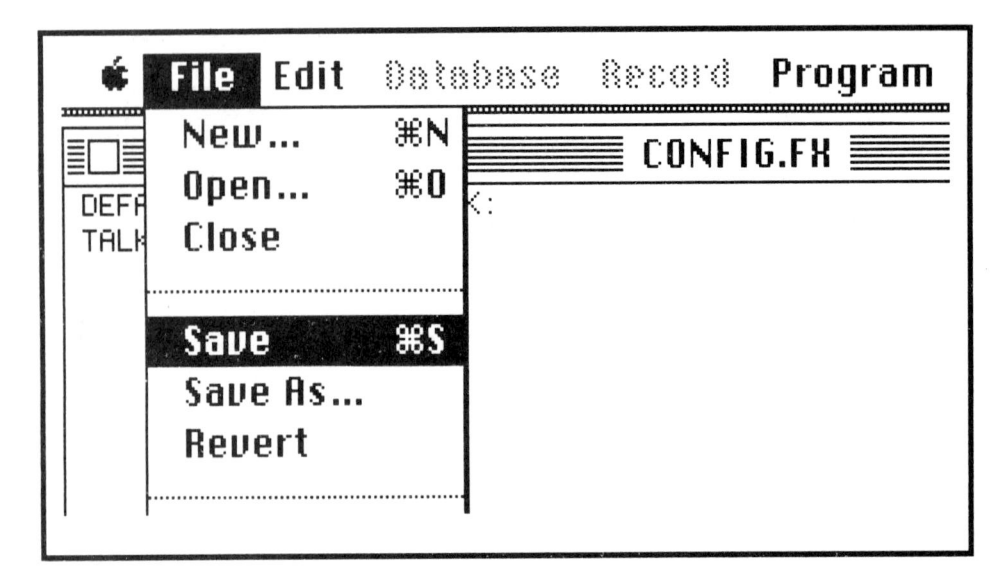

Figure 1-10. Save config.fx.

The first program

As you might expect, this will end your FoxBASE+/Mac session. To re-enter FoxBASE+/Mac, and begin programming, double-click on the book folder in the Fox folder. Because config.fx was created with FoxBASE+/Mac, FoxBASE+/Mac will be activated when you double-click on the config.fx document icon. To see if our efforts to make the HD40:FOX:BOOK: folder the default folder were successful, issue the following command in the command window:

DISPLAY STATUS

Your screen will include information similar to that found in Figure 1-11. Note that the Default disk drive: is HD40:FOX:BOOK: as we hoped. Note also that FoxBASE+/Mac is Waiting as evidenced by the message in the upper right corner of the screen. To continue, press the space bar.

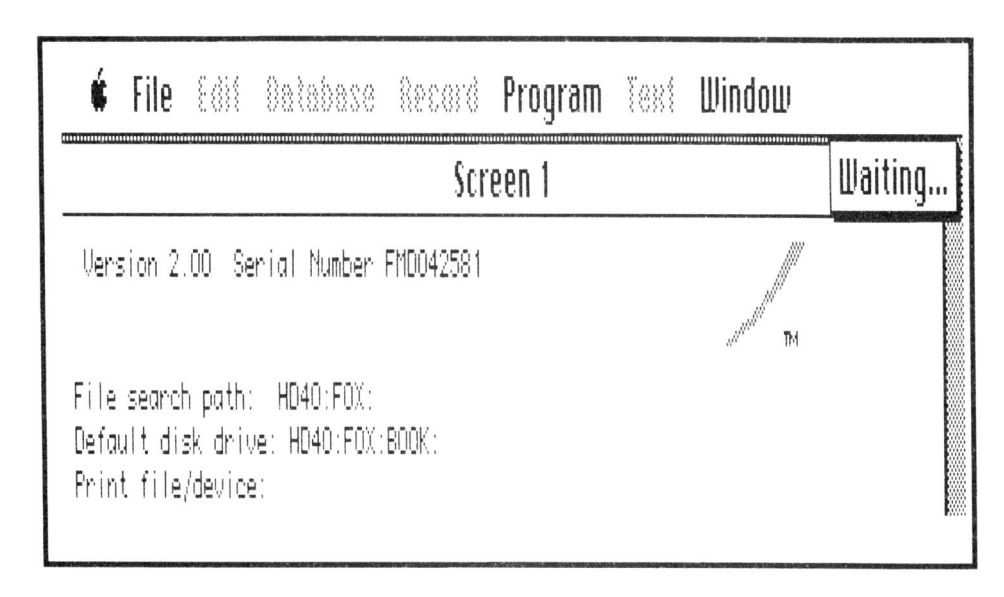

```
┌─────────────────────────────────────────────────────────┐
│  🍎 File  Edit  Database  Record  Program  Text  Window │
├─────────────────────────────────────────────────────────┤
│ ▓▓▓▓▓▓▓▓▓▓▓▓▓▓▓▓▓▓▓▓▓ Screen 1 ▓▓▓▓▓▓▓▓▓▓▓▓│ Waiting...│
├─────────────────────────────────────────────┴───────────┤
│                                                         │
│  Version 2.00  Serial Number FMD042581                  │
│                                                         │
│                                                     ™   │
│                                                         │
│  File search path:  HD40:FOX:                           │
│  Default disk drive: HD40:FOX:BOOK:                     │
│  Print file/device:                                     │
│                                                         │
└─────────────────────────────────────────────────────────┘
```

Figure 1-11. DISPLAY STATUS.

Now let's use the menus to create our first program file. Pull down the File menu, select the New option, and click on the Program radio button, as I have done in Figure 1-12. After you click OK, you will be presented with a screen similar to Figure 1-9, except that the program will be called Untitled.prg. All FoxBASE+/Mac program file names end in .prg. Note that you can resize the window and change the size, font, and style of the text in the program via the Text and Window menus.

Now let's write our first program. Please enter the following program statements in the Untitled.prg file:

```
* hello.prg
* first attempt at a simple dialog box
* Bring Screen 1 to the top of the
* desktop, and give it a heading
SCREEN 1 TOP HEADING "First Program"
CLEAR       && make the screen blank
* Now put the note on the screen
ALERT NOTE 1 "HELLO!"
RETURN      && return control to calling program
```

The first program

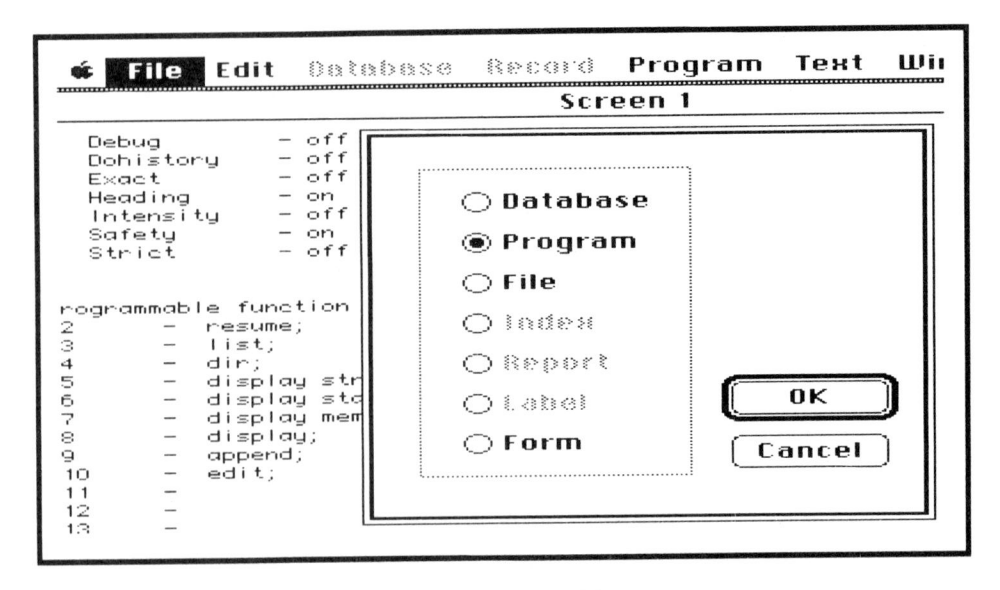

Figure 1-12. New program file via menus.

```
* EOF hello.prg
```

In case you did not heed my earlier advice to consult the manual regarding the FoxBASE+/Mac text editor, I will spend a paragraph hi-lighting some of the editor's features. You can cut and paste using [Command]+C to copy, [Command]+V to paste, and [Command]+X to cut selected text. You can change the font style and size of the text editor's window by pulling down the TEXT menu bar. You can move, resize, select, and close edit windows in standard Macintosh fashion. You can open multiple edit windows, and cut and paste between them. You can undo your last editing action by pressing [Command]+Z. You can find text by pressing [Command]+F. You can find more information about the editor by reviewing Chapter 4 of your FoxBASE+/Mac User's Guide.

When you try to save this Untitled.prg file, you will be presented with a dialog box like the one in Figure 1-13. Double-click on the BOOK folder, name your program hello.prg, and then save it. To run the program, pull down the Program menu, and select the Do hello.prg option as I have

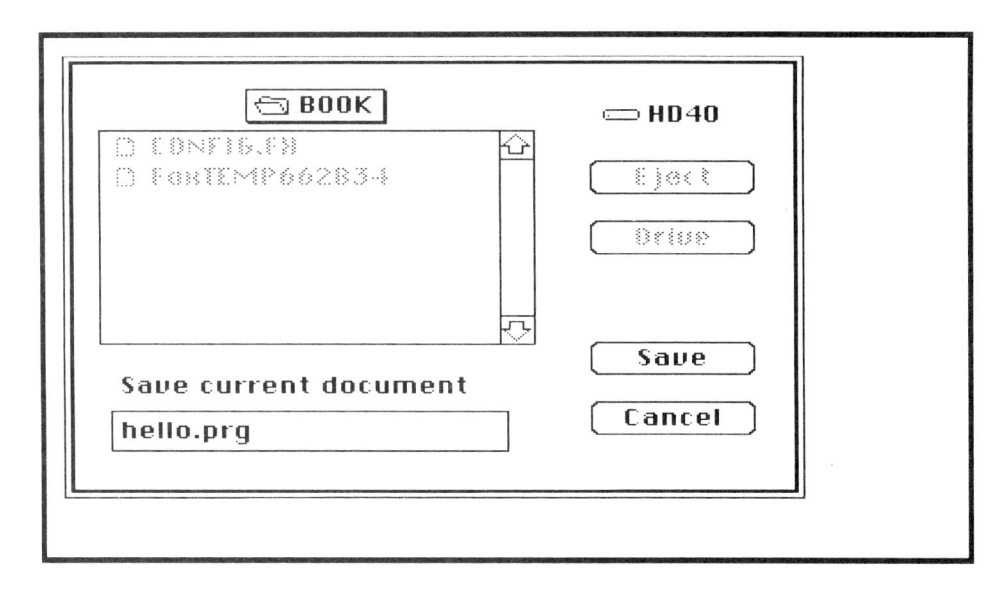

Figure 1-13. Save untitled.prg to hello.prg.

done in Figure 1-14. DOing hello should result in a screen that looks like Figure 1-15. Click on Continue, and you will be presented with a blank screen.

Note that when you elect to DO hello, FoxBASE+/Mac flashes a dialog on the screen while it compiles your program. This intermediate step is performed whenever a new program is run, or whenever an old program that has been changed since its last execution is run. Compilation will not take place when you subsequently DO hello, unless you have changed the program. Since compilation is fast and automatic, we have little interest in its operation at this point. So, let's return to hello.prg.

If you have made an error in typing the program, you will be presented with a screen that looks like Figure 1-16. This is FoxBASE+/Mac's signal that there is an error in the program. To correct the error, click on CANCEL, and recheck your typing. To assist you in correcting the program, FoxBASE+/Mac re-enters the hello.prg file and highlights the offending line of code. When the code is corrected, Do hello.prg again.

The first program

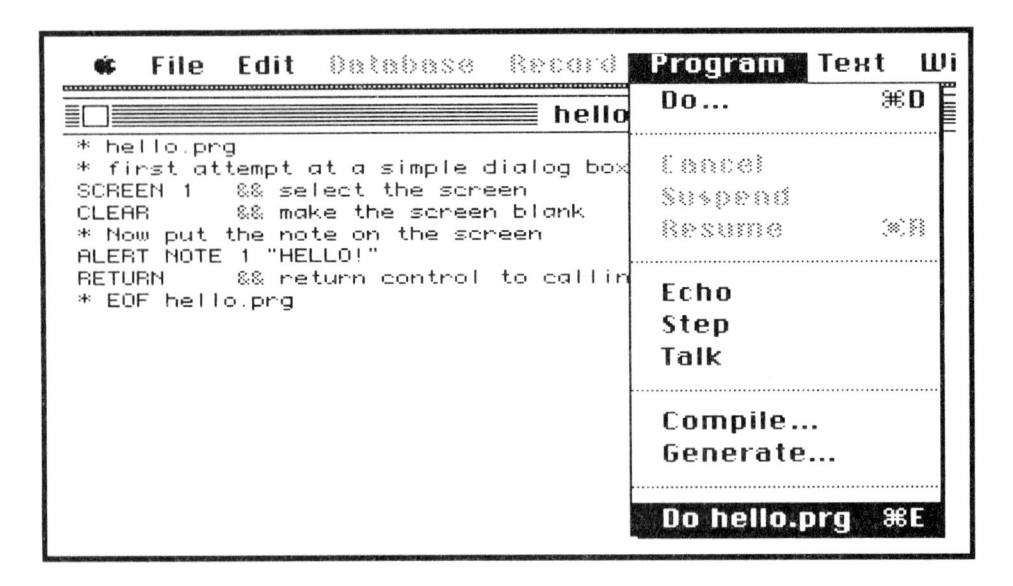

Figure 1-14. Do hello.prg via menus.

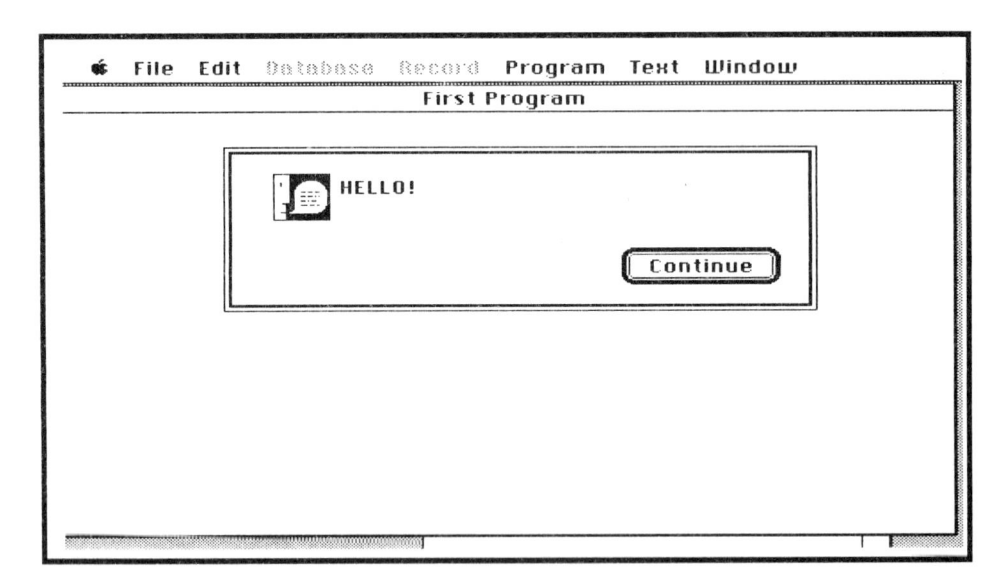

Figure 1-15. Results of hello.prg.

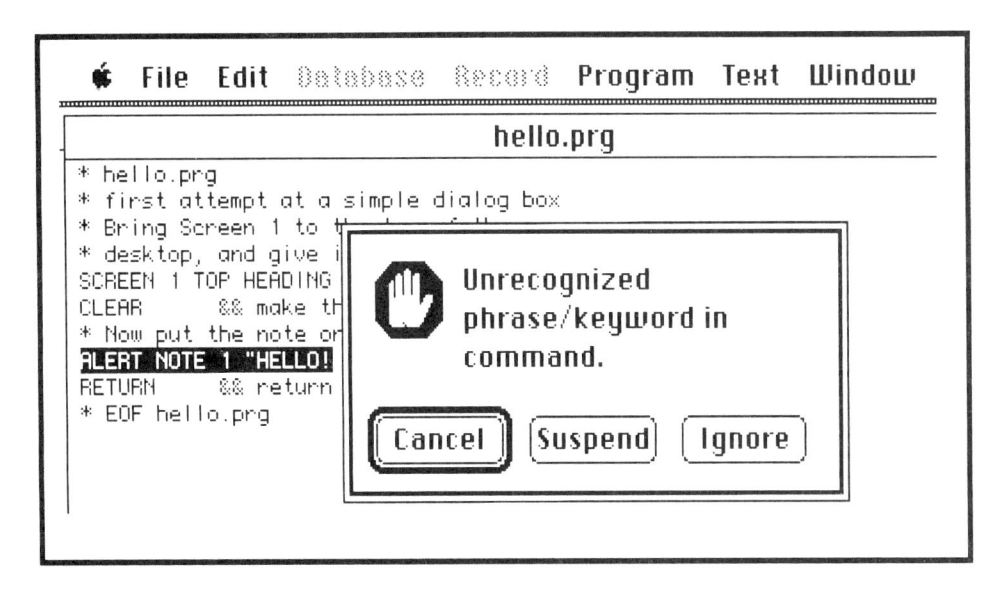

Figure 1-16. Result of flawed hello.prg.

Congratulations! You have written your first FoxBASE+/Mac program. Now let's see what you did!

The first four lines of the program are preceded with an asterisk (*). This identifies these lines as comments rather than instructions. FoxBASE+/Mac also treats any text that follows the double ampersand (&&) as a comment. FoxBASE+/Mac will ignore these comments when running the program. Well, if FoxBASE+/Mac ignores the comments, why include them?

Comments are included in program files for the benefit of the original programmer, and any programmers who might subsequently work on the program. Essentially, comments describe program instructions when those instructions might not be clear at a glance. In addition, some comments are always included in a program, no matter how clear the program instructions.

At Micro Endeavors, we always include the name of the program, a one-line description of the program, the name of the programmer, the date of creation, and the date of last update as comments at the beginning of the program. Also, an "* EOF program.prg" comment is included at the end of each program. There are other circumstances that always require comments, but we will leave a discussion of those circumstances for later, and move on to the rest of the hello.prg program.

FoxBASE+/Mac offers the programmer up to 9 screens in which to present or receive information to or from the user. The following command makes screen 1 the active screen, brings screen 1 to the top of the desktop, and gives it a heading:

`SCREEN 1 TOP HEADING "First Program"`

The command CLEAR removes any text from Screen 1. The CLEAR command operates on the currently active screen as selected by the SCREEN command.

The ALERT command takes a variety of arguments to produce dialog boxes that include icons, multiple user responses, and optional programmer controlled placement on the screen. With all its flexibility however, the ALERT command is still limited compared with the dialog boxes you can create for yourself, so this is the last time we will use the ALERT command. If you like, you can check your FoxBASE+/Mac manual for details on the use of the ALERT command.

The last instruction in hello.prg is RETURN. As we will see in detail in Chapter 7, the RETURN statement allows program control to return to the calling program. In this case, there is no calling program, we have interactively directed FoxBASE+/Mac to DO the hello.prg program. Therefore, control returns to the command window. To regain access to the hello.prg program, we can use the Window menu, and scroll to the last option to select the window in which the hello.prg program currently resides, or we can issue the following command from the command window:

```
MODI COMM hello
```

Note that MODI COMM is an abbreviation for MODIFY COMMAND. Since FoxBASE+/Mac allows us to abbreviate command words to the first four characters of the command, we will frequently use these abbreviations to reduce typing. Also, we have not included the .prg extension to the hello.prg file name. FoxBASE+/Mac adds .prg to the file name by default when using the MODIFY COMMAND and DO commands.

Finally, I have shown all FoxBASE+/Mac commands in upper case. FoxBASE+/Mac does not distinguish between upper and lower case letters in command words. However, I will continue to show commands in upper case to help you distinguish command words from other kinds of programming constructs.

FoxBASE+/Mac does not distinguish between upper and lower case command words.

Your first dialog box

Before moving on to the next chapter, let's make a somewhat less elegant, but much more flexible, dialog box. You should be editing the hello.prg file. Let's make a copy of hello.prg, and call it hello1.prg. To do so, select the Save As... option of the file menu as I have done in Figure 1-17. Then, name the new file hello1.prg as I have done in Figure 1-18. We will be doing a great deal of this copying throughout the rest of the book not only to save you time typing, but also to help you see how new concepts build on existing ideas.

Change your new hello1.prg program to read as follows:

```
* hello1.prg
* Our own dialog box!
* Bring Screen 1 to the top of the
* desktop, and give it a heading
SCREEN 1 TOP HEADING "First Program"
```

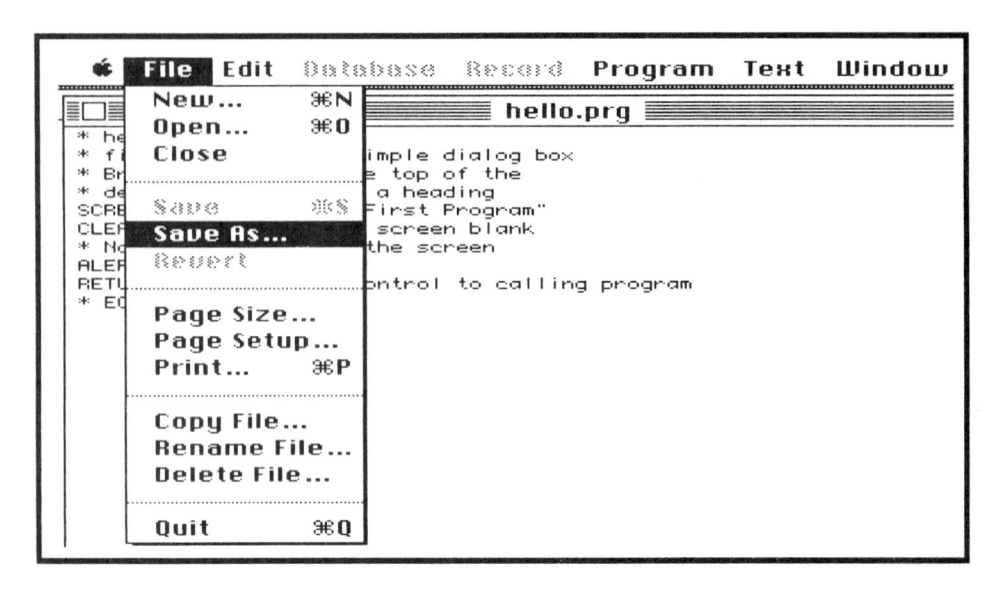

Figure 1-17. Save hello.prg as...

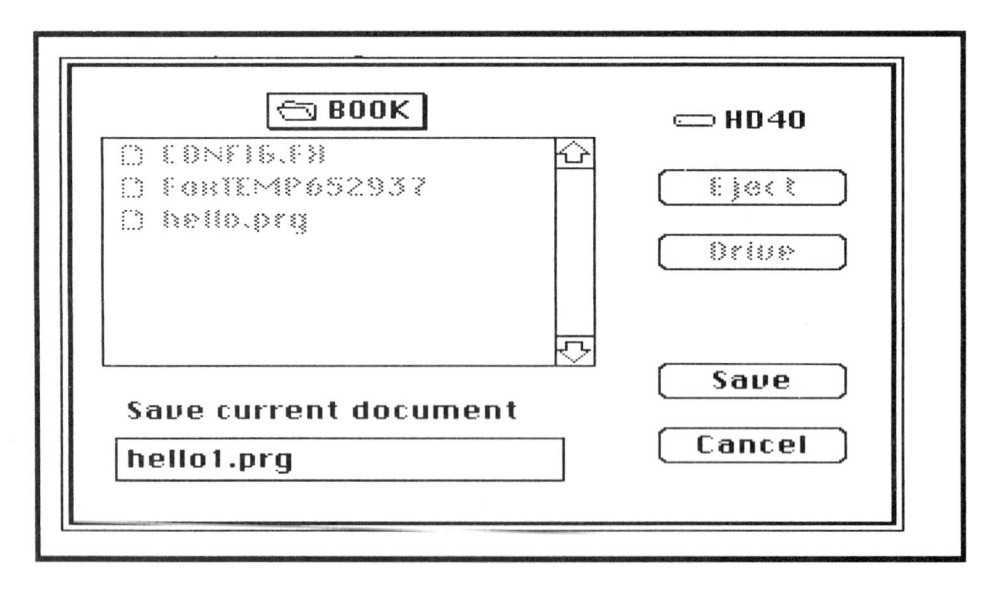

Figure 1-18. Save hello.prg as hello1.prg.

Chapter 1: Preparing the System

```
CLEAR         && make the screen blank
* Define screen number 2 as TYPE 1,
*         centered on the screen,
*         6 rows high by 40 columns wide,
*         with text displayed in 12 point Chicago FONT
SCREEN 2 TYPE 1 AT 0,0 SIZE 6,40 FONT "CHICAGO",12
CLEAR         && make screen 2 blank
SCREEN 2 TOP FIXED   && bring screen 2 to the top of the desktop
* Put a small picture of a fox in the box
@ 0,0 SAY 1 PICTURE "@* \P503" SIZE 5,5
* Put our message in the middle of the screen
@ 2,15 say "Hello!"
STORE 0 TO dummy
* Use the dummy variable to display a text button
@ 4,30 GET dummy PICTURE "@*v CONTINUE"
* Wait for the user to click on "CONTINUE"
READ
SCREEN 2 OFF  && remove our screen from the desktop
RETURN        && return control to calling program
* EOF hello1.prg
```

When you have made your changes, press [Command]+E. This will prompt you to save your changes, prior to compiling, and running your program. If you have created hello1.prg correctly, you will be presented with a screen like the one in Figure 1-19. Click on CONTINUE, and you will once again be presented with a blank screen 1.

Now let's review the hello1.prg program. The first six lines of hello1.prg are similar to the first six lines of hello.prg. After that however, things get interesting. FoxBASE+/Mac allows the programmer to use up to 9 screens onto which he can place and information for, and receive information from, the user. (Note: the number of screens that can actually be active simultaneously is limited by the amount of RAM available in your MAC.) As you might expect, the SCREEN command is the primary method of defining and using multiple screens in FoxBASE+/Mac.

In our example the following command creates a screen which we will use as a dialog box:

```
SCREEN 2 TYPE 1 AT 0,0 SIZE 6,40 FONT "CHICAGO",12
```

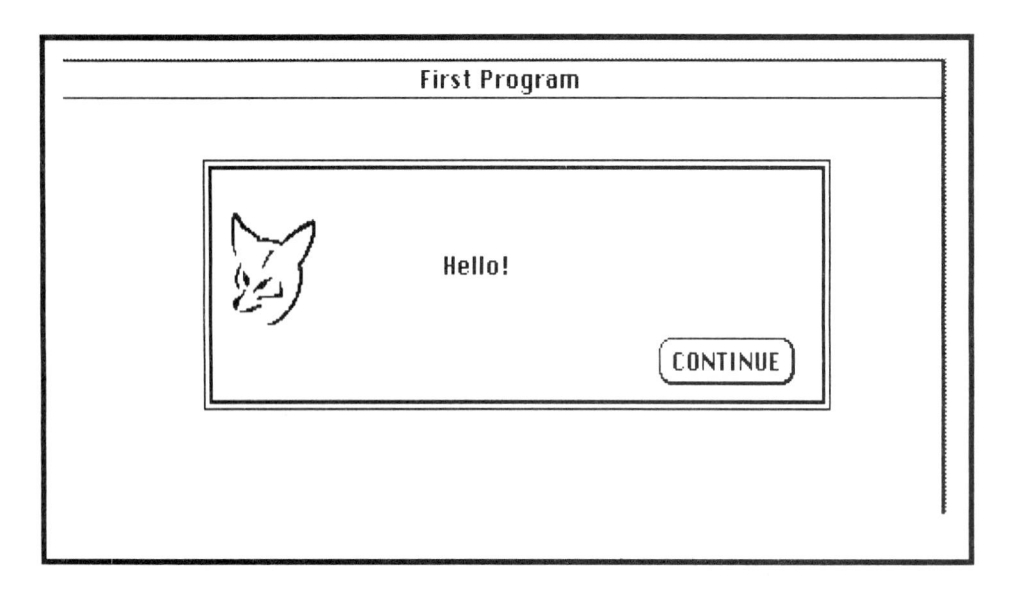

Figure 1-19. Result of hello1.prg.

This command defines screen 2 as TYPE 1. A FoxBASE+/Mac screen type 1 has no heading, no scroll bars, no zoom or close boxes, cannot be moved by the user, and cannot be resized by the user. As you can see, screen type 1 does a fairly complete job of forcing the user to respond to the programmer's dialog.

The AT clause of the SCREEN command allows the programmer to position his screen relative to the entire screen. The coordinates 0,0 are special however, and result in the automatic centering of the SCREEN.

The SIZE clause as used here defines the screen as 6 rows of 40 columns. A row is defined as the height of one character in the default type font and size, while a column is defined as the width of one character in the current default type font and size. We will talk further about rows and columns vs. pixels in the next chapter.

Finally, the clause FONT "CHICAGO",12 tells FoxBASE+/Mac that any text output to this screen should be displayed in 12 point CHICAGO, unless another type size or font is specifically chosen for a given text item.

There are several other clauses available in the screen command to affect headers, colors, etc., and we will encounter those later in the book. For now, let's see what else we did to create our own dialog box.

Note that we did not include a TOP clause in our first SCREEN 2 command. This is because we want to have a chance to erase the screen first, before showing it to the user. SCREENs can be used and reused, and the programmer must remember that the result of prior activity may still be present on any given screen. Therefore, we CLEAR screen 2 prior to placing it on top of the desktop.

When we do place screen 2 on top of the desktop, we include a new clause in the screen command, the FIXED clause. The FIXED clause prevents the user from clicking on another window or pulling down a menu. Since screen TYPE 1 prevents the user from manipulating the dialog window, and the FIXED clause prevents the user from manipulating any menus or other windows, the combination of screen type 1 and the FIXED clause does an effective job of forcing the user to respond to the programmer's dialog.

The @...SAY/GET commands are the most commonly used commands in FoxBASE+/Mac programming. Unfortunately, our first @...SAY command is slightly esoteric, so we won't go into great detail in describing its function. Suffice to say that this command puts a picture of a fox in our dialog box. You can substitute your own MacPaint or PICT file pictures if you like, but you will have to wait for Chapter 9 for the details.

The following command is more illustrative of most FoxBASE+/Mac @...SAY commands:

```
@ 2,15 SAY "Hello!"
```

This command directs FoxBASE+/Mac to place the word "Hello!" on row 2 of the current screen, starting with column 15. This variety of the

---

Your first dialog box

@...SAY command is the primary method of presenting information to the user. As we will see in the next chapter, there are many additional arguments that can be added to the @...SAY command to affect the positioning, content, color, font, and typographical style of the programmer's message.

The following command places a text button on the screen:

```
@ 4,30 GET dummy PICTURE "@*v CONTINUE"
```

However, the program will not wait for the user to take an action until the following command is issued two lines later:

```
READ
```

In many ways, the @...GET command is similar to the @...SAY command. However, while @...SAY only presents information to the user, @...GET accepts information from the user. In fact, the @...GET command is the primary method of accepting input from the user. In this case, we have restricted the user to clicking on the CONTINUE button, but the @...GET command is capable of much more, as we will see in subsequent chapters.

GETs are activated by the READ command.

Of particular importance however, is the idea that the READ command is required to activate the @...GET command. In other words, an @...GET command is like a firecracker, possessed of all the powder, chemicals, and packaging required to explode into brilliant action. But a firecracker can only explode when its fuse is lit, and an @...GET command can only accept information from the user when its fuse is lit by the READ command. We will explore the interdependence of these two commands more fully in the next chapter. Now however, let's finish our discussion of hello1.prg.

The following command removes screen 2 from the desktop, but does not change its definition, or its content:

```
SCREEN 2 OFF
```

When we want to use this dialog box again, we do not need to redefine the screen. Rather, we will be able to simply bring the screen to the top of the desktop and redisplay our messages and query our user. To completely remove screen 2 from memory, we would issue the following command:

```
SCREEN 2 DELETE
```

Finally, we end our hello1.prg program, as we did our hello.prg program, with a RETURN statement.

If you are new to programming, or new to FoxBASE+/Mac, or both, please take this opportunity to quit from FoxBASE+/Mac (type QUIT in the command window), and put this book down for a while. We have covered a great deal of ground in this first chapter, and your comprehension will be aided by an intermission. In fact, many readers find it helpful to read and review one chapter per day.

Whatever strategy you employ, we have reached the end of chapter At this point, you should be able to:

- Enter and exit FoxBASE+/Mac.

- Create and modify program files using menus or command window commands.

You should also understand the following commands:

```
CLEAR
SCREEN 1 TOP
RETURN
SCREEN 2 TYPE 1 AT 0,0 SIZE 6,40 FONT "CHICAGO",12
@ 2,15 SAY "Hello!"
```

Your first dialog box

If you don't understand any of these commands, please review this chapter before going on.

2. Beginning the User Interface

In the last chapter, we learned how to use the FoxBASE+/Mac editor to create programs, and we even devised a simple dialog box for our user. In this chapter, we will expand that dialog box slightly, and then move on to the design and implementation of a simple data entry screen.

Our primary goal will be to gather and validate data from the user. Along the way, we will investigate some of the variations of the @...SAY/GET and READ commands to create a Mac-like interface for our data entry screens.

Variables and constants

If you have QUIT from FoxBASE+/Mac, please re-enter the program by clicking on the config.fx file in the book folder. Our first program of this chapter will build on the hello1.prg program, so our first step will be to edit the hello1.prg file. This can be accomplished with the following command:

```
MODI COMM hello1
```

Now, as we did when we created hello1.prg, we will save this program as hello2.prg by using the SAVE AS... option of the file menu. (See Figure 1-17 if you need help.) Now make the changes necessary to produce the following program:

```
* hello2.prg
* Our own dialog box!
* Bring Screen 1 to the top of the
* desktop, and give it a heading
SCREEN 1 TOP HEADING "First Program"
CLEAR      && make the screen blank
* Define screen number 2 as TYPE 1,
*        centered on the screen,
```

```
*               6 rows high by 40 columns wide,
*               with text displayed in 12 point Chicago FONT
SCREEN 2 TYPE 1 AT 0,0 SIZE 6,40 FONT "CHICAGO",12
CLEAR          && make screen 2 blank
SCREEN 2 TOP FIXED  && bring screen 2 to the top of the desktop
* Put a small picture of a fox in the box
@ 0,0 SAY 1 PICTURE "@* \P503" SIZE 5,5
* Assign a value to the whoisit variable
STORE "George" TO whoisit
* Put our message in the middle of the screen
@ 2,15 SAY "Hello:"
@ 2,22 SAY
whoisit
STORE 0 TO dummy
* Use the dummy variable to display a text button
@ 4,30 GET dummy PICTURE "@*v CONTINUE"
* Wait for the user to click on "CONTINUE"
READ
SCREEN 2 OFF  && remove our screen from the desktop
RETURN        && return control to calling program
* EOF hello2.prg
```

When you have made your changes, press [Command]+E to save, compile, and run hello2.prg. The program should produce a screen like the one in Figure 2-01. Note that the word "George" is displayed on the screen next to the word "Hello." Let's see why.

All of the changes of interest in this program take place between lines 13 and 16. Note the use of the STORE command. This is one of several FoxBASE+/Mac commands that can assign a value to a variable. The other interesting line is as follows:

```
@ 2,22 SAY whoisit
```

This line is interesting because the word "whoisit" does not appear on the screen. Instead, the word "George" appears on the screen. If we wanted the word "whoisit" to appear on the screen, we would have placed quotations around whoisit. Because there are no quotes around whoisit however, FoxBASE+/Mac knows that the programmer wants to display the content of the variable named whoisit.

```
┌─────────────────────────────────────────────┐
│                First Program                │
├─────────────────────────────────────────────┤
│  ┌───────────────────────────────────────┐  │
│  │                                       │  │
│  │   [fox]     Hello:   George           │  │
│  │                                       │  │
│  │                       ( CONTINUE )    │  │
│  └───────────────────────────────────────┘  │
│                                             │
└─────────────────────────────────────────────┘
```

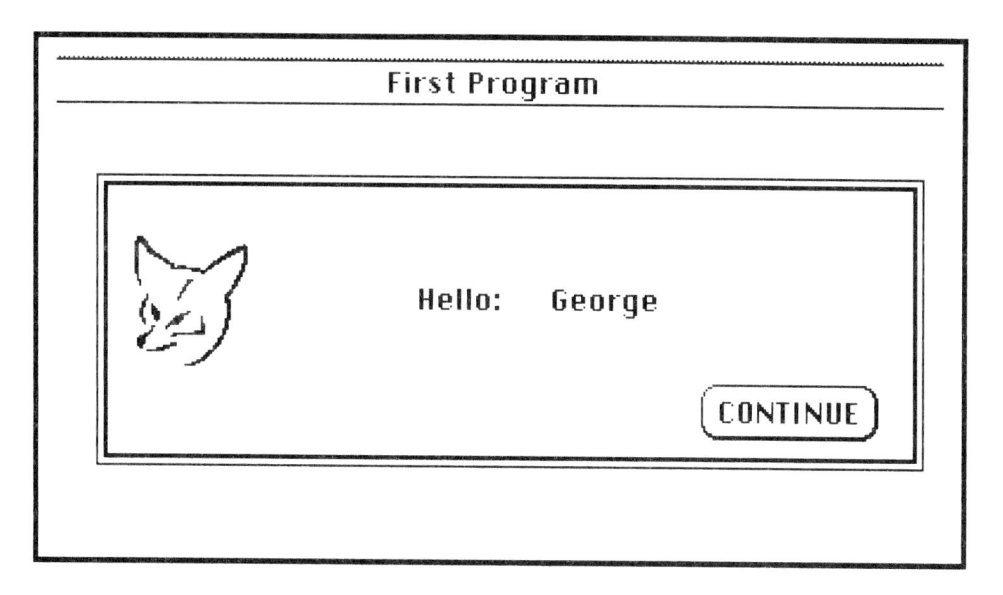

Figure 2-01. Results of hello2.prg.

Constants are unchanging.

The content of a variable can be changed.

In this program, the word "Hello:" is referred to as a <u>constant</u>. That is, the following line will <u>constantly</u> produce the word "Hello:"

    @ 2,15 SAY "Hello:"

On the other hand, the following line will produce <u>varying</u> results depending on the content of the whoisit <u>variable</u>:

    @ 2,22 SAY whoisit

To test this concept, change hello2.prg to use your name instead of "George". Then run the program, and note the result.

How does FoxBASE+/Mac know when an item is a constant or a vari-

---

Variables and constants   29

able? Character constants are surrounded by double quotes, or by single quotes, or by square brackets. Numeric constants start with a digit 0 through 9, or a decimal point, or a minus sign. Logical constants include .T., .F., .Y., and .N.. The periods are required. On the other hand, memory variables and field names start with a letter or an underscore.

We will revisit the concept of data types in Chapter 4. Until then, here are some sample FoxBASE+/Mac commands, with comments to denote whether FoxBASE+/Mac will treat the item in boldface as a variable or constant entity:

```
@ 5,5 SAY "GEORGE"   && CHARACTER CONSTANT
@ 5,5 SAY GEORGE     && VARIABLE
@ 5,5 SAY 1234       && NUMERIC CONSTANT
@ 5,5 SAY "1234"     && CHARACTER CONSTANT
@ 5,5 SAY M_1234     && VARIABLE
@ 5,5 SAY .F.        && LOGICAL CONSTANT
@ 5,5 SAY TFYN       && VARIABLE
```

The user's turn

Now it's time to let the user in on the fun. First, save hello2.prg as hello3.prg, and then adjust the program to look like this:

```
* hello3.prg
* Our own dialog box!
* Bring Screen 1 to the top of the
* desktop, and give it a heading
SCREEN 1 TOP HEADING "First Program"
CLEAR       && make the screen blank
* Define screen number 2 as TYPE 1,
*           centered on the screen,
*           6 rows high by 40 columns wide,
*           with text displayed in 12 point Chicago FONT
SCREEN 2 TYPE 1 AT 0,0 SIZE 6,40 FONT "CHICAGO",12
CLEAR       && make screen 2 blank
SCREEN 2 TOP FIXED && bring screen 2 to the top of the desktop
* Put a small picture of a fox in the box
@ 0,0 SAY 1 PICTURE "@* \P503" SIZE 5,5
* Assign blanks to the whoisit variable
```

```
STORE SPACE(10) TO whoisit
* Tell the user what to do
@ 1,10 SAY "Enter your name: "
* "Get" the whoisit variable
@ 1,col()+1 GET whoisit
* Activate the GET
READ
* Put our message in the middle of the screen
@ 3,10 SAY "Hello:"
* Put the user's name next to our message
@ 3,17 SAY whoisit
STORE 0 TO dummy
* Use the dummy variable to display a text button
@ 4,30 GET dummy PICTURE "@*v CONTINUE"
* Wait for the user to click on "CONTINUE"
READ
SCREEN 2 OFF   && remove our screen from the desktop
RETURN         && return control to calling program
* EOF hello3.prg
```

When you run hello3.prg you will be presented with a screen like Figure 2-02. When you begin to type your name, you will see a screen like Figure 2-03. When you press [Enter], or when you fill the whoisit variable with characters, you will be presented with a screen like Figure 2-04. Click on Continue to continue.

We will return to dialog creation later in the book, for now though it is time to begin creating more complex data entry screens. In the next program, we will ask the user for more information. The screen will be very plain, but this simplicity will make it easier to focus on new features. Please enter the following program:

```
* manygets.prg
* accept multiple inputs from the user
* Create some variables to hold the user's input
STORE SPACE(10) TO name
STORE SPACE(11) TO ssn
STORE 0 TO age
STORE SPACE(30) TO job
* Create a screen to accept the user's input
SCREEN 1 HEADING "Many Gets"
CLEAR   && make screen 1 blank
SCREEN 1 FONT "MONACO",12   && assign font type & size
```

The user's turn

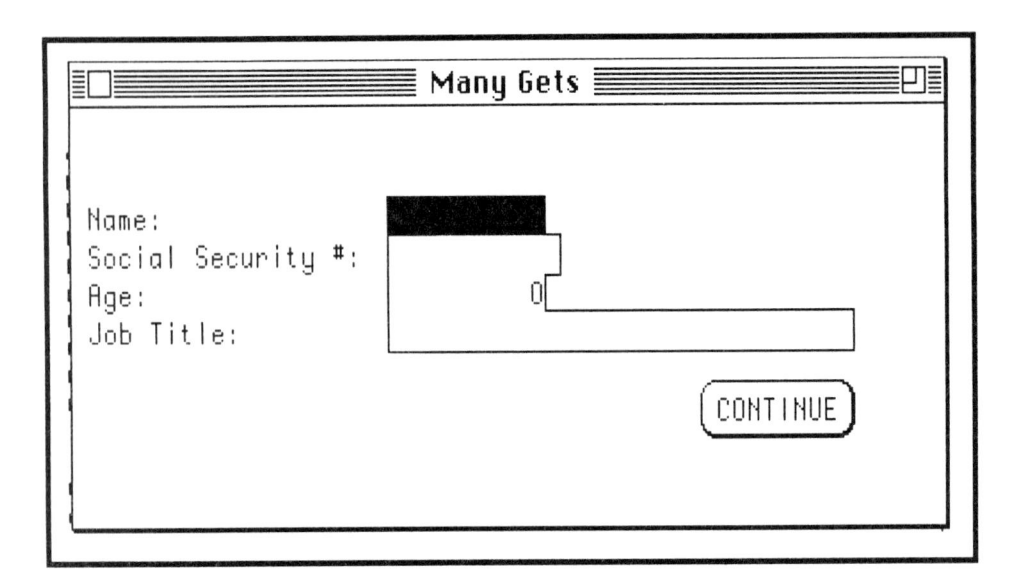

Figure 2-02. Start of hello3.prg.

Figure 2-03. Hello3.prg during entry.

Figure 2-04. Hello3.prg after entry.

```
SCREEN 1 TOP     && put screen 1 on top of desktop
SCREEN 1 SIZE 10,55   && 10 rows of 55 characters each
SCREEN 1 AT 0,0  && Center screen 1 on monitor
* Put some prompts on the screen
@ 2,0 SAY "Name: "
@ 3,0 SAY "Social Security #:"
@ 4,0 SAY "Age:"
@ 5,0 SAY "Job Title:"
* Now prepare screen locations for user input
@ 2,20 GET name
@ 3,20 GET ssn
@ 4,20 GET age
@ 5,20 GET job
* Activate all of the GETs
READ
RETURN
* EOF manygets.prg
```

When you [Command]+E to run manygets.prg, you will be presented with a screen like the one in Figure 2-05. Note the presence of the editing window beneath your screen 1.

The user's turn 33

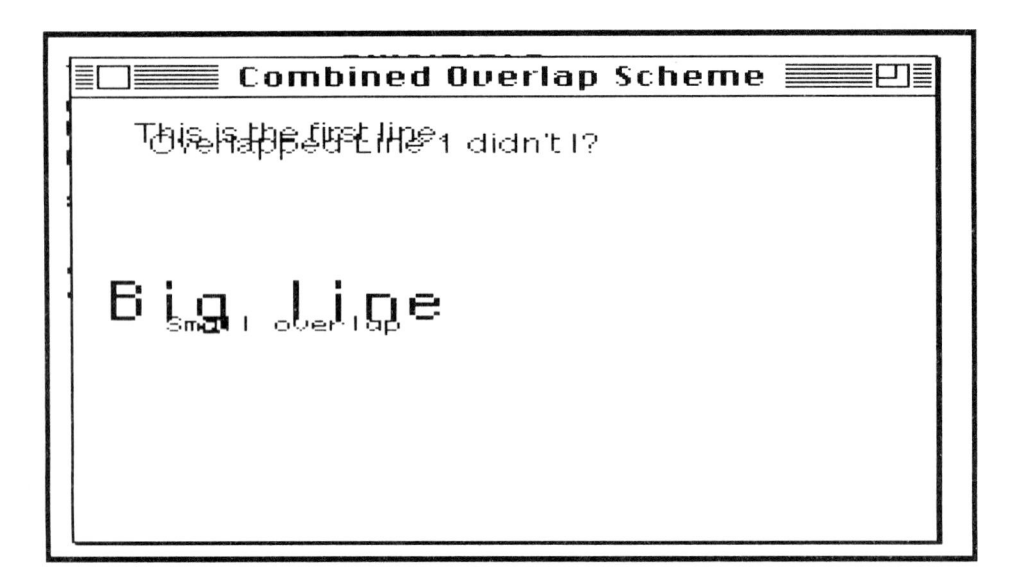

```
┌─────────────────────────────────────────────┐
│ ▓□▓   Combined Overlap Scheme   ▓▓□▓        │
│                                             │
│   This is the first line1 didn't I?         │
│     Overlapped line                         │
│                                             │
│                                             │
│      Big Line                               │
│       Small overlap                         │
│                                             │
│                                             │
└─────────────────────────────────────────────┘
```

Figure 2-05. Many gets.

To exit the manygets program, press [Enter] four times. To see how we can avoid this occurrence of the cluttered desktop problem, click on the edit window. This brings the edit window to the top. Now close the edit window by clicking the box in the upper left hand corner of the window. Now issue the following command from the command window:

`DO manygets`

This should provide you with a cleaner desktop. Now let's look at the manygets.prg program. From a programmer's point of view, the only news is the use of one READ to activate multiple gets. Also interesting is that the age variable, which is a numeric, will only allow numbers to be entered.

Full screen editing

Since this is our first program to READ multiple GETs, now is an appropriate time to discuss FoxBASE+/Mac's basic full-screen editing capabilities. Full-screen editing refers to the ways in which users can move around in a data entry screen.

The user can select a field to edit by clicking on the appropriate field. In addition, the user can use the arrow keys to move forward or back one field at a time. Further, the [Tab] and [Shift]+[Tab] keys can be used to move forward and back one field respectively. Also, the [Enter] key can be used to exit the READ, if SET STRICT is ON, or to move to the next field, if SET STRICT is OFF. (Note: Mac users may be more comfortable with SET STRICT ON, while PC users will be completely lost if SET STRICT is not OFF.) We have directed FoxBASE+/Mac to SET STRICT OFF in our config.fx file, and throughout the rest of this book we will assume that SET STRICT is OFF.

Finally, if a user fills a field on the screen with characters, the user will hear a bell if SET BELL is ON. Further, if SET CONFIRM is OFF, the system will advance to the next @...GET. If SET CONFIRM is ON, no advance will take place until the user presses [Enter]. By default, SET BELL is ON, and SET CONFIRM is OFF, and we will assume these settings throughout the rest of the book.

Regardless of the status of SET STRICT or SET CONFIRM, the user will exit the READ when [Enter] is pressed while editing the last field on the screen. Last here refers to the last GET issued in the program, **not to the last field on the screen!** Further, fields are processed in the order in which they appear in the program, not the order in which they appear on the screen.

To test the consequences of this last revelation, I suggest that you re-arrange the @...GET statements in manygets.prg as follows:

```
* manyget1.prg
* accept gets in non-screen order
* Create some variables to hold the user's input
STORE SPACE(10) TO name
STORE SPACE(11) TO ssn
```

Full screen editing

```
STORE 0 TO age
STORE SPACE(30) TO job
* Create a screen to accept the user's input
SCREEN 1 HEADING "Many Gets"
CLEAR   && make screen 1 blank
SCREEN 1 FONT "MONACO",12   && assign font type & size
SCREEN 1 TOP     && put screen 1 on top of desktop
SCREEN 1 SIZE 10,55    && 10 rows of 55 characters each
SCREEN 1 AT 0,0    && Center screen 1 on monitor
* Put some prompts on the screen
@ 2,0 SAY "Name: "
@ 3,0 SAY "Social Security #:"
@ 4,0 SAY "Age:"
@ 5,0 SAY "Job Title:"
* Now prepare screen locations for user input
@ 5,20 GET job
@ 3,20 GET ssn
@ 2,20 GET name
@ 4,20 GET age
* Activate all of the GETs
READ
RETURN
* EOF manyget1.prg
```

As you would expect, the screen for produced by manyget1.prg looks the same as the screen produced by manygets.prg. To see the difference between the two programs, use the [Tab] key to move among the fields.

Having satisfied yourself that I am telling you the truth about the processing of @...GET statements, you are ready to move on to the next issue in full-screen editing. In many Mac applications, it is customary for the user to click on a text button or picture button before moving on to the next screen.

Unfortunately, for this purpose, the user has many ways to exit from a READ in FoxBASE+/Mac. Here are just a few of those methods:

- Press [Enter] on last GET

- Press [Tab] on last GET

- Press [Shift]+[Tab] on first GET

- Fill the last GET

- Click on a text button

- Click on a picture button

- Press [Down-arrow] on last get

- Press [Up-arrow] on first get

- Press [Enter] on any get with SET STRICT ON

A Mac-like exit

To give our applications a Mac-like feel, we may wish to allow the user to keep READing a screen until the user clicks on a text-button or picture button that signifies that the user is finished with the screen. We need a technique that keeps both our GETs and our READ active until the user elects to exit the screen. Amazingly, the very next program in the book illustrates just such a technique:

```
* manyget2.prg
* Accept entry on same screen until user selects CONTINUE
* Create some variables to hold the user's input
STORE SPACE(10) TO name
STORE SPACE(11) TO ssn
STORE 0 TO age
STORE SPACE(30) TO job
* Create a screen to accept the user's input
SCREEN 1 HEADING "Many Gets"
CLEAR    && make screen 1 blank
SCREEN 1 FONT "MONACO",12   && assign font type & size
SCREEN 1 TOP   && put screen 1 on top of desktop
SCREEN 1 SIZE 10,55   && 10 rows of 55 characters each
SCREEN 1 AT 0,0   && Center screen 1 on monitor
* Put some prompts on the screen
@ 2,0 SAY "Name: "
```

```
@ 3,0 SAY "Social Security #:"
@ 4,0 SAY "Age:"
@ 5,0 SAY "Job Title:"
* Now prepare screen locations for user input
@ 2,20 GET name
@ 3,20 GET ssn
@ 4,20 GET age
@ 5,20 GET job
* setup a text button to signify completion
STORE 0 TO approved
@ 6,40 GET approved PICTURE "@*v CONTINUE"
* READ until approved
DO WHILE approved=0
   * Activate all of the GETs
   READ SAVE   && READ and keep GETs active
ENDDO   && wait until approved
CLEAR GETS   && deactivate GETs
RETURN
* EOF manygets.prg
```

The resultant screen, as seen in Figure 2-06 is about what you would expect. However, in running the program, you will note that the only way to exit the READ is to click on the CONTINUE button. The text button portion of the equation you have seen before, and we will discuss in detail later, but the DO WHILE, READ SAVE, and CLEAR GETS commands all deserve immediate attention.

The DO WHILE command will be discussed in greater detail in Chapter 3, so for now it is enough to understand that all of the commands between DO WHILE and ENDDO will be executed until the expression "approved=0" is made untrue by some action. Happily, when the user clicks on the text button, approved will be assigned the value 1. Since 1 does not equal 0, the expression "approved=0" will become untrue when the user clicks on the CONTINUE button.

Not only does the READ command activate the outstanding GETs, it also deactivates those GETs when the user exits the READ. A READ command with no outstanding GETs is a lonely, and useless, thing so we will make use of the READ SAVE command instead. This command activates processing of the outstanding GETs, but does not deactivate those GETs

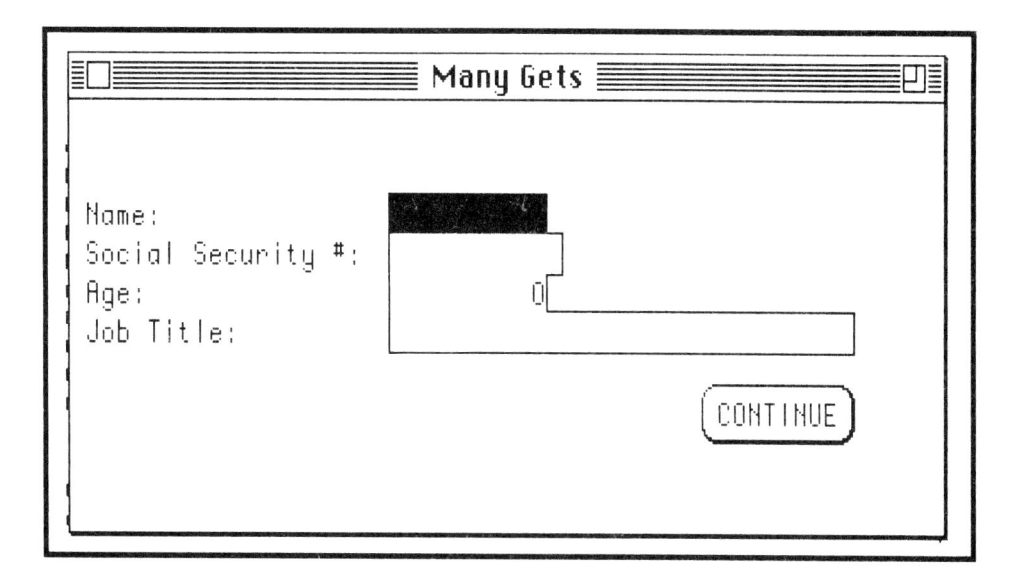

Figure 2-06. Many gets with continue.

when the user exits.

Since READ SAVE does not deactivate the outstanding GETs, we need to issue the CLEAR GETS command to prevent the outstanding GETS from being read by every subsequent READ SAVE command. In other words, don't turn your GETs on without eventually satisfying them with a READ, CLEAR GETS, or CLEAR command.

Of rows, columns, and pixels

Until now, we have used the concept of rows and columns to position our SAYs and GETs on the screen. This simple method of positioning information on the screen is a carry-over from FoxBASE+/Mac's PC-DOS heritage, where screens hold 25 rows of 80 characters in the same non-proportional spacing. Therefore, when picking a coordinate to begin a SAY or a GET, PC programmers choose between 0,0 and 24,79 to place their data.

The Macintosh however offers access to individual points or PIXELS on its screen. For example, on a Macintosh Plus, there are 342 vertical PIXELS by 512 Horizontal PIXELS. Any of these points can be used to position a screen. Subsequently, any of the points in the screen can be used to position the output of a SAY or GET.

Fortunately, FoxBASE+/Mac gives us a very natural method of utilizing PIXEL positioning, as demonstrated in the following program:

```
* pixel1.prg
SCREEN 1 HEADING "Pixel Addressing"
CLEAR    && make screen 1 blank
SCREEN 1 FONT "HELVETICA",12  && assign font type & size
SCREEN 1 TOP   && put screen 1 on top of desktop
SCREEN 1 SIZE 200,280 PIXELS && 200 by 280 pixels
SCREEN 1 AT 0,0   && Center screen 1 on monitor
@ PIXEL 20,20 SAY "This is the first line."
@ PIXEL 25,25 SAY "Overlapped Line 1 didn't I?"
@ PIXEL 100,10 SAY "Big line" FONT "MONACO",24
@ PIXEL 105,30 SAY "Small overlap" FONT "MONACO",9
* eof pixel1.prg
```

We simply add the PIXEL clause to the @...SAY/GET command, or to the SCREEN command, and our coordinates are interpreted as PIXELS rather than as rows and columns. Since pixel1.prg generates a screen that overlaps the edit window in which pixel1.prg resides, take this opportunity to click the edit window, and try your own PIXEL addressing. The [Command]+E command will allow you to run your program at any time, so this is an opportunity to practice adjusting your screen displays.

Note that FoxBASE+/Mac allows you to overlap information on the screen as shown in Figure 2-07. The STYLE clause can be used to modify the way in which overlapping objects are displayed on the screen. A simple example is shown in the following program:

```
* pixel2.prg
SCREEN 1 HEADING "Combined Overlap Scheme"
CLEAR    && make screen 1 blank
SCREEN 1 FONT "HELVETICA",12  && assign font type & size
```

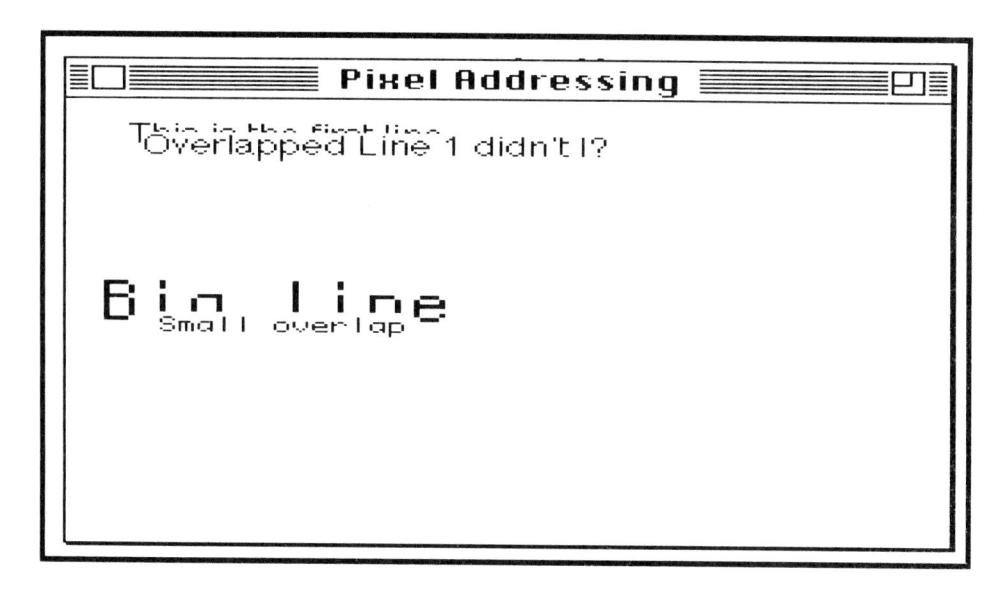

Figure 2-07. Pixel addressing.

```
SCREEN 1 TOP     && put screen 1 on top of desktop
SCREEN 1 SIZE 200,280 PIXELS && 200 by 280 pixels
SCREEN 1 AT 0,0  && Center screen 1 on monitor
@ PIXEL 20,20 SAY "This is the first line." STYLE 65536
@ PIXEL 25,25 SAY "Overlapped Line 1 didn't I?" STYLE 65536
@ PIXEL 100,10 SAY "Big line" FONT "MONACO",24 STYLE 65536
@ PIXEL 105,30 SAY "Small overlap" FONT "MONACO",9 STYLE 65536
* eof pixel2.prg
```

The result is shown in Figure 2-08. This demonstration of the STYLE clause illustrates its ability to affect the transfer mode of output. That is, it affects the way overlapping items are treated. The STYLE clause can also be used to affect the pen width of lines and boxes, the radius of the curvature of rounded boxes, the pen pattern of boxes, and the fill pattern of boxes. In addition, the STYLE clause plays an important part in directing output to a printer.

While we will investigate this last feature of the STYLE clause in Chapters 13 through 15, suffice to say that the STYLE clause allows objects to

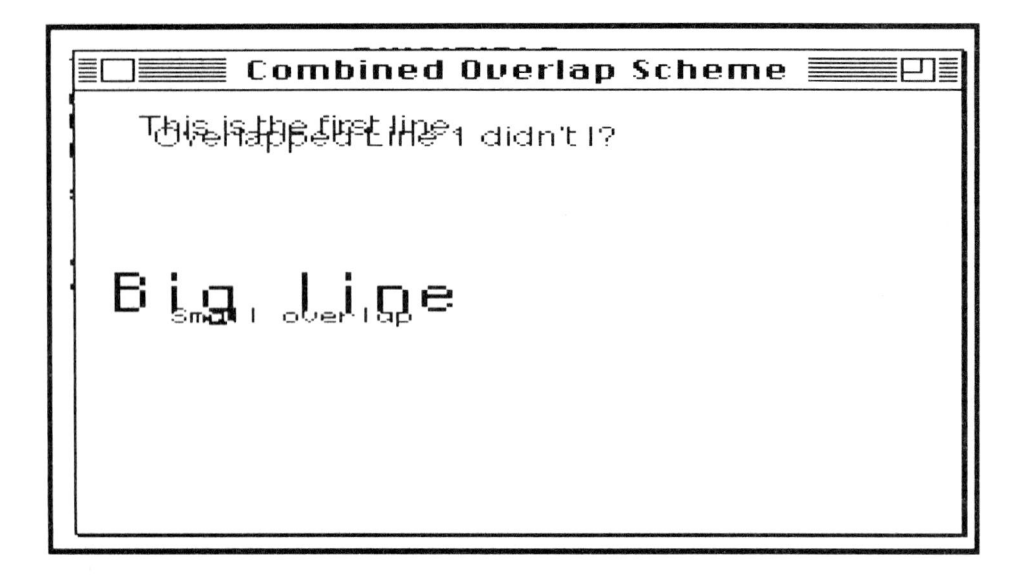

Figure 2-08. Combine overlap scheme.

overlap on printed output as well as on the computer screen.

More about pixels

While this capability of overlapping screen and printer objects is interesting and very flexible, most data entry operations do not benefit from overlapped SAYs or GETs. Further, because the number of pixels on a screen or monitor is greater than the number of rows and columns on a screen or monitor, it is more difficult to write programs that utilize PIXEL addressing than it is to write programs that utilize row and column addressing.

As a result, when using the same font for all of the content on one screen, many programmers depend on the row and column method of positioning to insure that their screens are readable. However, there are techniques that can be used to ameliorate some of the difficulty inherent in using PIXEL addressing when such addressing is necessary.

We will demonstrate the first of these techniques in the following reworking of the manyget2.prg program:

```
* manyget3.prg
* Use Pixels to increase line spacing
* Create some variables to hold the user's input
STORE SPACE(10) TO name
STORE SPACE(11) TO ssn
STORE 0 TO age
STORE SPACE(30) TO job
* Create a screen to accept the user's input
SCREEN 1 HEADING "Better Spacing"
CLEAR    && make screen 1 blank
SCREEN 1 FONT "MONACO",12   && assign font type & size
SCREEN 1 TOP    && put screen 1 on top of desktop
SCREEN 1 SIZE 10,55   && 10 rows of 55 characters each
SCREEN 1 AT 0,0   && Center screen 1 on monitor
* Determine size of current "ROW" of text
STORE VAL(SYS(1025))+VAL(SYS(1026))+VAL(SYS(1027)) ;
   TO newline
* Now add 4 pixels of "leading" to the line
STORE newline+4 TO newline
* Now determine column widths
STORE VAL(SYS(1028)) TO newcol
* Put some prompts on the screen
@ PIXEL newline*2,3 SAY "Name: "
@ PIXEL newline*3,3 SAY "Social Security #:"
@ PIXEL newline*4,3 SAY "Age:"
@ PIXEL newline*5,3 SAY "Job Title:"
* Now prepare screen locations for user input
@ PIXEL newline*2,20*newcol GET name
@ PIXEL newline*3,20*newcol GET ssn
@ PIXEL newline*4,20*newcol GET age
@ PIXEL newline*5,20*newcol GET job
* setup a text button to signify completion
STORE 0 TO approved
* Determine last "ROW" of screen
STORE VAL(SYS(1023))-newline-5 TO lastrow
* Determine size of button
STORE VAL(SYS(1030,"[ CONTINUE ]")) TO ;
   buttonwd
* Determine screen width
STORE VAL(SYS(1024)) TO scrwidth
* Put the button in the middle of the last "row"
* of the screen.
@ PIXEL lastrow,(scrwidth-buttonwd)/2 GET ;
```

```
    approved PICTURE "@*v CONTINUE"
* READ until approved
DO WHILE approved=0
  * Activate all of the GETs
  READ SAVE   && READ and keep GETs active
ENDDO  && wait until approved
CLEAR GETS   && deactivate GETs
RETURN
* EOF manygets.prg
```

The result of manyget3.prg is seen in Figure 2-09. The MONACO font, like many others, has no leading. That is, there is no space between the bottom of a descending character, (i.e. the letter "g"), on screen row 1 for example, and the top of an upper case letter on screen row 2. In short, the SAYs and GETs on our screen are too close together when placed on adjacent ROWs. To rectify this situation, we use several of FoxBASE+/Mac's more arcane functions to determine the size of rows and columns in the current font type and size.

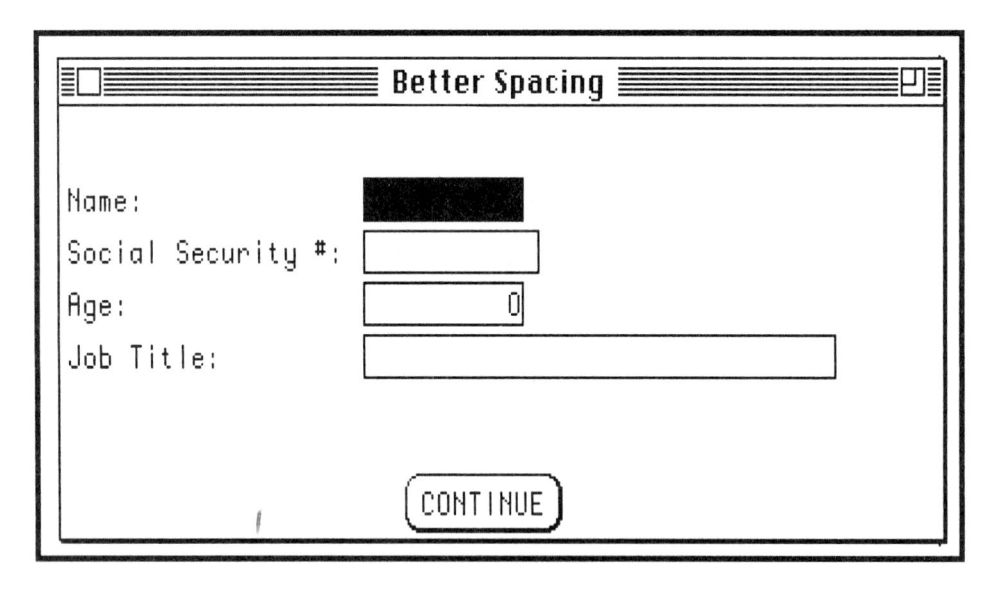

Figure 2-09. Better spacing through pixels.

These complicated-looking calculations are necessary because every font type and size can occupy a different number of vertical and horizontal pixels with a given character. Don't struggle overlong to understand the VAL() and SYS() functions, we will see them again in subsequent chapters when a discussion of their operation will be more appropriate. For now it is enough to understand the difference between rows and columns and PIXELS. Since row and column addressing is easier to type, and perhaps more frequently used by programmers, we will continue to use row and column addressing.

There are a number of interesting aspects to the manyget3.prg program in addition to its use of PIXELs. First, several lines end in a semi-colon. FoxBASE+/Mac will accept program lines up to 254 characters in length. However, most monitors, and the pages in this book, cannot display much more than 80 characters on a given line. While you can enter command lines that stretch on past the right side of the edit window using the horizontal scroll bar to see the ends of your lines, most programmers prefer to break long command lines into two or more continued lines. A semi-colon placed between clauses of a command line directs FoxBASE+/Mac to combine the next physical line with the current physical line to create a single program statement.

Next, manyget3.prg introduces several functions whose purpose it is to determine the size, in PIXELs, of various objects. Here is a brief summary of the functions that can be used in the pursuit of PIXEL sizing:

- SYS(1021) = number of vertical pixels on your monitor

- SYS(1022) = number of horizontal pixels on your monitor

- SYS(1023) = number of vertical pixels in the currently active screen or printer

- SYS(1024) = number of horizontal pixels in the currently active screen or printer

- SYS(1025) = number of vertical pixels from the bottom of the tallest non-descending character in the current font, to the top of that same character.

- SYS(1026) = number of vertical pixels from the bottom of a non-descending character to the bottom of a descending character in the current font.

- SYS(1027) = number of blank vertical pixels between rows in the current font.

- SYS(1028) = width, in pixels, of the letter "n" of the current font.

- SYS(1029) = width, in pixels, of the widest letter in the current font.

- SYS(1030,"characters") = width, in pixels of the specified character expression in the current font.

- SYS(1039) = vertical resolution of the printer

- SYS(1040) = horizontal resolution of the printer.

Now that we have developed a slightly more Mac-like rapport with our user, let's investigate some of the techniques available to insure that the user reciprocates by entering valid data. Prime among these tools is the use of the PICTURE clause of the @...GET command.

Picture templates

As we have already seen, the PICTURE clause can be used to create text buttons. It can also be used to create popups, text edit regions, scrolling lists, radio buttons, picture buttons and check boxes, but not by us. Not yet anyway. These options will be fully investigated in Chapter 10. At this point however, we are interested in the PICTURE clause's more modest capacity to control the input of users into variables and fields. To demonstrate this capability, save manyget2.prg as pict1.prg and modify the program to look like this:

```
* pict1.prg
* Demonstrate validation capabilities of
* PICTURE clause
* Create some variables to hold the user's input
STORE SPACE(10) TO name
STORE SPACE(11) TO ssn
STORE SPACE(14) TO phone
STORE 0 TO age
STORE SPACE(30) TO job
STORE 0.00 TO salary
* Create a screen to accept the user's input
SCREEN 1 HEADING "First Pictures"
CLEAR     && make screen 1 blank
SCREEN 1 FONT "MONACO",12  && assign font type & size
SCREEN 1 TOP   && put screen 1 on top of desktop
SCREEN 1 SIZE 10,55   && 10 rows of 55 characters each
SCREEN 1 AT 0,0   && Center screen 1 on monitor
* Put some prompts on the screen
@ 2,0 SAY "Name: "
@ 3,0 SAY "Social Security #:"
@ 4,0 SAY "Age:"
@ 5,0 SAY "Job Title:"
@ 6,0 SAY "Salary:"
* Now prepare screen locations for user input
* Use pictures to help validate data
@ 2,20 GET name PICTURE "@!A"   && Upper case, Alpha only
@ 3,20 GET ssn PICTURE "###-##-####"   && numbers with dashes
@ 4,20 GET age PICTURE "@B ###" && left justified 3 digits
* Next line capitalizes first letter of job
@ 5,20 GET job PICTURE "!XXXXXXXXXXXXXXXXXXXXXXXXXXXXX"
* Next line precedes salary with $ sign and
* places comma and decimal point in appropriate
* spaces
@ 6,20 GET salary PICTURE "$$$,$$$.$$"
* setup a text button to signify completion
STORE 0 TO approved
@ 6,40 GET approved PICTURE "@*v CONTINUE"
* READ until approved
DO WHILE approved=0
   * Activate all of the GETs
   READ SAVE  && READ but keep GETs active
ENDDO  && wait until approved
CLEAR GETS   && deactivate GETs
```

```
* Use simple ? to display content of variables
CLEAR
? name
? ssn
? age
? job
? salary
RETURN
* EOF pict1.prg
```

Data entry into the screen generated by pict1.prg might look like the screen in Figure 2-10. All of this formatting was accomplished through the use of the PICTURE clauses found in the @...GET commands located in lines 26 through 34. Since the techniques are obvious, we will move on to a discussion of nuclear waste disposal.

Just kidding. Let's look at each of the picture clauses in turn. First, we want the name to be entered in upper case. This command accomplishes

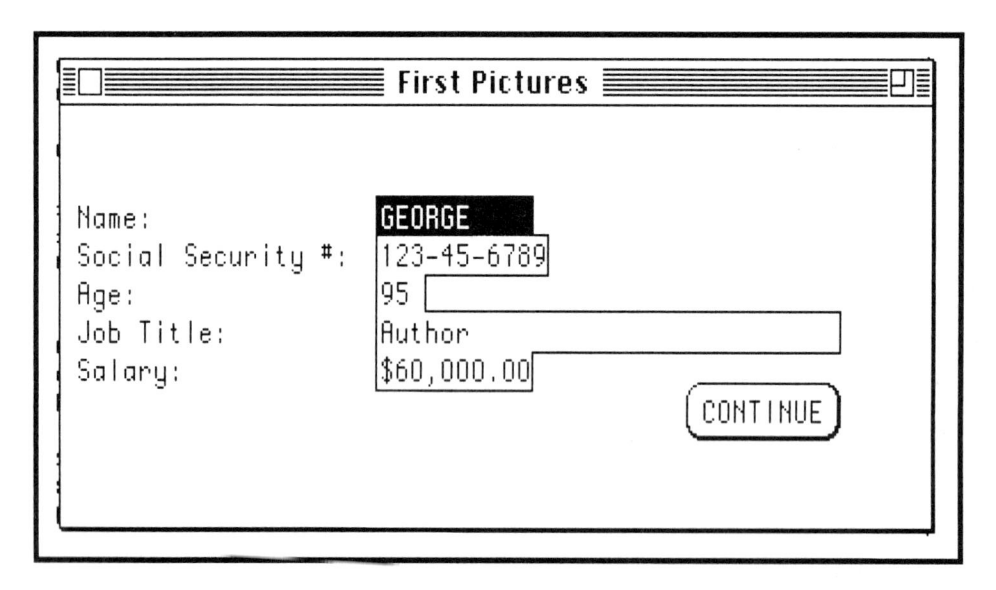

Figure 2-10. First picture entry.

our goal nicely:

```
@ 2,20 GET name PICTURE "@!"
```

Picture Functions start with @ and affect the entire GET.

The picture clause here is "@!", and this forces all letters a-z entered by the user to be stored and displayed as A-Z. However, name is 10 characters long, and we have only provided a 2 character picture. The "@" symbol, when used at the beginning of a picture clause, identifies a picture FUNCTION. Happily, a picture function acts on the entire GET, regardless of the GET's size or content. Without the picture function, we would have to use a command like the following to force upper case entry to the name field:

```
@ 2,20 GET name PICTURE "!!!!!!!!!!"
```

Picture Templates affect one character at a time.

Since this picture clause does not begin with an "@" symbol, it is known as a picture TEMPLATE. In a picture template, every character in the picture clause directly affects a single character of data entry. That is, the first character in the picture clause affects the first character entered or displayed in the GET, the second affects the second, and so on. The next picture clause is also a template:

```
@ 3,20 GET ssn PICTURE "###-##-####"
```

This template forces the user to enter digits or spaces, and adds two immutable dashes to the content and display of the ssn variable. By immutable I mean that the user cannot erase or overstrike those dashes.

Help for the programmer

Why do the dashes act differently than the "#" signs? Because the "#" signs are special template characters. You can find a list of special template characters, and special functions in your Commands and Functions manual, **or you can try the Help system!**

To access the help system, press [Command]+H. This will produce a screen like the one in Figure 2-11. Use the down scroll arrow to review help topics until you reach the @...SAY/GET topic as I have in Figure 2-12. Double-click on the @...SAY/GET topic and you will be presented with essentially the same information found in your Commands and Functions manual. You can reposition the Help screen by dragging the top of the window to its desired location, and you can resize the window by clicking on the small or large box in the lower right corner of the window. I have chosen to make the help window as large as possible in Figure 2-13. To gain access to the picture clause information, use the scroll bar to go to nearly the end of the @...SAY/GET help information.

This help is available to the programmer at almost any time during the

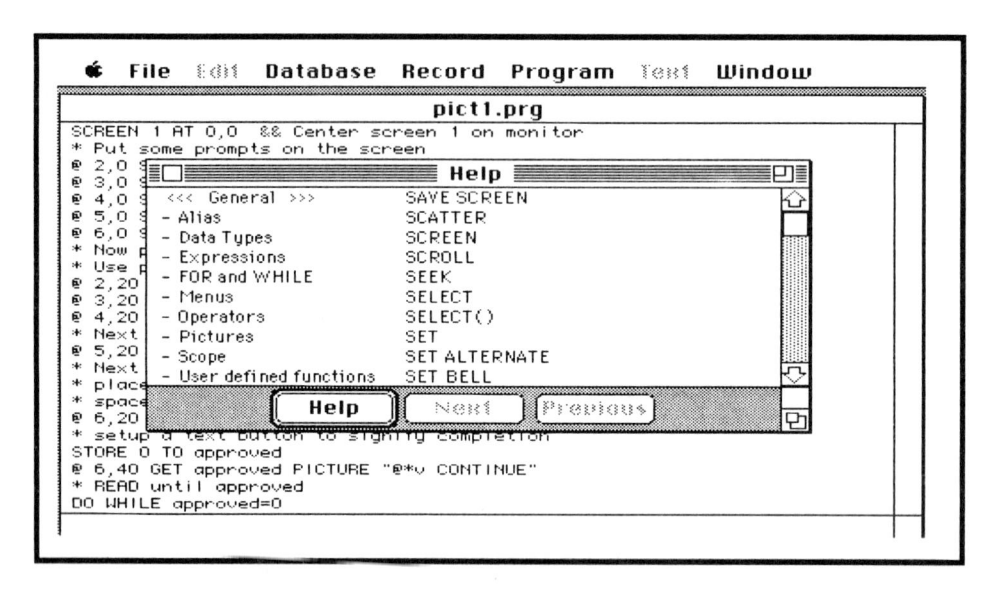

Figure 2-11. Help topics.

Chapter 2: Beginning the User Interface

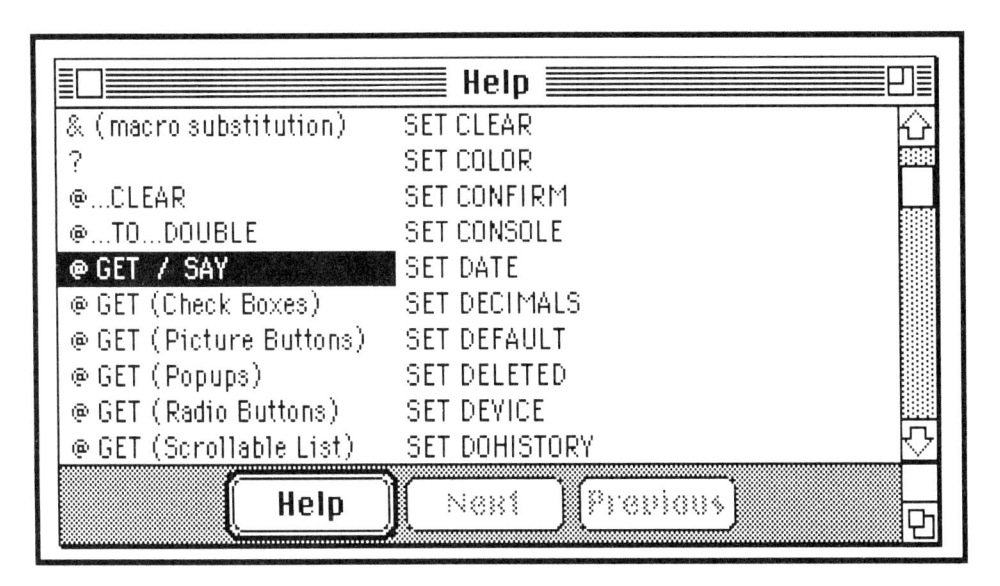

Figure 2-12. Selecting help for @...SAY/GET.

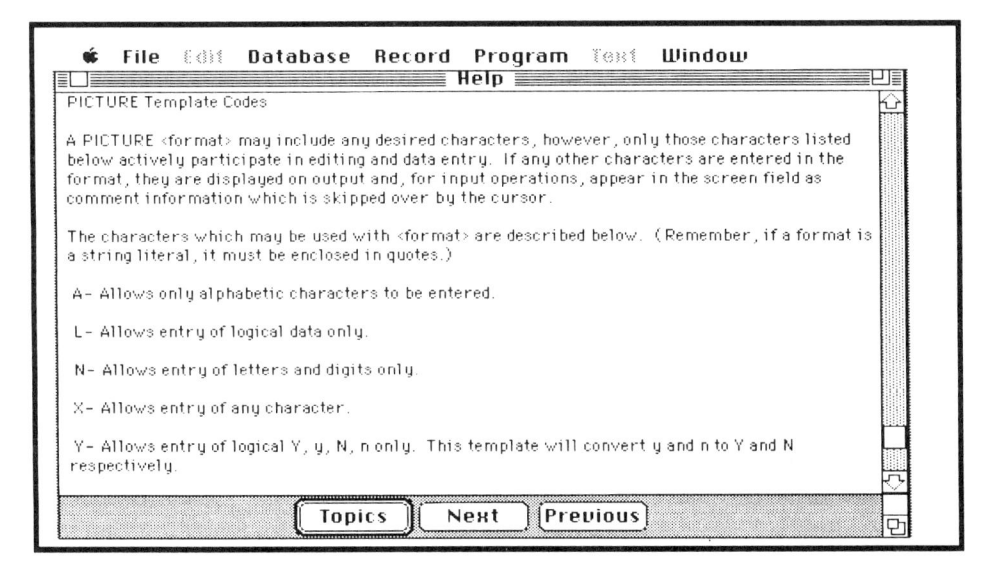

Figure 2-13. Help for picture clauses.

Help for the programmer

FoxBASE+/Mac session. Chapter 6 of your FoxBASE+/Mac User's Guide Utilities explains the techniques required to provide your users with help that pertains to your applications.

The next command combines both a picture clause function, and a picture clause template:

```
@ 4,20 GET age PICTURE "@B ###"
```

This combination directs FoxBASE+/Mac to receive and display the information in the age variable left justified, with up to three numeric characters. When you want to combine a function and a picture template, remember to put a space between the last character of the function, and the first character of the template. Since all of the picture clauses in pict1.prg are described with their own comments, we can move on to the last section of pict1.prg.

Effect of pictures on variables

In the last section of pict1.prg, we CLEAR the screen, then use a series of "?" commands to display the content of our variables. The result of these commands is reflected in Figure 2-14. Note that the ssn variable now contains two dashes. However, the salary variable contains no commas or dollar signs.

In general, picture clauses do not affect the content of numeric variables, (except for the placement of a decimal point). On the other hand, picture clauses usually do affect the content of character variables. We can inhibit this intrusion on the content of variables by the picture clause by using the "@R" picture clause function. Try this program for example:

```
* pict2.prg
* Demonstrate "@R" picture function
* Create some variables to hold the user's input
STORE SPACE(11) TO ssn
STORE SPACE(10) TO phone
```

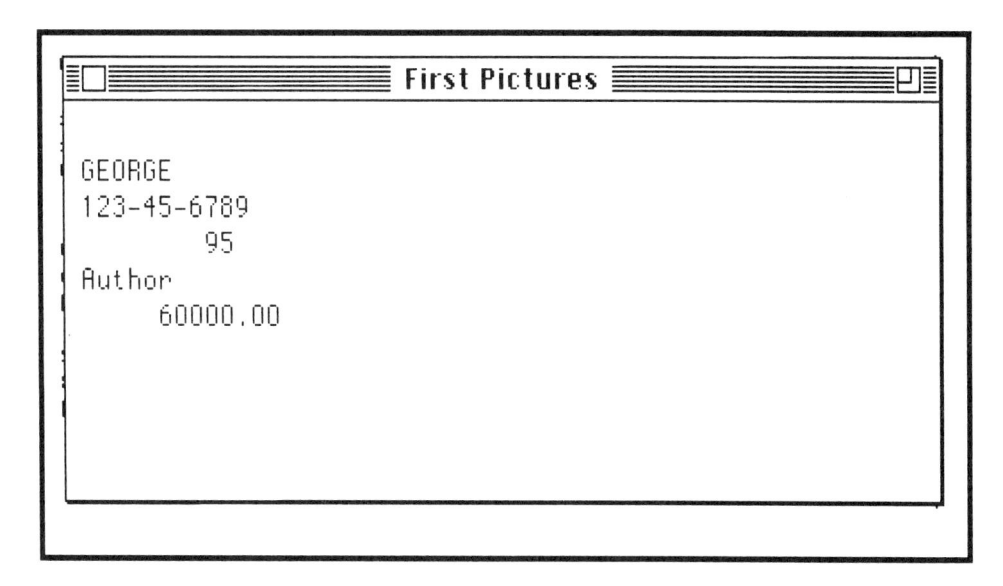

```
╔═════════════════ First Pictures ═════════════════╗
│                                                  │
│   GEORGE                                         │
│   123-45-6789                                    │
│           95                                     │
│   Author                                         │
│        60000.00                                  │
│                                                  │
╚══════════════════════════════════════════════════╝
```

Figure 2-14. Pict1.prg variable contents.

```
SCREEN 1 TOP HEADING "Second Picture"
CLEAR
@ 1,0 SAY "Phone:"
@ 2,0 SAY "SSN #:"
@ 4,0 SAY "Phone Alone"
@ 5,0 SAY "Phone PICT "
@ 7,0 SAY "SSN alone"
@ 8,0 SAY "SSN PICT "
@ 1,15 GET phone PICTURE "@R (###) ###-####"
@ 2,15 GET ssn PICTURE "###-##-####"
STORE 0 TO approved
@ 6,40 GET approved PICTURE "@*v CONTINUE"
* READ until approved
DO WHILE approved=0
  * Activate all of the GETs
  READ SAVE  && READ but keep GETs active
ENDDO  && wait until approved
CLEAR GETS  && deactivate GETs
@ 4,15 SAY phone
@ 5,15 SAY phone PICTURE "@R (###) ###-####"
@ 7,15 SAY ssn
@ 8,15 SAY ssn PICTURE "###-##-####"
RETURN
```

Effect of pictures on variables

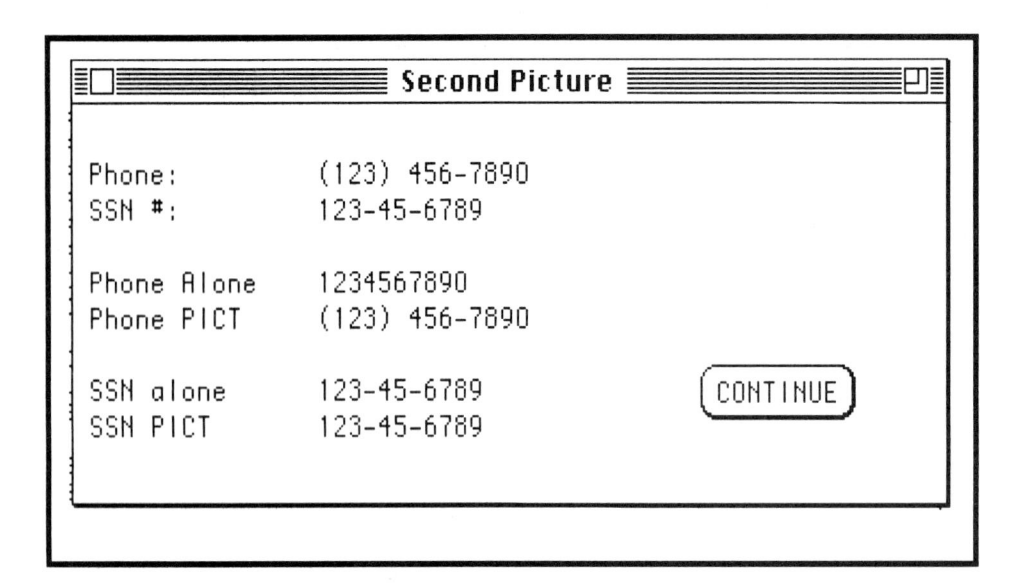

```
┌─────────────────────────────────────────────────────────┐
│ ▤□▤▤▤▤▤▤▤▤▤▤▤▤▤ Second Picture ▤▤▤▤▤▤▤▤▤▤▤▤▤▤□▤ │
│                                                         │
│   Phone:         (123) 456-7890                         │
│   SSN #:         123-45-6789                            │
│                                                         │
│   Phone Alone    1234567890                             │
│   Phone PICT     (123) 456-7890                         │
│                                                ┌────────┐│
│   SSN alone      123-45-6789                   │CONTINUE││
│   SSN PICT       123-45-6789                   └────────┘│
│                                                         │
└─────────────────────────────────────────────────────────┘
```

Figure 2-15. Pict2.prg "@R" picture clause.

```
* EOF pict2.prg
```

Pict2.prg will produce a screen similar to Figure 2-15 when you enter data, and click on CONTINUE. In essence, the @R picture function prevents non-template characters from being included in variables.

You can lookup all of the picture clause functions and template characters on-line via the help facility, or in your Commands & Functions manual.

3. Taking Control

As you have seen in the sample programs so far, FoxBASE+/Mac processes commands sequentially. That is, the first command in a program is executed first, the second command second, etc. This capability of executing a series of commands in the order in which they were entered by the programmer is sufficient to complete some very rudimentary tasks.

The calculator

Before we can start to accomplish significant work however, we will have to learn how to direct FoxBASE+/Mac to perform a task based on a condition. To demonstrate this conditional capability, I have constructed a simple calculator program, that we will slowly enhance to include all of FoxBASE+/Mac's conditional commands. Here is the first, non-conditional, version of the calculator program:

```
* calc1.prg
* adds two numbers
SCREEN 1 HEADING "Dumb Calculator"
CLEAR    && make screen 1 blank
SCREEN 1 FONT "MONACO",12   && assign font type & size
SCREEN 1 TOP    && put screen 1 on top of desktop
SCREEN 1 SIZE 10,55    && 10 rows of 55 characters each
SCREEN 1 AT 0,0    && Center screen 1 on monitor
* Use one STORE command to assign two variables
STORE 0 TO one,two
@ 2,0 SAY "First number:"
@ 4,0 SAY "Second number:"
@ 5,20 SAY "=========="
@ 6,0 SAY "Result:"
@ 2,20 GET one PICTURE "#######.##"
@ 4,20 GET two PICTURE "#######.##"
READ
* Use equal sign to assign value to one variable
result = one + two
@ 6,20 SAY result PICTURE "#######.##"
RETURN
```

`* EOF calc1.prg`

Calc1.prg generates a screen similar to Figure 3-01 after the user enters two numbers. Calc1.prg is most remarkable for what it does not do, and we will spend the rest of the chapter enhancing it. However, two commands lines do warrant attention. The first is:

`STORE 0 TO one,two`

This command assigns the same value to two variables. You can list as many variable names as will fit in one 254 character command line following the STORE command, provided you separate those variable names with commas. The second command of interest is:

`result = one + two`

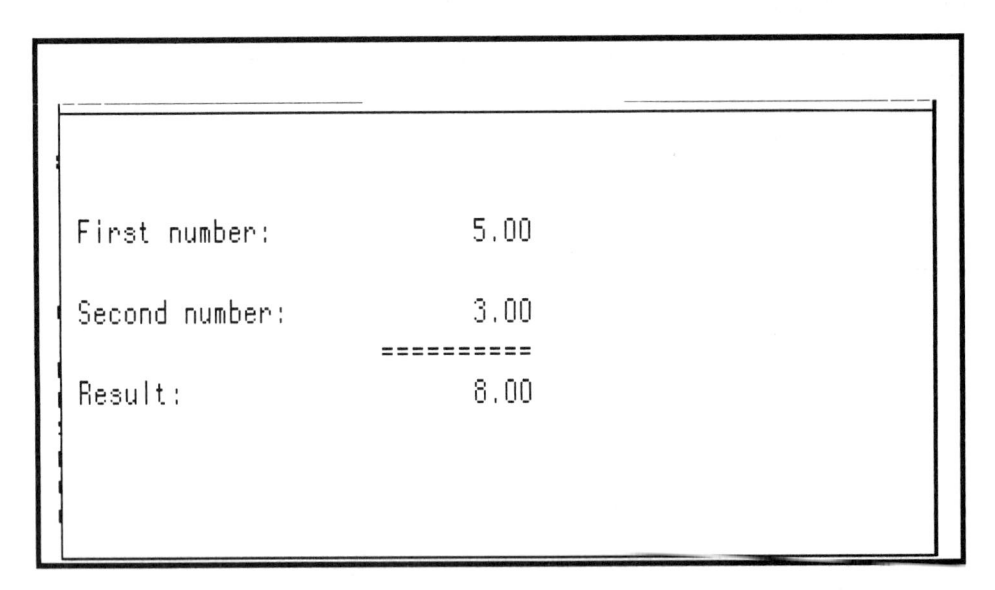

```
First number:              5.00

Second number:             3.00
                         ==========
Result:                    8.00
```

Figure 3-01. Dumb calculator.

This command directs FoxBASE+/Mac to assign the value of the variable named "one" plus the value of the variable named "two" to the variable named "result". This command is the functional equivalent of:

```
STORE one+two TO result
```

Since the first method saves typing, most programmers prefer it to the STORE command. The STORE command is therefore relegated to assigning the same value to more than one variable at a time.

DO WHILE

Now let's get back to the business of controlling our FoxBASE+/Mac programs. The first limitation of calc1.prg is that it requires the user to enter a DO calc1 command every time he or she wants to add two numbers. This is inefficient. So, the calc2.prg allows the user to add two numbers until the user enters zero for both numbers:

```
* calc2.prg
* adds two numbers until the user enters two 0s
SCREEN 1 HEADING "Dumb Calculator 2"
CLEAR   && make screen 1 blank
SCREEN 1 FONT "MONACO",12   && assign font type & size
SCREEN 1 TOP    && put screen 1 on top of desktop
SCREEN 1 SIZE 10,55   && 10 rows of 55 characters each
SCREEN 1 AT 0,0   && Center screen 1 on monitor
* Put some prompts on screen
@ 2,0 SAY "First number:"
@ 4,0 SAY "Second number:"
@ 5,20 SAY "=========="
@ 6,0 SAY "Result:"
STORE 99 TO one,two
DO WHILE one#0.OR.two#0
  STORE 0 TO one,two
  @ 2,20 GET one PICTURE "#######.##"
  @ 4,20 GET two PICTURE "#######.##"
  READ
  result = one + two
  @ 6,20 SAY result PICTURE "#######.##"
  WAIT
ENDDO && do until user enters 0s for both
```

```
CLEAR
RETURN
* EOF calc2.prg
```

The result of this program is reflected in Figure 3-02. Note the WAITING window in the upper right corner of the monitor. This is the result of the WAIT command in calc2.prg, which pauses program operation until the user presses a key, or clicks the mouse. Of more interest are the following two lines from calc2.prg:

```
STORE 99 TO one,two
DO WHILE one#0.AND.two#0
```

First, let's explore the DO WHILE command and its complementary command, ENDDO. DO WHILE loops contain the following parts:

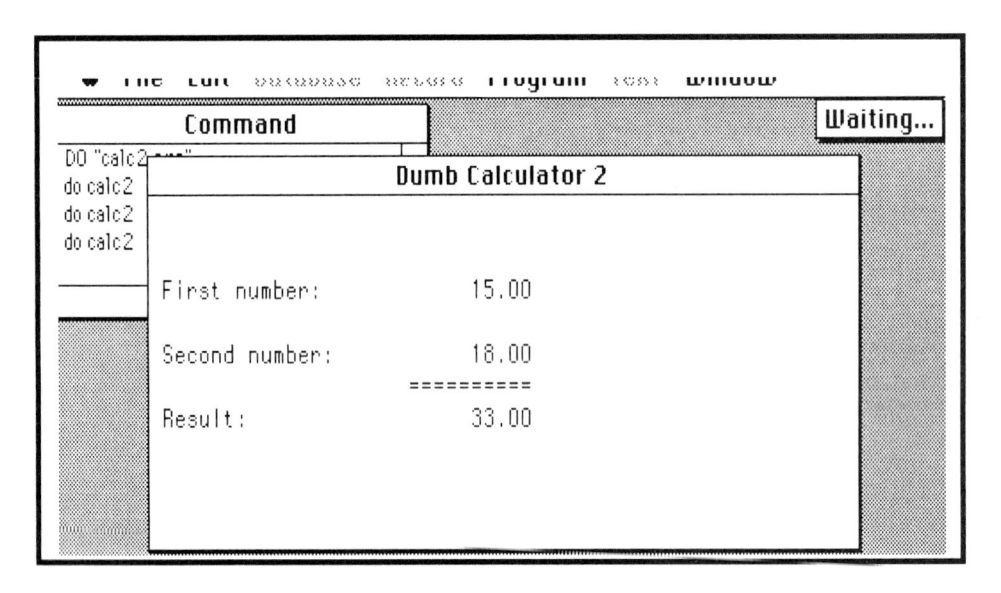

Figure 3-02. Continuous calculator.

```
1DO WHILE 2condition
3body of the loop containing
3any number of FoxBASE+ commands
4LOOP
5EXIT
6ENDDO
```

1. The DO WHILE command tells FoxBASE+ where the loop begins.

2. If the condition is true, the commands within the body of the loop (3), are executed. The condition is evaluated the first time FoxBASE+ encounters the DO WHILE command, and again when the corresponding ENDDO is encountered. When the condition becomes false, the program continues with the first command following the ENDDO command.

3. The body of the loop can contain any number of FoxBASE+ commands of any type.

4. The LOOP command is optional, and only used with DO WHILE loops. When the LOOP command is used, it immediately directs control of the program back to the current DO WHILE command. As a result, any commands coming after the LOOP command but before the ENDDO command will be ignored.

The indiscriminate use of the LOOP command can render a FoxBASE+ program unreadable by making it difficult to determine which commands inside a large DO WHILE loop are actually executed. We will investigate some legitimate uses of the LOOP command later.

5.The EXIT command is another optional command. It directs control of the program to the line following the ENDDO statement. We will investigate the use of the EXIT command in our next program.

6.Every DO WHILE command must have a corresponding ENDDO command. When the ENDDO command is encountered, control of the program is directed back to the DO WHILE command.

Before examining the use of the DO WHILE our calc2.prg in detail, let's look at a simpler program that can also shed light on the use of the DO WHILE command:

```
* dowhill.prg
* Simple count program to demonstrate
* the DO WHILE...ENDDO commands
SCREEN 1 TOP
CLEAR
x = 1
DO WHILE x <= 100
   ? x
   x = x + 1
ENDDO && count to 100
? "Dowhill.prg is finished!"
? "X now equals "
?? x
RETURN
* eof dowhill.prg
```

In the dowhill.prg program, x equals 1 the first time the DO WHILE command is encountered. As a result, the condition x<=100 is true, and the two commands inside the loop (the commands that come between the DO WHILE and ENDDO commands are considered to be inside the loop) are executed for the first time. By the time the ENDDO command is encountered for the first time, the command x = x + 1 has made x equal to 2. The ENDDO command transfers control of the program back to the DO WHILE command where the condition x <= 100 is evaluated again.

Since 2 is less than or equal to 100, the commands inside the loop are executed again. This process continues until x is equal to 101, at which point the condition x<=100 is false, and control of the program is transferred to the first line following the ENDDO. This simple program demonstrates that DO WHILE loops are designed to execute until some command or commands inside the loop cause the DO WHILE condition to become false. When the condition becomes false, the program continues with the line following the ENDDO.

When the dowhill.prg program is finished, you will be presented with

```
┌─────────────────────────────────────────────┐
│ ▤□  ═════════  Dumb Calculator 2  ═════  □▤ │
│           93                                │
│           94                                │
│           95                                │
│           96                                │
│           97                                │
│           98                                │
│           99                                │
│          100                                │
│  Dowhill.prg is finished!                   │
│  X now equals        101                    │
│                                             │
└─────────────────────────────────────────────┘
```

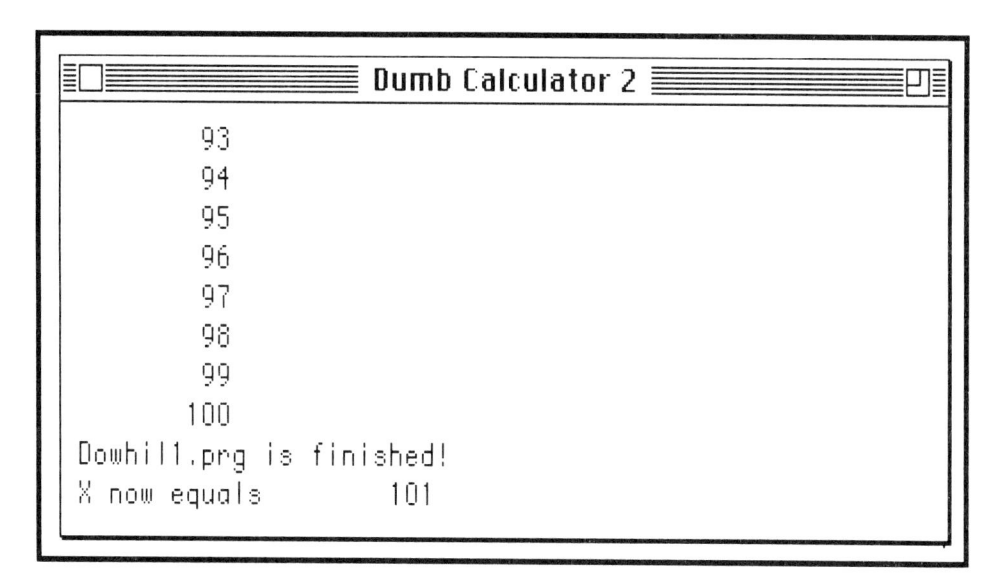

Figure 3-03. Count to 100.

a screen similar to Figure 3-03.

Priming and endless loops

Now back to the calc2.prg program. The conditional statement one#0.OR.two#0 is equivalent to "one does not equal 0 or two does not equal zero." That is, if either one or two does not equal zero, the condition is true.

By assigning the value of 99 to the variables one and two, we make the condition one#0.OR.two#0 true. In this way, we insure that the commands inside the DO WHILE...ENDDO construct are executed at least once.

This technique is known as priming the loop. Note that we immediately reset the values of one and two so that the user can enter his or her own values. If the user enters a zero in both variables, the condition one#0.OR.two#0 will be false, and control of the program will pass to the line following ENDDO, **when the ENDDO command is encountered!** Note that the DO WHILE...ENDDO construct is not exited immediately after the DO WHILE condition is made false. In this case, for example, the WAIT command is executed even though the DO WHILE condition is already false if the user has entered zeros.

The DO WHILE condition is only evaluated when its associated DO WHILE, ENDDO, or LOOP commands are executed.

An alternative to priming the loop is demonstrated in the calc2a.prg below:

```
* calc2.prg
* adds two numbers until the user enters two 0s
SCREEN 1 HEADING "Dumb Calculator 2"
CLEAR     && make screen 1 blank
SCREEN 1 FONT "MONACO",12   && assign font type & size
SCREEN 1 TOP    && put screen 1 on top of desktop
SCREEN 1 SIZE 10,55    && 10 rows of 55 characters each
SCREEN 1 AT 0,0    && Center screen 1 on monitor
* Put some prompts on screen
@ 2,0 SAY "First number:"
@ 4,0 SAY "Second number:"
@ 5,20 SAY "=========="
@ 6,0 SAY "Result:"
STORE 99 TO one,two
* Setup an endless loop
DO WHILE .T.
  STORE 0 TO one,two,finished
  @ 2,20 GET one PICTURE "#######.##"
  @ 4,20 GET two PICTURE "#######.##"
  @ 7,20 GET finished PICTURE "@*v FINISHED" FONT ,256
  READ
  IF finished = 1
    EXIT   && exit to line following ENDDO
  ENDIF && clicked on "FINISHED" text button
  result = one + two
  @ 6,20 SAY result PICTURE "#######.##"
  WAIT
ENDDO && do forever
SCREEN 1 OFF
CLEAR
```

```
RETURN
* EOF calc2.prg
```

The screen produced by the calc2a.prg is shown in Figure 3-04. Since .T. is a logical constant, the condition .T. will always be true. Therefore, the only way to stop the program from endlessly prompting the user for two numbers to add then is to include an EXIT command as one of the commands inside the loop. (Note to experienced programmers: Yes, you can also RETURN from inside a loop, but we won't discuss subroutines until later.)

If we execute an EXIT command every time we enter this DO WHILE loop however, we will have at most one iteration of the commands inside the loop. The solution to our dilemma lies in the second of FoxBASE+'s program control structures, the IF...ENDIF command.

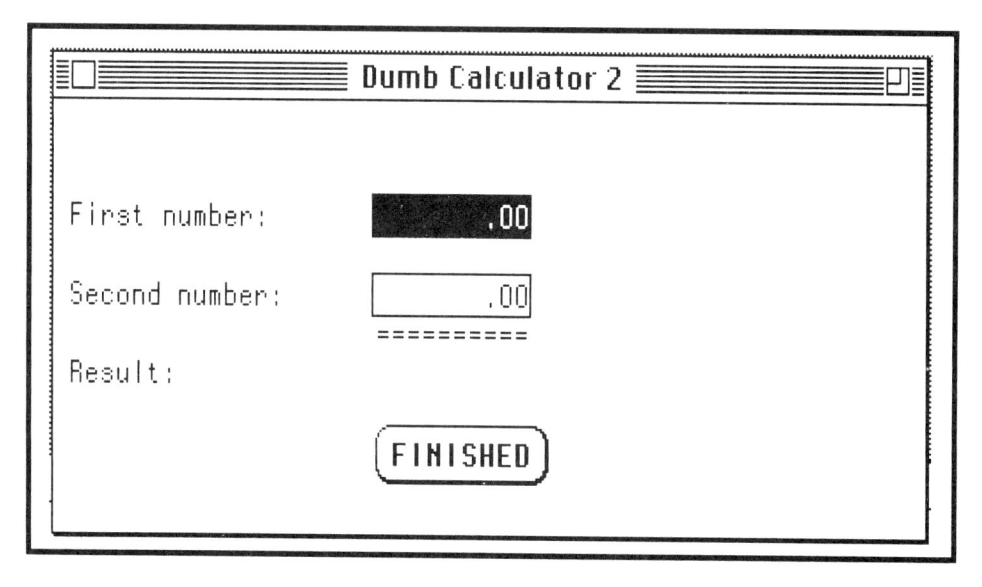

Figure 3-04. Finishable calculator.

Priming and endless loops

Note that we have added a new GET statement to the program. Not only does the FINISHED text button add a more Mac-like feel to our program, it offers an obvious way for us to determine whether the user wants to continue adding two numbers. All we have to do is see if the user clicked on the FINISHED text button. If he did, we want to exit the DO WHILE loop.

Consequently, we use the IF command to see the finished variable is equal to 1. If it is, the user has clicked on the FINISHED text button, and the program will execute the commands between the "IF finished = 1" and "ENDIF" commands.

In this case, the command EXIT will be executed. The EXIT command will cause control of the program to be immediately transferred to the first line following the ENDDO command. As a result, the commands that add the variables, display the result, and WAIT for the user, will be omitted when the user clicks on the FINISHED text button.

We see from these two versions of the calc2.prg that there are two primary methods of using a DO WHILE loop when we want to be sure that at least some of the commands inside the loop are executed at least once.

The method outlined in calc2.prg calls for the values in the DO WHILE condition to be primed so that the DO WHILE condition will be true at least once. The commands inside the loop will be responsible for changing the DO WHILE condition to false. When the condition is false, and the program encounters the ENDDO command, the program will continue with the next command after the ENDDO statement.

The method outlined in calc2a.prg calls for the use of an endless loop where the DO WHILE condition is always true. Here the programmer must include an EXIT command inside the loop to allow the program to continue. This EXIT command should be subject to some condition within the loop.

Which approach is better? Each method has its champions. The priming method can be more clear than the endless loop method because DO WHILE .T. is much less descriptive to a programmer than is DO WHILE one # 0 .AND. two # 0. Further, because the priming method requires no additional IF...ENDIF commands, it can result in more concise programs.

In our experience however, one good comment preceding the DO WHILE .T. statement will suffice for most programmers, thereby rendering the endless loop approach as readable as the priming method. Further, there is no need to artificially assign a value to a variable to enter an endless loop and this can considerably improve readability. Also, the EXIT command offers the flexibility of exiting the loop prior to encountering the ENDDO command, and this can enhance readability in large loop constructs. In some circumstances, the endless loop method can reduce the number of variables needed to perform a task, thereby rendering the program easier to maintain. Finally, the endless loop approach usually results in marginally faster programs.

For the rest of this book, we will use the endless loop approach whenever possible. This selection is mostly a matter of personal preference however, and many good programmers will counsel against the endless loop method. To each his own.

IF...ENDIF

The IF...ENDIF command that we encountered in calc2a.prg is another control structure, and one of the most common. Its use is straightforward. To use the IF command you need:

```
1. The IF statement itself.
2. A condition for the IF command to evaluate.
3. One or more FoxBASE+ commands to be executed if the condition
is true.
4. An ENDIF statement.
```

If the condition is true, the commands between the IF and the ENDIF will be executed. If the condition is false, the program will skip the commands between the IF and ENDIF, and continue with the command following the ENDIF.

Note that the ENDIF and ENDDO commands are both followed by what appear to be comments. FoxBASE+ allows programmers to place comments after the closing command of a control structure. For the DO WHILE control structure, ENDDO is the closing command. For the IF control structure, ENDIF is the closing command. As an aid to readability, we always place comments after closing commands. While this is helpful even in small programs, the practice is invaluable when dealing with large programs where the start and end of a control structure may be separated by several hundred lines of code.

Nested IFs

In the next incarnation of our calculator program, we wish to provide the user with options to perform addition, subtraction, multiplication, and division on two numbers. Further, we wish to allow the user to specify whether the result of the current operation should be accumulated for use in the next operation. All of this is accomplished in the calc3.prg program that follows:

```
* calc3.prg
* 5 function calculator
SCREEN 1 HEADING "Dumb Calculator"
CLEAR     && make screen 1 blank
SCREEN 1 FONT "MONACO",12  && assign font type & size
SCREEN 1 TOP   && put screen 1 on top of desktop
SCREEN 1 SIZE 10,55  && 10 rows of 55 characters each
SCREEN 1 AT 0,0   && Center screen 1 on monitor
* Put some prompts on screen
@ 2,0 SAY "First number:"
@ 4,0 SAY "Second number:"
@ 5,20 SAY "=========="
@ 6,0 SAY "Result:"
* Setup variables
STORE 0 TO one,two,result,finished
```

```
accum = .F. && default to do not accumulate
finished = 0  && not finished by default
thismath = 1  && addition by default
* Enter an endless loop
DO WHILE .T.
  * make the second number 0
  two=0
  * see if we are accumulating
  IF .NOT.accum  && not accumulating
    * make the first number 0 and allow
    * the user to edit the first number
    one=0
    @ 2,20 GET one PICTURE "#######.##"
  ELSE  && user wants to accumulate
    * assign the result of the previous
    * operation to the first number
    one=result
    * Display the first number, but do not
    * allow editing
    @ 2,20 SAY one PICTURE "#######.##"
  ENDIF && not accumulating
  * Always get the second number
  @ 4,20 GET two PICTURE "#######.##"
  * Use Radio buttons to determine the
  * operation to use
  @ 0,40 GET thismath PICTURE ;
  "@*Rv ADD;SUBTRACT;MULTIPLY;DIVIDE" FONT "MONACO",9
  * Use a Check box to see if the user wants to accumulate
  * the result of the next operation
  @ 6,40 GET accum PICTURE "@*C Accumulate"
  * Use a text button to see if the user is finished
  @ 7,20 GET finished PICTURE "@*v FINISHED" FONT ,256
  READ
  IF finished = 1
    * Clicked on finished
    EXIT && exit do while .t. loop
  ELSE && did not click on finished
    IF thismath = 1
      * chose to add
      result = one + two
    ELSE && not add
      IF thismath = 2
        * chose to subtract
        result = one - two
      ELSE && not subtract
        IF thismath = 3
          * chose to multiply
          result = one * two
```

Nested IFs 67

```
      ELSE && not multiply
        IF thismath = 4
          * chose to divide
          result = one / two
        ENDIF divide
      ENDIF multiply
    ENDIF subtract
  ENDIF add
ENDIF finished
* put the result on the screen
@ 6,20 SAY result PICTURE "#######.##"
ENDDO    && endless loop
CLEAR
RETURN
* EOF calc2.prg
```

You can see the screen generated by accumulating the result of multiplying 2 * 2 * 2 * 2 * 2 * 2 in Figure 3-05. In calc3.prg we have introduced the IF...ELSE...ENDIF control structure. We have also introduced the Radio Button and Check Box features of the FoxBASE+/Mac @...GET com-

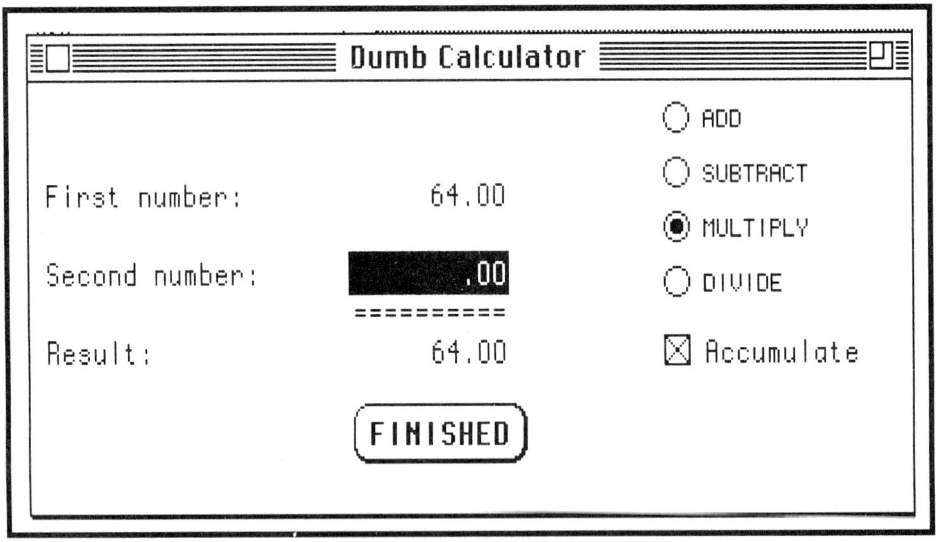

Figure 3-05. Four function calculator.

mand.

The IF...ELSE...ENDIF control structure allows us to choose between many possible conditions. In the IF...ELSE...ENDIF construct, the commands between the IF and the ELSE are executed if the condition is true. If the condition is false, the commands between the ELSE and the ENDIF command are executed.

As you can see from the listing of the calc3.prg program, it is possible to nest control structures. That is, it is possible, and common, to include one control structure within another. Because this activity can make the program hard to read, it is good programming technique to indent each conditional level of the program.

At Micro Endeavors we prefer two spaces per indent, but any number of spaces between 2 and 8 is acceptable. To facilitate this indenting process, you can direct the FoxBASE+/Mac editor to automatically indent the next program line to the current indent level when the programmer presses [Enter]. This is accomplished through the Preferences... option of the Edit menu when editing a program. Figure 3-06 shows the Edit Preference dialog with my personal preferences marked.

You can generate the indents by pressing the [Tab] key, or by pressing the [Space] bar twice. The [Tab] method allows you to outdent by pressing [Back-space] once, while the [Space] method requires two [Back-space] key presses. I prefer the [Space] method, but either will suffice.

The trace window

To see how this program works, I would like to introduce one of FoxBASE+/Mac's most valuable programming tools, the TRACE window. While the TRACE window is most often used to debug a program, it can also be used to illustrate the flow of a program. To effect this illustration, save Calc3.prg as calc3a.prg, and add the following commands to the calc3a.prg program:

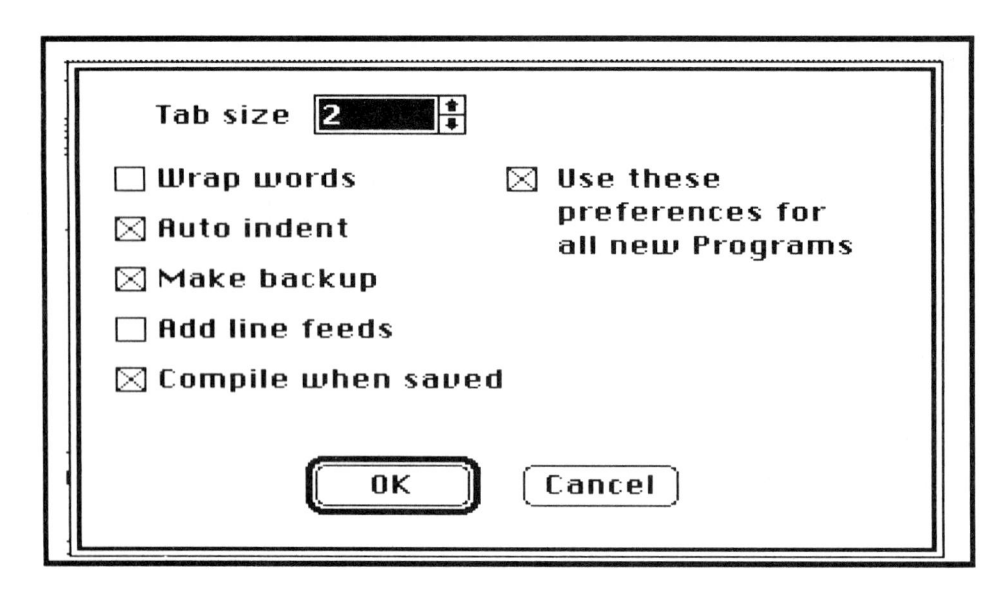

Figure 3-06. Edit preference dialog.

```
SET ECHO ON
SET STEP ON
```

Next, choose the TRACE option of the Window menu as we have done in Figure 3-07. This will produce a TRACE window, which you can drag to the lower left hand corner of the screen as I have in Figure 3-08. Be sure to leave all of the window controls on the screen, as we will need access to them later. Now, click the calc3a.prg window, and press [Command]+E to run the program.

Nothing happens! Don't panic, all is well. Click on the Trace window to bring it to the top of the desktop, as we have in Figure 3-09. Note the two buttons in the lower right corner of the Trace window. Also note that the calc3a.prg program appears in the Trace window, with one line hi-lighted.

Click on the resume button, and you can watch as each command in your calc3a.prg program is executed. When FoxBASE+/Mac reaches the fol-

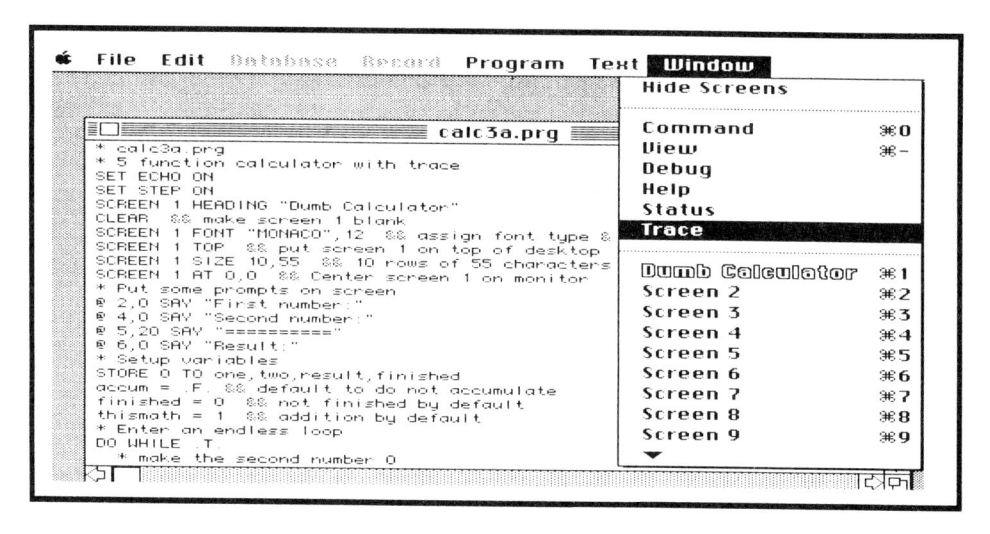

Figure 3-07. Trace from window menu.

lowing command, the Trace window will disappear:

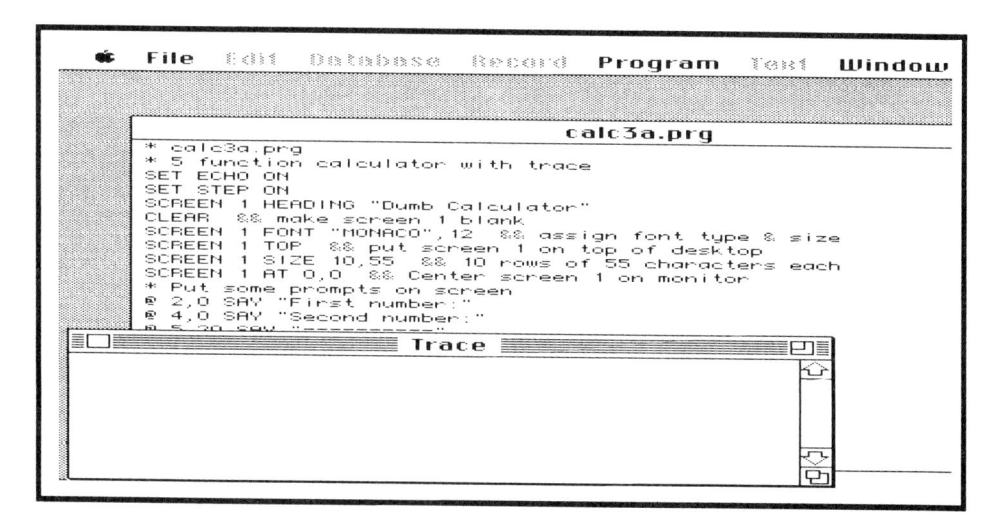

Figure 3-08. Trace window.

The trace window

```
┌─────────────────────────────────────────────────┐
│ ▤▤▤▤▤▤▤▤▤▤▤▤▤ Trace ▤▤▤▤▤▤▤▤▤▤▤▤▤ │
│   * calc3a.prg                              ⇧   │
│   * 5 function calculator with trace            │
│   SET ECHO ON                                   │
│   SET STEP ON                                   │
│   SCREEN 1 HEADING "Dumb Calculator"            │
│   CLEAR && make screen 1 blank                  │
│                           ( cancel ) ( resume ) │
└─────────────────────────────────────────────────┘
```

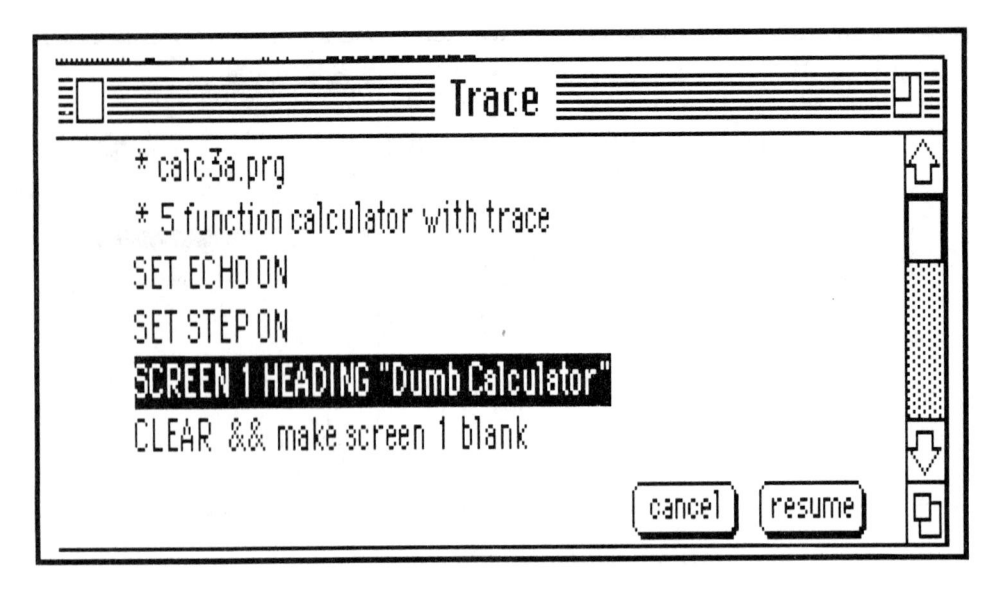

Figure 3-09. Active trace window.

SCREEN 1 TOP

Bring the Trace window forward by clicking on the Trace window or, if the Trace window is completely hidden, by choosing the Trace option of the Window menu as in Figure 3-07. This technique of stepping through a program is very helpful when working with programs that include multiple conditional statements.

You can step through the entire program, or you can click on the cancel button of the Trace window to cancel the program. When you are through, be sure to call up the command window and issue the following commands:

SET STEP OFF
SET ECHO OFF

This will turn off the STEP and ECHO processes so that subsequent programs will operate normally.

DO CASE...ENDCASE

Now it is time to visit the last of FoxBASE+/Mac's conditional constructs. To do so, edit the calc3.prg program, and save it as calc4.prg. Then change calc4.prg as follows:

```
* calc4.prg
* 5 function calculator with Do Case
SCREEN 1 HEADING "Dumb Calculator"
CLEAR    && make screen 1 blank
SCREEN 1 FONT "MONACO",12   && assign font type & size
SCREEN 1 TOP   && put screen 1 on top of desktop
SCREEN 1 SIZE 10,55   && 10 rows of 55 characters each
SCREEN 1 AT 0,0   && Center screen 1 on monitor
* Put some prompts on screen
@ 2,0 SAY "First number:"
@ 4,0 SAY "Second number:"
@ 5,20 SAY "=========="
@ 6,0 SAY "Result:"
* Setup variables
STORE 0 TO one,two,result,finished
accum = .F. && default to do not accumulate
finished = 0   && not finished by default
thismath = 1   && addition by default
* Enter an endless loop
DO WHILE .T.
  * make the second number 0
  two=0
  * see if we are accumulating
  IF .NOT.accum   && not accumulating
    * make the first number 0 and allow
    * the user to edit the first number
    one=0
    @ 2,20 GET one PICTURE "#######.##"
  ELSE  && user wants to accumulate
    * assign the result of the previous
    * operation to the first number
    one=result
    * Display the first number, but do not
    * allow editing
    @ 2,20 SAY one PICTURE "#######.##"
  ENDIF && not accumulating
  * Always get the second number
  @ 4,20 GET two PICTURE "#######.##"
  * Use Radio buttons to determine the
```

```
* operation to use
@ 0,40 GET thismath PICTURE ;
"@*Rv ADD;SUBTRACT;MULTIPLY;DIVIDE" FONT "MONACO",9
* Use a Check box to see if the user wants to accumulate
* the result of the next operation
@ 6,40 GET accum PICTURE "@*C Accumulate"
* Use a text button to see if the user is finished
@ 7,20 GET finished PICTURE "@*v FINISHED" FONT ,256
READ
DO CASE
   CASE finished = 1
      * Clicked on finished
      EXIT && exit do while .t. loop
   CASE thismath = 1
      * chose to add
      result = one + two
   CASE thismath = 2
      * chose to subtract
      result = one - two
   CASE thismath = 3
      * chose to multiply
      result = one * two
   CASE thismath = 4
      * chose to divide
      result = one / two
  ENDCASE && finished or math operation
  * put the result on the screen
  @ 6,20 SAY result PICTURE "#######.##"
ENDDO   && endless loop
CLEAR
RETURN
* EOF calc4.prg
```

This program accomplishes exactly the same result as does the calc3.prg program, but it does so with several fewer levels of indentation, and several fewer commands. In this book, and in our daily business, we use the DO CASE structure in lieu of nested IF statements whenever possible.

Every DO CASE structure consists of: a DO CASE statement; one or more CASE condition statements, each of which is usually accompanied by one or more FoxBASE+ commands; and an ENDCASE statement. To see how the CASE statement works, let's assume that the operator running the calc4a.prg program clicks on the Multiply option of the thismath radio button list.

When FoxBASE+ encounters the DO CASE statement, it evaluates the condition associated with the first CASE statement. Upon discovering that the condition finished = 1 is false, FoxBASE+ moves to the next CASE statement. Since the thismath does not equal 1, FoxBASE+ skips to the next CASE statement. When the condition thismath = 2 turns out to be false, FoxBASE+ moves to the next CASE statement.

This time however, the CASE condition is true, the Multiply button is the third Radio button associated with the thismath GET statement. As a result, FoxBASE+ begins performing the next command, which is result = one * two. FoxBASE+ will continue to execute commands until it encounters another CASE statement, or an ENDCASE statement. When FoxBASE+ encounters another CASE statement or the ENDCASE statement, it skips to the next line following the ENDCASE statement.

In this program then, the variable result is assigned the value of the variable one multiplied by the variable two. Then the program skips to the following command:

```
@ 6,20 SAY result PICTURE "#######.##"
```

(Of course, if you don't believe me, you could issue the SET STEP ON and SET ECHO ON commands to watch the program run in the trace window.)

Note that FoxBASE+ only looks for the first occurrence of a true CASE. If there is more than one true CASE, only the first one will be discovered.

What if none of the CASE conditions is true? If none of the CASE conditions are true, none of the commands between the DO CASE and the ENDCASE will be performed, unless you add an optional command to your DO CASE structure.

The optional command is the OTHERWISE command. The OTHERWISE command usually appears after the last CASE statement in a DO CASE structure. Simply put, if none of the CASE conditions is true, the commands that follow the OTHERWISE statement are executed. Here is a simple example that demonstrates the use of the OTHERWISE statement:

```
* docase1.prg
* Demonstrates the use of the OTHERWISE clause
SCREEN 1 TOP
CLEAR
x = 1
DO WHILE x<=10
   DO CASE
      CASE x=2
         ? "Two"
      CASE x=4
         ? "Four"
      CASE x=6
         ? "Six"
      CASE x=8
         ? "Eight"
```

```
╔═══════════════ Dumb Calculator ═══════════════╗

  Two          1  is not an even number.

               3  is not an even number.
  Four
               5  is not an even number.
  Six
               7  is not an even number.
  Eight
               9  is not an even number.
  Ten
```

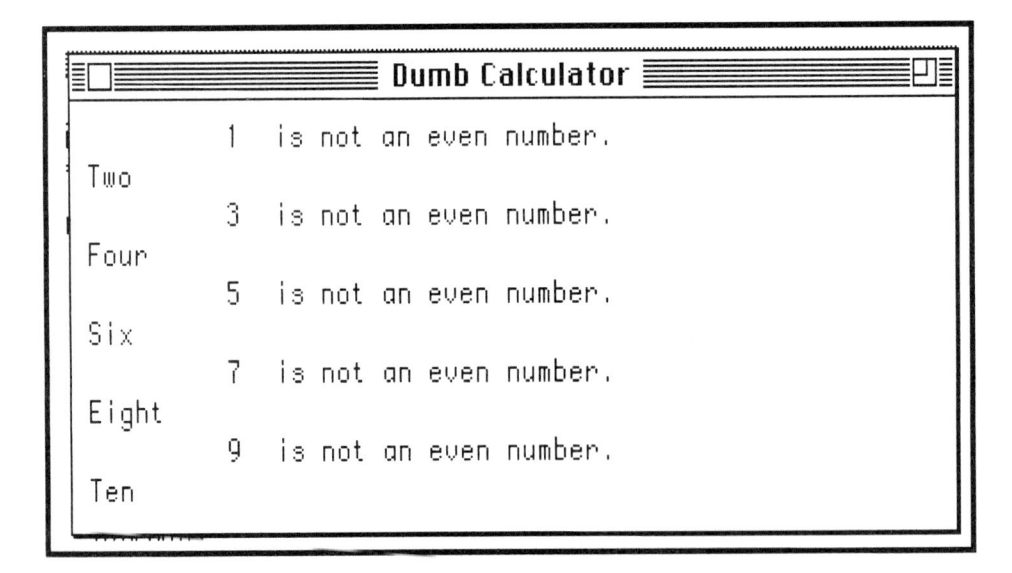

Figure 3-10. Otherwise command.

```
      CASE x=10
         ? "Ten"
      OTHERWISE
         * These commands will be executed if none of the
         * CASE conditions is true
         ? x," is not an even number."
   ENDCASE
   x=x+1
ENDDO
RETURN
* eof docase1.prg
```

The output from docase1.prg is shown in Figure 3-10. Note that the OTHERWISE clause is optional. There is nothing intrinsically wrong with the OTHERWISE command, but we prefer to process each potentiality with its own CASE statement whenever possible.

4. Data Types

In the first several chapters we have had some exposure to the idea of different data types. In subsequent chapters it will become increasingly important to be proficient in dealing with different data types. This short chapter is therefore dedicated to making clear the techniques used to compare, process, and convert not just numeric data as we did in the calc programs, but also date, logical, and character data types.

Comparing items

All of the relational operators can be used to compare two character items, or two date items, or two numeric items. Logical data items cannot be compared. What is a relational operator? Funny you should ask, since I just happen to have a list of FoxBASE+/Mac relational operators right here:

```
RELATIONAL OPERATORS
OPERATOR        DESCRIPTION
<<               Less than
>>               Greater than
=               Equal to
<<>>              Not equal to
#               Not equal to
<<=              Less than or equal to
>>=              Greater than or equal to
$               First string "in" second string
==              First character string equal to second
                character string.  (Note: when EXACT is SET
                ON, trailing blanks are significant to the
                comparison.)
```

One way of describing relational operators is to say that they accept two data items, and return a true or false value. So, for example, the following expression includes a relational operator, and is always false:

```
1234 = 1235
```

None of the relational operators can be used to compare items of different data types. Since it is frequently necessary to compare items of different data types, this could be a major problem. Fortunately, FoxBASE+/Mac provides a variety of tools for converting values of one data type to another data type. Most of these methods involve the use of functions. (Note: Don't confuse the following FoxBASE+/Mac functions with the PICTURE functions we discussed earlier. These functions play an entirely different role in program development than do the PICTURE functions.)

In general, FoxBASE+/Mac functions take one or more arguments, and return a value. It is important to understand that these functions don't actually change anything. They simply return a value. It is up to the programmer to make use of that returned value.

Mixing data types

Let's compare a numeric value to a character value. Here is the program segment:

```
* data1.prg
* demonstrrates a comparison of two different data types
* Define a screen
SCREEN 1 TOP SIZE 24,80 AT 0,0 FONT "MONACO",9
CLEAR
* assign a numeric constant to vnum
vnum = 123.67
* assign a character constant to the vletter variable
vletter = "17"
* Use the VAL function to compare the numeric variable
* vnum, with the VAL() of the character variable vletter
? vnum = VAL(vletter)
* Use the VAL() function to add the numeric value of the
* character variable vletter to the numeric variable vnum
vnum = vnum + VAL(vletter)
```

```
? vnum
* Display the name, type, and content of all current
* variables
DISPLAY MEMORY
WAIT
RETURN
*eof data1.prg
```

The output of data1.prg is reflected in Figure 4-01. The DISPLAY MEMORY command causes FoxBASE+/Mac to list all outstanding memory variable names, types, values, sizes, PUBLIC or PRIVATE status, and the program in which the variable was created. This command, in addition to its value in demonstrating the conversion of data types, is invaluable when debugging programs.

Note that we can't simply compare the variable vnum to the variable vletter because they are of different data types. The VAL() function returns a numeric value. In essence then, we are not comparing vnum to

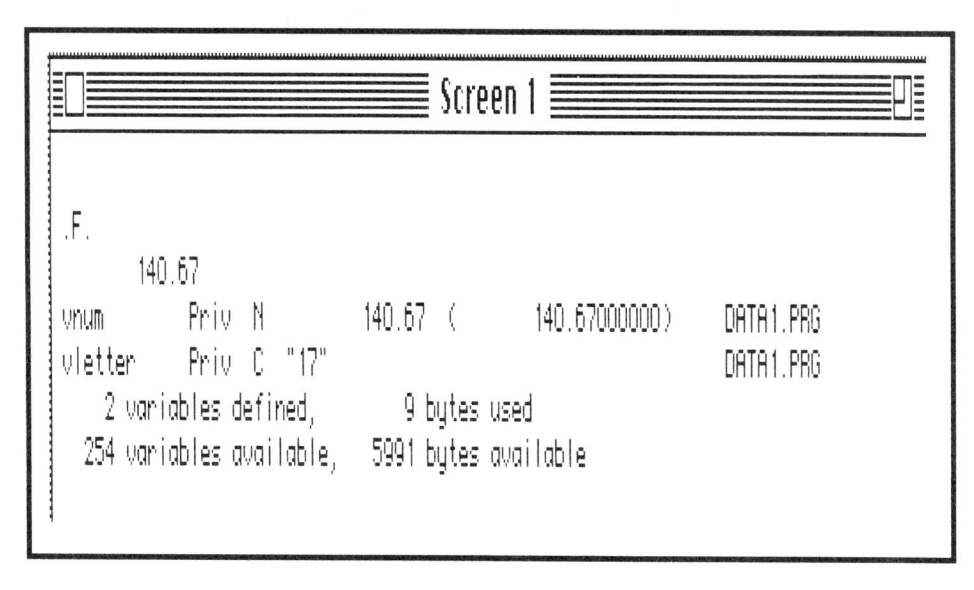

```
.F.
       140.67
vnum       Priv  N    140.67  (     140.67000000)    DATA1.PRG
vletter    Priv  C    "17"                           DATA1.PRG
     2 variables defined,      9 bytes used
   254 variables available,  5991 bytes available
```

Figure 4-01. Numeric vs. character.

Mixing data types

vletter, we are comparing vnum to the VAL() of vletter. Note that after we use the VAL() function, vletter is still a character type variable. The VAL() function does not change vletter.

If we want to change the data type of the vletter variable, we will need to issue a command like this:

```
vletter = VAL(vletter)
```

Our second data conversion program shows all of the ways to convert data types. Note that the efforts to convert dates to numerics and numerics to dates are not usually necessary. As we shall see after this program, FoxBASE+/Mac date items have special properties that allow them to be used directly with numeric items. Here is the second data conversion program:

```
* data2.prg
* demonstrrates a comparison of two different data types
* Define a screen
SCREEN 1 TOP SIZE 18,80 AT 40,0 FONT "MONACO",9
SCREEN 1 HEADING "ALL TYPES"
CLEAR
* number from character
oldvar = "87"
newvar = VAL(oldvar)
? oldvar,TYPE("oldvar"),newvar,TYPE("newvar")
* date from character
oldvar = "12/31/87"
newvar = CTOD(oldvar)
? oldvar,TYPE("oldvar"),newvar,TYPE("newvar")
* logical from character
oldvar = "Y"
newvar = oldvar = "Y"
? oldvar,TYPE("oldvar"),newvar,TYPE("newvar")
* character from number
oldvar = 765.893
newvar = STR(oldvar)
? oldvar,TYPE("oldvar"),newvar,TYPE("newvar")
* date from number
oldvar = 2447094
newvar = CTOD(SYS(10,oldvar))
? oldvar,TYPE("oldvar"),newvar,TYPE("newvar")
```

```
* logical from number
oldvar = 56
newvar = oldvar = 75
? oldvar,TYPE("oldvar"),newvar,TYPE("newvar")
* character from date
oldvar = CTOD("12/10/87")
newvar = DTOC(oldvar)
? oldvar,TYPE("oldvar"),newvar,TYPE("newvar")
* numeric from date
oldvar = CTOD("06/24/58")
newvar = VAL(SYS(11,oldvar))
? oldvar,TYPE("oldvar"),newvar,TYPE("newvar")
* logical from date
oldvar = CTOD("06/12/86")
newvar = oldvar = DATE()
? oldvar,TYPE("oldvar"),newvar,TYPE("newvar")
* numeric year from date
oldvar = DATE()
newvar = YEAR(oldvar)
? oldvar,TYPE("oldvar"),newvar,TYPE("newvar")
* numeric day of month from date
oldvar = DATE()
newvar = DAY(oldvar)
? oldvar,TYPE("oldvar"),newvar,TYPE("newvar")
* numeric day of week from date
oldvar = DATE()
newvar = DOW(oldvar)
? oldvar,TYPE("oldvar"),newvar,TYPE("newvar")
* numeric month from date
oldvar = DATE()
newvar = MONTH(oldvar)
? oldvar,TYPE("oldvar"),newvar,TYPE("newvar")
* character day of week from date
oldvar = DATE()
newvar = CDOW(oldvar)
? oldvar,TYPE("oldvar"),newvar,TYPE("newvar")
* character month from date
oldvar = DATE()
newvar = CMONTH(oldvar)
? oldvar,TYPE("oldvar"),newvar,TYPE("newvar")
RETURN
* data2.prg
```

(Note: If you ever need to know the type of a memory variable or database field, and you don't have the time or inclination to peruse all of the output from a DISPLAY MEMORY or DISPLAY STRUCTURE command, use the TYPE("memvar") function to determine the item's data type.)

The Debug window

The output from data2.prg can be seen in Figure 4-02. There is another way to watch the contents of variables change however, and that is through the use of the Debug window. To test this capability, pull down the Window menu. Then, select the Trace window. Next, move the Trace window to the lower left corner of the monitor as I have done in Figure 4-03.

Now, pull down the window menu, and select the Debug option. Move the Debug window toward the lower right corner of the screen as I have in Figure 4-04. Click in the left side of the Debug box, and type the variable name "oldvar". Press [Enter]. Type the name "newvar". Move the pointer

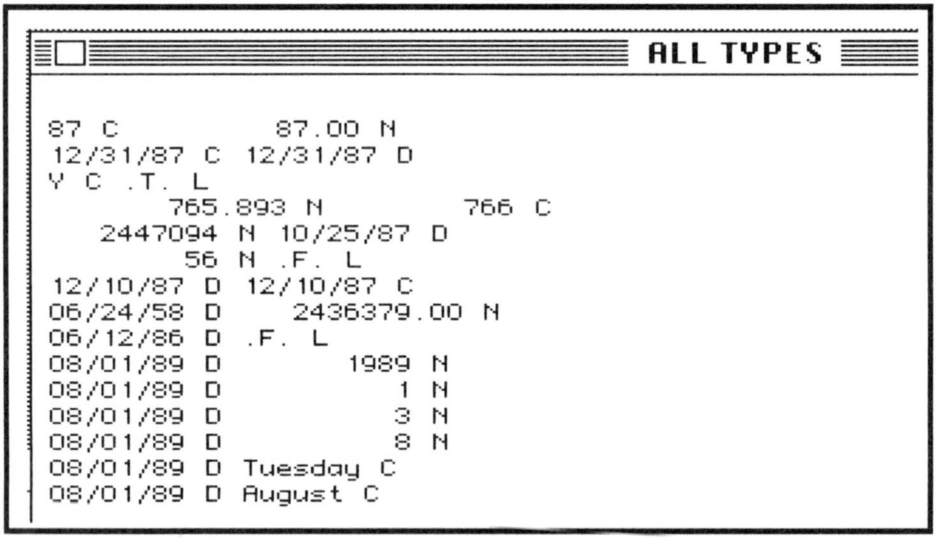

```
                                          ALL TYPES

 87 C              87.00 N
 12/31/87 C  12/31/87 D
 Y  C  .T. L
         765.893 N           766 C
      2447094 N  10/25/87 D
           56 N  .F. L
 12/10/87 D  12/10/87 C
 06/24/58 D       2436379.00 N
 06/12/86 D  .F. L
 08/01/89 D         1989 N
 08/01/89 D            1 N
 08/01/89 D            3 N
 08/01/89 D            8 N
 08/01/89 D  Tuesday C
 08/01/89 D  August  C
```

Figure 4-02. All types of data.

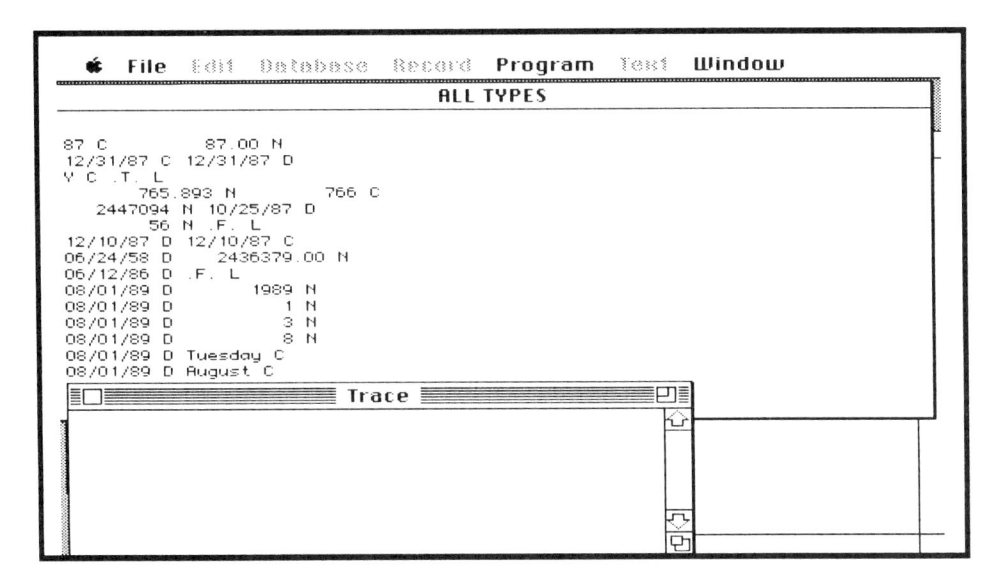

Figure 4-03. Open trace window.

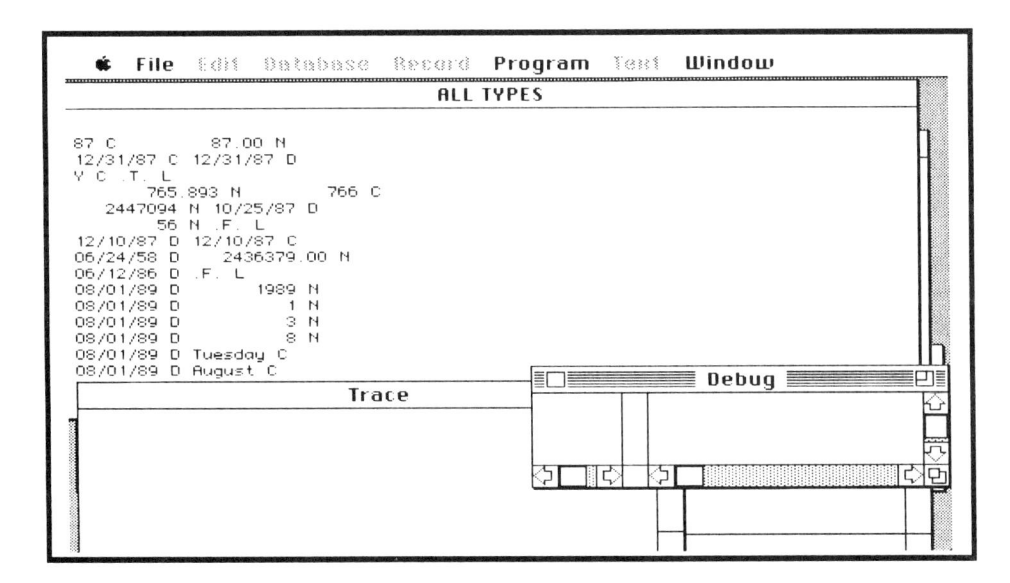

Figure 4-04. Open debug window.

The Debug window

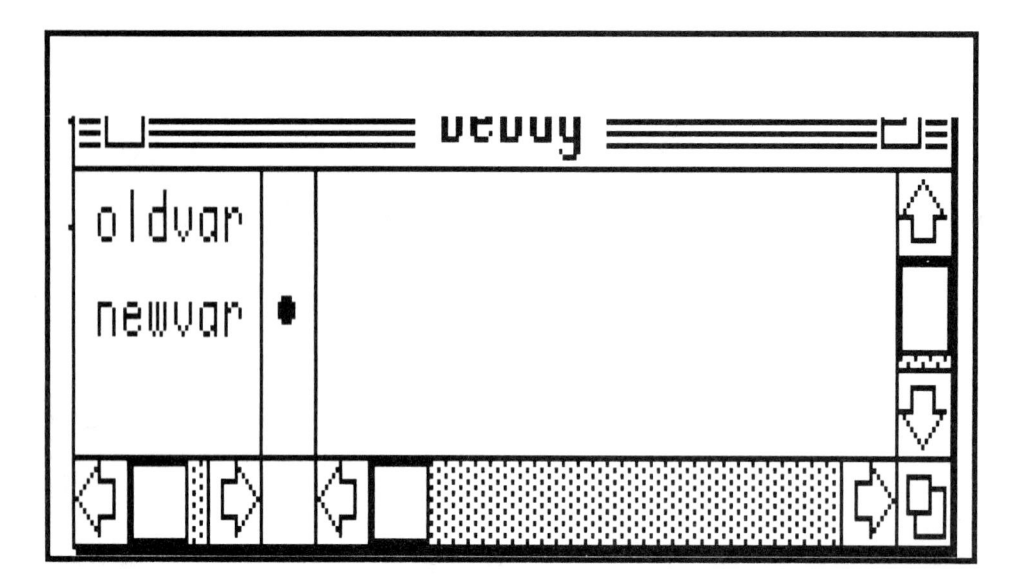

Figure 4-05. Filled debug window.

to the middle column of the debug window, and click next to the name "newvar". When you are finished you should have a debug window that looks like Figure 4-05.

Now bring up the command window, and enter this command:

```
DO data2
```

You will be presented with a confused screen similar to the one in Figure 4-06. Pull down the Window menu, and select the Debug window. Then pull down the Window menu, and select the Trace window. Click on the Debug window, and move it above the Trace window so that its contents show. This will give you a screen similar to Figure 4-07.

To continue the program, click on the Trace window, and then click on the resume button. Repeat these last two actions every time the Suspended message appears.

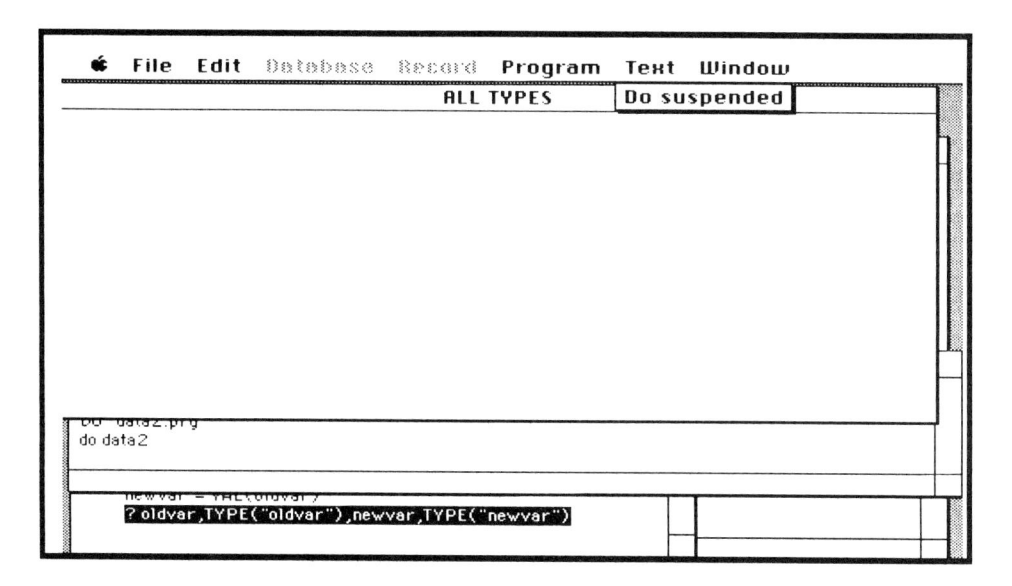

Figure 4-06. Confused data2.

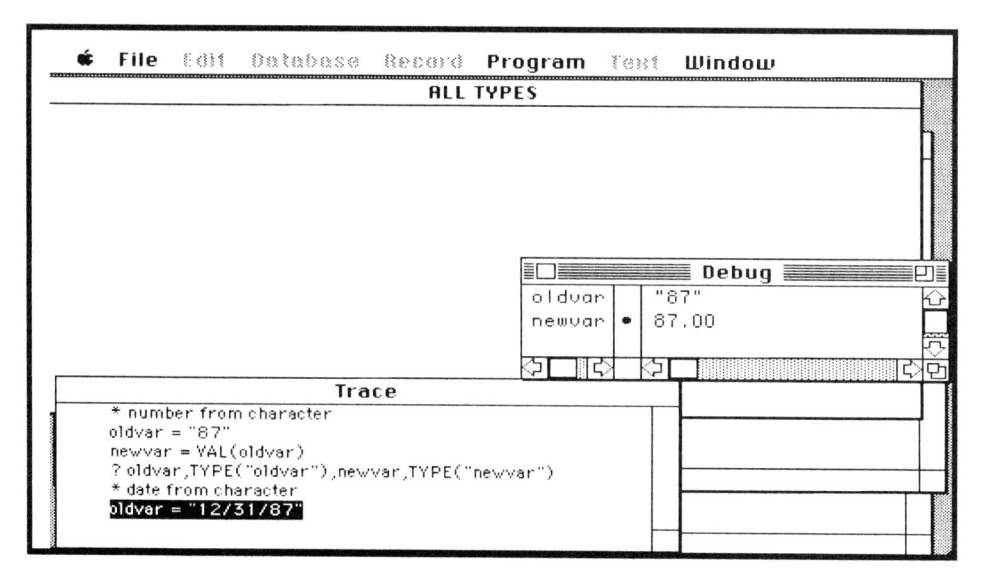

Figure 4-07. Trace & debug.

The Debug window

In this way you can watch each command in data2.prg execute in the Trace window, while you watch the content of the oldvar and newvar variables change in the debug window.

Why does the program stop after every command that changes the content of the newvar variable you ask? Because you directed FoxBASE+/Mac to suspend processing whenever the content of newvar is changed. This was accomplished when you clicked the center column of the debug window next to the newvar variable name. You can click this break-point off if you like, or just keep clicking on the resume button of the trace window until the data2.prg program finishes.

The Debug and Trace windows have application well beyond illustrating the creation of variables of different data types. For example, the Debug window allows you to enter any expression in the left column, not just variable names. Further, you can enter any number of expressions, and any number of these can include break-points. Obviously, the window can be scrolled horizontally and vertically, resized, and moved to facilitate viewing.

In addition, you can direct FoxBASE+/Mac to stop execution of a program at a specific line or lines in that program by holding the [Command] key and clicking on that line in the Trace window. This is in addition to the use of the SET STEP ON command, which allows you to execute one command at a time.

You can consult Chapter 6 of your User's Guide manual to obtain more information on the use of the Trace and Debug windows. For now however, close both windows so that we can resume our investigation of data types and their interactions.

The STR() function

There is no need to memorize the functions in the data2.prg program. Just remember that any time you need to compare or manipulate two or more data items of different types, you can usually find a function to do the job. Before we move on to date math, let's refine our use of one of the most common conversion functions, the STR() function.

The STR() function accepts a numeric value as an argument, and returns a character type value. The STR() function gives the programmer control over the length of the character value that is returned, and over the number of places to the right of the decimal point. The following program demonstrates the use of the STR() function:

```
* data3.prg
* Demonstrate the flexiblity of the STR() function
* initialaize a numeric variable
vnum = 345.671234
* use the STR() function to display the same numeric
* value in several different character formats
SCREEN 1 TOP HEADING "Flexible STR()"
CLEAR
SCREEN 1 SIZE 20,80 AT 0,0 FONT "Monaco",9
@ 1,0 SAY str(vnum)
@ 1,20 SAY "Default"
@ 2,0 SAY STR(vnum,5,0)
@ 2,20 SAY ",5,0"
@ 3,0 SAY str(vnum,5,2)
@ 3,20 SAY ",5,2"
@ 4,0 SAY str(vnum,15,6)
@ 4,20 SAY ",15,6"
@ 5,0 SAY str(vnum,15)
@ 5,20 SAY ",15"
@ 6,0 SAY str(vnum,15,1)
@ 6,20 SAY ",15,1"
oksofar = 1
@ 7,33 GET oksofar PICTURE "@*h OK SO FAR"
READ
* Clear from the 7th row of the screen to the bottom
@ 7,0 CLEAR
* now let the user demonstrate
@ 8,5 SAY "Value to convert: "
@ 9,5 SAY "Length of screen:"
@ 10,5 SAY "Decimal Places:"
DO WHILE .T.
   * defaults
   STORE 0.0000 TO show,size,decimals,finished
   @ 8,40 GET show
```

The STR() function

```
  @ 9,40 GET size PICTURE "##"
  @ 10,40 GET decimals PICTURE "##"
  @ 12,33 GET finished PICTURE "@*h FINISHED"
  READ
  IF finished = 1
    * Clicked finished button
    EXIT
  ENDIF && clicked finished button
  @ 14,0 SAY "Value                  = "+STR(show)
  @ 15,0 SAY "Size of string         = "+STR(size)
  @ 16,0 SAY "# of decimal places = "+STR(decimals)
  * Clear the 18th Row
  @ 18,0
  * Show the converted value
  @ 18,0 SAY "Conversion             = "+STR(show,size,decimals)
  WAIT
ENDDO while .t.
RETURN
* eof data3.prg
```

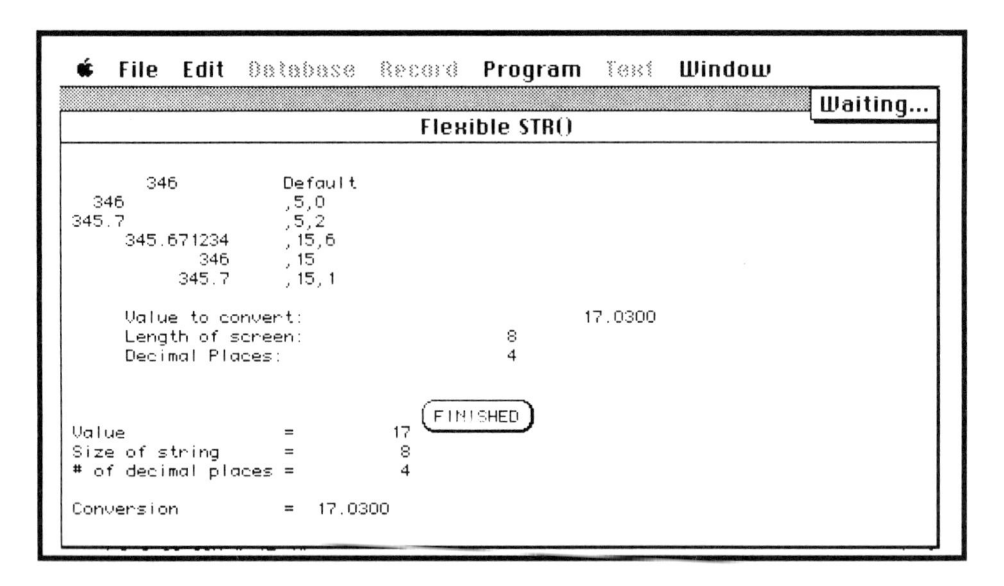

Figure 4-08. Flexible STR() function.

The result of a typical session with data3.prg is seen in Figure 4-08. We will make extensive use of the STR() function in future chapters, so take a minute to be sure that you understand its operation.

Date math

When we get to the chapters concerned with generating reports we will be particularly concerned with dates. It is frequently necessary to know how many days have elapsed between two dates. Unfortunately however, determining how many days are contained within a range of dates is tedious. Which months are involved? Any leap years involved? Fortunately, FoxBASE+/Mac does this work for us by allowing us to treat dates like numbers to perform addition and subtraction. Here is a simple program that demonstrates many of FoxBASE+/Mac's date math operations:

```
* date1.prg
* Demonstrate several date math capabilities
SCREEN 1 TOP
SCREEN 1 HEADING "Date Math"
SCREEN 1 SIZE 15,80 AT 0,0
DO WHILE .T.
  CLEAR
  * Initialize two date variables as null dates
  STORE CTOD("") TO billed,paid
  @ 5,5 SAY "Enter date of billing: " GET billed
  @ 7,5 SAY "Enter date of payment: " GET paid
  @ 9,5 SAY "Leave both dates blank to exit"
  READ
  * Then DOW() function returns the numeric day of the week
  * Sunday = 1, Saturday = 7. If DOW() returns a 0, the date
  * is either invalid, or blank.
  IF DOW(paid)=0.AND.DOW(billed)=0
    * Exit the endless loop
    EXIT
  ENDIF both dates blank
  DO CASE
    CASE billed+30 >= paid
      * bill less than 30 days old
```

```
         msg = "Current. Thank you."
      CASE billed+60 >= paid
         * bill less than 60 but more than 30
         msg = "Don't let it happen again"
      CASE billed+90 >= paid
         * bill less tan 90 but more than 60
         msg = "This is serious!"
      OTHERWISE
         * bill more than 90 days old
         msg = "You are in DEEP trouble!"
   ENDCASE
   * Determine the number of days between the billing
   * and the payment
   * Subtracting one date from another yields a numeric
   * value equal to the number of days between dates.
   howold = paid - billed
   * Tell them exactly how old the bill was
   @ 11,5 SAY "Bill was paid in "
   @ 11,22 SAY howold PICTURE "###"
   @ 11,26 say "days."
   * Tell them how you feel about this
   @ 13,5 SAY msg
   WAIT
ENDDO process choices
RETURN
* eof date1.prg
```

A typical output from the date1.prg program is seen in Figure 4-09. The use of blank dates to exit the screen is not very Mac-like, but it does serve to demonstrate a simple method for determining whether or not a data is blank.

Concatenating strings

Concatenation is a good cocktail party word that means "putting two character strings together." Fortunately, it is easier to concatenate two strings than it is to spell concatenation. Simply place a plus sign between two character items and you have concatenated two strings. Here is a program that demonstrates the concatenation process:

```
* concat1.prg
```

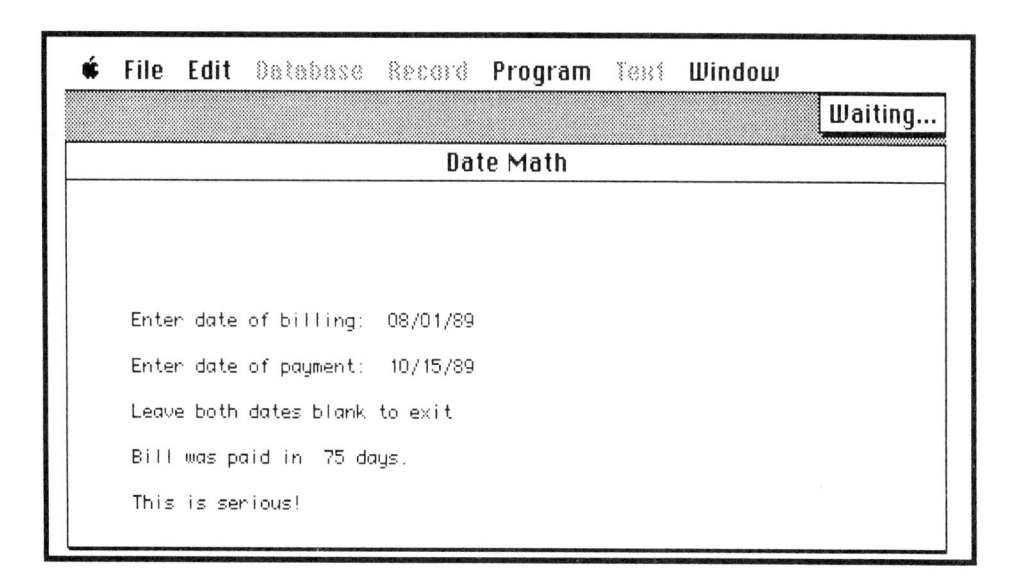

Figure 4-09. Date math.

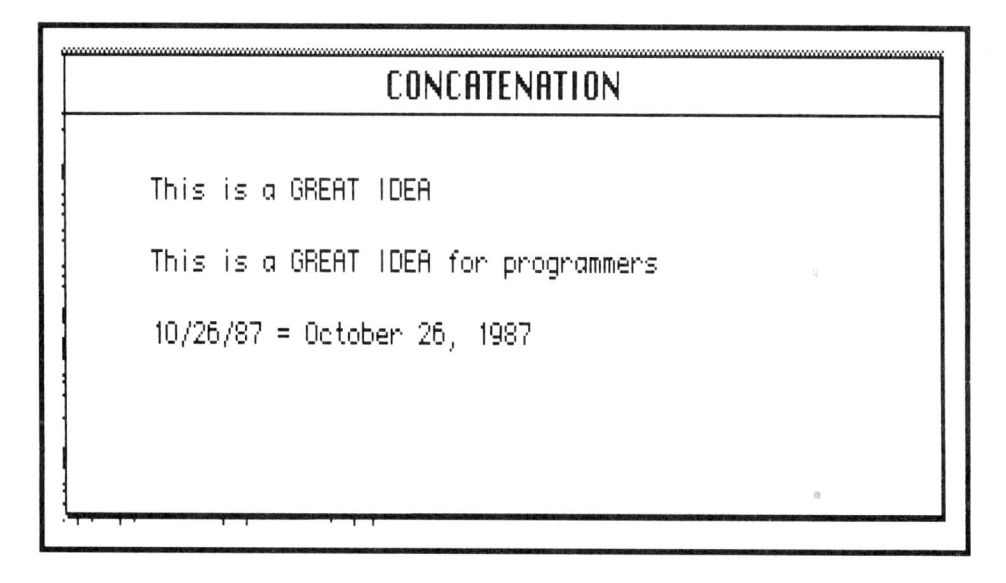

Figure 4-10. Concatenation.

Concatenating strings

```
* Demonstrate the concatenation process
SCREEN 1 TOP HEADING "CONCATENATION" FONT "MONACO",9
CLEAR
SCREEN 1 SIZE 10,60 AT 0,0
* simple concatenation
simple = "This is a " + "GREAT IDEA"
@ 1,5 SAY simple
* Concatenation using a variable
simple = simple + " for programmers"
@ 3,5 SAY simple
* initialize a date variable
today = CTOD("10/26/87")
* More complicated concatenation using date functions
words = CMONTH(today)+" "+STR(DAY(today),2)+;
   ", "+STR(YEAR(today),4)
@ 5,5 SAY DTOC(today) + " = " + words
WAIT
RETURN
* eof concat1.prg
```

The output from concat1.prg can be seen in Figure 4-10.

This concludes our primer on FoxBASE+/Mac data types and operators. In future chapters it may be helpful to refer to the programs in this chapter for: explanations of the various data conversion functions; demonstrations of date math; and the process involved in concatenating strings.

5. Database Management

The most outstanding benefit of working with the FoxBASE+ programming language is the built-in database management system that accompanies the language. In this chapter we will learn how to CREATE and INDEX database files that provide a place to store information.

Definition of terms

FoxBASE+/Mac features one structure that is used to store most of the information required for an application. This structure is called a database file. Since database files have the extension .dbf by default, these files are sometimes called dbf files.

We will investigate the following statement in detail shortly, but the main idea behind the composition of a database file can be expressed as follows:

DBFs consist of records, which consist of fields, which contain data.

All of the records in a given database file consist of the same fields. (Obviously, the content of the fields can differ from record to record.) Accordingly, when we design the structure of a database file, we are really describing the field names, field types, and field lengths to be used for every record in the database file.

Since it is usually easiest to learn by doing, let's CREATE a client database to contain the names, addresses, phone numbers and contacts for all of our clients. Our eventual goal will be to write a program that will allow us to load all of our clients into the database file, and then retrieve the information we need.

Our first step is to enter the following command in the command window:

```
CREATE client
```

After issuing this command, you will be presented with the dialog reproduced in Figure 5-01. At this point you are expected to enter the names, types, and lengths of the fields to be used for every record in the client dbf. Field names can be up to 10 characters in length, must begin with a letter, and can contain numbers, letters, and underscores. Each field must be assigned a CHARACTER, NUMERIC, DATE, LOGIC, or MEMO data type. (Note: MEMO fields have limited use in most applications since they are difficult to reference.) Please enter the field names, field types, and field lengths utilized in Figure 5-02.

When you have finished entering the field information, click on OK, listed above, press the Return key twice, and click on NO when you are

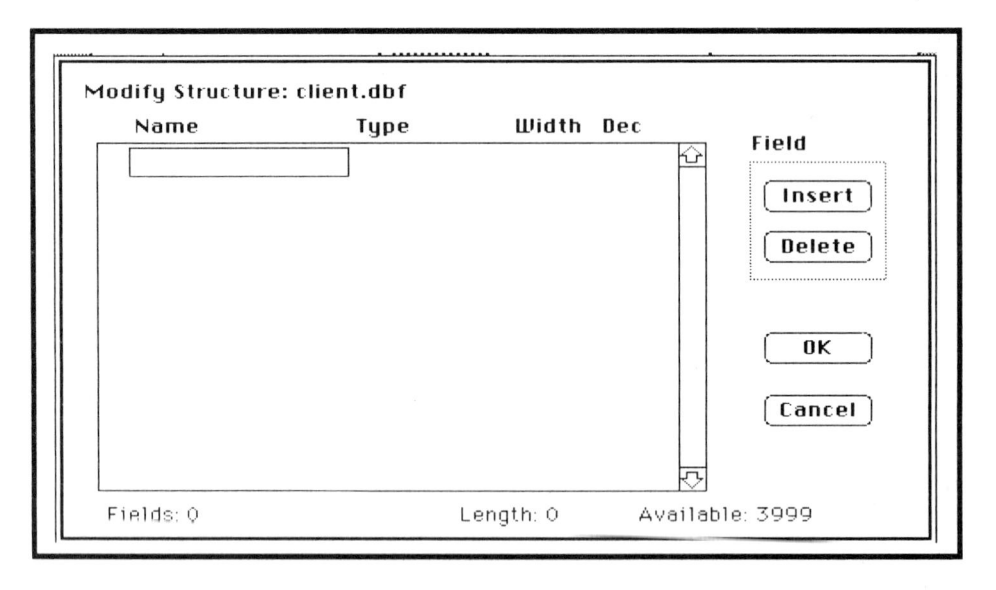

Figure 5-01. Creating a database.

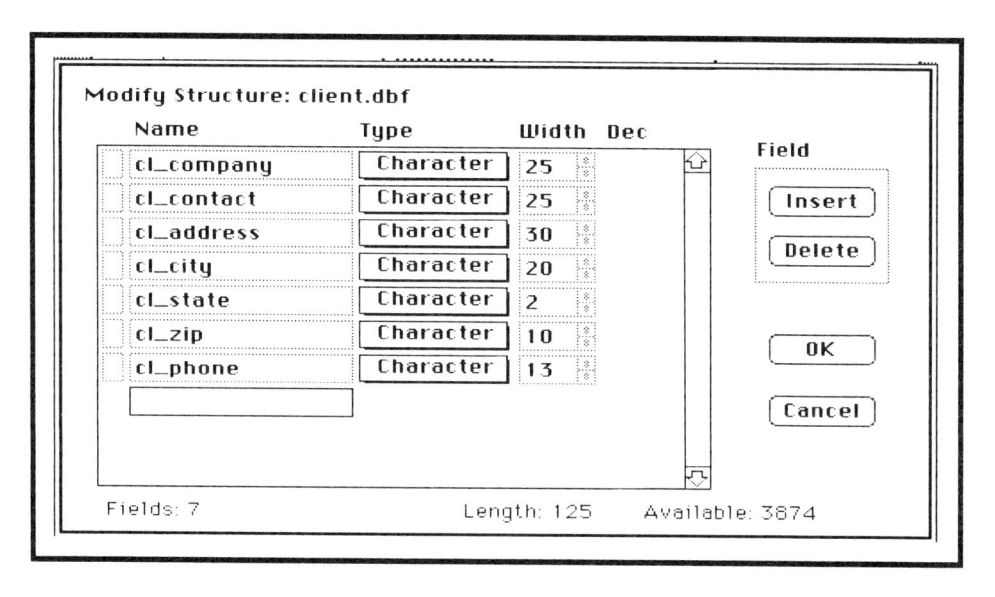

```
Modify Structure: client.dbf
    Name          Type         Width  Dec          Field
  cl_company    [Character]    25                [ Insert ]
  cl_contact    [Character]    25
  cl_address    [Character]    30                [ Delete ]
  cl_city       [Character]    20
  cl_state      [Character]    2
  cl_zip        [Character]    10                [   OK   ]
  cl_phone      [Character]    13
                                                 [ Cancel ]

  Fields: 7              Length: 125     Available: 3874
```

Figure 5-02. Client structure.

asked if you wish to Input data records now.

FoxBASE+/Mac imposes the following limitations on database structures/contents:

Definition of terms

DBF STRUCTURE/CONTENT LIMITATIONS

```
Maximum records per database:              1 BILLION
   (Note: Remember, you need enough disk
          space to hold the database)
Maximum characters per record:             4,000

Maximum fields per record:                 128

Maximum characters per field:              254    (Character)
   (Note: Numeric includes decimal point)  16     (Numeric)
                                           1      (Logical)
   (Note: Date=8 unless CENTURY is SET ON) 10     (Date)
                                           64,000 (Memo)

Maximum characters per index key:          100

Maximum database files:                    Unlimited

Maximum database files open concurrently:  10

Maximum index files open per database file: 7

Maximum length of field name:              10 characters

Field names start with A-Z, and may contain: A-Z, 0-9, and _
```

(Note to experienced programmers: FoxBASE+/Mac stores all data types as ASCII characters, and then converts numeric, logical, and date types as necessary.)

Notice that all of the field names in our client.dbf database file start with the characters "CL_". **This is not a FoxBASE+/Mac requirement.** This is a naming convention used by Micro Endeavors Inc. to help our programmers identify variable and field names in large applications. In this case, the "CL_" identifies all of these fields as residing in the client dbf file.

One of the problems inherent with large applications is the proliferation of field and variable names. Eventually it becomes difficult to determine which names refer to fields and which refer to variables. It also becomes difficult to determine which field names are associated with which database files.

We resolve this dilemma by starting every field name with a two character identifier unique to that database, followed by an underscore. Since none of our variable names include underscores as the third character in the name, our programmers can rapidly identify a field name as a field name. Further, since the starting characters of the field name are unique to the particular database file, our programmers can immediately identify the database file in which the field name is located.

You don't have to follow this naming convention, but we have found it to be a very useful tool, and we will follow it throughout the rest of the book.

Now that you have CREATEd a database it is time to learn how to put the database to USE. Here is simple program that prepares the database for use, adds a new record to the database, and lets the user change the content of the fields in the newly added database record:

```
* dbf1.prg
* USEs the client database, adds one record to the database,
* and allows the user to change the content of the newly
* added record.
SCREEN 1 SIZE 25,80 FONT "MONACO",9
SCREEN 1 HEADING "Add a Record To Client"
CLEAR
SCREEN 1 TOP AT 0,0
* Make the client database file available for processing
USE client ALIAS client
* Add one "blank" record to the client database
APPEND BLANK
* Use @..SAY...GET commands to allow the user to
* change the content of the newly added record.
CLEAR
@ 5,5 SAY "Company Name => " GET cl_company
@ 7,5 SAY "Contact ======> " GET cl_contact
@ 9,5 SAY "Address ======> " GET cl_address
@ 11,5 SAY "City =========> " GET cl_city
```

Definition of terms

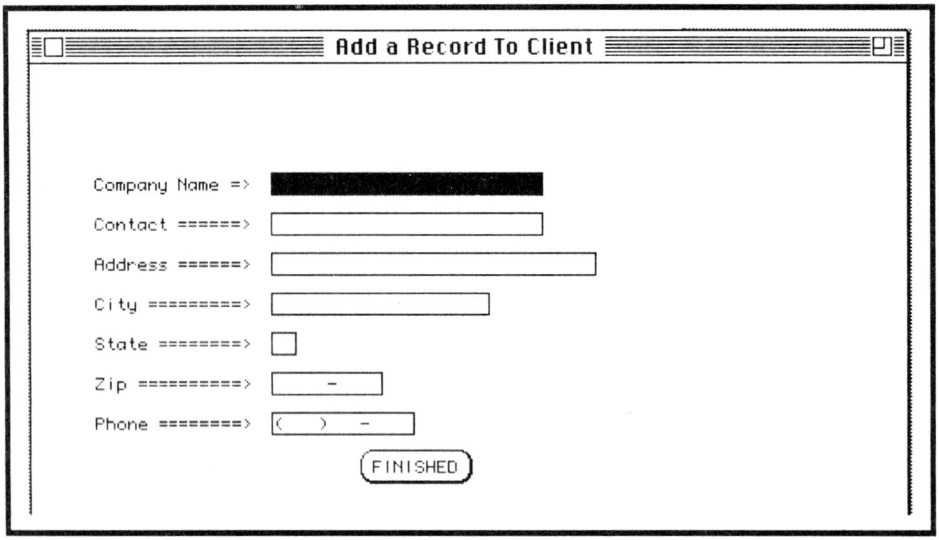

Figure 5-03. Simple file entry.

```
@ 13,5 SAY "State ========> " GET cl_state PICTURE "!!"
@ 15,5 SAY "Zip ==========> " GET cl_zip PICTURE "#####-####"
@ 17,5 SAY "Phone ========> " GET cl_phone PICTURE "(###)###-####"
* setup a dummy variable for local processing
dummy = 0
@ 18,30 GET dummy PICTURE "@*h FINISHED"
DO WHILE dummy=0
  READ SAVE
ENDDO until finished
CLEAR GETS
* Close the database file
USE
RETURN
*eof dbf1.prg
```

The excruciatingly simple data entry screen generated by dbf1.prg can be seen in Figure 5-03. Don't worry, we will create more professional data entry screens in subsequent chapters. For now, let's investigate the three new concepts presented in the dbf1.prg.

From earlier chapters you are familiar with the @...SAY...GET commands, but the USE and APPEND BLANK commands are new. The USE command opens the database file, and makes it available for use. Programmers familiar with other languages will note that FoxBASE+/Mac does not require a definition of the file structure every time a file is USEd. FoxBASE+/Mac automatically uses the field names, lengths, and types we CREATEd earlier.

The USE command does not require an ALIAS clause. However, when we begin working with more than one database file simultaneously, we will see how the ALIAS of a database can make programming easier by giving us another way to refer to a database. (Note: The ALIAS for a database does not have to be the same as the database name. In practice, the ALIAS for a database is usually not the same as the name of the database.) For now, remember to include an ALIAS with every USE command.

When issued with no clauses, the USE command has the effect of closing a database. Until a database is closed with one of the following commands, it remains available to all programs. That is, database files are not subject to the concepts of PUBLIC and PRIVATE status as are memory variables. Here are the commands that close a database:

```
USE
CLOSE DATABASES
CLOSE ALL
CLEAR ALL
QUIT
```

Of these commands, the USE command is the most selective in that it closes only one database file. The other commands close all open database files. At the end of this chapter we will discuss the methods of, and uses for, opening of more than one database file simultaneously.

Finally, the APPEND BLANK command adds an empty record to the end of the database file. It also positions the record pointer to the newly added

Definition of terms

record.

What is a record pointer?

We see in our sample program that we can GET fields in the same way that we can GET memory variables. But if we have a database file of 5,000 records for example, how does the GET command know which record is supplying the fields?

We have seen that we need to USE a database file in order to access the records in that file. In order to access the fields in a specific record, we need to tell FoxBASE+/Mac which record we want to work on. (Note: In FoxBASE+/Mac, only one record from a given dbf file may be active at any given moment.) FoxBASE+/Mac provides an abundance of commands to identify the record on which subsequent commands will act. The commands most frequently used to position the record pointer include:

```
APPEND BLANK
APPEND FROM
CONTINUE
COUNT
FIND
GO/GOTO
LOCATE
USE
SEEK<R>SKIP
```

As we progress in developing more advanced data entry programs we will make extensive use of these commands. (Note: Pay particular attention to the APPEND BLANK, SEEK, and SKIP commands as they are used more frequently than the others.) At this point it is only important to understand that FoxBASE+/Mac programmers need to identify the record to be worked on, and that FoxBASE+/Mac provides several commands to do the job under a variety of circumstances.

Since we have identified a way to choose a database, and a record within a database, all that remains is to identify the method of referring to a field in the current record. As you can see from the dbf1.prg, to refer to a specific field in the current record, simply refer to the field's name.

What is an index and why do we need it?

An INDEX is a file created by FoxBASE+/Mac based on the content of a specific database file. FoxBASE+/Mac uses a default extension of .idx for index files. Every serious FoxBASE+/Mac program will use at least one index file.

An index file serves two purposes. First, it makes its associated database file appear to be in order based on an index key. If we were writing a program to keep track of phone numbers for example, we could use an index to make the entries in the database file appear to be in order by last name, regardless of the order in which we made the entries.

DATABASE FILE: STUDENTS.DBF

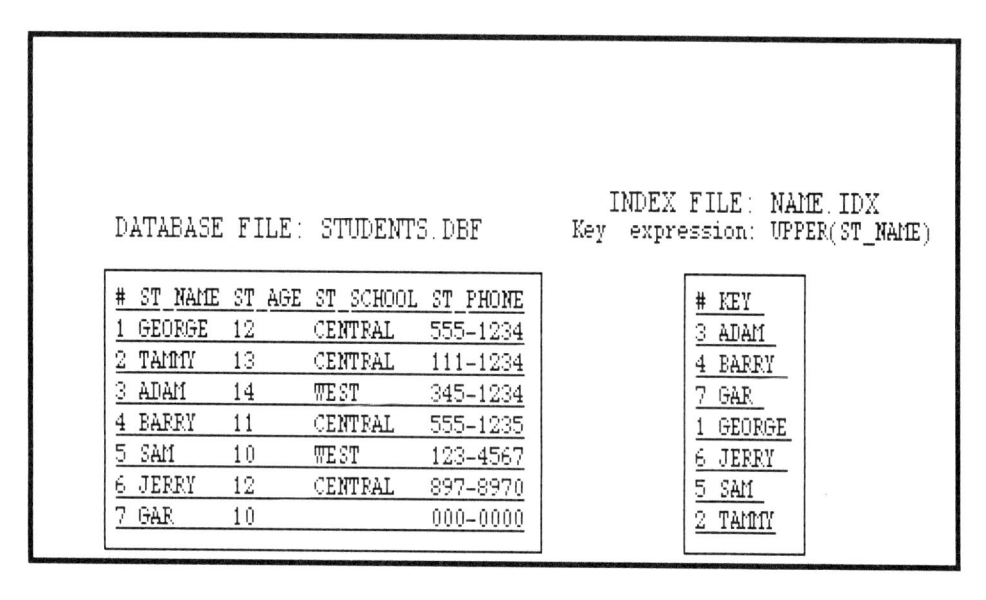

#	ST_NAME	ST_AGE	ST_SCHOOL	ST_PHONE
1	GEORGE	12	CENTRAL	555-1234
2	TAMMY	13	CENTRAL	111-1234
3	ADAM	14	WEST	345-1234
4	BARRY	11	CENTRAL	555-1235
5	SAM	10	WEST	123-4567
6	JERRY	12	CENTRAL	897-8970
7	GAR	10		000-0000

INDEX FILE: NAME.IDX
Key expression: UPPER(ST_NAME)

#	KEY
3	ADAM
4	BARRY
7	GAR
1	GEORGE
6	JERRY
5	SAM
2	TAMMY

Figure 5-04. Conceptual presentation of an index.

Second, an index file allows the very rapid, typically less than 1/4 of a second, retrieval of any record in the database, regardless of our current position in the database.

The secret of the index file's popularity is that it accomplishes the goals stated above, **without changing the content of the original database.** The effort required to insert or remove records at the beginning or middle of a database file would result in unacceptable delays in adding, editing, or deleting records. Also, when the database file needs to be sequenced in different ways for different operations, it is often not feasible to generate multiple copies of a large database.

The FoxBASE+/Mac indexing scheme allows the addition, deletion, and modification of records, without changing the physical sequence of the records in the database file. This is accomplished by maintaining a separate index file for an associated database file. For every record in the database file, the index file contains an entry consisting of an index key, and a pointer to the physical record in the database file.

To help us conceptualize the relationship between an index file and the database file on which it is based, let's examine the drawing in Figure 5-04.

In this table we show the content of a student database, along with a representation of how an index works. (Note: FoxBASE+/Mac uses a sophisticated B+ tree indexing scheme to create and maintain its index files. This conceptual representation of the content of an index file is provided only to further your understanding of the use of index files.) In this example, the database file contains 7 records. Each record contains the name, age, school, and phone number for one student.

As you can see, the records in the student database file were entered in no particular order. When we used FoxBASE+/Mac to create the index file name.idx however, we directed it to use the UPPER() case value of the st_name field as the key expression. As a result, the records in the name.idx index file are placed in order by the value of the st_name field

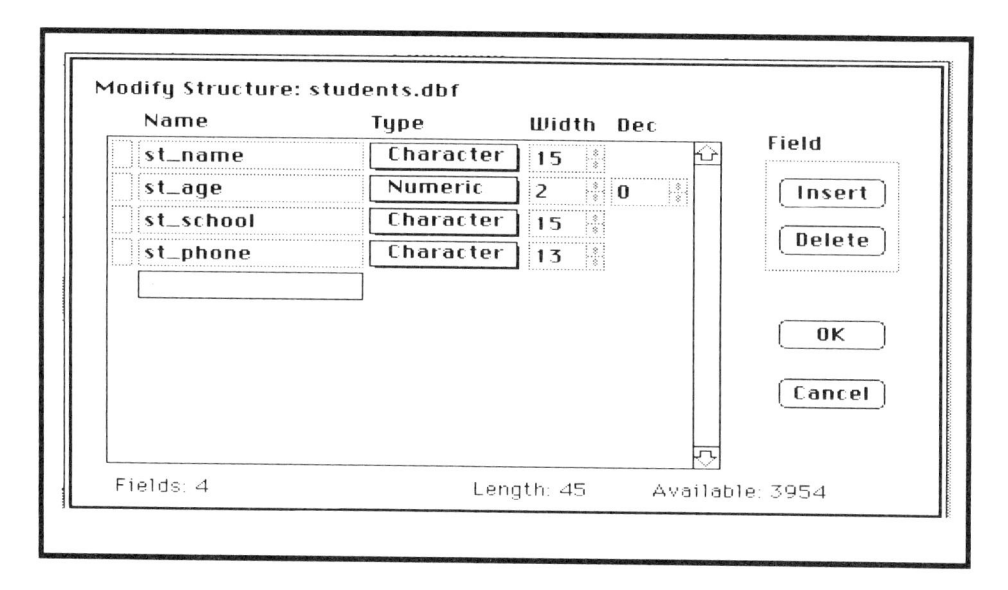

Figure 5-05. Student.dbf.

in the students.dbf database file. Note that the records in the index file consist only of the key expression and a number that points to a record in the database file. Shortly we will see how to use the index file in conjunction with the database file to make the database file appear to be sequenced in name order. First however, let's follow the steps necessary to create the student.dbf and name.idx files.

From the command window, issue the following command:

CREATE students

Use the field names, types, and lengths found in Figure 5-05. (In case you are wondering, you use the mouse to click on the data type column to enter a data type other than character.) When you have finished entering the fields for students.dbf, click on OK, and elect not to Input data records now.

What is an index and why do we need it?

Using an index file to make records appear in order

Now we can create the name.idx index file with the following command:

`INDEX ON st_name TO name.idx`

Now we can put some records in the database. We will use the following program to enter information:

```
* dbf2.prg
* Add records until the user selects not to add anymore
SCREEN 1 SIZE 25,80 AT 0,0 FONT "MONACO",9
CLEAR
SCREEN 1 TOP HEADING "Student Entry"
* Put some prompts on the screen
@ 5,5 SAY "Name:"
@ 7,5 SAY "Age:"
@ 9,5 SAY "School:"
@ 11,5 SAY "Phone:"
* Use the students.dbf file with the name.idx index
USE students ALIAS stu INDEX name
DO WHILE .T.
  * make up some memory variables to hold user input
  mst_name=SPACE(15)
  mst_age=0
  mst_school=SPACE(15)
  mst_phone=SPACE(13)
  * Create a memory variable for local control
  action = 0
  @ 13,10 GET action PICTURE "@*h ADD;EXIT"
  @ 5,25 GET mst_name
  @ 7,25 GET mst_age
  @ 9,25 GET mst_school
  @ 11,25 GET mst_phone
  DO WHILE action = 0
    READ SAVE
  ENDDO until they choose an action
  CLEAR GETS
  DO CASE
    CASE action = 1
      ** chose to add record
      * Create a blank record
      APPEND BLANK
      * Put memory variables into fields in this record
```

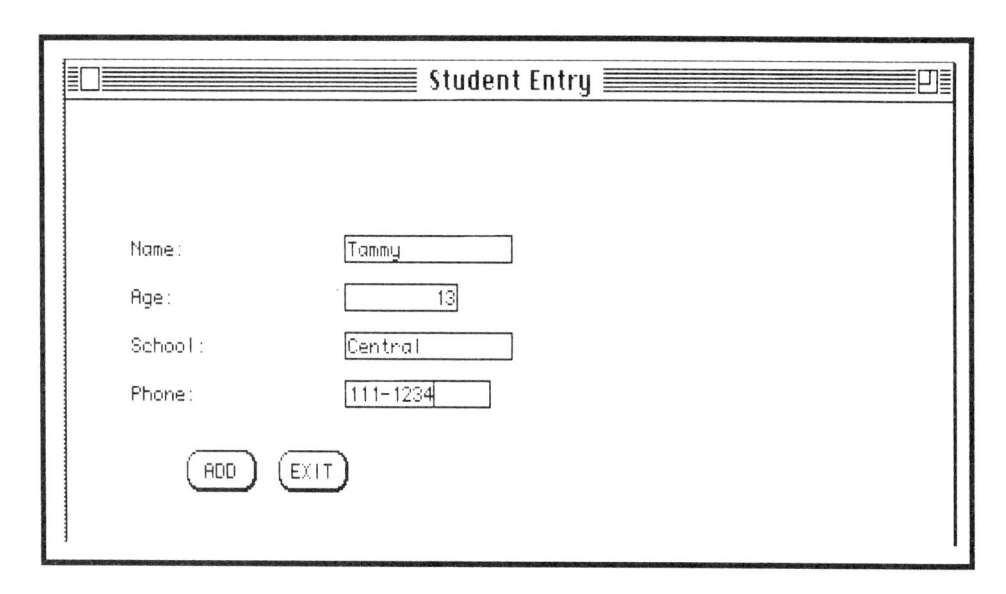

Figure 5-06. Student entry.

Record#	st_name	st_age	st_school	st_phone
3	Adam	14	West	345-1234
4	Barry	11	Central	555-1235
7	Gar	10		000-0000
1	George	12	Central	555-1234
6	Jerry	12	Central	897-8970
5	Sam	10	West	123-4567
2	Tammy	13	Central	111-1234

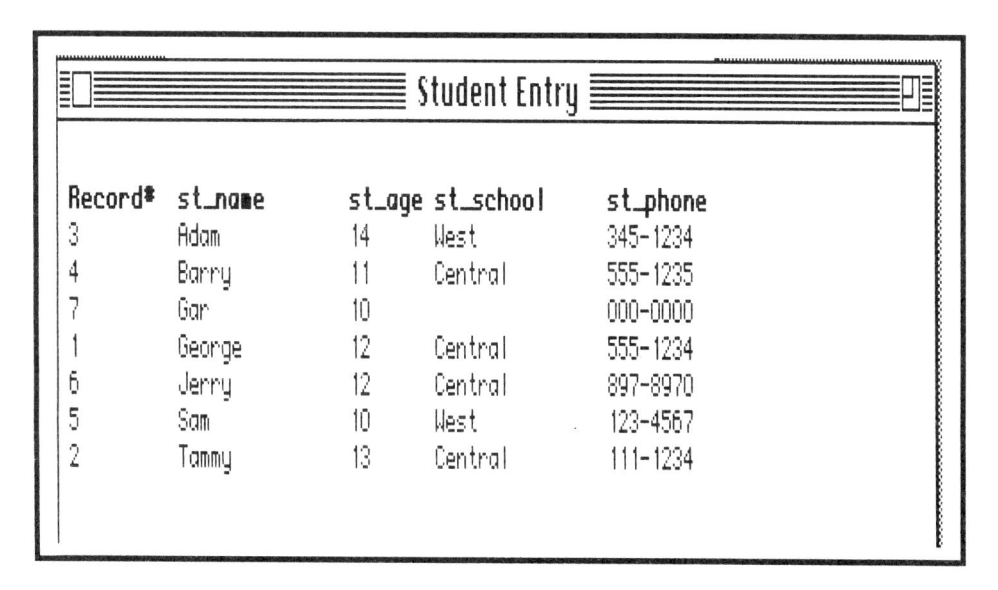

Figure 5-07. Indexed student list.

Using an index file to make records appear in order

```
      REPLACE st_name WITH mst_name
      REPLACE st_age WITH mst_age
      REPLACE st_school WITH mst_school
      REPLACE st_phone WITH mst_phone
    CASE action = 2
      ** chose to exit
      EXIT
  ENDCASE what action was taken
ENDDO process requests to add records
CLEAR
RETURN
*eof dbf2.prg
```

When you DO the dbf2.prg, enter the name, age, school, and phone number information listed in the index table above. A sample entry is displayed in Figure 5-06. To add an entry, click the Add text button, to finish entering students, click the exit button.

```
                          Student Entry

   Record#  st_name        st_age st_school   st_phone
   3        Adam           14     West        345-1234
   4        Barry          11     Central     555-1235
   7        Gar            10                 000-0000
   1        George         12     Central     555-1234
   6        Jerry          12     Central     897-8970
   5        Sam            10     West        123-4567
   2        Tammy          13     Central     111-1234

   Record#  st_name        st_age st_school   st_phone
   1        George         12     Central     555-1234
   2        Tammy          13     Central     111-1234
   3        Adam           14     West        345-1234
   4        Barry          11     Central     555-1235
   5        Sam            10     West        123-4567
   6        Jerry          12     Central     897-8970
   7        Gar            10                 000-0000
```

Figure 5-08. Unindexed student list.

When you are finished, issue the following command from the command window:

`LIST`

This should present you with a screen that looks like the one found in Figure 5-07.

Notice the record numbers in the first column of the display. These record numbers refer to the physical location of the records in the students.dbf. The students.dbf appears to be in order by name, but we know that the physical layout of the records has not changed. To prove that the records in the students.dbf have not been rearranged, let's turn the index off by issuing the following command from the command window:

`SET INDEX TO`

Now let's LIST the students.dbf again with:

`LIST`

You should get a screen that looks like the one in Figure 5-08.

The preceding series of screens, commands, and programs have been designed to demonstrate that INDEXing a file does not change the sequence of the records in a database file. Further, we have discovered that when we added records to the student database, the name.idx index file was **updated automatically.** This automatic updating took place only because we included the clause "INDEX name.idx" when we USEd the students.dbf.

It is important to note that indexes will only be updated when specifically referred to with one of the following commands:

```
USE database INDEX indexfile
SET INDEX TO indexfile
INDEX ON key TO indexfile
```

Using an index file to make records appear in order

To put it another way, it is possible, but not usually desirable, to add, edit, or delete records in a database file without updating an associated index file. This is accomplished by neglecting to activate the index file.

Keeping a database in more than one sequence

It is possible to activate up to 7 index files for each active database file. This is often done when a program is required to search for data based on different keys. For example, in addition to maintaining the students file in order by name, we may want the students file to be maintained by school+name. The following program demonstrates one potential use for a dual indexing of this kind:

```
* dbf3.prg
* Demonstrates the creation and use of multiple indexes
SCREEN 1 SIZE 25,80 AT 0,0 FONT "MONACO",9
CLEAR
SCREEN 1 TOP HEADING "Student Listings"
* Open database file
USE students ALIAS stu
* Check for the existence of the index files
IF .NOT.FILE('name.idx')
   * Generate an index based on name
   INDEX ON st_name TO name
ENDIF missing name.idx file
IF .NOT.FILE('schname.idx')
   * Generate an index based on school+name
   INDEX ON st_school+st_name TO schname
ENDIF missing school+name index file
* Activate both index files
* Note that the Name index file will be the MASTER index
* Therefore, any SEEKs or movement through the students
* database file will be based on the name.idx index.  The
* schname.idx index file will be updated by any changes to
* the students.dbf file however.
SET INDEX TO name,schname
* Process requests to see the file in either name or school+name
* order
DO WHILE .T.
   CLEAR
   * Use text buttons to get user choice
   @ 5,5 SAY "Order of display menu"
```

```
    ordchoice=0
    @ 7,5 GET ordchoice PICTURE "@*h NAME;School+Name;EXIT"
    READ
    DO CASE
      CASE ordchoice=1
        * display in name order
        * Use SET ORDER command to make sure the name.idx is
        * the master index.
        SET ORDER TO 1
        CLEAR
        LIST
        ? "These students are in name order"
        WAIT
      CASE ordchoice=2
        * display in school+name order
        * Use the SET ORDER command to make the schname.idx index
        * the maseter index
        SET ORDER TO 2
        CLEAR
        LIST
        ? "These students are listed in school+name order"
        WAIT
      CASE ordchoice=3
        * exit
        EXIT
      ENDCASE ordchoice
ENDDO process requests to see the file in order
* Close the student database and all associated index files
USE
RETURN
*eof dbf3.prg
```

The dbf3.prg program has introduced the FILE() function, the SET INDEX TO command, and the SET ORDER TO command. It has also introduced the concept of a master index when more than one index is active for a database file. Let's discuss each new item in order.

The FILE() function returns a logical true value if the file name provided exists in the current path. This function is often used at the beginning of an application to verify that all necessary files exist before beginning operations. In this case, we use the FILE() function to determine whether or not we need to recreate the name.idx and schname.idx index files.

The SET INDEX TO command allows the programmer to activate one or more (up to 7) indexes for a database file that is already in USE. When multiple indexes are activated, each is separated by a comma.

The SET ORDER TO command is used to tell FoxBASE+/Mac which of the currently active index files is to be treated as the master index. When more than one open index is associated with an open database file, it makes sense that FoxBASE+/Mac needs some way to determine which of the open indexes is to provide the order in which records are to appear.

In the absence of the SET ORDER TO command, FoxBASE+/Mac assumes that the first index listed with the USE...INDEX or SET INDEX TO command is the master index. The SET ORDER TO command allows the programmer to quickly designate any one of the open indexes as the master index file.

Using the SEEK command to find records quickly

Aside from making database records appear in a specified sequence without changing the physical sequence of the records in the database, the use of index files also enables lightning fast searches based on index keys. Let's assume that our students database file grows to include 20,000 students. Even given the great speed of FoxBASE+/Mac, a simple sequential search of the file could take several seconds. (Note: A sequential search starts with the first record in the file and moves forward one record at a time until a match is found.) Larger files could result in sequential search times of several minutes.

In many applications, such a delay in processing time is unacceptable. If our 20,000 record student file were indexed by name however, and we knew the student's name, we could use the SEEK command to find the appropriate student record in less than 1/4 of a second. Let's see how this might work in a program:

```
* dbf4.prg
* Demonstrate the use of the SEEK command
SCREEN 1 SIZE 25,80 AT 0,0 FONT "MONACO",9
CLEAR
SCREEN 1 TOP HEADING "Student Seeks"
* Open the students database with both indexes
* Note that the name.idx index is the MASTER index
USE students ALIAS stu INDEX name,schname
DO WHILE .T.
  CLEAR
  namelook=SPACE(15)
  action = 0
  @ 10,15 SAY "Enter name here: " GET namelook
  @ 9,55 GET action PICTURE "@*v LOOKUP;EXIT"
  DO WHILE action = 0
    READ SAVE
  ENDDO until user takes action
  CLEAR GETS
  IF action=2
    * exit
    EXIT
  ENDIF blanks
  * look for a record with this name in the st_name field
  SEEK namelook
  * If the SEEK was successful, FOUND() will return a
  * true value
  IF FOUND()
    * Show the student's age and wait for a key
    @ 14,25 SAY "Student's age is "+STR(st_age,2)
    WAIT
  ELSE   && student was not found
    * Msg and wait for a key
    @ 14,25 SAY "Student not found."
    WAIT
  ENDIF found the student's name
  *
ENDDO process requests to SEEK student names
* Close the student database and its indexes
USE
RETURN
* eof dbf4.prg
```

In the dbf4.prg our goal is to quickly find a particular student's record, and display the student's age. Note that capitalization is important when entering student names to SEEK. This is known as case sensitivity. After we have studied the new concepts in the dbf4.prg we will return to the topic of case sensitivity. For now, type the names you want to SEEK exactly as you entered them earlier.

The new concepts presented in dbf4.prg are the use of the SEEK command and the FOUND() function. The SEEK command requires a constant, variable, or expression to be sought. (Note: When we begin using multiple database files simultaneously, we will discuss the use of fields from one database file as SEEK arguments in another database file.) In this case, we have supplied the memory variable namelook.

The SEEK command also requires the current database file to be open with an active index file. Using a sophisticated searching algorithm, the SEEK command quickly checks the file to see if any record has a key that begins with the content of the SEEK expression. In this case, because the active master index is indexed on st_name, the SEEK command looks for a record whose st_name field contains the same value as the namelook memory variable.

If the SEEK is successful, the record pointer is set to the appropriate record. If the SEEK is unsuccessful, the record pointer will be set **beyond the last record in the file**, and FOUND() will return a false value.

We could check the success or failure of the SEEK command with the EOF() function rather than the FOUND() function. The EOF() function returns a true value if the record pointer for the current file is set beyond the last record in the file. Therefore, the statements:

```
IF FOUND()
```

and

```
IF .NOT.EOF()
```

are functionally equivalent in this instance. Many dBASE programmers will be more familiar with the EOF() method because the FOUND() function was added to the dBASE language rather recently. We choose to use the FOUND() function because it is more english-like and therefore more intelligible.

Who cares about upper and lower case letters?

While it is not unknown for an application to require case sensitivity, far more often it is desirable to have the system ignore the difference between upper and lower case letters. To facilitate this blissful ignorance, we will need to perform two conversions. First, the index key for the name.idx must be made to be all upper case letters. This can be accomplished with the following command:

```
INDEX ON UPPER(st_name) TO name
```

Note that the content of the st_name field will not be altered by forcing an index key to use the upper case value of the st_name field. The content of the st_name field will appear in all upper case letters only in the name.idx index file. Now of course we need to be certain that the item associated with the SEEK command is also converted to upper case.

In the dbf4.prg program, this goal can be accomplished in either of two ways. First, the programmer could force the operator to enter only upper case letters through the use of the PICTURE clause as follows:

```
 @ 12,25 SAY "Enter name here ==>> " GET namelook PICTURE "@!"
```

The other option would allow the user to enter upper and lower case letters, and then ignore them in the SEEK command by adding the UPPER() function to the SEEK command as follows:

```
SEEK UPPER(namelook)
```

The choice is a matter of programming style and personal preference. We usually prefer to force the user to enter upper case letters.

Using multiple database files simultaneously

FoxBASE+/Mac allocates 10 work areas for use with database files. In other words, we can USE one database file in each of 10 different work areas. We identify the work area in which we wish to toil with the SELECT command.

In subsequent chapters we will have extensive practice in the simultaneous manipulation of multiple database files. For now, we will content ourselves with a cursory look at the mechanics of opening more than one database at a time. We will also try our hand at SELECTing one of several open database files for processing.

Since we have already created two database files, one with indexes, let's use both files in one program:

```
* dbf5.prg
* Demonstrates the use of more than one database file
* simultaneously.  Also shows how to SELECT one of the
* open database files for processing.
* Close any open databases, and clear any current
* memory variables.  In essence, create a "clean slate."
CLEAR ALL
SCREEN 1 SIZE 25,85 AT 0,0 FONT "MONACO",9
CLEAR
SCREEN 1 TOP HEADING "Multiple Open Files"
* Select the first of 10 possible work areas
SELECT 1
* Open the students file with indexes
USE students ALIAS stu INDEX name,schname
* Select the second of 10 possible work areas
SELECT 2
* Open the client database for use in the second area
USE client ALIAS cli
* Process requests to shift between work areas
DO WHILE .T.
   CLEAR
   * Display the currently selected work area number
   @ 1,5 SAY "Selected: "
   @ 1,20 SAY SELECT()
   * Display the alias of the currently selected work area
```

```
@ 3,5 SAY "Alias: "
@ 3,20 SAY ALIAS()
* Display the database file name for the currently selected
* work area
@ 5,5 SAY "DBF: "
@ 5,20 SAY DBF()
* Display the first index for the currently selected work area
@ 7,5 SAY "1st ndx: "
@ 7,20 SAY NDX(1)
* Display key for first index for the currently selected
* work area
@ 8,5 SAY "1st key: "
@ 8,20 SAY SYS(14,1)
* Display the current record number for the currently selected
* work area
@ 10,5 SAY "Rec #: "
@ 10,20 SAY RECNO()
* Display the number of records in the database file in the
* currently selected work area
@ 11,5 SAY "# recs: "
@ 11,20 SAY RECCOUNT()
* Display the number of fields in the database file in the
* currently selected work area
@ 12,5 SAY "# fields: "
@ 12,20 SAY FCOUNT()
* Display the size of the records in the database file in the
* currently selected work area
@ 14,5 SAY "Rec size: "
@ 14,20 SAY RECSIZE()
* Display the name of the first field in the database file in
* the currently selected work area
@ 16,5 SAY "1st field: "
@ 16,20 SAY FIELD(1)
@ 17,0
* Display the content of the current record in the currently
* selected work area
DISPLAY
* Give the operator a menu of options

dbf5choice=1
@ 22,0 GET dbf5choice PICTURE ;
"@*h Student File;Client File;Exit"
READ
DO CASE
  CASE dbf5choice=1
    * select students work area
    SELECT stu
  CASE dbf5choice=2
```

```
      * select client work area
      SELECT cli
    CASE dbf5choice=3
      * exit
      EXIT
  ENDCASE dbf5choice
ENDDO requests to shift between work areas
* Close all open database files and their open indexes
CLOSE DATABASES
RETURN
* eof dbf5.prg
```

The results of dbf5.prg can be seen in Figure 5-09. In addition to a plethora of new FoxBASE+/Mac functions, the dbf5.prg introduces the proper usage of the SELECT command. The new functions can be researched in the FoxBASE+/Mac manual since most are rarely used in applications, but the SELECT command bears closer examination.

There are four methods for SELECTing from one of FoxBASE+/Mac's 10 work areas. First you can provide the number of the work area as in:

SELECT 1

Second, you can refer to the work areas as A-J as in:

SELECT B

Third, you can use the ALIAS (Note: If no ALIAS is specified when the database is put in USE, FoxBASE+/Mac uses the name of the database file in USE for an ALIAS.) for the database file that is open in the work area as in:

SELECT stu

Fourth, you can SELECT the lowest numbered unused work area with the following command:

SELECT 0

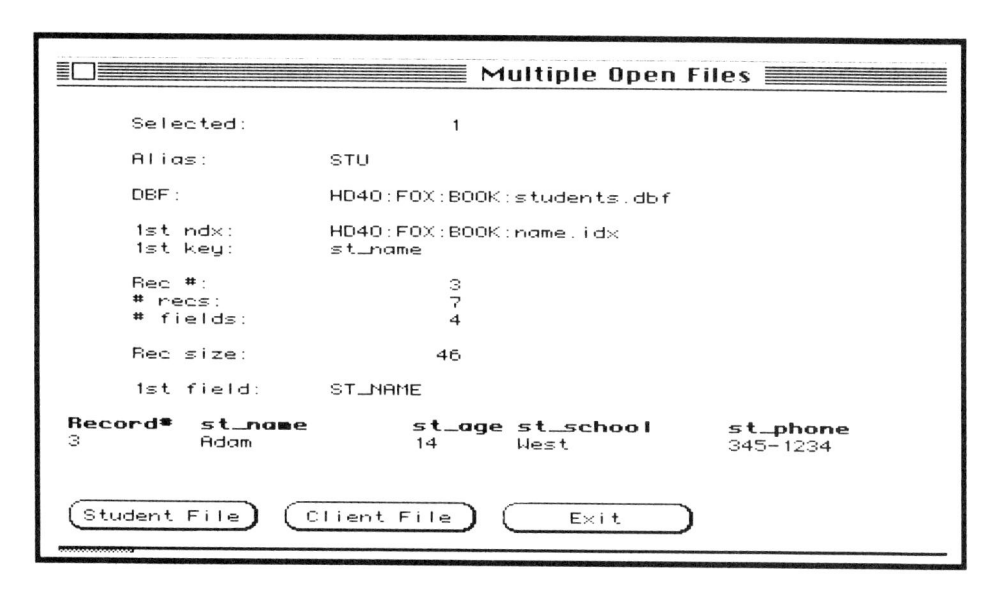

Figure 5-09. Multiple open files.

The dbf5.prg doesn't accomplish much with its newly discovered power of SELECTing work areas. But dbf5.prg does prepare us to make more productive use of the SELECT command in subsequent chapters.

One final note about the dbf5.prg program. Instead of issuing a single USE command at the end of the program as we did in the other dbf.prg programs, we have included a CLOSE DATABASES command. This command has the same result as SELECTing each of the active work areas and issuing individual USE commands for each.

Using multiple database files simultaneously

6. Menus and System Design

Event-driven vs. Menu-driven

You may have heard Macintosh programs referred to as event-driven. Traditional data processing applications, on the other hand, are often referred to as menu-driven. Both phrases refer to the ways in which users choose activities.

In the traditional menu-driven scheme, the user chooses an option from a menu, at which point the user will be presented with either another menu, or with an operation. It may take several menu selections to get to an operation (a series of menus is often called a tree), and once the operation begins, it must either be completed or aborted, it cannot be suspended while another operation is performed.

Further, once the user chooses from a series of menus, the user must backup through those same menus to perform another activity. In other words, if the user chose from seven different menus to arrive at an operation, the user will be required to make seven more choices to return from the operation to his original place in the application.

Conversely, users of Macintosh-based, event-driven programs are typically treated to a variety of activity selecting options. More importantly, it is usually possible to move from one activity to another, **and back,** without fighting through a menu tree.

This contrast is roughly analogous to two messengers, one of whom delivers messages in a mountainous area, and another who makes deliveries in a flatland. The mountain messenger must carefully wind his way through a maze of passages, peaks, and valleys, never able to see more than one turn ahead. Furthermore, this messenger must always return to the top of the tallest mountain to receive his next message for delivery. This is the menu-driven messenger.

The flatlander on the other hand, can walk in a straight line to any delivery point. In addition, he can see all of his delivery points from the doorstep of any other delivery point, and (magically) every delivery point is equidistant from any other delivery point. Finally, his messages are radioed to him from a central dispatch. This is the ultimate event-driven messenger.

It seems from these analogies that event-driven processing is better than menu-driven processing, and it is, for the user. For the programmer however, event-driven processing adds a substantial amount of complexity. For this reason, most programs are written as a combination of both schema, with the trade-offs centering on program cost and complexity versus ease of use.

FoxBASE+/Mac provides us with the tools to create event-driven programs, and I will attempt to instruct you in their use throughout the rest of the book. To facilitate this effort, I will break user options into two categories.

Local vs. activity options

The first category I will call local options. These options affect the current operation, and usually take the form of Text Buttons or Picture Buttons. The selection of one of these options will change the way the current operation takes place, but will not cause the program to perform an entirely different operation. Examples of these local options include the FINISHED button, CONTINUE button, and the Accumulate check box found in the calculator and hello programs in earlier chapters.

The second category I will call activity options. These options usually take the form of menus on the menu bar, and represent the opportunity to switch from operation to operation. For example, while entering invoices, a data entry operator might pull-down a report menu from the menu bar, and elect to print an aged accounts receivable report.

So then, the user of our programs can select local options by clicking on Text Buttons, Check Boxes, Radio Buttons, or Picture Buttons, and that same user can select activity options by pulling-down menus. We have already seen some examples of local option selection, and more of these will be forthcoming in the chapters on data entry. This chapter will deal with the mechanics of creating and responding to pull-down menus.

There is another way that users of most Macintosh applications can choose an activity however, and that is by manipulating windows. Happily, FoxBASE+/Mac gives the programmer the opportunity to create resizable, movable, and closable windows. More importantly, it offers a method to respond to the user's manipulation of those windows. It also offers a method of preventing the user from manipulating those windows.

In Chapter 11 we will investigate the nuances of window activity tracking. For now however, we will consider window manipulation to be too sophisticated a programming task for our purposes. In some of our programs therefore, we will use SCREEN TYPE 4, and add the LOCK clause to create windows that cannot be resized and cannot be closed by the user. Note that SCREEN TYPE 4 does allow the user to move the window on the desktop.

Mastering menus

I realize that this is one of the longest uninterrupted stretches of text in the book. Don't worry, the programs are just around the corner. In fact, because systems design in FoxBASE+/Mac requires a thorough mastery of the MENU commands, we will put the entire concept of event-driven systems on hold until next chapter while we master the mechanics of menu creation.

Here is a simple program that demonstrates the mechanics of menu creation:

```
* menu1.prg
* First try at a pull-down menu
* Uses "delimited string" method
* Create Menu BAR options
MENU BAR "Data Entry;Reports;Utilities"
* Now "fill" each bar with options
MENU 1,"Customers;Invoices;Inventory"   && Data Entry
MENU 2,"Sales;Receivables;Inventory"    && Reports
MENU 3,"Quit;Cancel"
* Create a variable to hold the options
whatchoice=""
* Now tell FoxBASE+/Mac what to do when a user makes
* a selection from the menu
ON MENU whatchoice=STR(MENU(0),2)+STR(MENU(1),2)
* Put screen 1 on the desktop
SCREEN 1 TYPE 4 LOCK TOP SIZE 24,80
CLEAR
@ 13,15 SAY "Please select a menu option."
* Now process menu selections
DO WHILE whatchoice#" 3 1"   && Until Quit
   * Menu activity can only occur during a READ or WAIT,
   * so we will conjure up a nonsense READ to
   * facilitate our menu demonstration
   STORE SPACE(10) TO nonsense
   @ 14,20 GET nonsense
   * reset the whatchoice variable
   whatchoice=""
   READ
   * Now display any menu activity
   @ 15,0
   @ 15,1 SAY "Last menu selection: " + whatchoice
ENDDO until user quits
* Turn menu system off
ON MENU
RETURN
* eof menu1.prg
```

When you run the menu1.prg program you will be presented with a screen like the one found in Figure 6-01. After you select the Invoices option from the Data Entry menu, you will see a screen like the one in

```
      File    Edit  Data Entry  Reports  Utilities
                    Customers    Screen 1
                    Invoices
                    Inventory




              Please select a menu option.
```

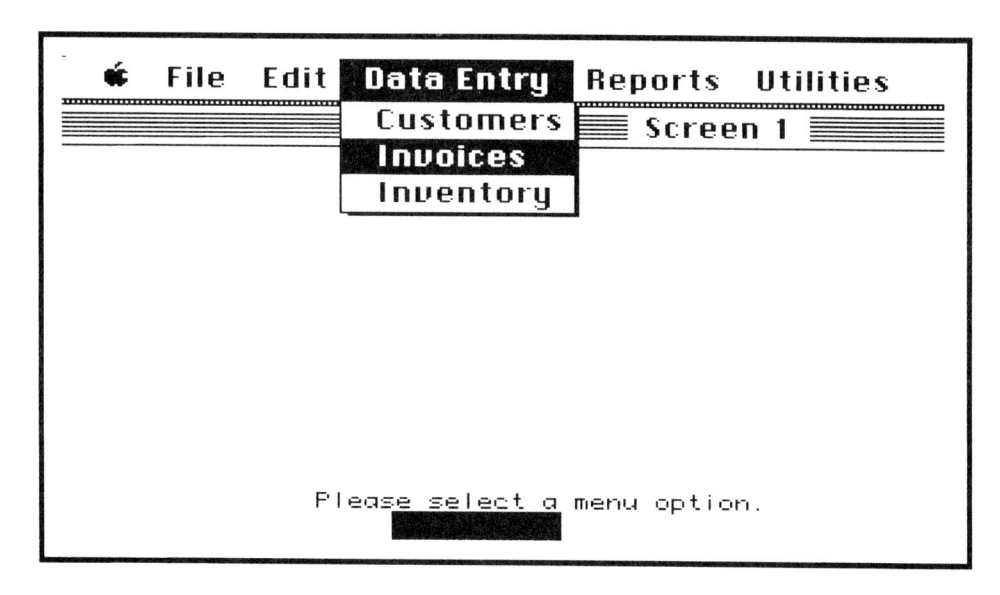

Figure 6-01. First menu selection.

Figure 6-02. To exit the program, choose the Quit option of the Utilities menu.

In Figure 6-03, I have taken the screen in Figure 6-01, and annotated it for our use. Note that the Apple, File, and Edit menus are not replaced by our three menus. While we can change the content of these menus, we cannot remove them from the desktop. The items "Data Entry", "Reports", and "Utilities" are called Menu Bars. The items "Customers", "Invoices", and "Inventory" are called menu options. Now that we are speaking the same language, let's examine the menu1.prg program more carefully.

Before learning what menu1.prg does, please understand what it does not do. Nothing in the menu1.prg actually causes a menu bar to pull down and present its options. It is up to the user to drag down a menu bar, and click one of its options. It is also up to the programmer to check for a menu selection following a READ.

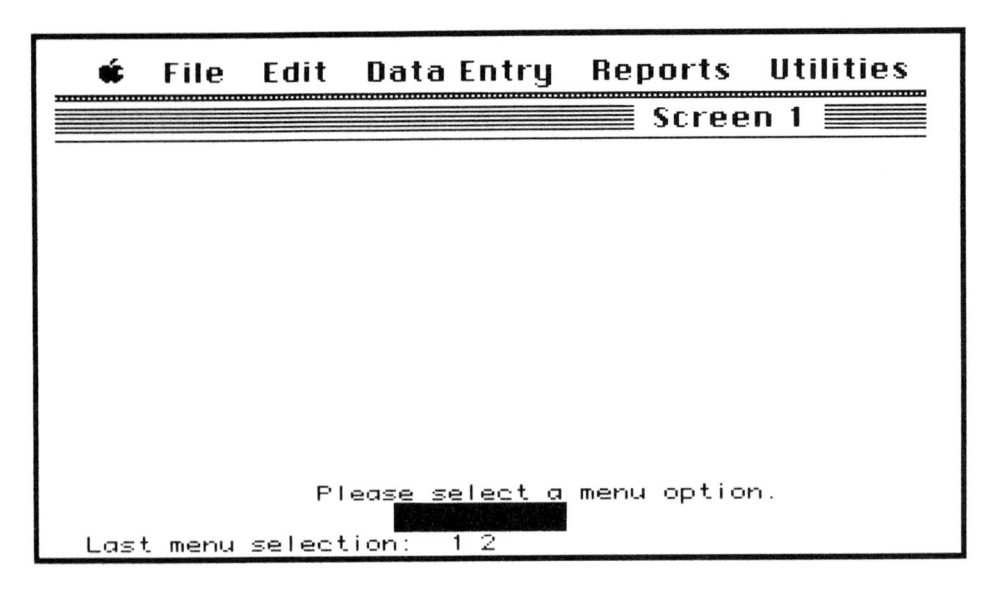

Figure 6-02. Result of 1st menu selection.

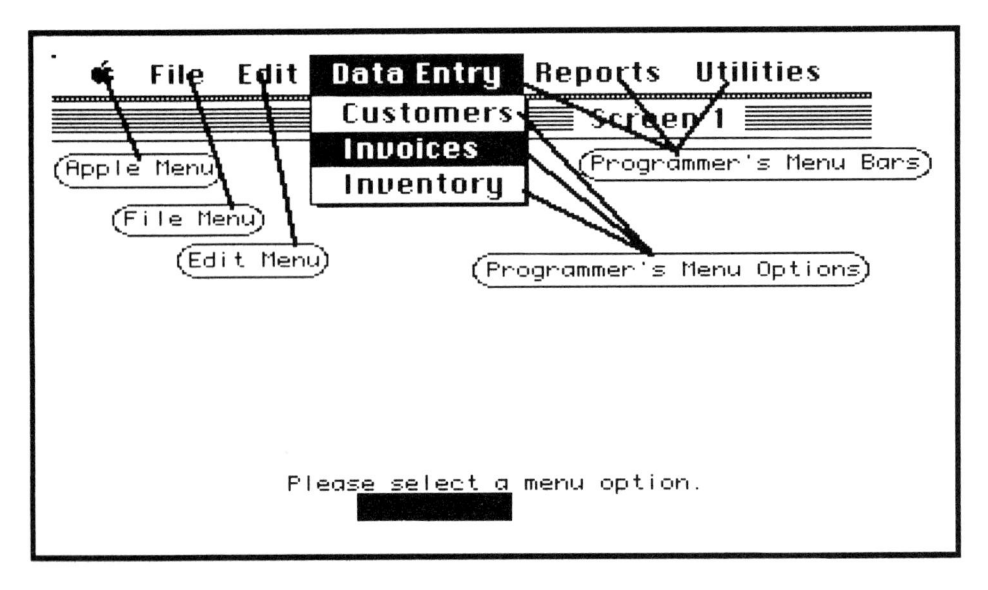

Figure 6-03. Annotated menu selection.

The steps required to create a menu system are as follows:

- Create Menu Bars with the MENU BARS command.

- Create Menu Options with the command MENU.

- Use the ON MENU command to tell FoxBASE+/Mac what to do with a menu selection.

- Prepare for the possibility of a menu selection following a READ command.

The following command fills the menu bar starting to the right of the permanent EDIT menu:

```
MENU BAR "Data Entry;Reports;Utilities"
```

Each bar name is separated by a semi-colon. If too many bars are assigned, no error will result, but the user will not be able to access the excess bars.

Assigning options to each of the menu bars is accomplished can be accomplished with a command like the following:

```
MENU 3,"Quit;Cancel"
```

Once again, the semicolon is used to separate multiple options. The number 3 in this example tells FoxBASE+/Mac to place this list of options in the 3rd menu bar. If you define more options than will fit on your screen, any additional options will be available to the user via a scroll arrow at the bottom of the menu bar list.

Recognizing a menu hit

The following command instructs FoxBASE+/Mac to assign the STR() of the functions MENU(0) and MENU(1) to the variable whatchoice:

```
ON MENU whatchoice=STR(MENU(0),2)+STR(MENU(1),2)
```

After this command has been issued, FoxBASE+/Mac will respond to a user's selection of a menu option by ending the current READ or WAIT operation, and by updating the content of the whatchoice variable. This situation will remain in effect until another ON MENU command is issued, or until a QUIT command is issued.

The MENU(0) function returns the number of the menu bar selected. The Apple menu is -2, the File menu is -1, the Edit menu is 0, and our first programmer defined menu is 1. The MENU(1) function returns the number of the option chosen from that menu bar.

Having told FoxBASE+/Mac what to do with a menu hit, it is up to us to determine what to do with FoxBASE+/Mac's response to a menu hit. In this case, we don't do much. We simply display the result of the user's menu access.

It may be that no menu access took place. For example, run the menu1.prg program, and press [Enter] instead of making a menu selection. This results in a display of the now empty whatchoice variable.

Submenus

The next program demonstrates the use of submenus:

```
* menu2.prg
* Submenus
* Uses "delimited string" method
* Create Menu BAR options
MENU BAR "Data Entry;Reports;Utilities"
* Now "fill" each bar with options
MENU 1,"Customers;Invoices;Inventory"   && Data Entry
MENU 2,"Sales;Receivables;Inventory"    && Reports
MENU 3,"Quit;Cancel"
```

```
* Now create a submenu for each of the
* Report menu options
MENU 2,"Cost List;Price List",3
MENU 2,"Salesmen;YTD Sales",1
MENU 2,"Overdue Accounts;Aging;Receipts",2
* Create a variable to hold the options
whatchoice=""
* Now tell FoxBASE+/Mac what to do when a user makes
* a selection from the menu
ON MENU whatchoice=STR(MENU(0),2)+STR(MENU(1),2)
* Put screen 1 on the desktop
SCREEN 1 TYPE 4 LOCK TOP SIZE 24,80
CLEAR
@ 13,15 SAY "Please select a menu option."
* Now process menu selections
DO WHILE whatchoice#" 3 1"   && Until Quit
  * Menu activity can only occur during a READ or WAIT,
  * so we will conjure up a nonsense READ to
  * facilitate our menu demonstration
  STORE SPACE(10) TO nonsense
  @ 14,20 GET nonsense
  * reset the whatchoice variable
  whatchoice=""
  READ
  * Now display any menu activity
  @ 15,0
  @ 15,1 SAY "Last menu selection: " + whatchoice
ENDDO until user quits
* Turn menu system off
ON MENU
RETURN
* eof menu2.prg
```

The screen in Figure 6-04 reflects the output of menu2.prg as the user is about to select the Aging sub-option from the Receivables option of the Reports bar, for the second time. Note that this action will result in a MENU(0) return of 6. Since we only put 3 menu bars on the desktop, this seems to be an anomaly.

Unfortunately, this is just FoxBASE+/Mac's rather awkward method of dealing with sub menu selection. Looking back to the program listing for menu2.prg, we see that the Aging sub-menu is the sixth menu option list created by the program. This is how FoxBASE+/Mac determines what

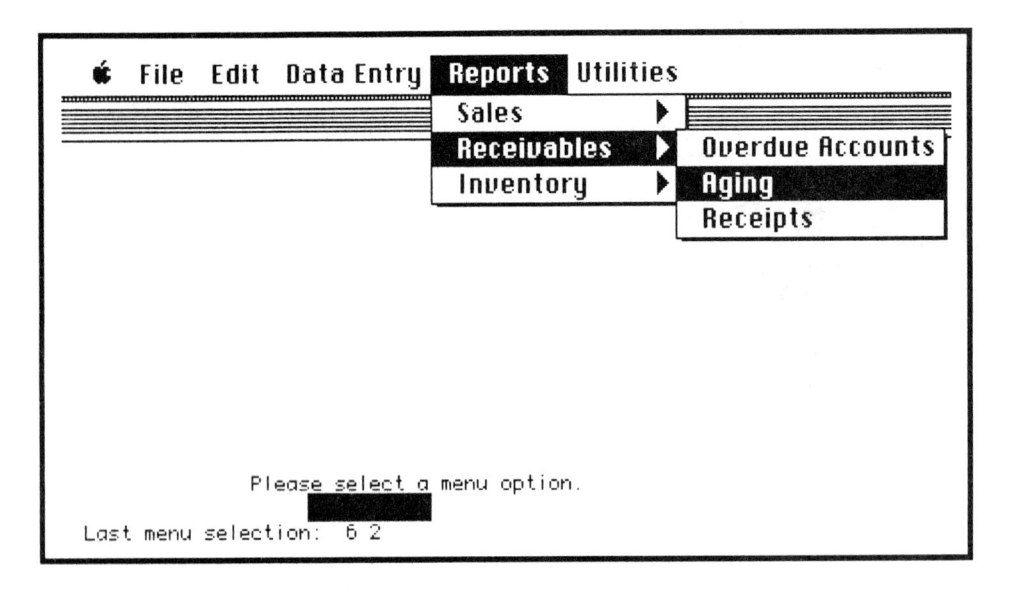

Figure 6-04. Submenus.

number is returned by MENU(0) to reflect the menu bar chosen. Please use the menu2.prg to experiment with the selection of suboptions.

Arrays vs. Delimited strings in menus

Users familiar with older versions of FoxBASE+/Mac may be wondering, "What happened to all of those arrays I used to need to create menus?" It is still possible to create menu systems using arrays. And, as we shall see, it is often beneficial to use arrays of bars/options instead of strings of bars/options. However, the use of strings of semi-colon delimited lists requires much less typing, and is therefore easier to teach. For your reference, here is the menu2.prg rewritten to use arrays:

```
* menu3.prg
* Submenus
* Uses array method
* Create Menu BAR options
DIMENSION ktopbar(3)
```

```
ktopbar(1)="Data Entry"
ktopbar(2)="Reports"
ktopbar(3)="Utilities"
MENU BAR ktopbar
* Now "fill" each bar with options
DIMENSION kdataopts(3)
kdataopts(1)="Customers"
kdataopts(2)="Invoices"
kdataopts(3)="Inventory"
MENU 1,kdataopts   && data entry
DIMENSION krepoopts(3)
krepoopts(1)="Sales"
krepoopts(2)="Receivables"
krepoopts(3)="Inventory"
MENU 2,krepoopts
DIMENSION kutilopts(2)
kutilopts(1)="QUIT"
kutilopts(2)="CANCEL"
MENU 3,kutilopts
* Now create a submenu for each of the
* Report menu options
DIMENSION sub1(2)
sub1(1)="Cost List"
sub1(2)="Price List"
DIMENSION sub2(2)
sub2(1)="Salesmen"
sub2(2)="YTD Sales"
DIMENSION sub3(3)
sub3(1)="Overdue Accounts"
sub3(2)="Aging"
sub3(3)="Receipts"
MENU 2,sub1,2,3
MENU 2,sub2,2,1
MENU 2,sub3,3,2
* Create a variable to hold the options
whatchoice=" "
* Now tell FoxBASE+/Mac what to do when a user makes
* a selection from the menu
ON MENU whatchoice=STR(MENU(0),2)+STR(MENU(1),2)
* Put screen 1 on the desktop
SCREEN 1 TYPE 4 LOCK TOP SIZE 24,80
CLEAR
@ 13,15 SAY "Please select a menu option."
* Now process menu selections
DO WHILE whatchoice#" 3 1"   && Until Quit
   * Menu activity can only occur during a READ or WAIT,
   * so we will conjure up a nonsense READ to
   * facilitate our menu demonstration
```

```
    STORE SPACE(10) TO nonsense
    @ 14,20 GET nonsense
    * reset the whatchoice variable
    whatchoice=""
    READ
    * Now display any menu activity
    @ 15,0
    @ 15,1 SAY "Last menu selection: " + whatchoice
ENDDO until user quits
* Turn menu system off
ON MENU
RETURN
* eof menu3.prg
```

Creating and using arrays

For those readers who are not familiar with arrays, the following definition may be helpful:

Arrays are groups of memory variables that have the same name, and are distinguishable only by their element reference.

Arrays are created with the DIMENSION or PUBLIC commands, each of which defines the number of elements in each array. (Note: If you try to DIMENSION an existing array or memory variable, you will generate an error. It is therefore helpful to always issue a RELEASE arrayname command prior to issuing a DIMENSION command.) Each element can be treated as an individual memory variable by using the array name and the element number as follows:

```
DIMENSION arr(5)    && Create array with 5 elements
arr = 0     && Store the number 0 to all five elements
arr(1) = 128   && store 128 to the first element
STORE 3 TO arr(3),arr(4),arr(5)    && assign the number 3 to
elements 3, 4, and 5
```

FoxBASE+/Mac supports both one and two dimensional arrays. Arrays can contain up to 32,767 elements of mixed data types. Elements that are of character type use the same pool of string space as do standard character type memory variables. That is, each character element consumes 7 bytes of string space plus the number of characters contained in the character element. This pool size is governed by the MVARSIZ setting in the config.fx file.

Numeric, Date, and Logical array elements do not use any of the available memory pool. They do however use system memory. Arrays cannot be passed as parameters, but individual array elements can be passed as parameters. Array elements cannot be expanded via the ampersand (&) macro expansion operator.

Let's interrupt our discussion of menus long enough to provide a simple example of the use of an array. In the following program, the goal is to place a word on the screen that matches a numeric value between 0 and 9 entered by a user. Here is the program:

```
* array.prg
* Demonstrates the use of a small array
SCREEN 1 SIZE 5,80 FONT "MONACO",9
SCREEN 1 AT 0,0 TOP LOCK TYPE 4
CLEAR
* Setup 10 element array
DIMENSION numwords(10)
* Fill the individual array elements
numwords(1)="Zero"
numwords(2)="One"
numwords(3)="Two"
numwords(4)="Three"
numwords(5)="Four"
numwords(6)="Five"
numwords(7)="Six"
numwords(8)="Seven"
numwords(9)="Eight"
numwords(10)="Nine"
DO WHILE .T.
   thisnum = 0
   @ 2,20 SAY "Enter number or 0 to exit ==>> " ;
   GET thisnum PICTURE "#"
   READ
   * Display the appropriate word.  Note how the element
   * reference can be an expression as well as a numeric
```

Creating and using arrays

```
*  constant.   Variables can also be used as element references.
@ 4,0
@ 4,20 SAY numwords(thisnum+1)
IF thisnum = 0
   EXIT
ENDIF 0
ENDDO Process requests for num words
* EOF array.prg
```

Each element in an array can be of any legal data type, and can contain any legal value. We will use arrays more extensively in later chapters, but for now, let's resume our investigations of the mechanics of menu creation.

Fancy menu displays

FoxBASE+/Mac provides several options in defining individual menu options and sub options. The following program demonstrates most of these options:

```
* menu4.prg
* Fancy menu options using both delimited strings
* and arrays
* Create Menu BAR options
MENU BAR "Data Entry;Reports;Utilities"
* Now "fill" each bar with options
MENU 1,"Customers;Invoices;Inventory"  && Data Entry
DIMENSION kbarrepo(9)
kbarrepo(1)="/CCost" && [Command]+C shortcut
kbarrepo(2)="/PPrice List" && [Command]+P shortcut
kbarrepo(3)="(-" && seperator line
kbarrepo(4)="<ISalesmen" && italicized
kbarrepo(5)="<OYTD Sales" && Outline
kbarrepo(6)="(-" && separator line
kbarrepo(7)="<BOverdue Accounts" && Bold Face
kbarrepo(8)="<U<SAging" && Underline / Shadow
kbarrepo(9)="(Receipts" && Inactive
MENU 2,kbarrepo   && Reports
MENU 3,"Quit;Cancel"
* Create a variable to hold the options
whatchoice=""
```

```
* Now tell FoxBASE+/Mac what to do when a user makes
* a selection from the menu
ON MENU whatchoice=STR(MENU(0),2)+STR(MENU(1),2)
* Put screen 1 on the desktop
SCREEN 1 TYPE 4 LOCK TOP SIZE 24,80
CLEAR
@ 13,15 SAY "Please select a menu option."
* Now process menu selections
DO WHILE whatchoice#" 3 1"  && Until Quit
   * Menu activity can only occur during a READ or WAIT,
   * so we will conjure up a nonsense READ to
   * facilitate our menu demonstration
   STORE SPACE(10) TO nonsense
   @ 14,20 GET nonsense
   * reset the whatchoice variable
   whatchoice=""
   READ
   * Now display any menu activity
   @ 15,0
   @ 15,1 SAY "Last menu selection: " + whatchoice
ENDDO until user quits
* Turn menu system off
ON MENU
RETURN
* eof menu4.prg
```

You can see the output of menu4.prg in Figure 6-05. Choosing the Overdue Accounts option of the Reports bar returns 2 and 7 for the bar and option selections respectively. This illustrates that divider lines, even though inactive, are still counted when determining the number of the option selected.

Descriptive menu systems

Note that we have used both the array and the delimited string methods of menu option definition in the menu4.prg program. Even though the delimited string method is often easier to type than the array method, the array method does help overcome one significant weakness in the FoxBASE+/Mac menu selection process.

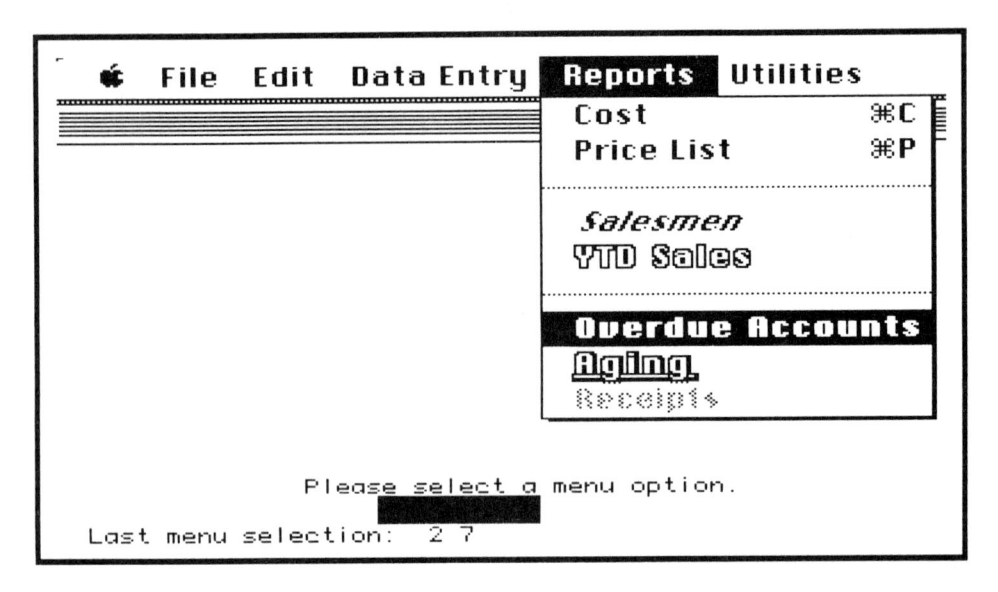

Figure 6-05. Fancy menu options.

The problem lies in the values returned by MENU(0) and MENU(1). Always numeric, these values can be cryptic when seen out of context in a program. In other words, it is of little value to know that the user selected bar 2, option 7, if we don't know what those numbers represent. It would be much nicer to know that the user chose the Reports bar, and the Overdue Accounts option.

Happily, there is a solution, and it is presented in the menu5.prg and sysmenu.prg programs that follow:

```
* menu5.prg
* First use of ON MENU DO
* Uses array method
* Create Menu BAR options
DIMENSION ktopbar(4)
ktopbar(1)="Data Entry"
ktopbar(2)="Reports"
ktopbar(3)="Utilities"
ktopbar(4)="Customer Sub-menu"
* Now "fill" each bar with options
```

```
DIMENSION kfileopt(2)   && File menu
kfileopt(1)="Flush Buffers"
kfileopt(2)="Close all Files"
DIMENSION keditopt(2)   && Edit menu
keditopt(1)="Edit"
keditopt(2)="Delete"
DIMENSION kapple(1)   && Apple Menu
kapple(1)="About My Program"
DIMENSION kdataopt(3)   && Data Entry
kdataopt(1)="Customers"
kdataopt(2)="Invoices"
kdataopt(3)="Inventory"
DIMENSION kcustsub(3)
kcustsub(1)="Lookup"
kcustsub(2)="Purge"
kcustsub(3)="Edit"
DIMENSION krepoopt(9)   && Reports
krepoopt(1)="Cost /C" && [Command]+C shortcut
krepoopt(2)="Price List /P" && [Command]+P shortcut
krepoopt(3)="(-"  && seperator line
krepoopt(4)="Salesmen <I" && italicized
krepoopt(5)="YTD Sales <O" && Outline
krepoopt(6)="(-" && separator line
krepoopt(7)="Overdue Accounts <B" && Bold Face
krepoopt(8)="Aging <U<S" && Underline / Shadow
krepoopt(9)="(Receipts" && Inactive
DIMENSION kutilopt(2)
kutilopt(1)="QUIT"
kutilopt(2)="CANCEL"
* Now load the arrays into the menu system
MENU BAR ktopbar,3 && only three bars
MENU -2,kapple  && Insert to Apple menu
MENU -1,kfileopt && Overwrite File menu
MENU  0,keditopt && Add to end of Edit menu
MENU  1,kdataopt && data entry
MENU  2,krepoopt && Reports
MENU  3,kutilopt && utilities
MENU  1,kcustsub,3,1 && Sub menu of data entry
* Create variables to hold results of menu hit
PUBLIC kmnbar,kmnopt,kmnhit
STORE .F. TO kmnhit
STORE "" to kmnbar,kmnopt
* Now tell FoxBASE+/Mac to DO the sysmenu.prg
* program when a menu selection is made.
* Sysmenu.prg will load the appropriate info into
* the kmnbar,kmnopt,kmnhit variables
ON MENU DO sysmenu WITH MENU(0),MENU(1)
* Put screen 1 on the desktop
```

Descriptive menu systems

```
SCREEN 1 TYPE 4 LOCK TOP SIZE 24,80
CLEAR
@ 13,15 SAY "Please select a menu option."
* Now process menu selections
DO WHILE !(kmnbar="UTIL".AND.kmnopt="QUIT")   && Until Quit
   * Menu activity can only occur during a READ or WAIT,
   * so we will conjure up a nonsense READ to
   * facilitate our menu demonstration
   STORE SPACE(10) TO nonsense
   @ 14,20 GET nonsense
   * reset kmnhit
   kmnhit=.F.
   READ
   * Now display any menu activity
   @ 15,0 CLEAR
   IF kmnhit
      @ 15,1 SAY "Last menu bar: "+kmnbar
      @ 16,1 SAY "Last menu opt: "+kmnopt
   ELSE
      @ 15,1 SAY "No menu selection made!"
   ENDIF menu selection used to exit READ
ENDDO until user quits
* Turn menu system off
ON MENU
RETURN
* eof menu5.prg
```

```
* sysmenu.prg
* Places results of menu selections into
* kmnbar, kmnopt, kmnhit variables
* whatbar = MENU(0)
* whatopt = MENU(1)
PARAMETERS whatbar,whatopt
DO CASE
   CASE whatbar = -3
      * user changed screens
      kmnbar="SCREEN"
      kmnopt="CHANGE"
   CASE whatbar = -2
      * Apple menu
      kmnbar="APPLE"
      kmnopt=kapple
   CASE whatbar = -1
      * File menu
      kmnbar="FILE"
      kmnopt=UPPER(kfileopt(whatopt))
```

```
      CASE whatbar = 0
        * Edit menu
        kmnbar="EDIT"
        kmnopt=UPPER(keditopt(whatopt))
      OTHERWISE
        * User selected one of the standard, programmer
        * generated menus
        * Use the numeric value of whatbar to place the content
        * of the appropriate ktopbar() array into a variable
        kmnbar = UPPER(ktopbar(whatbar))

        * Now see what array has the option text
        DO CASE
          CASE UPPER(kmnbar) = "DATA ENTRY"
            kmnopt = kdataopt(whatopt)
          CASE UPPER(kmnbar) = "REPORT"
            kmnopt = krepoopt(whatopt)
          CASE UPPER(kmnbar) = "UTILITIES"
            kmnopt = kutilopt(whatopt)
          CASE UPPER(kmnbar) = "CUSTOMER SUB"
            kmnopt = kcustsub(whatopt)
        ENDCASE kmnbar
        kmnopt = UPPER(kmnopt)
ENDCASE what kind of menu bar was selected
IF whatbar >= -2
  * set hit flag to true
  kmnhit = .T.
ENDIF not a screen change
RETURN
* eof sysmenu.prg
```

Figure 6-06 shows both the selection process, and the result of choosing the second option from the first submenu defined in the current menu system. If the last sentence seems cryptic, try remembering that the customer sub menu is the fourth menu bar, and that the purge option is the second option on that sub menu.

If you follow the guidelines demonstrated in menu5.prg and sysmenu.prg, and the explanations that follow, you won't have to remember any numbers. You'll just have to remember the phrases "Customer Sub-menu" and "Purge."

Descriptive menu systems

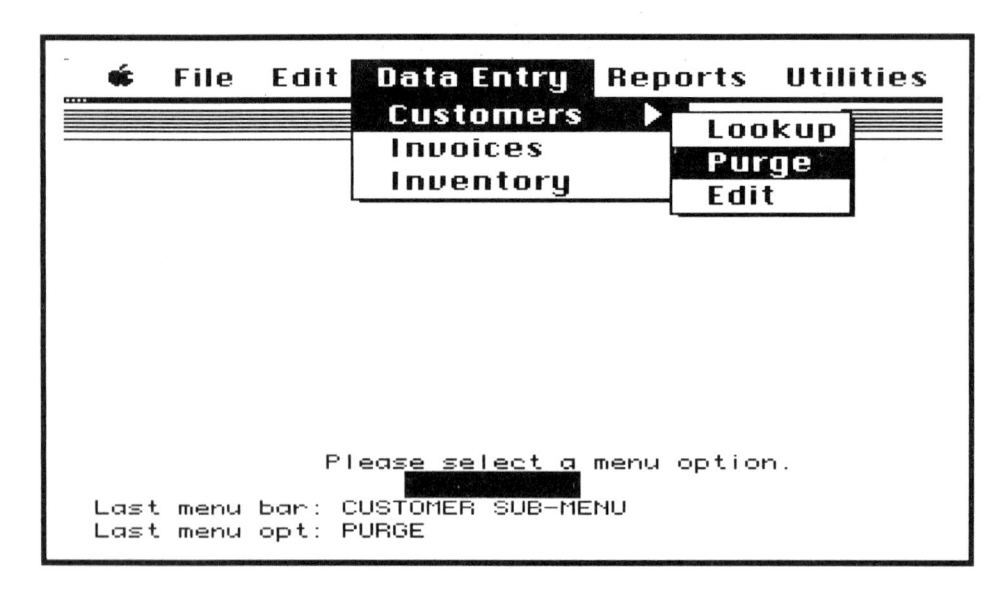

```
     File    Edit   Data Entry   Reports   Utilities
                    Customers  ▶  ┌─────────┐
                    Invoices      │ Lookup  │
                    Inventory     │ Purge   │
                                  │ Edit    │
                                  └─────────┘




                    Please select a menu option.
     Last menu bar: CUSTOMER SUB-MENU
     Last menu opt: PURGE
```

Figure 6-06. Descriptive menu returns.

To create a descriptive menu system, use arrays to define your menu bars and options. In the array used for bars, include all of the titles to be displayed on the menu bar, and then include the names of any submenus, in the order in which those submenus will be attached to the menu system. This part of the technique is demonstrated in the menu5.prg program.

Next, create a program like sysmenu.prg. Here it will be necessary to remember the names of the arrays used to fill each menu bar with options, so it is best to use descriptive array names as I have done in menu5.prg. The first DO CASE structure is designed to handle those menu systems where the programmer has installed options into the Apple, File, or Edit menus. (The -3 return from MENU(0) has a special meaning, which we will review in the later chapters on advanced data entry.)

The second DO CASE structure is designed to handle selection of one of the options from one of the programmer's menu bars. Note that we convert the options to UPPER() case, so that we needn't remember how the actual option is capitalized in the menu system.

Finally, adapt your programs to evaluate descriptive menu selection values, as we have in the following command in menu5.prg:

```
DO WHILE !(kmnbar="UTIL".AND.kmnopt="QUIT")
```

Contrast this "DO WHILE user doesn't Quit" statement with this equivalent from a non-descriptive menu system:

```
DO WHILE !(kmnbar=3.AND.kmnopt=1)
```

At this point, you know how to create programs and menu systems, but I haven't yet shown you how to integrate these tools to create an application. I will remedy this deliberate oversight in the very next chapter.

Descriptive menu systems

7. System Design

More on event-driven applications

As we discussed in the last chapter, Macintosh programs usually feature an event-driven user interface. To refine our understanding of the terms menu-driven and event-driven, I have included Figures 7-01 and 7-02.

Both Figures reflect the user and program effort required to perform two tasks in succession. In the menu-driven approach, the user is required to make 3 selections to arrive at the first task and, more importantly, is required to make 4 more selections to access the second task. In the event-driven approach, the user is only required to make at most 2 selections to access two tasks.

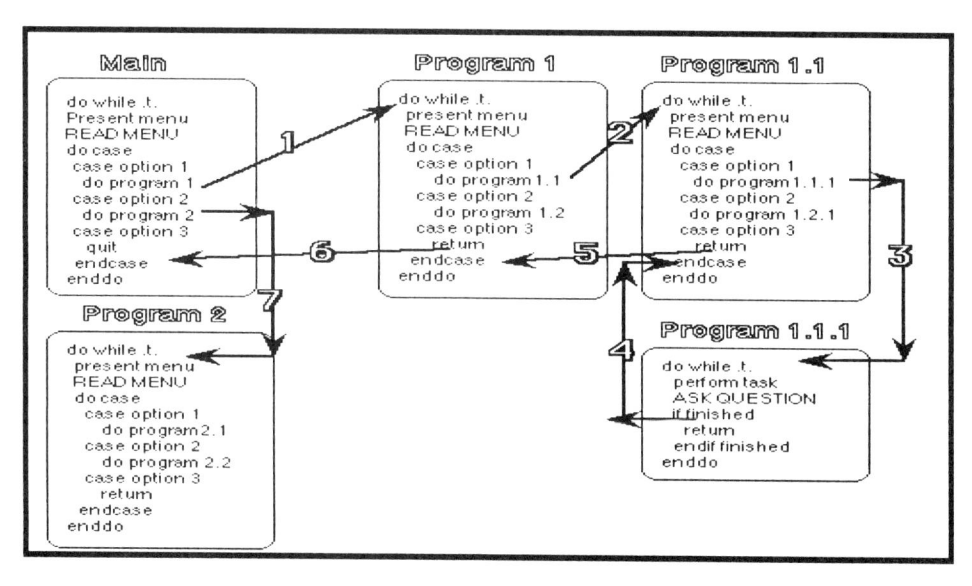

Figure 7-01. Menu driven program flow.

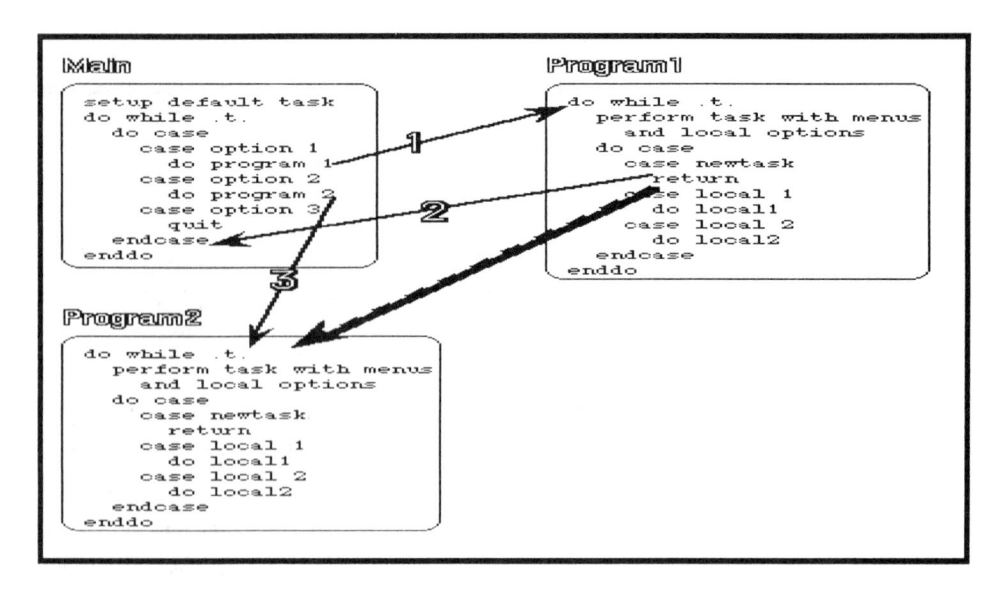

```
Main                              Program1
 setup default task                do while .t.
 do while .t.                        perform task with menus
   do case                             and local options
     case option 1                   do case
       do program 1                    case newtask
     case option 2                       return
       do program 2                    case local 1
     case option 3                       do local1
       quit                            case local 2
   endcase                               do local2
 enddo                              endcase
                                  enddo

Program2
 do while .t.
   perform task with menus
     and local options
   do case
     case newtask
       return
     case local 1
       do local1
     case local 2
       do local2
   endcase
 enddo
```

Figure 7-02. Event driven program flow.

Note that the event-driven approach includes a return to the main program that is similar to the returns found in the menu-driven approach. Of key importance however, is the thick line pointing from program 1 to program 2 in Figure 7-02. This line reflects the user's impression that the switch from one task to another is a one-step process. In other words, the user is not aware of any returns, he believes that the path from one task to another is a straight line.

This makes for fine theoretical discussion, but how do we implement such a system in FoxBASE+/Mac? There are many possible solutions, but this chapter will demonstrate one of the best.

We need three kinds of programs to implement our event-driven approach in FoxBASE+/Mac. First, we need a menu handling program like the sysmenu.prg that made its debut in the last chapter. Next we need a main program. This program is responsible for performing a task based on the user's last menu selection. Finally, we need a series of task programs to accomplish the work of the application.

Creating a main program

The sysmenu.prg program will suffice for now as our menu handling program, and subsequent chapters will concentrate on programs to perform common database management tasks. All that is left is a main menu program, and for that we turn to the following program listing:

```
* main.prg
* Sample main menu program
* SET environment
SET TALK OFF
SET SCORE OFF
SET STAT OFF
SET VIEW OFF
SET BELL ON
SET STRICT ON
SET CONFIRM OFF
SCREEN 1 TOP
* Setup menu system
DIMENSION ktopbar(4)
ktopbar(1)="Data Entry"
ktopbar(2)="Reports"
ktopbar(3)="Utilities"
ktopbar(4)="Customer Sub-menu"
* Now "fill" each bar with options
DIMENSION kdataopt(3)   && Data Entry
kdataopt(1)="Customers"
kdataopt(2)="Invoices"
kdataopt(3)="Inventory"
DIMENSION kcustsub(3)
kcustsub(1)="Lookup"
kcustsub(2)="Purge"
kcustsub(3)="Edit"
DIMENSION krepoopt(9)   && Reports
krepoopt(1)="Cost /C" && [Command]+C shortcut
krepoopt(2)="Price List /P" && [Command]+P shortcut
krepoopt(3)="(-"   && seperator line       '
krepoopt(4)="Salesmen <I" && italicized
krepoopt(5)="YTD Sales <O" && Outline
krepoopt(6)="(-" && separator line
krepoopt(7)="Overdue Accounts <B" && Bold Face
krepoopt(8)="Aging <U<S" && Underline / Shadow
krepoopt(9)="(Receipts" && Inactive
DIMENSION kutilopt(2)
```

```
kutilopt(1)="QUIT"
kutilopt(2)="CANCEL"
* Now load the arrays into the menu system
MENU BAR ktopbar,3 && only three bars
MENU 1,kdataopt  && data entry
MENU 2,krepoopt  && Reports
MENU 3,kutilopt  && utilities
MENU 1,kcustsub,3,1 && Sub menu of data entry
* end of menu setup
* Setup default task
kmnbar = "REPORTS"  && menu bar
kmnopt = "AGING"    && option
kmnhit = .F.   && has a menu option been selected
* Activate menu system
ON MENU DO sysmenu WITH MENU(0),MENU(1)
* At this point you may wish to use any databases
* that will remain in use throughout the application
* Now begin the application
DO WHILE .T.
  * what menu bar was selected
  DO CASE
    CASE kmnbar = "DATA ENTRY"
      * Which data entry option was selected
      DO CASE
        CASE kmnopt = "INVOICES"
          DO standard WITH kmnbar + "/" + kmnopt
        CASE kmnopt = "INVENTORY"
          DO standard WITH kmnbar + "/" + kmnopt
      ENDCASE data entry option
    CASE kmnbar = "REPORTS"
      DO CASE
        CASE kmnopt = "COST"
          DO standard WITH kmnbar + "/" + kmnopt
        CASE kmnopt = "PRICE"
          DO standard WITH kmnbar + "/" + kmnopt
        CASE kmnopt = "SALESMEN"
          DO standard WITH kmnbar + "/" + kmnopt
        CASE kmnopt = "YTD SALES"
          DO standard WITH kmnbar + "/" + kmnopt
        CASE kmnopt = "OVERDUE ACCOUNTS"
          DO standard WITH kmnbar + "/" + kmnopt
        CASE kmnopt = "AGING"
          DO standard WITH kmnbar + "/" + kmnopt
        CASE kmnopt = "RECEIPTS"
          DO standard WITH kmnbar + "/" + kmnopt
      ENDCASE report option
    CASE kmnbar = "UTILITIES"
      DO CASE
```

```
        CASE kmnopt = "QUIT"
          * exit from FoxBASE+/Mac
          QUIT
        CASE kmnopt = "CANCEL"
          * Turn off menu system
          ON MENU
          MENU BAR
          * cancel program execution
          CANCEL
      ENDCASE utilities option
    CASE kmnbar = "CUSTOMER SUB-MENU"
      DO CASE
        CASE kmnopt = "LOOKUP"
          DO standard WITH kmnbar + "/" + kmnopt
        CASE kmnopt = "PURGE"
          DO standard WITH kmnbar + "/" + kmnopt
        CASE kmnopt = "EDIT"
          DO standard WITH kmnbar + "/" + kmnopt
      ENDCASE customer sub-menu option
  ENDCASE menu bar
  ** set the menu hit flag to false
  kmnhit = .F.
ENDDO endless loop for entire application
```

Remember to adjust the sysmenu.prg program to accommodate your menu bars and array names. The standard.prg program is an attempt to demonstrate most of the key activities that need to take place in a task portion of an application. Obviously, the actual content of these kinds of programs will vary widely from the sample content of standard.prg, but most will include the types of activities denoted by triple asterisk ("***") comments in the following program listing:

```
* standard.prg
* Sample program featuring some of the standard activities
* found in a "task" portion of an application
* message = name of task for the purposes of the book only
PARAMETERS message
*** Create screen(s) for use by this program
SCREEN 1 SIZE 8,80 TYPE 8 FONT "MONACO",9
CLEAR
SCREEN 1 TOP AT 50,10 HEADING message
*** Use any local databases required
* USE customer
```

Creating a main program

```
*** setup any local memory variables
PRIVATE option,name
STORE 0 TO option
STORE SPACE(10) TO name
*** Display screen prompts
@ 2,3 SAY "Enter stuff here:"
*** begin local processing
DO WHILE .T.
  *** reset local options
  option = 0
  *** GET info from user
  @ 2,30 GET name
  @ 5,0 GET option PICTURE "@*h SAVE;DELETE;NEXT;PREVIOUS"
  *** set the menu hit flag to false
  *** READ user's input until local or menu option selected
  DO WHILE option = 0.and.(!kmnhit)
    READ SAVE
  ENDDO wait for local option or menu hit
  CLEAR GETS
  *** Check for menu hit
  IF kmnhit
    *** exit from this task
    EXIT
  ENDIF menu hit
  *** check for local activity
  DO CASE
    CASE option = 1
      DO stub WITH "Save"
    CASE option = 2
      DO stub WITH "Delete"
    CASE option = 3
      DO stub WITH "Next"
    CASE option = 4
      DO stub WITH "Previous"
  ENDCASE local activity
ENDDO local processing
*** close any local databases
*** remove any temporary work files
*** clear the desktop of any local screens
RETURN     && return control to calling program
* eof standard.prg
```

Modular programs and stubs

Typical applications include many programs like standard.prg, each performing a specific task. This technique is often referred to as modular programming. As you can see by the use of the stub.prg program in standard.prg, tasks can perform other tasks. Here is the listing for stub.prg:

```
* stub.prg
* Used as a "place-holder" for tasks that have
* not yet been programmed
PARAMETERS message
*
PRIVATE oldscreen
oldscreen = VAL(SYS(1034))
SCREEN 8 TYPE 1 AT 0,0 SIZE 6,40 FONT "CHICAGO",12
CLEAR       && make SCREEN 8 blank
SCREEN 8 TOP   && bring SCREEN 8 to the top of the desktop
@ 1,15 say message
@ 2,15 say "is not yet available."
STORE 0 TO dummy
* Use the dummy variable to display a text button
@ 4,30 GET dummy PICTURE "@*v CONTINUE"
* Wait for the user to click on "CONTINUE"
READ
SCREEN 8 OFF  && remove our screen from the desktop
* put the other screen back on top
SCREEN oldscreen TOP
RETURN     && return control to calling program
* eof stub.prg
```

When writing programs, it is usually best to identify as many of the options and tasks in the application as possible. Then, once these have been identified, you can begin to write each individual module. Until all of the modules are completed however, it is often helpful to save the place of unfinished portions of the program with a program stub. The stub.prg program can be used for such a purpose.

Watching program execution with trace

When you DO the main.prg program you will see how the user is shielded from the actions of the main.prg program. As far as the user can tell, all activities are a single menu option away. To get a better understanding of how FoxBASE+/Mac reacts to the user's attempt to switch tasks, open the Debug window from the Window menu, and position it at the bottom of the screen. Next, expand the Debug window to hold 5 expressions at once. Then, insert the expressions seen in the left side of the Debug window in Figure 7-03. Don't forget to click on the center column of the Debug window next to the SYS(16) expression in the Debug window.

The SYS(16) function returns the name of the currently active program. In our example, the user has selected the NEXT text button from within the standard.prg program. Take a moment to experiment with other activities, especially the use of pull-down menus.

DOing programs

In the above examples, we have made use of such heretofore unexplained

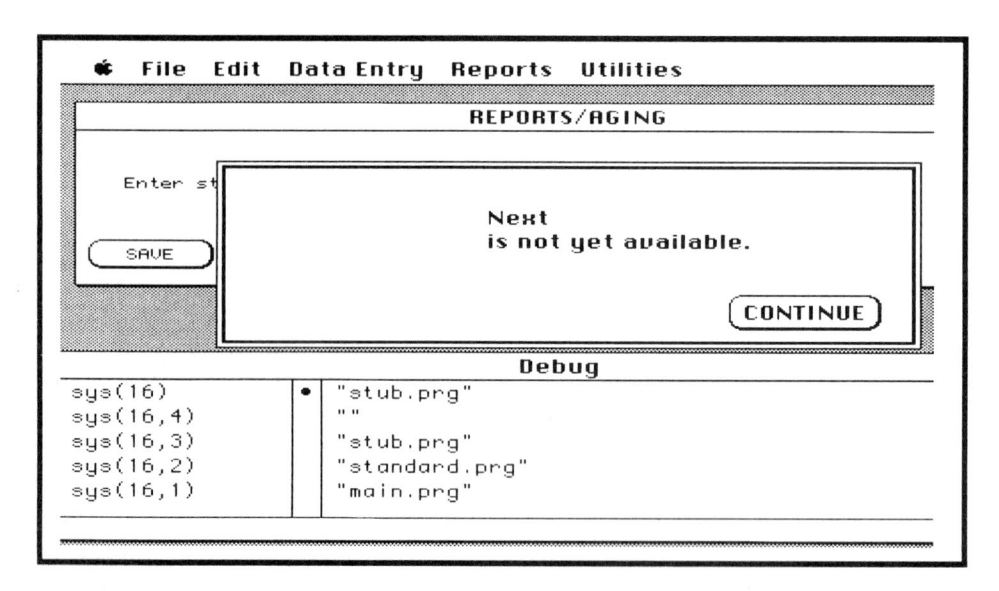

Figure 7-03. Debugging Multiple DO's.

commands as PARAMETERS, DO, DO ... WITH, and PRIVATE. These commands are all related to the DOing of programs. Since this activity is central to any significant application, I will use the rest of the chapter to explain the characteristics of the FoxBASE+/Mac DO command.

In the examples above, the program main.prg can be referred to as the DOing program, and standard.prg can be referred to as one of the DOne programs. Programmers have a curious vocabulary however, and most programmers would refer to main.prg as the calling program, and to maintain.prg as one of the called programs. To retain our standing in the programming community, and to insure that you share the vocabulary of most professionals in the field, we will use called and calling to refer to programs that DO other programs and are DOne by other programs respectively. (Note: called programs are also referred to as subroutines.)

The action of DOing one program from another is commonly referred to as the nesting of one program in another. This nesting generates a hierarchy of called and calling programs where a called program is said to occupy a position one level lower than the program that called it.

(Note: There is no prescribed limit to the number of levels of program nesting that can be accomplished with the DO command. In practice however, it is rare to see more than 10 levels of nesting.)

Public and private memory variables

Generally, when you define a variable in FoxBASE+/Mac, the variable stays active until you RETURN from the program, CANCEL the program, or QUIT from the program. Variables that behave in this way are known as PRIVATE variables. PUBLIC variables on the other hand remain active until they are specifically released with the RELEASE, CLEAR MEMORY, or CLEAR ALL commands, or until you QUIT. A variable is PRIVATE unless declared PUBLIC.

FoxBASE+/Mac imposes a limit of between 256 and 3600 (Note: The actual number is selected by entering a command in the config.fx file. See the FoxBASE+/Mac manual for details.) simultaneously active memory variables. While this number is more than enough for most applications, the automatic RELEASE of PRIVATE memory variables relieves the programmer of the burden of manually RELEASing the memory variables. In fact, in most applications it is unnecessary to include any RELEASE or CLEAR MEMORY commands at all.

Another benefit to the PRIVATE/PUBLIC treatment of memory variables is the ability to reuse memory variable names without danger of unintentionally affecting an unrelated part of the application. After all, coming up with 1,500 unique variable names can be difficult.

Rather than explaining all of the conditions that dictate the PUBLIC or PRIVATE status of a memory variable, let's check the results of a few sample programs:

```
* pubpriv.prg
* Demonstrates the public or private nature of variables
screen 1 TOP SIZE 26,80 FONT "MONACO",9 AT 0,0
SCREEN 1 HEADING "PUBLIC / PRIVATE"
CLEAR
CLEAR MEMORY && start with no memory variables
george = 17
tom = 18
dick = 19
DISPLAY MEMORY
* Run the pubpriv1.prg (Which displays memory)
DO pubpriv1
* Show status of memory variables after pubpriv1
DISPLAY MEMORY
WAIT
* Notice that the harry variable assigned in pubpriv1 is no
* longer active.  Also notice that pubpriv1 was able to change
* the value of the dick variable.
CLEAR
* Run the pubpriv2.prg (Which displays memory)
DO pubpriv2
* Show status of memory variables after pubpriv2
DISPLAY MEMORY
```

```
WAIT
* Notice that the harry variable assigned in pubpriv2 is still
* active.  Also notice that the content of the dick variable was
* unchanged by the pubpriv2.prg
* eof pubpriv.prg
```

```
* pubpriv1.prg
* Helps the pubpriv.prg demonstrate the PUBLIC or PRIVATE status
* of variables
harry = 21
dick = 22
* Show memory status at this point
DISPLAY MEMORY
RETURN
*eof pubpriv1.prg
```

```
* pubpriv2.prg
* Helps the pubpriv.prg demonstrate the PUBLIC or PRIVATE status
* of variables
* Use the PRIVATE command to prevent any changes to the
* dick variable in pubpriv2.prg from affecting the dick
* variable as it currently exists.
PRIVATE dick
* Use the PUBLIC command to make the harry variable available
* to the pubpriv.prg
PUBLIC harry
harry = 21
dick = 5
* Show memory status at this point
DISPLAY MEMORY
RETURN
*eof pubpriv2.prg
```

The results of these programs are shown in Figures 7-04 and 7-05. Notice the effect of the PUBLIC and PRIVATE commands on the content of the dick and harry variables. Pubpriv1.prg and pubpriv2.prg contain the same assignment statements, but the use of the PRIVATE and PUBLIC commands in the pubpriv2.prg protect dick from modification, and allow harry to remain active when control is returned to pubpriv.prg.

Public and private memory variables

As your programs become so large that you cannot remember the names of all of your memory variables, you will grow to appreciate the ability to hide existing variables from the processes of a called program. In the interim, let's investigate the process of DOing a program WITH PARAMETERS.

Parameter passing

In the course of writing many large applications, you will identify many instances where the same process is repeated over and over, differing only in the name and content of the variables on which it acts. You could write the same lines of code over and over again, or you could create a library of subroutines to perform these common tasks.

One of the most common tasks is the centering of a line of text in a screen. This is particularly difficult when trying to use a font different than the

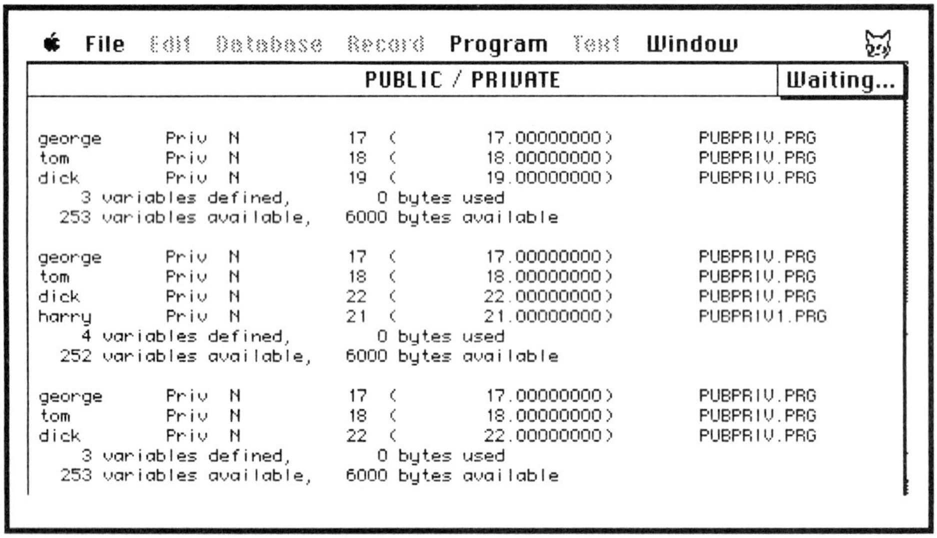

Figure 7-04. Pubpriv and pubpriv1.

```
                               PUBLIC / PRIVATE                      Waiting...

harry        Pub    N       21  (         21.00000000)
george       Priv   N       17  (         17.00000000)    PUBPRIV.PRG
tom          Priv   N       18  (         18.00000000)    PUBPRIV.PRG
dick         Priv   (hidden) N       22  (         22.00000000)  PUBPRIV.PRG
dick         Priv   N        5  (          5.00000000)    PUBPRIV2.PRG
      5 variables defined,        0 bytes used
    251 variables available,   6000 bytes available

harry        Pub    N       21  (         21.00000000)
george       Priv   N       17  (         17.00000000)    PUBPRIV.PRG
tom          Priv   N       18  (         18.00000000)    PUBPRIV.PRG
dick         Priv   N       22  (         22.00000000)    PUBPRIV.PRG
      4 variables defined,        0 bytes used
    252 variables available,   6000 bytes available
```

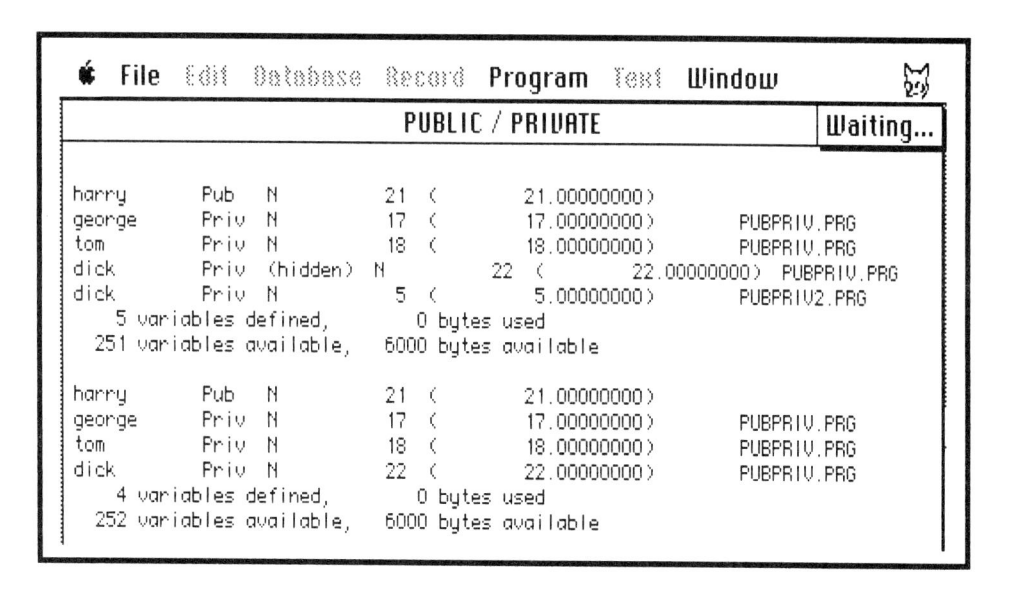

Figure 7-05. Pubpriv2.

default font for the screen. The following program handles these problems nicely:

```
* lbcenter.prg
* centers a line of text in a window
* Assumes that screen 9 is unused by the application
** mrow = row or pixel vertical positioning (numeric)
** msg = text to be centered
** fntname = font
** fntsize = size of font (numeric)
** options = B = boldface
**           I = italic
**           U = underline
**           O = outline
**           S = shadow
**           W = wait for keystroke
**           P = use PIXELS for vertical positioning
**           L = Ring a bell
**           F = Old screen was "FIXED"
* Sample Usage: DO lbcenter WITH 20,"Enter data","",0,""
PARAMETERS mrow,msg,fntname,fntsize,options
PRIVATE msgwidth,effects,oldscreen,mcol,scrnwidth
```

Parameter passing

```
options=UPPER(options)
* Identify any special effects
effects = 0
IF "B"$options
  effects = 256
ENDIF boldface
IF "I"$options
  effects = effects + 512
ENDIF italics
IF "U"$options
  effects = effects + 1024
ENDIF underline
IF "O"$options
  effects = effects + 2048
ENDIF outline
IF "S"$options
  effects = effects + 4096
ENDIF shadow
* See if we need to account for a message size other than
* the current window's current
IF ""#fntname.OR.0#fntsize.OR.effects#0
  oldscreen = VAL(SYS(1034)) && number of current screen
  * Use screen 9 as a scratch pad to see how big the msg is
  SCREEN 9 FONT fntname,fntsize+effects SIZE 5,5 PIXELS
  msgwidth = VAL(SYS(1030,msg))
  SCREEN 9 OFF  && remove scratch screen from desktop
  IF "F"$options  && Old screen was "FIXED"
    SCREEN oldscreen FIXED
  ELSE && old screen was not fixed
    SCREEN oldscreen
  ENDIF && old screen was fixed
ELSE  && use standard sizing
  msgwidth = VAL(SYS(1030,msg))
ENDIF non-standard sizing
scrnwidth = VAL(SYS(1024))  && Horizontal PIXELS in screen
mcol = (scrnwidth - msgwidth) / 2
IF .NOT."P"$options
  * The mrow parameter is in ROWS, which need to be
  * converted to pixels
  mrow = mrow * (VAL(SYS(1025))+VAL(SYS(1026))+VAL(SYS(1027)))
ENDIF did not send in PIXELS
IF ""#fntname.OR.0#fntsize.OR.effects#0
  @ PIXEL mrow,mcol SAY msg FONT fntname,fntsize+effects ;
  STYLE 65536
ELSE
  @ PIXEL mrow,mcol SAY msg STYLE 65536
ENDIF not the default font for this window
IF "L"$options
```

```
   * Ring a bell
   ?? CHR(7)
ENDIF ring a bell
IF "W"$options
   WAIT
ENDIF wants to pause for the user
RETURN
 * EOF lbcenter.prg
```

The following program demonstrates several uses of the lbcenter.prg program:

```
* docenter.prg
* Demonstrates the use of the lbcenter program
SCREEN 1 TOP SIZE 25,80 AT 0,0 FONT "MONACO",9
SCREEN 1 HEADING "Centering some Text"
CLEAR
DO lbcenter WITH 2,"This is the first test","HELVETICA",18,"L"
DO lbcenter WITH 3,"This is the second test","HELVETICA",10,"BL"
DO lbcenter WITH 4,"This is the third test","CHICAGO",12,"UIB"
DO lbcenter WITH 6,"This is the fourth test","HELVETICA",10,"OSB"
DO lbcenter WITH 88,;
"This is the fifth test, on the 8th line","MONACO",9,"BP"
DO lbcenter with 12,"This is standard text","",0,""
RETURN
* EOF docenter.prg
```

The nicely centered text generated by lbcenter.prg via docenter.prg can be seen in Figure 7-06.

The benefit of the standard library approach is reduced keystrokes for the programmer. With one command, the programmer can center a message of any font type, size or style, and wait for the user to enter a keystroke. When used throughout a large application, this savings can translate to several hundred lines of code.

The user also benefits from the standard library approach through the development of improved screen displays. In general then, the creation and use of subroutines to replace the repetitive entry of common commands results in improved programs.

The mechanics of lbcenter.prg

The first command line in the lbcenter.prg program is a PARAMETERS command. This command catches values and or variables passed to lbcenter.prg via the DO lbcenter WITH... command in docenter.prg. Not all subroutines include PARAMETERS commands, but if the PARAMETERS command is included, it must be the first command line in the subroutine.

Note that we **must pass the correct number of PARAMETERS** to the called program. That is, the number of arguments that follows the WITH clause in the calling program must equal the number of arguments that follows the PARAMETERS statement in the called program.

Figure 7-06. Some centered messages.

It is also important to note that any variables listed on the PARAMETERS line are automatically declared PRIVATE. In the case of the lbcenter.prg program this means that existing variables (if any) named mrow, msg, fntname, fntsize, or options, will be hidden from lbcenter.prg. This will insure that lbcenter.prg will not unintentionally change the value of any existing variable. For the same reason, we expressly declare the effects, mcol, msgwidth, scrnwidth, and oldscreen variables as PRIVATE variables.

In addition to the PARAMETERS command, the lbcenter.prg also utilizes several FoxBASE+/Mac functions. The first of these functions is the UPPER() function. UPPER() accepts a character string as an argument, and returns the upper case value of that character string. For example, UPPER("abcd") returns "ABCD". Since FoxBASE+/Mac distinguishes between upper and lower case letters when comparing character items, the UPPER() function is frequently used to ignore case differences.

The second new function is the CHR() function, which returns the ASCII character equivalent of a numeric value. The ASCII character 7 causes the computer to make a sound that passes for the ringing of a bell. This function can be used to output special characters to the printer and or screen, but for now just understand that requesting the value of CHR(7) will result in the computer ringing the bell.

The VAL() function returns the numeric value of a string. The SYS(1034) function returns the number of the current screen as a string. This function is frequently used to allow the programmer to return to the current screen after performing some activity on another screen.

The SYS(1030,"") function returns the number of pixels used by a string in the current screen's default font type, font size, and font style. The SYS(1024) function returns the number of horizontal pixels in the current screen. The SYS(1025) through SYS(1027) functions return the ascent, descent, and leading of the default font in the current screen.

Notes on creating common subroutines

When used throughout a large application, the use of the lbcenter.prg (and programs like it) will save the programmer thousands of keystrokes. Just as importantly, lbcenter.prg will continue to save those keystrokes throughout the programmer's career because it can be used without modification in virtually any application. One of the results of this decrease in keystrokes will be a reduction in programming time. Another result will be a reduction in errors generated by typos! Finally, because all of the messages will look alike and act alike, the user will view the program as easier to use.

The good programmer is constantly on the lookout for opportunities to reduce typing, improve reliability, and increase consistency in his or her programs by adding to his or her library of frequently used portable programs. When creating these generic programs, keep the following principles in mind:

- Make the programs as generic as possible. Do so by limiting the items to be worked with to those items passed as PARAMETERS, and by keeping assumptions about the current working environment to a minimum.

- Use the PRIVATE command for any new variables introduced in the subroutine. This will protect the value of existing variables that coincidentally have the same name as variables used in the subroutine.

- Make sure all of the options are useful. Extraneous options or options that are used infrequently make it more difficult for the programmer to remember how to activate the commonly used aspects of the program.

- Keep the typing required to DO the program to a minimum. Whenever possible, calculate needed information from within the program rather than requiring the programmer to pass an additional parameter.

- Resist the temptation to significantly alter an existing generic program. Write a new one if necessary, but remember, a change to a generic program might require the re-coding of several hundred lines in a large application.

- Use some naming convention to identify all of your library programs. We begin our library program names with "lb" for library.

Changing variables with subroutines

As we saw with the pubpriv2.prg program, we can change the value of an existing variable from within a subroutine. But if we are creating a generic program, we might not know the name of the variable to be changed. How then can we change the content of a variable without knowing the variable's name?

Watch how the value of the variables tom and george change in the following programs:

```
* mystery.prg
* Demonstrate the changing of a "blind" variable
SCREEN 1 TOP SIZE 20,80 FONT "MONACO",9 AT 0,0
SCREEN 1 HEADING "Mystery"
CLEAR
george = 17
tom = 319
@ 5,5 SAY "George starts as "+STR(george)
@ 6,5 SAY "Tom starts as "+STR(tom)
* DO the subroutine with a variable
DO mystery1 WITH george
@ 8,5 SAY "George is "+STR(george)+;
" after being passed to mystery1."
* Now change the tom variable
DO mystery1 WITH tom
@ 9,5 SAY "Tom is "+STR(tom)+;
" after being passed to mystery1."
```

```
RETURN
*eof mystery.prg
```

```
* mystery1.prg
* Demonstrates the changing of a variable without referencing
* the variable name.
PARAMETERS mysteryvar
* Change the value of whatever variable was passed
mysteryvar = mysteryvar + 7
RETURN
*eof mystery1.prg
```

The results from mystery.prg can be seen in Figure 7-07. If we pass the name of a variable to a subroutine, and that subroutine changes the value of the variable named with the PARAMETER statement, the value of the original variable will be changed. What if we prefer not to change the content of the variable? Here is an interesting trick demonstrated in a rewrite of mystery.prg:

```
* mystery2.prg
* Demonstrate a technique for protecting the content of
* a parameter passed to a subroutine
SCREEN 1 TOP SIZE 20,80 FONT "MONACO",9 AT 0,0
SCREEN 1 HEADING "Mystery"
CLEAR
george = 17
tom = 319
@ 5,5 SAY "George starts as "+STR(george)
@ 6,5 SAY "Tom starts as "+STR(tom)
* DO the subroutine with an expression instead of a variable
DO mystery1 WITH george+0
@ 8,5 SAY "George is "+STR(george)+;
" after being passed to mystery1 as part of an expresson."
* Now use the tom variable in an expression
DO mystery1 WITH tom+0
@ 9,5 SAY "Tom is "+STR(tom)+;
" after being passed to mystery1 as part of an expression."
RETURN
*eof mystery2.prg
```

The results from mystery2.prg can be found in Figure 7-08. The mystery1.prg program cannot change the content of the george and tom variables because the variables were not passed as parameters. That is, mystery1 is not aware of the use of the george variable when called with a command like the following:

```
DO mystery1 WITH george + 0
```

In this case, FoxBASE+/Mac first calculates the value of the expression, then passes that value to the mystery1.prg program as a constant, not as a variable.

We have seen that we can explicitly run a program using the DO command. We have also seen that we can DO a program when the user chooses a pull-down menu option via the ON MENU DO command. A third way to execute a FoxBASE+/Mac program is as a USER DEFINED FUNCTION.

User Defined Functions are commonly referred to as UDFs, and are far less complicated than their reputation suggests. In fact, you already know how to create UDFs, because UDFs are simply programs that return a value. Here is a sample UDF that helps simplify the common task of asking the user a question:

```
* lbq.prg
* Simplifies standard user queries
* Best used as a UDF
** msg = "Note to user"
** options = Options delimited with semi-colon
** prgopts = options for operation of lbq
**           F = Reset current screen as Fixed
PARAMETERS msg,options,prgopts
PRIVATE maxwidth,choice,retval,xx,oldscreen
oldscreen = VAL(SYS(1034))   && save current screen number
* Create a "modal" dialog screen
SCREEN 8 FONT "HELVETICA",12
CLEAR
* Calculate proper width of dialog box
maxwidth = MAX(LEN(msg),LEN(options))+30
```

Changing variables with subroutines

```
SCREEN 8 SIZE 5,maxwidth AT 0,0
* Use the lbcenter procedure to center our message
DO lbcenter WITH 2,msg,"HELVETICA",12,"B"
* Note, use the following command for a faster, less
* fancy display
** DO lbcenter WITH 2,msg,"",0,""
IF "F"$prgopts
   SCREEN 8 TOP TYPE 1FIXED
ELSE
   SCREEN 8 TOP TYPE 1 LOCK
ENDIF && FIXED window
* Now get the user's selection
choice = 1
@ PIXELS 50,0 GET choice PICTURE "@*h "+options SIZE  532,80
READ
SCREEN 8 OFF
SCREEN oldscreen TOP
* See if they hit the menu
IF choice = 0
   ** return a null if user exited without selection a
   ** text button
   retval = ""
ELSE  && did not hit the menu
   * Now use the SUBSTR() function to determine a descriptive
   * representation of the user's selection
   xx=1
   retval = options+";"
   do while xx<choice
      retval = SUBSTR(retval,AT(";",retval)+1)
      xx=xx+1
   ENDDO && get to the selected option
   retval = UPPER(LEFT(retval,AT(";",retval)-1))
ENDIF hit the menu
* Now, "return" the value to calling expression
RETURN retval
* eof lbq.prg
```

The only difference between lbq.prg and the other programs you have written so far is the extra argument following the RETURN statement. To see how lbq.prg, or any other UDF, might be used, enter the following program:

```
* udftest.prg
* Test the ways in which User Defined Functions can be used
```

```
                    ≡ Mystery ≡

        George starts as        17
        Tom starts as          319

        George is              24 after being passed to mystery1.
        Tom is               326 after being passed to mystery1.
```

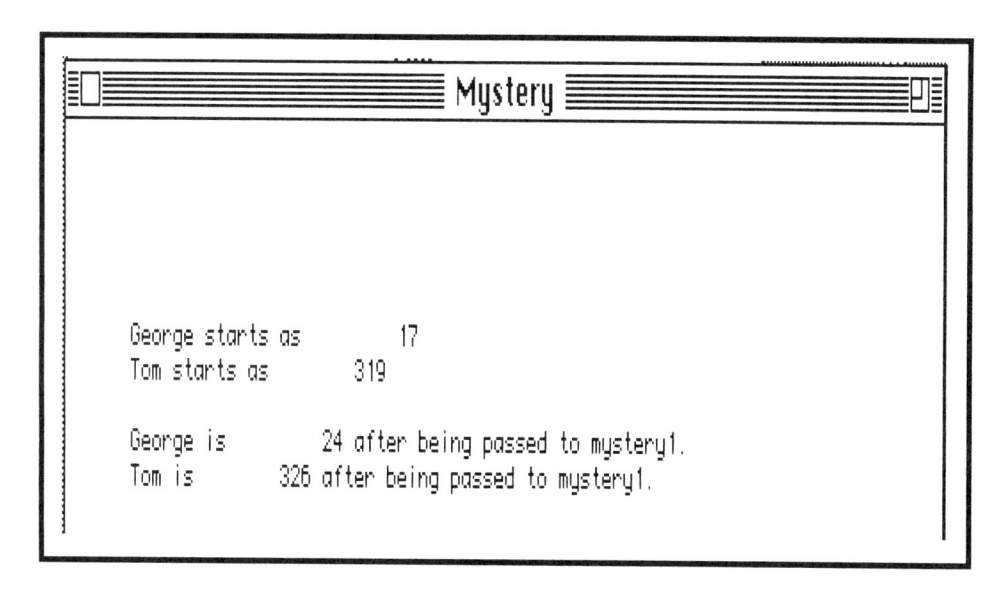

Figure 7-07. Mystery variables.

```
SCREEN 1 TOP TYPE 8 FONT "MONACO",9
SCREEN 1 SIZE 24,80
CLEAR
* Use UDF in IF statement
IF lbq("Do you want to do this?","Yes;No","F")="YES"
  ? "You asked for it."
ELSE
  ? "You didn't ask for it!"
ENDIF wants it
* Use UDF in a DO WHILE statement
xx=1
DO WHILE lbq("Do this again?","No;Yes","F")="YES"
  @ 15,5 say "You have done this "+LTRIM(STR(xx))+;
  " times."
  xx=xx+1
ENDDO still wants to do this
* Use UDF in an assignment statement
ok = lbq("Is it ok to do this?","Yes;No","F")
@ 17,5 SAY ok
* eof udftest.prg
```

The results from a sample running of udftest.prg can be seen in Figure

Changing variables with subroutines

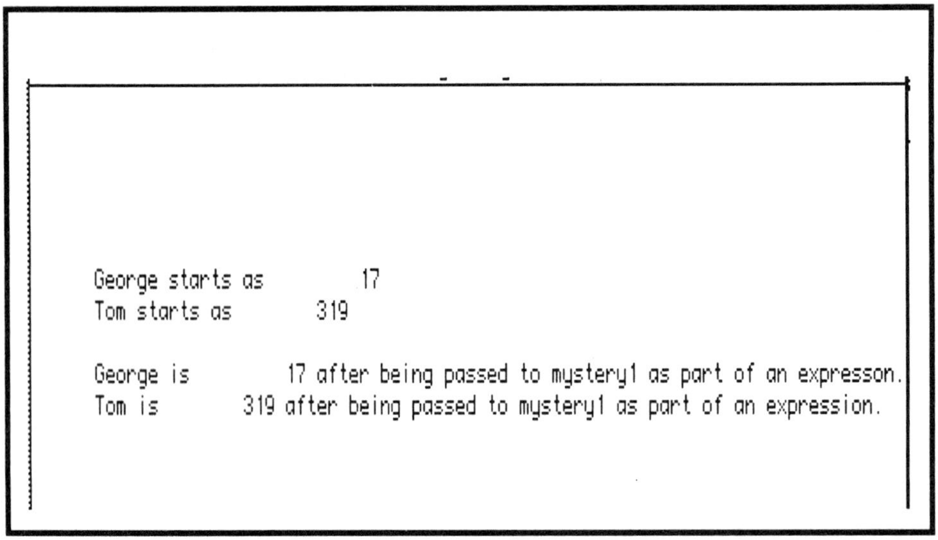

```
George starts as      17
Tom starts as         319

George is             17 after being passed to mystery1 as part of an expresson.
Tom is                319 after being passed to mystery1 as part of an expression.
```

Figure 7-08. Mystery variables 2.

7-09. Conspicuous by its absence from the examples in udftest.prg is an @...SAY UDF() command. UDFs cannot be used as the object of an @...SAY command. They can be used with any of the following FoxBASE+/Mac commands however:

STORE
REPLACE
IF
DO WHILE
CASE
?
LIST
DISPLAY

In addition, UDFs can be used as arguments in VALID clause expressions. VALID clauses are examined more fully in Chapter 10.

One note about the use of UDFs vs. procedures. Like all other FoxBASE+/Mac functions, UDFs return a value, **but they do not change**

the content of any variables passed as parameters! This is an important difference since, except for this discrepancy, UDFs can be used as regular programs or as functions interchangeably. (Note: When a UDF is used as a regular program called via a DO...WITH command, the argument following the RETURN in the UDF is ignored.)

Looking ahead

By the time you reach this point in the book, you will have mastered the usage of most of the important FoxBASE+/Mac commands. This state of affairs is akin to the author who is possessed of a large vocabulary, but who has no experience in crafting portions of a book. Accordingly, in the next chapter, we will begin to draw upon your expertise with the FoxBASE+/Mac language to create working programs.

The goal of the next and subsequent chapters is to demonstrate the ways in which your current skills are commonly used to generate working programs. As we progress in these chapters, we will also investigate more advanced commands and functions.

To insure that all of our programs have the necessary PUBLIC variables, system SETtings, and full menu selections, I have developed the following "bk" programs. These programs are designed to run all of the programs in the rest of the book. Further there is an option in the menu to MODIFY a program. This feature allows you to write each program as needed, without leaving the "bk" programs. Here are the programs:

```
* bkmain.prg
* Main menu program for book programs
* SET environment
SET TALK OFF
SET SCORE OFF
SET STAT OFF
SET SAFE OFF
SET VIEW OFF
SET BELL ON
SET STRICT OFF
SET CONFIRM OFF
```

```
SET ESCAPE ON
* Setup menu system
DIMENSION ktopbar(4)
ktopbar(1)="Data Entry"
ktopbar(2)="Reports"
ktopbar(3)="Utilities"
ktopbar(4)="Query"
* Now "fill" each bar with options
DIMENSION kdataopt(6)   && Data Entry
kdataopt(1)="Inventory"
kdataopt(2)="FoxForm Inventory"
kdataopt(3)="Inventory With Lookup"
kdataopt(4)="Employee Maintenance"
kdataopt(5)="Correspondence"
kdataopt(6)="Z Correspondence"
DIMENSION kqueropt(10) && Query menu
kqueropt=""
DIMENSION krepoopt(11)   && Reports
krepoopt(1)="Crrepo1"
krepoopt(2)="Zrrepo1"
krepoopt(3)="Stat"
krepoopt(4)="Stat1"
krepoopt(5)="Non-Grouped Subtotals"
krepoopt(6)="Snaked 2 column report"
krepoopt(7)="Repo1 Students"
krepoopt(8)="Repo1a Sorted Students"
krepoopt(9)="Repo1b Totaled Students"
krepoopt(10)="Repo1c Subtotaled Students"
krepoopt(11)="Vidrents Video Rentals"
DIMENSION kfileopt(4)
kfileopt(1)="MODIFY PROGRAM /M"
kfileopt(2)="CREATE DATABASE"
kfileopt(3)="INDEX"
kfileopt(4)="FoxForm SCREENS"
DIMENSION kutilopt(3)
kutilopt(1)="EXIT /E"
kutilopt(2)="BOOK INFO /B"
kutilopt(3)="QUIT /Q"
* Now load the arrays into the menu system
MENU BAR ktopbar,4 && only four bars
MENU 1,kdataopt    && data entry
MENU 2,krepoopt    && Reports
MENU 3,kutilopt    && utilities
MENU 4,kqueropt && User defined queries
MENU -1,kfileopt   && file menu
MENU OFF -3,1      && screen change flag
MENU OFF 4 && turn the query menu off
* end of menu setup
```

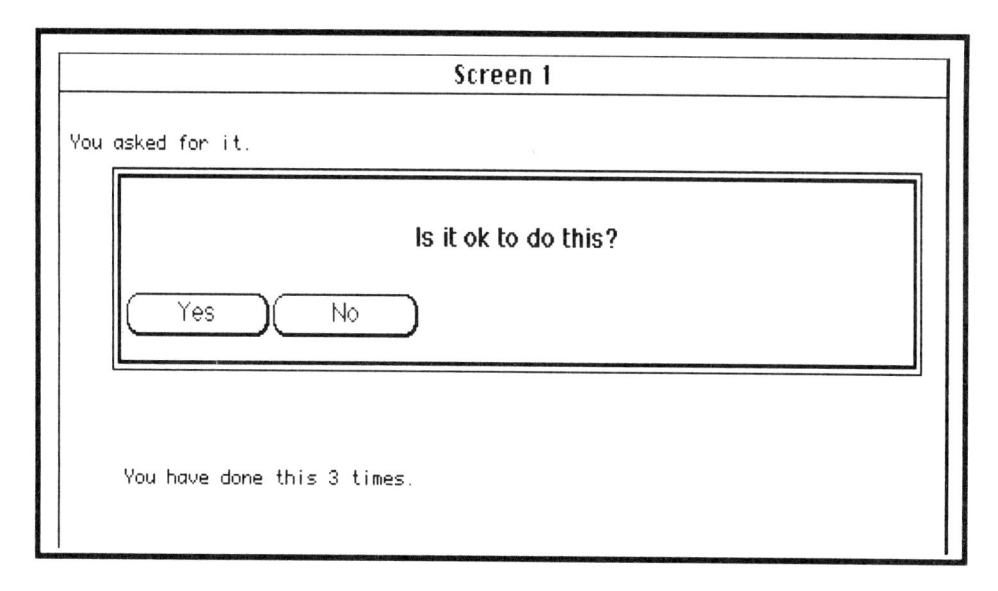

```
┌─────────────────────────────────────────────┐
│                  Screen 1                   │
│ You asked for it.                           │
│   ┌─────────────────────────────────────┐   │
│   │                                     │   │
│   │         Is it ok to do this?        │   │
│   │                                     │   │
│   │      ╭─────╮    ╭─────╮             │   │
│   │      │ Yes │    │ No  │             │   │
│   │      ╰─────╯    ╰─────╯             │   │
│   │                                     │   │
│   └─────────────────────────────────────┘   │
│                                             │
│   You have done this 3 times.               │
│                                             │
└─────────────────────────────────────────────┘
```

Figure 7-09. Lbq.prg UDF.

```
* Declare PUBLIC variables
PUBLIC kmnbar,kmnopt,kmnhit,kfb,kfi,kfu,kfo,kfs
* Setup variables for typographical styles
kfb = 256  && boldface
kfi = 512  && italic
kfu = 1024 && underline
kfo = 2048 && outline
kfs = 4096 && shadow
* Setup default task
kmnbar = "UTILITIES"  && menu bar
kmnopt = "BOOK INFO"  && option
kmnhit = .F.   && has a menu option been selected
badopt=.F. && bad option selected in bkmain
* Activate menu system
ON MENU DO sysmenu1 WITH MENU(0),MENU(1)
* Trap errors
ON ERROR DO bkerror WITH ERROR(),MESSAGE(),MESSAGE(1),SYS(16)
* Now begin the application
DO WHILE .T.
  * what menu bar was selected
  DO CASE
    CASE kmnbar = "REPORTS"
      * save menu numbers to vars
      curbar=MENU(0)
```

Looking ahead

```
      curopt=MENU(1)
      * Turn this menu option off
      MENU OFF curbar,curopt
      DO CASE
         CASE kmnopt="CRREPO1"
            DO crrepo1
         CASE kmnopt="ZRREPO1"
            DO zrrepo1
         CASE kmnopt="STAT1"
            DO stat1
         CASE kmnopt="STAT"
            DO stat
         CASE kmnopt="NON-GROUPED"
            DO subtot
         CASE kmnopt="SNAKE"
            DO snake
         CASE kmnopt="REPO1C"
            DO repo1c
         CASE kmnopt="REPO1B"
            DO repo1b
         CASE kmnopt="REPO1A"
            DO repo1a
         CASE kmnopt="REPO1"
            DO repo1
         CASE kmnopt="VIDRENTS"
            DO vidrents
      ENDCASE which report
      * Turn this menu option back on
      MENU ON curbar,curopt

   CASE kmnbar = "DATA ENTRY"
      * Save menu numbers to vars
      curbar=MENU(0)
      curopt=MENU(1)
      * Turn this menu option off
      MENU OFF curbar,curopt
      * Which data entry option was selected
      DO CASE
         CASE kmnopt = "INVENTORY WITH LOOKUP"
            DO ilentr
         CASE kmnopt = "INVENTORY"
            DO iventr
         CASE kmnopt = "FOXFORM INVENTORY"
            DO iventrx
         CASE kmnopt = "EMPLOYEE MAINTENANCE"
            DO prempl
         CASE kmnopt = "CORRESPONDENCE"
            DO crmain
```

```
        CASE kmnopt = "Z CORRESPONDENCE"
          * Enhanced correspondence
          DO zrmain
        OTHERWISE
          ** bad option selected somehow
          badopt=.T.
      ENDCASE data entry option
      * Turn this menu option back on
      MENU ON curbar,curopt
    CASE kmnbar = "REPORTS"
      DO CASE
        OTHERWISE
          ** bad option selected somehow
          badopt=.T.
      ENDCASE report option
    CASE kmnbar = "UTILITIES"
      DO CASE
        CASE kmnopt = "QUIT"
          IF lbq("Do you want to quit?","NO;YES","F")="YES"
            * exit from FoxBASE+/Mac
            QUIT
          ELSE
            kmnbar = "UTIL"
            kmnopt = "BOOK"
          ENDIF wants to quit
        CASE kmnopt = "EXIT"
          * Turn off menu system
          ON MENU
          MENU BAR
          * cancel program execution
          CANCEL
        CASE kmnopt = "BOOK INFO"
          * Book info
          kmnhit = .F.
          DO WHILE !kmnhit
            DO lbq WITH "Please select a menu Choice.","OK",""
          ENDDO wait for a menu hit
        OTHERWISE
          ** bad option selected somehow
          badopt = .T.
      ENDCASE utilities option
    CASE kmnbar = "FILE"
      * file menu
      MENU BAR
      ON MENU
      DO CASE
        CASE kmnopt = "MODIFY"
          * Allow programmer to modify a program
```

Looking ahead   171

```
      CLEAR PROGRAM
      MODIFY COMMAND
    CASE kmnopt = "CREATE"
      * Allow programmer to create a database
      CREATE
      CLOSE DATA
    CASE kmnopt = "INDEX"
      * Allow programmer to index a file
      * Get the dbf name
      thisdbf = GETFILE("F+DB","Pick a DBF to index")
      if ""#thisdbf  && selected a dbf
        * Open the database
        USE &thisdbf.
        * Get the index file name
        thisidx=PUTFILE("Index to create","","")
        IF ""#thisidx   && selected an index name
           * Get the index expression
           GETEXPR "Enter index key" TO thiskey
           IF ""#thiskey
              INDEX ON &thiskey TO &thisidx
           ENDIF expression
        ENDIF index
      ENDIF dbf
      CLOSE DATA
    CASE kmnopt="FOXFORM SCREENS"
      * generate a screen
      MODIFY SCREEN
      * generate a program from the screen
      GENERATE
    OTHERWISE
      badopt=.T.
  ENDCASE file menu
  IF .NOT.badopt
     kmnbar = "UTILITIES"
     kmnopt = "BOOK INFO"
  ENDIF picked a valid file option
  MENU BAR ktopbar,4 && only four bars
  MENU 1,kdataopt  && data entry
  MENU 2,krepoopt  && Reports
  MENU 3,kutilopt && utilities
  MENU 4,kqueropt && queries
  MENU -1,kfileopt  && file menu
  ON MENU DO sysmenu1 WITH MENU(0),MENU(1)
OTHERWISE
   ** bad menu bar selected somehow
   DO lbq WITH kmnbar+" menu bar is invalid.","CONTINUE","F"
   kmnbar = "UTILITIES"
   kmnopt = "BOOK INFO"
```

```
  ENDCASE menu bar
  IF badopt
    DO lbq WITH kmnopt+" option of "+kmnbar+;
    " is invalid.","CONTINUE","F"
    kmnbar = "UTILITIES"
    kmnopt = "BOOK INFO"
    badopt=.F.
  ENDIF bad option selected
  kmnhit = .F.
ENDDO endless loop for entire application
* eof bkmain.prg
```

```
* bkerror.prg
* Sample error trapping routine for book program
PARAMETERS errnum,errmsg,errcomm,errprg
PRIVATE oldscreen
oldscreen = VAL(SYS(1034))
SCREEN 8
CLEAR
SCREEN 8 SIZE 10,80 FONT "MONACO",9 AT 0,0
SCREEN 8 TYPE 1 FIXED TOP
SET TALK OFF
SET PRINT OFF
SET DEVICE TO SCREEN
SET CONSOLE ON
@ 1,0 SAY "Error has occurred."
@ 2,0 SAY "Error #:"+STR(errnum,5)
@ 3,0 SAY "Error msg:"+errmsg
@ 4,0 SAY "Caused by:"+errcomm
@ 6,0 SAY "In Program:"+errprg
WAIT
SCREEN 8 OFF
SCREEN oldscreen TOP
CLOSE DATABASES
** Set menu options to get another menu selection
kmnbar = "UTILITIES"
kmnopt = "BOOK INFO"
** Return all the way to bkmain
RETURN TO MASTER
* eof bkerror.prg
```

```
* sysmenu1.prg
* Places results of menu selections into
* kmnbar, kmnopt, kmnhit variables
```

Looking ahead

```
* whatbar = MENU(0)
* whatopt = MENU(1)
PARAMETERS whatbar,whatopt
DO CASE
   CASE whatbar = -3
     * user changed screens
     kmnbar="SCREEN"
     kmnopt="CHANGE"
   CASE whatbar = -2
     * Apple menu
     kmnbar="APPLE"
     kmnopt=kapple
   CASE whatbar = -1
     * File menu
     kmnbar="FILE"
     kmnopt=UPPER(kfileopt(whatopt))
   CASE whatbar = 0
     * Edit menu
     kmnbar="EDIT"
     kmnopt=UPPER(keditopt(whatopt))
   OTHERWISE
     * User selected one of the standard, programmer
     * generated menus
     * Use the numeric value of whatbar to place the content
     * of the appropriate ktopbar() array into a variable
     kmnbar = UPPER(ktopbar(whatbar))
     * Now see what array has the option text
     DO CASE
        CASE UPPER(kmnbar) = "DATA ENTRY"
           kmnopt = kdataopt(whatopt)
        CASE UPPER(kmnbar) = "REPORT"
           kmnopt = krepoopt(whatopt)
        CASE UPPER(kmnbar) = "UTILITIES"
           kmnopt = kutilopt(whatopt)
        CASE UPPER(kmnbar) = "QUERY"
           kmnopt = kqueropt(whatopt)
     ENDCASE kmnbar
     kmnopt = UPPER(kmnopt)
ENDCASE what kind of menu bar was selected
IF whatbar >= -2
   * set hit flag to true
   kmnhit = .T.
ENDIF not a screen change
RETURN
* eof sysmenu1.prg
```

The use of ON ERROR trapping is discussed in detail in Chapter 16. For now, it is enough to know that it traps errors in our programs.

Once you have created the bkmain.prg and bkerror.prg programs listed above, you can begin every book oriented session of FoxBASE+/Mac by DOing bkmain.

For the rest of the book, all programs are expected to be called by a DO statement in the bkmain.prg program!

When you run the bkmain.prg program for the first time, you will find that none of the menu options works. That is because you have not yet created the programs that bkmain.prg is DOing! To modify a program while running bkmain.prg, select the MODIFY option of the file menu. (Note: All of the programs listed in The Dynamics of FoxBASE+/Mac Programming are available on diskette from Micro Endeavors. Call 215 449-4690.)

8. Single File Data Entry

In this chapter we will begin to put your newly acquired FoxBASE+/Mac skills to work in developing data entry programs. While this effort will entail the introduction of several new functions and commands, the majority of the chapter will be devoted to the examination of the ways in which simple operations are combined to create a full-featured data entry program.

To accomplish this goal, we will develop a skeleton program that includes most of the operations found in single-file data entry programs. This skeleton program is suitable for use in virtually all FoxBASE+/Mac programs. In addition, we will develop several single-function programs that will be useful in all FoxBASE+/Mac programs.

When you have finished this chapter, you will be able to begin writing your own programs to enter, store, and modify data. In subsequent chapters we will learn how to generate reports from the data you have entered, for now it is time to get started on our data entry section.

What should our data entry program do?

Experience has shown that most data entry consists of the following activities:

1. Displaying existing records.

2. Adding new records.

3. Looking up existing records using key fields.

4. Looking up existing records using non-key fields.

5. Editing existing records.

6. Deleting records.

7. Moving forward or backward in the file some number of records.

In this chapter we will concentrate on data entry screens that operate on one record at a time. Subsequent chapters will deal with multiple record and multiple file entry from one data entry screen.

We have chosen an inventory item entry screen to be the sample application for this chapter. Note however, that the skeleton, and many of the individual activity programs, are applicable to most programming situations. We choose the inventory example because it is easy to understand, but the programs could easily be applied to customer files, contact lists, contributor lists, publications, phone calls, etc.

The programs that follow require these database file structures and indexes:

```
DATABASE AND INDEX FILES FOR SAMPLE DATA ENTRY PROGRAM

Structure for database: IVITEM.DBF

Field  Field Name  Type        Width    Dec
   1   IV_ID       Character     10
   2   IV_DESC     Character     30
   3   IV_ONHAND   Numeric        5
   4   IV_PRICE    Numeric        7       2
** Total **                      53

Master index file: IVITEM.IDX   Key: IV_ID
       Index file: IVDESC.IDX   Key: UPPER(IV_DESC)
```

The skeleton

The iventr.prg program contains the logic needed to implement the 7 activities listed above. Each of the individual activities will be contained in their own .prg file.

There are three fundamental reasons for using a skeleton program like iventr.prg to call all of the various activities rather than including all of the commands in one program. First, because the skeleton program is not encumbered by the details of all of the data entry activities, the skeleton program will provide an excellent description of the logic of the data entry program. Second, the individual programs will be easier to understand and fix if necessary. Third, we will be able to develop the data entry screen one activity at a time, rather than all at once.

Here then is a data entry skeleton that you can use in most of your programs:

```
* iventr.prg
* Sample data entry skeleton.
* Adaptable to most programs
SCREEN 1 SIZE 10,80 FONT "MONACO",9
CLEAR
SCREEN 1 AT 0,0 TOP HEADING "Inventory Item Entry"
* Open database file with indexes
USE ivitem INDEX ivitem,ivdesc ALIAS item
* Place prompts on the screen
@ 0,24 SAY "Item id:"
@ 2,20 SAY "Description:"
@ 4,23 SAY "# onhand: "
@ 6,26 SAY "Price:"
* Loop to process requests for data entry
DO WHILE .T.
   * reset local option variable
   entchoice=0
   * Check to see if there is a record to display
   * EOF() will only be true if there are no records
   * on the file.  All activities will leave EOF() false
   * if there is at least one record on file.
   IF EOF()   && no records on file
     * Tell user the bad news
     DO lbcenter WITH 7,"There are no records on file.","",0,""
     * Offer to add a record via text button
     * Optionally, user may select a menu option
     @ 7,37 GET entchoice PICTURE "@*h ADD"
     READ
   ELSE && at least one record on file
```

The skeleton

```
      * Allow user to edit this record, and/or
      * select an action using the iventr2.prg UDF
      entchoice=iventr2()
   ENDIF no records on file
   * Identify activity to be performed
   DO CASE
      CASE kmnhit
         * menu hit encountered
         kmnhit = .F. && reset menu flag
         SELECT item
         USE   && close the inventory database
         RETURN
      CASE entchoice=1
         * Add or find new record
         DO iventrn
      CASE entchoice=2
         * Move forward one record
         DO iventrm WITH "F"
      CASE entchoice=3
         * Move back one record
         DO iventrm WITH "B"
      CASE entchoice=4
         * Lookup by description
         DO iventrl
      CASE entchoice=5
         * Delete or recall record
         DO iventrd
   ENDCASE entchoice
ENDDO requests for data entry
* eof iventr.prg
```

(Note: We always begin all file names in an application with the same two letters. This makes it easy to copy and backup the files. For the purpose of these sample programs, we use "iv" to indicate that these programs belong to the inventory application.)

After we have placed the appropriate prompts on the screen, we then check to see if there are any records in the database. Never assume that there is at least one record in a file. Even if the user has been working with the program for some time, there is always the chance that the user will delete all of the records in the file in order to start over. The EOF() function will return a true value if there are no records in the file.

Note that if there are no records on the file, we give the user only one local option. The option to Add a new record.

If there is at least one record on file, we use the iventr2.prg program as a UDF to assign a local option to the entchoice variable.

In the DO CASE structure of the iventr.prg program, the following command checks to see if the user has selected a menu option:

```
CASE kmnhit
```

Don't forget that the user can pick a menu option during most READ operations!

Generating the data entry items

Now it is time to investigate the programs that are called by iventr.prg to flesh out this skeleton of a data entry program. The first program that we encounter in iventr.prg is iventr2.prg the function of which is to display and edit the content of an item. This is the program:

```
* iventr2.prg
* Edits the content of the current inventory item
PRIVATE localopt
@ 0,33 GET iv_id
* Prevent the user from changing the key field
CLEAR GETS
* Setup local option
localopt=0
* Check to see if the record is marked for deletion
IF DELETED()
   * Put  note on screen for user
   @ 1,53 SAY "(DELETED)"
   @ 7,0 GET localopt PICTURE "@*h ADD;NEXT;PREVIOUS;LOOKUP;RECALL"
ELSE
   * Remove any existing DELETED message
   @ 1,53 CLEAR TO 1,62
   @ 7,0 GET localopt PICTURE "@*h ADD;NEXT;PREVIOUS;LOOKUP;DELETE"
ENDIF record marked for deletion
@ 2,33 GET iv_desc
```

```
@ 4,33 GET iv_onhand PICTURE "##,###"
@ 6,33 GET iv_price PICTURE "$$$.##"
DO WHILE localopt=0.AND.(!kmnhit)
  READ SAVE
ENDDO until option or menu hit
CLEAR GETS
RETURN localopt
* eof iventr2.prg
```

The combination of iventr.prg and iventr2.prg create the screen shown in Figure 8-01.

One important idea presented by the iventr2.prg is the notion that the key field of a record is never directly changed by the user. To explain the importance of this idea, let's imagine that this series of sample programs is a part of a larger inventory control program.

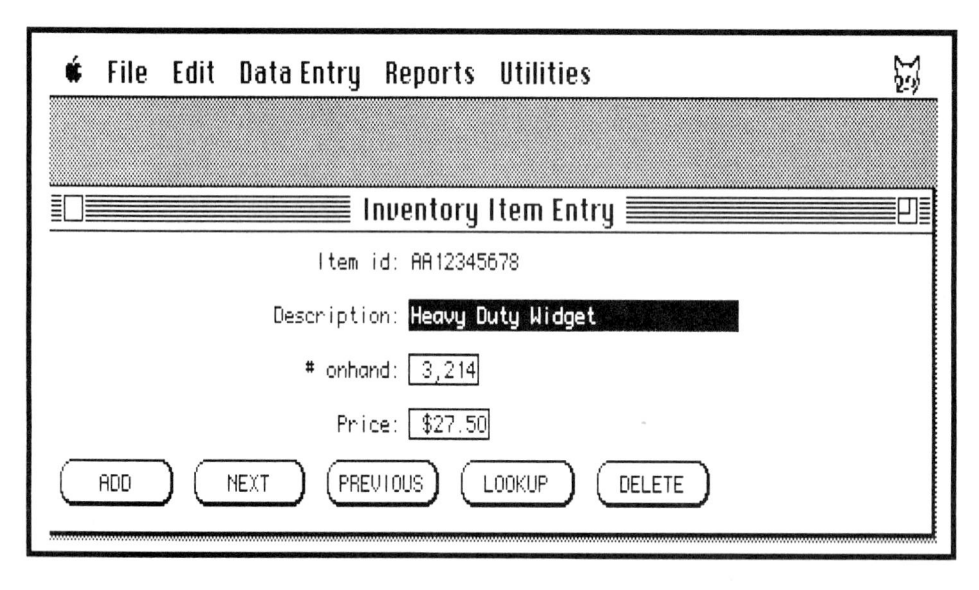

Figure 8-01. Main inventory item screen.

In such an application, it is important that every inventory item have a unique id number, otherwise it would be impossible to determine how many of an item had been sold, purchased, or wasted. We can take precautions against the addition of an inventory item that has the same id number as an existing item (and we will in the iventrn.prg), but if we let the user change an existing id number, that user might change an item's id number to be the same as another item's id number.

This concept of protecting unique id numbers by preventing the user from directly changing the content of a key field is common in database applications.

The DELETED() function is also new to us. The DELETED() function returns a true value if the current record has been marked for deletion. The concept of marking a record for deletion is new, and bears investigation.

When you CREATEd databases in earlier chapters, you may have noticed that the size of the records in the databases was always one character greater than the sum of the sizes of the fields. This occurs because FoxBASE+/Mac includes an extra field in every database to designate a record as DELETED() or not DELETED().

As we shall see later in this chapter, a record is marked for deletion by issuing a DELETE command. However, the marked record is not physically removed from the file until a PACK command is issued. As a result, a marked record can be unmarked by issuing a RECALL command.

Adding a new item or SEEKing an existing id number

Since the rest of the iventr2.prg has nothing new to teach us, we can move ahead to a program that allows the user to add a new item, at the same time the user is prevented from duplicating an existing id number. The iventrn.prg that follows accomplishes this feat by SEEKing the user's prospective id number and, if the id number is found, simply returning to iventr.prg to allow the display and editing of the existing inventory item. In this way, no existing id number can be duplicated in the inventory file. Here is the code:

```
* iventrn.prg
* Add a new record or find an item by item id
PRIVATE newkey,thisrec,ans,option,oldscreen
oldscreen=VAL(SYS(1034))
* Setup a memory variable to accept the id to SEEK
newkey = SPACE(10)
* Save our place in the file in case the new key is not found,
* and the user does not want to add a new record
IF .NOT. EOF()
   * Save the record number
   thisrec = RECNO()
ELSE  && no current record
   thisrec = 0
ENDIF there is a current record
* Tell the user what to do, and get the new key
SCREEN 3 SIZE 5,60 TYPE 4 LOCK AT 240,60
CLEAR
SCREEN 3 TOP HEADING "New Inventory Item" FIXED
DO WHILE .T.
   @ 1,0 SAY "Enter id to add or lookup here:"
   @ 1,COL()+1 GET newkey PICTURE "@! AA99999999"
   option = 0
   @ 2,15 GET option PICTURE "@*h LOOKUP;CANCEL"
   DO WHILE option=0
     READ SAVE
   ENDDO wait for action
   CLEAR GETS
   * Note that the id must be two upper case letters
   * followed by 8 numbers
   * See if the user chose to cancel
   IF newkey # SPACE(10).AND.option#2
      * Check to see if the item is already on file
      SEEK newkey
      IF .NOT.FOUND()
         * See if the user wants to add a new item
         IF lbq(newkey+" is not on file.","ADD;RETRY","F")="RETRY"
            * See if there is a current record
            IF thisrec#0
               * Return the record pointer to its position prior
               * to the unsuccessful SEEK
               GOTO thisrec
            ENDIF there is a current record
         ELSE  && wants to add the new item
```

```
         * Add a blank record to the file
         APPEND BLANK
         * Fill the key field with the memory variable
         REPLACE iv_id WITH newkey
         EXIT
       ENDIF doesn't want to add the item
     ELSE && found it!
       * Exit with the record pointer set on this record
       EXIT
     ENDIF found the item
   ELSE &&
     * Chose to cancel, or left key field blank
     EXIT
   ENDIF did not leave new key blank
ENDDO process lookup requests
SCREEN 3 OFF
SCREEN oldscreen TOP
RETURN
* eof iventrn.prg
```

A typical two step addition of a record is shown in Figures 8-02 and 8-03.

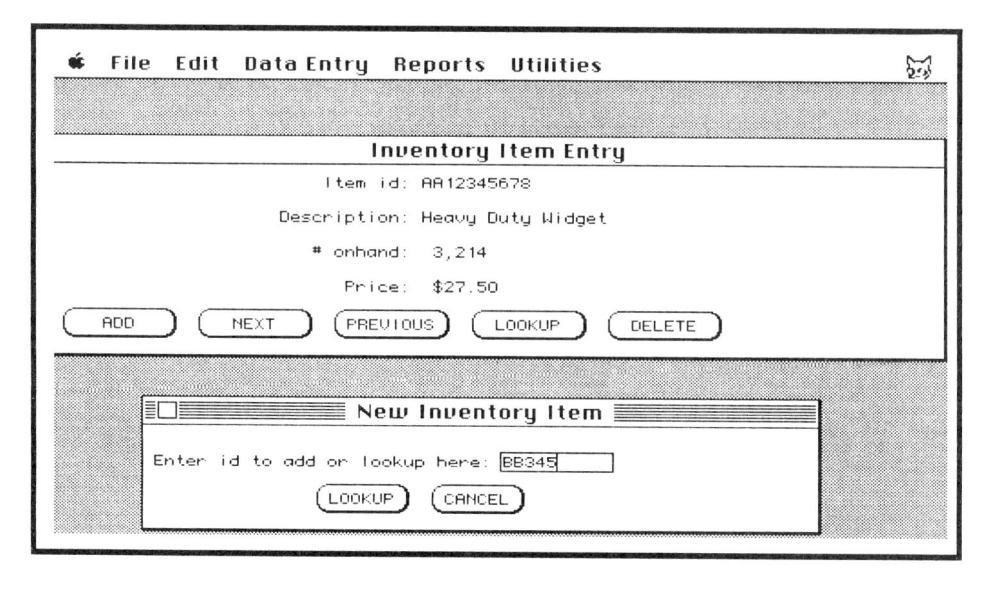

Figure 8-02. Add inventory item screen.

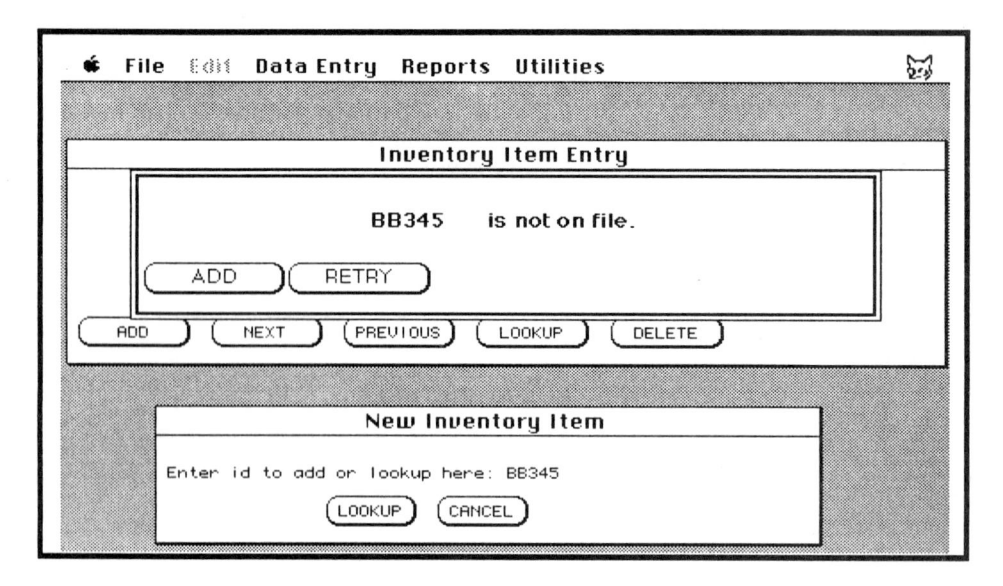

Figure 8-03. Second part of add item.

The process of saving our place in the file has application in many programs as we shall see. In the iventrn.prg program this process gives us a graceful way to return the user to his or her current spot in the file in the event that the user enters a new id number, but does not wish to add a new inventory item.

The GOTO command is the command used to return us to our previous position should something go awry in the user's efforts to add or lookup an inventory id. The GOTO thisrec command positions the record pointer on the record number stored in the thisrec variable.

An important feature of the GOTO command is that it is not affected by index files; it operates directly with the record numbers in the database file. That is, GOTO 7 places the record pointer on the seventh record in the database file, not the seventh record from the top of the index file.

There are two more variations of the GOTO command that will be most valuable when we begin working with reports. They are the GOTO TOP, and GOTO BOTTOM forms of the command.

GOTO TOP places the record pointer on the first record in the file. However, unlike a GOTO 1 command, GOTO TOP is affected by open indexes, and will place the record pointer on the record that is first in the current master index. If no index is open, GOTO TOP and GOTO 1 will produce the same result.

GOTO BOTTOM will place the record pointer on the last record in the file. If an index is open, the record pointer will be placed on the record that is last in the current master index file.

One of the keys to writing user friendly software is to provide the user with a way to back-track in the event of a mistake. Accordingly, the iventrn.prg allows the user to abort the process of adding a new inventory item by selecting CANCEL or by leaving the newkey variable blank. This is accomplished by only SEEKing the newkey variable IF newkey#SPACE(10).AND.option#2.

If the user does enter a prospective id number, the system SEEKs the content of that variable in the ivitem index. If the newkey is found, the program will not prompt the user to add a new record, but rather return to the iventr.prg program, where the newly found record will be processed. This is the key piece of logic that prevents the duplication of inventory id numbers.

If the SEEK is unsuccessful, the user is queried before a record is added. This accommodates the user who sought to lookup an existing inventory item, only to discover that the item is not on file, or that the user made an error in entering the newkey value.

After gaining the user's assurance that a new record is to be added, the iventrn.prg adds a blank record to the file, replaces the key field with the newly verified unique id, and then allows the user to edit the non-key fields by returning to the iventr.prg program. This APPEND BLANK / REPLACE WITH / RETURN for processing sequence is common to most applications. In fact, this is frequently the only time the programmer will allow a key field to be altered in an application.

Editing the current record

As in most FoxBASE+/Mac applications, iventr.prg EDITS the current record by default. Since we have already discussed the workings of the iventr2.prg, let's take this opportunity to note the usefulness of the iventr2.prg subroutine.

We use this program to display the content of the current record, to edit the content of the current record, and to edit the content of a newly added record. As a result, if we need to add a field to the inventory file, we will only need to change the iventr2.prg subroutine.

Moving forward or back in the file

The purpose of the iventrm.prg program is to allow the user to move forward or back one record in the file. This process of scrolling through a file is very common, and can usually be accomplished with the following program:

```
* iventrm.prg
* Move forward or back one record
* direction = F for forward, B for back
PARAMETERS direction
PRIVATE thisrec
direction = UPPER(direction)
* Save our current position
thisrec = RECNO()
IF direction = "F"
   SKIP
ELSE   && backup
   SKIP -1
ENDIF forward
* Check to see if we moved beyond the first or last
* record in the file
IF BOF() .OR. EOF()
   * Ring a bell and then return the record pointer to its
```

```
   * position prior to the unsuccessful SKIP
   ?? CHR(7)
   GOTO thisrec
ENDIF moved too far
RETURN
* eof inventrym.prg
```

This program introduces us to the SKIP command, and the BOF() function. The EOF() and BOF() functions are important to this scrolling routine to prevent the user from SKIPping out of the file. For example, if the user is already on the first record of the file or index, and chooses to move back one record, the record pointer will be placed above the first record in the file. In the same way, if the user is on the last record of the file or index, and chooses to move forward one record, the record pointer will be placed below the last record in the file.

If the pointer is above the first record in the file, BOF() will return a true value. If the pointer is below the last record in the file, EOF() will return a true value. In either case, the iventrm.prg puts the record pointer back to its position prior to the SKIP.

The SKIP command on the other hand, is used extensively in most applications. The SKIP command directs FoxBASE+/Mac to move the record pointer a given number of records. If the number of records to be moved is negative, the record pointer moves back toward the top of the file, otherwise the record pointer moves forward, toward the bottom of the file.

Unlike the GOTO command, the SKIP command is affected by open indexes. If an index is open in the current work area when a SKIP command is issued, FoxBASE+/Mac will move forward or back the required number of records in the current master index, before assigning the record pointer to a record in the database file.

Using a secondary key to lookup items

Moving forward or back in the file

The next program called by iventr.prg allows the user to lookup inventory items using the description of the item as a key. Since the program will not be verifying the uniqueness of an inventory id, the user will not be allowed to add new inventory items based on description. The iventrl.prg accomplishes these tasks in the following manner:

```
* iventrl.prg
* Lookup the item by description
* Do not allow the user to add a record
PRIVATE newdesc,thisrec,ans,option,oldscreen
oldscreen=VAL(SYS(1034))
* Make the description index the master index
SET ORDER TO 2
* Setup a memory variable to accept the description to SEEK
newdesc = SPACE(LEN(iv_desc))
* Save our place in the file in case the description is not found
thisrec = RECNO()
* Tell the user what to do, and get the description
SCREEN 3 SIZE 5,70 TYPE 4 LOCK AT 240,40
CLEAR
SCREEN 3 TOP HEADING "Lookup Inventory Item" FIXED
  @ 1,0 SAY "Enter description to lookup here:"
  @ 1,COL()+1 GET newdesc
  option = 0
  @ 2,15 GET option PICTURE "@*h LOOKUP;CANCEL"
  DO WHILE option=0
    READ SAVE
  ENDDO wait for action
  CLEAR GETS
  * See if the user left the description
  IF newdesc # SPACE(LEN(newdesc)).AND.option#2
    * Remove any spaces from the end of the description
    newdesc = TRIM(newdesc)
    * Convert the memory variable to upper case to match the
    * index expression "UPPER(iv_desc)"
    newdesc = UPPER(newdesc)
    * Look for a description that begins with the content of
    * the newdesc memory variable
    SEEK newdesc
    IF .NOT.FOUND()
      * Tell the user this one is not on file
      DO lbq WITH newdesc+" is not on file.","CONTINUE","F"
      * Look for the closest match
      nearly = RECNO(0)
      IF nearly = 0  && beyond last record in file
```

```
         GOTO BOTTOM
      ELSE
         GOTO nearly
      ENDIF beyond last record in file
    ENDIF did not find  the item
  ENDIF did not leave new description blank or cancel
SCREEN 3 OFF
SCREEN oldscreen TOP
* Make the item id index the master index
SET ORDER TO 1
RETURN
* eof iventrl.prg
```

As you might suspect, this program bears a close resemblance to the iventrn.prg program which SEEKS inventory items by item id. This similarity is demonstrated in Figure 8-04. As stated above however, the big difference lies in the user's inability to add new items based on item description.

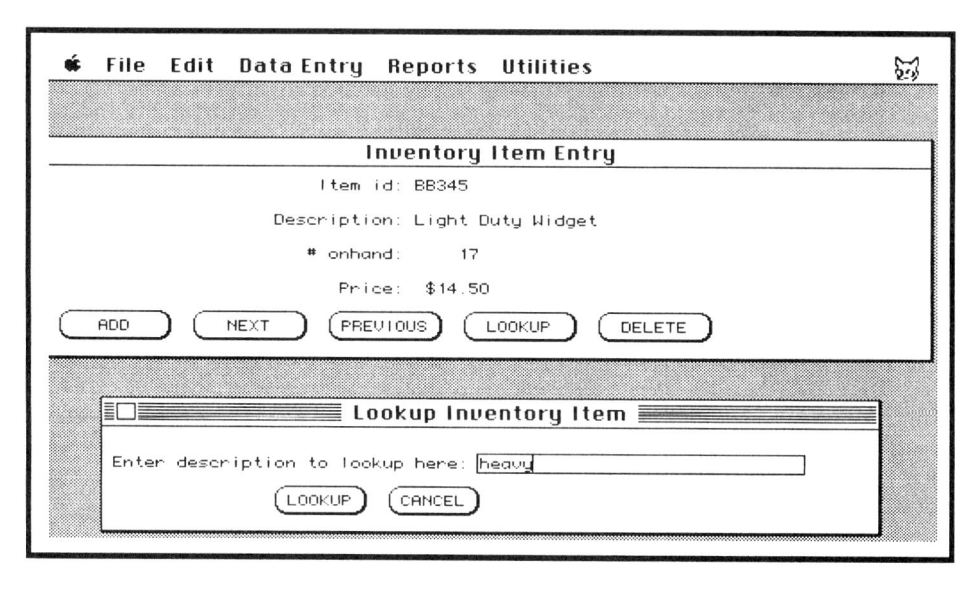

Figure 8-04. Lookup item by description.

Moving forward or back in the file

The first difference between the iventrl.prg and iventrn.prg is the master index used by each. In the iventrl.prg we need to SET ORDER TO 2 to make the ivdesc.idx index the master index. We must also remember to reset the proper order of the indexes prior to exiting the iventrl.prg program.

The iventrl.prg program introduces three new functions, and a new concept in SEEKing values in a character-based index key. The new functions are LEN(), TRIM(), and RECNO(0). LEN() returns a numeric value that represents the length of a character string. Therefore, the statement:

```
newdesc = SPACE(LEN(iv_desc))
```

creates a variable with the name newdesc, containing a number of spaces equal to the length of the iv_desc field. Accordingly, the following statement accurately checks for a newdesc variable which contains only spaces, regardless of the length of the newdesc variable:

```
IF newdesc # SPACE(LEN(newdesc))
```

The TRIM() function returns a string with no trailing spaces. For example, if a string consists of the letters "ABCD" followed by 10 spaces, the TRIM() of that string would equal "ABCD", with no spaces.

We TRIM() the newdesc variable so that the user does not need to enter a complete description to find a matching record. This technique works because the SEEK command only compares as many characters as are in the item being sought to the index key. For example, the following command would find the first inventory item whose description begins with the letter A, regardless of the rest of the description.

```
SEEK "A"
```

The following command however, would only find inventory items whose description consisted solely of a single letter A.

SEEK "A   "

It is usually not a good idea to use the TRIM() function when SEEKing unique id numbers. However, for the reasons outlined above, most SEEKs on non-unique keys are performed using the TRIM() value of a character expression.

The RECNO(0) function is useful when the user isn't sure of the exact content of an index key. When a SEEK fails, RECNO(0) returns the record number of the record that would follow the SEEK key, if that key existed in the file. If the SEEK key would be the last key in an indexed file, RECNO(0) returns a 0.

The idea of using a secondary index file to allow SEEKs based on a key other than the unique id for a record is common to many applications. For example, a customer file might include an index for the unique customer id, and a secondary index for the customer's name. This arrangement would allow the user to lookup a customer's record without knowing the customer's unique id number.

Deleting and recalling records

The final program included in our sample single-file data entry program is the iventrd.prg the function of which is to delete or recall records. Here is the code:

```
* iventrd.prg
* Delete or recall the current record
IF DELETED()
  * Unmark this record
  RECALL
ELSE  && not already deleted
  * Mark this record for deletion
  DELETE
ENDIF record marked for deletion
RETURN
* eof iventrd.prg
```

As we discussed earlier in this chapter, FoxBASE+/Mac marks records for deletion. These records are not actually removed from the file until a PACK command is issued.

In other words, the removal of a record from a database file is a two step activity. Since the PACKing of a file requires the reindexing of all index files, and since the PACK operation itself can be time consuming when operating on large files, it is usually best to make the PACKing of a file a separate operation.

In the interim, if you would prefer not to allow your users to RECALL a DELETED() record, you can SET DELETED ON to make most FoxBASE+/Mac commands, including SKIP and SEEK, ignore DELETED() records.

Looking ahead

This sample data entry program can be adapted to most applications by changing the names of the programs, and the content of the programs called by iventr.prg. In chapter 10 we will investigate some common methods of enhancing this simple data entry program to include lookup tables, lookups based on the content of any field, handling non-unique key applications, and a one step method of handling the deletion of records.

9. FoxForm Automates Screen Creation

What took you so long?

You may be wondering why the chapter on automatic screen generation appears this late in the book. There are two primary reasons for this. First, I am not a strong proponent of FoxForm usage by any programmer, and my reasons for this prejudice are outlined at the end of this chapter.

Second, the ultimate result of a FoxForm session is the generation of a series of @...SAY...GET commands. This capability is of little value however if the programmer doesn't understand the function of the @...SAY...GET commands. Therefore, by exposing you to many of the features of the @...SAY...GET commands earlier in the book, I hoped to make it easier for you to put FoxForm to work.

What does FoxForm do?

Essentially, FoxForm allows the user to paint a screen by placing objects on a screen. The location and characteristics of these objects are stored by FoxForm in a .scx file. This information, along with commands written in a special template programming language, is then used by the FoxBASE+/Mac GENERATE command to generate a .prg file.

To make these concepts a little less abstract, let's see how we might have used FoxForm to help create the inventory item data entry programs from chapter 8. Remembering that FoxForm helps to generate @...SAY...GETS, which of the "iv" programs might best be created with FoxForm?

Using FoxForm

If you guessed iventr2.prg, give yourself a pat on the back. Then, issue the following command from the command window:

```
MODIFY SCREEN iventr3
```

You will be presented with a screen like the one in Figure 9-01. The icons on the left
side of the window represent tools for creating the following types of commands:

```
1.@ PIXEL 5,5 SAY "This is text."

2.@ PIXEL 5,5 TO 5,90 STYLE 31    && a straight line

3.@ PIXEL 5,5 TO 55,90 STYLE 3871   && a box
```

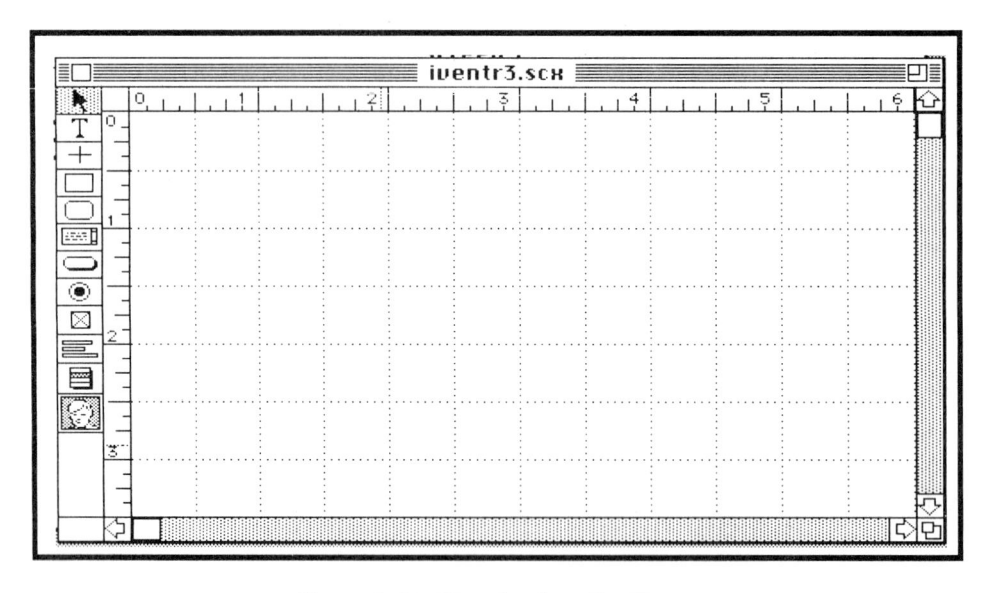

Figure 9-01. First look at FoxForm.

196 Chapter 9: FoxForm Automates Screen Creation

```
4.@ PIXEL 5,5 TO 55,90 STYLE 28447 && a box with rounded edges

5.@ PIXEL 5,5 GET iv_memo SIZE 40,90 SCROLL && text edit region

6.@ PIXEL 5,5 GET m1 PICTURE "@*h CONTINUE"  && text button

7.@ PIXEL 5,5 GET m1 PICTURE "@Rh GOOD;FAIR;POOR" && radio button

8.@ PIXEL 5,5 GET m1 PICTURE "@*c Alive?" && check box

9.@ PIXEL 5,5 GET m1 && regular GET statement

10.@ PIXEL 5,5 GET m1 PICTURE "@^ GOOD;FAIR;POOR" && popup

11.@ PIXEL 5,5 GET m1 PICTURE "@* \P503" && Picture button
```

The fifth or Text Region tool can also be used to generate a command like the following:

```
@ PIXEL 5,5 GET m1 FROM array SIZE 125,180 && scrollable list
```

To specify the size, font, color, shape, and sequence of an object, use the Object and Form menus. Since we want to recreate the iventr2.prg program, we first need to adjust the size of the screen. To do so, choose the Screen... option of the Form menu. Next, adjust the settings on the screen setup dialog to mirror those found in Figure 9-02.

When you have saved those settings, use the Text tool to generate a screen that looks like the one in Figure 9-03. (To move the individual text items, use the pointer found in the upper left corner of the window.) Since the fields that belong on the inventory item entry screen reside in the ivitem database, we will place that database in USE.

To do so, press [Command]+0, and enter the following command:

```
USE ivitem ALIAS item
```

Next, use the field tool, (#8 from the top), to place fields on the screen

Using FoxForm

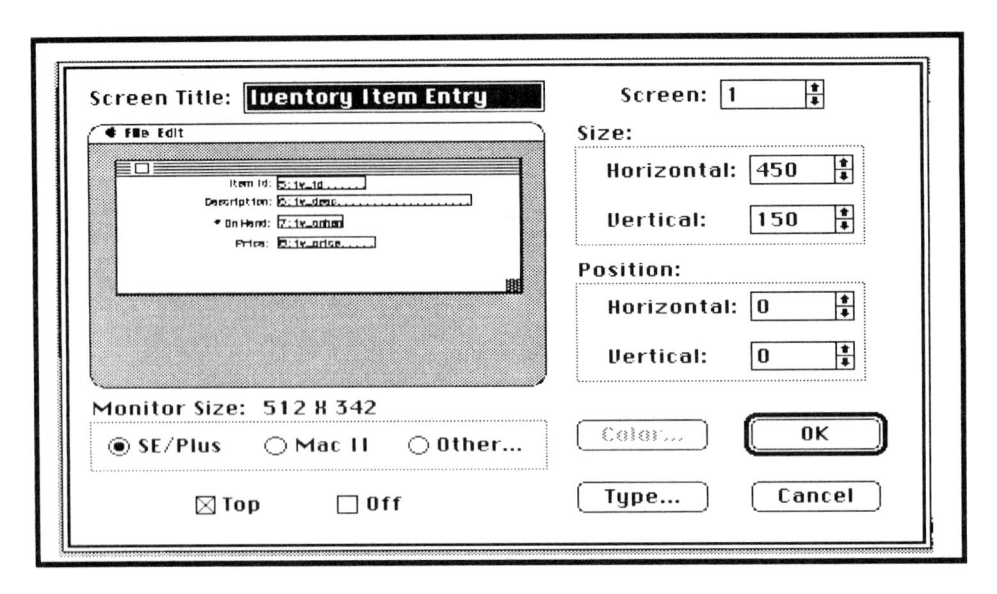

Figure 9-02. Screen setup.

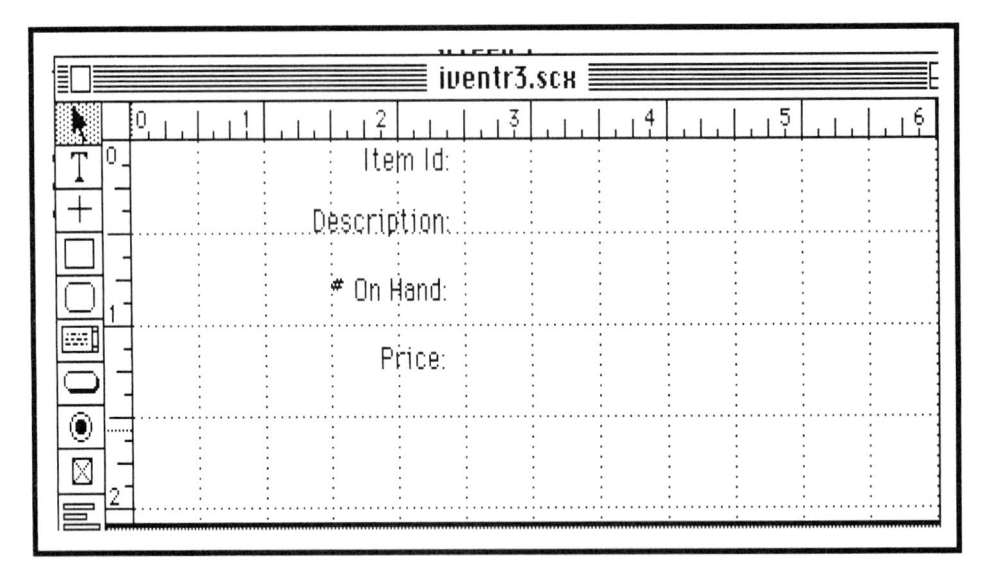

Figure 9-03. Text entries in FoxForm.

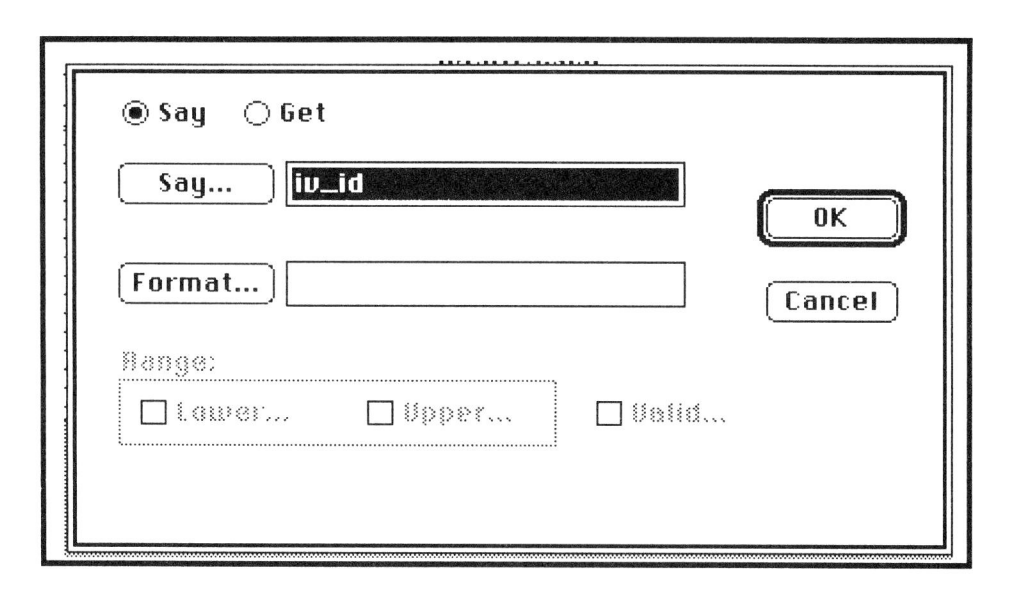

Figure 9-04. Iv_id in FoxForm.

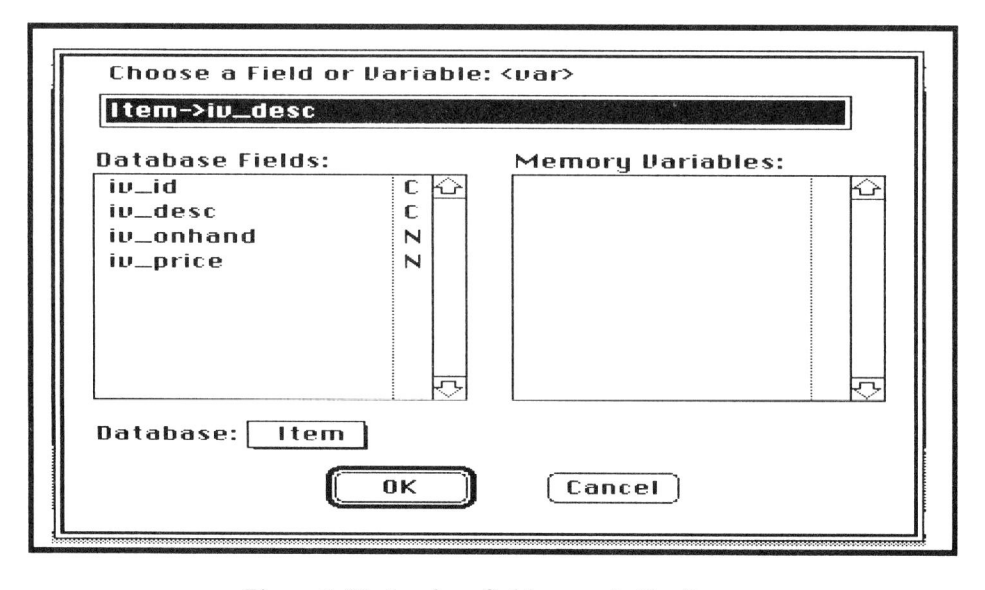

Figure 9-05. Lookup field name in FoxForm.

Using FoxForm

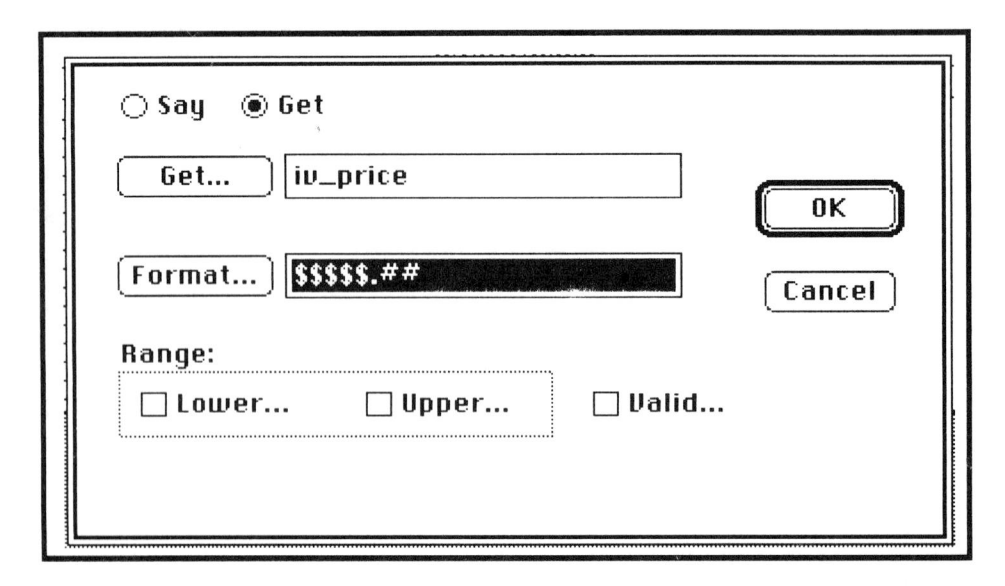

Figure 9-06. Picture format in FoxForm.

next to the appropriate prompt. In Figure 9-04 I have filled in the field dialog with information for iv_id. If you forget the name of a field, click the SAY or GET text button of the field dialog to obtain a dialog like the one in Figure 9-05. Place the rest of the fields on the screen, and include a picture format like the one in Figure 9-06.

Generating a program

Your finished screen should look like the one in Figure 9-07. Use the Save option of the File menu to save your work, then use the Generate option of the Program menu to create a program based on the screen information you have designed. Select the Format File option of the generate dialog as I have in Figure 9-08. **Be sure to change the name of the output file from iventr3.fmt to iventr3.prg** as I have done in Figure 9-09.

Exit from FoxForm by closing the FoxForm window, and modify the iventr3.prg program. You will see code similar to the following:

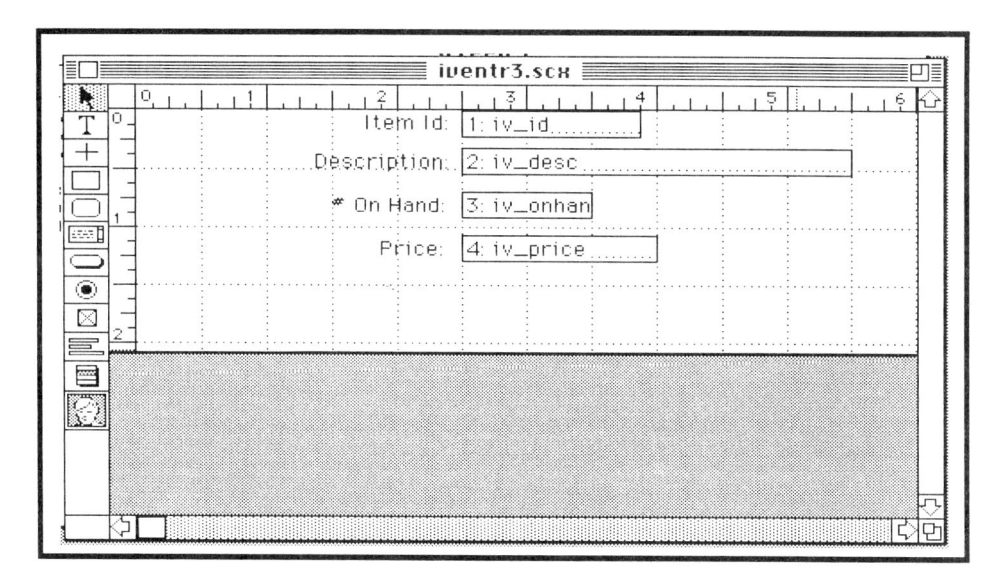

Figure 9-07. Completed inventr3.scx.

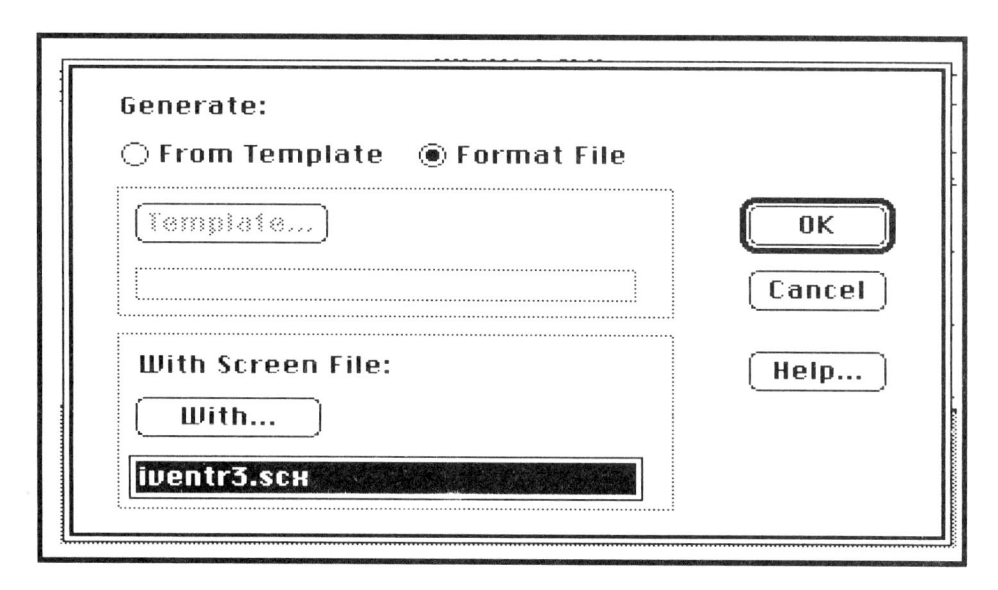

Figure 9-08. Generate dialog.

Generating a program

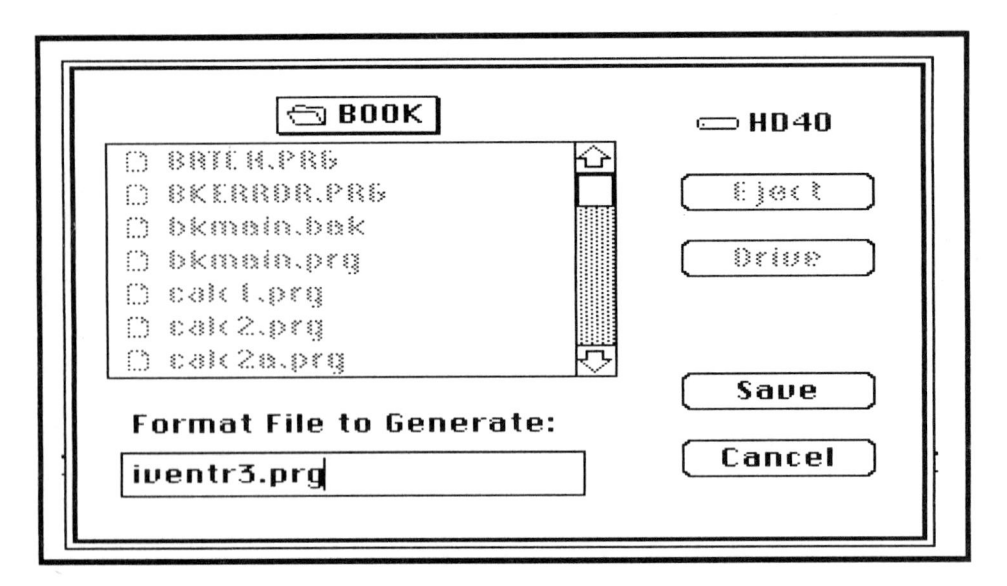

Figure 9-09. File to generate.

```
* Program.: iventr3.prg
* Date....: 8/20/89
* Version.: FoxBASE+/Mac, revision 1.10
* Notes...: Format file iventr3
*
SCREEN 1 TYPE 0 HEADING "Inventory Item Entry" AT 0,0 SIZE 150,450 PIXELS  FONT "Geneva",12 COLOR 0,0,0,-1,-1,-1 TOP
@ PIXELS 12,125 SAY "Item Id:" STYLE 65536 FONT "Geneva",12 COLOR 0,0,0,-1,-1,-1
@ PIXELS 36,98 SAY "Description:" STYLE 65536 FONT "Geneva",12 COLOR 0,0,0,-1,-1,-1
@ PIXELS 63,107 SAY "# On Hand:" STYLE 65536 FONT "Geneva",12 COLOR 0,0,0,-1,-1,-1
@ PIXELS 90,134 SAY "Price:" STYLE 65536 FONT "Geneva",12 COLOR 0,0,0,-1,-1,-1
@ PIXELS 13,182 SAY iv_id STYLE 0 FONT "Geneva",12 SIZE 15,97 COLOR 0,0,0,-1,-1,-1
@ PIXELS 36,182 GET Item->iv_desc STYLE 0 FONT "Geneva",12 SIZE 15,214 COLOR 0,0,0,-1,-1,-1
@ PIXELS 63,182 GET iv_onhand STYLE 0 FONT "Geneva",12 SIZE 15,70 COLOR 0,0,0,-1,-1,-1
@ PIXELS 90,182 GET iv_price STYLE 0 FONT "Geneva",12 PICTURE "$$$$$.##" SIZE 15,106 COLOR 0,0,0,-1,-1,-1
*
* EOF: iventr3.prg
```

Using FoxForm-generated programs

Now we need to adjust the iventr program to accommodate the new version of iventr2.prg. Here is the code:

```
* iventrx.prg
* Sample data entry skeleton.
* Uses the FoxForm Generated iventr3.prg program
* Adaptable to most programs
```

```
SCREEN 1
CLEAR
* Open database file with indexes
USE ivitem INDEX ivitem,ivdesc ALIAS item
* Loop to process requests for data entry
DO WHILE .T.
  * reset local option variable
  entchoice=0
  * Check to see if there is a record to display
  * EOF() will only be true if there are no records
  * on the file.  All activities will leave EOF() false
  * if there is at least one record on file.
  IF EOF()                              && no records on file
    * Tell user the bad news
    DO lbcenter WITH 7,"There are no records on file.","",0,""
    * Offer to add a record via text button
    * Optionally, user may select a menu option
    @ 7,37 GET entchoice PICTURE "@*h ADD"
    READ
  ELSE                                  && at least one record on file
    * Put field gets on screen
    do iventr3
    * Check to see if the record is marked for deletion
    IF DELETED()
      * Put  note on screen for user
      @ 0,53 SAY "(DELETED)"
      @ 7,0 GET entchoice PICTURE "@*h ADD;NEXT;PREVIOUS;LOOKUP;RECALL"
    ELSE
      * Remove any existing DELETED message
      @ 0,53 CLEAR TO 0,62
      @ 7,0 GET entchoice PICTURE "@*h ADD;NEXT;PREVIOUS;LOOKUP;DELETE"
    ENDIF record marked for deletion
    DO WHILE entchoice=0.AND.(!kmnhit)
      READ SAVE
    ENDDO until option or menu hit
    CLEAR GETS
  ENDIF no records on file
  * Identify activity to be performed
  DO CASE
    CASE kmnhit
      * menu hit encountered
      kmnhit = .F.                      && reset menu flag
      SELECT item
      USE                               && close the inventory database
      RETURN
    CASE entchoice=1
      * Add or find new record
      DO iventrn
```

```
      CASE entchoice=2
         * Move forward one record
         DO iventrm WITH "F"
      CASE entchoice=3
         * Move back one record
         DO iventrm WITH "B"
      CASE entchoice=4
         * Lookup by description
         DO iventrl
      CASE entchoice=5
         * Delete or recall record
         DO iventrd
   ENDCASE entchoice
ENDDO requests for data entry
* eof iventrX.prg
```

In addition to DOing iventr3 instead of iventr2, we have:

- **allowed iventr3.prg to design Screen 1** because programs generated with the standard FoxForm format option include their own screen setups.

- **Put the READ statement in iventrx.prg** to allow the use of the READ SAVE command.

- **Put the entchoice local options in iventrx.prg** so that we can control which local options are presented based on whether or not there are any records on file.

We could have changed the iventr3.prg program to mirror the iventr2.prg program, and thereby left iventr.prg intact. However, any changes made directly to iventr3.prg would be overwritten the next time FoxForm was used to change the inventory item screen.

In other words, to use the default FoxForm format file generator in lieu of hand-generated screens, observe the following rules:

- Change the name of the output file from .fmt to .prg

- Allow the generated program to set the screen characteristics.

- Place the GET(s) for local options in the calling program.

- Place the READ SAVE in the calling program.

If, on the other hand, you would prefer to generate programs that resemble the original iventr2.prg program, you can use the FoxCode template programming language to generate virtually any FoxBASE+/Mac program you like based on a screen layout. The FoxCode template programming language has a syntax and structure all its own, and a discussion of this programming language is beyond the scope of this book. To read more about the FoxCode language, consult your FoxBASE+/Mac FoxReport - FoxForm - FoxCode manual.

Aside from the changes listed above, note that our modular design of iventr.prg has allowed us to use a new screen layout without changing the routines to add new records, lookup records by description, move forward or back, and delete or recall records. This flexibility is the reason for modular program design.

Pros of using FoxForm

I mentioned in the opening of this chapter that I am not a strong proponent of FoxForm usage. There are several advantages to the use of FoxForm however, including these:

- It is easier to completely fill every pixel with information in a very busy screen using FoxForm than by writing the program by hand.

- It is much easier to mix different fonts on the same screen using FoxForm.

- It is easier to move items around on a screen using FoxForm that to do so by hand.

- FoxForm eliminates most of the typing associated with @...SAY...GET commands and, as a result, virtually eliminates program bugs caused by typos.

- FoxForm makes it easy to remember how to assign fonts, styles, and colors to individual items by presenting most options in clickable lists.

- FoxForm makes it easy to import picture file data to the resource file for use as a picture button or icon.

Many programmers find these arguments completely persuasive and, therefore, use FoxForm to generate all of their data entry screens.

Cons of using FoxForm

In spite of the benefits mentioned above, I believe that FoxForm is not a necessary part of most program development. Here are my reasons:

- Changes made to the output file directly are overwritten any time that file is re-generated by FoxForm/FoxCode.

- Because FoxForm generates all of its @...SAY...GETs in PIXELs, it is difficult to add items to the screen from other programs.

- Because FoxForm uses PIXEL addressing for all of its @...SAY...GETs, FoxForm generated screens are difficult to use under FoxPro and FoxBASE+ in PC-DOS environments.

- Because of the flexibility of positioning items on the screen, it is often difficult to line up items horizontally and vertically using FoxForm.

- Because FoxForm requires at least 3 files per screen, and as many as 6 files per screen, there are more files to keep track of in an application.

- While the point and click method of assigning colors, fonts, pictures, valid clauses, and the like is helpful to the novice, experienced programmers find this method more time consuming than simply typing the associated commands directly into a program file.

- The default FoxForm Format file template generates STYLE, COLOR, SIZE, and FONT clauses for every @...SAY...GET statement. This makes the output program larger, slower, and harder to read than a program that used those clauses only where needed.

- To effectively use the FoxForm/FoxCode product as a program generator requires learning a new programming language. This language is sufficiently different from FoxBASE+/Mac to make learning it a significant challenge for most FoxBASE+/Mac programmers.

- Making even a small change to a FoxForm generated program is a multi-step process requiring the loading of FoxForm, changing of objects, and generation of programs. The manual method requires only one action to effect a change.

- FoxForm does not allow the programmer to specify a font for an entire screen.

It should be said that most of my objections can be ameliorated by sophisticated use of the FoxCode programming language. Therefore, if you can live with the limitations of the default templates, or if you are willing to invest the time in learning the FoxCode programming language, FoxForm may be a more viable programming tool for you than it is for me.

10. Enhanced Data Entry

This chapter is filled with new commands and new ideas, most of which are designed to validate input from the user. Along the way, we will use several commands that give FoxBASE+/Mac programs a mac-like interface including the creation of check boxes, radio buttons, scrollable lists, pop-ups, and others.

Unlike previous chapters where I presented you with a program, and then modified it to include each new idea, this chapter will present you with a series of complete programs. As a result, you may find yourself typing commands that you don't understand. Don't panic, I will explain all of the features in the employee programs to follow before leaving this chapter.

The programs

To demonstrate the data validation techniques available in FoxBASE+/Mac, I have chosen a sample employee maintenance program. This program will give the user the option to Add, Edit, Delete, Lookup, and Search employee records. The program is called from the Employee Maintenance option of the Data Entry menu in the bkmain.prg program. The database and index information is contained in Figures 10-01 and 10-02, the programs are as follows:

```
* prempl.prg
* Main program for employee maintenance
* Open database containing project names
USE prproj INDEX prproj ALIAS proj
* Create an array to hold the project names
RELEASE projarr
DIMENSION projarr(100)
LOCATE FOR pj_status="O"  && Find the first open project
projqty=1   && current projarr element reference
* Load project names into projarr
DO WHILE projqty<100.AND.(.NOT.EOF())
```

```
╔═════════════════════════════════════ Employee Information ═╗
 Structure for database:       HD40:FOX:BOOK:prempl.dbf
    Field   Field Name    Type           Width    Dec
       1    em_name       Character         25
       2    em_address    Character         25
       3    em_city       Character         25
       4    em_state      Character          2
       5    em_zip        Character         10
       6    em_phone      Character         13
       7    em_age        Numeric            2
       8    em_salary     Numeric            6
       9    em_title      Character         10
      10    em_gender     Numeric            1
      11    em_fistat     Numeric            1
      12    em_wagetp     Numeric            1
      13    em_proj       Character         15
      14    em_comm       Memo              10
      15    em_loctax     Logical            1
      16    em_sttax      Logical            1
      17    em_fedtax     Logical            1
      18    em_ssn        Character         11
 ** Total **                                161
 Index: HD40:FOX:BOOK:prempls.idx   Key = em_ssn
 Index: HD40:FOX:BOOK:prempln.idx   Key = UPPER(em_name)
```

Figure 10-01. Structure for prempl.dbf.

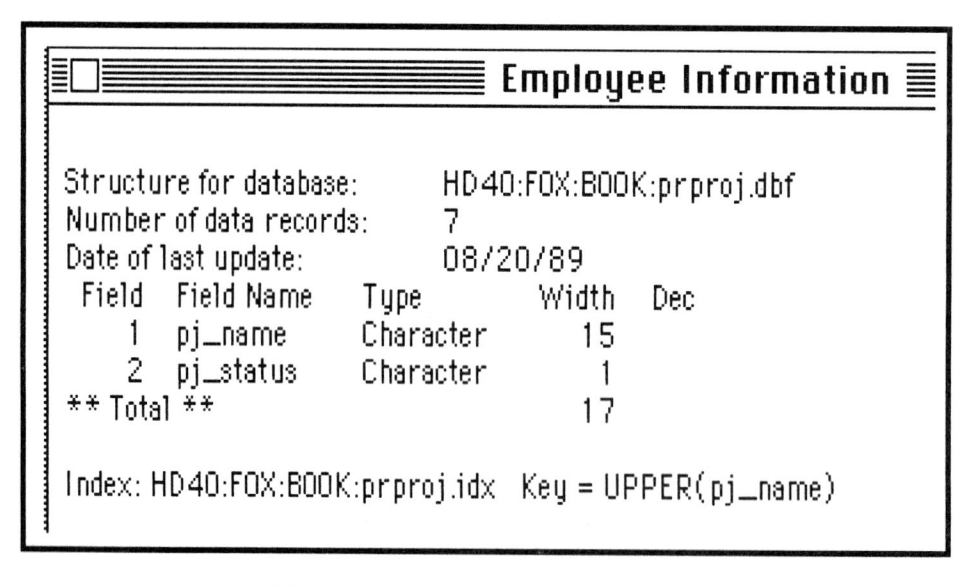

```
╔═════════════════════════════════════ Employee Information ═╗

 Structure for database:    HD40:FOX:BOOK:prproj.dbf
 Number of data records:    7
 Date of last update:       08/20/89
    Field   Field Name    Type         Width     Dec
       1    pj_name       Character      15
       2    pj_status     Character       1
 ** Total **                              17

 Index: HD40:FOX:BOOK:prproj.idx   Key = UPPER(pj_name)
```

Figure 10-02. Structure for prproj.dbf.

```
    * Load field content into array element
    projarr(projqty)=TRIM(UPPER(pj_name))
    projqty=projqty+1
    CONTINUE && Find the next open project
ENDDO load project names into array
* Make last element invalid in case the employee
* has not been assigned an open project
projarr(projqty)="**INVALID**"
* Create a memory variable to reference the
* projarr array
thisproj=projqty
* Close the project database
USE
* Setup a string for use with Age popup
agestr="18;19;20;21;22;23;24;25;26;27;28;29;30;"+;
"31;32;33;34;35;36;37;38;39;40;41;42;43;44;45;46;"+;
"47;48;49;50;51;52;53;54;55;56;57;58;59;60;61;62;"+;
"63;64;65"
* Open main database file with indexes
USE prempl INDEX prempln,prempls ALIAS empl
* Place prompts on the screen
DO prempl1
* Put some options in the query menu
kqueropt(1)="NEW"
kqueropt(2)="Current"
* Load query options in menu system
MENU 4,kqueropt,2
* Turn Query menu on
MENU ON 4
MENU OFF 4,2 && No current query
* Setup new query string
emplquery=""
* Loop to process requests for data entry
DO WHILE .T.
   * reset local option variable
   entchoice=0
   IF EOF()  && no records on file
     * Tell user the bad news
     DO lbcenter WITH 21,"There are no records on file.",;
     "",12,"BOI"
     * Offer to add a record via text button
     * Optionally, user may select a menu option
     @ 22,37 GET entchoice FONT ,12+kfo ;
     PICTURE "@*h ADD"
     READ
     * clean our message from the screen
     @ 21,0 CLEAR
   ELSE && at least one record on file
```

The programs

```
      * Allow user to edit this record, and/or
      * select an action using the prempl2.prg UDF
      entchoice=prempl2()
   ENDIF no records on file
   * Identify activity to be performed
   DO CASE
      CASE kmnhit
         * menu hit encountered
         kmnhit = .F. && reset menu flag
         IF kmnbar="QUERY"
            * DO the query program
            DO premplq WITH kmnopt,emplquery
            IF ""#emplquery
               * Turn "Current" option of
               * query menu ON
               MENU ON 4,2
            ENDIF && not an empty query string
         ELSE && not a query
            SELECT empl
            USE    && close the inventory database
            Kqueropt=""
            MENU OFF 4 && turn query menu off
            RETURN
         ENDIF && requested a query
      CASE entchoice=1
         * Add or find new record
         SET ORDER TO 2   && index by ssn
         DO prempln
         SET ORDER TO 1   && index by name
      CASE entchoice=2
         * Move forward one record
         DO iventrm WITH "F"
      CASE entchoice=3
         * Move back one record
         DO iventrm WITH "B"
      CASE entchoice=4
         * Lookup by name
         DO prempll
      CASE entchoice=5
         * Delete or recall record
         DO iventrd
   ENDCASE entchoice
ENDDO requests for data entry
* eof iventr.prg
```

```
* prempll.prg
```

```
* Displays fixed prompts for prempl employee maintenance
SCREEN 1 SIZE 24,80 FONT "geneva",10 AT 36,10
CLEAR
SCREEN 1 TYPE 4 LOCK TOP HEADING "Employee Information"
* Put a box around personal info
* Use black pen, 2 pixels wide, fill box with light grey,
* curve the box slightly
@ 0,0 TO 07,40 STYLE 15+32+1024+8192
@ 01,02 SAY "Name:"
@ 02,02 SAY "Address:"
@ 03,02 SAY "City:"
@ 04,02 SAY "State:"
@ 05,02 SAY "Zip:"
@ 06,02 SAY "Phone:"
* Put a box around age etc. info
* Use black pen, 2 pixels wide, fill box with light grey,
* curve the box slightly
@ 0,41 TO 07,79 STYLE 15+32+1024+8192
@ 01,43 SAY "SSN:"
@ 02,43 SAY "Salary:"
@ 03,43 SAY "Title:"
@ 05,43 SAY "Age..."
@ 05,51 SAY "Sex..."
@ 05,65 SAY "Status..."
* Put a box where wage type radio buttons will go
* Use black pen, 1 pixel wide
@ 08,0 TO 10,79 STYLE 15+16
@ 12,0 SAY "Current project..."
@ 12,20 SAY "Enter comments..."
* Put a box where tax check boxes will go
@ 12,51 to 20,79 STYLE 15+192   && black pen, 12 pixels wide
* Center an Inverted heading in the box
mboxwide = VAL(SYS(1028))*29
mboxstart = VAL(SYS(1028))*51
mrow = (VAL(SYS(1025))+VAL(SYS(1026))+VAL(SYS(1027)))*12+7
SCREEN 1 FONT "GENEVA",12+2048
msize = VAL(SYS(1030," TAXES "))
mcol = (mboxstart+(mboxwide/2))-(msize/2)
@ PIXELS mrow,mcol SAY " TAXES "    && STYLE 458752
SCREEN 1 FONT "GENEVA",10
RETURN
* eof prempl1.prg
```

```
* prempl2.prg
* Gets info about employees for prempl.prg
PRIVATE thisage,xx,localopt
```

The programs

```
@ 1,53 SAY em_ssn SIZE 1,15 FONT ,9+256
* Make the user enter a name, default message
@ 1,11 GET em_name VALID em_name#SPACE(25)
@ 2,11 GET em_address VALID ;
  lbval1(em_address#SPACE(25),"The address is blank!")
@ 3,11 GET em_city
@ 4,11 GET em_state PICTURE "!!" VALID ;
  prstchk(em_state)
@ 5,11 GET em_zip SIZE 1,12 PICTURE "#####-####"
* Don't allow spaces in the phone number, no message
@ 6,11 GET em_phone SIZE 1,16 PICTURE ;
  "(###)###-####"  VALID ;
  IIF(!" "$em_phone, .t., 0)
* Determine the location of the age in the popup string
thisage = MAX(1,MIN(48,em_age-17))
* Use a memory variable as part of a picture clause
@ 6,43 GET thisage PICTURE "@^ "+agestr SIZE 1,2
@ 6,51 GET em_gender SIZE 1,7 PICTURE "@^ Male;Female"
@ 6,65 GET em_fistat SIZE 1,8 PICTURE "@^ Single;Married;Head"
* Prior three GETs use popup lists to validate data entry
@ 2,53 GET em_salary SIZE 1,11 PICTURE "$$$,$$$.##"
* Force a title, provide programmer's message
@ 3,53 GET em_title SIZE 1,12 VALID ;
  lbval(em_title#SPACE(10),"Title cannot be blank!")
* The next line generates 4 radio buttons
@ 9,1 GET em_wagetp PICTURE ;
  "@*Rh SALARIED;TEMPORARY/UNION;TEMPORARY;HOURLY"
* Next 3 lines generate check boxes
@ 14,55 GET em_loctax PICTURE "@*c Local Taxes"
@ 16,55 GET em_sttax PICTURE "@*c State Taxes"
@ 18,55 GET em_fedtax PICTURE "@*c Federal Taxes"
* Determine the project for this employee
DO CASE
  CASE em_proj=SPACE(LEN(em_proj)) && empty project
    thisproj=projqty   && assign "**INVALID**"
  CASE em_proj#projarr(thisproj)
    * Current project array element does not
    * match the employee's project field
    * Try to find a match
    thisproj=1
    DO WHILE thisproj<projqty.AND.em_proj>projarr(thisproj)
      thisproj=thisproj+1
    ENDDO less than last array and no match
    * If no match, thisproj will equal projqty, and
    * therefore current project will be "**INVALID**"
ENDCASE project
@ 12,0 GET thisproj FROM projarr,projqty SIZE 6,18
@ 13,20 GET em_comm SIZE 8,30 SCROLL
```

```
* Setup local option
localopt=0
* Check to see if the record is marked for deletion
IF DELETED()
  @ 21,0 GET localopt FONT ,12+kfo ;
  PICTURE "@*h ADD;NEXT;PREVIOUS;LOOKUP;RECALL"
ELSE
  @ 21,0 GET localopt FONT ,12+kfo ;
  PICTURE "@*h ADD;NEXT;PREVIOUS;LOOKUP;DELETE"
ENDIF record marked for deletion
* Setup a validation loop
DO WHILE .T.
  * Wait for local option or menu hit
  DO WHILE localopt=0.AND.(!kmnhit)
    READ SAVE
  ENDDO wait for menu hit or local action
  * Check full screen validations
  valmsg=""
  DO CASE
    CASE em_wagetp=4.AND.em_salary>27.50
      * Hourly employee making more than 27.50
      valmsg = "Maximum hourly wage is $27.50"
    CASE " "$em_phone
      * bad phone number
      valmsg = "Phone number must be complete.;"
    CASE em_name=SPACE(LEN(em_name))
      * blank name
      valmsg = "Name cannot be blank"
    CASE em_title=SPACE(LEN(em_title))
      * blank title
      valmsg = "Title cannot be blank."
  ENDCASE recheck all validations
  IF ""#valmsg
    * some error took place
    * Use ALERT so as not to disturb GETs
    ALERT 1 STOP valmsg,"Please correct."
    localopt = 0
    kmnhit = .F.
  ELSE  && no errors
    EXIT && validation loop
  ENDIF either not hourly or acceptable hourly wage
ENDDO validation looop
CLEAR GETS
* Put calculated fields back in database
REPLACE em_age WITH thisage+17
REPLACE em_proj WITH projarr(thisproj)
return localopt
* eof prempl2.prg
```

The programs

```
* lbval1.prg
* Uses @...PROMPT to get user choice from within a
* VALID clause UDF
** Isvalid = expression passed by valid clause
** valmsg = message to be displayed in ALERT boxlbval
PARAMETERS isvalid,valmsg
PRIVATE ans,oldscreen
* note that the expression passed by the valid clause
* is automatically evaluated and placed in the isvalid
* variable
IF isvalid && true expression
   RETURN .t.  && allow exit from this get
ELSE && false expression
   oldscreen = VAL(SYS(1034))
   * Create a "modal" dialog screen
   SCREEN 8 FONT "HELVETICA",12
   CLEAR
   SCREEN 8 SIZE 7,40 AT 0,0
   DO lbcenter WITH 1,"WARNING!","",0,"OB"
   DO lbcenter WITH 3,valmsg,"",0,""
   DO lbcenter WITH 4,"How do you wish to proceed?","",0,""
   @ 6,0 PROMPT "RETRY"
   @ 6,10 PROMPT "USE_AS_IS"
   ans=1
   MENU TO ans
   SCREEN oldscreen TOP
   IF ans < 2
     * wants to retry
     RETURN 0
   ELSE
     * wants to use invalid entry
     RETURN .T.
   ENDIF wants to retry
ENDIF && true expression
* EOF lbval1.prg
```

```
* lbval.prg
* Programmer defined valid messages
** Isvalid = expression passed by valid clause
** valmsg = message to be displayed in ALERT boxlbval
PARAMETERS isvalid,valmsg
* note that the expression passed by the valid clause
* is automatically evaluated and placed in the isvalid
* variable
```

```
IF isvalid && true expression
  RETURN .t.  && allow exit from this get
ELSE && false expression
  ALERT STOP 1 valmsg
  RETURN 0  && stay in this GET
ENDIF && true expression
* EOF lbval.prg
```

```
* prempll.prg
* Lookup the item by customer name
* Do not allow the user to add a record
PRIVATE newname,thisrec,ans,option,oldscreen
oldscreen=VAL(SYS(1034))
* Setup a memory variable to accept the customer name to SEEK
newname = SPACE(LEN(em_name))
* Save our place in the file in case
* the customer name is not found
thisrec = RECNO()
* Tell the user what to do, and get the customer name
SCREEN 3 SIZE 5,70 TYPE 4 LOCK AT 240,40
CLEAR
SCREEN 3 TOP HEADING "Lookup Employee Name" FIXED
  @ 1,0 SAY "Enter customer name to lookup here:"
  @ 1,COL()+1 GET newname
  option = 0
  @ 2,15 GET option PICTURE "@*h LOOKUP;CANCEL"
  DO WHILE option=0
    READ SAVE
  ENDDO wait for action
  CLEAR GETS
  * See if the user left the customer name
  IF newname # SPACE(LEN(newname)).AND.option#2
    * Remove any spaces from the end of the customer name
    newname = TRIM(newname)
    * Convert the memory variable to upper case to match the
    * index expression "UPPER(iv_desc)"
    newname = UPPER(newname)
    * Look for a customer name that begins with the content of
    * the newname memory variable
    SEEK newname
    IF .NOT.FOUND()
      * Tell the user this one is not on file
      DO lbq WITH newname+" is not on file.","CONTINUE","F"
      * Look for the closest match
      nearly = RECNO(0)
      IF nearly = 0  && beyond last record in file
        GOTO BOTTOM
```

The programs

```
         ELSE
            GOTO nearly
         ENDIF beyond last record in file
      ENDIF did not find  the item
   ENDIF did not leave new customer name blank or cancel
SCREEN 3 OFF
SCREEN oldscreen TOP
RETURN
* eof prempll.prg
```

```
* prempln.prg
* Add a new record or find an item by SSN
PRIVATE newkey,thisrec,ans,option,oldscreen
oldscreen=VAL(SYS(1034))
* Setup a memory variable to accept the SSN to SEEK
newkey = SPACE(11)
* Save our place in the file in case the new key is not found,
* and the user does not want to add a new record
IF .NOT. EOF()
   * Save the record number
   thisrec = RECNO()
ELSE  && no current record
   thisrec = 0
ENDIF there is a current record
* Tell the user what to do, and get the new key
SCREEN 3 SIZE 5,60 TYPE 4 LOCK AT 240,60
CLEAR
SCREEN 3 TOP HEADING "New Employee" FIXED
DO WHILE .T.
   @ 1,0 SAY "Enter SSN to add or lookup here:"
   @ 1,COL()+1 GET newkey PICTURE "###-##-####"
   option = 0
   @ 2,15 GET option PICTURE "@*h LOOKUP;CANCEL"
   DO WHILE option=0
      READ SAVE
   ENDDO wait for action
   CLEAR GETS
   * Note that the id must be two upper case letters
   * followed by 8 numbers
   * See if the user chose to cancel
   IF newkey # "   -  -    ".AND.option#2
      * Check to see if the item is already on file
      SEEK newkey
      IF .NOT.FOUND()
         * See if the user wants to add a new item
         IF lbq(newkey+" is not on file.","ADD;RETRY","F")="RETRY"
```

```
            * See if there is a current record
            IF thisrec#0
               * Return the record pointer to its position prior
               * to the unsuccessful SEEK
               GOTO thisrec
            ENDIF there is a current record
         ELSE && wants to add the new item
            * Add a blank record to the file
            APPEND BLANK
            * Fill the key field with the memory variable
            REPLACE em_ssn WITH newkey
            EXIT
         ENDIF doesn't want to add the item
      ELSE && found it!
         * Exit with the record pointer set on this record
         EXIT
      ENDIF found the item
   ELSE &&
      * Chose to cancel, or left key field blank
      EXIT
   ENDIF did not leave new key blank
ENDDO process lookup requests
SCREEN 3 OFF
SCREEN oldscreen TOP
RETURN
* eof prempln.prg
```

```
* premplq.prg
* Builds and/or uses a query
PARAMETERS newuse,curquery
newuse=upper(newuse)
SELECT empl
IF newuse="NEW"
   IF lbq("Do you want a new query?","No;Yes","")="YES"
      ** let the user build an expression
      GETEXPR "Enter the employee query..." TO curquery ;
      TYPE "L;Not a proper query expression." ;
      DEFAULT curquery
   ENDIF wants to make a new query
ENDIf asked for new
* Set the filter
SELECT empl
SET FILTER TO &curquery.
GOTO TOP
* Setup titles for browse
m1="Employee Query "+LEFT(curquery,25)
```

The programs

```
m2="SSN;NAME;TITLE;ADDRESS;CITY;ST:2;ZIP;WAGE TYPE;"+;
"SALARY;AGE:2;COMMENT:7;PROJECT:15;SEX:3;LOCAL;FEDERAL;STATE"
* Now browse the file with the filter set
BROWSE FIELDS em_ssn,em_name,em_title,em_address,;
em_city,em_state,em_zip,em_wagetp,em_salary,em_age,em_comm,;
em_proj,em_gender,em_loctax,em_sttax,em_fedtax ;
HEAD m1,m2 NOMODIFY NOMENU NOAPPEND ;
AT 0,0 SIZE 200,VAL(SYS(1024)) FONT "MONACO",9
* When they exit the browse, turn the filter off
SET FILTER TO
RETURN
* eof premplq.prg
```

Many of the techniques demonstrated in these programs use portions of more than one program. Therefore, rather than examine each program line by line as we have in previous chapters, we will examine the entire set of programs technique by technique.

APPENDing records directly

Before we begin our discussion of the programs, we need some data in the prproj.dbf file. After creating the prproj.dbf database, and creating the prproj.idx index, issue the following commands:

```
USE prproj INDEX prproj ALIAS proj
APPEND
```

Then, enter the data found in Figure 10-03. This method of directly APPENDing records, without the use of a program or format file, is not viable for end users, but programmers often use it to enter sample data.

The VALID clause

The 6th line of prempl2.prg contains the following line of code:

```
@ 1,11 GET em_name VALID em_name#SPACE(25)
```

```
Record#   pj_name        pj_status
1         MacBook        0
2         Fox Dev Conf   0
3         Foxpro Beta    0
4         Fox Column     0
5         FoxPro Book    0
6         Fox Utilities  0
7         FoxGraph Beta  0
```

Figure 10-03. Data for prproj.dbf.

This demonstrates the simplest use of the very powerful VALID clause. In essence, the VALID clause of this @...GET command will not let the user enter all spaces in the em_name field. In other words, when the user is positioned in the em_name field, and has entered all spaces, or when the em_name field originally contained all spaces and the user has not changed that content, the user will not be allowed to leave the em_name field. That is, the user will not be allowed to select a menu option, click on a local text button, or press [Enter] to exit the field.

If the user does attempt one of these actions while the em_name field contains all blanks, he will be presented with a screen like the one in Figure 10-04. When the user clicks or presses a key, the em_name field will be reset to its previous content, and the user will still be positioned in the em_name field.

Now that we know what a standard VALID clause does, let's see how we write a VALID clause. The expression supplied for the VALID clause by the programmer must return a logical true or false, or a number. In our example, the expression em_name#SPACE(25) will return a true or false value. If the expression returns a true value, the user will be allowed to leave the em_name field to edit another field, exit the READ via text button, or exit the READ via menu selection. If the logical expression returns false value, the default message in screen 10-04 will be presented.

If the VALID expression returns a numeric value, the user will be moved among the current GETs based on the value returned. That is, if the expression returns a numeric 2, the user will be advanced two fields from the current field. If the expression returns a negative 2, the user will be moved back 2 GETs from the current field. Most importantly, no error message will be displayed.

Since the default error message is less than informative, we may want to avoid it use altogether. The following command from prempl2.prg accomplishes this task:

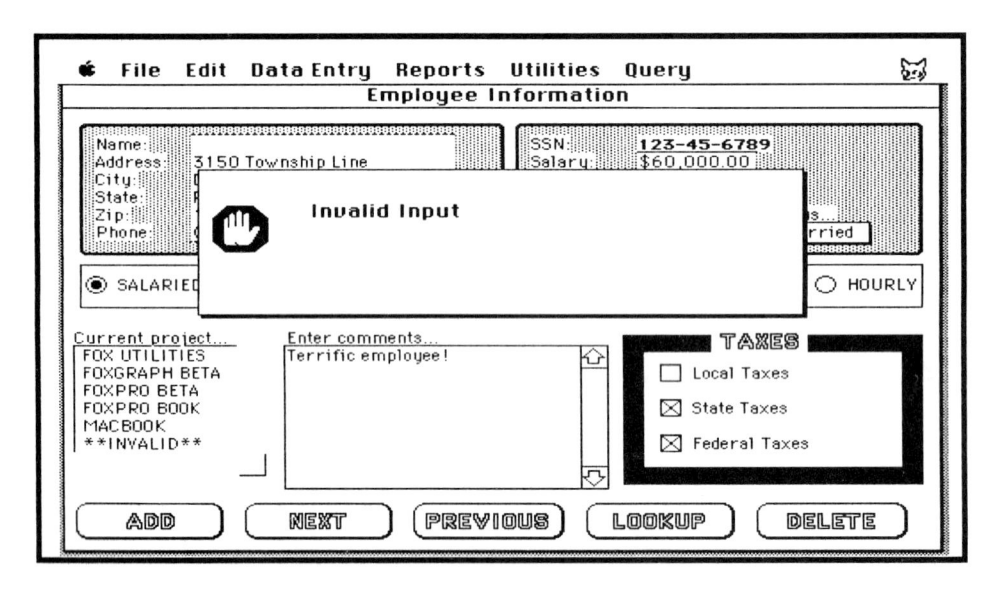

Figure 10-04. Standard valid clause.

```
@ 6,11 GET em_phone SIZE 1,16;
  PICTURE "(###)###-####";
  VALID IIF(!" "$em_phone,.t.,0)
```

The IIF() function returns the 2nd argument if the first argument is true. It returns the 3rd argument if the first argument is false. Translated then, the VALID expression reads, "IF there is no space in em_phone, return logical true, otherwise return numeric 0."

Therefore, when invalid data is entered, this VALID expression will return numeric 0, and the user will move 0 GETs from his current position. Further, no error message will be presented.

You can test this VALID clause by entering or leaving a space in the em_phone field.

If you like the idea of providing an error message, but don't like the default message, try using a UDF as part of a VALID clause as I have done in the following line from prempl2.prg:

```
@ 3,15 GET em_title SIZE 1,12 VALID ;
  lbval(em_title#SPACE(10),"Title cannot be blank!")
```

The UDF lbval.prg returns a logical TRUE if the first parameter evaluates to TRUE. If the first parameter evaluates as FALSE, lbval.prg uses an ALERT statement to display the programmer's message, and then lbval.prg returns a numeric 0 to force the user to enter a valid content. Figure 10-05 is an example of the dialog created by the lbval.prg when em_title is left blank.

Of note is the use of the FoxBASE+/Mac ALERT command in lbval.prg. The reason I use ALERT instead of lbq.prg or other home-made dialog is that UDFs in VALID clauses may not contain any of the following commands:

The VALID clause

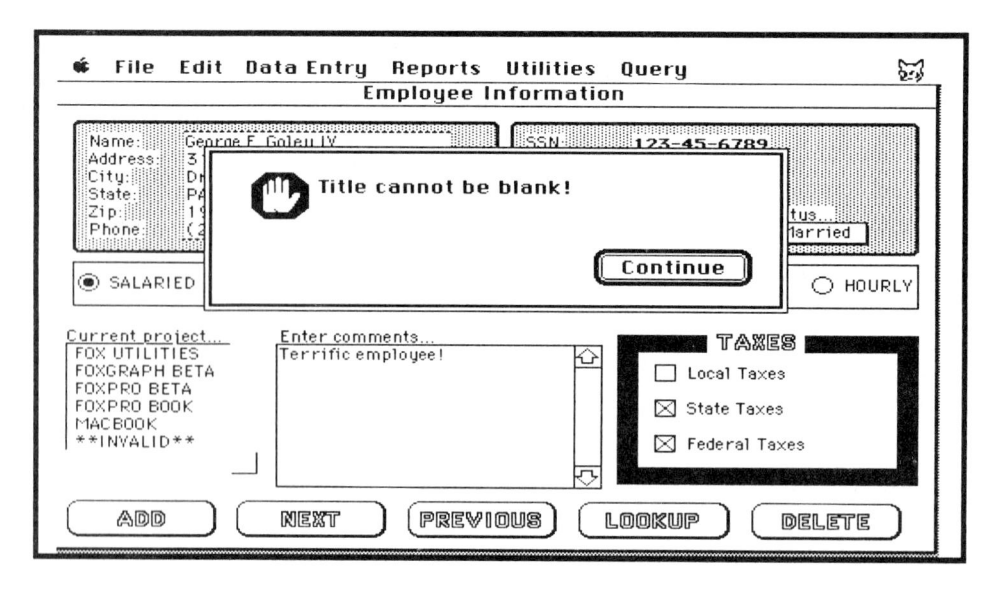

Figure 10-05. UDF valid clause message.

```
READ
@...GET
CLEAR GETS
CLEAR
SET FORMAT
```

If you do need to obtain information from the user from within a VALID clause UDF, try one of the following commands/functions:

```
ACCEPT
WAIT
INKEY(0)
ALERT
@...PROMPT/MENU TO
```

The last command combination is used to create rather plebian menus in FoxBASE+ under PC DOS. The command combination is not covered in the FoxBASE+/Mac manual because Fox Software sees no use for the ugly, by Macintosh standards, interface generated by @...PROMPT.

However, since @...PROMPT does not disturb outstanding GETs, it is perfect for use in complicated VALID clause UDFs. The following line of code in prempl2.prg causes lbval1.prg to generate the screen in Figure 10-06:

```
@ 2,11 GET em_address VALID ;
lbval1(em_address#SPACE(25),"The address is blank!")
```

Another common use of a VALID clause UDF is to allow the user to select from a list of options. The variations here are endless, but the prstchk.prg UDF demonstrates the basic techniques. First, present the user with some options. This can be done with a BROWSE command, an @...PROMPT/MENU TO command, or other command that does not interfere with open GETs. Next, use the KEYBOARD command to type

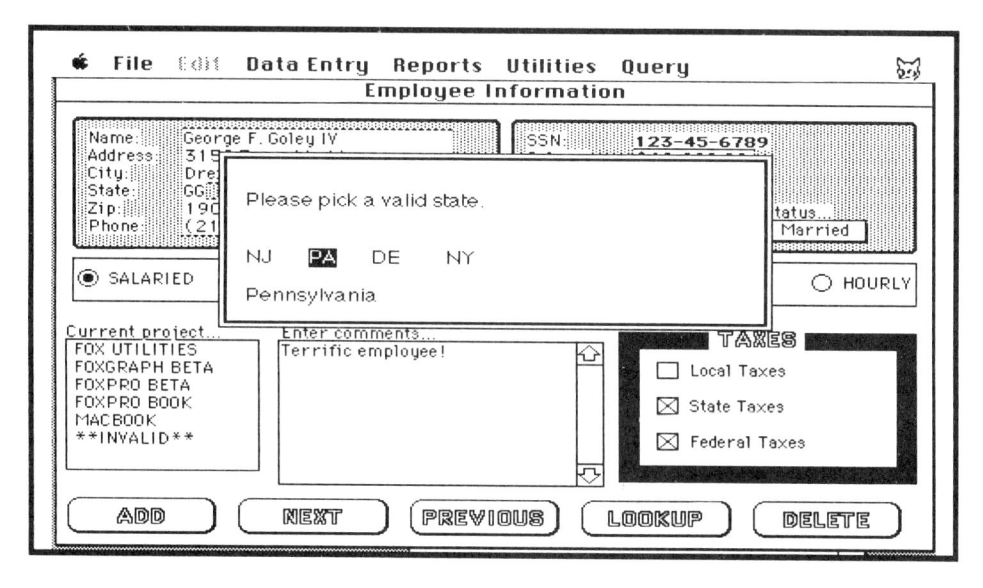

Figure 10-06. Multiple choice valid UDF.

The VALID clause   225 characters into the keyboard buffer as though the user had typed them himself. Finally, issue a RETURN 0 command to insure that the KEYBOARDed data goes to the correct field. Figure 10-07 shows a sample screen generated by the entry of an invalid state. Here is the associated command from prempl2.prg:

```
@ 4,11 GET em_state PICTURE "!!" VALID ;
prstchk(em_state)
```

Validation loops

There are two circumstances under which a VALIDated GET can be left with an invalid content. First, the user could press the [Escape] or [Clear] button during editing. This action automatically exits the READ, and avoids any VALID clauses. Second, the user exits the screen without ever entering the VALIDated GET. Both of these potentialities, and several others, can be resolved with a validation loop like the one found in prempl2.prg.

In general, a validation loop consists of a DO WHILE .T. loop around a READ SAVE loop. When the READ SAVE loop is exited, all of the validation is double checked. If everything is valid, or if the programmer wants to allow some kinds of invalid data, or if the programmer wants to allow the user to abort a READ, the validation loop is exited. Otherwise, the program displays some messages, and continues editing the screen.

The pop-up edit

One way to insure that the user enters valid data is to give him only valid choices. This is the aim of the pop-up field. The following command in prempl2.prg generates a popup for the employee's filing status:

```
@ 6,65 GET em_fistat SIZE 1,8 PICTURE "@^ Single;Married;Head"
```

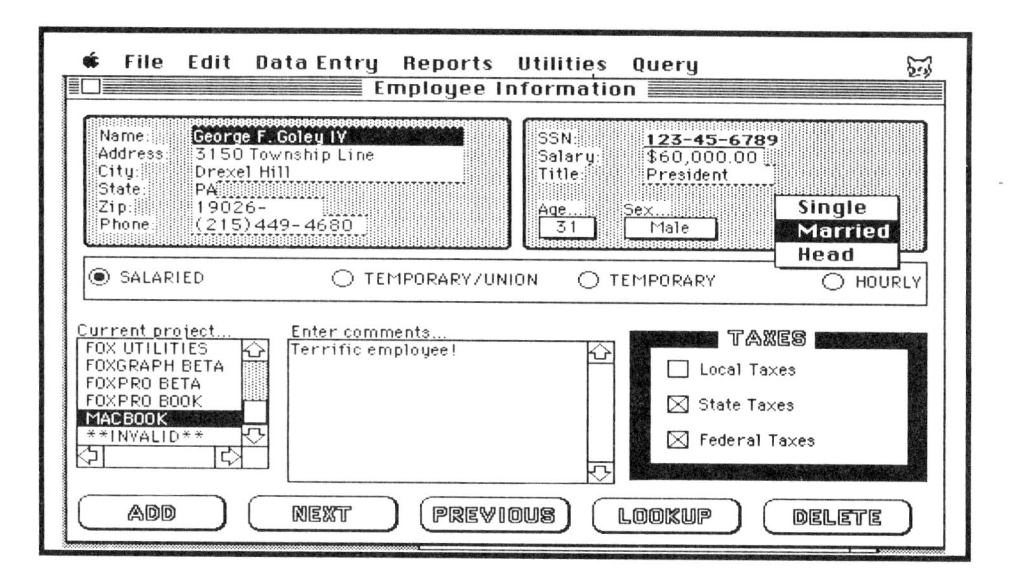

Figure 10-07. Pop-ups.

The user will not be allowed to type in this field. Rather, when the user positions the pointer on this field, the finger symbol will appear, and the three valid choices will pop up, as they have in Figure 10-08. The only limit to the number of available choices is that they must fit within the FoxBASE+/Mac limit of 254 characters per character string. Choices are separated by semi-colons. The characters "@^" in the PICTURE clause tell FoxBASE+/Mac to treat the choices as a pop-up menu.

Note that em_fistat is a numeric field. This accommodates the numeric return generated by popup gets. In other words, when the user selects Single, em_fistat will receive a value of numeric 1. If the user selects Married, em_fistat will equal 2, and so on.

Popups are best used for static selections like sex, movie rating, etc.

Note that we use a memory variable to hold the result of the AGE GET. This is so that we can store the actual age of the employee in the em_age

The pop-up edit

field of the prempl database. Also note that the agestr variable is setup in the prempl.prg program.

Experiment with the popups in the employee maintenance screen to see how they might best be used in your applications.

Check boxes

Check boxes, like the one generated by the following command from prempl2.prg, are used for Yes/No type data.

```
@ 14,55 GET em_sttax PICTURE "@*c State Taxes"
```

The characters "@*c" in the PICTURE clause tell FoxBASE+/Mac to treat this field as a check box. The user can click the box on or off. If the variable or field is logical, true will be placed in the field when the box is clicked on. If the field is numeric, 1 for on or 0 for off will be placed in the field.

Radio buttons

Radio buttons are generated by commands like the following from prempl2.prg:

```
@ 9,1 GET em_wagetp PICTURE ;
"@*Rh SALARIED;TEMPORARY/UNION;TEMPORARY;HOURLY"
```

The characters "@*R" in the PICTURE clause tell FoxBASE+/Mac to treat the field as a series of radio buttons. The letter "h" following the "@*R" indicates that the buttons are to placed horizontally on the screen. A "v" in lieu of the "h" would position the radio buttons vertically.

As with the pop-ups, multiple options are separated by a semi-colon. Also, as with popups, the value returned from this GET is numeric, with 1 indicating the selection of the SALARIED radio button.

Radio buttons are used with small, static lists of data where all of the options need to be displayed at all times.

The number of radio button options is limited by both screen size and the FoxBASE+/Mac character string limitation.

Scrolling lists

One of the requirements for this particular employee maintenance program is the ability to track the current project for a given employee. To effect this feature, I have elected to present the user with a scrollable list of open tasks. The user will then select the task, and that task will be assigned to the employee.

The following command from prempl2.prg initializes the scrollable list, but this is only the tip of the iceberg from which the task assignment feature comes:

```
 @ 12,0 GET thisproj FROM projarr,projqty ;
SIZE 6,18
```

This command tells FoxBASE+/Mac to create a scrollable list. The upper left corner of the list will begin at row 12, column 0 of the current screen. The number of the item chosen by the user will be placed in the numeric variable thisproj. The items in the list will be comprised of the elements from the projarr array. The number of elements included in the list will be determined by the value of the numeric variable projqty. The SIZE clause dictates that the list will occupy 6 rows of 18 characters each in the current font of the current screen.

The scrollable list will include vertical and horizontal scroll bars, and will allow the user to select an element by scrolling the list, and clicking on the desired item.

Scrollable lists are best used for medium sized lists of data.

If the list of items is very short, consider popups or radio buttons instead of scrollable lists. If the list of items is very long, remember that every element in an array takes up system memory. Further, while the limit of 32,767 array elements is not very constricting, remember that any character elements must fit in the available string memory pool. Finally, even if the programmer can spare enough memory to create a huge array, the user may not be thrilled with the prospect of scrolling through 1000+ items to find his selection.

In our case, the items in the scrollable list are dynamic. That is, the number and name of the open projects change from day to day. As a result, we cannot simply store the number placed in the thisproj variable in the em_proj field.

Rather, we need to store the name of the project identified by the thisproj item in the em_proj field. This is accomplished with the following command taken from the prempl2.prg program:

```
REPLACE em_proj WITH projarr(thisproj)
```

Here we have used the value of the thisproj variable to refer to the projarr() array element chosen by the user.

Well, storing the content of the user's selection from a scrollable list rather than the number of the item is a fairly simple matter. But how do we get the available items into the scrollable list in the first place? And how do we identify the current value in the scrollable list?

The following lines from the prempl.prg program are used to load the currently open project names into the projarr array for use in the scrollable list:

```
* Open database containing project names
USE prproj INDEX prproj ALIAS proj
* Create an array to hold the project names
RELEASE projarr
DIMENSION projarr(100)
LOCATE FOR pj_status="O" && Find the first open project
projqty=1  && current projarr element reference
* Load project names into projarr
DO WHILE projqty<100.AND.(.NOT. EOF())
   * Load field content into array element
   projarr(projqty)=TRIM(UPPER(pj_name))
   projqty=projqty+1 && prepare to use next array element
   CONTINUE  && find next open project
ENDDO load project names into array
* Make last element invalid in case the employee
* has not been assigned an open project
projarr(projqty)="**INVALID**"
* create a memory variable to reference the
* projarr array
thisproj=projqty
* Close the project database
USE
```

Note that this program only accommodates up to 99 open projects. To allow for more open projects, increase the size of the projarr() array, and increase the limit on the projqty variable in the DO WHILE loop. If you decide to increase the number of open projects that can be stored in the projarr array, you may need to provide more character string memory by adjusting the MVARSIZ command in the config.fx file.

The LOCATE and CONTINUE commands are not specific to scrollable list usage. They are used to process records that meet a condition. In this case, they insure that only open project names are placed in the projarr array.

As to the problem of identifying an employee's current project assignment, the following code from prempl2.prg does the job:

Scrolling lists

```
* Determine the project for this employee
DO CASE
  CASE em_proj=SPACE(LEN(emproj)) && empty project
    thisproj=projqty  && assign "**INVALID**"
  CASE em_proj#projarr(thisproj)
    * Current project array element does not
    * match the employee's project field
    * Try to find a match
    thisproj=1
    DO WHILE thisproj<=projqty.AND.em_proj>projarr(thisproj)
      thisproj=thisproj+1
    ENDDO less than last array and no match
ENDCASE project
```

Our problem is that thisproj must be a numeric value. However, we are storing the actual project name in the em_proj field of the prempl.dbf database. To resolve this problem we use the preceding piece of code to find the number of the array element that has the same project name as the em_proj field.

Obviously, if we were using a static array for a scrollable list, we could simply store the number of the array element in the database, and avoid this step. (Note to advanced programmers: Since the project names in projarr are stored in alphabetical order, you could substitute a binary search algorithm for the simple sequential search listed above.)

Text edit ranges

It is often desirable to include comments or descriptions of items in databases. In our example, we want to provide space for comments for each employee. By creating a field with a memo data type, and accessing it with a command like the following taken from prempl2, we can provide for virtually unlimited comments per employee:

```
@ 13,20 GET em_comm SIZE 8,30 SCROLL
```

The fact that em_comm is a memo field tells FoxBASE+/Mac to provide a text edit region for the field. The SIZE 8,30 portion of the command generates a box that is 8 rows high by 30 characters wide. The content of the em_comm field will be word wrapped to fit in this region. Because we included the SCROLL clause in this @...GET command, a scroll bar will be placed on the right side of the region to allow the user to easily access portions of the em_comm content that do not fit in the 8 by 30 box.

Memo fields have many advantages when storing a variable amount of information for each record, or when storing a large amount of information for each record. First, unlike character fields, memo fields take up only as much disk space as it takes to store the actual content of the field. That is, a 100 character character field will consume 100 characters of disk space for every record in the database, even if most of the fields are empty!

A memo field on the other hand will consume 10 characters of disk space plus the number of characters actually input to the field for each record in the database. In this example, if the average number of characters is 50, and there are 10,000 records in the database, the 100 character character field would consume 1,000,000 characters of disk space, while the memo field would consume approximately 600,000 characters of disk space.

Second, when records need to store large amounts of information, full records of correspondence for each record for example, the 254 character limit on the size of character fields renders them useless. Conversely, memo field size is limited only by available disk space.

Memo fields also have several disadvantages compared with character fields however. First, functions designed to change the content of character strings do not work with memo fields. That is, you cannot use SUBSTR(), or UPPER(), or STUFF() or most other string functions with memo field data. The only exception is the AT() function which can be used to search a memo field for the position of a given character string. Future versions of FoxBASE+/Mac promise to resolve these problems, and add such enhancements to memo field handling as the ability to directly import text files to memo fields.

Second, memo fields are exceedingly difficult to print without the help of the FoxForm report generator.

Third, memo fields are stored in separate .dbt files. This makes for more work in maintaining files, and leads to slower processing.

Because of these disadvantages, and others, memo fields are usually appropriate only when the content of the field is likely to exceed 254 characters.

Queries

Our sample application calls for the ability to query the employee database. In our case, we want the user to be able to define his or her own query, and then present the user with a list of employees that match the user's query.

To accomplish our goal we first must provide the user with a Query option. Since this is obviously a local activity, a text button would seem the logical mechanism for acknowledging the user's desire to query.

However, menus can also be used for local options, and I will take this opportunity to describe the technique. First we need to define the Query menu. This menu has been defined in the bkmain.prg and sysmenu1.prg programs listed at the end of Chapter 7.

We need to activate the menu for use in employee maintenance however, and the following lines from prempl.prg do the job nicely:

```
* Put some options in the query menu
kqueropt(1)-"NEW"
kqueropt(2)="Current"
* Load query options in menu system
MENU 4,kqueropt,2
* Turn Query menu on
MENU ON 4
MENU OFF 4,2 && No current query
```

Next, we need to perform some local process when the user selects an option from the Query menu. These lines from prempl.prg accomplish this goal:

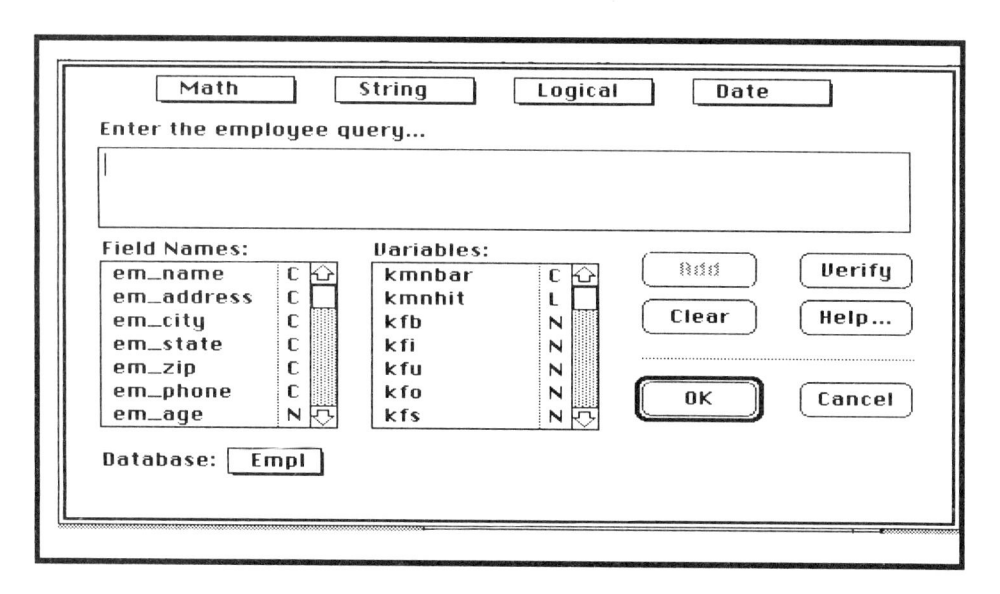

Figure 10-08. GETEXPR at work.

Queries

```
CASE kmnhit
   * menu hit encountered
   kmnhit = .F. && reset menu flag
   IF kmnbar="QUERY"
      * DO the query program
      DO premplq WITH kmnopt,emplquery
      IF ""#emplquery
         * Turn "Current" option of
         * query menu ON
         MENU ON 4,2
      ENDIF && not an empty query string
   ELSE && not a query
```

Now of course, we need to let the user design a query. The premplq.prg contains the following powerful command:

```
GETEXPR "Enter the employee query..." TO curquery ;
TYPE "L;Not a proper query expression." ;
DEFAULT curquery
```

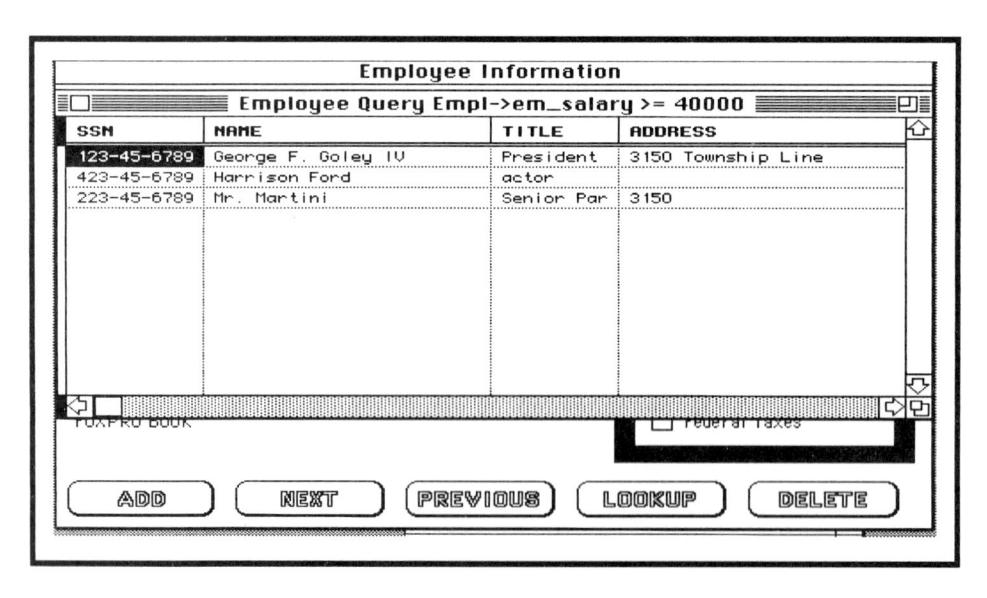

Figure 10-09. BROWSE expensive employees.

This single command creates the dialog found in Figure 10-09. From here the user can:

- click on a field name to include that field name in the query.

- select a database from among the open databases by clicking the popup next to the Database: prompt.

- select a variable from the list of active memory variables.

- select a Math, String, Logical, or Date operator and/or function from the popups at the top of the dialog.

- obtain help for using the GETEXPR dialog.

- verify an expression.

- directly type in any valid query.

For example, if you use the scroll bar on the field names list, you can scroll down to the em_salary field. Click on em_salary. Next, pull down the Logical popup at the top of the dialog. Select the greater than or equal to option. Finally, type the number 40000. You will have generated the following expression:

```
Empl->em_salary >= 40000
```

To verify your expression, click on Verify. To save the expression, click on OK. You will be presented with a screen like the one in 10-10. Now let's review the GETEXPR command that created all of this interaction with the user. For your convenience, here is the command again:

```
GETEXPR "Enter the employee query..." TO curquery ;
TYPE "L;Not a proper query expression." ;
DEFAULT curquery
```

"Enter the employee query..." will be the prompt above the expression box in the GETEXPR dialog. The expression will be saved as a character string TO curquery. The "L;" portion of the command directs GETEXPR to force the user to enter a Logical expression. The "Not a proper query expression." message will be displayed if the user enters an invalid expression. Finally, the "DEFAULT curquery" portion of the command directs GETEXPR to use the current content of curquery as the default expression.

Now that we have created a query, we need to do something to present the user with a list of those records that match the query. The following command from premplq.prg insures that only records matching the expression are displayed:

```
SET FILTER TO &curquery.
```

Until this command is counteracted, by closing the database or issuing another SET FILTER TO command, most FoxBASE+/Mac commands that access records in the prempl.dbf file will ignore any records that do not match the expression in curquery.

About the BROWSE command

In general, the BROWSE command provides us with a tabular view of a database. Among the most flexible commands in FoxBASE+/Mac, BROWSE offers an impressive selection of options for displaying database information.

The following commands in premplq.prg are responsible for creating the BROWSE window seen in Figure 10-10:

```
* Setup titles for BROWSE
m1="Employee Query "+LEFT(curquery,25)
m2="SSN;NAME;TITLE;ADDRESS;CITY;ST:2;ZIP;WAGE TYPE;"+;
"SALARY;AGE:2;COMMENT:7;PROJECT:15;SEX:3;LOCAL;FEDERAL;STATE"
* Now BROWSE the file with the filter set
BROWSE FIELDS em_ssn,em_name,em_title,em_address,;
em_city,em_state,em_zip, em_wagetp,em_salary,em_age,em_comm,;
em_proj,em_gender, em_loctax,em_sttax,em_fedtax ;
HEAD m1,m2 NOMODIFY NOMENU NOAPPEND ;
AT 0,0 SIZE 200,VAL(SYS(1024)) FONT "MONACO",9
```

The FIELDS clause of the BROWSE command determines which fields will be displayed, and the order in which they will be displayed. The HEAD clause uses the content of the m1 variable as the header for the window. The HEAD clause uses the content of the m2 variable to determine the headers for each field in the window. Each field header is separated by a semi-colon. If a colon is included, the number following the colon is used to determine the width of the field display.

The NOMODIFY clause prevents the user from changing the content of any of the records. The NOMENU clause prevents the user from selecting a menu option while BROWSing. The NOAPPEND clause prevents the user from adding records while BROWSing.

The AT 0,0 clause positions the BROWSE window in the middle of the screen. The SIZE 200,VAL(SYS(1024)) clause creates a window that is 200 PIXELs high, and as wide as the current screen. The FONT "MONACO",9 clause makes the BROWSE window use the Monaco 9 point font.

The user can use the standard BROWSE window controls to resize the window, resize any of the field columns, display the content of memo fields, split the BROWSE window vertically, and scroll both horizontally and vertically in the BROWSE window. When the user closes the BROWSE window, control returns to the premplq.prg program.

About the BROWSE command

Note that when the user exits the BROWSE, the record pointer in the prempl.dbf file remains where the user positioned it during the BROWSE session.

Screen layouts

In addition to the sophisticated data validation techniques displayed above, I have included a few techniques to improve the appearance of our data entry screen. Most of these techniques are located in the prempl1.prg program.

I generated the prempl1.prg program without using the FoxForm screen painter. However, as you can see from the amount of PIXEL calculating I had to do to line up boxes and headers, FoxForm might have come in handy on this job.

First among the fancy screen techniques is the use of boxes. Boxes are often used to group items on the screen for the user. For example, it is quite common to draw boxes around a series of Radio Buttons so that the user realizes that the buttons are related.

FoxBASE+/Mac offers a great deal of flexibility in implementing boxes. For example, the following command from prempl1.prg creates a box with a black, 2 pixel wide border, a light gray background, and slightly rounded corners:

```
@ 0,0 TO 07,40 STYLE 15+32+1024+8192
```

The @...TO command creates a box. The STYLE clause of the @...TO command makes the box interesting! Your FoxBASE+/Mac Commands & Functions manual provides detailed explanations of the various STYLE values and their effect. Unfortunately, it does not provide any examples as to the STYLE clause's usage.

There are five different attributes that you can affect by using the STYLE clause. The first four attributes affect boxes drawn with the @...TO command, while the fifth attribute affects most objects generated with the @ command. Here are the attributes:

- Pen Pattern = pattern of the border of the box.

- Pen Width = width of the border of the box.

- Fill Pattern = the pattern of the area inside the box.

- Radius = the curvature of the corners of the box.

- Transfer mode = the manner in which the object overlays other objects occupying the same position on the screen or printer.

Each attribute has 16 possible settings. To select a setting for an one of these attributes, we add a number to the STYLE clause. For example, the numbers affecting the Pen Pattern are 0, 1, 2, 3, 4, 5, 6, 7, 8, 9, 10, 11, 12, 13, 14, and 15, so we will add one of these numbers to the STYLE clause to denote the border pattern for the box.

The next attribute in the STYLE clause is the Pen Width which can be selected by adding 0, 16, 32, 48, 64, 80, 96, 112, 128, 144, 160, 176, 192, 208, 224, or 240 to the STYLE clause. For example, to create a box that has a black border 7 pixels wide, we would issue the following command:

```
@ 5,5 TO 10,30 STYLE 15+112
```

The next attribute is the Fill Pattern, and this attribute is selected by adding a number between 0 and 3840 in increments of 256. So, to create a box that has a light gray border, 2 pixels wide, that is filled with black, we would issue a command like the following:

```
@ 5,5 TO 10,30 STYLE 4+32+3840
```

The fourth attribute is the Radius, or amount of curvature of the corners of the box. This attribute is selected by adding a number between 0 and 61440 in increments of 4096. To create a box with a black border that is 3 pixels wide, that is filled with gray, and has slightly rounded corners, we would issue a command like the following:

```
@ 5,5 TO 10,30 STYLE 15+48+2048+8192
```

The last attribute is the transfer mode, which determines the manner in which objects overlap. This attribute is selected by adding a number between 0 and 983040 in increments of 65536. The following command would cause the word "George" to combine with any objects already on the screen at position 5,5 through 5,10:

```
@ 5,5 SAY "George" STYLE 65536
```

The following command would cause the word "George" to overwrite any objects already on the screen at positions 5,5 through 5,10:

```
@ 5,5 SAY "George"
```

Tips for using STYLE

If you include a STYLE clause when generating a box, remember to include both a pen pattern and a pen width value, otherwise the box will have no border.

The values for the five attributes can be derived from the following formula: (selection * 16 ^ attribute) where selection is a number between 0 and 15, and where attribute is a number between 0 and 4. For example, the following commands both generate a box with a black, 2 pixel wide border, with a gray background, and very rounded corners:

```
@ 5,5 TO 10,30 STYLE 15+32+2048+57344
@ 5,5 to 10,30 STYLE (15*16^0)+(2*16^1)+(8*16^2)+(14*16^3)
```

```
Structure for database: HD40:FOX:BOOK:ivsupp.dbf
Number of data records:   4
Date of last update:     09/01/89
Field  Field Name   Type         Width   Dec
    1  su_code      Character        6
    2  su_company   Character       25
** Total **                         32

Index: HD40:FOX:BOOK:ivsupp.idx
Key: su_code
```

Figure 10-10. Structure for ivsupp.dbf.

Try saving the value of common STYLEs in memory variables for later use. For example, if you often generate a box with a gray background, black 2 pixel border, and gray background, you might issue the following command in the main program of your system:

`kbox1 = 15+32+2048+8192`

Later in the application, you could generate a box with the aforementioned attributes with the following command:

`@ 5,5 TO 13,50 STYLE kbox1`

If you have trouble remembering the sequence of attributes for the STYLE command, try remembering the nonsense word "PWiFeRT." This word might help you remember P for Pattern, W for width, F for fill, R for radius, and T for transfer.

Tips for using STYLE

Finally, the only time the STYLE clause is truly necessary in a FoxBASE+/Mac program is to insure that overlapping objects do not cause a page eject while printing. In other words, you will usually include the following STYLE clause in the @...SAY commands of printout routines:

```
STYLE 65536
```

Other than this use, the STYLE clause is for decoration only. Therefore, consider writing your program without STYLE clauses first. Then, when you have time, you can go back and decorate your screens.

Lookups for validation

After reviewing our inventory data entry programs, your boss decides that each inventory item should be assigned a supplier code. Further, she thinks that it would be a good idea to provide the data entry operator with a list of suppliers if the operator enters an invalid supplier code. Finally, the entry of a valid supplier code should result in the display of the supplier's company name.

The first thing we need to effect these changes is a supplier database. The information for ivsupp.dbf is found in Figure 10-11. Next we need to adjust the iventr.prg program to provide a prompt and screen space for the supplier code, and to open the ivsupp.dbf database. Here is the iventr.prg after adjustments, and renamed as ilentr.prg:

```
* ilentr.prg
* Sample data entry skeleton.
* Adaptable to most programs
* Allows for use of lookups
SCREEN 1 SIZE 12,80 FONT "MONACO",9
CLEAR
SCREEN 1 AT 0,0 TOP HEADING "Inventory Item Entry"
* Open database file with indexes
SELECT 1
USE ivitem INDEX ivitem,ivdesc ALIAS item
SELECT 2
```

```
USE ivsupp INDEX ivsupp ALIAS supp
SELECT item
* Place prompts on the screen
@ 0,24 SAY "Item id:"
@ 2,20 SAY "Description:"
@ 4,23 SAY "# onhand: "
@ 6,26 SAY "Price:"
@ 8,23 SAY "Supplier:"
* Loop to process requests for data entry
DO WHILE .T.
  * reset local option variable
  entchoice=0
  * Check to see if there is a record to display
  * EOF() will only be true if there are no records
  * on the file.  All activities will leave EOF() false
  * if there is at least one record on file.
  IF EOF()  && no records on file
    * Tell user the bad news
    DO lbcenter WITH 8,"There are no records on file.","",0,""
    * Offer to add a record via text button
    * Optionally, user may select a menu option
    @ 9,37 GET entchoice PICTURE "@*h ADD"
    READ
  ELSE && at least one record on file
    * Allow user to edit this record, and/or
    * select an action using the iventr2.prg UDF
    entchoice=ilentr2()
  ENDIF no records on file
  * Identify activity to be performed
  DO CASE
    CASE kmnhit
      * menu hit encountered
      kmnhit = .F. && reset menu flag
      SELECT item
      USE   && close the inventory database
      RETURN
    CASE entchoice=1
      * Add or find new record
      DO iventrn
    CASE entchoice=2
      * Move forward one record
      DO iventrm WITH "F"
    CASE entchoice=3
      * Move back one record
      DO iventrm WITH "B"
    CASE entchoice=4
      * Lookup by description
      DO iventrl
```

Lookups for validation

```
      CASE entchoice=5
         * Delete or recall record
         DO iventrd
      ENDCASE entchoice
   ENDDO requests for data entry
   * eof ilentr.prg
```

Next, we need to adjust the iventr2.prg program to display the supplier company name, and to validate the entry of a new supplier code. Here is the program:

```
* ilentr2.prg
* Edits the content of the current inventory item
PRIVATE localopt
@ 0,33 GET iv_id
* Prevent the user from changing the key field
CLEAR GETS
* Setup local option
localopt=0
* Check to see if the record is marked for deletion
IF DELETED()
   * Put  note on screen for user
   @ 1,53 SAY "(DELETED)"
   @ 9,0 GET localopt PICTURE "@*h ADD;NEXT;PREVIOUS;LOOKUP;RECALL"
ELSE
   * Remove any existing DELETED message
   @ 1,53 CLEAR TO 1,62
   @ 9,0 GET localopt PICTURE "@*h ADD;NEXT;PREVIOUS;LOOKUP;DELETE"
ENDIF record marked for deletion
@ 2,33 GET iv_desc
@ 4,33 GET iv_onhand PICTURE "##,###"
@ 6,33 GET iv_price PICTURE "$$$.##"
@ 8,45 && remove any previous supplier name
IF iv_supp#SPACE(6)
   * Lookup the supplier company name in the supplier file
   SELECT supp
   SEEK item->iv_supp
   IF FOUND()
      @ 8,45 SAY su_company
   ELSE
      @ 8,45 SAY "**Invalid Supplier**"
   ENDIF valid supplier
   SELECT item
ENDIF not a blank supplier
```

Chapter 10: Enhanced Data Entry

```
* Provide lookup capability for iv_supp via the
* ilsuppv.prg UDF
@ 8,33 GET iv_supp PICTURE "@!" ;
VALID ilsuppv(item->iv_supp)
DO WHILE localopt=0.AND.(!kmnhit)
  READ SAVE
ENDDO until option or menu hit
CLEAR GETS
RETURN localopt
* eof iventr2.prg
```

Finally, we need to supply a VALID UDF program as follows:

```
* ilsuppv.prg
* Validates supplier code for ilentr2.prg
PARAMETERS thissupp
PRIVATE result
IF thissupp#SPACE(LEN(thissupp))
  SELECT supp
  SEEK thissupp
  IF FOUND()   && entered a valid supplier code
    @ 8,45 SAY su_company && put company name on screen
    result = .T.
  ELSE
    @ 8,45 && clear any company name from screen
    * Find closest match to user's entry
    thisrec=RECNO(0)
    IF thisrec=0
      GOTO bottom
    ELSE
      GOTO thisrec
    ENDIF
    * Use BROWSE to allow user to scroll through
    * the supplier file
    BROWSE nomodify noappend nomenu
    * "Type" the correct code for the user
    KEYBOARD su_code
    * Make sure typing goes in the iv_supp field
    result = 0
  ENDIF
ELSE && entered blanks
  result = .T.   && blanks are allowed
ENDIF did not enter blanks
SELECT item && return to the current work area
RETURN result
```

Lookups for validation

```
* eof ilsuppv.prg
```

Note that none of the other iv*.prg programs needed to be changed. Also note that all of the techniques utilized in ilsuppv.prg were used earlier in the correspondence programs.

11. Multi-File Data Entry

In this chapter we will develop a simple, multi-file data entry screen. The sample program will provide a method of tracking telephone correspondence with customers, but the principles can be applied to any application that has parent records to which multiple child records are related. Familiar examples include: multiple invoices per customer; multiple items per invoice; multiple paychecks per employee; multiple contractors per construction site; multiple checks per checking account. Obviously, the list is endless.

Our correspondence tracking system will offer the user the opportunity to add, edit, delete, and move among customer records. More importantly, the system will also give the user the opportunity to add, edit, delete, and move among the correspondence records related to a given customer. Before we can write our correspondence programs however, we need to understand the concept of related files.

Relationships

In our example, we will have multiple customers in the customer file. In addition to the name and address info stored in the customer file, we wish to keep track of our correspondence with each customer.

One solution would be to create multiple correspondence fields in the customer file. This method has several disadvantages. First, since every record in the customer database has the same fields, any customer that did not fill all of his correspondence fields would be wasting valuable disk space. Second, and more importantly, we would be severely limited in the number of calls we could track since database records can contain no more than 128 fields.

The solution is to create a correspondence file. Each record in this file will contain the chronicle of one phone call. This method reduces wasted space by only using disk space when a call is actually made. Further, since a database file can contain in excess of 1 Billion records, this method allows the tracking of a virtually unlimited number of calls per customer.

At this point in our discussion, we have created two distinct, separate, databases. To link these two database files together, we need the two databases to share a common piece of information.

Further, the shared piece of information must be capable of connecting each correspondence record to one, and only one, customer record. In our example, we will use a unique customer id as the shared piece of information.

The customer id will be unique in the customer file. That is, no two customers can have the same id. Further, **each correspondence record for a given customer will share the same customer id.** This last observation is central to all multi-file processing. When relating multiple records in a child file to single records in a parent file, all of the children related to the same parent record will share the same id.

At this point, we have two databases. The customer database, where every record has a unique customer id, and the correspondence database where every record associated with the same customer contain's that customer's id.

All that is left is to create an index file for the correspondence database so that we can quickly find the correspondence records for a given customer. The database files and indexes for the correspondence tracking system can be found in Figure 11-01.

Note that in addition to providing fast lookups of correspondence records via the SEEK command, the crcorr.idx index also groups all of the correspondence records for a given customer together. That is, the index key values for all twenty of ABC Company's phone calls will be the same. As a result, the index will make those records appear to be next

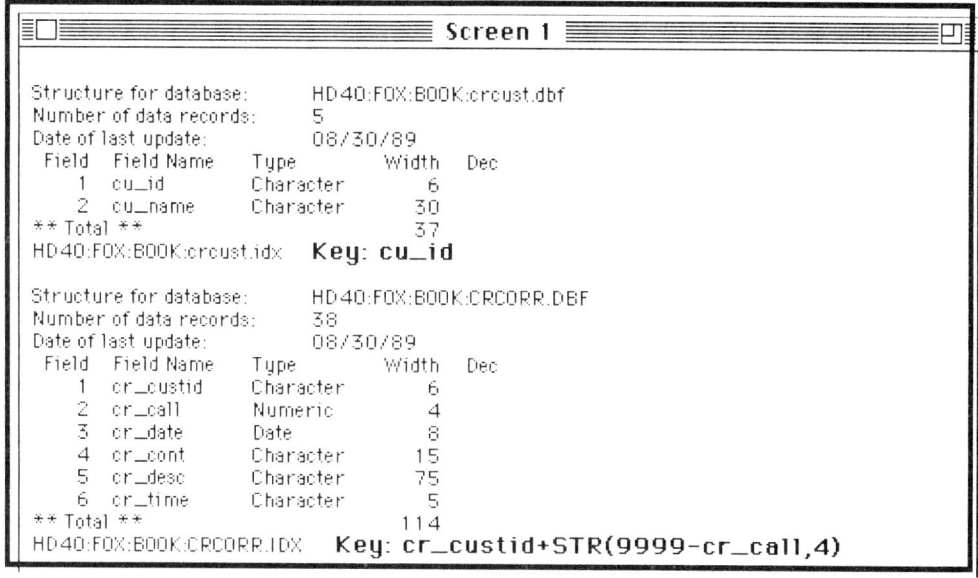

```
┌─────────────────────────────────────────────────────────┐
│≣□≣≣≣≣≣≣≣≣≣≣≣≣≣≣≣≣ Screen 1 ≣≣≣≣≣≣≣≣≣≣≣≣≣≣≣≣≣□│
├─────────────────────────────────────────────────────────┤
│ Structure for database:    HD40:FOX:BOOK:crcust.dbf     │
│ Number of data records:    5                            │
│ Date of last update:       08/30/89                     │
│   Field  Field Name    Type          Width    Dec       │
│     1    cu_id         Character       6                │
│     2    cu_name       Character      30                │
│ ** Total **                           37                │
│ HD40:FOX:BOOK:crcust.idx   Key: cu_id                   │
│                                                         │
│ Structure for database:    HD40:FOX:BOOK:CRCORR.DBF     │
│ Number of data records:    38                           │
│ Date of last update:       08/30/89                     │
│   Field  Field Name    Type          Width    Dec       │
│     1    cr_custid     Character       6                │
│     2    cr_call       Numeric         4                │
│     3    cr_date       Date            8                │
│     4    cr_cont       Character      15                │
│     5    cr_desc       Character      75                │
│     6    cr_time       Character       5                │
│ ** Total **                          114                │
│ HD40:FOX:BOOK:CRCORR.IDX   Key: cr_custid+STR(9999-cr_call,4) │
└─────────────────────────────────────────────────────────┘
```

Figure 11-01. Structures for correspondence.

to each other in the correspondence application.

In reviewing Figure 11-01, you will notice that the field names containing the linking information are different in the two databases. This is an important difference between FoxBASE+/Mac and some other database management systems. In FoxBASE+/Mac, all that matters is that the data is shared between the two files, and that the child file is indexed by that shared data. Field names are of no consequence in this matter.

Note the use of the expression STR(9999-cr_call,4) in the crcorr.idx key. This little trick makes the records appear in descending order of call number. As each correspondence record is entered, it is assigned a new call number. Since we wish to see the most recent call for a given customer first, we index the file in descending order of call number.

To test the descending order trick, try generating the following test program:

Relationships

```
* desc.prg
* Demonstrates the descending order trick
SCREEN 1 TOP SIZE 24,50 FONT "Monaco",9
CLEAR
xx=1
DO WHILE xx<=20
  ? xx,STR(9999-xx,4)
  xx=xx+1
ENDDO
* eof desc.prg
```

Correspondence overview

The CR system will display the current customer record in one screen. Simultaneously, the most recent call for this customer will be displayed in a second screen.

Options to add, delete, move forward, or move backward a customer will be provided in the first screen. The second screen will provide these same options for correspondence related to the current customer only.

The user will be allowed to switch between customer and correspondence maintenance by clicking on the appropriate screen. At all times the user will be allowed to select a menu option from the menu system.

Correspondence programs

The correspondence programs can be called from the correspondence option of the Data Entry menu of the bkmain.prg program. Before listing the code for all of the programs, here is a brief synopsis of each:

- CRMAIN.PRG: Control program for correspondence tracking. Creates screens, opens databases, and creates memory variables for the other routines. Also selects customer or correspondence tracking based on the screen selected by the user.

- CRCUST.PRG: Controls customer maintenance. Also displays the most recent call for this customer in the correspondence screen. Calls appropriate crcust?.prg program based on a user text button selection, or returns to crmain.prg if the user selected a menu option or clicked on the correspondence screen.

- CRCUSTA.PRG: Adds one customer.

- CRCUSTD.PRG: Deletes a customer, **and all of it's related correspondence.**

- CRCORR.PRG: Controls correspondence maintenance. Calls appropriate crcorr?.prg program based on a user text button selection, or returns to crmain.prg if the user selected a menu option or clicked on the customer screen.

- CRCORR2.PRG: Displays and or edits current correspondence record.

- CRCORRA.PRG: Adds one correspondence record. Assigns the current customer id to the new correspondence record. Determines and assigns next call number for this customer. Reuses blank records if possible.

- CRCORRD.PRG: Erases one correspondence record. Positions correspondence file record pointer on next call for the current customer.

- CRSCROLL.PRG: Moves one correspondence record forward or back. Insures that only records for the current customer are displayed.

Here is the crmain.prg program:

```
* crmain.prg
* Correspondence entry program
* Allows entry of history of correspondence by customer.
* Setup memory variables for screen numbers
scrcust = 1
scrcorr = 2
```

```
* Setup customer screen
SCREEN scrcust FONT "MONACO",12 SIZE 5,60 AT 40,30
CLEAR
SCREEN scrcust TOP TYPE 4 HEAD "CUSTOMER"
* Put prompts up for customer screen
@ 1,0 SAY "  Customer id:"
@ 2,0 SAY "Customer name:"
SCREEN scrcorr FONT "MONACO",9 SIZE 9,82 AT 160,2
CLEAR
SCREEN scrcorr TOP TYPE 4 HEAD "CORRESPONDENCE"
@ 1,0 SAY "       Date: "
@ 2,0 SAY "       Time: "
@ 3,0 SAY "       Call: "
@ 4,0 SAY "    Contact: "
@ 5,0 SAY "Description: "
* Open databases
SELECT 1
USE crcust INDEX crcust ALIAS cust
SELECT 2
USE crcorr INDEX crcorr ALIAS corr
* Make the customer screen current
SCREEN scrcust TOP LOCK
MENU ON -3,1  & enable screen switching!
DO WHILE .T.
  curscreen = VAL(SYS(1035))
  DO CASE
    CASE kmnhit
      * user selected a menu option
      EXIT
    CASE curscreen = scrcust
      * user clicked on customer screen
      SCREEN scrcust TOP LOCK
      DO crcust
    CASE curscreen = scrcorr
      * user clicked on correspondence screen
      SCREEN scrcorr TOP LOCK
      DO crcorr
  ENDCASE what are we working on
ENDDO process
SELECT corr
USE
SELECT cust
USE
RETURN
* eof crmain.prg
```

You have seen most of the commands in crmain.prg before, however these two might be new to you:

```
MENU ON -3,1
curscreen = VAL(SYS(1035))
```

Under normal circumstances, if a user clicks on one screen while READing information on another, the READ is not exited, and processing will not resume until the user re-selects the initial screen. The MENU ON -3,1 command directs FoxBASE+/Mac to treat the selection of another screen as a Menu hit. This causes the current READ to be exited, and allows the programmer to determine what screen the user has selected.

The way we determine the currently active screen is by calling the SYS(1035) function. This function returns a string with the number of the currently active screen. We convert the string to a numeric value with the VAL() function.

In short, if the user is READing information on the customer screen when he clicks on the correspondence screen, the MENU ON -3,1 command will cause the READ to be exited. When we check the SYS(1035) function, we will see that the user selected the correspondence screen. As a result, we will direct FoxBASE+/Mac to DO crcorr.prg.

Look for this feature in both the crcorr.prg and crcust.prg programs. In fact, here is the crcust.prg program now:

```
* crcust.prg
* Processes customers for crmain.prg
PRIVATE localopt
DO WHILE .T.
  SCREEN scrcorr
  @ 1,13 CLEAR && clean correspondence screen
  localopt=0
  SCREEN scrcust TOP LOCK
  SELECT cust
  IF EOF()
    @ 1,15 CLEAR TO 2,50
    @ 3,20 GET localopt PICTURE "@*h ADD"
```

Correspondence programs

```
    ELSE
      @ 1,15 SAY cu_id
      SCREEN scrcorr  && corr screen active
      SELECT corr   && corr work area
      SEEK cust->cu_id   && seek the current customer's id
      IF FOUND() && at least one record for this customer
         DO crcorr2 WITH "SAY"
      ENDIF at least one record for this customer
      SELECT cust && customer work area
      SCREEN scrcust TOP LOCK && return to customer screen
      @ 2,15 GET cu_name
      IF DELETED()
         @ 3,10 GET localopt PICTURE "@*h ADD;RECALL;FWD;BACK"
      ELSE && not deleted
         @ 3,10 GET localopt PICTURE "@*h ADD;DELETE;FWD;BACK"
      ENDIF customer is deleted
   ENDIF no customers on file
   DO WHILE localopt=0.AND.VAL(SYS(1035))=scrcust.AND.;
      !kmnhit
      READ SAVE
   ENDDO wait for local option, screen switch, or menu hit
   CLEAR GETS
   DO CASE
      CASE VAL(SYS(1035))#scrcust.OR.kmnhit
         * screen switch or menu hit
         RETURN
      CASE localopt=1 && add
         * add a customer
         DO crcusta
      CASE localopt=2 && delete or recall
         IF DELETED()
            RECALL
         ELSE
            * delete the customer
            DO crcustd
         ENDIF already deleted
      CASE localopt=3 && forward
         SKIP
         IF EOF()
            ?? CHR(7)
            GOTO BOTTOM
         ENDIF already at the bottom
      CASE localopt=4 && backward
         SKIP -1
         IF BOF()
            ?? CHR(7)
            GOTO TOP
         ENDIF already at the top
```

```
    ENDCASE what did the user do to exit the read
ENDDO process customer requests
* eof curcust.prg
```

Look familiar? Most of crcust.prg is old news to readers of chapters 8 through 10. However, the following lines might be unfamiliar:

```
SCREEN scrcorr && corr screen active
SELECT corr    && corr work area
SEEK cust->cu_id && seek the current customer's id
IF FOUND() && at least one record for this customer
   DO crcorr2 WITH "SAY"
ENDIF at least one record for this customer
SELECT cust && customer work area
```

In essence, these 7 lines of code lookup the most recent call for this customer. If the customer has at least one correspondence record, the crcorr2.prg program is called to display that record.

The next lines of interest are as follows:

```
DO WHILE localopt=0.AND.VAL(SYS(1035))=scrcust.AND.;
!kmnhit
   READ SAVE
ENDDO wait for local option, screen switch, or menu hit
```

This loop recognizes that the user can exit by pressing a text button, in which case localopt would not equal 0, or by clicking on another screen, in which case VAL(SYS(1035)) would not equal scrcust, or by selecting a menu option, in which case kmnhit would be true. Note that text buttons exit READs by default, while the MENU ON -3,1 command in crmain.prg is required to exit the READ due to a screen change, and the sysmenu1.prg program is responsible for changing the value of the kmnhit variable when a menu option is selected.

The routines to add and delete customers are as follows:

```
* crcusta.prg
```

Correspondence programs

```
* Adds or looks up a customer for crcust
memid = SPACE(6)
@ 3,0 CLEAR
@ 3,0 SAY "Enter new id: " GET memid PICTURE "@!"
READ
@ 3,0 CLEAR
IF memid#SPACE(6) && did not leave blank
   SELECT cust
   SEEK memid
   IF !FOUND() && not a duplicate
     APPEND BLANK
     REPLACE cu_id WITH memid
   ENDIF not a duplicate
ENDIF did not leave blank
RETURN
* eof crcusta
```

```
* crcustd.prg
* Deletes a customer AND ASSOCIATED CORRESPONDENCE!
* In a real program, you would ask the user to
* verify that he wants to delete this customer
* First, erase all correspondence for the customer
SELECT corr
SEEK cust->cu_id && look for first corr for this customer
DO WHILE FOUND() && correspondence on file
   REPLACE cr_custid WITH "",cr_call WITH 0,;
   cr_desc WITH "",cr_date WITH CTOD(""),;
   cr_time WITH "",cr_cont WITH ""
   SEEK cust->cu_id && look for the next corr record
ENDDO while correspondence on file for this cust
* Now delete this customer
SELECT cust
DELETE
* Note that the correspondence is gone for good,
* but the customer can be RECALLed
RETURN
* eof crcustd.prg
```

The crcusta.prg program is unremarkable, but the crcustd.prg program provides a new method of deleting records. By replacing the fields that make up the index key, (cr_custid and cr_call) with empty values, we essentially disconnect the correspondence records from their related customer record. These records can be re-used, as evidenced in the crcorra.prg program.

The crcorr.prg program follows:

```
* crcorr.prg
* Process correspondence records for a given customer
PRIVATE localopt
SCREEN scrcorr TOP LOCK
DO WHILE .T.
  * Clear the work area
  @ 1,13 CLEAR
  localopt = 0
  SELECT corr
  @ 6,0 CLEAR
  IF EOF().OR.cr_custid#cust->cu_id && no records for this customer
    * only add option is available
    @ 6,30 GET localopt ;
    PICTURE "@*v ADD"
  ELSE && use all options
    DO crcorr2 WITH "GET"
    @ 6,10 GET localopt PICTURE "@*h ADD;DELETE;FORWARD;BACK"
  ENDIF no records
  READ
  DO CASE
    CASE kmnhit.OR.VAL(SYS(1035))#scrcorr
      @ 6,0 CLEAR
      RETURN
    CASE localopt=1 && add
      * add the new record
      DO crcorra
    CASE localopt=2 && delete
      DO crcorrd
    CASE localopt=3 && forward
      DO crscroll WITH "FORWARD"
    CASE localopt=4 && back
      DO crscroll WITH "BACK"
  ENDCASE
ENDDO
RETURN
* eof crcorr.prg
```

This program is very similar to the standard data entry programs we have already seen. Indeed, most of the new features are hidden in the crcorra.prg, crcorrd.prg, crcorr2.prg, and crscroll.prg programs. One new concept is evidenced in the following line from crcorr.prg:

```
IF EOF().OR.cr_custid#cust->cu_id
```

First, it is not enough to know whether there are any records in the correspondence file. The program must determine whether there are any records on file for the current customer. If there are any records on file for this customer, the crcust.prg program will already have found that record, and so the IF condition above will be true.

Second, cust-> work area identifier deserves some explanation. When working with more than one database simultaneously, any reference to a field that is not contained in the current work area, must be prefaced with a work area identifier. Please see Chapter 5 for more details about work areas.

The display or edit of the current correspondence record is accomplished with the following program:

```
* crmain2.prg
* Displays or gets correspondence records
PARAMETERS action
action=UPPER(action)
@ 1,13 SAY cr_date
@ 2,13 SAY cr_time
@ 3,13 SAY cr_call PICTURE "####"
IF action="SAY"
   @ 4,13 SAY cr_cont
   @ 5,13 SAY cr_desc SIZE 1,68
ELSE
   @ 4,13 GET cr_cont
   @ 5,13 GET cr_desc SIZE 1,68
ENDIF say
RETURN
* eof crcorr2.prg
```

Note that crcust.prg passes the parameter "SAY" to crcorr2.prg while crcorr.prg passes the parameter "GET".

The routines to add and delete correspondence records are as follows:

```
* crcorrd.prg
* Deletes one correspondence record
* See where you will go when this record is gone
currec=RECNO()
* See if the next record is ok
SKIP
IF EOF().OR.cr_custid#cust->cu_id
  * Try the record before this one
  GOTO currec
  SKIP -1
  IF BOF().OR.cr_custid#cust->cu_id
    * no more on file!
    newrec=0
  ELSE && use record before this one
    newrec=RECNO()
  ENDIF no records
ELSE && next record is ok
  newrec=RECNO()
ENDIF next record is not for this customer
GOTO currec
* Erase this record
REPLACE cr_custid WITH "",cr_call WITH 0,;
cr_date WITH CTOD(""),cr_time WITH "",;
cr_desc WITH "",cr_cont WITH ""
IF newrec#0   && at least one record available
  GOTO newrec
ENDIF at least one record available
RETURN
* eof crcorrd.prg
```

```
* crcorra.prg
* Adds one correspondence record
* Find "newest" correspondence
SELECT corr
SEEK cust->cu_id
IF FOUND()
  * Calculate next call number
  newcall = cr_call+1
ELSE && no calls for this customer
  newcall = 1
ENDIF at least one call for this customer
* Look for an empty correspondence record
SEEK SPACE(6)
IF !FOUND() && no empty records on file
  * Create a new correspondence record
```

Correspondence programs

```
    APPEND BLANK
ENDIF no empty records on file
* Put customer number in to "link" this call to
* this customer
REPLACE cr_custid WITH cust->cu_id
* Put new call number in to "sequence" the call
REPLACE cr_call WITH newcall
* Put time and date in for display
REPLACE cr_date WITH DATE(), cr_time WITH TIME()
RETURN
* eof crcorra.prg
```

Note that both programs accommodate the creation and reuse of empty records. Further, note that crcorra.prg immediately places the current customer's id in the newly created correspondence record. There is no option for the user to edit this field, indeed this field is not even displayed. This insures that a correspondence record will always be related to one and only one customer record.

Here is the last of the correspondence programs:

```
* crscroll.prg
* Scrolls the detail screen for crcorr
PARAMETERS direction
PRIVATE xx
direction = UPPER(direction)
SELECT corr
currec=RECNO()
IF direction = "BACK"
   SKIP -1
ELSE && forward toward end of file
   SKIP
ENDIF back toward top of the file
IF cr_custid#cust->cu_id.OR.BOF().OR.EOF()
   * Can't move that way
   ?? CHR(7)
   GOTO currec
ENDIF can't move
RETURN
* eof crscroll.prg
```

Note that the crscroll.prg program will not let the user move to a

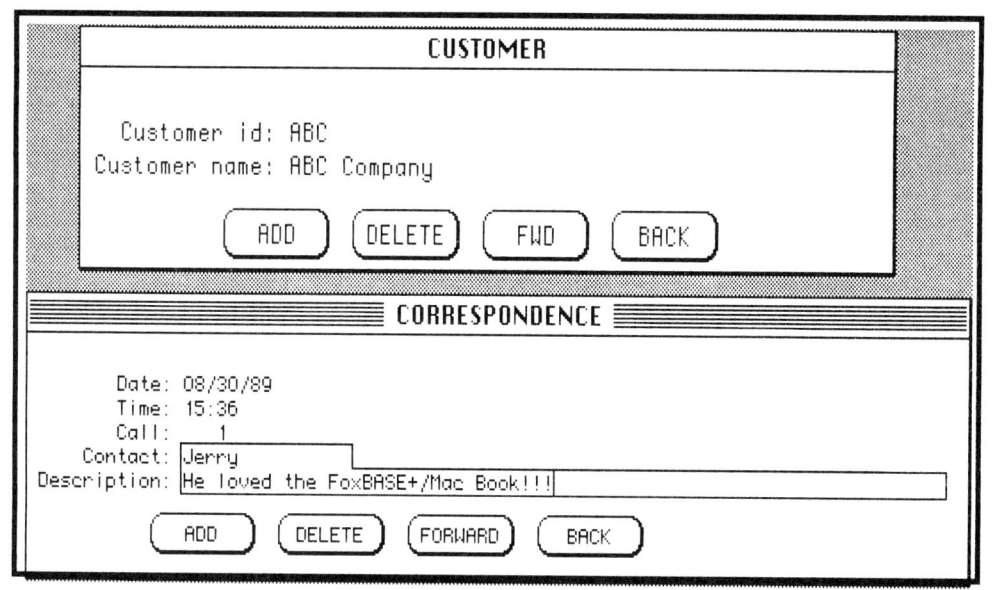

Figure 11-02. Sample Correspondence.

correspondence record that is not related to the current customer. It accomplishes this by comparing the shared data between the correspondence record and the current customer record.

A sample run of the correspondence application appears in Figure 11-02. Note that the screens are small, contain relatively little information, and have substantial room between them on the desktop. Using the techniques in this chapter, you could create applications with more than two screens, with many data entry elements on each screen, and with all manner of Mac-like user interface objects.

12. Enhanced Multi-file Data Entry

I confess. The first draft of the chapter on Multi-file data entry included a much more sophisticated user interface than the one found in the correspondence programs. Filled with calculated PIXEL addressing, invisible buttons, scrolling lists of data, and arrays of record numbers, the first version was much slicker than the correspondence program.

It was also much larger. About 50% larger to be exact. Further, most of the code revolved around PIXEL addressing, and scrolling the correspondence screen so that multiple records could be in view at the same time. I finally decided that this window dressing was immaterial to the main concepts of multi-file data entry. So I rewrote the programs to emphasize relating multiple child records to a single parent record. The result is contained in the previous chapter.

However, I was still left with a rather slick, if imposing, supply of multi-file data entry programs. I could just forget about the slick version. I could try to write another 20+ page chapter on the use of all of the various tools in the slick version (with a commensurate delay in the book's publication). Or I could just provide the code to the slick version, and let you decide whether you need to invest the time required to learn about PIXEL addressing, screen scrolling, and invisible buttons.

As you may have surmised, I opted for the third solution. To whet your appetite for advanced multi-file programming technique, I have included Figure 12-01. Before diving in however, consider that none of these techniques are absolutely vital to the development of normal data entry screens. Further, note that the zr programs all include the same activities as their cr program counterparts. Finally, both the cr and the zr programs use the crcust.dbf and crcorr.dbf databases and indexes.

Here are the programs:

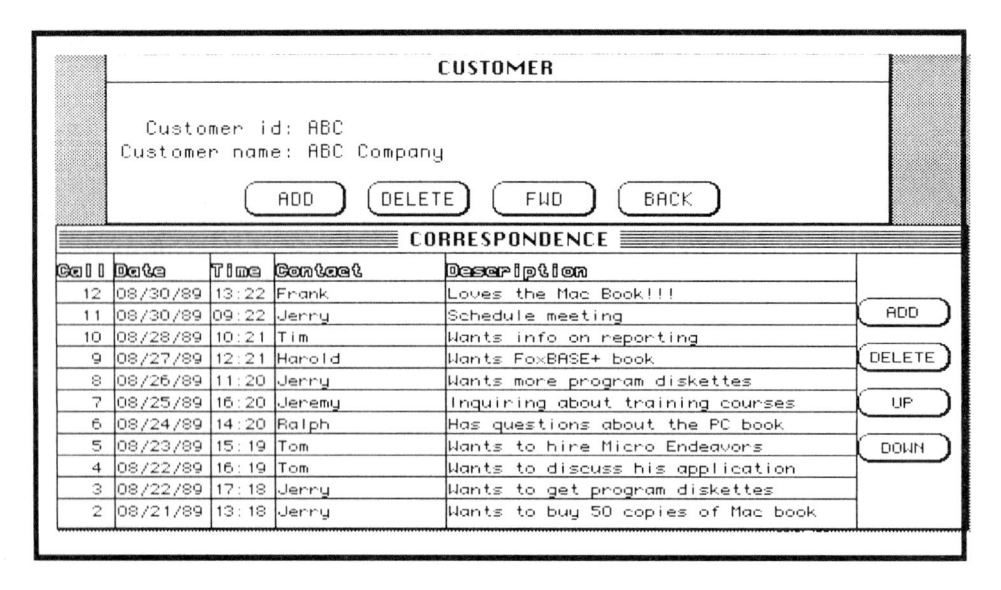

Figure 12-01. Enhanced correspondence screen.

```
* zrmain.prg
* Correspondence entry program
* Allows entry of history of correspondence by customer.
* Setup memory variables for screen numbers
scrcust = 1
scrcorr = 2
* Setup customer screen
SCREEN scrcust FONT "MONACO",12 SIZE 5,60 AT 40,30
CLEAR
SCREEN scrcust TOP TYPE 4 HEAD "CUSTOMER"
* Put prompts up for customer screen
@ 1,0 SAY "  Customer id:"
@ 2,0 SAY "Customer name:"
SCREEN scrcorr FONT "MONACO",9 SIZE 15,82 AT 150,2
CLEAR
SCREEN scrcorr TOP TYPE 4 HEAD "CORRESPONDENCE"
* Make some memory variables for easier pixel addressing
rgmg = VAL(SYS(1024))-60   && location of right margin
wide = VAL(SYS(1028))      && width of "n" in current font
high = VAL(SYS(1023))      && height of screen in pixels
scrwide = VAL(SYS(1024))   && width of screen in pixels
thinover = 15+16+65536     && black, 1 pixel high, overwrite style
* Next line calculates the number of pixels in a "row"
```

```
* for the current font
pixrow = VAL(SYS(1025))+VAL(SYS(1026))+VAL(SYS(1027))/3+3
bline = VAL(SYS(1026))+1 && spot for horizontal lines
colcall = 1
coldate = wide*5+3   && column for date
coltime = wide*14+3  && column for time
colcont = wide*20+3  && column for contact
coldesc = wide*36+3  && column for description
* Setup an array for use by correspondence programs
RELEASE arrcorr
DIMENSION arrcorr(11)
arrcorr=0
* Open databases
SELECT 1
USE crcust INDEX crcust ALIAS cust
SELECT 2
USE crcorr INDEX crcorr ALIAS corr
* Make the customer screen current
SCREEN scrcust TOP LOCK
MENU ON -3,1
DO WHILE .T.
   curscreen = VAL(SYS(1035))
   DO CASE
     CASE kmnhit
       * user selected a menu option
       EXIT
     CASE curscreen = scrcust
       * user clicked on customer screen
       SCREEN scrcust TOP LOCK
       DO zrcust
     CASE curscreen = scrcorr
       * user clicked on correspondence screen
       SCREEN scrcorr TOP LOCK
       DO zrcorr
   ENDCASE what are we working on
ENDDO process
SELECT corr
USE
SELECT cust
USE
RETURN
* eof zrmain.prg
```

```
* zrcust.prg
* Processes customers for crmain.prg
PRIVATE localopt
```

```
DO WHILE .T.
  SCREEN scrcorr
  DO zrcorr1 && paint empty correspondence screen
  localopt=0
  SCREEN scrcust TOP LOCK
  SELECT cust
  IF EOF()
    @ 1,15 CLEAR TO 2,50
    @ 3,20 GET localopt PICTURE "@*h ADD"
  ELSE
    @ 1,15 SAY cu_id
    SCREEN scrcorr
    SELECT corr
    SEEK cust->cu_id
    arrcorr=0
    DO zrcorr2 WITH "SAY",1,11
    SELECT cust
    SCREEN scrcust TOP LOCK
    @ 2,15 GET cu_name
    IF DELETED()
      @ 3,10 GET localopt PICTURE "@*h ADD;RECALL;FWD;BACK"
    ELSE && not deleted
      @ 3,10 GET localopt PICTURE "@*h ADD;DELETE;FWD;BACK"
    ENDIF customer is deleted
  ENDIF no customers on file
  DO WHILE localopt=0.AND.VAL(SYS(1035))=scrcust.AND.;
    !kmnhit
    READ SAVE
  ENDDO wait for local option, screen switch, or menu hit
  CLEAR GETS
  DO CASE
    CASE VAL(SYS(1035))#scrcust.OR.kmnhit
      * screen switch or menu hit
      RETURN
    CASE localopt=1 && add
      * add a customer
      DO zrcusta
    CASE localopt=2 && delete or recall
      IF DELETED()
        RECALL
      ELSE
        * delete the customer
        DO zrcustd
      ENDIF already deleted
    CASE localopt=3 && forward
      SKIP
      IF EOF()
        ?? CHR(7)
```

```
            GOTO BOTTOM
         ENDIF already at the bottom
      CASE localopt=4 && backward
         SKIP -1
         IF BOF()
            ?? CHR(7)
            GOTO TOP
         ENDIF already at the top
   ENDCASE what did the user do to exit the read
ENDDO process customer requests
* eof zrcust.prg
```

```
* zrcusta.prg
* Adds or looks up a customer for crcust
memid = SPACE(6)
@ 3,0 CLEAR
@ 3,0 SAY "Enter new id: " GET memid PICTURE "@!"
READ
@ 3,0 CLEAR
IF memid#SPACE(6) && did not leave blank
   SELECT cust
   SEEK memid
   IF !FOUND() && not a duplicate
      APPEND BLANK
      REPLACE cu_id WITH memid
   ENDIF not a duplicate
ENDIF did not leave blank
RETURN
* eof zrcusta.prg
```

```
* zrcustd.prg
* Deletes a customer AND ASSOCIATED CORRESPONDENCE!
* In a real program, you would ask the user to
* verify that he wants to delete this customer
* First, erase all correspondence for the customer
SELECT corr
SEEK cust->cu_id && look for first corr for this customer
DO WHILE FOUND() && correspondence on file
   REPLACE cr_custid WITH "",cr_call WITH 0,;
   cr_desc WITH "",cr_date WITH CTOD(""),;
   cr_time WITH "",cr_cont WITH ""
   SEEK cust->cu_id && look for the next corr record
ENDDO while correspondence on file for this cust
* Now delete this customer
SELECT cust
DELETE
```

```
* Note that the correspondence is gone for good,
* but the customer can be RECALLed
RETURN
* eof zrcustd.prg
```

```
* zrcorr.prg
* Process correspondence records for a given customer
PRIVATE localopt
SCREEN scrcorr TOP LOCK
* Create an array to hold selection of invisible buttons
RELEASE invbutt
DIMENSION invbutt(11)
* Make all invisible buttons "unselected"
invbutt=0
DO WHILE .T.
  * Put up invisible buttons
  curitem = 0
  xx=1
  DO WHILE xx<=11.AND.arrcorr(xx)#0
    IF invbutt(xx)#0  && User has selected this invisible button
      SELECT corr
      GOTO arrcorr(xx)
      DO zrcorr2 WITH "GET",xx,xx
      curitem = xx
      invbutt(xx)=0
    ELSE  && unselected button
      @ PIXEL xx*pixrow+2,colcall GET invbutt(xx) ;
      PICTURE "@* \F" size pixrow+1,rgmg
    ENDIF user wants to edit this one
    xx=xx+1
  ENDDO put buttons up
  localopt = 0
  IF arrcorr(1)=0 && no records for this customer
    * only add option is available
    @ PIXEL 0,rgmg+1 CLEAR TO high,scrwide
    @ PIXEL pixrow*2,rgmg+1 GET localopt ;
    PICTURE "@*v ADD"
  ELSE && use all options
    @ PIXEL pixrow*2,rgmg+1 GET localopt ;
    PICTURE "@*v ADD;DELETE;UP;DOWN"
  ENDIF no records
  READ OFF
  DO CASE
    CASE kmnhit.OR.VAL(SYS(1035))#scrcorr
      RETURN
    CASE localopt=1 && add
      * add the new record
```

```
      DO zrcorra
      * Redraw the screen
      DO zrcorr2 WITH "SAY",1,11
      * Set invbutton to edit this record
      invbutt=0
      invbutt(1)=1
    CASE localopt=2 && delete
      * See if an item has been chosen
      IF curitem = 0
        ALERT 1 STOP "Please select a correspondence to delete."
      ELSE && already positioned on the record in question
        * delete
        DO zrcorrd
      ENDIF no item selected
    CASE localopt=3 && up
      DO zrscroll WITH "UP"
    CASE localopt=4 && down
      DO zrscroll WITH "DOWN"
  ENDCASE
ENDDO
RETURN
* eof zrcorr.prg
```

```
* zrcorr1.prg
* Paints blank screen for correspondence
SCREEN scrcorr
CLEAR
* Put the headers for the correspondence on screen
@ PIXEL pixrow,colcall SAY "Call" FONT ,9+2048
@ PIXEL pixrow,coldate SAY "Date" FONT ,9+2048
@ PIXEL pixrow,coltime SAY "Time" FONT ,9+2048
@ PIXEL pixrow,colcont SAY "Contact" FONT ,9+2048
@ PIXEL pixrow,coldesc SAY "Description" FONT ,9+2048
* Put vertical lines on screen
@ PIXEL 0,coldate-2 TO high,coldate-2
@ PIXEL 0,coltime-2 TO high,coltime-2
@ PIXEL 0,colcont-2 TO high,colcont-2
@ PIXEL 0,coldesc-2 TO high,coldesc-2
@ PIXEL 0,rgmg TO high,rgmg   && right hand border
RETURN
* eof zrcorr1.prg
```

```
* zrmain2.prg
* Displays or gets correspondence records
```

```
PARAMETERS action,start,end
PRIVATE mrow
mrow=start
action=UPPER(action)
SELECT corr
DO WHILE mrow<=end.AND.cr_custid=cust->cu_id
  * Put a horizontal line one pixel below the previous line
  @ PIXEL mrow*pixrow+bline,0 TO ;
  mrow*pixrow+bline,rgmg STYLE thinover
  * Put the three "look only" fields up for this record
  @ PIXEL (mrow+1)*pixrow+1,colcall SAY cr_call
  @ PIXEL ROW(0),coldate SAY cr_date
  @ PIXEL ROW(0),coltime SAY cr_time
  IF action="SAY"
    @ PIXEL ROW(0),colcont SAY cr_cont
    @ PIXEL ROW(0),coldesc SAY cr_desc PICTURE "@S35"
    arrcorr(mrow)=recno()
    IF start#end
      SKIP
    ENDIF not a one record display request
  ELSE
    * Put up the gets
    @ PIXEL ROW(0),colcont GET cr_cont
    @ PIXEL ROW(0),coldesc GET cr_desc PICTURE "@S35"
  ENDIF
  mrow=mrow+1
ENDDO display the requested number of records
* Reset array of record numbers if screen is unfilled
DO WHILE mrow<=end
  arrcorr(mrow)=0
  mrow=mrow+1
ENDDO reset array of record numbers
RETURN
* eof zrcorr2.prg
```

```
* zrcorra.prg
* Adds one correspondence record
* Find "newest" correspondence
SELECT corr
SEEK cust->cu_id
IF FOUND()
  * Calculate next call number
  newcall = cr_call+1
ELSE && no calls for this customer
  newcall = 1
ENDIF at least one call for this customer
* Look for an empty correspondence record
```

```
  SEEK SPACE(6)
  IF !FOUND() && no empty records on file
    * Create a new correspondence record
    APPEND BLANK
  ENDIF no empty records on file
  * Put customer number in to "link" this call to
  * this customer
  REPLACE cr_custid WITH cust->cu_id
  * Put new call number in to "sequence" the call
  REPLACE cr_call WITH newcall
  * Put time and date in for display
  REPLACE cr_date WITH DATE(), cr_time WITH TIME()
  RETURN
  * eof zrcorra.prg
```

```
* zrcorrd.prg
* Deletes one correspondence record
* See where you will go when this record is gone
currec=RECNO()
* See if the next record is ok
SKIP
IF EOF().OR.cr_custid#cust->cu_id
  * Try the record before this one
  GOTO currec
  SKIP -1
  IF BOF().OR.cr_custid#cust->cu_id
    * no more on file!
    newrec=0
  ELSE && use record before this one
    newrec=RECNO()
  ENDIF no records
ELSE && next record is ok
  newrec=RECNO()
ENDIF next record is not for this customer
GOTO currec
* Erase this record
REPLACE cr_custid WITH "",cr_call WITH 0,;
cr_date WITH CTOD(""),cr_time WITH "",;
cr_desc WITH "",cr_cont WITH ""
DO zrcorr1 && paint blank correspondence screen
IF newrec=0   && no more recs for this customer
  * Set arrcorr array
  arrcorr = 0
ELSE
  GOTO newrec
  DO zrcorr2 WITH "SAY",1,11
ENDIF no record to go to
```

273

```
RETURN
* eof zrcorrd.prg
```

```
* zrcust.prg
* Processes customers for crmain.prg
PRIVATE localopt
DO WHILE .T.
  SCREEN scrcorr
  DO zrcorr1 && paint empty correspondence screen
  localopt=0
  SCREEN scrcust TOP LOCK
  SELECT cust
  IF EOF()
    @ 1,15 CLEAR TO 2,50
    @ 3,20 GET localopt PICTURE "@*h ADD"
  ELSE
    @ 1,15 SAY cu_id
    SCREEN scrcorr
    SELECT corr
    SEEK cust->cu_id
    arrcorr=0
    DO zrcorr2 WITH "SAY",1,11
    SELECT cust
    SCREEN scrcust TOP LOCK
    @ 2,15 GET cu_name
    IF DELETED()
      @ 3,10 GET localopt PICTURE "@*h ADD;RECALL;FWD;BACK"
    ELSE && not deleted
      @ 3,10 GET localopt PICTURE "@*h ADD;DELETE;FWD;BACK"
    ENDIF customer is deleted
  ENDIF no customers on file
  DO WHILE localopt=0.AND.VAL(SYS(1035))=scrcust.AND.;
    !kmnhit
    READ SAVE
  ENDDO wait for local option, screen switch, or menu hit
  CLEAR GETS
  DO CASE
    CASE VAL(SYS(1035))#scrcust.OR.kmnhit
      * screen switch or menu hit
      RETURN
    CASE localopt=1 && add
      * add a customer
      DO zrcusta
    CASE localopt=2 && delete or recall
      IF DELETED()
        RECALL
```

```
      ELSE
        * delete the customer
        DO zrcustd
      ENDIF already deleted
    CASE localopt=3 && forward
      SKIP
      IF EOF()
        ?? CHR(7)
        GOTO BOTTOM
      ENDIF already at the bottom
    CASE localopt=4 && backward
      SKIP -1
      IF BOF()
        ?? CHR(7)
        GOTO TOP
      ENDIF already at the top
  ENDCASE what did the user do to exit the read
ENDDO process customer requests
* eof zrcust.prg
```

```
* zrscroll.prg
* Scrolls the detail screen for zrcorr
PARAMETERS direction
PRIVATE xx
direction = UPPER(direction)
SELECT corr
IF direction = "DOWN"
  * Goto the first record on the screen
  IF arrcorr(1)=0
    * no records on screen
  ELSE  && at least one record on screen
    GOTO arrcorr(1)
    SKIP -1
    IF cr_custid=cust->cu_id.AND.!BOF()
      * Found one!
      SCROLL PIXEL pixrow*2-11,0,high,rgmg-1,-pixrow
      * Reset the arrcorr array
      xx=11
      DO WHILE xx>1
        arrcorr(xx)=arrcorr(xx-1)
        xx=xx-1
      ENDDO shuffle down
      * Note: crcorr2 will place the record number in
      * arcorr(1)
      DO zrcorr2 WITH "SAY",1,1
      @ PIXEL 0,coldate-2 TO high,coldate-2
      @ PIXEL 0,coltime-2 TO high,coltime-2
```

```
         @ PIXEL 0,colcont-2 TO high,colcont-2
         @ PIXEL 0,coldesc-2 TO high,coldesc-2
      ELSE && already at the top
        ?? CHR(7)
      ENDIF found one
   ENDIF at least one on screen
ELSE && direction must be up
   * Goto the last record on the screen
   IF arrcorr(11)=0 && not a full screen
     ?? CHR(7)
   ELSE
     * Goto last record on the screen
     GOTO arrcorr(11)
     SKIP
     IF cr_custid=cust->cu_id.AND.!EOF()
       * Found one!
       * Reset the arrcorr array
       xx=1
       DO WHILE xx<11
         arrcorr(xx)=arrcorr(xx+1)
         xx=xx+1
       ENDDO shuffle up
       SCROLL PIXEL pixrow*3-9,0,high,rgmg-1,pixrow
       * Note crcorr2 will place the record number in
       * arcorr(11)
       DO zrcorr2 WITH "SAY",11,11
       @ PIXEL 0,coldate-2 TO high,coldate-2
       @ PIXEL 0,coltime-2 TO high,coltime-2
       @ PIXEL 0,colcont-2 TO high,colcont-2
       @ PIXEL 0,coldesc-2 TO high,coldesc-2
     ELSE  && no more
        ?? CHR(7)
     ENDIF found one
ENDIF DOWN
RETURN
* eof zrscroll.prg
```

13. Reports

One of the primary goals of most database management applications is to generate useful reports. Accordingly, the goal of this chapter is to help you generate useful reports. To accomplish this goal, we will examine the following topics:

- The use of the printer instead of the screen for output.

- The generation of page breaks, headers, and page numbers.

- The sequencing of reports with indexes or by SORTing.

- The selection of records based on a criteria using the LOCATE, CONTINUE, and SET FILTER TO commands demonstrated in earlier chapters.

- The creation of totals and subtotals.

In subsequent chapters we will investigate the creation of multi-file and multi-column reports, as well as the use of the FoxReport report generator. However, the basic concepts demonstrated in this chapter are prerequisites for the more advanced topics in the next two chapters. As a result, it is important to enter the report programs in this chapter so that you can become familiar with standard report writing logic.

Preliminaries

Reports require data. Rather than generating entire applications to fill database with information, and wasting pages showing lists of sample data however, we will depend on you to fill the sample databases referenced in this chapter with information. You can write small data entry applications like the ones shown in chapter 8, or you can use the APPEND command directly from the command window.

When used without a clause, the APPEND command uses a default data entry screen to allow the operator to create new records. This approach is unacceptable for inclusion in sophisticated programs because it provide the programmer with too little control over the screen and the validation of input. However, the bare APPEND command is helpful when programmers are trying to fill their database with test data for the purpose of testing report programs.

When you need to change the data in some or your test records, you can use the EDIT command in the same way that you use the bare APPEND command. The EDIT command features the same strengths and weaknesses as the bare APPEND command.

Every report needs lbrepo.prg

Our first report will list all of the information in the students database by last name. Sometimes called a file dump because all of the information in the file is printed, this type of report is required by most applications.

Here is the code for the first report:

```
* repo1.prg
* First report
* Call the lbrepo.prg UDF to setup the printer, check
* printer status, etc.
DO WHILE lbrepo("First Student Report")
  * Open the student database with the name.idx to present the
  * database in st_name order.
  * The name.idx index is assumed to exist and to be indexed on
  * st_name.
  SELECT 1
  USE students INDEX name.idx ALIAS stu
  * Make sure you are on the first record of the file
  SELECT stu
  GOTO TOP
    * Preset the page and line numbers, and the time of the report
```

```
  page = 1
  repline = 99
  reptime = TIME()
  * Print the first page header
  DO repo1h WITH page,repline,reptime
  * Process all records in the students file
  DO WHILE .NOT. EOF()
    * Check for a page break
    IF repline > 57
      * Print a page header
      DO repo1h WITH page,repline,reptime
    ENDIF need another page
    * Print one record
    @ repline,5 SAY st_name
    @ repline,25 SAY st_age
    @ repline,30 SAY st_school
    @ repline,50 SAY st_phone
    * Move to next record
    SKIP
    * Move to next line on page
    repline = repline + 1
  ENDDO process all records in the file
  * Close students.dbf
  SELECT stu
  USE
ENDDO while wants to print
RETURN
* eof repo1.prg
```

The first new idea in repo1.prg is the use of the lbrepo.prg UDF. The lbrepo.prg UDF will be used in most of our report programs, so here is the listing:

```
* lbrepo.prg
* Standard screen for report prompting
* Sample usage:
**   DO WHILE lbrepo("Report name")
**       commands to print report
**   ENDDO while lbrepo
PARAMETERS repdesc
PRIVATE localopt
SET DEVICE TO SCREEN
SET PRINT OFF && end any prior print jobs
SET PRINTER TO
```

Every report needs lbrepo.prg

```
SCREEN 1 TOP TYPE 4 FONT "monaco",9
SCREEN 1 HEAD "Print "+repdesc
SCREEN 1 SIZE 5,70 AT 0,0 LOCK
CLEAR
@ 1,1 SAY "Please select a menu option, or choose "+;
 "one of the text buttons below."
localopt=0
@ 2,2 GET localopt PICTURE ;
"@*h SET PAGE;SET PRINTER;GO PRINTER;GO FILE"
DO WHILE localopt<3 .AND. !kmnhit
  READ SAVE
  DO CASE
    CASE localopt=1
      * call page setup dialog
      null=SYS(1037)
    CASE localopt=2
      * call print dialog
      null=SYS(1038)
    CASE localopt=3
      * Wants to print to printer
      SET PRINTER TO
    CASE localopt=4
      * Wants to print to file
      thisfile=PUTFILE("Name of Printer file",;
      "","txt")
      SET PRINTER TO &thisfile
  ENDCASE
ENDDO until print or menu
CLEAR GETS
IF localopt>2
  * wants to print
  CLEAR
  @ 2,1 SAY "Printing: "+repdesc FONT ,12+kfo
  * Prepare to check for missing printer
  ON ERROR prnerr=ERROR()
  prnerr=0
  SET DEVICE TO PRINT
  * Return to standard error trapping
  ON ERROR DO bkerror WITH ERROR(),MESSAGE(),MESSAGE(1),SYS(16)
  IF prnerr#0
    * Message, and don't print
    ALERT 1 STOP "Printer is not ready. Report aborted."
    RETURN .F.
  ELSE
    RETURN .T.
  ENDIF an error occurred
ELSE
  RETURN .F.
```

```
ENDIF wants to print
* eof lbrepo.prg
```

This little program performs several common report program services. First, lbrepo.prg makes sure that the output of any @...SAY commands is directed to the screen by issuing the following command:

`SET DEVICE TO SCREEN`

Next, lbrepo.prg flushes any current print job to the printer by issuing the following command:

`SET PRINT OFF`

Next, lbrepo.prg provides the user with a screen that includes a title that describes the current report. The content of the title is determined by the message passed to lbrepo.prg by the calling program.

Next, lbrepo.prg alerts the user of the opportunity to select a menu option from the standard menu bar. Then, lbrepo.prg provides four local options, and waits for the user to select a local option or a menu option.

The first of the four local options offers the opportunity to set the page layout. This is accomplished via the SYS(1037) function, which calls forward the familiar Macintosh page setup dialog. The SYS(1037) function returns "0" if the user selects cancel, "1" if the user selects OK, and "-1" if there is an error.

The second option uses the SYS(1038) function to call forward the standard Macintosh printer setup dialog. SYS(1038) returns the same values as SYS(1037).

The third option is the most common selection, and allows the user to begin printing the report. The fourth option uses the PUTFILE() function to prompt the user for a file name, and then directs FoxBASE+/Mac to send all output destined for the printer to the file named by the user.

Every report needs lbrepo.prg

Next, if the user has chosen to print the report, lbrepo.prg uses the following set of commands direct the output of @...SAY commands to the printer, and to see if the printer is available for printing:

```
ON ERROR prnerr=ERROR()
prnerr=0
SET DEVICE TO PRINT
* Return to standard error trapping
ON ERROR DO bkerror WITH ERROR(),MESSAGE(),MESSAGE(1),SYS(16)
IF prnerr#0
  * Message, and don't print
  ALERT 1 STOP "Printer is not ready. Report aborted."
  RETURN .F.
ELSE
  RETURN .T.
ENDIF an error occurred
```

SET DEVICE TO PRINT directs the output of @...SAY commands to the printer. Also, when the command SET DEVICE TO PRINT is issued, FoxBASE+/Mac tries to prepare the printer for output. If the printer is unavailable, an error is generated. The command ON ERROR prnerr=ERROR() traps this error, and causes the number of the error to be placed in the prnerr variable.

Therefore, if no error occurred when FoxBASE+/Mac tried to prepare the printer, prnerr will still equal 0, and the lbrepo.prg UDF will return a TRUE value. However, if an error occurs when FoxBASE+/Mac tries to prepare the printer, (e.g. the printer is not turned on or is out of paper), prnerr will not equal 0, and lbrepo.prg will return a FALSE value.

Note that if the user has exited the DO WHILE local option loop by selecting a menu option, lbrepo.prg will return a false value. Further, our bkmain.prg program will be able to see the newly selected menu bar and menu option when the report program returns control.

Returning to repo1.prg, we see how the lbrepo.prg UDF works with most report programs. The first time the DO WHILE lbrepo() command is encountered, lbrepo is entered, and the user is given the opportunity to print the report, or select a menu option. If lbrepo returns a false value because the user selected another menu option, the commands inside the DO WHILE lbrepo() loop will not be executed, and our event driven program will proceed with the option selected by the user.

If the user chose to print, lbrepo.prg will have directed output of the @...SAY commands to the printer, and the commands inside the DO WHILE lbrepo() loop will be executed. Then, when the program hits the ENDDO associated with the DO WHILE lbrepo() command, the lbrepo() program will be reentered, and lbrepo will SET DEVICE TO SCREEN, and SET PRINTER OFF, thereby ending the print job.

Note that if the command SET DEVICE TO SCREEN is not issued, all subsequent efforts to send messages to the screen via the @...SAY command would send messages to the printer instead. Further, nothing will print on the printer until the SET PRINTER OFF command is issued.

The first report

Now that we understand the mechanics of directing information to the printer, let's see how the repo1.prg program collects and disseminates that information.

After placing the student file in USE, repo1.prg prepares to process all records in the students file by issuing the following commands:

```
GOTO TOP
DO WHILE .NOT. EOF()
```

The command, DO WHILE .NOT.EOF(), is familiar to FoxBASE+/Mac programmers because some version of the command is included in virtually every report program written in FoxBASE+/Mac. This loop statement, combined with a SKIP command, causes the program to process records one at a time until the bottom of the file is reached. (Note: EOF() stands for "End Of File.")

The next new idea in the repo1.prg program is the handling of new pages. The number of lines on a page is determined by the font and point size used by the printer.

FoxBASE+/Mac uses the default font and point size of the current screen to setup a default font and point size for the printer.

Based on the font and point size, we know how many lines will fit on one page. In our example, we have chosen to print up to 57 lines per page. We keep track of the current printer line in the variable repline.

That is, after every line of the report, we add 1 to the value of repline. Then, before printing any new line in the report, we check the current printer line with the following command:

```
IF repline > 57
```

If repline is greater than 57, indicating that it is time for a new page, we call the following program to generate a page header, increment the page number counter, and establish the next line for record information:

```
* repo1h.prg
* Prints page header for repo1.prg
PARAMETERS page, line, time
@ 1,0 SAY "Date "+DTOC(DATE())
rephead = "List of all Students by name"
* Center the header on the first line of the page
@ 1,42-LEN(rephead)/2 SAY rephead
@ 1,72 SAY "Page "+LTRIM(STR(page))
@ 2,0 SAY "Time "+time
* Put column headers on page
@ 4,5 SAY "Name"
@ 4,25 SAY "Age"
@ 4,30 SAY "School"
@ 4,50 SAY "Phone"
@ 5,5 SAY "===="
@ 5,25 SAY "==="
@ 5,30 SAY "======"
@ 5,50 SAY "====="
* Set current print line
```

```
line = 6
* Increment the page counter
page = page + 1
RETURN
* eof repo1h.prg
```

The final service that repo1h.prg provides is the execution of a page eject on the current printer. This is accomplished by sending a row coordinate to the printer that is less than the current printer row. For example, if the program reaches the 58th line on the first page of the report, and still has more records to print, the IF repline > 57 statement will be triggered, and the repo1h.prg program will be called.

Since the first @...SAY statement in repo1h.prg directs output to row 1, and since row 1 is less than the current printer position of row 58, a page eject is issued, and printing resumes on the next page.

Note that this automatic page eject feature can be overridden by including a STYLE clause with any @...SAY commands directed to the printer. When a STYLE clause is included with an @...SAY command that is directed to the printer, the content of the @...SAY command will be placed on the current page, regardless of the coordinates of any previous @...SAY commands. In the following example, the words "George", "Tom", and "Harry", would be printed on three separate pieces of paper:

```
SET DEVICE TO PRINT
 @ 5,5 SAY "GEORGE"
 @ 4,5 SAY "TOM"
 @ 3,5 SAY "HARRY"
```

In the following example, the same words would all appear on the same piece of paper:

```
SET DEVICE TO PRINT
 @ 5,5 SAY "GEORGE" STYLE 0
 @ 4,5 SAY "TOM" STYLE 65536
 @ 3,5 SAY "HARRY" STYLE 65536
```

The first report

If you do include a STYLE clause with each of your printed @...SAYs, you will need to issue an EJECT command to explicitly direct the printer to begin printing on a new page.

Of fonts and layouts

As stated above, the default font and point size for the currently active screen will be used as the defaults for printed output. Therefore, FoxBASE+/Mac will use the size of the current default font and point size to determine the location of rows and columns when @...SAY commands do not use PIXEL addressing.

This arrangement works well when the programmer selects a nonproportional font such as Monaco or Courier. However, problems can arise when the programmer mixes fonts and point sizes on the same report, or uses a non-proportional font.

In a nonproportional font, all of the characters consume the same amount of horizontal space. Proportional fonts however, use different amounts of horizontal space for different size characters. Try the following commands from the command window to get a better feel for proportional vs. nonproportional spacing:

```
SCREEN 1 TOP SIZE 20,80 FONT "MONACO",9
CLEAR
 @ 5,5 SAY "MMMMMM" FONT "MONACO",9
 @ 6,5 SAY "iiiiii" FONT "MONACO",9
 @ 8,5 SAY "MMMMMM" FONT "GENEVA",9
 @ 9,5 SAY "iiiiii" FONT "GENEVA",9
```

Note that the capital "M" and lower case "i" take up the same amount of horizontal space in the nonproportional Monaco font, while the two letters use significantly different amounts of vertical space in the proportional Geneva font.

As you can imagine, the use of proportional fonts can make it very difficult for the programmer to line up columns of information. My suggestion is to use nonproportional fonts in those reports that include columns of information.

Alternatively, you could leave extra space between columns, or use PIXEL addressing to position your output. The remainder of the reports in this chapter and the next chapter use the nonproportional Monaco font and row and column addressing.

Programmers interested in using multiple fonts and point sizes on the same page will want to investigate the PROW(0), PCOL(0), SYS(1023), SYS(1024), SYS(1039), SYS(1040), SYS(1025), SYS(1026), and SYS(1027) functions.

The case of SORTing vs. INDEXing

Our first modification of the repo1.prg program will involve the use of the SORT command to produce a report sequenced by st_name. Though this method will involve extra programming, it often provides superior performance compared to the use of a file with an open index.

In an earlier chapter we created an index file to make the students.dbf appear to be in order by name. In the first version of repo1.prg we used that index file to provide the same service for our report program. An alternative to the use of an updated index file is illustrated in the following version of repo1a.prg:

```
* repo1a.prg
* Demonstrates the use of the SORT command
* Call the lbrepo.prg UDF to setup the printer, check
* printer status, etc.
DO WHILE lbrepo("SORTed Student Report")
  * Open the student database
  USE students ALIAS stu
  * SORT the students database
  SORT ON st_name TO newstu
```

```
* Open the database created by the SORT
USE newstu ALIAS stu
* Direct output of @...SAY commands to printer
SET DEVICE TO PRINTER
* Make sure you are on the first record of the file
SELECT stu
GOTO TOP
* Preset the page and line numbers, and the time of the report
page = 1
repline = 99
reptime = TIME()
* Print the first page header
DO repolh WITH page,repline,reptime
* Process all records in the students file
DO WHILE .NOT. EOF()
   * Check for a page break
   IF repline > 57
      * Print a page header
      DO repolh WITH page,repline,reptime
   ENDIF need another page
   * Print one record
   @ repline,5 SAY st_name
   @ repline,25 SAY st_age
   @ repline,30 SAY st_school
   @ repline,50 SAY st_phone
   * Move to next record
   SKIP
   * Move to next line on page
   repline = repline + 1
ENDDO process all records in the file
* Close the temporary database file
SELECT stu
USE
* Remove the temporary file
ERASE newstu.dbf
ENDDO lbrepo
RETURN
* eof repola.prg
```

As you can see, this method requires extra work on the programmer's part. It also requires more disk space than the use of an open index, and if offers less flexibility in determining the sequence of the records. If SORTing has all of these shortcomings, why bother with the practice at all?

The answer is performance. Simply put, SKIPping through an unindexed file is much faster than SKIPping through an indexed file. Therefore, in most circumstances, it is faster to create a SORTed file and process that SORTed file, than it is to simply process an unSORTed file with an active index. Before we discuss the pros and cons of each method, however, let's investigate the main differences between the two approaches.

INDEXing creates an .idx file that is meant to be used in conjunction with a database file. That .idx file will be updated by any alterations to its associated database file, provided the index file is open at the time of the alteration.

SORTing creates an entirely new .dbf file that contains copies of records from the original database file. The records in the database file created by the SORT command will be sequenced in accordance with the arguments supplied in the SORT command. For example, the newstu.dbf database in the repo1a.prg program will contain all of the records that are contained in the students.dbf, but the records in the newstu.dbf database will be in order by st_name. Unlike the .idx file created by the INDEX command, the new database file created by the SORT command will be unaffected by any alterations made to the database file from which the new database file was created.

The advantages of SORTing are:

- Substantially increased speed for sequential processing.

- No need to keep an extra index open during data entry, thereby improving data entry speed.

- It is easier to SORT in descending order than it is to index in descending order.

- In multiuser environments it is often advantageous to allow one user to process a SORTed version of a file, while allowing another user to process another SORTed version of the file, while allowing another user to enter data into the original version of the file.

The disadvantages of SORTing are:

- Greater use of disk space. This can be critical with large databases since FoxBASE+/Mac often requires as much as three times the disk space consumed by the original file to create a SORTed version of the file.

- Inability to use expressions in the SORT argument. This means that files can only be SORTed on fields, not calculations or parts of fields as is possible with INDEXing.

- Extra programming is required.

The increase in speed realized by the SORT method id most commonly encountered when:

- The database file is larger than 100 records.

- There is plenty of disk space available.

- The records in the original database are substantially out of order.

- The report excludes some records based on a condition.

The selection of the most efficient method is only critical in applications that deal with large database files. In smaller files FoxBASE+/Mac will implement both methods so quickly that the difference will be negligible. To save typing then, most of our examples will use the INDEX file method of report processing.

The mechanics of SORTing

SORTing on multiple fields is a matter of listing the fields in question and then separating those fields with commas. In the following example, the students.dbf is sorted by school and then by student name:

```
USE students
SORT ON st_school,st_name TO schname
```

When a report only requires the values of a few of the fields in a large database, the following type of command can be used to create a SORTed file that contains only the fields required for the report:

```
SORT ON st_school,st_name TO schname FIELDS ;
st_age,st_school
```

This command would create an schname.dbf file that includes only the st_age and st_school fields.

SORTing in descending rather than ascending order is accomplished by adding a /D switch to individual fields in the fields list as follows:

```
SORT ON st_name,st_age/D TO nameage
```

This command would create a nameage.dbf file in ascending name by descending age order.

The SORT command can be directed to ignore case differences by adding the /C switch as follows:

```
SORT ON st_name/C TO updown
```

These and other SORT command options are discussed in the FoxBASE+/Mac manual.

Totals and statistics

Adding totals and other statistics to the report program is a matter of declaring and maintaining a few extra memory variables. For example, let's assume that we want the report to include a summary of the number of students, the average age of the students, the age of the youngest student, and the age of the oldest student. Here is the repo1.prg program modified to include these statistics:

```
* repo1b.prg
* Demonstrate totals
* Call the lbrepo.prg UDF to setup the printer, check
* printer status, etc.
DO WHILE lbrepo("Student Totals")
  USE students INDEX name.idx ALIAS stu
  * Make sure you are on the first record of the file
  SELECT stu
  GOTO TOP
  * Preset the page and line numbers, and the time of the report
  page = 1
  repline = 99
  reptime = TIME()
  * Print the first page header
  DO repo1h WITH page,repline,reptime
  * Setup variables for statistics
  STORE 0 TO oldest,avgage,number
  STORE 99999 TO youngest
  * Process all records in the students file
  DO WHILE .NOT. EOF()
    * Check for a page break
    IF repline > 57
      * Print a page header
      DO repo1h WITH page,repline,reptime
    ENDIF need another page
    * Calculate number of students printed
    number = number + 1
    * Calculate avgage by accumulating total ages
    * We will get the average by dividing avgage by number
    * at the end of the report
    avgage = avgage + st_age
    * Calculate oldest
    oldest = MAX(oldest,st_age)
    * Calculate youngest
    youngest = MIN(youngest,st_age)
```

```
      * Print one record
      @ repline,5 SAY st_name
      @ repline,25 SAY st_age
      @ repline,30 SAY st_school
      @ repline,50 SAY st_phone
      * Move to next record
      SKIP
      * Move to next line on page
      repline = repline + 1
   ENDDO process all records in the file
   * Print totals
   @ repline,0 SAY REPLICATE("=",80)
   repline = repline + 1
   @ repline,0 SAY "Number of students: "
   @ repline,PCOL()+1 SAY number PICTURE "##,###"
   @ repline,40 SAY "Average Age: "
   @ repline,PCOL()+1 SAY avgage/number PICTURE "##.##"
   @ repline+1,0 SAY "Youngest student: "
   @ repline+1,PCOL()+1 SAY youngest PICTURE "##"
   @ repline+1,40 SAY "Oldest student: "
   @ repline+1,PCOL()+1 SAY oldest PICTURE "##"
   SELECT stu
   USE
ENDDO lbrepo
RETURN
* eof repolb.prg
```

This program demonstrates the usual steps required to generate totals for a report. Those steps are:

- Assign some variables to hold the values for the totals.

- As each record is accessed, use some value in the record to accumulate totals.

- When all records have been processed, print the totals.

Processing selected records

If you are using the open index method of placing records in the correct sequence, the issuance of a SET FILTER TO command following the opening of the database file will suffice to prevent unwanted records from being reported. If, for example, the report should only list those students who are at least 12 years old, the following command would secure the desired result:

`SET FILTER TO st_age >= 12`

Using this method it is important to remember that **the SET FILTER TO command only takes effect when the record pointer is moved.** The repo1.prg program already accommodates this idiosyncracy by issuing a GOTO TOP statement before printing begins.

If you are using the SORT method of placing records in the correct sequence you could use the SET FILTER TO command, or you could add a conditional expression to the SORT command. The following SORT command would produce a newstu.dbf file that contains only those students who are at least 12 years old:

`SORT ON st_name TO newstu FOR st_age >= 12`

If your conditions are too complicated to fit on one line, you could combine a LOCATE/CONTINUE command with the SET FILTER TO or SORT...FOR commands to expand the degree of selectivity. Or, you could issue several SORT...FOR commands. Finally, if you conditions are too complicated still, you could use a series of nested IF...ENDIF statements to prevent the printing of unwanted records.

Let the user choose

In Chapter 10 I introduced the GETEXPR command. This command calls forth a dialog box that allows your user to use field names, FoxBASE+/Mac functions, variable names, and all of the FoxBASE+/Mac operators to create conditional statements. The resultant expression is stored in a memory variable that you can use. For example, the following commands would allow the user to create his own criteria for printing students:

```
GETEXPR "Which students should be printed?" TO ;
memvar TYPE "L;Invalid criteria"
SET FILTER TO &memvar.
```

See Chapter 10 for screen shots of GETEXPR at work. If the user does not select a criteria, memvar will be blank.

Subtotals

Reports are frequently required to include subtotals as well as totals. For example it would not be unusual to request that the student report list the students by school, with subtotals after each school listing. To simplify matters, the report will only need to total and subtotal the number of students. The following program uses the schname.idx index and a nested DO WHILE loop to accomplish these goals:

```
* repo1c.prg
* Demonstrates subtotals
* Call the lbrepo.prg UDF to setup the printer, check
* printer status, etc.
DO WHILE lbrepo("Student Subtotals")
   * Open the student database with the schname.idx to present the
   * database in st_school+st_name order.
   USE students INDEX schname.idx ALIAS stu
   * Make sure you are on the first record of the file
   SELECT stu
   GOTO TOP
   * Preset the page and line numbers, and the time of the report
   page = 1
   repline = 99
   reptime = TIME()
   * Setup variables for total statistics
   number = 0
   * Print the first page header
   DO repo1hc WITH page,repline,reptime
   * Process all records in the students file
   DO WHILE .NOT. EOF()
      * Print the name of the school
```

```
      @ repline,0 SAY st_school
      repline = repline + 1
      * Setup subtotals for this school
      scnumber = 0
      thisschool = st_school
      * Process all students for this school
      DO WHILE st_school=thisschool .AND. (.NOT.EOF())
         * Check for a page break
         IF repline > 57
            * Print a page header
            DO repolhc WITH page,repline,reptime
         ENDIF need another page
         * Calculate subtotals
         scnumber = scnumber + 1
         * Print one record
         @ repline,25 SAY st_name
         @ repline,45 SAY st_age
         @ repline,50 SAY st_phone
         * Move to next record
         SKIP
         * Move to next line on page
         repline = repline + 1
      ENDDO process all for this school
      * Accumulate report totals
      number = number + scnumber
      * Print subtotals for this school
      @ repline,3 SAY "# students for "+TRIM(thisschool)+" = "
      @ repline,PCOL()+1 SAY scnumber PICTURE "@B ##,###"
      repline = repline + 2
   ENDDO process all records in the file
   * Print report totals
   @ repline,3 SAY "Total students = "
   @ repline,PCOL()+1 SAY number PICTURE "@B ##,###"
   SELECT stu
   USE
ENDDO lbrepo
RETURN
* eof repol.prg
```

Because the records in the students.dbf index schname.idx appear in order by school and then by name, students from the same school will be grouped together. Therefore, we can setup a loop like the following to process all of the students for a school:

```
DO WHILE st_school=thisschool .AND.(.NOT.EOF())
```

In other words, we know that when a record is encountered that represents a new school, all of the records for the current school have been processed. This grouping of items to be subtotaled is the essence of generating subtotals in reports.

The mechanics of generating subtotals in reports usually include the following steps:

- Setup variables to hold report grandtotals

- Setup a loop to process all of the records in the file.

- Assign null values to subtotal variables

- Assign the value of the field or expression that represents the current group to a memory variable.

- Setup a loop to process records until the field or expression in the current expression becomes different from the value stored in the group memory variable, or until the end of the file is reached.

- Print a record.

- Accumulate subtotal information.

- When the group loop is complete, print the subtotals, and use the subtotals to accumulate grandtotals.

- When all of the records in the file have been processed, print the report grand totals.

What about subsubtotals and beyond? The formula remains the same with multiple levels of subtotals. Each subtotal group receives a DO WHILE loop, and a set of subtotal variables. After the ENDDO statement for each level of subtotals, print the subtotals and accumulate values for the next higher level of subtotals.

Regardless of the number of levels of subtotals however, there is usually only one SKIP or CONTINUE command in the program, and that command is included in the lowest level DO WHILE loop.

14 Advanced Reporting

In this chapter we will expand your knowledge of common reporting techniques. As in Chapter 13, there will be relatively few new commands to learn. Rather, the emphasis will be placed on organizing the commands you already know to produce more sophisticated reports.

Specifically, you will learn how to:

- Use the descriptions in a lookup table to make a simple report more descriptive.

- List all of the children of a record in a parent file in a report.

- Send special control characters to the printer to produce special printing effects.

- Generate statistics with single FoxBASE+ commands.

- Print multi-column reports that snake up and down the page.

- Generate subtotals when records in a file are not grouped by subtotal category.

Using the content of lookup tables

In Chapter 10 we investigated the use of lookup tables to improve data validation. In this section we will investigate ways to use those lookup tables to enhance our simple reports.

Frequently, programmers are called upon to generate reports that perform lookups. For example, in our inventory program, each inventory item is given a supplier id number. That id number is validated in the supplier file. Our report specifications call for a listing of inventory items by inventory id, with the name of the supplier in place of the supplier id number.

The next three sample programs demonstrate ways to accomplish this goal. The first program uses commands with which we are familiar to SELECT and SEEK our way to an acceptable report. The second and third programs introduce the SET RELATION TO command and the IIF() and EOF() functions to accomplish the same result with less programming.

Here is the first example:

```
* ivrepo.prg
* First version of item list with supplier name
* Uses SELECT /SEEK method
* Open data files
SELECT 1
USE ivitem INDEX ivitem ALIAS item
SELECT 2
USE ivsupp INDEX ivsupp ALIAS supp
* Note: Add your own code for page headers, page breaks, etc.
repline = 6
SET DEVICE TO PRINT
SELECT item
* Process all items in id number order
DO WHILE .NOT. EOF()
   * Print info for item
   @ repline,0 SAY iv_id
   @ repline,10 SAY iv_desc
   * SEEK supplier for this item
   SELECT supp
   SEEK item->iv_supp
   * Print supplier's name
   IF .NOT.EOF()
      @ repline,50 SAY su_company
   ELSE   && this item's supplier is not in supplier file
      @ repline,50 SAY "INVALID SUPPLIER"
   ENDIF found this item's supplier in the supplier file
   SELECT item
   repline=repline+1
   SKIP
ENDDO
CLOSE DATABASES
```

```
EJECT
SET DEVICE TO SCREEN
SET PRINT OFF && end print job
RETURN
* eof ivrepo.prg
```

Note that we have omitted the steps for pagination. As promised, this first method introduces no new commands or functions. The second method introduces the use of the SET RELATION TO command, which can often be used in place of the SELECT and SEEK commands. Here is the second attempt:

```
* ivrepo1.prg
* Second version of item list with supplier name
* Uses SET RELATION TO method
* Open data files
SELECT 1
USE ivitem INDEX ivitem ALIAS item
SELECT 2
USE ivsupp INDEX ivsupp ALIAS supp
* Setup relationship
SELECT item
SET RELATION TO iv_supp INTO supp
* Activate relation
GOTO TOP
* Note: Add your own code for page headers, page breaks, etc.
repline = 6
SET DEVICE TO PRINT
* Process all items in id number order
DO WHILE .NOT. EOF()
  * Print info for item
  @ repline,0 SAY iv_id
  @ repline,10 SAY iv_desc
  * Use relation to perform "invisible" seek and then
  * reference the supp field with the supp-> alias identifier
  IF .NOT. EOF(2)
    @ repline,50 SAY supp->su_company
  ELSE && invisible SEEK in supp work area was unsuccessful
    @ repline,50 SAY "INVALID COMPANY"
  ENDIF invisible SEEK in supp work area was successful
  repline=repline+1
  SKIP
ENDDO
CLOSE DATABASES
```

Using the content of lookup tables

```
EJECT
SET DEVICE TO SCREEN
SET PRINT OFF && end print job
RETURN
* eof ivrepo1.prg
```

If you understand that the first and second versions of the ivrepo.prg program perform exactly the same function, you will understand the use of the SET RELATION TO command. Simply put, a SET RELATION TO command uses the content of the current record in a file to perform an invisible SEEK in a database that is open in another work area. This invisible SEEK is performed each time the record pointer is repositioned in the master file.

In the ivrepo1.prg program, we instruct FoxBASE+ to perform an invisible SEEK in the supp-> work area using the content of the it_supp field in the current record of the item file, every time we reposition the record pointer in the item file. We accomplish this with the following command:

```
SET RELATION TO iv_supp INTO supp
```

By taking advantage of this command, we have effectively removed these three commands from the ivrepo.prg program:

```
SELECT supp
SEEK item->iv_supp
SELECT item
```

There is one other difference between the ivrepo.prg and ivrepo1.prg programs. In ivrepo1.prg, the EOF() function includes an argument. EOF(2) refers to the 2nd work area. Since we are performing an invisible SEEK in the 2nd or "supp->" work area every time we move the record pointer in the item file, we can test the EOF(2) function to see if the invisible SEEK was successful. (Note: The FOUND() function can be used in the same way.)

We can further reduce the number of commands in the ivrepo1.prg by using the "immediate IF" function, IIF(). The IIF() function is featured in the following program:

```
* ivrepo2.prg
* Third version of item list with supplier name
* Uses SET RELATION TO method
* Uses IIF() and EOF(area) functions to conditionally print
* the supplier name
* Open data files
SELECT 1
USE ivitem INDEX ivitem ALIAS item
SELECT 2
USE ivsupp INDEX ivsupp ALIAS supp
* Setup relationship
SELECT item
SET RELATION TO iv_supp INTO supp
* Activate relation
GOTO TOP
* Note: Add your own code for page headers, page breaks, etc.
repline = 6
SET DEVICE TO PRINT
* Process all items in id number order
DO WHILE .NOT. EOF()
   * Print info for item
   @ repline,0 SAY iv_id
   @ repline,10 SAY iv_desc
   * Use IIF() and EOF() functions to conditionally print
   * supplier name
   @ repline,50 SAY IIF(EOF(2),"INVALID SUPPLIER",supp->su_company)
   repline=repline+1
   SKIP
ENDDO
CLOSE DATABASES
EJECT
SET DEVICE TO SCREEN
SET PRINT OFF   && end print job
RETURN
* eof ivrepo2.prg
```

The IIF() function requires a logical expression, followed by a comma, followed by an expression of any data type, another comma, and a third expression of any data type. If the logical expression is true, IIF() returns

Using the content of lookup tables

the value of the first second expression. If the logical expression is false, IIF() returns the value of the third expression.

The IIF() function saves time and space by taking the place of an IF...ELSE...ENDIF construct. **More importantly, IIF() can be used in FoxReport Generated reports!** We will investigate FoxReport in the next chapter, but now it is time to study another aspect of multifile reporting

All my children (and other relations)

We spent much of Chapter 11 studying the ways in which files are related. The understanding taken from that chapter will pay dividends again as we attempt to print reports that list all of the children for a given parent record.

To return to our correspondence application, one report that should be generated by the program is a listing of correspondence in order by customer and date. The following program demonstrates the technique that not only applies to this report, but to most applications that include related files:

```
* crrepo1.prg
* Report of correspondence by customer and by date
DO WHILE lbrepo("Simple Correspondence")
  SELECT 1
  USE crcust INDEX crcust ALIAS cust
  SELECT 2
  USE crcorr INDEX crcorr ALIAS corr
  SELECT cust
  GOTO TOP
  * Use a small point size to fit everything
  SCREEN 1 FONT "MONACO",9
  * Preset the page and line numbers, and the time of the report
  page = 1
  repline = 99
  reptime = TIME()
  * Print the first page header
  DO crrepo1h WITH page,repline,reptime
  * Process all records in the customer file
  DO WHILE .NOT. EOF()
```

```
      IF repline > 59
        DO crrepo1h WITH page,repline,reptime
      ENDIF need page head
      * Print customer information
      @ repline,0 SAY cu_id
      @ repline,10 SAY cu_name
      repline = repline + 1
      * SEEK the first correspondence record for this customer
      SELECT corr
      SEEK cust->cu_id
      * Process all correspondence for this customer
      DO WHILE cr_custid = cust->cu_id .AND. (.NOT. EOF())
        IF repline > 59
          DO crrepo1h WITH page,repline,reptime
        ENDIF need page head
        @ repline,5 SAY cr_date
        @ repline,15 SAY cr_cont
        @ repline,37 SAY LEFT(cr_desc,40)
        repline = repline+1
        * Move to the next correspondence record
        SKIP
      ENDDO process all correspondence for this customer
      * Draw a line to separate customers
      @ repline,0 TO repline,80 STYLE 15+16+65536
      repline = repline + 1
      * Move to the next customer record
      SELECT cust
      SKIP
   ENDDO process all customer files
ENDDO while wants to print
RETURN
* eof crrepo1.prg
```

```
* crrepo1h.prg
* Header for crrepo1.prg
PARAMETERS page, line, time
@ 1,0 SAY "Date "+DTOC(DATE())
rephead = "Correspondence by customer by date"
* Center the header on the first line of the page
@ 1,42-LEN(rephead)/2 SAY rephead
@ 1,72 SAY "Page "+LTRIM(STR(page))
@ 2,0 SAY "Time "+time
* Put column headers on page
@ 4,0 SAY "Customer"
@ 5,5 SAY "Date"
@ 5,15 SAY "Contact"
```

```
@ 5,37 SAY "Description"
@ 6,5 TO 6,9 DOUBLE
@ 6,15 TO 6,22 DOUBLE
@ 6,37 TO 6,48 DOUBLE
* Set current print line
line = 8
* Increment the page counter
page = page + 1
RETURN
* eof crrepo1h.prg
```

The formula for this kind of multi-file report is as follows:

- Open the parent and child files.

- Be certain that the child file is indexed on the field that links child records to their associated record in the parent file.

- Use a DO WHILE loop to process the records in the parent file.

- For each parent record, perform a SEEK in the child file.

- Use a DO WHILE loop to process all of the records in the child file that are associated with the current record in the parent file.

- Move to the next record in the parent file.

This formula requires that the files to be linked via an index, and that the index be open during processing.

The inclusion of data from more than two files is accomplished with the same sort of PRINT / SELECT / SEEK / PRINT / SKIP sequence as demonstrated in the crrepo1.prg program. For example, an invoice printing program might utilize the following logic:

- SELECT invoice file.

- LOCATE an open invoice.
- SELECT customer file.
- SEEK customer number from invoice file.
- SAY customer name, address, contact, etc.
- SELECT invoice file.
- SAY invoice number, date, reference, etc.
- SELECT item file.
- SEEK this invoice number.
- DO WHILE items associated with this invoice.
- SAY item number, description, qty, price.
- Accumulate invoice totals in memory variables.
- SAY invoice totals.
- SELECT invoice file.
- CONTINUE to next open invoice.

Beautiful printouts

The preceding crrepo1.prg report is functional, but it hardly produces the kind of output mac users have come to expect. Surprise! Here is a version of the correspondence report that utilizes multiple point sizes, bold face, and ruling lines around and throughout the report:

```
* crrepo1.prg
* Report of correspondence by customer and by date
DO WHILE lbrepo("Fancy Correspondence")
SELECT 1
USE crcust INDEX crcust ALIAS cust
SELECT 2
USE crcorr INDEX crcorr ALIAS corr
SELECT cust
GOTO TOP
* Use a small point size to fit everything
SCREEN 1 FONT "GENEVA",6
* Preset the page and line numbers, and the time of the report
page = 1
repline = 99
reptime = TIME()
* Print the first page header
DO zrrepo1h WITH page,repline,reptime
* Process all records in the customer file
DO WHILE .NOT. EOF()
  IF repline > 100
    DO zrrepo1h WITH page,repline,reptime
  ENDIF need page head
  * Print customer information
  @ repline,2 SAY cu_id STYLE 0
  @ repline,11 SAY cu_name STYLE 0 FONT ,6+256
  * SEEK the first correspondence record for this customer
  SELECT corr
  SEEK cust->cu_id
  IF .NOT.FOUND()
    repline=repline+1
  ELSE
    * Process all correspondence for this customer
    DO WHILE cr_custid = cust->cu_id .AND. (.NOT. EOF())
      IF repline > 100
        DO zrrepo1h WITH page,repline,reptime
      ENDIF need page head
      @ repline,46 SAY cr_call PICTURE "####" STYLE 65536
      @ repline,56 SAY cr_date STYLE 65536
      @ repline,66 SAY cr_time STYLE 65536
      @ repline,78 SAY cr_cont STYLE 65536
      * The SIZE clause in the next command will cause the
      * content of cr_desc to be "word-wrapped" onto
      * two lines.
      @ repline,101 SAY cr_desc SIZE 2,75 STYLE 65536
      repline = repline+2
      * Move to the next correspondence record
      SKIP
```

```
      ENDDO process all correspondence for this customer
    ENDIF no correspondence for this customer
    IF repline<=100
      * Draw a line to separate customers
      @ repline,1 TO repline,174 STYLE 15+16+65536
      repline = repline + 1
    ENDIF still on the page
    * Move to the next customer record
    SELECT cust
    SKIP
ENDDO process all customer files
ENDDO while wants to print the report
RETURN
* eof crrepo1.prg
```

```
* crrepo1h.prg
* Header for crrepo1.prg
PARAMETERS page, line, time
IF page>1
  EJECT
ENDIF not the first page
* Box printout
@ 0,0 TO 100,175 STYLE 15+48+(4*16^3)+65536
* Draw vertical bars
@ 4,45 to 100,45 STYLE 15+16*16+65536
@ 4,55 TO 100,55 STYLE 15+16*16+65536
@ 4,65 TO 100,65 STYLE 15+16*16+65536
@ 4,77 TO 100,77 STYLE 15+16*16+65536
@ 4,100 TO 100,100 STYLE 15+16*16+65536
@ 1,2 SAY "Date "+DTOC(DATE()) STYLE 65536
rephead = "Correspondence by customer by date"
* Center the header on the first line of the page
@ 1,82-LEN(rephead)/2 SAY rephead STYLE 65536
@ 1,167 SAY "Page "+LTRIM(STR(page)) STYLE 65536
@ 2,2 SAY "Time "+time STYLE 65536
* Put column headers on page
@ 5,2 SAY "Customer"style 65536 FONT ,12
@ 5,46 SAY "Call" STYLE 65536 FONT ,12
@ 5,56 SAY "Date" STYLE 65536 FONT ,12
@ 5,66 SAY "Time" STYLE 65536 FONT ,12
@ 5,78 SAY "Contact" STYLE 65536 FONT ,12
@ 5,101 SAY "Description" STYLE 65536 FONT ,12
@ 6,1 TO 6,174 STYLE 15+32+65536
* Set current print line
line = 8
* Increment the page counter
```

```
    page = page + 1
    RETURN
    * eof crrepo1h.prg
```

All of the commands should be familiar to you if you reviewed Chapter 10. Note that I have selected the Monaco font again. This nonproportional font makes it much easier to line items up in columns than does a proportional font like Helvetica. See the last chapter for a brief discussion of proportional and nonproportional fonts.

If you elect to use the line and box drawing capabilities provided by the @...TO command on your reports, remember to include a STYLE command **with every @...SAY statement in the report!** If you neglect to do so, your report will force a page eject every time a row or vertical PIXEL coordinate is referenced that is higher on the page than the last row or vertical PIXEL referenced by the report. If you need clarification of this concept, remove the STYLE clause of any of the @...SAY commands in the zrrepo1.prg program.

The remainder of the reports in this chapter will not take advantage of the FoxBASE+/Mac's ability to mix fonts, and produce line graphics on a printout. Instead, the rest of the reports in this chapter will concentrate on standard reporting requirements. If you like, you are welcome to adjust these programs to produce more Mac-like output.

Single command statistics

FoxBASE+ offers the following commands that generate statistics without the need for a DO WHILE loop:

AVERAGE
COUNT
SUM

Of these commands, the SUM command is the most versatile. For example, let's query the students file for the number of students, total age, and average age. Here is the program:

```
* stat.prg
* Use of the SUM command
SCREEN 1 SIZE 7,50 AT 0,0 TYPE 4
SCREEN 1 HEAD "Stat.prg" TOP
USE students ALIAS stu
SUM 1,st_age TO number,totage
CLEAR
@ 1,5 SAY "# of students = "
@ 1,COL()+1 SAY number PICTURE "##,###"
@ 2,5 SAY "Average age of students = "
@ 2,COL()+1 SAY totage/number PICTURE "##.##"
@ 5,0 SAY "Please select a menu option..."
* Force a menu hit
DO WHILE !kmnhit
   WAIT ""
ENDDO
RETURN
* eof stat.prg
```

Here is a sample program that uses the SUM command to generate subtotals:

```
* stat1.prg
* Use of the SUM command for subtotals
DO WHILE lbrepo("Stat1")
   * Prevent unwanted messages from being displayed
   SET TALK OFF
   USE students INDEX schname ALIAS stu
   GOTO TOP
   repline = 6
   DO WHILE .NOT. EOF()
      thisschool = st_school
      SUM 1,st_age TO number,totage WHILE st_school = thisschool
      * print subtotals
      @ repline,0 SAY thisschool
      @ repline,20 SAY number PICTURE "##,###"
      @ repline,40 SAY totage/number PICTURE "##,###"
      repline = repline + 1
   ENDDO process all students
```

Single command statistics

```
ENDDO while wants to print
RETURN
* eof stat1.prg
```

By now you should know how to generate page breaks and page headers. Note the use of the WHILE clause. The WHILE clause can also be used with the AVERAGE, COUNT, SORT, REPLACE, LOCATE, and other commands to process records WHILE a condition is true.

Subtotals on non-grouped records

Assume that a report is needed that lists the movies in a movie store by title. At the end of the report, the manager wants a summary of each category of movie including the number of rentals, and the number of movies for each category. Since the manager is constantly adding new categories and deleting old ones, we will need a method that allows for an unlimited number of categories.

Our approach will be to create a temporary work file called subtot.dbf. This file will contain fields for category name, number of movies, and number of rentals. The file will be indexed by category name. The use of this temporary work file is demonstrated in the following programs:

```
* subtot.prg
* Demonstrates calculation of non-grouped subtotals
* Open main file
DO WHILE lbrepo("Non-grouped Subtotals")
  SELECT 1
  USE movie INDE title ALIAS movie
  * Open temporary file
  SELECT 2
  USE subtot ALIAS subtot
  * Remove existing records
  ZAP
  * Recreate temporary work file index
  INDEX ON sb_cat TO subtot
  page = 1
  repline = 99
  reptime = TIME()
```

```
SET DEVICE TO PRINT
DO subtoth WITH page,repline,reptime
* Process movie list
SELECT movie
GOTO TOP
DO WHILE .NOT. EOF()
  IF repline > 59
    DO subtoth WITH page,repline,reptime
  ENDIF need a page break
  @ repline,5 SAY mv_title
  @ repline,25 SAY mv_cat
  @ repline,35 SAY mv_rentals
  * Accumulate subtotals
  SELECT subtot
  SEEK movie->mv_cat
  IF .NOT. FOUND()
    APPEND BLANK
    REPLACE sb_cat WITH movie->mv_cat
  ENDIF first time for this category
  REPLACE sb_count WITH sb_count + 1
  REPLACE sb_rentals WITH sb_rentals + movie->mv_rentals
  * Process next movie record
  SELECT movie
  SKIP
  repline = repline + 1
ENDDO process all movies
repline = repline + 1
* Setup variables for grand totals
STORE 0 TO allcount,allrents
* Print subtotals
SELECT subtot
GOTO TOP
DO WHILE .NOT. EOF()
  IF repline > 59
    DO subtoth WITH page,repline,time
  ENDIF need page break
  @ repline,0 SAY "Category: "+sb_cat
  @ repline,PCOL()+5 SAY "Movies: "
  @ repline,PCOL()+1 SAY sb_count PICTURE "##,###"
  @ repline,PCOL()+5 SAY "Rentals: "
  @ repline,PCOL()+1 SAY sb_rentals PICTURE "##,###"
  * Accumulate grand totals
  allcount = allcount + sb_count
  allrents = allrents + sb_rentals
  repline = repline + 1
  SKIP
ENDDO process all subtotals
* Print Grand totals
```

Subtotals on non-grouped records

```
    @ repline,0 SAY "Report Grand Totals:"
    @ repline,PCOL()+5 SAY "Movies: "
    @ repline,PCOL()+1 SAY allcount PICTURE "##,###"
    @ repline,PCOL()+5 SAY "Rentals: "
    @ repline,PCOL()+1 SAY allrents PICTURE "##,###"
ENDDO while wants to print
CLOSE DATABASES
RETURN
* eof subtot.prg
```

```
* subtoth.prg
* Prints page header for subtot.prg
PARAMETERS page, line, time
@ 1,0 SAY "Date "+DTOC(DATE())
rephead = "Movie list with subtotals by category"
* Center the header on the first line of the page
@ 1,42-LEN(rephead)/2 SAY rephead
@ 1,72 SAY "Page "+LTRIM(STR(page))
@ 2,0 SAY "Time "+time
* Put column headers on page
@ 4,5 SAY "Title"
@ 4,25 SAY "Category"
@ 4,35 SAY "Rentals"
@ 5,5 SAY "====="
@ 5,25 SAY "========"
@ 5,35 SAY "======="
* Set current print line
line = 6
* Increment the page counter
page = page + 1
RETURN
* eof subtoth.prg
```

The steps demonstrated above are:

- Use a subtotal file indexed on a field containing the names of the groups to be subtotaled.

- Process the records in the master file.

- For each record in the master file, accumulate a subtotal in the subtotal file.

- When all master file records have been printed, print the subtotal records.

Multi-column "snaked" reports

Staying with our video store motif for a moment, let's try to design a report that will generate a two column listing of movies by title. The movies should proceed in order down the left column, and continue again at the top of the right column. To accomplish this, we will place one page worth of movies in an array, then go back and print the array. Here is the program:

```
* snake.prg
* Prints a two column list of movie titles
DO WHILE lbrepo("Snaked Report")
  * Open movie file with index by title
  SELECT 1
  USE movie INDEX title ALIAS movie
  * Setup array to hold one page of movies
  DIMENSION mv(110)
  * Preset the page and line numbers, and the time of the report
  page = 1
  repline = 99
  reptime = TIME()
  GOTO TOP
  SET DEVICE TO PRINT
  DO WHILE .NOT. EOF()
    * Reset page array
    mv = " "
    numonpage = 1
    * Fill page array
    DO WHILE numonpage <= 110 .AND. (.NOT.EOF())
      mv(numonpage) = mv_title
      SKIP
      numonpage = numonpage + 1
    ENDDO process on page worth of movies
    * Print entire page
    @ 1,0 SAY "Date "+DTOC(DATE())
    rephead = "Multi-column move list"
```

```
   * Center the header on the first line of the page
   @ 1,42-LEN(rephead)/2 SAY rephead
   @ 1,72 SAY "Page "+LTRIM(STR(page))
   @ 2,0 SAY "Time "+reptime
   * Put column headers on page
   @ 4,0 SAY "TITLE"
   @ 4,40 SAY "TITLE"
   @ 5,0 SAY "====="
   @ 5,40 SAY "====="
   prnarr = 1
   repline = 6
   * Print page array
   DO WHILE prnarr <= 55
      @ repline,0 SAY mv(prnarr)
      @ repline,40 SAY mv(prnarr+55)
      repline = repline + 1
      prnarr = prnarr + 1
   ENDDO print a page
  ENDDO process all movies
ENDDO while wants to print
RETURN
* eof snake.prg
```

If you want to make the columns even, work with the prnarr, prnarr, and numonpage variables. If you need more than two columns, use a bigger array with the same concept.

15. FoxReport

The FoxReport program is well documented in both the Tutorial and in the FOXREPORT/FOXFORM/FOXCODE manual. However, there are a few tips worth passing on.

Lining up

First among these tips is the use of nonproportional fonts for columnar reports. As we discussed in Chapter 12, proportional fonts like Helvetica, Times Roman, and Geneva use different widths for different characters. As a result, it is virtually impossible to line up columns of information. Especially difficult is the alignment of decimals in columns of numeric data. Therefore, use nonproportional fonts like Courier and Monaco to produce columns of information.

Directly modifying .frx files

FoxReport generates a .frx file based on the information you provide. The information contained in this .frx file includes the font and point size for all of the items in the report, as well as all grouping, totaling, and other information.

Obviously, you can change the content and or layout of a report by issuing a MODIFY REPORT command, but did you know that you could directly modify the content of the .FRX file with a MODIFY FILE command?

Since FoxReport does such a good job of allowing the creation of reports by simply painting a screen with objects, you may be wondering why anyone would want to risk ruining a report by directly modifying the .frx file.

The first reason is the limitation on point sizes. In FoxReport, the smallest point size available is 9. By directly modifying the .frx file you can lower the point size to 6 or lower. (Note: 6 point Monaco provides about 100 lines of 175 very readable characters on a LaserWriter page.)

To modify the point size of an individual item, find the first number following the font name. This number is the point size plus any bold face, underline, or other special effects number. (See the FoxBASE+/Mac Commands and Functions Manual under @...SAY command.) Change the number to match your desired point size.

Using reports in programs

Using a FoxReport generated report from within one of your programs is a simple matter, as demonstrated in the following program:

```
* vidrents.prg
* Prints vidrents.frx
SELECT 1
USE video ALIAS video
SUM times_rent TO totrents
STORE 0 TO subrents
SET INDEX TO video1
DO WHILE lbrepo("Video Rentals")
   SCREEN 1 TOP
   SCREEN 2 OFF FONT "GENEVA",12
   REPORT FORM vidrents TO PRINT
ENDDO lbrepo
SELECT video
USE
RETURN
* eof vidrents.prg
```

This program runs a report that uses the video.dbf which accompanied your copy of FoxBASE+/Mac. As you can see, the REPORT FORM command is very easy to use. Note that you can add a FOR and/or WHILE clause to the command to include only certain records from the file. In addition, you can use the SET FILTER TO and SORT methods outlined in Chapter 13 to restrict the content of the report.

Of course the vidrents.prg program is of little value without a vidrents.frx, and so I have included a screen shot of the vidrents.frx layout in Figure 15-01. The report generates a listing of movies by class, and makes use of a video1.idx index file. The key expression for video1.idx is type+title.

In addition to providing subtotals of rentals by movie type, and a grand total of all rentals for all movies, the report includes the following interesting features:

- The percentage of total rentals represented by each group.

- The percentage of total rentals represented by each movie.

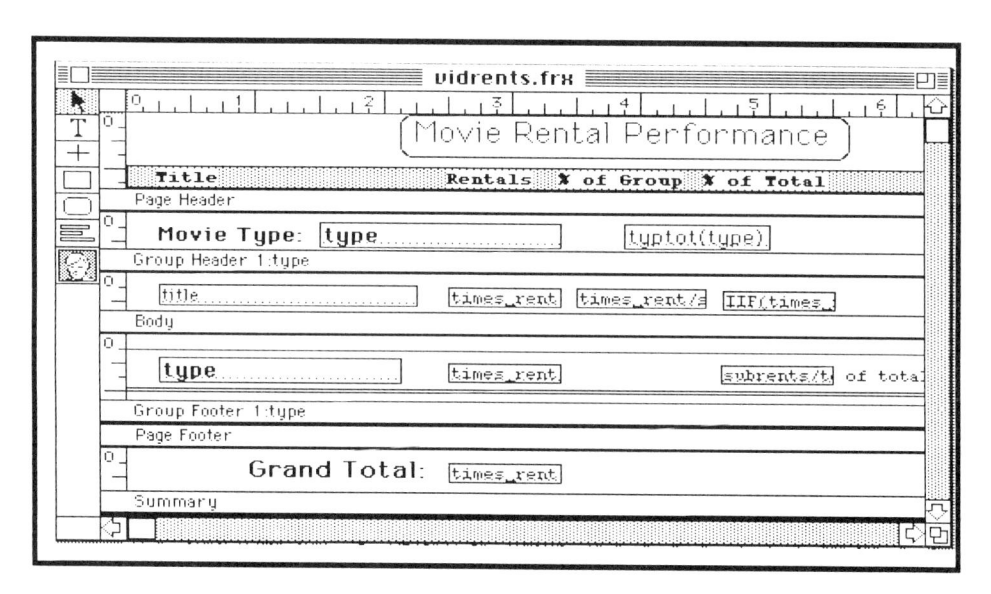

Figure 15-01. Vidrents.frx design on screen.

Using reports in programs

- The percentage of rentals for this group represented by each movie.

- Any movie accounting for more than 5% of the total rentals of all movies will have that percentage displayed in bold face print.

Using memory variables in reports

Calculating the percentage of total rentals for each movie was fairly simple. I placed the following expression in a field under the header "% of Total":

```
times_rent/totrents*100.00
```

Of course I included a format of "###.###" to make the content print properly. More importantly, before every run of the vidrents.frx report, I issue the following command from the vidrents.prg program:

```
SUM times_rent TO totrents
```

While percentages are often useful in reports, the important thing to understand about this example is the use of memory variables. In short, you can use memory variables in FoxReport expressions, provided you make sure those memory variables are available when the report is run.

Using IIF() in reports

Taking a break from the vidrents.frx report for a moment, consider the available field in the video.dbf database. A logical field, available is .T. when the movie is available for rental, and .F. when the movie is unavailable. A report that lists a .T. or .F. under a column named "Available" lacks style however, so we need to way to use the content of the available field to generate a "YES" if the movie is available or a "NO" if the movie is unavailable.

The following report field would do the trick:

```
IIF(available,"YES","NO")
```

See Chapter 14 for an extended visit with the IIF() function. When you have finished, make a note to use the IIF() function whenever you need to print one of two values depending on a condition.

Returning to the vidrents.frx report, you will notice that the report prints "% of Total" figures in bold for any movie that has accounted for more than 5% of the total movie rentals. Well, the IIF() function can be used to print one of two values, but there seems to be no direct method for printing in one of two type styles.

A little work with the IIF() function and the OR MODE, provides a delightful solution. In the exact same location on the report, I placed the following two expressions:

```
IIF(times_rent/totrents*100>5,times_rent/totrents*100.00,"")
IIF(times_rent/totrents*100<=5,times_rent/totrents*100.00,"")
```

I tagged the first expression to be printed in boldface, while the second expression was left in plain text. Both expressions were tagged with the OR option of the MODE selection under the Object menu. The first expression means, "If the percentage is greater than 5, print the percentage, otherwise, print nothing." The second expression means, "If the percentage is less than or equal to 5, print the percentage, otherwise print nothing."

This technique of overlapping mutually exclusive expressions, can be used to conditionally assign any typographical characteristic to a position on a report. If you neglect to select the OR option of the MODE selection however, this overlap will cause a page eject, rather than the desired conditional printing.

Programs inside reports

We still have one feature to accommodate before our vidrents.frx report is complete. The ability to determine an individual movie's percentage of that movie type's total rentals seems beyond the capability of Fox-Report.

However, FoxReport offers a feature that makes it possible to accommodate virtually any report requirement. Specifically, FoxReport allows the inclusion of UDFs in report specifications. In other words, you can write programs that will be run inside the report.

In our example, we need to calculate the total number of rentals for the current movie type, before we print the first movie type. Accordingly, I have placed the following field in the Group header:

```
* typtot.prg
* Provides group subtotals for percentages "inside"
* the vidrents.frx
PARAMETERS curtype
PRIVATE spot
spot = RECNO()
SUM times_rent TO subrents WHILE type=curtype
GOTO spot
RETURN ""
* eof typtot.prg
```

The typtot.prg may not be much to look at, but its use demonstrates just one way to exploit the power of UDFs inside a report form. First note that typtot.prg returns nothing. Therefore, nothing prints when the report gets to the typtot(type) field. In other words, you can write UDFs to perform almost any function without worrying about cluttering your report with unwanted information.

In our case, the typtot.prg resets the value of the subrents variable every time a new movie type is encountered. The timing of the execution of typtot.prg is handled by the Grouping feature of FoxReport.

Secure that typtot.prg has assigned the correct value to subrents, we can use the variable subrents in subsequent report fields to calculate percentages for individual movies, and for the movie type as a group. Note that subrents, like any other variable used in a report, **must exist prior to running vidrents.frx!**

UDFs can be used for all manner of purposes inside a report including:

- Translating abbreviated fields into their full descriptive content.

- Performing lookups in multiple database files. This is especially helpful when more than 10 databases are required for a report.

- Setting up memory variables for use by other report fields.

When using UDFs, remember that FoxReport processes records just like a DO WHILE...SKIP...ENDDO construct from Chapter 13. In fact, a close review of Chapters 13 and 14 will prove invaluable in creating your own report form UDFs.

16. Multiuser

The number one question I receive from readers of my columns and books goes something like this: "I have written a program that works well for one user. How do I make it multiuser?"

The answer the reader is looking for is something like, "Just SET MULTIUSER ON!" The answer the reader gets is, "It depends!"

General Considerations

A full-scale investigation of multiuser application design and implementation using FoxBASE+/Mac would fill an entire book, and indeed I hope to spend some time on such a project in the not too distant future. Such a book would explain in detail all of the many and varied schemes for allowing more than one user to share the programs and data in the same application at the same time.

I have only set aside one chapter in this book to address the issue, so I will restrict our discussions to the most immediate and practical concerns of multiuser programming. In other words, this chapter will help you with the mechanics of file and record locking, but the intricacies of multiuser system design will have to wait for another book.

There are two general approaches to multiuser programming. In the rest of the chapter we will investigate each by reviewing sample programs. These reviews will introduce you to the following concepts:

- Exclusive or shared use of database files.

- Record locking.

- File locking.

- Error trapping and recovery.

- Creating temporary files in a multiuser environment.

The easy way out

Most of the grunt-work of multiuser programming involves attempting to lock records and files before changing the content of those records or files. If the programmer fails to perform these locking efforts, FoxBASE+/Mac will generate an error, and abort the offending command.

However, since we can use the ON ERROR command to trap FoxBASE+/Mac errors, we can address the locking considerations after the fact. First though, we need to understand the ON ERROR command. Here is a sample ON ERROR command:

```
ON ERROR DO muerror WITH ERROR(), ;
  MESSAGE(), MESSAGE(1), SYS(16)
```

After this command is issued, the generation of a FoxBASE+/Mac error will cause FoxBASE+/Mac to stop processing the current program file, and begin processing the muerror.prg program. In addition, the values of several functions will be passed to muerror.prg as parameters.

Every error that can be generated by FoxBASE+/Mac has a unique number associated with it. This unique number is returned by the ERROR() function. Further, each error has a description associated with it. The description of the current error is returned by the MESSAGE() function. Note that if no error has occurred, ERROR() returns 0, and MESSAGE() returns "". To finish our discussion of the sample ON ERROR command, the MESSAGE(1) command returns the text of the command that caused the error, and SYS(16) returns the name of the program in which the error-generating command resides.

Because we know what each error number represents, and because we can include all of the appropriate locking techniques in the muerror.prg, all we need is a way to reissue the offending command after we have put the proper locks in place. The RETRY command fits the bill, as we shall see in the following program listing:

```
* muerror.prg
* Traps errors
PARAMETERS errnum,errmsg,errcomm,errprg
PRIVATE tries
tries=0
DO CASE
   CASE errnum = 108 .AND. errmsg = "APPEND BLANK"
      * Someone else tried to APPEND BLANK at the same time as this
      * user.
      RETRY   && try the append blank again
   CASE errnum = 108
      * Someone else has the file locked, or at least one
      * record in the file locked, when a program tried to
      * change the content of multiple records in the file
      DO WHILE tries<=1000
        IF FLOCK()
           RETRY
        ENDIF got it!
        tries=tries+1
      ENDDO wait until file can be locked
   CASE errnum = 109
      * A command tried to change the content of a single record
      * by automatically locking the record. Unfortunately, the
      * record was already locked by another user.
      DO WHILE tries<=1000
        IF RLOCK()
           RETRY
        ENDIF got it!
        tries=tries+1
      ENDDO wait until this record can be locked
   CASE errnum = 130
      * Either a REPLACE command, or a READ command that acts on
      * GETS that refer to database fields was issued when the
      * record involved was not locked.
      DO WHILE tries<=1000
        IF RLOCK()
           RETRY
        ENDIF got it!
        tries=tries+1
```

```
      ENDDO wait until this record can be locked
ENDCASE errors
* problem was not resolved
CLOSE DATABASES
ALERT 8 STOP "System halted because of ( "+errmsg+;
" ) caused by command ( "+errcomm+;
" ) in program  ( "+errprg+" )"
RETURN TO MASTER
* eof muerror.prg
```

Each case statement handles one error. If the effort to correct the error succeeds, muerror.prg directs FoxBASE+/Mac to RETRY to command. If the effort to correct the error fails, muerror.prg closes all databases, and issues a RETURN TO MASTER command to return control to the first program in the application.

To activate the muerror.prg, include the following commands at the beginning of your main program:

```
SET EXCLUSIVE OFF
ON ERROR DO muerror WITH ERROR(), ;
 MESSAGE(),MESSAGE(1),SYS(16)
```

Surprisingly, this very simple solution to a very complex problem actually works for some applications. If you have written a simple application that works in a single user environment, and that will be used by only 2 or 3 users simultaneously, and that utilizes only a few databases, and that uses few or no related databases, this technique might work for you.

The biggest problems with this approach are:

- No provision is made for UNLOCKing LOCKed records or files.

- Using this method, it is difficult to distinguish between tasks that can be safely aborted, and those that must be completed.

- Programs that use this method will run more slowly than programs using explicit file and record locks.

For the remainder of this chapter we will concentrate on the tools available to FoxBASE+/Mac who wish to include explicit file and record locking in their multiuser applications.

Editing a LOCKed record

Most of our sample data entry programs included a series of @...GET statements, followed by a READ statement. FoxBASE+/Mac Multiuser requires any record whose fields are accessed by a GET during a READ to be locked. For example, here is a version of the inventory entry screen that will function in a multiuser environment:

```
* iventr2m.prg
* Edits the content of the current inventory item
* Multiuser version using GET field/READ method
PRIVATE localopt
@ 0,33 GET iv_id
* Prevent the user from changing the key field
CLEAR GETS
@ 2,33 GET iv_desc
@ 4,33 GET iv_onhand PICTURE "##,###"
@ 6,33 GET iv_price PICTURE "$$$$.##"
* See if we can lock this record
IF !RLOCK()
   * Can't lock this record!
   ALERT 1 NOTE "Sorry. Cannot lock this record."
   * Deactivate the GETS associated with this record
   CLEAR GETS
ENDIF unable to lock this record
* Setup local option
localopt=0
* Check to see if the record is marked for deletion
IF DELETED()
   * Put  note on screen for user
   @ 1,53 SAY "(DELETED)"
   @ 7,0 GET localopt PICTURE "@*h ADD;NEXT;PREVIOUS;LOOKUP;RECALL"
ELSE
   * Remove any existing DELETED message
   @ 1,53 CLEAR TO 1,62
```

```
    @ 7,0 GET localopt PICTURE "@*h ADD;NEXT;PREVIOUS;LOOKUP;DELETE"
ENDIF record marked for deletion
DO WHILE localopt=0.AND.(!kmnhit)
   READ SAVE
ENDDO until option or menu hit
CLEAR GETS
FLUSH    && Make sure everyone can "see" our changes
UNLOCK   && Remove the lock we may have put on this record
RETURN localopt
* eof iventr2m.prg
```

The RLOCK() function performs two tasks. First, it tries to place a record lock on the current record. Second, it returns a true or false value to indicate whether or not it was successful.

Note that the locked record requirement only applies to READs that utilize GETs of fields. In this example, localopt is a memory variable, and therefore can be READ even though the current record is not locked.

The FLUSH command directs FoxBASE+/Mac to write all database related information to the disk. This allows everyone using the application to see the changes we have made to the current record the next time they access the record.

The UNLOCK command removes the latest RLOCK() or FLOCK() from the current work area. This allows other users to work with this record.

Editing a record in memory variables

Using the method described above, the current record would be locked until the user moves to another record, or chooses another activity. As a result, no other user could make changes to the locked record, nor could any other user lock the entire database file, so long as this user is editing this record.

These restrictions can be troublesome in many applications, so many programmers prefer the record locking method demonstrated in the iventr2z.prg program that follows:

```
* iventr2z.prg
* Edits the content of the current inventory item
* Multiuser version using STORE/REPLACE method
PRIVATE localopt
@ 0,33 GET iv_id
* Prevent the user from changing the key field
CLEAR GETS
* Put field values into memory variables
STORE iv_desc TO mivdesc
STORE iv_onhand TO mivonhand
STORE iv_price TO mivprice
@ 2,33 GET mivdesc
@ 4,33 GET mivonhand PICTURE "##,###"
@ 6,33 GET mivprice PICTURE "$$$$.##"
* Setup local option
localopt=0
* Check to see if the record is marked for deletion
IF DELETED()
   * Put  note on screen for user
   @ 1,53 SAY "(DELETED)"
   @ 7,0 GET localopt PICTURE "@*h ADD;NEXT;PREVIOUS;LOOKUP;RECALL"
ELSE
   * Remove any existing DELETED message
   @ 1,53 CLEAR TO 1,62
   @ 7,0 GET localopt PICTURE "@*h ADD;NEXT;PREVIOUS;LOOKUP;DELETE"
ENDIF record marked for deletion
DO WHILE localopt=0.AND.(!kmnhit)
   READ SAVE
ENDDO until option or menu hit
CLEAR GETS
* See if we can lock this record
IF !RLOCK()
   * Can't lock this record!
   ALERT 1 NOTE "Sorry. Cannot lock this record."+;
   " CHANGES NOT SAVED!!!"
ELSE
   * Put changed values of variables back into fields
   REPLACE iv_desc WITH mivdesc,iv_onhand WITH mivonhand,;
   iv_price WITH mivprice
   FLUSH  && Make sure everyone can "see" our changes
   UNLOCK  && Remove the lock we may have put on this record
ENDIF unable to lock this record
```

Editing a record in memory variables

```
RETURN localopt
* eof iventr2m.prg
```

In this method, the programmer first stores the values of the fields to be edited in memory variables. These memory variables are then READ without locking the record. This allows other users to lock this record or file.

When the user has finished changing the data, the programmer attempts to lock the record, and REPLACE the fields with their new values.

One potential problem to be overcome when using this method occurs when two users change the same record. Since the record is not locked when the STORE commands are issued, the user cannot be guaranteed of working with the most current version of the record. Further, any changes made to the record while the user is editing the memory variables, will go unnoticed by the user. Finally, when the user exits the screen, his changes may overwrite any changes made by other users.

There are a variety of methods available to ameliorate these problems, but an investigation of these methods will have to wait for another book.

Waiting for a lock

If you wish to direct FoxBASE+/Mac to continually try to lock a record indefinitely, or for a specified length of time, try substituting the following UDF for RLOCK():

```
* lblockr.prg
* Attempts to lock a record
* desc = description of record
* tries = number of times to try before returning .F.
*         if tries = 0, try forever
PARAMETERS desc,tries
PRIVATE xx
IF !RLOCK()
  oldscreen = VAL(SYS(1034))
```

```
   SCREEN 9 TOP SIZE 5,50 FONT "MONACO",12
   CLEAR
   SCREEN 9 TYPE 1 FIXED AT 0,0
   @ 2,0 SAY "Trying to lock: "+desc
   IF tries#0
     @ 3,0 SAY "Press any key to abort..."
   ENDIF
   @ 4,0 SAY "Number of tries:"
   xx=1
   DO WHILE !RLOCK().AND.(tries=0.OR.xx<tries)
     xx=xx+1
     IF INKEY(.5)#0.AND.tries#0
       EXIT
     ENDIF pressed a key
     @ 4,17 SAY xx PICTURE "#,###"
   ENDDO wait for lock or number of tries
   SCREEN 9 OFF
   SCREEN oldscreen
ENDIF unable to lock
RETURN RLOCK()
* eof lblockr.prg
```

When the programmer uses this UDF instead of RLOCK(), the user will be presented with a screen explaining the delay when an RLOCK() fails. By passing a 0 for the number of tries, the programmer can direct the system to wait forever. Alternatively, the lblockr() will try to lock the current record every 1/2 second for the number of tries indicated.

If the lblockr() UDF fails to lock the record in the specified number of tries, or if the user presses any key to abort the lock attempt, lblockr() will return a .F. value.

Multiple record processing

Commands like REPLACE ALL, DELETE ALL, and APPEND FROM add or change more than one record in the current database. As a result, the file must be locked prior to issuing one of these commands. This program segment will give you the idea:

```
IF FLOCK()
   REPLACE ALL amount WITH amount*1.1
ELSE
   ALERT 1 NOTE "Can't lock file. No replacements performed!"
ENDIF
```

Obviously, you could substitute a UDF for FLOCK() in the same way that I suggested you replace RLOCK() with lblockr.prg.

Adding records in a multiuser environment

When attempting to add records in a multiuser environment, you must always prepare for the possibility that APPEND BLANK might fail. Here is the iventrn.prg program rewritten to accommodate a multiuser environment:

```
* iventrnm.prg
* Add a new record or find an item by item id
* Multiuser version
PRIVATE newkey,thisrec,ans,option,oldscreen
oldscreen=VAL(SYS(1034))
* Setup a memory variable to accept the id to SEEK
newkey = SPACE(10)
* Save our place in the file in case the new key is not found,
* and the user does not want to add a new record
IF .NOT. EOF()
   * Save the record number
   thisrec = RECNO()
ELSE   && no current record
   thisrec = 0
ENDIF there is a current record
* Tell the user what to do, and get the new key
SCREEN 3 SIZE 5,60 TYPE 4 LOCK AT 240,60
CLEAR
SCREEN 3 TOP HEADING "New Inventory Item" FIXED
DO WHILE .T.
   @ 1,0 SAY "Enter id to add or lookup here:"
   @ 1,COL()+1 GET newkey PICTURE "@! AA99999999"
   option = 0
   @ 2,15 GET option PICTURE "@*h LOOKUP;CANCEL"
   DO WHILE option=0
      READ SAVE
```

```
      ENDDO wait for action
      CLEAR GETS
      * Note that the id must be two upper case letters
      * followed by 8 numbers
      * See if the user chose to cancel
      IF newkey # SPACE(10).AND.option#2
         * Check to see if the item is already on file
         SEEK newkey
         IF .NOT.FOUND()
            * See if the user wants to add a new item
            IF lbq(newkey+" is not on file.","ADD;RETRY","F")="RETRY"
               * See if there is a current record
               IF thisrec#0
                  * Return the record pointer to its position prior
                  * to the unsuccessful SEEK
                  GOTO thisrec
               ENDIF there is a current record
            ELSE  && wants to add the new item
               ** Be sure there is an ON ERROR to RETRY this
               ** APPEND BLANK in case it fails!
               APPEND BLANK
               * STILL HAVE TO LOCK THE RECORD AFTER APPENDING IT!
               IF RLOCK()
                  * Fill the key field with the memory variable
                  REPLACE iv_id WITH newkey
                  UNLOCK
                  EXIT
               ELSE
                  ALERT 1 STOP "Could not lock record. Try again."
                  IF thisrec#0
                     * Return the record pointer to its position prior
                     * to the unsuccessful SEEK
                     GOTO thisrec
                  ENDIF there is a current record
               ENDIF able to lock this record
            ENDIF doesn't want to add the item
         ELSE && found it!
            * Exit with the record pointer set on this record
            EXIT
         ENDIF found the item
      ELSE &&
         * Chose to cancel, or left key field blank
         EXIT
      ENDIF did not leave new key blank
ENDDO process lookup requests
SCREEN 3 OFF
SCREEN oldscreen TOP
RETURN
```

Adding records in a multiuser environment

```
* eof iventrn.prg
```

Note that an ON ERROR routine must be included to trap the rare instance when an APPEND BLANK runs into another user APPENDing BLANK at precisely the same time. The APPEND BLANK command would also fail if another user had FLOCKed the file.

Finally, note that the iventrnm.prg has to lock the record it just APPENDed prior to performing a REPLACE in that record.

Major surgery

The following program segment is fine for use in a single user environment, but unacceptable in a multiuser environment:

```
USE ivitem ALIAS item
PACK
```

ZAP, PACK, REINDEX, INSERT, and MODIFY STRUCTURE all require exclusive use of the database file in question. Since you will be unable to USE a database exclusively if any other user has the database in USE, you need to prepare for potential failure. Here is a program segment that uses a UDF for this purpose:

```
IF lbexcl("ivitem ALIAS item")
   PACK
ENDIF
```

Here is the lbexcl.prg UDF:

```
* lbexcl.prg
* Tries to open a file for exclusive use
PARAMETERS thisfile
PRIVATE errnum,tries
errnum=0
ON ERROR errnum=ERROR()
tries=0
```

```
DO WHILE tries<=10
  errnum=0
  USE &thisfile EXCLUSIVE
  IF errnum=0
    RETURN .T.
  ENDIF
  tries=tries+1
ENDDO
ALERT 1 NOTE "Could not open file for exclusive "+;
"use. Try again later."
RETURN .F.
* eof lbexcl.prg]
```

Unfortunately, the only way to know if you can open a database file for exclusive use is to try, and then see if you succeeded. The checking is performed via the ON ERROR command. Note that if you have a general ON ERROR routine, that routine should be reset with an ON ERROR command at the end of the lbexcl.prg UDF.

Temporary work files

In a single user environment, the following program segment is perfectly acceptable:

```
USE students
SORT ON st_name TO temp
LIST
```

In a multiuser application, this program segment does not work because more than one user may try to create a file called temp.dbf at the same time. Or, a user may try to create a temp.dbf file while another user is already using a file called temp.dbf. The solution stems from the use of the SYS(3) function, which returns a unique file name. Here is a program segment that takes advantage of SYS(3) to create temporary work files suitable for multiuser applications:$ITemporary work files;

```
tmpfile=SYS(3)
USE students
SORT ON st_name TO &tmpfile.
USE &tmpfile. EXCLUSIVE
LIST
USE && close the temp file
ERASE &tmpfile.
```

Index

!

&&	17
*	17
.dbf	95
.dbt	234
.frx	317
.idx	103
.prg	195
.scx	195
.T.	63
=	56
@...GET	24
multiuser	329
sequence	35
using memory variables for multiuser	330, 331
@...PROMPT/MENU TO	224
@...SAY	23
to printer	285
@...TO	240, 310

A

ALERT	18, 223
ALIAS	118
ALIAS clause	101
APPEND	220, 278
APPEND BLANK	101, 102, 187
multiuser	336
APPEND FROM	102, 333

Apple menu 125, 128
ARRAY
    limits 230
array element 132
array.prg 133
Arrays 130, 131, 132, 315
arrays of record numbers 265
ASCII character 159
asterisk 17
AT()
    with memo field 233
automatic page eject 285
automatically indent 69
AVERAGE 310

B

bkerror.prg 173
bkmain.prg 167
BOF() 189
break-point 88
BROWSE 225, 238

C

calc1.prg 55
calc2.prg 57
calc2a.prg 62
calc3.prg 66
calc4.prg 73
called 151
calling 151
CANCEL 151

CASE 74
case sensitivity 114, 115
Centered text 155
Check boxes 228
child file 306
child records 249
CHR() 159
CHR(7) 159
CLEAR 18
CLEAR ALL 101, 151
CLEAR GETS 38, 39
CLEAR MEMORY 151
CLOSE ALL 101
CLOSE DATABASES 101, 119
close the edit window 34
columns, ...39, 41
command window
    inserts from menu system 8
Command+0 10
Command+E 21
    See: **DO**
commands
    abbreviating 19
    in upper case 19
comments 17
    following ENDDO,ENDIF 66
Compiling
    Automatic by FoxBASE+/Mac 15
concat1.prg 92
Concatenation 92
config.fx 10
    Starting FoxBASE+/Mac with 12
constants 27, 29
    character 30
    logical 30
    numeric 30

Index

CONTINUE 102, 231, 294, 298
Copying an existing program 19
correspondence programs 252
COUNT 102, 310
crcorr.prg 259
crcorr2.prg 260
crcorra.prg 261
crcorrd.prg 261
crcust.prg 255
crcusta.prg 257
crcustd.prg 258
CREATE 96, 105
crmain.prg 253
crrepo1.prg 304
crrepo1h.prg 305
crscroll.prg 262

D

data entry programs 177
data1.prg 80
data2.prg 82
data3.prg 89
database 95
Date math 91
date1.prg 91
DBF STRUCTURE/CONTENT LIMITATIONS 98
dbf1.prg 99
dbf2.prg 106
dbf3.prg 110
dbf4.prg 113
dbf5.prg 116
Debug option 84
Debug window 84, 85, 87, 150

Delete
    using REPLACE 258
DELETE ALL 333
DELETED() 183, 194
desc.prg 252
descending indexes 251
descriptive menu system 140
DIMENSION 132
DISPLAY MEMORY 84
DISPLAY STATUS
    Default drive 12
DISPLAY STRUCTURE 84
DO 18, 151
    WITH clause 158
DO CASE 73, 74, 75, 77
DO WHILE 38, 57, 59
    endless loop 64
    primed loop 64
DO WHILE .NOT.EOF() 283
DO WHILE lbrepo() 283
docase1.prg 76
docenter.prg 157
double ampersand 17
dowhil1.prg 60

E

EDIT 278
Edit menu 125, 128
ELSE 69
ENDCASE 73, 74, 75, 77
ENDDO 38, 58, 59
ENDIF 63, 66
endless loop 64

EOF() 114, 180, 189, 283, 300
EOF(2) 302
ERASE 338
ERROR() 326
Event-driven 121, 143
exclusive use 336
EXIT 59, 63

F

field lengths 96
Field names 96
Field type 96
fields 95
File menu 125, 128
FILE() 111
FIND 102
FLOCK() 330, 334
FLUSH 330
Font
    default for printer 286
FOUND() 114, 302
FoxBASE+/Mac text editor 14
FoxCode 205
FoxForm 195, 196, 198, 200, 202, 204, 206
    Rules for using in programs 204
    Tools 196
FoxReport 317, 318, 320, 322
    calculations in 320
    conditional type styles 321
    memory variables in 320
    OR MODE for overlapping objects 321
    preventing output to screen 318
    Smaller point sizes in 317

UDF usage in 322, 323
using IIF() 320
full-screen editing 35

G

GENERATE 195
GET
  outstanding..38
  satisfying...39
GETEXPR...236, 294
GO/GOTO 102
GOTO..186
GOTO BOTTOM 187
GOTO TOP 186, 294
Grouping feature of FoxReport 322
Grouping records by Indexing 250

H

hello.prg..13
hello1.prg..19
hello2.prg..27
hello3.prg..30
Help 49, 51

I

IF 63, 65
IIF()..223, 300, 303, 320, 321
ilentr.prg 244

Index 345

ilentr2.prg 246
ilsuppv.prg 247
immediate if
   See: **IIF()**
indenting programs 69
index 287
INDEX CLAUSE 109
INDEX file 103
INDEX ON 106, 115
INSERT
   multiuser..336
invisible buttons 265
invisible SEEK 302
IVDESC.IDX 178
iventr.prg 179
iventr2.prg 181
iventr2m.prg 329
iventr2z.prg 331
iventr3.prg 202
iventrd.prg 193
iventrl.prg 190
iventrm.prg 188
iventrn.prg 184
iventrnm.prg 334
iventrx.prg 202
IVITEM.DBF 178
IVITEM.IDX 178
ivrepo.prg 300
ivrepo1.prg 301
ivrepo2.prg 303

K

key expression 105

key field
    unchangeable 182
KEYBOARD 225
keyboard shortcut
    Command+0 for command window 10
    Command+E 21
    Command+H 50

L

LaserWriter 318
lbcenter.prg 155
lbexcl.prg 336
lblockr.prg 332
lbq.prg 163
lbrepo.prg 278, 279, 281
lbval.prg 216, 223
lbval1.prg 216
leading 44
LEN() 192
LIST 109
LOCATE 102, 231, 294
LOCK clause 123
Lookups 244, 245, 247, 257, 299
Loop
    See: **Do While**

M

main program 144, 145, 147
main.prg 145
manyget1.prg 35
manyget2.prg 37

Index

347

manyget3.prg 43
manygets.prg 31
master index 111
memo field 233
Memory Variagles,limits 152
MENU 127
    Check following READ 127
MENU BARS 127, 129
menu handling program 144
menu hit 127
MENU ON -3,1 255
MENU(0) 128, 136
MENU(1) 128
MENU(1). 136
Menu-driven 121
menu1.prg 124
menu2.prg 128
menu3.prg 130
menu4.prg 134
menu5.prg 136
menus
    divider lines 135
    Enhanced display 134
    using to create programs 13
MESSAGE() 326
MESSAGE(1) 326
Micro Endeavors 3
MODI COMM 19
MODIFY COMMAND 19
MODIFY FILE 10, 317
MODIFY REPORT 317
MODIFY SCREEN 196
MODIFY STRUCTURE
    multiuser 336
modular programming 149
muerror.prg 327

multiple database files	116, 117, 119
multiple records on screen	265
multiplying	68
Multiuser	325, 326, 328, 330, 332, 334, 336, 338
MVARSIZ	133
mystery.prg	161
mystery1.prg	162
mystery2.prg	162

N

naming convention	98
nested DO WHILE	295
Nested IF	66, 67
nonproportional font	286, 310
nonproportional fonts	317

O

ON ERROR	175, 282, 326, 337
ON MENU	127, 128
OTHERWISE	75
overlapping objects on screen	40

P

PACK	183, 194
multiuser	336
Page breaks	284
page eject	285
Parameter	154, 155, 157

PARAMETERS 151, 158
parent file..306
parent records..249
pict1.prg 47
pict2.prg 52
PICTURE clause 46
Picture Functions..49
Picture templates 46, 47, 49
PIXEL addressing 265
    functions to use when printing 287
PIXEL clause..40
pixel1.prg 40
pixel2.prg 40
pixels..39, 41
    Functions for calculating 159
pop-up 226, 227
Preferences... option of the Edit 69
prempl.prg 209
prempl1.prg 212
prempl2.prg 213
prempll.prg 217
prempln.prg 218
premplq.prg 219
Primed loop 64
Printer error trapping 282
PRIVATE 81, 101, 151, 153, 160
    program disk 3
Program diskette 175
Program Listing
    array.prg 133
    bkerror.prg..173
    bkmain.prg 167
    calc1.prg 55
    calc2.prg 57
    calc2a.prg 62
    calc3.prg 66

calc4.prg	73
concat1.prg	92
crcorr.prg	259
crcorr2.prg	260
crcorra.prg	261
crcorrd.prg	261
crcust.prg	255
crcusta.prg	257
crcustd.prg	258
crmain.prg	253
crrepo1.prg	304
crrepo1h.prg	305
crscroll.prg	262
data1.prg	80
data2.prg	82
data3.prg	89
date1.prg	91
dbf1.prg	99
dbf2.prg	106
dbf3.prg	110
dbf4.prg	113
dbf5.prg	116
desc.prg	252
docase1.prg	76
docenter.prg	157
dowhil1.prg	60
hello.prg	13
hello1.prg	19
hello2.prg	27
hello3.prg	30
ilentr.prg	244
ilentr2.prg	246
ilsuppv.prg	247
iventr.prg	179
iventr2.prg	181
iventr2m.prg	329

iventr2z.prg	331
iventr3.prg	202
iventrd.prg	193
iventrl.prg	190
iventrm.prg	188
iventrn.prg	184
iventrnm.prg	334
iventrx.prg	202
ivrepo.prg	300
ivrepo1.prg	301
ivrepo2.prg	303
lbcenter.prg	155
lbexcl.prg	336
lblockr.prg	332
lbq.prg	163
lbrepo.prg	279
lbval.prg	216
lbval1.prg	216
main.prg	145
manyget1.prg	35
manyget2.prg	37
manyget3.prg	43
manygets.prg	31
menu1.prg	124
menu2.prg	128
menu3.prg	130
menu4.prg	134
menu5.prg	136
muerror.prg	327
mystery.prg	161
mystery1.prg	162
mystery2.prg	162
pict1.prg	47
pict2.prg	52
pixel1.prg	40
pixel2.prg	40

prempl.prg	209
prempl1.prg	212
prempl2.prg	213
prempll.prg	217
prempln.prg	218
premplq.prg	219
pubpriv.prg	152
pubpriv1.prg	153
pubpriv2.prg	153
repo1.prg	278
repo1a.prg	287
repo1b.prg	292
repo1c.prg	295
repo1h.prg	284
snake.prg	315
standard.prg	147
stat.prg	311
stat1.prg	311
stub.prg	149
subtot.prg	312
subtoth.prg	314
sysmenu.prg	138
sysmenu1.prg	173
typtot.prg	322
udftest.prg	164
vidrents.prg	318
zrcorr.prg	270
zrcorr1.prg	271
zrcorr2.prg	271
zrcorra.prg	272
zrcorrd.prg	273
zrcust.prg	267, 274
zrcusta.prg	269
zrcustd.prg	269
zrmain.prg	266
zrrepo1.prg	308

Index

zrrepo1h.prg 309
zrscroll.prg 275
Program nesting..151
program stub 149
Proportional font..286
proportional fonts 317
prproj.dbf 220
prproj.idx 220
PUBLIC 81, 101, 132, 151, 153
pubpriv.prg 152
pubpriv1.prg 153
pubpriv2.prg 153
PUTFILE() 281

Q

QUIT 11, 101, 151

R

Radio buttons 228
READ 24, 128
    Exiting from by user 36
    multiple gets 34
READ SAVE..38
RECALL 183, 194
RECNO(0) 192, 193
record pointer 102, 189
records 95
REINDEX
    multiuser...336
Relating Databases 249
relational operators 79

RELEASE 132, 151
REPLACE 187
REPLACE ALL 333
repo1.prg 278
repo1a.prg 287
repo1b.prg 292
repo1c.prg 295
repo1h.prg 284
REPORT FORM 318
Reports
    boldface..307
       multiple fonts..307
       ruling lines 307
resume button 70
RETRY 327
RETURN 18, 151
reuse of empty 262
RLOCK() 330
rows..39, 41

S

Save As...19
Saving a new .prg file..14
SCREEN 18, 21
    AT clause 22
    FIXED 23
    FONT 22
    LOCK clause 123
    row size 22
    SIZE clause 22
    TOP 23
    TYPE 22
SCREEN TYPE 4 123

screens
    limited by RAM 21
scrolling data entry 265
Scrolling lists 229, 231
SEEK 102, 112, 113, 115, 183, 185, 187, 192, 250, 300
    Using TRIM() 192
SELECT 116, 300
semi-colon for long commands 45
semicolon to separate multiple menu options 127
SET BELL 35
SET CONFIRM 35
SET DEFAULT TO 5
SET DELETED 194
SET DEVICE TO PRINT 282
SET DEVICE TO SCREEN 281, 283
SET ECHO OFF 72
SET ECHO ON 70
SET EXCLUSIVE OFF 328
SET FILTER 238
SET FILTER TO 293
SET INDEX TO 109, 111
SET ORDER 192
SET ORDER TO 111
SET PRINT OFF 281
SET PRINTER OFF 283
SET RELATION TO 300, 302
SET STEP OFF 72
SET STEP ON 70, 88
SET STRICT 35
skeleton program 179
SKIP 102, 189, 283, 289, 298
snake.prg 315
SORT 287, 291
    descending 291
SPACE() 187, 192
standard.prg 147

stat.prg 311
stat1.prg 311
STORE 28, 56
STR() 88, 89
string memory pool 133
stub.prg 149
STUFF()
    with memo field 233
STYLE
    for boxes 240
    for printing 310
    to prevent automatic page eject 285
STYLE clause 40
submenus 128
subroutines 151
SUBSTR()
    with memo field 233
subtot.prg 312
Subtotals 295, 297
subtoth.prg 314
SUM 320
SUM 310
SYS() 45
SYS(1021) 45
SYS(1022) 45
SYS(1023) 45
SYS(1024) 45, 159, 239
SYS(1025) 46, 159
SYS(1026) 46
SYS(1027) 46, 159
SYS(1028) 46
SYS(1029) 46
SYS(1030,"") 159
SYS(1030,"characters") 46
SYS(1034) 159
SYS(1035) 255

SYS(1037)
    page dialog 281
SYS(1038)
    printer setup 281
SYS(1039) 46
SYS(1040) 46
SYS(16) 150, 326
sysmenu.prg 138
sysmenu1.prg 173
system memory 133

T

Temporary work files 337
Text edit ranges 232, 233
Trace option 72
trace window 69, 71
TRIM() 192
TYPE("memvar") 84
typtot.prg 322

U

UDF 163, 181, 279
    commands used with 166
    lblockr for record locks 333
udftest.prg 164
unique id 183, 187
UNLOCK 328, 330
UPPER() 104, 159
    with memo field 233
USE 99
    INDEX CLAUSE 109

USE 102
USER DEFINED FUNCTION...163

V

VAL() 45, 81, 159
VALID
   default message 220
   Input from user in UDF 224
   Invalid UDF commands 223
   no message...223
   UDF for message 223
   User's defeating 226
VALID clause...220, 221, 223, 225
Variables 27, 29
   changing with subroutines..161, 163, 165
vidrents.prg 318
View window 8

W

WAIT 58, 128
WHILE clause 312
work area identifier 260
work areas..116

Z

ZAP
   multiuser..336
zrcorr.prg..270

zrcorr1.prg 271
zrcorr2.prg 271
zrcorra.prg 272
zrcorrd.prg 273
zrcust.prg 267, 274
zrcusta.prg 269
zrcustd.prg 269
zrmain.prg 266
zrrepo1.prg 308
zrrepo1h.prg 309
zrscroll.prg 275

Management of Electronics Assembly

Management of Electronics Assembly

Design, development, production, test

IAN OAKES

NEWNES

Newnes
An imprint of Butterworth-Heinemann Ltd
Linacre House, Jordan Hill, Oxford OX2 8DP

PART OF REED INTERNATIONAL BOOKS

OXFORD LONDON BOSTON
MUNICH NEW DELHI SINGAPORE SYDNEY
TOKYO TORONTO WELLINGTON

First published 1992

© Ian Oakes 1992

All rights reserved. No part of this publication may be reproduced in any material form (including photocopying or storing in any medium by electronic means and whether or not transiently or incidentally to some other use of this publication) without the written permission of the copyright holder except in accordance with the provisions of the Copyright, Designs and Patents Act 1988 or under the terms of a licence issued by the Copyright Licensing Agency Ltd, 90 Tottenham Court Road, London, England W1P 9HE. Applications for the copyright holder's written permission to reproduce any part of this publication should be addressed to the publishers

British Library Cataloguing in Publication Data
A catalogue record for this book is available from the British Library

ISBN 0 7506 0071 3

Typeset and produced by Co-publications, Loughborough
Printed and bound in Great Britain by
Thomson Litho Ltd, East Kilbride, Scotland

Contents

Preface vii

Acknowledgements ix

1 Pupose of management 1
    The financial framework 1
    Accounts 4
    Measuring company performance 6
    Liquidity 8
    Management's role 10

2 Planning in electronics manufacture 13
    Market share 14
    Business strategy 14
    Electronics manufacturing — quality 15
    Manufacturing as a process 17
    Materials resource planning 18
    Just-in-time 21
    Optimized production technology 25
    Cost allocations 26
    Quality systems 28
    Product reliability 31
    Process optimization 33

3 Component technologies 35
    Evolution and revolution 35
    A choice of manufacturing technique 44
    Surface mount technology 48

Contents

4	Design of assemblies	59
	Structured software design	64
	Design using computer-aided design	67
	Printed circuit board layout	75
	Designing for assembly	82
5	Assembly production	87
	Printed circuit boards	87
	Printed circuit board manufacture	91
	Justification of surface mounted technology	102
	Electronics assembly	104
	Design guidelines for leaded auto-insertion	105
	Surface mounted component placement machines	111
6	Soldering assemblies	115
	Soldering basics	116
	Solder	117
	Flux	118
	Soldering processes	121
	Solder paste or adhesive application	127
	Cleaning of assemblies after soldering	129
	Testing of electronics assemblies	130
7	Test methods and strategies	133
	Faults	134
	Test and inspection applications	137
	Test methods	142
	Test strategies	153
8	Computer integrated manufacture	156
	Open systems interconnect	157
	Manufacturing automation protocol	159
	Data exchange standards	159

Glossary   164

References and further reading   173

Index   175

Preface

"Nothing gets done, until somebody sells something"

That's an adage you hear often enough in the electronics manufacturing industry (in others, too, for that matter). In many respects, it's true. For without a marketplace, there's little point in making anything. If somebody wants to buy something, though, somebody has to sell it. And to sell it, there must be some way of making it.

But if you don't actually have the product on your market-stall — ready to hand over to the person who's giving you the money, how can you justify being able to sell it in the first place?

Of course, this is an age-old problem. It's the main reason why manufacturers build up stocks of product prior to selling. Otherwise, when demand hits you for your product, you've no product to sell, have you?

These days, though, stocks of products mean lost revenue. Worse still, stocks of products effectively mean you as a manufacturer have invested money which, at best, you *might* see returned as profit; at worst, on the other hand, may liquidate you!

Manufacturing as a business

In the real world, manufacturers make things to make a profit. Otherwise, there is no point in making things at all. So, it's a manufacturer's business to see the business is profitable.

To do this properly the business must be under control. Every aspect of the business — personnel, industrial equipment, working procedures and, particularly, finance, must be controlled. That is, in essence, what this book is about — control.

Managers control or, at least, they are expected to control. Whether managers do their job effectively or not is a matter of contention. In many cases it is difficult to see if they do their job well. Often a manufacturer's insolvency is the first outside indication of bad managerial practices. By this point, of course, it is too late to repair the damage done.

Mind your own business

Many managers are tied up within their businesses and do not get the chance to look at things in perspective. What this book hopes to achieve, is simply to make the managers look at their businesses from the outside in; to see things which aren't so apparent when you're in the thick of it.

Armed with the knowledge presented here and perhaps with a little luck, managers can manage effectively so that when somebody sells something, what's supposed to happen — does.

Perhaps the old addage should be rewritten —

"Nothing gets done, until somebody manages something"

Acknowledgements

Many people have helped me in the course of researching, writing and producing this book. However, I would particularly like to thank the following:

Mr J Spanton
Mr P Macready
Miss K Bellamy
Prof F Arthur
Mr K Brindley
Mrs B Buckley
Dr P Ingham

Their help has been invaluable.

1 Purpose of management

Like all businesses, electronics and all areas involved in manufacture of electronics products is based on sound control — control over personnel, control over work procedures, control over safety and so on. Areas to be controlled by management often vary from business to business. Yet one area within any and, indeed, all businesses requires control in a virtually identical way — whatever the business. It is the financial area of any business which needs to be controlled thus.

Without sound financial control, no business is safe. *With* sound financial control, on the other hand, each part of a company can progress as planned, secure in the knowledge it has the required monetary backing.

While no one can deny importance of controlling other areas within the business domain, it remains the *prime* purpose of management to maintain sound control over a company's financial situation.

The financial framework

This chapter introduces some of the elements of financial management and how they relate to investment in computer-aided design and advanced manufacturing techniques.

Without an understanding of *why* companies invest and how they *judge* those investments, managers and users cannot expect to play their full part in achieving the full benefits of modern manufacturing methods.

As a consequence, one of our main objectives in this chapter is to define those terms which are used in financial management. Many of these terms are used quite loosely by those who don't understand them, but the definitions here are specific. By way of defining these terms, we relate them, practically, to typical accounting methods.

Purpose of management

Funds flow

Financial management is concerned with the task of ensuring that monies provided by lenders, owners and customers are sufficient and are used profitably and effectively to fund a company's operation. Figure 1.1 shows the major sources and application of funds.

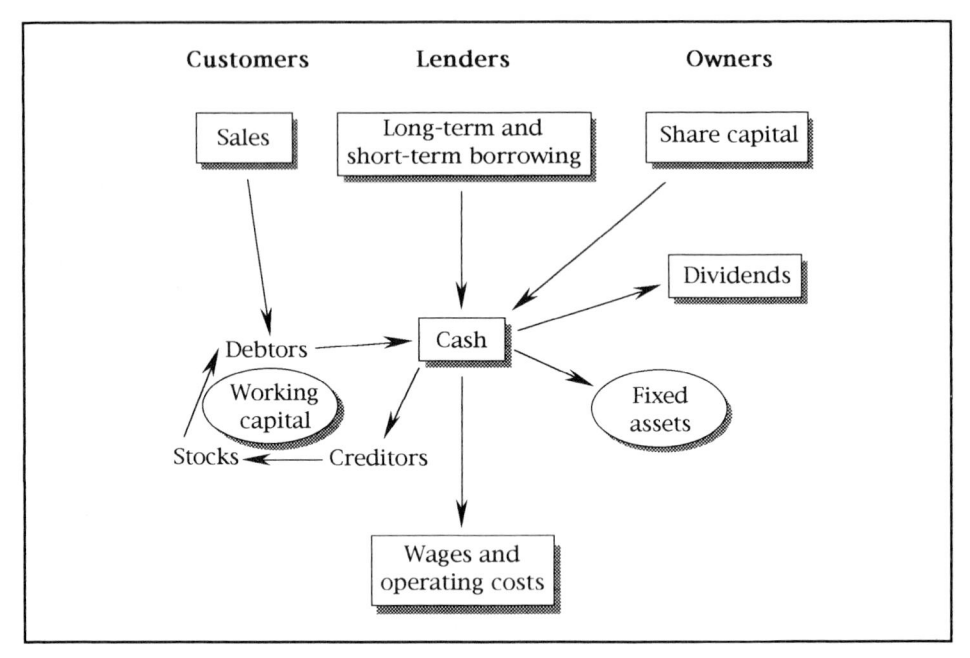

Figure 1.1 *Flow of funds model for business, showing major sources and applications of funds in a company's operation*

There are two major types of expenditure that have to be managed for a firm to remain in business. These are:

- those required for the company to operate on a day-to-day basis (wages, materials, dividends, interest, and so on) — called **working capital**
- those required to provide the plant and machinery necessary to carry out the business on a long-term basis — called **investments**.

Working Capital

This is the difference between the money owed to creditors such as suppliers of materials and the cash and assets that can easily be converted to cash. Examples of these are bank balances, monies owed by customers, finished goods, and so

The financial framework

on. We can specifiy working capital by the expression:

working capital = current assets - current liabilities.

Current generally means within the next twelve months. There must be sufficient working capital to cover the period between the suppliers being paid, the products being sold and the customer paying. This period varies from industry to industry and product to product and is usually measured in months.

Current ratio

The ratio between current assets and current liabilities, expressed as:

$$\text{current ratio} = \frac{\text{current assets}}{\text{current liabilities}}$$

is called the current ratio and indicates the liquidity of a business. This is considered further in the section on measuring company performance, later in this chapter.

Investments

Investments are the employment of capital over a longer term than the next 12 months and may be funded from a number of sources such as working capital, lenders or owners. Each of the sources has its costs and benefits.

Working capital

Consideration needs to be given as to what uses, other than investment, this money could be put to. The current ratio and the cash needs in the near future must be borne in mind before committing money to a long-term investment.

Working capital in a profitable company is available but the use of the money for investment relative to other business needs has to be considered.

Lenders

Costs of this form of funding are largely in the interest charges levied by lenders and the repayment over a defined period. The requirement to pay interest and the need for lenders to recoup their money in a given time is sometimes a problem, especially in the early days of a company when cashflow is a major concern.

Lenders, whether providing money on overdraft, as a bank loan or by means of loan stock, need to safeguard their investment. This means that they will not only judge the creditworthiness of the company on its past, present and

Purpose of management

predicted performance but may also demand security for their money in the form of a mortgage on assets.

Shareholders' funds

This method of raising investment capital involves the cost of issuing extra shares in the company, and that of providing a satisfactory return to the owners. It is a complex and costly system. One advantage is that the money raised itself does not have to be repaid. However, the investment and management of the working capital needs to be good enough to attract investors to move their money from elsewhere.

Shareholders supply funding as a matter of faith, though in the case of large companies the largest shareholders are often companies themselves who may prove as hard to impress as other lenders.

Dependent on circumstances, it is usual to consider forms of funding in the order shown here. There is also, however, a small number of mechanisms for raising investment capital, including hire-purchase, leasing and so on which are only loosely based on the above sources, and which are not usually classed in these groups.

Provision of capital for investments involves greater issues than whether the investment is an improvement in technology and it is usual to produce a financial justification. This involves a cost/benefit analysis which includes a comparison between using the money this way and investing it for the interest.

Accounts

In order that shareholders of companies can form a view of how well the managers are using their money, companies produce a number of financial reports.

The most important of these are the *profit and loss accounts* showing how profitable or otherwise the company is and the *balance sheet* which details where the money has come from and where it has gone.

Profit and loss account

This is a record of the results of trading, usually over a 12-month period. It details the revenue generated by sales and other activities and the expenses incurred in operating the business. The basic purpose of the profit and loss account is to simply state a company's profit over the period. It is expressed:

   net profit = total revenues − total expenses

This account, while showing how profitable the operations are, gives no indication as to the liquidity of the business; nor does it show how much the business is worth in asset terms. Many a profitable company has been declared bankrupt because it has insufficient current assets to pay its creditors on time. A company clearly needs to make profits to secure its future, but it also needs to ensure it has sufficient cash flow to survive the present.

Balance sheet

A balance sheet is a snapshot of the disposition of funds in a business. It gives information as to the sources of funding and how those funds have been used. It separates assets into *fixed* and *current* categories and lists the sources of the funding for them.

Fixed assets

These are assets which cannot readily be converted back to cash. Examples are buildings and plant and machinery.

Current assets

These are assets it is realistic to consider as being convertible to cash within 12 months. They may be made up of tangible goods or they may be formed by money owed by debtors or, indeed, cash itself in the form of bank balances. They can also include intellectual property such as patents or copyrights that can be expected to yield income or be saleable.

Current liabilities

These are liabilities (generally in the form of debts to others) that fall due for payment within the next 12 months.

Net current assets

Net current assets of a company are given by the expression:

> net current assets = current assets − current liabilities

Capital employed

This is given by the expression:

> capital employed = fixed assets + net current assets

Purpose of management

Fixed assets usually comprise the majority of the *capital employed*, and are funded by long-term finance. This is commonly in the form of shares but it may include long-term loans from other sources. These creditors are in general the last to be paid, after the current creditors, in the event of the company ceasing to trade.

Measuring company performance

The profit and loss account, together with the balance sheet, are the key sources of information for evaluating company performance.

A number of standard ratios are used to express company performance in terms of its:

- profitability
- liquidity
- capital structure and gearing
- activity and efficiency.

Summaries of the accounts of Bloggs Electronics are used throughout, to illustrate these ratios.

Profitability

A statement of actual profit made by a business is not in itself a measure by which one can compare companies (or investments). It needs to be related to the size of the business or how much money it cost to achieve that profit. One method is to calculate the *return on capital employed* (ROCE). This can be done in more than one way and the two most common methods consider the net capital employed and the shareholders' capital employed. These are illustrated in Tables 1.1 (net capital employed) and 1.2 (shareholders' capital employed).

Table 1.1 shows that every pound invested as capital employed in the company was used to generate 22 pence profit in 1992. Table 1.2, on the other

Table 1.1 Using *net capital employed* to calculate the *return of capital employed*. Taken from Bloggs Electronics' accounts for the three-year period from 1990 to 1992

	1990 £1000s	1991 £1000s	1992 £1000s
Profit before taxation and interest	69.5	85	89
Capital employed	300	400	410
Return on capital employed	23%	21%	22%

Measuring company performance

Table 1.2 Using *shareholders' capital employed* to calculate the *return of capital employed*. Taken from Bloggs Electronics' accounts for the three-year period from 1990 to 1992

	1990 £1000s	1991 £1000s	1992 £1000s
Profit after taxation	40	45	46
Shareholders capital employed	235	250	260
Return on capital employed	17%	18%	18%

hand, shows that for every pound of shareholders' money the business generated 18 pence profit which was then available for distribution to shareholders in 1992.

It is the distribution of this post-tax profit as dividends that provides the shareholders with their returns on investment.

The rate of return is known as the *yield* or *payout*. This ratio is, of course, dependent on the price paid for the share and is quoted in the financial press with the share price. The history of yield is also of importance and so we'll consider a three-year period as with the earlier examples and assume that shares were purchased at each year end. The balance sheet of Table 1.3 shows the total dividend yield.

Table 1.3 Total *dividend yield* over the three-year period from 1990 to 1992. Taken from Bloggs Electronics' accounts

	1990 £1000s	1991 £1000s	1992 £1000s
Total dividends	30	30	36
Total number of shares	600	600	600
Dividend per share (p)	5	5	6
Market price per share (p)	100	150	125
Dividend yield	5%	3%	4%

Whilst it can be seen that the return is much lower than could have been earned from a Building Society account, the example serves to illustrate the other major attraction to the shareholder, the *capital value* of the share. In the example the share price has risen 25% over the same period.

Purpose of management

Shareholders invest for two main purposes: either *income* (the dividends) or *capital growth* (the share price). Many factors affect whether an investor wants income or capital growth but the Board of a company must be aware of the effect investments have on both the share price and the dividend level.

Liquidity

There are two main ratios concerned with the ability of a business to pay its debts: the *current ratio* and the *liquid ratio*. Current ratio is given by the expression:

$$\text{current ratio} = \frac{\text{current assets}}{\text{current liabilities}}$$

This is a simple ratio and indicates the state of a company's finances. Too high a ratio would suggest that money is being 'hoarded' in the form of high stocks or bank balances or maybe even that there are large amounts of money owed by customers.

Whether money could be more profitably employed elsewhere than tied up in stock or bank accounts (say, in investment in the business) or whether customers should be allowed large amounts of credit are among the issues a company has to consider in management of its working capital.

A stricter measure of the ability of a business to meet its commitments is the *liquid ratio*, which is similar to the *solvency ratio* except that the only current assets considered as readily convertible (that is, liquid) are cash and debtors. It is given by the expression:

$$\text{liquid ratio} = \frac{\text{cash + debtors}}{\text{current liabilities}}$$

Capital structure and gearing

Relative size of a company's liabilities to the capital employed is known as *gearing*. The higher the gearing the less flexibility there is to raise more capital for investment. Gearing also indicates how hard the company has to work its assets just to service its loans, that is, before any money is available for investors.

In the electronics manufacturing sector gearing approaching 50% is considered large, as investments do not usually yield large profits.

In the property and building sectors, on the other hand, large capital outlays are needed at the outset and investments can yield very high returns indeed.

Following our Bloggs Electronics example, Table 1.4 shows the company's gearing. The figures reflect the additional £85,000 debenture (loan) raised in 1991 without the increase of the company share capital.

Liquidity

Table 1.4 Gearing of Bloggs Electronics, over the three-year period from 1990 to 1992

	1990 £1000s	1991 £1000s	1992 £1000s
Long-term borrowings	65	150	150
Capital employed	300	400	410
Gearing	22%	38%	37%

These ratios show that less than half the external funding used for the business was obtained from outside. It should be remembered that loans are usually interest bearing and so reduce the amount of profit available to shareholders.

So far the examples have looked at how profitable the business is, the margin between its debts and current assets and the ratios of debts to owners' capital. The final ratios in this set concern the efficiency with which the business uses funds.

Efficiency and activity

There are various ways in which these can be expressed or measured; the two considered here are *profit margin* and *asset turnover*.

Profit margin

This is used to indicate the efficiency (profitability) of the core activity ie, sales, and is given by the expression:

$$\text{profit margin} = \frac{\text{gross profit}}{\text{sales}}$$

Once again, our Bloggs Electronics example provides an illustration. Table 1.5 shows profit margin over the three-year period.

These figures indicate that sales have declined in their profitability. This may be due to many factors; tight competition may force reduced prices, say, or increases in the business costs create debts which cannot be fully recovered by price rises.

Asset turnover

This expresses the number of times the total value of the assets utilized has been covered by sales. Asset turnover of a company is given by the expression:

Purpose of management

$$\text{asset turnover} = \frac{\text{sales}}{\text{capital employed}}$$

Once again the accounts of Bloggs Electronics provide an example of asset turnover, in Table 1.6.

Table 1.5 Profit margin for Bloggs Electronics over the three-year period from 1990 to 1992

	1990 £1000s	1991 £1000s	1992 £1000s
Gross profit	69.5	85	89
Sales	480	560	690
Gross profit margin	14%	15%	13%

Table 1.6 Asset turnover, according to the accounts of Bloggs Electronics over the three-year period from 1990 to 1992

	1990 £1000s	1991 £1000s	1992 £1000s
Sales	480	560	690
Capital employed	300	400	410
Asset turnover	1.6	1.4	1.7

Management's role

Investment in computer-aided engineering systems and other advanced manufacturing plant increases fixed assets and thence the capital employed. In turn, an increase in capital employed adversely affects the major standard business ratios.

For this reason, management needs to consider carefully the benefits claimed for investments and, more important, to ensure that when investment is made the savings actually materialize.

Savings may take the form of reduced cost for material and labour affecting the gross profit, or of reduced development times, faster or higher production rates, or a combination of these to increase sales and thus asset turnover.

In some cases the benefit of the improvement in plant is to provide sales of totally or radically improved products.

Management's role

Management's task is an increasingly complex one: not purely to increase profit but to do so in a way that maintains or improves the quality of those profits, as measured by the business criteria explained earlier.

The main financial objective of management and possible actions to achieve the management function are illustrated in Figure 1.2. Finally, Bloggs Electronics' accounts, as a summary of results, are given in Table 1.7.

Financial management — an overview of main strategies

Aim — to increase profitability (ie, to improve return on capital employed)

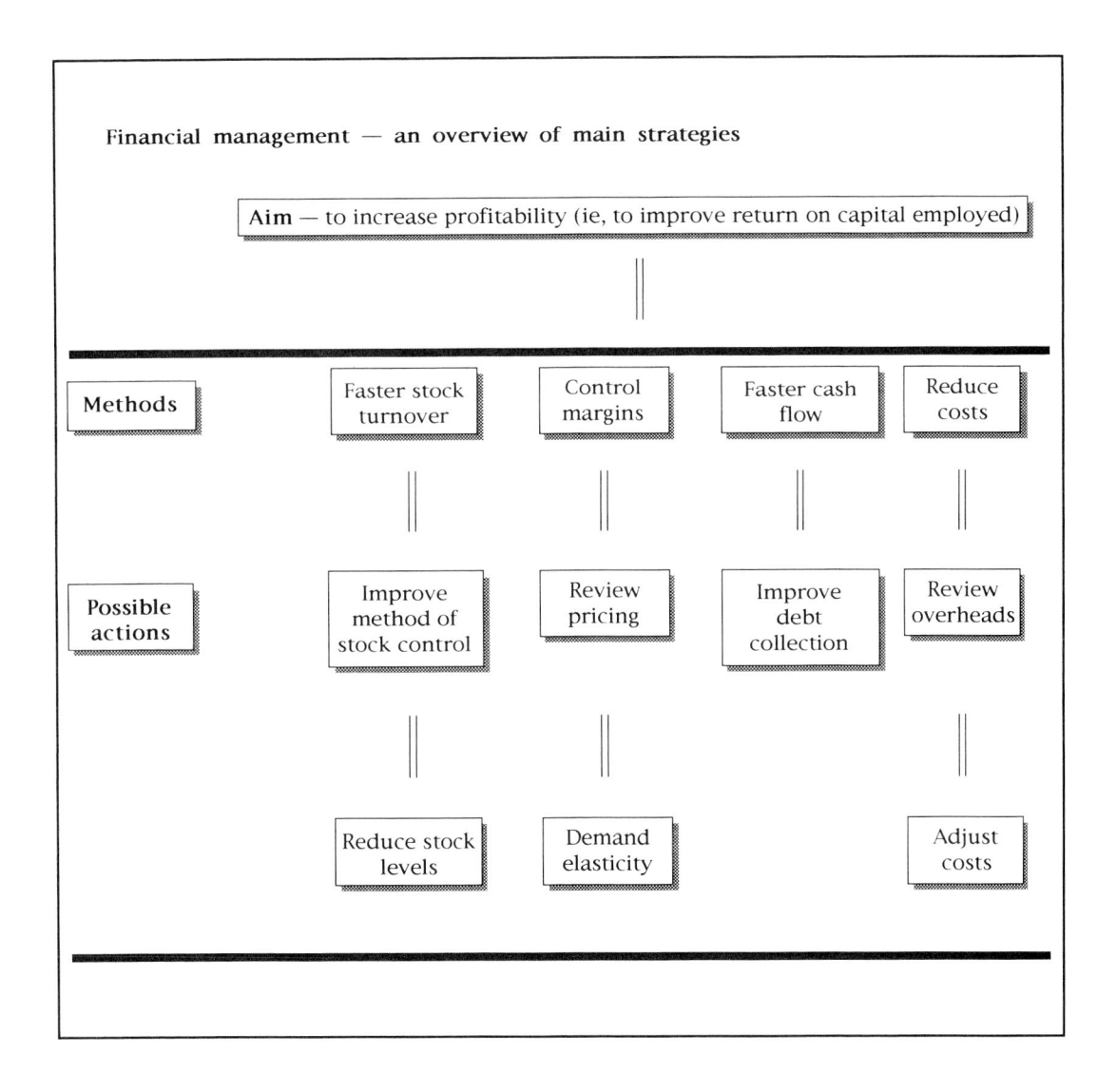

Methods	Faster stock turnover	Control margins	Faster cash flow	Reduce costs
Possible actions	Improve method of stock control	Review pricing	Improve debt collection	Review overheads
	Reduce stock levels	Demand elasticity		Adjust costs

Figure 1.2 *Showing the management function in finance, together with methods and possible actions to achieve its aim*

Purpose of management

Table 1.7 Bloggs Electronics' accounts over the three-year period from 1990 to 1991

Summary of results

	Year ending 31 December		
	1990 £1000s	1991 £1000s	1992 £1000s
Sales	480	560	690
Profits before tax	63	70	74
Tax	23	25	28
Profits after Tax	40	45	46
Dividends	30	30	36
Retained profits	10	15	10
Share capital (600,000 shares @ £0.25)	150	150	150
Retained profit	85	100	110
Shareholders' funds	235	250	260
10% debentures	65	150	150
Capital employed	300	400	410
Market price per share at 31 December	£1	£1.50	£1.25
Debt interest	6.5	15	15
Profits before tax	63	70	74
Add back debt interest	6.5	15	15
Profits before interest and tax	69	85	89

2 Planning in electronics manufacture

Rate of change in technology is mirrored to some extent in the market demand for its products. As design and manufacturing techniques have improved, the customers' expectations have also grown, not only in terms of the sophistication of the product but also its price and speed of delivery.

Product lifetimes are also decreasing; some products now have a lifespan of as little as 12 months and many are in the 12- to 24-month band. With such short product lives, product development and manufacture cycles have also become compressed and the margin for error is drastically reduced.

Constraints of reduced cost, reduced product lead times and the customer's increasing demand for ever higher quality makes *right first time* a survival strategy rather than a slogan. Manufacturers are faced by a dilemma which worsens rapidly with time (see Figure 2.1).

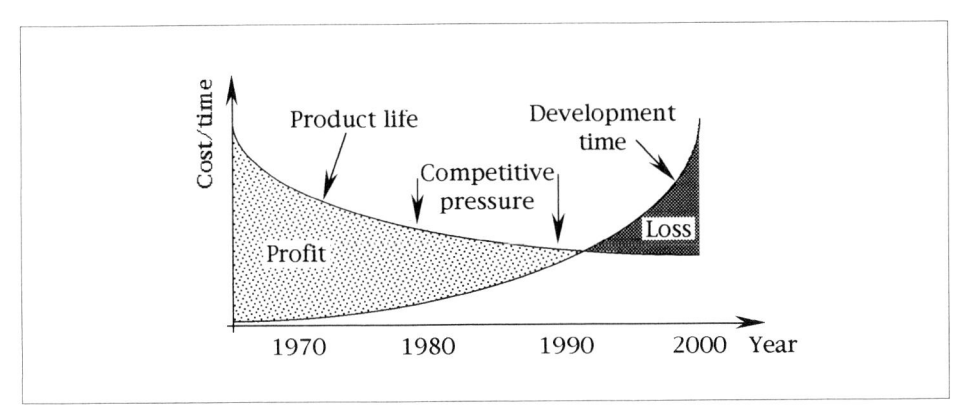

Figure 2.1 *The electronics assembly manufacturer's dilemma*

Market share

The marketplace (customers, plus the competition) defines the problem companies have to solve.

Market share simply goes to those companies that can meet the demand for a product and — unless they have a unique product (rare) — they must fight for this share with others. Thus there are no absolutes in meeting the demand — competition determines the standards. In a nutshell, to meet a demand, modern businesses must face up to and overcome certain challenges, including:

- raise product quality
- introduce new and improved products with reduced lead times
- attain higher productivity and reduced costs
- improve information for the company *and* customers
- improve flexibility — learn to adapt to change.

Despite the growth in national markets, much of the demand is being lost to imports, demonstrating that the challenges *can* be met.

Key product-related elements in meeting market challenges and obtaining a market share include:

- price
- functionality
- quality
- other attributes (form, style, ease of use and so on).

Meeting the challenge to companies

The key issues facing companies are how to provide these basic requirements of high quality, high value-for-money and so on, along with increased complexity and sophistication in very short timescales.

All this has to be managed whilst ensuring that the business remains profitable.

Business strategy

A business needs to define the strategy on which it intends to rely to achieve its business objectives. The strategy needs to be formulated in such a way that it will endure with time and provide direction as financial and product decisions are being made. Some of the crucial issues that such a statement should address include:

- product volume, variety and specifications
- organization
- personnel and training

- capital equipment requirements
- commitment to advanced product technology
- broad computer-integrated manufacture (CIM) implementation timetable
- technology requirements for integrated design, manufacture and test.

These possible points for specific direction can be used to create a company's **strategic statement** which everyone throughout the organization should be aware of. A business strategy is not just for Board members — in fact, it should be aimed more at other personnel.

It is the financial and business environment that provides the reason for — and the pressures on — *good* electronics design and manufacturing. Following this, we need to be aware what *good* electronics design and manufacturing is! This chapter concerns itself with good electronics manufacturing, while Chapter 4 details the requirements of good electronics design.

Electronics manufacturing — quality

The constraints of cost and time as well as the complexity of today's products mean that the required standard of the product can longer be achieved by examining and correcting the finished item.

The Japanese, using theories defined by an American, Dr W Edwards Deming, [#1] in 1948 and originally ignored in the US, have demonstrated that quality needs to run *throughout* the product design and manufacturing operations.

To achieve this the business needs an overall quality strategy to include all of its operations. Each of these operations then requires its own local detailed strategy.

Deming's involvement in quality began with his fundamental study of statistics. He then extended this statistical work to control quality. He was invited to Japan after World War II to advise on sampling techniques — unrelated to manufacturing industries. At that time, Japan was prepared to study in depth what had to be done to rebuild the country as an industrial force and to rid it of the poor reputation Japanese goods had.

Deming's management philosophy is based on the foundations of *total quality* (see later) and the behaviour of variation. This, however, is closely linked to the statistical control of processes, combined with a vital extra component concerned with establishing the best environment in which these concepts can flourish.

Figure 2.2 illustrates the elements of a quality strategy based on Deming's work, showing the links between design and manufacture.

Total quality management

There is an extension of the work of Deming, coupled with that of Dr Joseph M Juran, 1988 [#2], based on the concept that companies should be seeking to constantly improve their products and service. It is interesting to note that, while Japan followed this concept closely, most other countries ignored it until Japan proved it to be viable.

Juran founded the Juran Institute in the USA in 1979. He is a contemporary of Deming and also worked in Japan. Like Deming he too contributed in no small way to the post-war Japanese industrial revolution. He is recognized as a pioneer and visionary in the field of quality and has published several related books.

A fundamental premise behind Juran's message is that quality does not happen by accident — it must be planned. His emphasis is on management's ability to manage quality, rather than technology improvements or statistical manipulation.

Deming's and Juran's principles suggest manufacturers follow a number of principles, including:

- use of statistical evidence to check that quality is being built-in
- emphasis on staff training
- provision of good leadership
- removal of fear and barriers to improvement
- fostering of pride in workmanship.

This extension of Deming's and Juran's work is called **total quality management**. Rather than being just a simple business device, it is a *cultural environment* which places its emphasis on people rather than mechanisms. Rather than overriding the quality system shown in Figure 2.2 and its elements, it is complementary to it.

In essence, total quality management is a philosophy that seeks to help and enable people to identify and solve problems at the source.

The basic model is of 'customer-supplier' where everyone is both a customer and supplier to someone else: in particular, each time information or material is passed from one person or process to the next. In order to make those exchanges useful it is necessary for both parties to understand exactly what is required and to meet those requirements.

Total quality benefits

Benefits of total quality management include:

- self or in-line inspection to identify problems during the process rather than at the end — this enables faster and more cost effective correction
- improved understanding between design and manufacturing, of each other's capabilities and requirements — leading to products designed for ease of manufacture
- increased use of computer-aided engineering (CAE) systems with inherent in-built rules and checks, to produce designs requiring fewer engineering changes during production — a valuable contribution in this area
- elimination of waste — not only of material, but any operation that does not add value to the product.

Manufacturing as a process

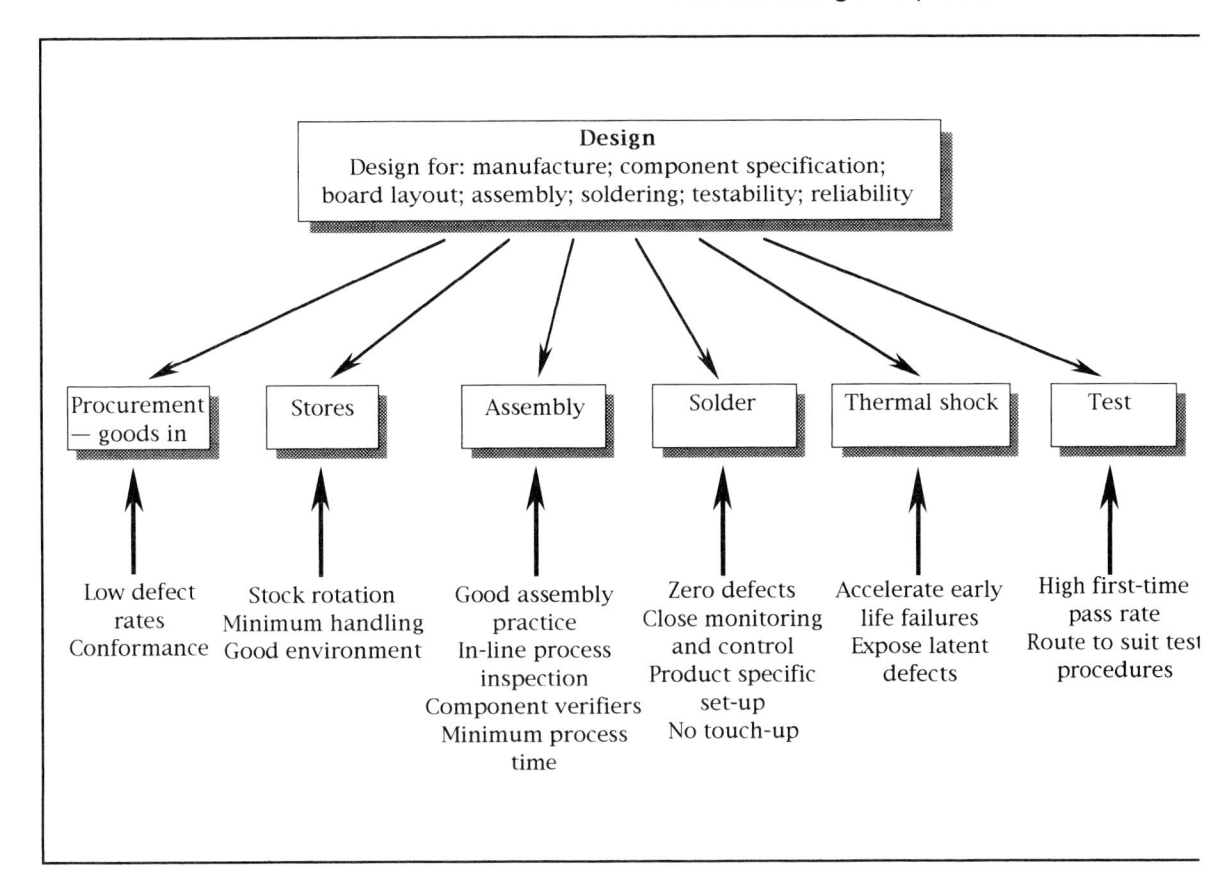

```
                    ┌─────────────────────────────────────────────────┐
                    │                    Design                       │
                    │ Design for: manufacture; component specification;│
                    │ board layout; assembly; soldering; testability;  │
                    │                  reliability                     │
                    └─────────────────────────────────────────────────┘
```

Procurement — goods in	Stores	Assembly	Solder	Thermal shock	Test
Low defect rates Conformance	Stock rotation Minimum handling Good environment	Good assembly practice In-line process inspection Component verifiers Minimum process time	Zero defects Close monitoring and control Product specific set-up No touch-up	Accelerate early life failures Expose latent defects	High first-time pass rate Route to suit test procedures

Figure 2.2 *Links between design and manufacture stages of electronics assemblies, in an overall quality strategy*

Manufacturing as a process

The manufacturing process needs a management system to control and direct it. A complex information network is required to monitor and provide data on subjects such as demand, design, material requirements and the operations required on those materials. It is largely a matter of defining and controlling business information flow although thought needs to be given, also, to technical ways in which information flow can be improved.

Figure 2.3 is a basic schematic of such a system. From this it can be seen there are several interconnecting modules and all need continuous development to increase the sophistication. Without good, accurate and timely information, the financial and business targets will be all the more difficult to achieve.

Planning in electronics manufacture

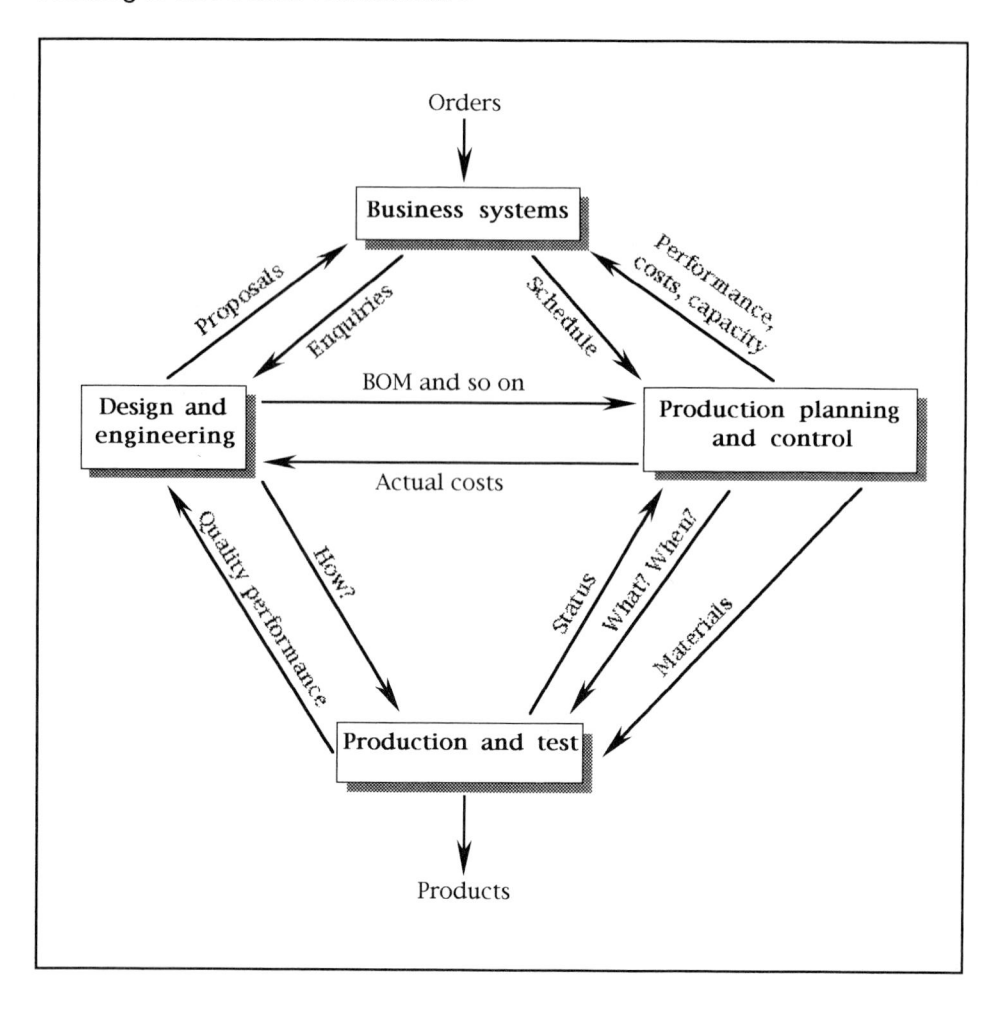

Figure 2.3 *A management system suitable to control and direct the manufacturing processes of electronics assembly*

Materials resource planning

The need for companies to improve reponse times and reduce manufacturing costs has led to the development of **manufacturing resource planning** (MRP) systems, based on conventional computer planning and data processing networks.

The first generation of such systems, conceived and developed by Oliver Wight, concerned itself with materials *requirement* planning and has become known simply as MRP I [Orlicky, 1975 #5][New, 1973 #6].

Materials resource planning

Present systems (MRP II), on the other hand, have evolved to provide computer-based planning and scheduling tools that link and relate information on the product, suppliers and customers by means of a central database.

A manufacturing resource planing system relies on an accurate database containing information on materials, availability, specifications, capacity and forecasts. This, along with any other relevant data, is used to calculate and plan a production schedule. It can also provide feedback to the database on revised stock levels, purchasing requirements and so on. The tight interlinking of the various data sources allows for a consequently tighter control on work in progress and stock as well as providing for more accurate delivery estimates, shorter planning cycles and faster lead times.

Figure 2.4 is a conceptual model of an MRP II system showing the importance of a centralized database. Parts of this model are now described.

Materials requirements planning

Seeks to simulate the manufacturing process to formulate minimum supply levels to achieve the lowest inventory consistent with the sales forecast.

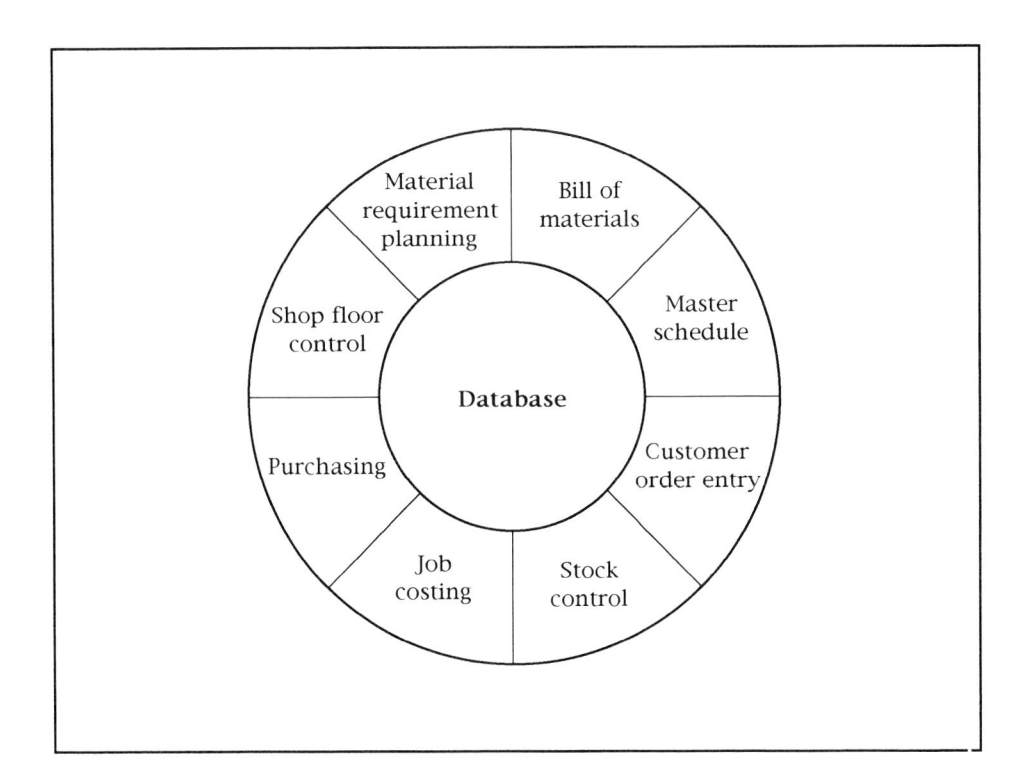

Figure 2.4 *A model for materials resource planning*

Planning in electronics manufacture

Bill of materials (BOMs)

This is similar to a parts list but usually extended to include tooling, test and manufacturing information. Integration with computer-aided engineering (CAE) system tools can reduce the data entry and accuracy problems associated with the conversion of parts lists into bills of materials and their maintenance.

Master schedule

The production plan that tries to make the most effective use of resources to meet the long-term corporate objectives. Application of the forecast demand to the capacity model enables bottlenecks to be identified and analyzed.

Shop floor control

Tracks work in progress for feedback to the master schedule.

Customer order entry

Customers' orders are entered into the system then tracked through to dispatch.
   Orders are aggregated with marketing information to provide the forecast demand.

Purchasing

Generates order documents and provides for entry of material receipts into stock.

Stock control

Used to maintain an up-to-date record of stock levels based on usage and material receipts.

Job costing

Calculates costs either based on bills of materials and routings or from information generated during the manufacturing process. The costs can be actual, standard or average.
   MRP II systems address the problems related to multiple incompatible information sources that are all too common in manual systems. These include:

- stock control — unmatched to demand thus shortages and excesses
- deliveries — uncertain delivery times
- work in progress — excessive work in progress levels

- productivity — low
- production — unforecast peaks and troughs
- paper work — excessive, contributing to high overheads and confusion
- data — inconsistent, dated and inaccurate
- product change control — ineffective.

A complete and successful MRP II implementation is judged by the accuracy of its information. A class A MRP II implementation is defined as:

- inventory record accuracy — 96% or better
- vendor delivery performance — 95% or better
- master production scheduling and materials resource planning time periods — less than one week
- routing accuracy — 95% or better
- master schedule performance — 95% or better
- bill of materials accuracy — 95% or better.

The importance of understanding how an MRP II system interacts with all the operations, is reflected in the requirement that, to achieve class A status, at least 80% of the employees have received material resource planning training.

Figure 2.5 is a view of a basic MRP II system illustrating the data provided to and from the functional elements. This is simplified, and readers should understand that data flows around a real system are more complex.

To achieve the benefits of a comprehensive MRP II system requires considerable planning and analysis. It must also be seen as a collection of tools to help and not become an obstacle because it has not developed with the business.

Just-in-time

Material resource planning systems are designed to plan for economic production based on sales forecasts. Usually items are made for stock in anticipation of demand.

Just-in-time (JIT) systems, on the other hand, derive their name from their aim to make a product when it is needed — not before, and not later.

Unlike materials resource planning, the just-in-time system includes the delivery chain. As soon as the product is completed, it is delivered, even if this means 40 or 50 deliveries per day. The savings on holding inventory outweigh the costs of transport.

What the system requires over and above technology is greater attention to people. Strong bonds are required between suppliers and customers as well as between members of the company. Total quality management is, indeed, essential if just-in-time is to work. Major elements of the JIT philosophy include:

- flow — treat the whole business as a flow process rather than batch-orientated
- quality — implement total quality control so the customer, internal or external, always receives 100% quality

Planning in electronics manufacture

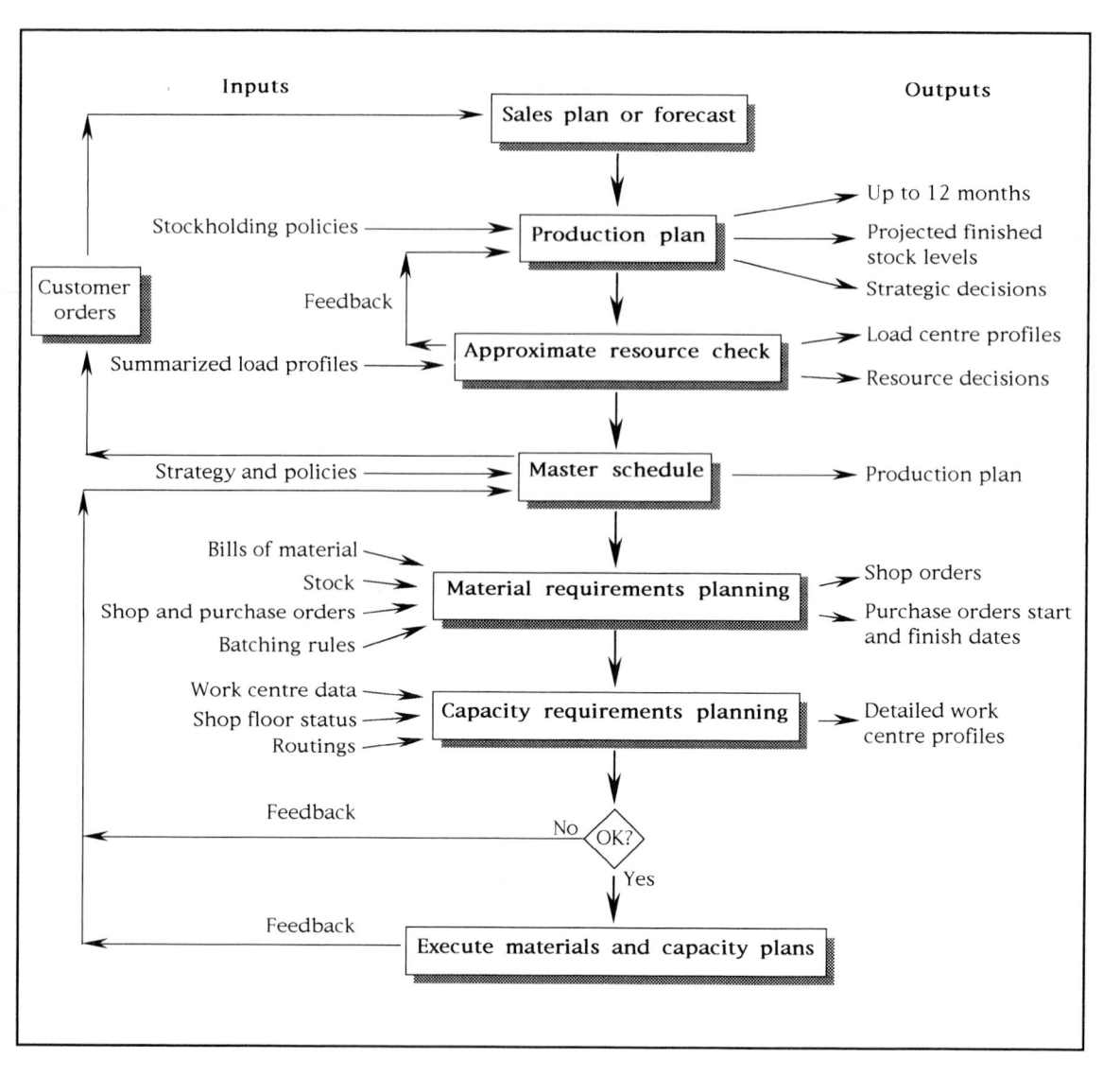

Figure 2.5 *Showing a comprehensive MRP II system*

- waste — eliminate waste by using the absolute minimum of equipment, labour, space and time to add value to a product.

To be able to run successfully a just-in-time system, the whole process has to be seen as one continuous flow. It needs to be smooth and so waste and defective items must be eliminated. Everybody has to play their part — it cannot be *someone else's job*, hence the need for people development.

To ensure the smoothest, most responsive process, just-in-time systems need to be simple. This is achieved by:

- reducing material movement
- eliminating queues
- minimizing set-up times
- simplifying flow and movement
- developing the flexibility of operators
- designing products for ease of manufacturing.

Just-in-time systems are based, essentially, on a concept of *pulling work through* on a customer-demand basis as opposed to *pushing work through* based on forecasts (as in materials resource planning).

The *pull* environment rapidly shows up bottlenecks and disruptions. Effort can immediately be applied to remove the disruption. Systems cannot have high inertia, queues or lack of flexibility, otherwise they simply do not function at all.

Just-in-time work flow

Just-in-time embodies the **kanban** principle for controlling its flow. The term kanban simply refers to a signal from a downstream activity, that indicates an output is required from an upstream process. Thus it is a manufacturing *pull signal*, instructing the upstream process to make another item. Kanban signals can be issued through electronic data communication means, printed cards, or simple word-of-voice.

A kanban card tells you:

- how many parts are needed
- the part name and number
- where they come from
- where they go to.

The kanban card is often fixed to a box that will carry the required parts — for this reason the box can be regarded as a kanban in itself.

When a kanban arrives empty at a machine it tells the machine operator how many to make — and no more! Usually, empty boxes are exchanged for full ones.

Designing the kanban system in this way ensures that:

- lead time is kept to a minimum
- only one journey is made to bring empty containers and take full containers.

It can be appreciated that a kanban box is simply a recirculating works order, so eliminates paperwork, yet ensures that the right parts are delivered in the right amounts to the right place — at the right time. Simple, but extremely effective.

The ultimate downstream activity is customer-demand: a fact which makes the system *make to order*. In turn, this has the effect of reducing batch sizes to a minimum. The ultimate *upstream* activities, on the other hand, are formed by design processes and materials supplies, which is why excellent communications and relationships with both suppliers and designers are so vitally important. A manufacturer implementing a just-in-time philosophy in the workplace has to consider outside suppliers and designers as part of the overall system.

Suppliers and designers, on the other hand, as part of the total just-in-time manufacturing process have to understand and appreciate the capabilities and limitations of the system, so they are able to respond positively, cooperatively and rapidly to the kanban signals they receive in normal operation.

Just-in-time guidelines

There are a few guidelines which should be remembered when considering, implementing, or operating a just-in-time manufacturing system. These guidelines include:

- identify the regular runner
- level the schedule to make products daily, and sell products daily
- reduce any changeover times on machines
- carefully design the system, simulate it and document it
- train the people to use it
- monitor and improve the system, regularly auditing against the manufacturing strategy.

In design, simplicity and modularity of a just-in-time system are important, hence reducing component counts and types. Vendors need to appreciate the importance of just-in-time deliveries of their products and, perhaps, irregular batch sizes. To achieve this, businesses must concentrate on building up their relationships rather than encourage competition purely on price amongst their suppliers.

Figure 2.6 is a schematic of just-in-time production flow.

MRP and JIT comparisons

Materials resource planning systems attempt to plan on a global basis and, as such, are complex. This complexity and inherent inertia make it difficult to operate in a demand-driven market subject to constant change.

Just-in-time philosophy, on the other hand, forms a simpler, low-inertia system, giving faster response times. Its full benefits, however, can only be realized if considerable effort in establishing and maintaining customer-supplier relationships is undertaken.

Both require computer planning, simulation and management tools and both benefit from integration with computer-aided engineering tools.

Table 2.1 provides a comparison of MRP II and JIT manufacturing systems.

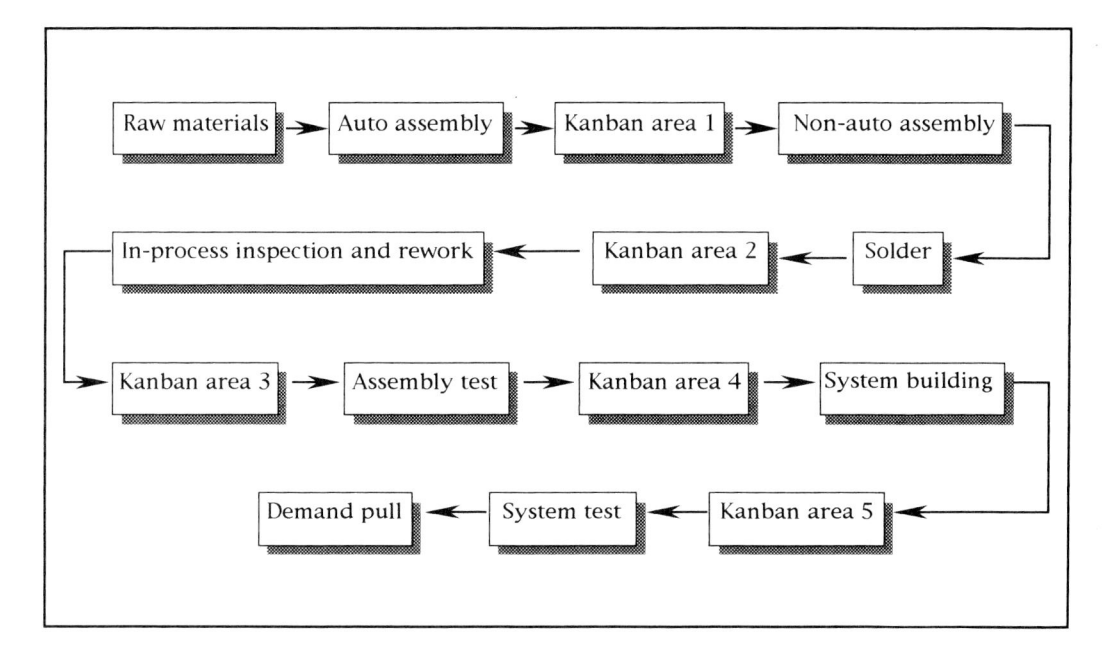

Figure 2.6 *A just-in-time production flow*

Optimized production technology

Whereas materials resource planning focuses on planning resource requirements, and just-in-time focuses on creating flow, optimized production technology (OPT) is concerned with the creation of a precise, achievable production schedule — minute-by-minute if necessary.

The principle was formulated by Moshe Eliyaku Goldratt, an Israeli physicist, and has been implemented in around 300 sites world-wide [Aggarwal, #7].

Concentrates on costs

The goal of manufacturing is to make money and operations in an optimized production technology system are expressed in terms of money. Cost calculations in the manufacturing process are defined in the following ways:

- throughput — the rate at which money is generated through sale
- inventory — money invested in purchasing things intended for sale
- operating expense — the comparison of cost of sales and profitability with budget.

Table 2.1 A comparison of MRP II and just-in-time manufacturing systems

Factor	MRP II — push	JIT — pull
Organizational impact	total company	total company
Planning	extensive	limited
Computer systems	complex, large	simple, smaller
Simulation	extensive	limited
Control	sophisticated	simple
Parameters	fixed	variable
Scheduling	push	pull
Responsiveness	sluggish — weeks	fast — hours
Summary	extensive planning: restrictive and inflexible	limited planning: execution simple and flexible

The analysis of an optimized production technology system is one of identifying bottlenecks or *constraints* in it. For this reason the evolving theory is called the *theory of constraints*.

A bottleneck is defined as a *resource constraint* when capacity is less than or equal to demand. Bottlenecks constrain work-flow, leading to excessive inventories and delivery problems in the production sequence.

By controlling and managing constraints, production itself is managed. If production at the bottleneck is increased, *throughput* increases; if, on the other hand, production of a non-constrained resource is increased then *inventory* is increased. Further, by assuming a bottleneck is going to occur and, indeed, planning on it happening, it can be buffered from prior and later operations taking place. Thus, saleable throughput can be optimized while the correct priorities are achieved.

The aim of management in an optimized production technology system is to synchronize activities of all resources to that of the most constrained resource, thereby to reduce waste and unproductive inventory. The synchronized plan is then used to drive a material requirements system such as MRP I.

Cost allocations

The total quality management philosophy of considering the whole company as one process, along with significant reductions in the labour content of products, is changing the way in which costs are allocated and considered.

In Japan, for example, industrial engineers spend up to 90% of their time

Cost allocations

trying to reduce set-up times and costs. In the UK, on the other hand, up to 75% of the time is spent trying to reduce labour costs, although *labour only accounts for around 10% of the average company's costs*. The typical UK company's attempts to minimize labour costs are illustrated in Figures 2.7a and b.

The usefulness of the conventional accounting separation of costs into direct and indirect is now being challenged. It is the whole company's ability to earn money that is important and costs are costs, after all, however incurred.

Concentration on direct costs has motivated companies to strive for maximum efficiency in the use of production equipment and labour. As a result, the science and skills of work measurement are most highly developed in this area and underdeveloped elsewhere.

Improving efficiency is beneficial but the long-term aim must be for a reduction or elimination of all *unnecessary* costs. All activities in a business that do not add value to a product cause avoidable cost.

The most common form of non-value-added activity is handling, be it transfer of material or information. Handling often requires that an item has to be converted in its presentation, packaging or its contents, before use. Computer-aided design (CAD), computer networks, material handling, fabrication and tracking systems can provide significant benefits in reducing these costs.

Inventory in accounting terms raises the capital value of a company and can enhance its ability to raise capital, in that it is less 'volatile' than cash. Its disadvantage is that it raises the capital employed and so reduces profitability and other important business ratios. It also costs money to keep (accommodation, storekeeping and so on). Reducing inventory levels requires a well-planned and synchronized process.

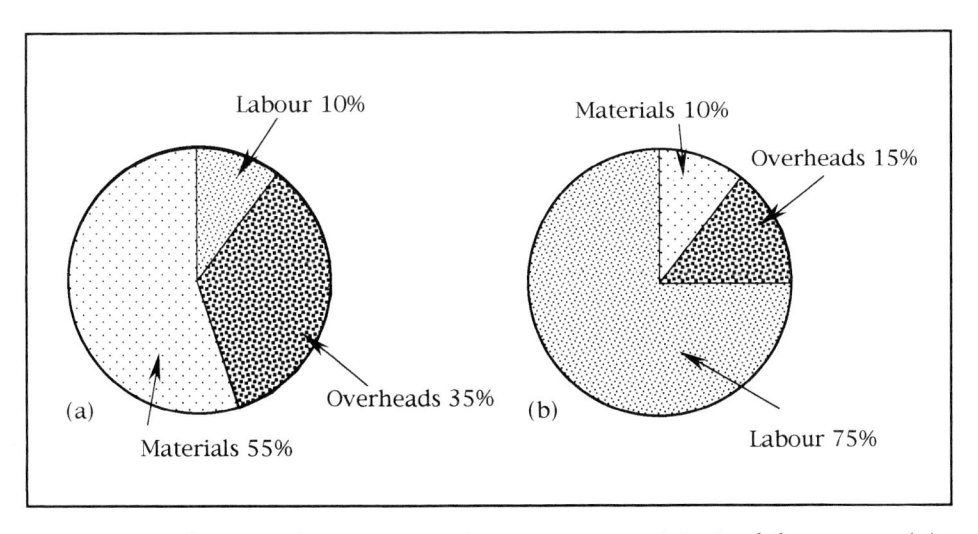

Figure 2.7 *The typical UK company's attempts to minimize labour costs (a) showing costs as a direct proportion of a company's total costs (b) showing time spent reducing costs as a direct proportion of a company's total time*

Quality systems

It should be clear from the previous sections that, in a successful business, quality is not simply a measurement of whether a product conforms to its specification — it is, rather, an involvement of all the processes to ensure that the product satisfies the customer. Thus any quality control procedures must be able to ensure a product is reliable and fit for its function.

While the actual level of quality a product has is primarily a matter to be decided on by the manufacturer, there are national, regional, and worldwide recommendations which should be followed closely if products of the highest standards are to be made. In the United Kingdom, the principal standard covering the quality process is British Standard BS 5750. There are many such standards worldwide. The EEC's equivalents are ISO 9001 and EN 9001.

Quality standards typically require a framework of records and procedures that are directed at ensuring the conformance of the end product to its specification. Major elements required in a quality system approved to BS 5750, for example, include:

1. documented system
2. efficient organization
3. self-audit
4. planning
5. work instructions
6. records
7. analysis of errors
8. control of design
9. control of documentation and change
10. control of test facilities and calibration
11. control of sub-contractors and raw materials
12. control of manufacturing
13. formal testing before delivery
14. marking
15. packaging and transport
16. training organization
17. control of defective items.

If these elements are effectively organized and controlled by a company, then products manufactured or services provided should be of good quality.

Software quality

Trends in product designs are leading to a predominance of software over hardware in the end product, in the approximate ratio of 60%/40%. Quality assurance of software is therefore more crucial than ever to the overall product design and manufacturing process.

Quality systems

Analysis has shown that the majority (around 60%) of software faults arise during the requirements capture stage and subsequent planning. These arise, generally, due to ambiguities in the use of natural language in specifications and the difficulty in specifying all possible paths through the resulting software code. Figure 2.8 illustrates the software quality problem.

Faults due to incorrect coding are often difficult to isolate, because it is rarely possible to test products exhaustively (ie, test each output obtained from a product for every possible input combination) simply due to the high number of possible conditions.

There are aids, fortunately, to assist in writing software; among them are systems designed specifically to improve the quality of software. These include:

- formal requirements specification languages
- structured design methods
- automatic code generators.

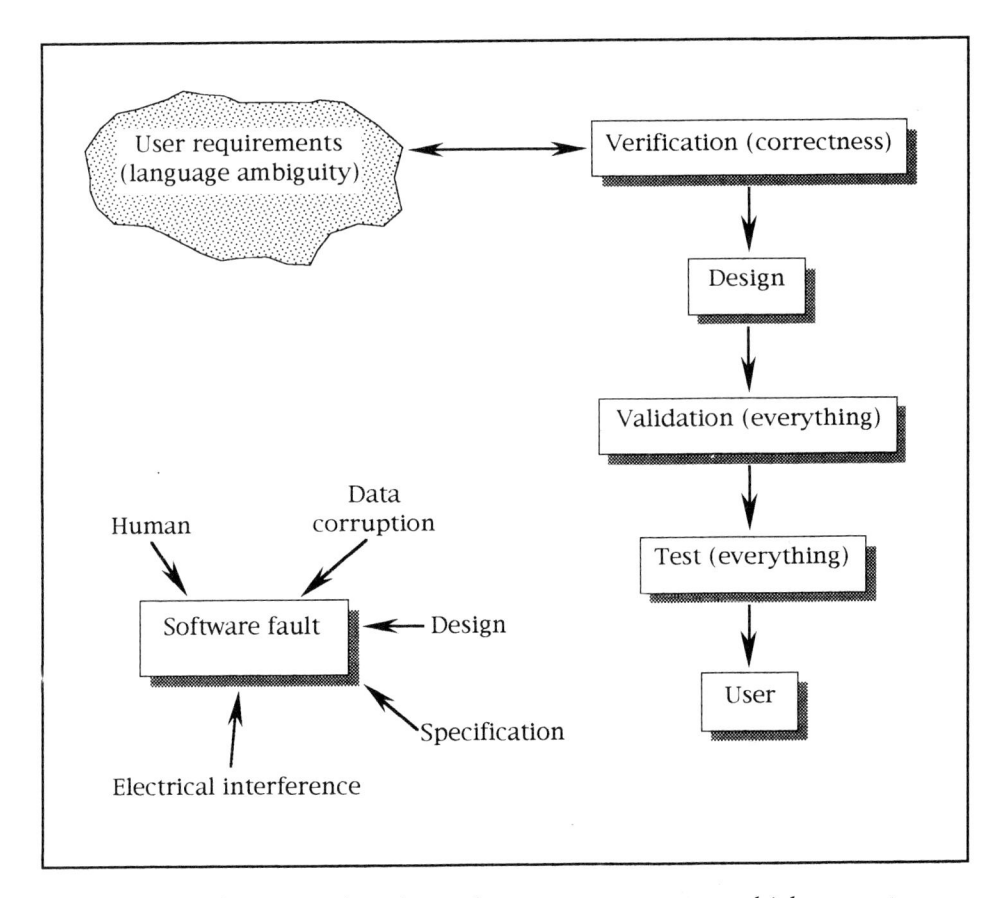

Figure 2.8 *Software quality depends on many processes which are not always considered sufficiently in design stages*

Planning in electronics manufacture

Formal requirements specification

This is a notation based on natural language, which is supplemented by diagrams and tables. It is appropriate for expressing software requirements definition because this must be understood by both the client and the contractor. Albeit useful as the basis of a system contract, however, a specification written in natural language leaves a great deal to be desired.

It is sometimes suggested that formal specification languages should be used initially to express system requirements but that this, in turn, should lead to an unambiguous requirements specification written in a more formal language. Such an unambiguous specification is ideal as the basis of a contract as it leaves no room for argument between client and contractor about system functionality. Unfortunately, most users would not understand a specification written in a formal specification language so are unlikely and unwilling to accept it as a contract basis.

A variation on this theme is **model-based specification**. This is a technique relying on formulation of a model of the proposed system, using well-understood mathematical entities. Entities such as sets and functions are commonly used in model-based specifications, as they are the most easily understood mathematical expressions for clients to come to terms with. System operators within the model are specified by defining how they affect the overall system model.

A well-known model-based specification notation is Z. This is a specification language first suggested by Abrial in 1980, later developed at the University of Oxford by Hayes in 1987. Z is based on typed set theory, because sets are mathematical entities whose semantics are formally defined.

Structured design methods

A methodical approach to software design is offered by structured methods, which are basically sets of notations and guidelines about how to create a software design.

The term *structured methods* is a little misleading in that it suggests some kind of repeatable method whereby two designers, given the same specification, would generate the same design. In fact, these methods are really just standard notations and embodiments of good practice. By following them and applying their guidelines a reasonable design should result, but the designer's creativity is still required to decide on system decomposition and to ensure that the design adequately captures the system specification.

Automatic code generators

The design representations from formal requirements specification languages and structured design methods are translated into a programming language which, ultimately, produces machine-executable instructions. Generally this is done automatically in a number of ways, including:

- static program analyzers — these are software tools which scan the source text of a program and detect possible faults and anomalies. They do not require the program to be executed. They may be used as part of a verification process, to complement error detection facilities provided by the language compiler. As well as checking syntax, static analyzers also check that no parts of the program are unreadable
- automatic verification — the notion of a mathematically formal verification of program correctness is an attractive one, but the amount of work involved is probably not a cost-effective technique to validate large software systems. However, some efforts have been made to develop software tools to reduce this effort. Complete automated program verifiers do not exist, but current theorem provers can develop a proof and help check proofs which have been developed.

Other tool developments include notations which have introduced the idea of self-checking code where verification tool activation and program execution are integrated. The programmer includes verification information in the program and, during execution, this is automatically checked. If the verification tool signals a potential inconsistency, program execution may be suspended or some other exception-handling mechanism may be activated.

Product reliability

Quality considerations do not end with the sale of a product or service. They continue into the warranty period and beyond, either because of legal requirements or to ensure repeat business.

Reliability is the ability of the product to continue to conform to its specification after manufacture. It is designed in — it does not happen by accident.

BS 5760 is the UK standard for the framework of procedures designed to ensure that a product has and meets its designed reliability.

There are many methods used for predicting reliability of a product, ranging from calculations that sum the reliability of every component to an analysis of the ways in which the product can fail. Figure 2.9 emphasises the work to be done in the design stage, viewed as part of the overall development of an electronic product.

At the design stage, specification of materials and components and the conditions under which they will operate are vitally important when trying to achieve the required level of reliability. Heat is a major failure accelerator for components and computer-aided design systems are particularly useful in helping to design the correct thermal environment, especially with the ongoing pressure to reduce physical size of products.

Planning in electronics manufacture

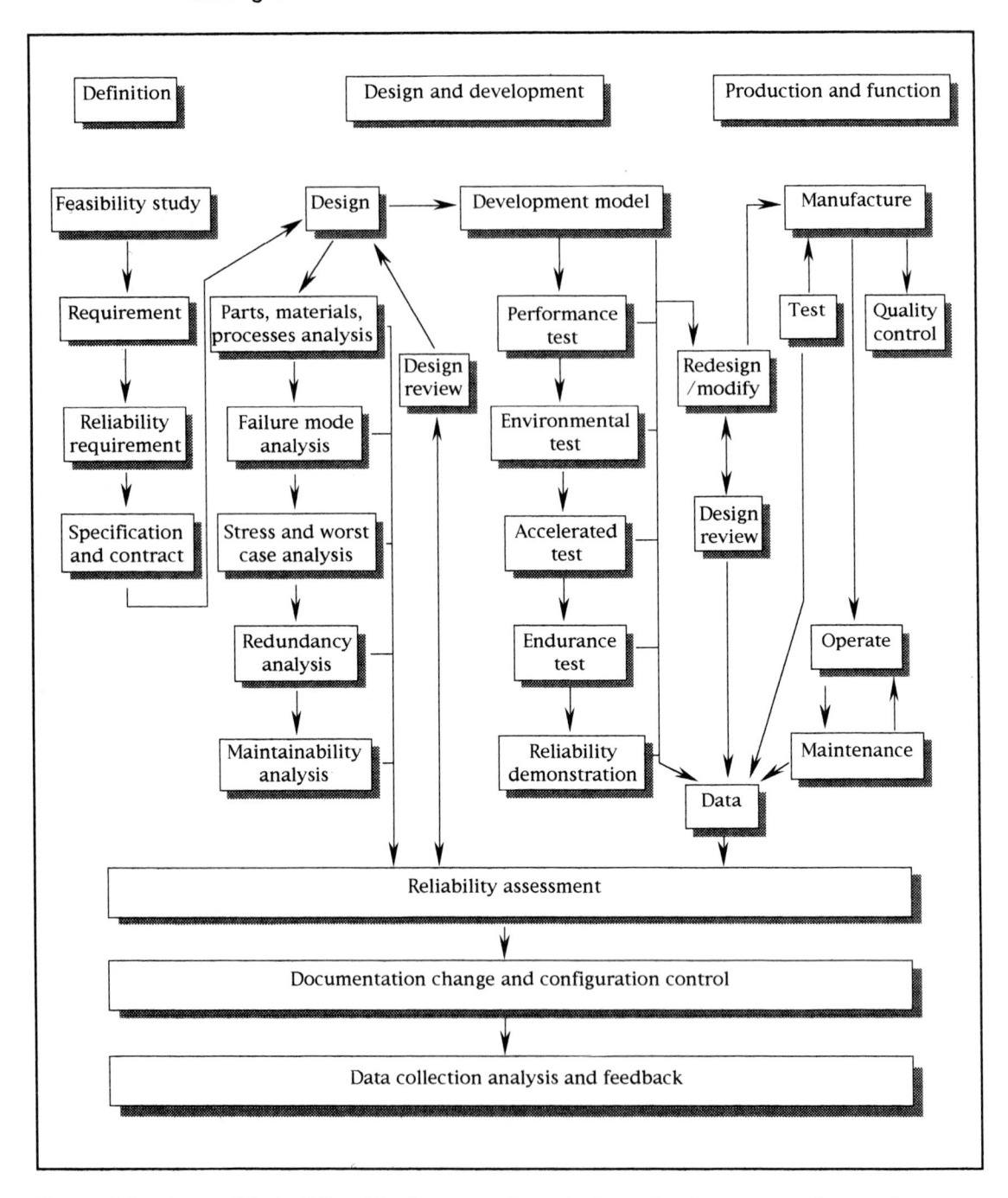

Figure 2.9 *A possible building block approach to design, development and manufacture of an electronic product*

Process optimization

A process is set up to achieve certain objectives, but most systems will exhibit variations in the specification of the resultant product, whether it be tolerance on a component or the standard of workmanship. To ensure overall conformance to specification these variations need to be monitored and controlled for optimum cost and quality; if they are too restricted then cost and throughput are at risk.

Key parameters in a process must be identified before they can be monitored and controlled. It is for the development of methods of identifying these parameters that Dr Genuchi Taguchi [#4] is known. Taguchi presents industry with a philosophy as well as a series of techniques for the optimization of products and processes at early stages before manufacturing starts. In effect, Taguchi turns engineers away from traditional concepts of producing products to specified tolerance limits, to a philosophy based on quantifying progressive quality loss the further away from the nominal.

Taguchi's technique is based on the work of an English statistician, Sir Ronald Fisher. His work, published in *The Design of Experiments*, in 1935, is a documentation describing the rational planning of experiments rather than the detailed analysis of experimental results.

Fisher's rigorous approach requires a factorial number of experiments to determine the effect of each parameter, and to establish the key ones. Taguchi simplified this approach to one of establishing the key parameters by such techniques as brainstorming.

Variables and their interactions are defined, then experiments are run to determine their exact effects. These results are consequently used to establish the control parameters for *statistical process control* in which measurements of the variations indicate trends. From these trends, parameters can be identified and adjusted when the control parameters are reached.

Experiments also produce data on the effects of setting tolerance limits tighter than required by the process.

Figure 2.10 (over) is a flow diagram illustrating the overall Taguchi process.

Planning in electronics manufacture

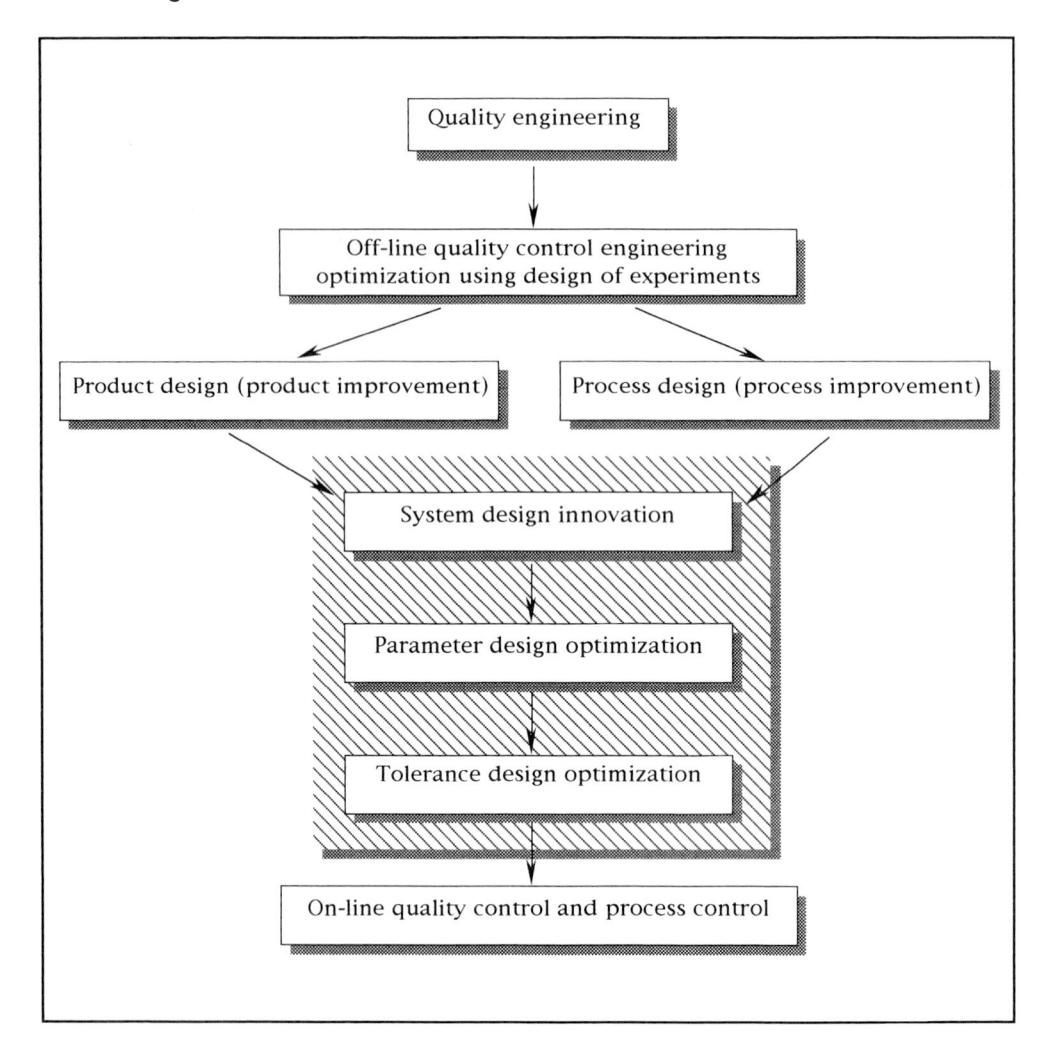

Figure 2.10 *The Taguchi process optimization approach as a flow diagram*

3 Component technologies

On average, component prices fall, year-by-year. On the other hand, printed circuit board prices rise, equally steadily. Quite naturally, therefore, there is a strong argument to both increase complexity of components (so that fewer components are required in any given circuit) and decrease printed circuit board area (by making components more complex *and* by increasing component density on the board).

This chapter first takes us through an overview of how technology within the electronics industry is changing, with particular reference to microprocessor developments and surface mount techniques. Then, we consider the main component types in common use within the industry. Finally the chapter discusses how these component types affect printed circuit board design and production methods.

Evolution and revolution

Throughout the history of electronics manufacture, there have been some notable component developments. Many of these developments are reasonably natural evolutionary steps, from one type of technique to another. Nevertheless, without these logical and progressive evolutionary steps, *revolutions* in manufacturing such as miniaturization and dramatic quality increases could never have been obtained. Nowadays, we almost take for granted the power and complexity of battery-powered products such as notebook computers and pocket televisions, where just a few years ago products with their power and complexity were much larger, much less reliable and, if batteries to power them *could* have been obtained, were certainly not transportable without a fork-lift truck. Table 3.1 shows revolutionary steps in the history of electronics products, in terms of devices, active functions, size, power consumption and reliability.

Component technologies

Table 3.1 Revolutionary steps in electronics in terms of devices

	Valves	Transistors	Integrated circuits	VLSI/ULSI
Characteristics	Amplifiers	Binary logic	Micro-computers and memory	Application-specific ICs
Active functions per device	1	1	$10^4 - 10^5$	$10^6 - 10^8$
Physical size per active function	1	10^{-2}	10^{-5}	10^{-7}
Power consumption per active function	1	10^{-3}	10^{-5}	10^{-6}
Reliability per 100 active functions	1	$10^3 - 10^4$	$10^9 - 10^{10}$	$10^{12} - 10^{13}$
Year	1900	1950	1960	1980
Consequential influences on man's environment	Communications	Computing	Low-cost computing	Artificial intelligence

Growth of system complexity and technology trends

The trend is towards ever higher levels of complexity in hardware and software. Some developmental trends associated with electronics evolutions are shown in Figure 3.1. The design and manufacturing implications of such trends are profound.

For example, as integration levels have risen, the numbers of connection terminations or pins on integrated circuits have risen correspondingly. Resultant problems of interconnection have imposed increasing demands on printed circuit board technology. The problem is expressed by *Rent's rule*, which asserts — the number of input and output pins required on an integrated circuit increases with the number of gates raised to the power of s, with s typically 0.6.

More integration means more tracks on printed circuit boards and a subsequent increasing demand for board area to accommodate them.

The need to minimize propagation delays means that integrated circuits must be kept close together so that, in practice, multi-layered printed circuit boards may be required. Up to 40 or so layers of interconnected tracks are possible in

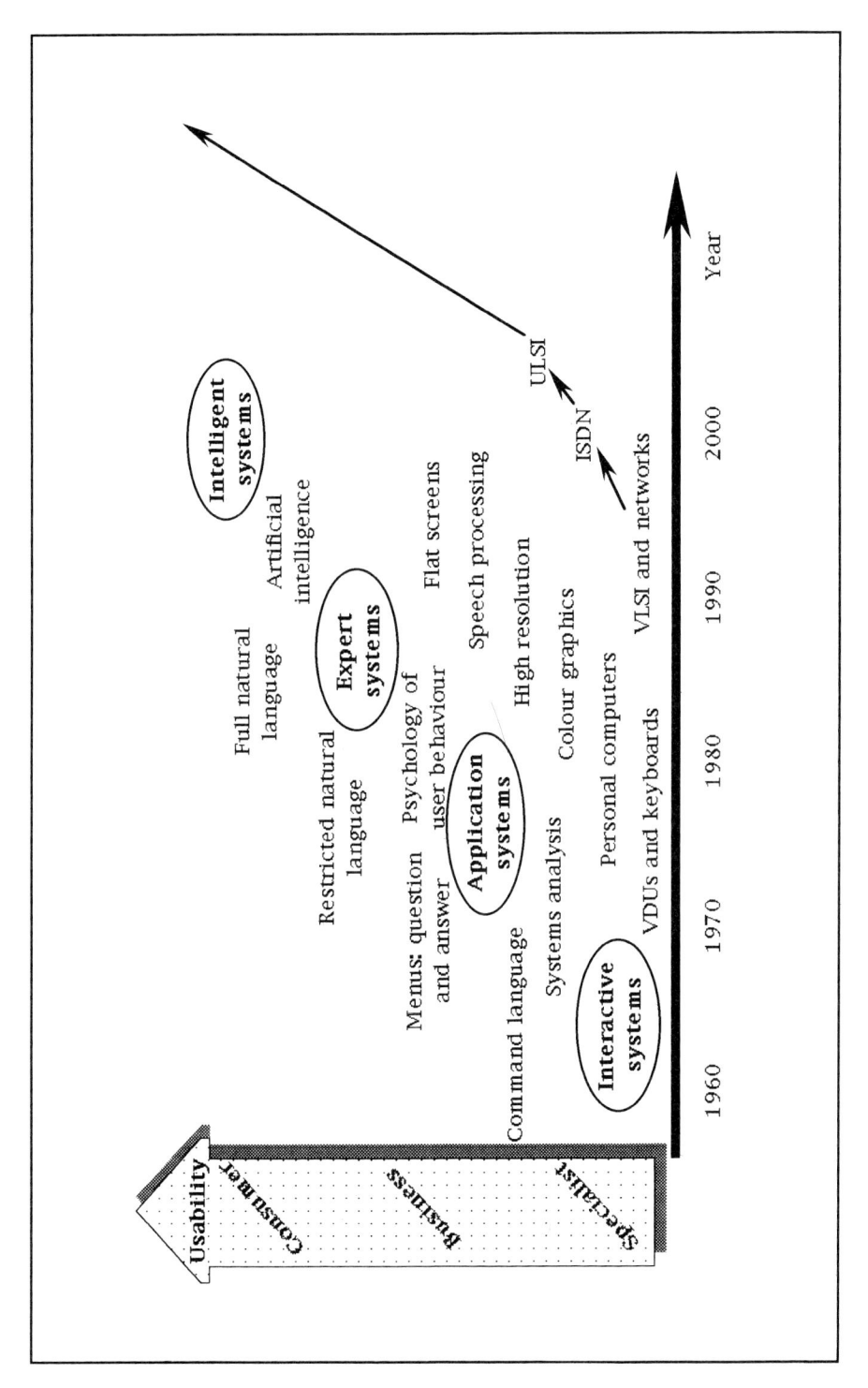

Figure 3.1 Developmental trends associated with evolutions in electronics

Component technologies

such multi-layered printed circuit boards. However, boards with 60 layers have been successfully produced. Multi-layered boards with these numbers of layers are, naturally, very expensive to manufacture.

Microprocessor development

An approximate history of the microprocessor device is shown in Table 3.2. Developments in such complex devices depend on semiconductor process technology enabling more than 350,000 transistors to be fabricated on a single silicon chip.

Clock speeds well in excess of 20 MHz are now typical. A 32-bit address bus enables access to 4 gigabytes of direct memory. Improved system architectures, RISC (reduced instruction set computer) techniques, co-processor implementations and reducing memory costs are all significant trends. Parallel processing developments, employing new architectures (best known being the transputer) will be increasingly applied.

Custom silicon options

Application-specific integrated circuits (ASICs), designed and manufactured for specific purposes, are now making significant inroads into product designs.

Table 3.2 A history of microprocessor developments

Year	Development
1971	4-bit microprocessor (4004)
1972	first 8-bit microprocessors (8008, 8080)
1974	4 kilobyte DRAMs
1978-80	first 16-bit microprocessors. 64 kilobyte DRAMs
1980-83	first 32-bit microprocessors second generation 16-bit microprocessors
1985	32-bit microprocessors readily available 256 kilobyte SRAMs
1986	second generation 32-bit microprocessors 1 megabyte DRAMs

Best known 32-bit microprocessors include:
   Motorola MC68020/30
   Intel 80386
   National Semiconductor NS32032/332

ASICs provide very substantial competitive and technical benefits, for products manufactured in medium to large-scale numbers. Options available for custom devices are shown in Table 3.3, along with a comparison of main parameters of device types. Increasing power, reducing costs and increasing requirements of powerful CAD systems are all likely to increase use of ASICs significantly.

Table 3.3 Custom silicon options — application-specific devices

Application-specific integrated circuit

Device parameter	Semi-custom		Custom	
	Erasable programmable logic device (EPLD)	Gate array	Standard cell	Full custom
Design cost	very low	low	medium	high
Design cycle time	hours-days	days-weeks	weeks-months	months
Complexity (gates)	very low (2000)	low (20,000)	medium-high (200,000)	medium-high (200,000)
Volume unit costs	very high	high	low	very low
Design security	low	high	very high	very high

Surface mount technology

The higher speeds and functionalities of new products employing, say, 32-bit and ASIC technologies, require new interconnect and packaging technologies — simply to ensure that such devices can be mounted on a printed circuit board in as compact a way as economically possible. Printed circuit board techniques have risen to the challenge producing many important manufacturing variations to do the job. One of the most versatile and economic manufacturing techniques is **surface mount technology** (SMT), in which components are assembled onto the surface of a printed circuit board substrate. This technique is growing in popularity as it provides a reliable interconnection method, with reasonable economic incentive.

Surface mount technology is a combination of hybrid manufacturing techniques (in which components are manufactured or assembled directly on a substrate) and conventional printed circuit board techniques. Conventional printed circuit board techniques allow assembly of components with interconnecting leads (called **leaded components**), and these leads push through holes in the printed circuit board, to be soldered on the opposite side. For this reason manufacture of conventional printed circuit boards with leaded components is often known as **through-hole technology**. Surface mount technology, on the other hand, uses components with *no* leads (called **leadless**

Component technologies

components), simply *placing* them on the surface of the printed circuit board, soldering them on the *same* side. Actually, the term *leadless* is something of a misnomer, as some surface mounted components do have leaded terminations, however small. For most purposes, though, the term is perfectly acceptable. Figure 3.2 illustrates how the two manufacturing techniques differ.

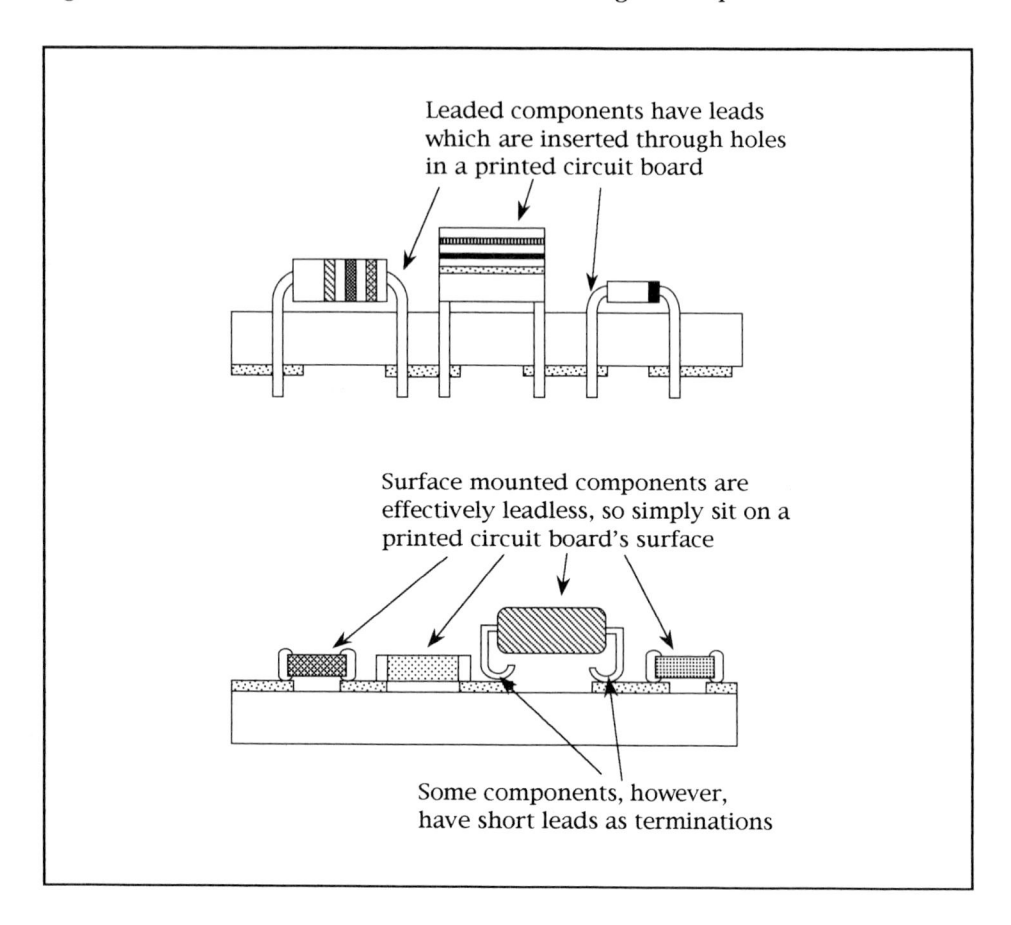

Figure 3.2 *Leaded (through-hole) and leadless (surface mounted) technologies. While all surface mounted components are officially classed as leadless, some do in fact have short terminations*

Leadless components are also known as **surface mounted components** (SMCs), or **surface mounted devices** (SMDs). Examples of outlines of several types of package used for leadless components are shown in Figure 3.3. Generally, size of leadless components is much smaller than size of their leaded counterparts. This, in itself, gives surface mounted printed circuit boards the advantage of being much smaller than through-hole printed circuit boards, for

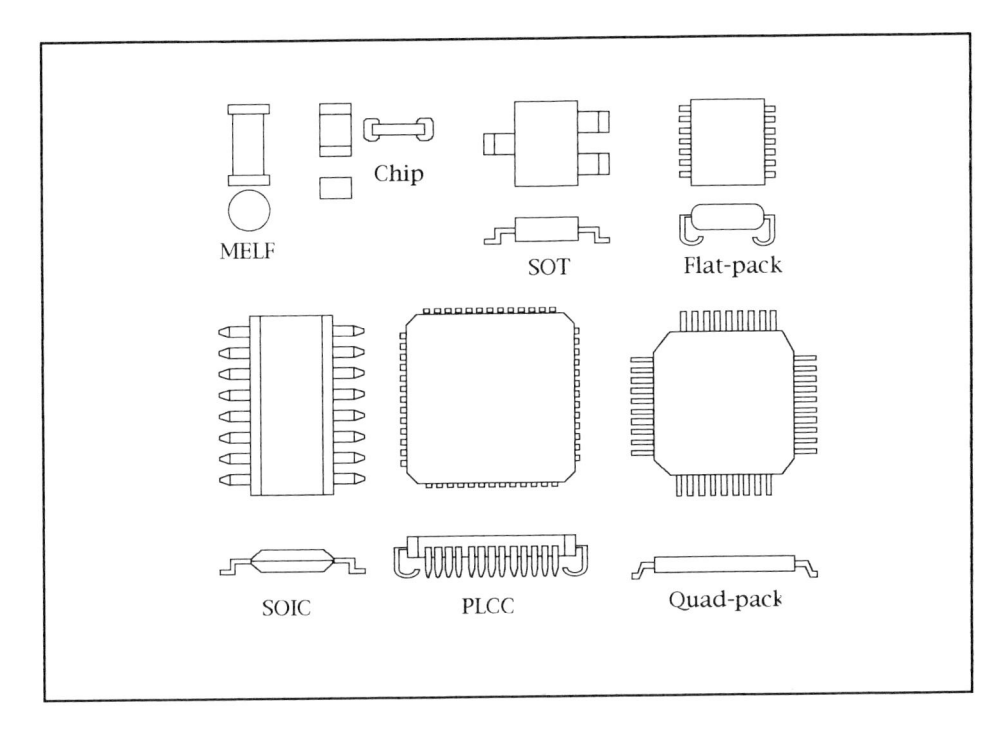

Figure 3.3 *Typical surface mounted component outlines*

the same amount of circuit complexity. However, part of the concept of surface mounted technology is that integrated circuit packages themselves can become much more miniaturized (because lead termination pins are smaller and much more closely packed) and bonding methods of attaching devices to printed circuit boards can use much smaller terminations on the board. Developments in packaging and bonding technologies push the limits of miniaturization further and further.

Applications for gallium arsenide devices

With frequencies of special categories of analog circuits approaching 100 GHz and some digital circuits approaching 10 gigabit s^{-1}, limits of silicon technology are being reached. A semiconductor technology based on gallium arsenide could well start to dominate during the next decade. Relative application areas for silicon and gallium arsenide devices are shown in Figure 3.4. Table 3.4 lists characteristics of semiconductors based on the two technologies.

As is apparent, gallium arsenide has semiconducting properties offering better performance than silicon. These include electron mobility some five times better than silicon, providing higher speeds and extended frequency response. The energy bandgap is 0.3 eV higher, allowing higher temperature operation.

Component technologies

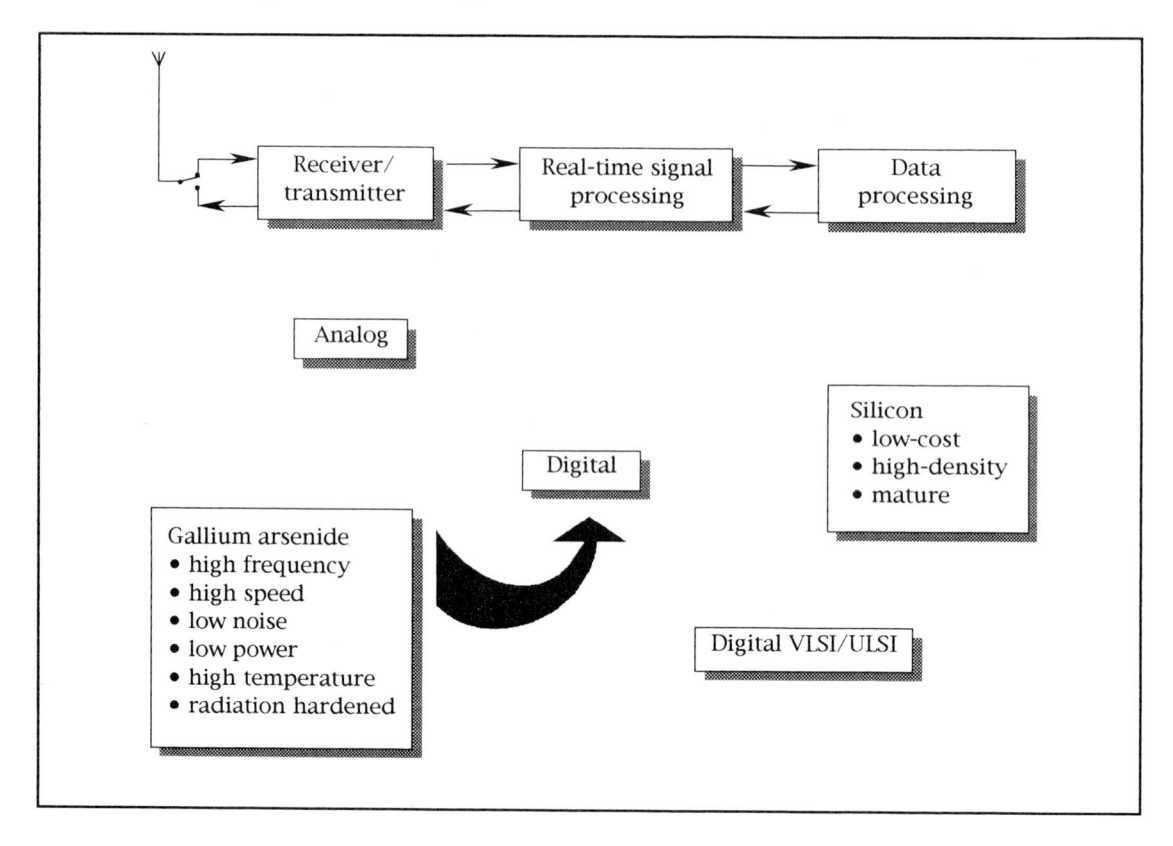

Receiver/transmitter → **Real-time signal processing** ↔ **Data processing**

Analog

Digital

Gallium arsenide
- high frequency
- high speed
- low noise
- low power
- high temperature
- radiation hardened

Silicon
- low-cost
- high-density
- mature

Digital VLSI/ULSI

Figure 3.4 *Relative application areas for silicon and gallium arsenide semiconductors*

Table 3.4 Comparisons between silicon and gallium arsenide semiconductors

Preferred semiconductor	Relative maturity	Maximum frequency	Minimum noise	Maximum speed	Minimum power	Maximum complexity
MEDFET GaAs	2	1	1	1	2	2
MEEFET GaAs	3	2	2	2	3	1
Bipolar Si	1	2	3	2	3	3
MOSFET Si	1	3	4	3	4	4

Notes:
1 = high
2 = medium
3 = low
4 = unsuitable for high frequency applications

Its fabrication technique allows for improved device isolation and lower capacitance. Gallium arsenide also has properties which allow it to be used in the form of lasers and photodetectors. It is thus possible to envisage integrated optoelectronic devices which can be interconnected by optical fibres.

Optical technology

Relative data rate capacities for various transmission media are indicated in Figure 3.5. A major development over recent years has been optical fibre systems for realizing very high data rates over telephone and data networks. Current systems are capable of transmitting data at over 560 gigabyte s^{-1} over a single fibre. Translated into telecommunications channels, this represents over 8400 telephone conversations able to take place simultaneously over that optical fibre link. Current developments in optical fibres indicate much higher data rates will become the norm.

Developments in communications systems will play an important role in enabling design and manufacturing functions to be organized on a world basis.

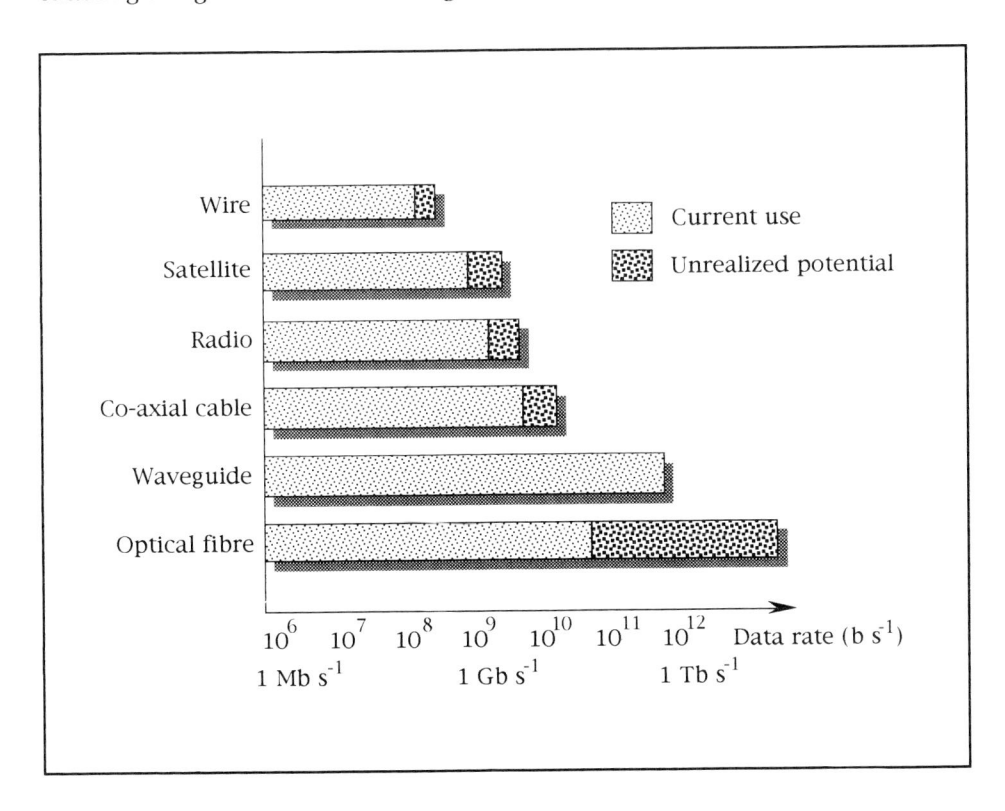

Figure 3.5 *Data rate capacities of transmission media, showing current use and unrealized potential*

Component technologies

There are many other developments in optical technologies. Use of optical discs, for example, as mass storage devices promises to be of particular interest and enormous potential.

Optical technology has many uses currently unrealized.

Vertical integration

From all this, we can see that technology evolution is a vertically integrated process. It starts with an organization's marketing department — identifying future opportunities to maximize added value. This establishes the necessary research and development programmes which generate new materials, processes and products to meet marketplace needs.

A need for long-term strategic planning is clear. Only in such a well-planned and structured environment can successful new products be engineered. After all, it was such an approach which generated microprocessors and VLSI devices in the first place.

Overall, a building block structure for both hardware and software can be followed. Such a structure is shown in Figure 3.6. This permits maximum gain from existing plant and systems, while facilitating a transition to information-based systems of the future.

A choice of manufacturing technique

There are many factors determining which components we use in a particular product. These may be summarized in a list which includes:

- reliability
- cost
- availability
- standards
- size and weight
- assembly and rework
- performance
- interconnection capability
- power rating
- temperature and voltage stability.

All are important, though none alone holds the key to choice of a particular component type.

For example, the average price of an integrated circuit has fallen consistently, year-by-year, while cost per unit area of printed circuit board rises in almost inverse proportions. Viewed on a cost per interconnection (Table 3.5) basis it becomes apparent that we have to use more complex integrated circuits, while using less complex (relatively) printed circuit boards.

A choice of manufacturing technique

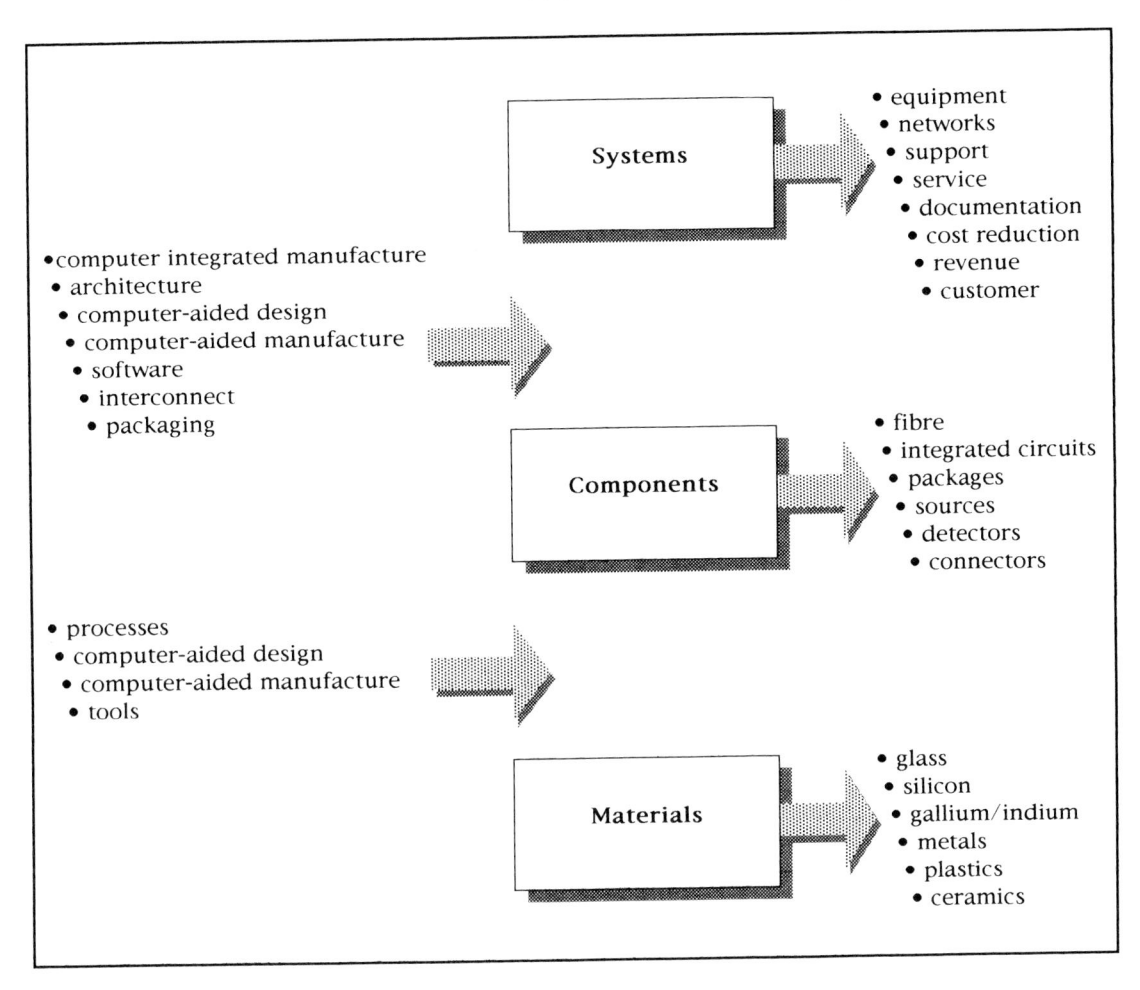

- computer integrated manufacture
- architecture
- computer-aided design
- computer-aided manufacture
- software
- interconnect
- packaging

→ **Systems** →
- equipment
- networks
- support
- service
- documentation
- cost reduction
- revenue
- customer

→ **Components** →
- fibre
- integrated circuits
- packages
- sources
- detectors
- connectors

- processes
- computer-aided design
- computer-aided manufacture
- tools

→ **Materials** →
- glass
- silicon
- gallium/indium
- metals
- plastics
- ceramics

Figure 3.6 *A possible building block structure to guide hardware and software development*

Table 3.5 Relative costs of interconnections between various manufacturing technologies

Manufacturing technology	Cost per interconnect (cents)
Printed circuit boards	0.03 to 0.12
Hybrids	0.005 to 0.02
LSI	0.004
VLSI	0.0001

Component technologies

Lead count requirements for products such as 32-bit microprocessors cannot be met satisfactorily by the standard 2.54 mm lead pitch dual-in-line package. As lead count increases, long internal lead lengths increase resistance and inter-lead capacitance. This limits device performance, to a maximum dual-in-line leadout of around 68 pins for plastic packages. Current easily-reproducible chip line widths of such devices are about 1 μm. Initiatives worldwide have resulted in line widths being reduced to about 0.3 μm, giving 64 megabits of memory on a single integrated circuit — but this is about the limit of conventional silicon technology.

The need to improve performance and interconnect efficiency is resulting in more products being designed using surface mount components and application-specific integrated circuits. Finer track width and spacing on printed circuit boards is a natural development.

So what are these components we use in modern electronic products? And how much further can they be developed to match our manufacturing requirements? It's possible to classify component types according to their main production methods, and there are some four methods which we are interested in:

- thin film circuits — complete circuits fabricated on ceramic substrates
- thick film circuits — as above, but less expensive and more flexible
- silicon hybrids — miniaturized printed circuit boards built on silicon wafers
- surface mount technology.

We can now study these in detail.

Thin film circuits

Basic process steps of thin film circuits are:

(1) Substrate is cleaned and placed in an evaporator, where residual surface contamination is removed by ion etching. A thin layer of resistive material, usually nichrome but sometimes tantalum nitride, is then evaporated onto the substrate. Thickness of the evaporated layer is sufficient for all resistive values required in the circuit to be formed from it. If no resistors but only conductors are to be used on the circuit, the nichrome is still deposited — but to a thickness of only a few nanometres. A thin layer of copper is then deposited over the nichrome, and the substrate is removed from the evaporator

(2) Subsequent processing uses photo-imaged resists to delineate first tracks, then resistors. Track conductors are outline masked with photoresist. They are then electroplated to required thickness with copper or gold. Resist is then removed and further photolithographic and etching stages are used to define resistors.

In a straightforward comparison between conventional printed circuits, thin film circuits have excellent track definition — tracks of less than 50 μm width are easily constructable. They offer excellent high frequency performance, too. On the other hand, resistors on a thin film circuit have different geometries, depending on their required value. This is so because the evaporated nichrome making up the resistors has a uniform thickness, so resistance value depends on a component's surface area.

Thick film circuits

Thick film circuits are less expensive and more flexible than thin film counterparts. The circuit is screen-printed onto a substrate with special inks developed as conductors, resistors and dielectrics. After printing each component the system is fired in a kiln — hence the basic technology can only be used with ceramic substrates. Polymer thick film developments (see later), on the other hand, use low firing temperatures compatible with organic substrates.

Thick film inks for ceramic substrates are composed of metal and oxide powders, glass powders and a suitable organic carrier of resin and solvent. After initial printing the organic components are burnt out at a relatively low temperature prior to firing at 850° to 900°C to melt the glass and form a permanent bond. The most common conductor used in thick film circuits is a palladium-silver mixture, fired in air. Presence of palladium in the material alleviates two of silver's tendencies which would otherwise prevent its use:

- to migrate across the substrate surface under influence of an electric field
- to dissolve into molten solder.

Thick film resistors cover a range from 0.1 Ω to 1000 MΩ. Most resistive inks are based on ruthenium oxide. After printing and firing, trimming of resistors to obtain accurate values is carried out by laser. In this way tolerances of less than 0.1% are achieved.

Polymer thick film circuits

Polymer thick film technology combines the economic benefits and flexibility of thick film technology with standard printed circuit board materials such as glass-reinforced epoxy resin laminate, polyester and polyimide. New thick film conductor and resistor materials are now available that are based on polymers instead of glass for which the firing and curing temperature is only around 150° to 300°C. Polymer thick film techniques allow a possibility of a cheaper additive method of printed circuit fabrication, rather than the usual subtractive method of etching copper laminate.

Advantages of film circuits of all types — thin film, thick film, polymer thick film — are:

- efficient use of raw material due to an additive rather than a subtractive process
- integration of resistors within the interconnection pattern
- ability to produce readily a two-layered interconnection pattern on one side of a substrate, without requiring holes through the substrate
- suitability for linear circuits, with precision resistors, high voltage and high power handling characteristics.

Component technologies

Silicon hybrids

Much research currently is into silicon hybrids. They hold great promise for the future. At its simplest a silicon hybrid is essentially a miniaturized printed circuit board, built on a silicon wafer. Like any printed circuit board it is made up of layers of metal separated by a suitable dielectric. Unlike a conventional printed circuit board, however, a silicon hybrid is built using integrated circuit fabrication techniques. The principal dielectric is polyimide. Polyimide is an established feature of integrated circuit manufacture where it is used for planarizing (ie, producing a flat surface on an integrated circuit chip — it is used as an alternative to silicon dioxide).

A cross-section of a typical silicon hybrid is shown in Figure 3.7. Manufacture starts with the growth of an oxide film on a silicon substrate. This is followed by a metal ground plane, followed by layers of polyimide and metallization. Typically, a silicon hybrid has some four layers of metallization (ie, ground, power and two signal planes) although more are possible if required.

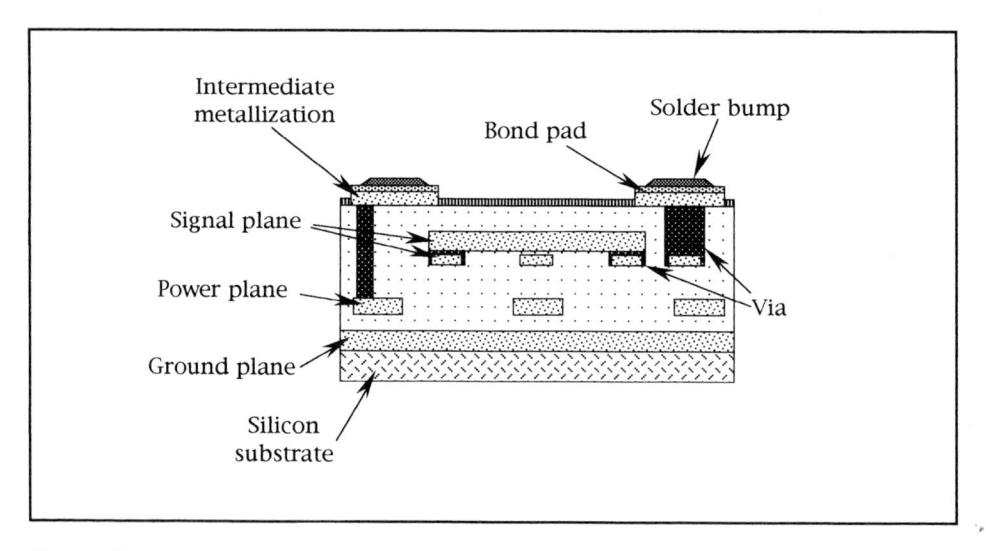

Figure 3.7 *Cross-section of a silicon hybrid circuit*

Surface mount technology

While all three technologies described here are important in their own ways, applications are usually quite specific and only minorities of product groups can be expected to be manufactured using them. On the other hand, surface mounted technology promises to be used more widely than even conventional printed circuit board.

Already, more than 50% of components used in electronics manufacture are surface mounted varieties. In Western Europe, growth of use of surface mount

Surface mount technology

technology is expected to remain at around 150% for the foreseeable future, which leads us to the inevitable conclusion that it won't be long before conventional leaded components aren't used at all. Indeed, as manufacturers demand more complex and more specific integrated circuits, there is already an increased trend towards use of surface mount components, simply because leaded components cannot perform the functions required.

Surface mount component outlines

All but a handful of surface mount component outlines are standardized. Package standards are based on JEDEC (Joint Electronics Devices Engineering Council) and IEC (International Electrotechnical Commission) specifications. The main surface mount component styles are now described.

Chips — passive components with rectangular prism shapes.

SOIC — small outline integrated circuit — available in up to 28-pin versions on a standard 1.27 mm lead pitch. SOICs are the most efficient device in terms of board area for low pin count (up to 16 pin) integrated circuits. They are easy to design into high-density printed circuit board track layouts.

VSOIC — very small outline integrated circuit — as SOICs but with up to 56 pins at a 0.762 mm lead pitch.

SOT — small outline transistor — these are single transistors, in three main types of package:

- SOT 23, used in a wide range of general applications and able to dissipate about 200 milliwatts in free air
- SOT 89, able to dissipate up to 500 milliwatts
- SOT 194, able to dissipate up to 4 watts with a suitable heatsink.

SOD — small outline diode — cylindrical diode packages. SOD 80 is limited to power dissipation of 250 milliwatts.

MELF — metal electrode face bonded packages — single device packages for power dissipation up to 2 watts.

Component technologies

LCCC — leadless ceramic chip carrier (refers to integrated circuit chip, not a passive surface mounted component chip) — an integrated circuit with all leads and excess packaging material discarded, bonded into a ceramic base, with connections made with fine wires to metallizations brought out to solderable contact pads. Pad pitch is 1.27 mm and versions from 18 to over 156 terminals are available.

PLCC — plastic leaded chip carriers — integrated circuits bonded into plastic bases, with connections of fine wires brought out to metallizations of small compliant leads. Lead pitch is 1.27 mm.

Flatpacks (FPs) and quad-flatpacks (QFPs) — integrated circuits with leadframes co-planar with the package body. Flatpacks have two in-line rows of terminations, while quad-flatpacks have four rows of terminations. Lead pitch varies typically with lead count:

- 64-pin devices typically have a lead pitch of 1 mm
- 80-pin devices have a lead pitch of 0.8 mm
- 100-pin are 0.65 mm
- 200-pin are 0.55 mm.

TAB — taped automated bonded — integrated circuits in a taped form, without protective packaging, intended for punching out of the tape for direct mounting on a printed circuit board.

Surface mount component lead terminations

There are only four main lead terminations for surface mounted components. These are:

- rigid two-terminal devices (chips, MELF, and so on)
- rigid multi-terminal devices (LCCCs)
- gull-wing terminations (SOICs, QFPs and so on)
- J-lead terminations (PLCCs and so on).

These are illustrated in Figure 3.8 a to d. While all these termination types allow soldered joints to be made to acceptable levels, there are significant differences between the first two and the last two. Two-terminal and multi-terminal devices with rigid terminations allow no movement between component and printed circuit board. Gull-wing and J-lead terminations, on the other hand, provide compliant joints (compliancy is built-in with their short lead terminations) which allow some small movement between component and board.

Surface mount technology

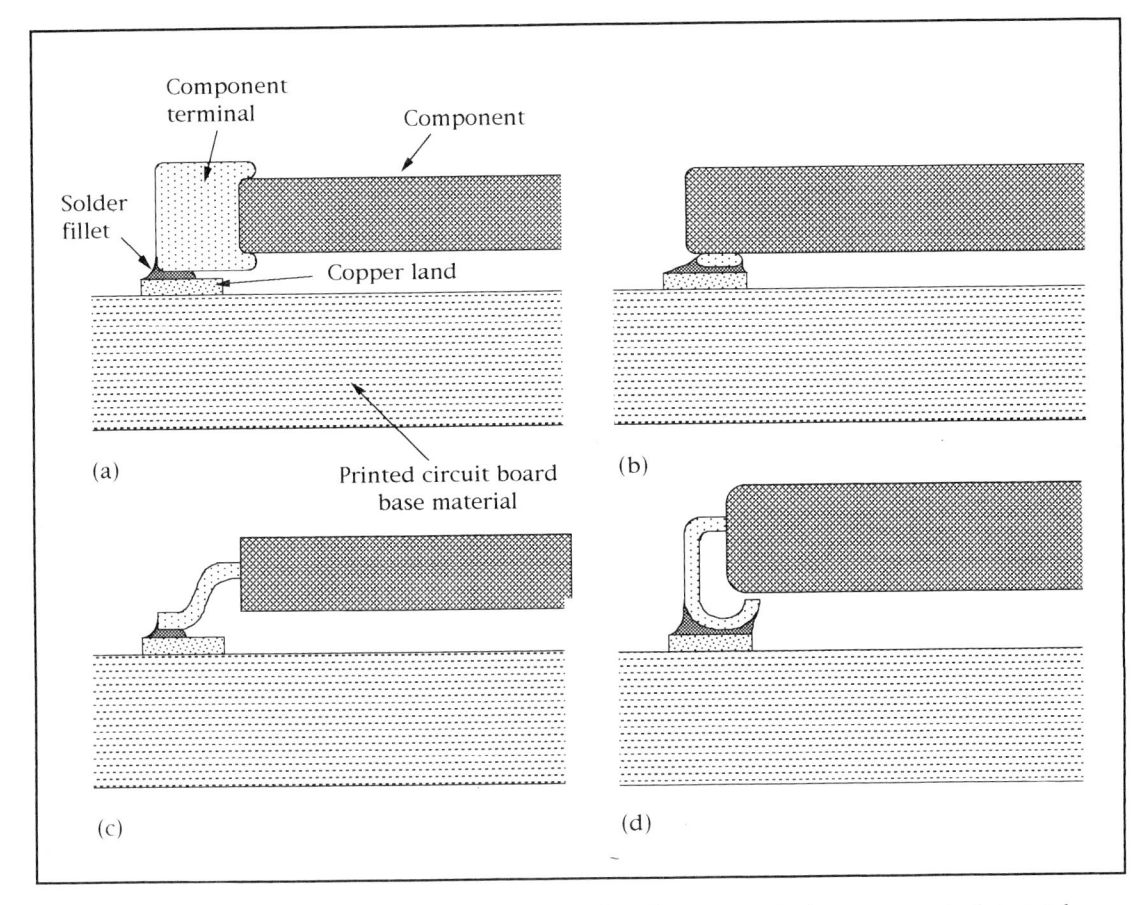

Figure 3.8 *The four main lead terminations of surface mounted components (a) rigid, two-terminal (b) rigid, multi-terminal (c) compliant, gull-wing terminal (d) compliant, J-lead terminal*

Movement between component and board can result in joint failure, in two main ways: thermal mismatch between component and board; and mechanical stress due to movement of the board relative to component, say, by bending. Given that most assemblies are suitably mounted so that mechanical stresses cannot be passed on unduly to printed circuit boards, the main problem regarding a choice between rigid and compliant terminations is one of thermal mismatch between component and board.

Mismatch of coefficients of thermal expansion

Any differences in thermal coefficients of expansion between a component and the printed circuit board base material will mean, on heating prior to soldering,

Component technologies

that both component and board expand (Figure 3.9a) then, on cooling after soldering, component and circuit board shrink by different amounts. If the amount is great enough, stresses are set up which pull copper tracks underneath the component terminals from the board's surface (Figure 3.9b).

How much this effect limits use of surface mounted components depends initially on the type of component. Components whose terminals form rigid joints, for example, suffer most from this effect, as there is no compliance built-in to the arrangement.

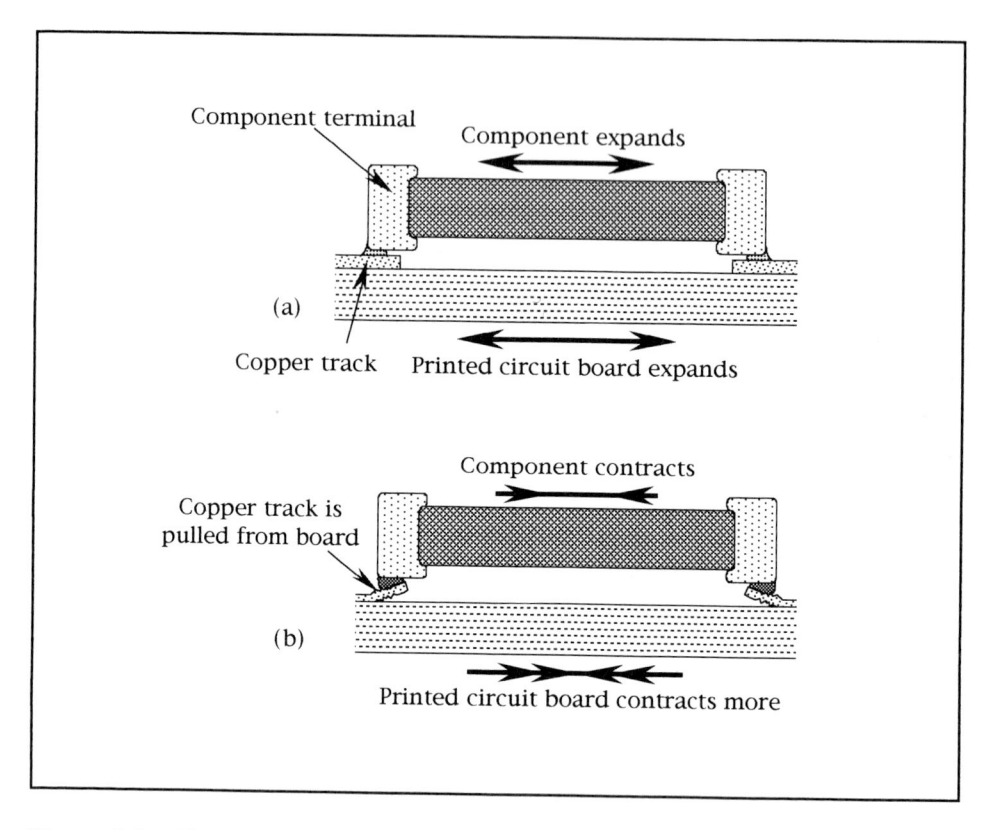

Figure 3.9 *Showing effects of mismatch of thermal expansions, when soldering surface mounted components to a printed circuit board*

A general rule-of-thumb is used when soldering rigid jointed surface mounted components (generally those commonly called *chip* components) to epoxy resin-bonded, glass fibre reinforced circuit boards; this allows use of components up to about 6 mm in length. Many surface mounted components are within this size limit, so copper track remains unaffected by thermal coefficient of expansion mismatch.

Many other rigid surface mounted components (leadless ceramic chip carriers form the main group), on the other hand, are larger than 6 mm. Such rigid jointing of these components to epoxy resin-bonded, glass fibre reinforced circuit board is not, therefore, possible and in the long run an ultimate solution can only be in use of printed circuit board base materials with thermal coefficients of expansion matching those of rigid components (eg, ceramic, metal-bonded).

On the other hand, compliant jointed surface mounted components larger than 6 mm do not suffer from any thermal coefficient mismatch problem, simply because the short terminations themselves flex as components and boards contract differently.

Small outline diodes (SODs), small outline transistors (SOTs), small outline integrated circuits (SOICs), very small outline integrated circuits (VSOICs), tape automated bonded integrated circuits (TABs), flatpacks, plastic leaded chip carriers and so on are all components having compliant terminations. As surface mounted components are known for their advantage of being *leadless*, this is something of a backward step, not to mention a misnomer, but does form a short-term solution to a tricky problem.

In effect, compliant joints illustrate a successful short-term method of enabling surface mounted components, in quasi-leaded form, to be used with cheaply produced circuit board materials. In the long term, though, the only solution to enable *pure* leadless surface mounted assembly must be to develop cheap and easy manufacture of thermally-matched circuit boards, or to develop newer bonding processes.

Taped automated bonded integrated circuits

There is increasing interest in and use of taped automated bonded integrated circuits. As devices they feature high numbers of input and output terminations within an extremely small surface area. Indeed, the TAB packaging and interconnect technique is the fastest growing one in the world. Main application areas for TAB include high volume commodity production, smartcards and any assembly where a high lead count integrated circuit is required.

Prior to TAB, a manufacturer's only other alternative was to wire-bond integrated circuit chips directly to printed circuit boards. This is a tricky job. Further, wire-bonded integrated circuit chips require 150% larger bonding pads than TAB requires, so TAB chips may be smaller, with greater numbers of leadouts. Other benefits of TAB include better electrical properties (less propagation delay and smaller signal distortion) resulting from shorter leads and larger cross-sectional area. TAB interconnects have profiles only one-third those of wire-bonded chips, so TAB devices can be used in thinner applications (a smartcard, for example). Heat conduction is better as taped leads have greater heat dissipation. TAB interconnects are more rugged mechanically, coping with high vibration and g-force environments. TAB leads have higher bond strengths

Component technologies

than wire-bond leads. TAB provides superior lead separation over wire-bond, which reduces problems caused by wire sag and shorting that occur with small wire-bonded dice. But perhaps TAB's biggest advantage over wire-bonded integrated circuit chips is the fact that TAB devices can be fully tested and burnt-in on the taped reel, before assembly. This greatly reduces the number of packaged, non-functional integrated circuit chips.

Basic steps in fabrication of a TAB package are illustrated in Figure 3.10, where it can be seen that blank polyimide tape is punched, then layered with metal foil and resist prior to etching. An integrated circuit chip is positioned and bonded to the tape which is then ready for use. Bonding is undertaken at the fabrication

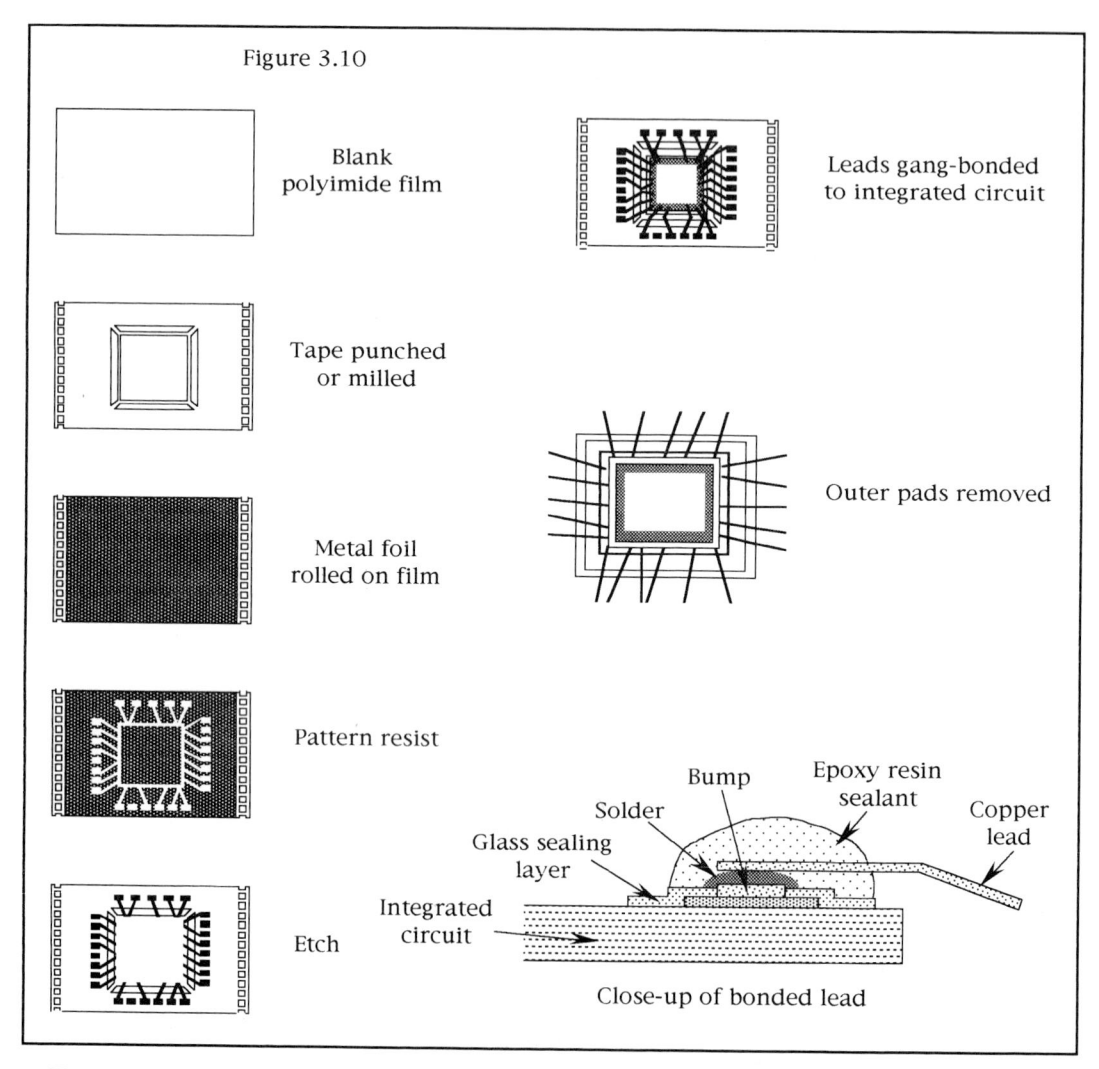

Figure 3.10 *Processes in manufacture of taped automated bonded devices*

Surface mount technology

stage — a fact which alleviates any necessity for the assembly manufacturer to do the job. In effect, TAB allows a basic integrated circuit chip to be mounted directly onto the printed circuit board, with fairly simple soldering techniques and *without* having to wire bond the integrated circuit directly.

Figure 3.10 also shows a cross-section of a typical TAB integrated circuit's bonded lead. Here an addition of thick metal — called a **bump** — has been applied to the chip bond pad to provide a platform for bonding. In TAB devices featuring bumps, bond pad geometries should be designed so that the passivation opening is smaller than the metal bond pad. Bump size itself must be thicker than the opening, but smaller than the bond pad metal — in this way the opening is sealed in the bump process, preventing problems of corrosion in use. Bumping also helps prevent damage in the subsequent bonding process.

Bonding of TAB integrated circuit chips to printed circuit board conductors is undertaken at the manufacture stage by one of three processes:

- thermocompression (heat at 300°C and compression)
- ultrasonic bonding (ultrasonic energy heats the bond area)
- thermosonic bonding (heat and ultrasonic energy heat the bond area).

Problems have been encountered when gang-bonding integrated circuits with high lead-counts, simply because it is difficult to maintain perfectly flat bonding surfaces. These problems can be overcome by bonding each lead separately, in a process known as single-point TAB (SPT). Considerably lower bonding forces are required in SPT manufacture; a fact which results in less damage to the integrated circuit dice.

As we've seen, TAB packaging has the advantage of being extremely thin. In situations where even the thickness of the lowest profile chip carrier is unacceptable, TAB techniques allow integrated circuits to be successfully mounted directly onto a printed circuit board. By indenting the printed circuit board to suit, even the thickness of the basic integrated circuit can be eliminated — the integrated circuit is protected in the process, too (shown in Figure 3.11).

After assembly the TAB device is encapsulated to protect the delicate connections.

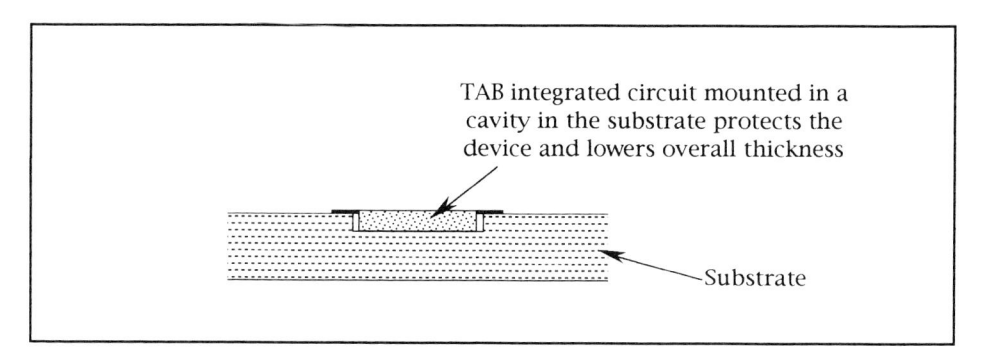

Figure 3.11 *Mounting an inverted TAB device in a cavity in the substrate*

Component technologies

Hierarchical interconnection technology

Where printed circuit assembly by surface mounted technology alone is insufficient to keep size small enough, manufacturers are looking to value added techniques to reduce system size. One such technique is **hierarchical interconnect technology** (HIT), which features up to eight child boards parallel-mounted on one side of a mother board; the mother board is either a standard double Eurocard-sized board, or a daughter board. Child boards act as the core of the system, and are designed to meet basic metric dimensional standards. Connections are via all four edges of a child board with north-south edges used for data and east-west used for control.

Basic elements of a hierarchical interconnect technology system are shown in Figure 3.12. The connector system comprises low-profile receptacles accepting child boards with zero insertion force to a specification which includes a pin count of 130 to 140 at 0.05 mm pitch, contact resistance up to 20 mΩ and minimum 100 insertion life. Daughter boards accommodate both DIN and HIT backplane connectors.

Development was initiated by the UK Department of Trade and Industry, with a consortium of connector companies including McMurdo, Ferranti and ITT Cannon. Initial impetus to create such an interconnect solution arose from problems, both economic and technical, stemming from surface mounted technology manufacture. Cost of producing double Eurocard-sized surface mounted technology assemblies is expected to rise by at least a factor of ten over the next few years, purely because of assembly complexity. Part of the problem arises because the more complex an assembly is, the more difficult it is to test. If traditional assembly and test procedures are used while assemblies become more complex, test times of over 10 hours and prohibitive quality cost risks are likely.

One of the main benefits in test of using hierarchical interconnect technology is the elimination of the need for in-circuit testing of a complete assembly using bed-of-nails fixtures. By splitting a complex assembly up into several constituent parts, and testing each part separately prior to mounting on a mother board, there is no requirement to do other than a functional test on the whole assembly.

Surface mounted component reliability

Surface mounted components have a higher reliability than their leaded counterparts. Typical reliability figures of surface mounted components are listed in Table 3.6, in terms of failures in time standard (FITs) of 10^9 hours. Examples of typical failure rates can only be approximate, but high reliability equipment often has failure rates of around 50 FITs, while consumer electronic products have failure rates between about 100 to 1000 FITs.

Surface mount technology

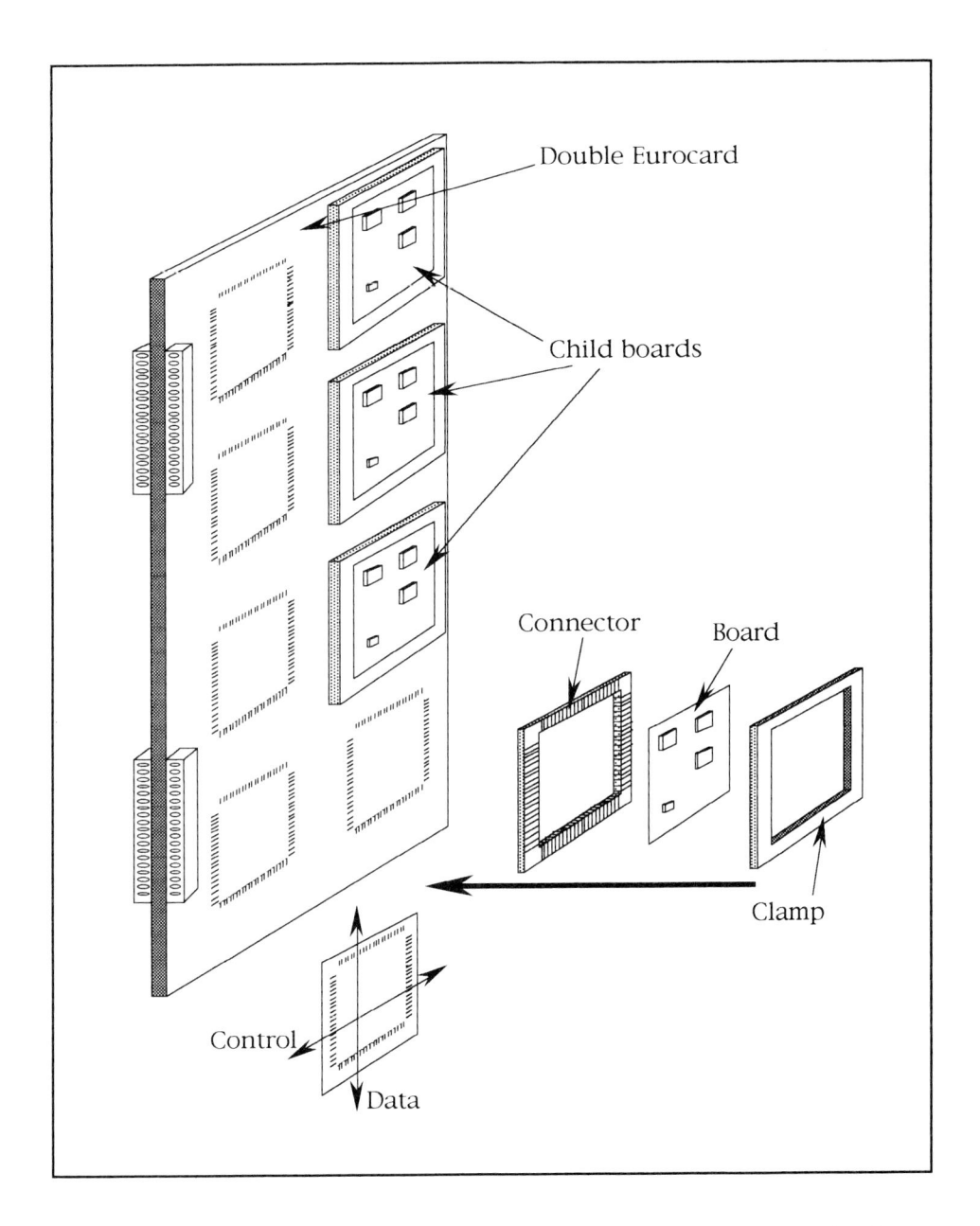

Figure 3.12 *Showing principles of the hierarchical interconnect technology. Up to eight child boards may be mounted on each side of a double-sided mother board. Child boards are clamped onto connectors prior to mounting*

Component technologies

Table 3.6 Surface mounted component reliability in terms of FITS (failures in time standard of 1 in 10^9 hours). Typical high-quality component failure rates at 55°C are listed

Component	Failures hr^{-1}	FITs
Chip resistors	<10^{-9}	1
Chip capacitors	<10^{-9}	1
SOTs	1×10^{-8}	10
SOICs	1×10^{-8}	10
PLCCs	5×10^{-8}	50

Note: reliabilities of components and assemblies are functions of temperature, humidity and electrical overstress and the compatibility of the substrate and component combination

Reliability prediction techniques are available based on data contained in many publications, including:

- Mil-Hdbk 217D
- BTs HRD4
- CNET
- Bell
- NTT
- Inspec
- MoD
- Stack

Prediction techniques should, ideally, be incorporated at a product's design stage, typically in a computer-aided design (CAD) process. Failure models involve multiplying the base failure rate of each component by the appropriate environmental, quality and complexity factors and the quantity of each component type, then adding the results. Such a method, though, only takes into account mechanical component failures, and cannot include failures created by design faults or software errors.

Mathematically, system failure probability is:

$$\lambda_s = \sum_{i=1}^{n} N_i \lambda_j$$

where: $\lambda_j = \lambda_b \Pi_t \Pi_q \Pi_e \Pi_c$
N_i = quantity of the i-th part
λ_b = base failure rate for the i-th part
Π_t = temperature weighting factor for the i-th part
Π_q = quality factor for the i-th part
Π_e = environmental factor
Π_c = complexity factor for the i-th part.

4 Design of assemblies

Most assemblies are designed following **top-down design** principles, in which all design work stems from a customer's original requirement. Top-down design is known to help reduce mistakes while facilitating completion of the design task on time and within budget.

Basic steps within the top-down design philosophy are shown in Figure 4.1. Main steps vary with products to be designed, but all include most of the following stages.

Customer requirement

The very first stage in any design must be a **customer requirement** — a description of the required product's function — which must be defined carefully. Additional information should identify what freedoms or constraints exist for the designer eg, if a particular type of microprocessor has to be used.

System design

Next follows **system design** — also known as **top-level design** — which is concerned with examination of the customer's requirements. Here, the task is confirmed as suitable to proceed with, and those parts which required modification are identified. Parts which need to be modified are referred back to the customer, perhaps repeatedly, until agreement is reached on a final product description which forms a specification on which the design proceeds.

The system design stage may require a feasibility study to answer questions arising which cannot be answered easily. Often feasibility studies amount to technical queries relating to a product's potential design. Often, also, feasibility studies may involve input from marketing departments to define non-technical

Design of assemblies

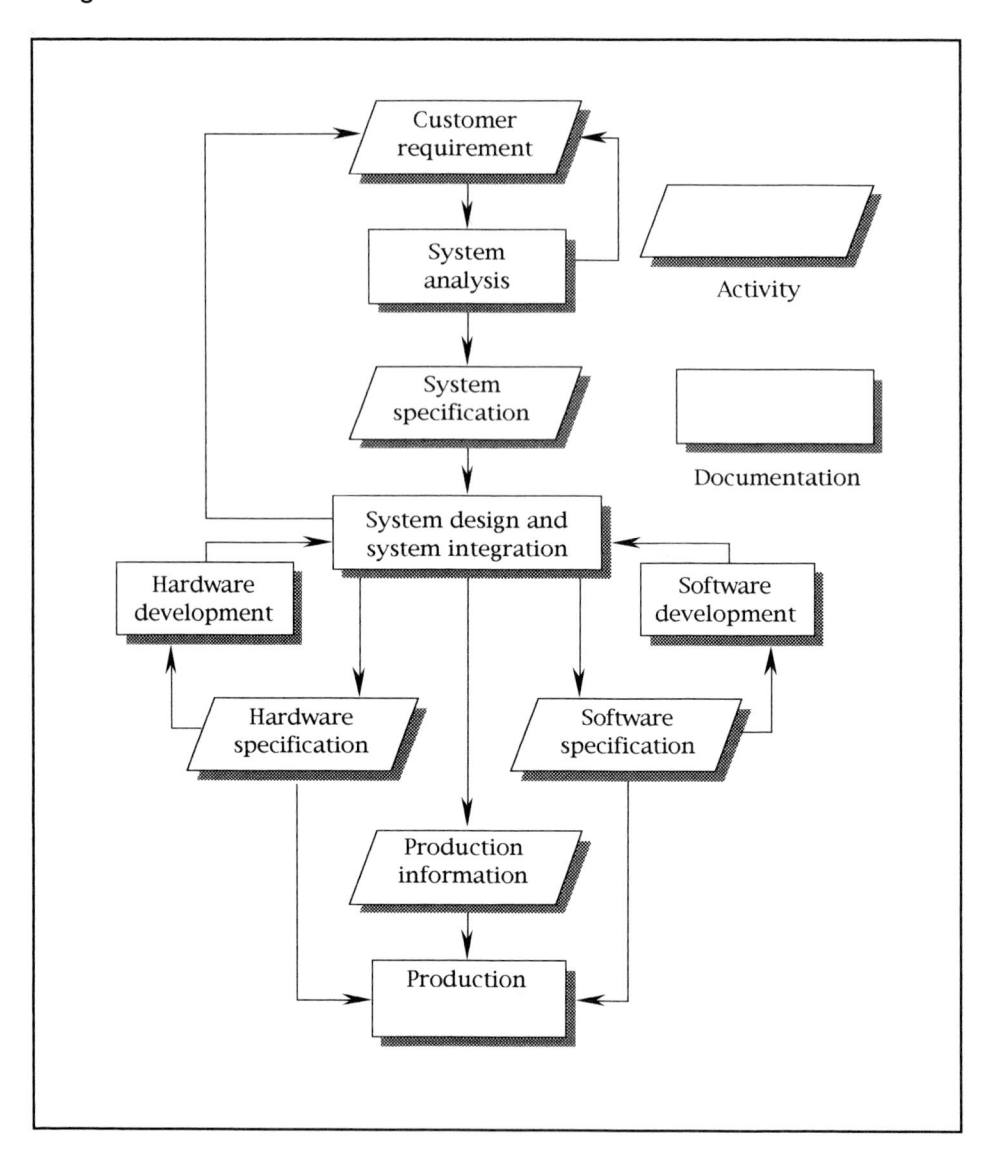

Figure 4.1 *Top-down design as a flow diagram*

aspects of the product. Computer simulation can be a valuable tool at this point.

Decisions can now be taken which partition the overall design into sub-specifications concerning hardware and software. Sub-specifications, particularly those involving software, are often broken down further into sub-tasks or modules. Interfaces between modules must be carefully structured to facilitate design changes and modifications.

By conclusion of the system design stage, a project plan concerning manpower resources and so on should be defined. As a result, further sub-tasks may emerge and be specified. Tasks concerned with detailed software and hardware design now start.

It cannot be overstressed how important documentation of the work and proper use of test results are to overall control of the whole project.

System integration

The next stage involves **system integration** in which all modules of the design are carefully tested, then brought together. Correspondingly, interactions between hardware and software must be checked. Useful aids in testing and debugging hardware include the oscilloscope and logic analyzer. Microprocessor projects are often tested using in-circuit emulators.

It is this stage which usually identifies problems in those modules which have not been adequately specified at earlier stages.

While here we have considered system design and system integration as being two separate stages they are, in fact, more usually undertaken in parallel and often boundaries between the two stages are difficult to identify.

Hardware design

The purpose of any electronic circuit is to provide specified electrical outputs in response to particular electrical inputs. An output may be needed to control an electric motor, or to drive a loudspeaker, for example. Inputs may come from a variety of sources such as a microphone, measuring instrumentation, or even a computer keyboard. The electronic circuit in between inputs and outputs merely processes incoming information to give the required outputs.

The process of hardware design is illustrated in Figure 4.2. Design of electronic circuits is similar to many design tasks and, simplified, is a matter of a designer choosing, arranging and interconnecting available components to achieve the specified performance. Input/output interfaces, displays and controls, power supplies, buffering circuits for protection, analog circuits, digital circuits and so on, are all examples of hardware design. Trade-offs concerning choice of components can be important from a cost reduction and performance point of view during this phase of a design. There is, naturally, more to this than meets the eye, however.

A typical, moderately complex digital electronic design problem might proceed in the following stages:

1 a formal system specification is derived from knowledge of the behaviour required and the way the system might need to interact with other systems
2 the system is then divided or partitioned into well-defined and convenient subsystems

Design of assemblies

```
                          ┌─────────────────┐
                          │  System design  │
                          └─────────────────┘
                           ↑              ↓
         Details, modifications      Revised
            of specification         specification
```

Hardware development
- microcomputer validation
- input/output methods
- input/output interface
- analog design
- test procedures
- power supplies
- protection circuits
- displays and controls
- mechanical design
- value engineering

Hardware
- specification
- documentation

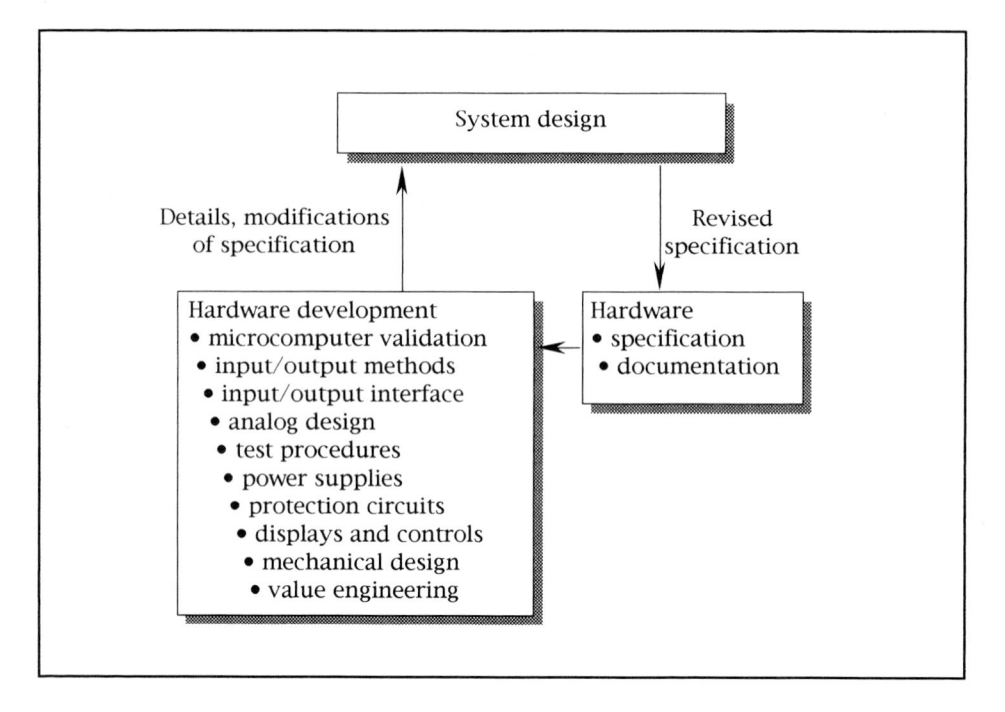

Figure 4.2 *Hardware design process, as a flow diagram*

3 partitioning continues until the blocks are small enough for a designer to be able to define each block's structure in terms of convenient logic functions such as gates, flip-flops and so on
4 if necessary this logic description is then sub-divided further until it is a realizable circuit of components that are available in the chosen technology, whether discrete components on a printed circuit board, the available logic blocks of a semi-custom integrated circuit, or a combination of both
5 the circuit is then implemented, either as a layout for a printed circuit board, or an integrated circuit.

Many of the above processes can be done on computer-aided design systems as, increasingly, data in product manufacture becomes available for assembly and test purposes.

There are several problems in this simple hierarchy of design procedures that can be solved by simulation, and several different kinds of process are called for.

Behavioural simulation

In stage 1, the designer must check that the defined system specification is a true reflection of what is required, and that there are no unforeseen problems. This is conveniently achieved by testing the 'behaviour' of a computer model based on the specification. In effect, the specification must be represented as a model with the same inputs and output that the real system will have, so that its output response can be examined under an appropriate variety of realistic input conditions. This is commonly termed **behavioural simulation**. Its purpose is simply to find out whether the specification does what is expected.

After completing stage 2, it is necessary to check that the partitioned system still behaves in the correct manner. This again can be done by means of a behavioural simulation in which each subsystem is represented by its own self-contained behavioural model. The results of this simulation can be compared with that of the overall system to ensure that the proposed combination of subsystem specifications meets the original system specification.

Once the system has been partitioned sufficiently, the structure of each block can be designed in terms of standard logic functions. To check that it still meets the specification established by the previous stages of behavioural simulation, each block's structure can be simulated at a number of levels.

Circuit simulation

The most detailed picture is obtained from **circuit simulation**, using programs such as SPICE, in which the circuit is described in terms of transistors and other physical components that form the final layout. SPICE, incidentally, is the most widely used circuit simulation software. Originally developed at the University of California at Berkeley, it now has many variants such as DSPICE, PSPICE, HSPICE, USPICE and others from commercial sources.

Unfortunately, circuit analysis programs like SPICE are very slow and require considerable computer resources. They may be impractical to use for the whole circuit or even a moderately complex digital integrated circuit. Hence digital designers commonly use simpler models for components and signals which although less accurate give an adequate prediction in a small fraction of the time.

Logic simulation

However, a much more significant simplification is to model all signals in the circuit as binary logic values, 0 and 1. The circuit can be described in terms of transistor switches, simple logic elements such as gates, or more complex components like flip-flops, counters and registers. This type of structural modelling is commonly called **logic simulation**. Such logic simulation is very often used to verify the function and basic performance of hardware designs.

Making a physical prototype to test a design is not always possible or convenient. Even in cases where prototyping is possible, simulation is usually cheaper, quicker, easier and more reliable. This last point is because component parameters are much more controllable in a computer model and not subject to the random variations experienced by physical prototypes.

Design of assemblies

It is the ability to simulate which raises a computer-aided design system above the level of being a mere drafting aid and enables it to play these active roles in all types of electronic design.

Resources for the complete spectrum of electronic design activities comprise both the appropriate software packages to perform design activities and the hardware platform on which to run this software.

Items of hardware used in electronic design can include:

- the digital computing resource itself; which may range from personal computers, through stand-alone workstations specifically designed for computer-aided design and manufacture activities, to general-purpose computers
- visual display units to display graphic and alphanumeric information, either in monochrome or colour
- keyboards for entering alphanumeric commands and data into the system
- printers and plotters for layout details
- magnetic tape or floppy disk units to store design data.

The simplest hardware resource is the stand-alone personal computer. Often, additional hardware in the form of co-processors are incorporated, to enhance graphic or simulation capabilities. However, while performance of personal computers continually increases, cost of workstations is also dropping, making them increasingly competitive with enhanced personal computer systems.

Structured software design

Use of structured software design methodologies should result in the following attributes:

- correct — the product does what it is intended to do
- efficient — it features good use of time and memory
- well-documented — it has clear and up-to-date documentation
- maintainable — changes can be made easily as required
- usefulness — it can be enhanced and maximized
- reliability — it should behave correctly at all times and under all variations

- timeliness — it should be delivered on time.

The software life cycle

Stages in the development of software-based systems are shown in Figure 4.3. Development comprises the following main phases (although other minor phases exist, too):

- analysis
- design

Structured software design

- implementation and testing
- integration and testing
- operation and maintenance.

Analysis

This phase identifies the need for a computerized system. It considers the benefits, feasibility in relation to resources, cost, time and additional resources required. As such it leads on to a requirements analysis phase which forms a detailed determination of the user's requirements.

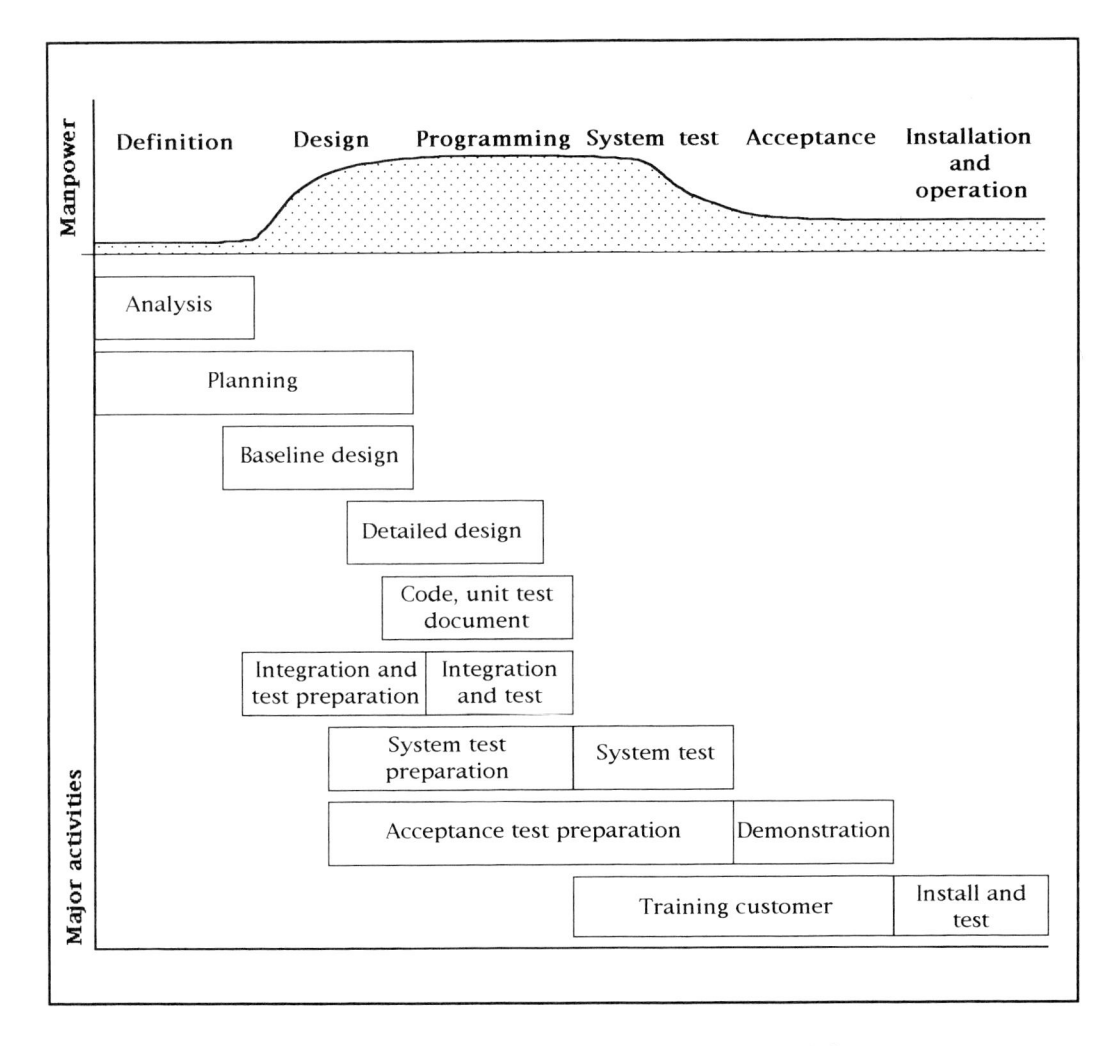

Figure 4.3 *Development of software-based systems occurs in definite stages*

Design of assemblies

From this phase, a document known as the **software requirements document** (SRD) is prepared. The document should include:

- an introduction — a description of the system needs
- special hardware requirements — a description of any special hardware and its interfaces
- the conceptual model — a high-level system view showing major services provided by the software and detailing their relationships with each other
- functional requirements — a description of the services provided for the user
- non-functional requirements — constraints the software has to operate under
- maintenance — should describe the fundamental assumptions upon which the system is based and describe anticipated changes due to hardware evolution and changing user needs
- tail-end sections — glossary of terms, index, references and so on.

A useful guideline on software specification preparation is British Standard BS 6719.

Design

Software design can be defined as the problem-solving process which derives a software solution to satisfy a given set of requirements. The process represents the functions of each software system in a form which may be transformed readily to one or more computer programs.

Several phases of iteration and refinement are likely to obtain a design product which satisfies a specification, and is also of high quality. Any design must be based on a set of systematic techniques ie, a methodology. Structured design methodologies have been proposed whose general principles are:

- to divide a system into modules, classifying it in some way
- to arrange modules into a hierarchy
- to represent this hierarchy
- to show communications between modules
- to show a smooth progression from principles at the top level to finest details at the bottom.

If these or similar principles are followed, the resultant design has:

- readability
- small module size
- modular independence
- understandability in terms of inputs and outputs
- close association between design and requirement.

Implementation and testing

Program modules specified in the design phase are transformed into a set of programs or program units which are to be written in a programming language during the implementation and testing phase. Each unit is tested individually to ensure it meets its specification. The program design can be derived from the functions performed by the program or it can be derived from the data to be processed.

Testing involves exercising the program using data similar to the real data the program is designed to execute. At the same time program outputs should be observed, and any program errors or inadequacies noted. From these errors and inadequacies corrective actions can be identified.

All functions, all modules, all units and all interfaces must be tested.

Integration and testing

During the integration and testing phase all individual program units are integrated and tested as a complete system. This ensures that the software requirements have all been met. Prerequisites for this stage are the individual tested units and an integration test plan.

A good approach is to build the integrated system in increments, having a phased release of some units. This avoids over-complex integration tests and allows for identification of problems.

Operation and maintenance

This phase involves correcting errors not discovered in earlier phases, as well as making improvements to operational features. As a consequence, maintenance can mean going back to any stage of the software life cycle.

Changes and improvements must be seen to 'ripple through' life cycle phases, thus ensuring that subsequent problems which may be created by them are located. Changes and improvements must not simply be implemented at code level and results ignored.

Design using computer-aided design

Use of computer-aided design (CAD) in any design process is essential to the reduction of iterations around the design loop. Where product complexity is not great, reiterations may not form much of a problem. But where product complexity *is* great, iterations can take up most of a designer's time if not aided by computer. While errors can never be eliminated, even where computer-aided design is used, at least they can be minimized — design errors found after production has started, of course, add to cost and time penalties.

A full computer-aided design process is shown in Figure 4.4, here including use of computer simulation. Some systems include thermal modelling and vibration analysis stages, too. Mechanical computer-aided design systems can, in some cases, be integrated with electronic computer-aided design systems to

Design of assemblies

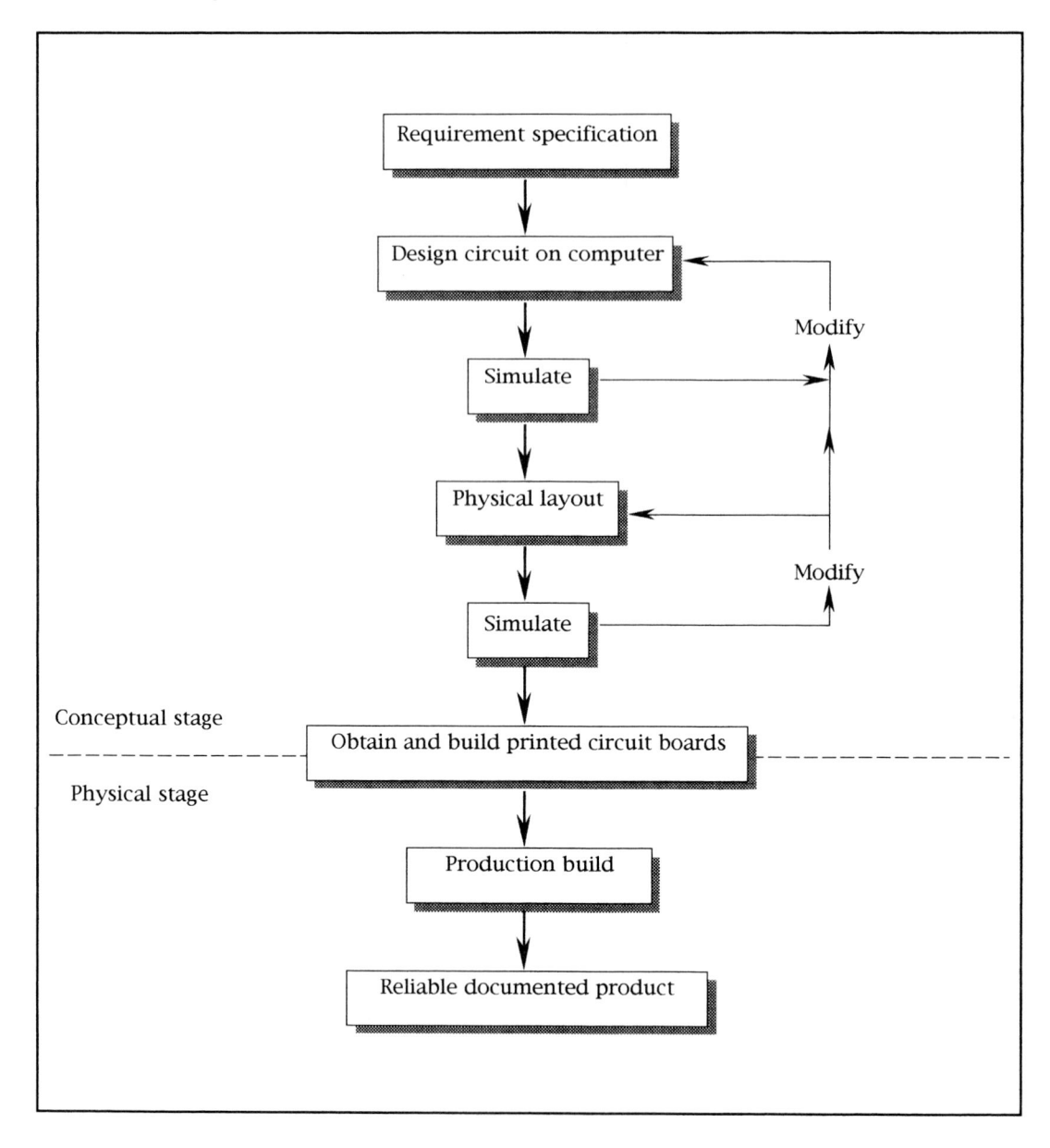

Figure 4.4 *Computer-aided design processes*

provide physical tolerance checking within an enclosure and the transfer of common mechanical information.

Computer-aided design provides the source for assembly and test information. As a product's design is undertaken, the computer-aided system contains all relevant information relating to the product and so can be an integral part of assembly of the product, and subsequent testing.

Manufacturing requirements must be built in to the computer-aided design database, with design release and modification control procedures carefully designed for the specific environment.

Computer-aided design environment

Key features of an automated design environment are shown in Figure 4.5. Several important features of any computer-aided design system are now considered.

Circuit capture

For printed circuit boards, the main method of data entry is the use of conventional circuit symbols. For application-specific integrated circuit design, behavioural or functional descriptions of a circuit are translated by software into primitive circuit elements related to the target component technology.

Most systems provide multi-sheet facilities, enabling circuits to be created from block diagram down or detailed circuit diagram up.

This approach, using signal names to indicate connections as well as visible point-to-point connections, lends itself to major system design by teams of people, rather than just single designer use. Documentation can be easily checked and data outputs for system rack and panel information generated.

Design partitioning — deciding on component technologies to be used, manufacturing details and so on — are best done after simulation. Initial tasks concentrate on circuit functionality.

Any computer-aided design system should enable management of all components used, ensuring that the final circuit has the correct pin and package information. This process is known as **back annotation**.

Circuit capture makes available three important outputs:

- documentation which is well-presented, to company standards
- information in digital format for the next stage of design
- information which is electrically correct.

Simulation

Simulation is a computer-aided design process which allows designers to check that circuits designed will function according to their specifications, meeting parameters defined *by* the specifications. Simulators work in a variety of modes, each of which is designed to test circuit performance depending on possible parameter variations.

Design of assemblies

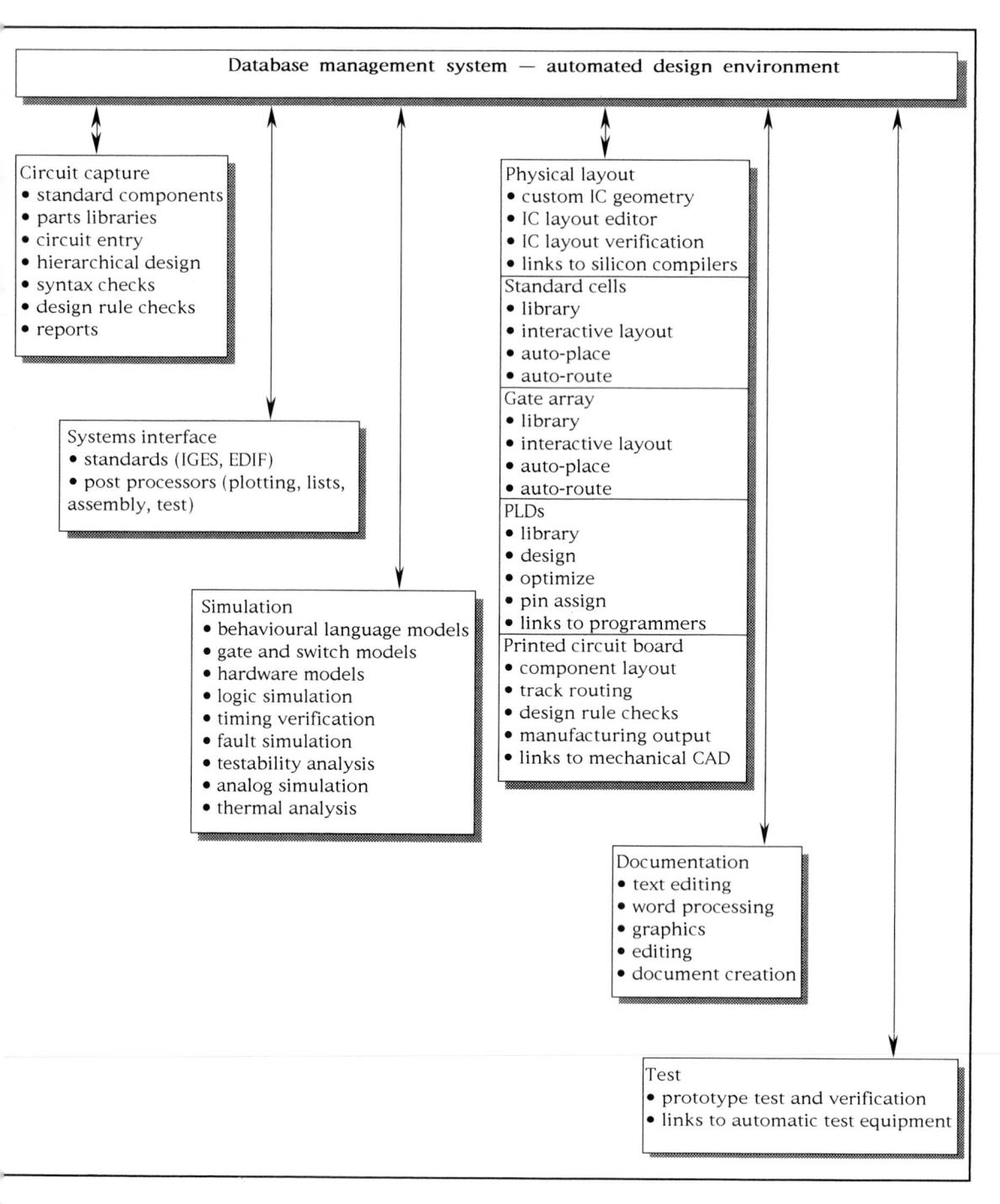

Database management system — automated design environment

Circuit capture
- standard components
- parts libraries
- circuit entry
- hierarchical design
- syntax checks
- design rule checks
- reports

Systems interface
- standards (IGES, EDIF)
- post processors (plotting, lists, assembly, test)

Simulation
- behavioural language models
- gate and switch models
- hardware models
- logic simulation
- timing verification
- fault simulation
- testability analysis
- analog simulation
- thermal analysis

Physical layout
- custom IC geometry
- IC layout editor
- IC layout verification
- links to silicon compilers

Standard cells
- library
- interactive layout
- auto-place
- auto-route

Gate array
- library
- interactive layout
- auto-place
- auto-route

PLDs
- library
- design
- optimize
- pin assign
- links to programmers

Printed circuit board
- component layout
- track routing
- design rule checks
- manufacturing output
- links to mechanical CAD

Documentation
- text editing
- word processing
- graphics
- editing
- document creation

Test
- prototype test and verification
- links to automatic test equipment

Figure 4.5 *A computer-aided design environment*

Simulation can also be used (and is being so, increasingly) to ensure that designs can be tested after manufacture — by writing test programs and response data in the form of simulations.

Analog simulation software tools are available which provide functions directly equivalent to such test equipment as signal generators, oscilloscopes, voltmeters and power sources, frequency sweepers and spectrum analyzers. Functions within simulations also allow users to create effects of component tolerance, power supply variations, temperature and so on, giving users the ability to test possible physical variations a final product might encounter.

Logic simulation employs a user-generated input pattern in the form of timing diagrams, truth tables or a stimulus file. The simulator then evaluates the effect of each specific input variation on the logic circuit, using information about device functionality obtained from a software model.

As well as variations in correct operation, simulation is used to create specific faults. Fault simulation can be carried out by setting each node to open circuit, stuck-at-zero, or stuck-at-one conditions. The simulation process is repeated for each fault. Outputs will indicate faults which cannot be found and the percentage fault coverage. Additionally, diagnostic information, giving confidence in the degree of design verification and fault diagnostics at test, is provided.

Timing verification allows the effect of propagation delay and other time-related parameters to be evaluated. Glitches and race conditions which may occur in practice can be highlighted.

Thermal simulation allows the designer to check power dissipation and power distribution within the circuit.

Layout

It is at this stage that manufacturing requirements should be incorporated. Any mechanical considerations in a design must be specified and considered before laying out track and designing the printed circuit board. Efficient component placement on the printed circuit board is essential to allow proper track routing. For example, if automatic assembly is to be used to place or insert components onto a printed circuit board, a design must incorporate the necessary insertion footprints and component orientations. There are many factors which need to be considered here.

Default design data, for example, should include information about printed circuit board dimensions, tooling holes, clearances, pad and hole dimensions and so on.

Auto-placement software attempts to place each component on a grid position, obeying certain rules about layer usage where surface mounted components are concerned. First components placed are usually integrated circuits. Other components are typically added afterwards. An interactive layout procedure, demanding relevant information from the designer at specific intervals, is often used to optimize placement. Typically, analog circuits are placed in a totally interactive way.

Design of assemblies

One of the aims of placing in computer-aided design is to minimize track lengths — this helps keep propagation delays to a minimum. Further, devices such as memory arrays require components to be placed in-line, to facilitate daisy-chaining of tracks. Interconnected components should be grouped together — for example, bus drivers should be close to their associated connector. Exchanges of equivalent gates between packages and equivalent pins within gates or packages are often incorporated, to improve placing.

Surface mounted technology imposes special placement requirements. For example, certain variations of surface mounted technology feature components positioned on both sides of a printed circuit board. Consequently, a placement system must be able to do this. Each component must be able to be placed on either side of the printed circuit board, the system mirroring connection-pad pattern and component outline as necessary.

Following placement, computer-aided design systems then route tracks between components to make up the circuit. Track routing usually incorporates a combination of interactive and automatic tools. Routing strategies commonly include memory router and random-search pattern approaches.

Rip-up routers use a random-search pattern approach, routing connections until one is blocked by a previously routed connection. The connection is then 'ripped up' and a new one is attempted. If the new route is considered better than the old one it is retained. If the new route is not considered better, the old route is restored and the previous connection is re-routed. One by one, connections are made this way until the whole printed circuit board track layout is complete.

Auto-routers are limited in their abilities. They work to fixed rules, and rarely achieve track layout solutions as good as a manually produced one. An interactive approach is often better.

At the end of this stage, considerable mechanical information is available: hole sizes and positions, printed circuit board profiles and component positions.

Documentation

A common feature of computer-aided design systems is the inclusion of documentation facilities. These are often incorporated and integrated throughout the various design stages of the system. Thus, any circuit update is automatically revised within the whole manufacturing process, not just at one particular stage.

A key documentation output from a computer-aided design system is photo-plotted artwork. Most common types of photo-plotters are flat-bed units, while scanning types utilizing a modulated laser beam are becoming more common.

Silicon compilers

Cost-effective design of complex VLSI devices would be virtually impossible without powerful computer-aided design systems with software enabling high

Design using computer-aided design

level descriptions of complex circuit elements to be translated automatically into logic gate descriptions in a process known as **silicon compiling**.

Silicon compilers have functions similar to those of software compilers. They translate high-level descriptions of circuit elements, such as ROM or microprocessor cores, into low-level representations which can be organized as the primitive elements in an integrated circuit's basic layout. In essence, the designer only needs to concentrate on a top-level representation of a design. The silicon compiler deals with everything below this, as shown in Figure 4.6.

A lever effect is generated. Complexity of VLSI systems is now within the orbit of a single designer, with very quick lead times. Complex integrated circuits these days contain over 100,000 transistors. With silicon compilers this will increase over the next few years, to possibly 10,000,000 transistors on a single integrated circuit.

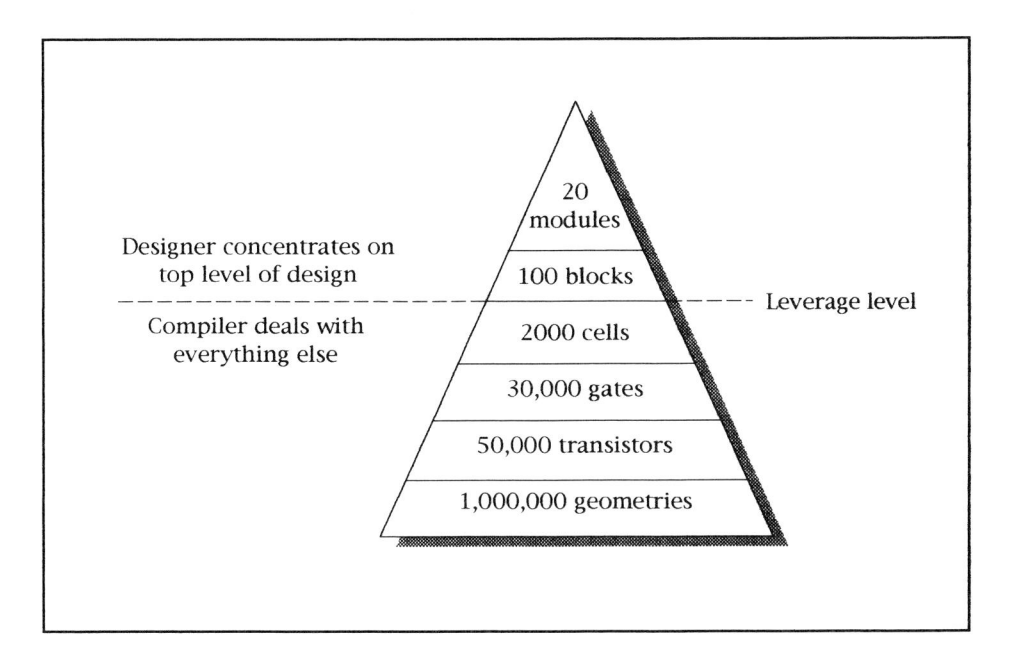

Figure 4.6 *Showing the leverage level below which a silicon compiler is used to design complex circuits*

An integrated computer-aided design environment

A typical integrated computer-aided design environment is shown in Figure 4.7. Such a system ensures that all data concerning the manufacturing environment, from first proposals through to final product, is correlated efficiently. Further, integrity of data within a system is vital to the accuracy and reliability of a design. Without total computer-aided control over these data files, there is often

Design of assemblies

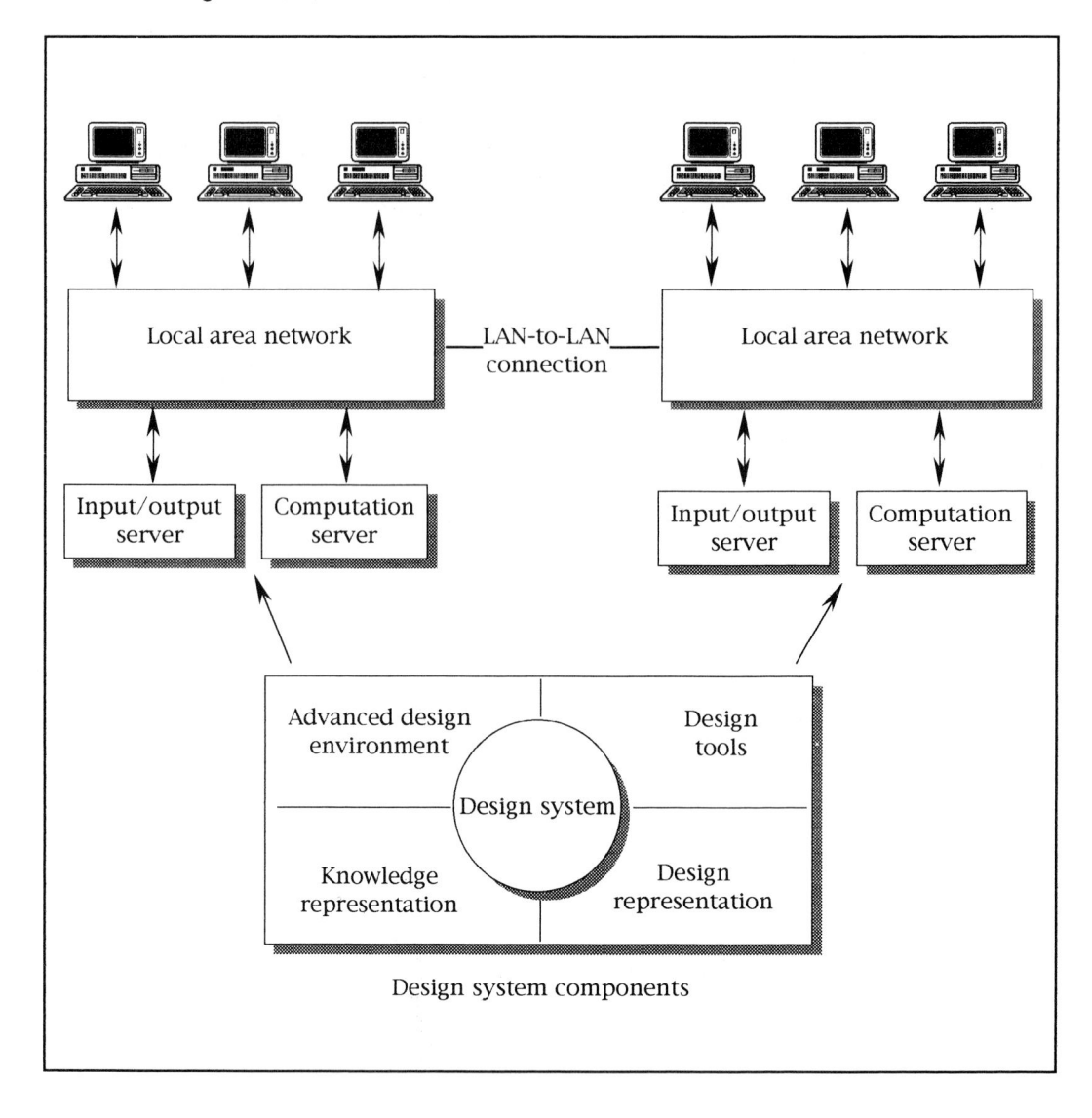

Figure 4.7 *An integrated computer-aided design environment*

a huge financial overhead simply monitoring all manufacturing aspects. In a manual system, proper correlation can never be assured, and there is always a fear of incorrect data.

Computer-aided design system suppliers often provide standard data and information about components. Designers merely have to input company-specific information such as stock reference numbers, auto-insertion footprints, orientation restrictions, pad and hole dimension preferences.

Printed circuit board layout

Things that go wrong in practice

While the manufacturing environment and the processes which take place in it are far from simple, we can consider some aspects of it which cause problems in a practical situation. These are mainly human interface problems which can contribute to cost escalation, late delivery and a loss of market share, so are most definitely to be avoided. Summarized, they are:

- poorly defined specifications, based on marketing wish lists rather than market research
- market projections which totally over- or under-estimate a sales profile. As a consequence, an organization's whole approach to design and manufacture is affected, and may be entirely wrong
- designers who think money grows on trees, have tunnel vision and who have an arrogant attitude to manufacturing processes
- insufficient thought given at design stages to power supplies, enclosure hardware, components to be used (for example, preferred types which can be second-sourced and which are approved for use in the manufacturing processes and markets to be sold into) and testability
- poor control of software, resulting in confusion about the issue of upgrades
- over-engineering, resulting in cost escalation
- insufficient time spent on value engineering
- fuzzy project management which fails to control interfaces between separate design functions.

Printed circuit board layout

This section is a straightforward collection of design hints, aimed at indicating good practices when designing printed circuit boards layouts. These practices aim to minimize circuit noise and crosstalk effects.

Switching effects

Gates switching on and off in a circuit take current from the power supply. Decoupling capacitors are used to provide a charge reservoir to smooth resulting transients on the power supply rail. If, however, inductances due to long track lengths are too high, the resulting voltage swings on the power supply rail can be considerable. This is an effect which results in noise, which affects circuit operation. The ground induction situation is illustrated in Figure 4.8.

When gate A switches low, the transient ground current flows clockwise to the ground pin of gate D, also (as it acts through inductance Lx) appearing as a spike on the ground pin of gate B. If gate B's output is low the positive spike on its

Design of assemblies

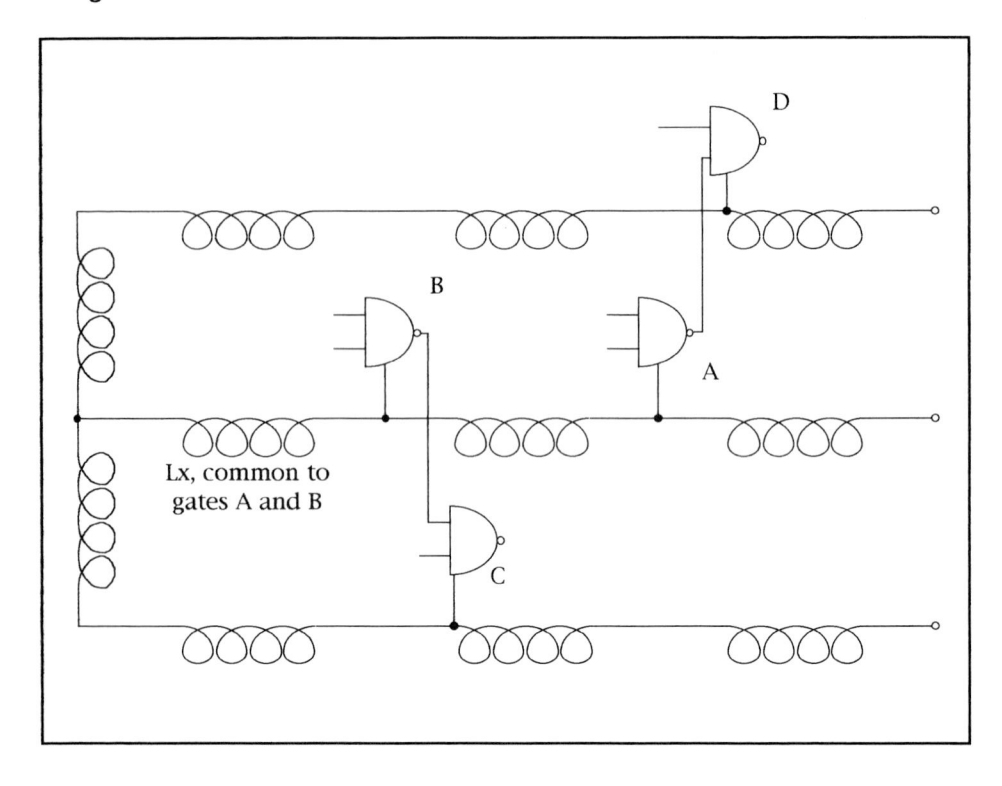

Figure 4.8 *Ground induction switching effects*

ground pin appears on the output. Gate B's output appears on gate C's input and, if the spike is greater than gate C's noise margin, gate C switches and propagates the pulse to other circuit parts.

The first requirement of a power distribution system must therefore be low inductance between integrated circuits and decoupling capacitors. This is of general importance, but is a priority with high-speed devices such as Schottky TTL integrated circuits.

Decoupling capacitors

Decoupling capacitors must maintain the power supply rail within, say, 50 mV of its nominal voltage. Typically, a 100 nF capacitor for each pair of packages should be provided. A brief calculation proves this (refer to Figure 4.9).

Say inductance of the track (L) is 30 nH, and decoupling capacitor C must supply +5 V at 50 mA during the switch rise time (say, 1.5 ns). Voltage drop across L:

$$= -L\,di/dt$$

Printed circuit board layout

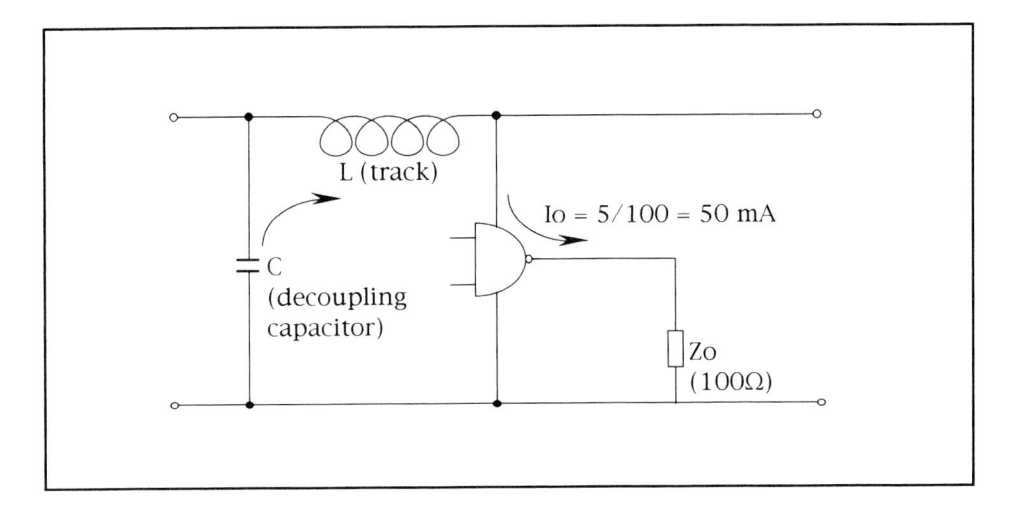

Figure 4.9 *Calculation of decoupling capacitor*

$= 30 \times 10^{-9} \times 50 \times 10^{-3} / 1.5 \times 10^{-9}$
$= 1$ volt (with one gate switching).

If we assume that local demand is for 10 gates switching and demand lasts 10 ns, then:

$i = C dv/dt$
$0.5 = C \times 50 \times 10^{-3} / 10 \times 10^{-9}$.

Which gives a value of $C = 100$ nF. Thus a decoupling capacitor of this value provides sufficient decoupling for about two packages.

Bad layout practice

Figure 4.10 shows a layout which has long track distances between power supply rails (therefore high inductance), and decoupling capacitors. In particular, a signal from A to B, say, has a return line of long distance. A fast step therefore tends to use adjacent signal lines as returns, resulting in induction of transient noise in these signal lines.

A further problem is that an input to part B takes a long time to settle with a consequent reduction in system speed.

Another problem with high inductive paths concerns radio-frequency emissions. A 20 MHz clock buffer sinks some 16 mA at full fan-out. A spectral analysis of this signal shows that it contains a 4 mA component at 100 MHz. Impedance of, say, 100 mm of track is about 50 Ω, giving 200 mV of radio-frequency potential, which develops between the integrated circuit's ground pin and the power supply's ground return. This gives an emitted signal strength of 5.6 $\mu V\ m^{-1}$, at a distance of 10 m (about 200 times specified limits).

Design of assemblies

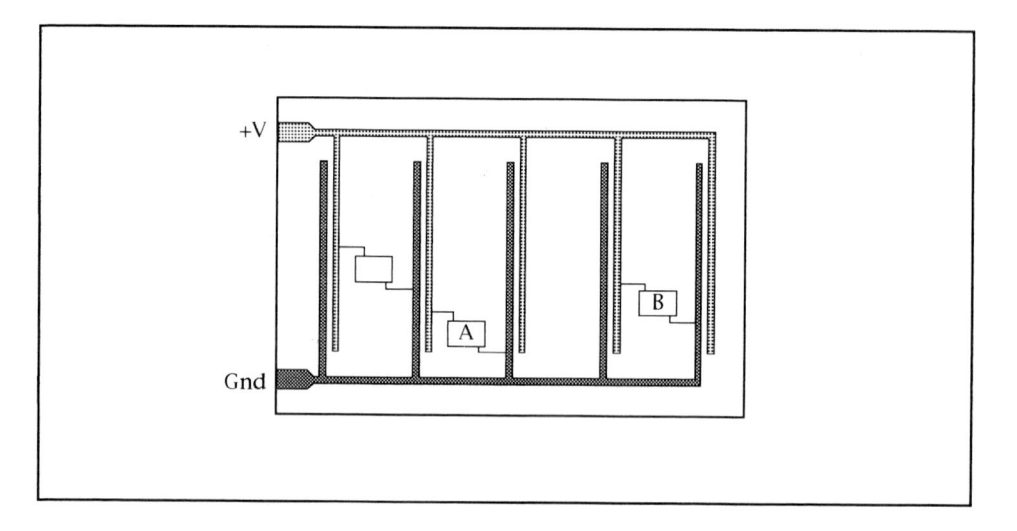

Figure 4.10 *Track layout with long track distances between power supply rails. This can result in transient noise induction in signal lines*

Good layout practice

A feature of digital circuits (unlike analog circuits) is the multiplicity of signal paths from various points on a printed circuit board. In a digital circuit each signal path must have an adjacent return path. One way of achieving this is to provide a ground plane on one side of the printed circuit board, which has the disadvantage that all other connections must be made on the other side alone. Another method is to use a multi-layered printed circuit board, with one of the layers devoted to being a ground plane, and others devoted to power supply planes and signal routing layers. Multi-layered printed circuit boards are expensive, however, although many companies are indicating an increasing preference to go to this expense. In certain cases, higher cost of a multi-layered board can be partially, if not totally, offset by reduced lead times using computer-aided design systems and the consequent simplicity of the approach.

A layout avoiding the cost of a multi-layered printed circuit board is shown in Figure 4.11, which enables a ground grid to be laid out so that a signal line is never more than 25 mm away from its return path. This layout reduces the common ground inductance of any two packages and thus minimizes the ground spike occurring at the ground pin of one package due to the transient ground current of another package. The power rails are run as close together as possible along the columns of the integrated circuit packages and are interconnected at the top and bottom of the printed circuit board. These provide return paths for signals travelling parallel to them.

Meanwhile, ground pins of the packages are connected together from left to right, which provides return paths for signals travelling across the board. Thin

Printed circuit board layout

track (as used for signal lines) is used for this. A tantalum bead decoupling capacitor is used for each pair of integrated circuits. A large capacitor, located where the power supply voltage enters the printed circuit board, is also advisable. This smooths current demands over a time period of more than 3 ns, which the tantalum bead decoupling capacitors cannot meet. Ground connections are brought out at regular intervals across the printed circuit board edge connector. These provide return paths for signals travelling on and off the printed circuit board.

Such a practice also helps to reduce radio-frequency emissions, although not to the extent to which ground planes reduce them.

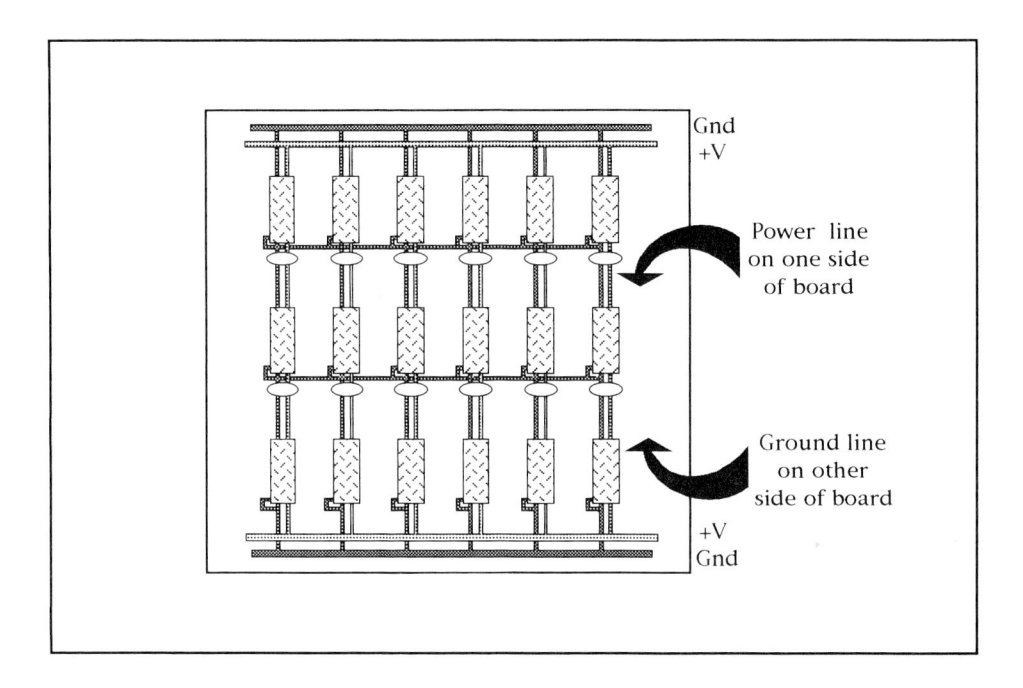

Figure 4.11 *Reducing ground inductance by laying out components in this way can eliminate the need of a multi-layered printed circuit board*

Crosstalk

Occurring when electrical energy is coupled between two signal paths, crosstalk is a function of the types of lines and their lengths.

It is a problem particularly where two closely spaced signal tracks run parallel for a distance long enough for crosstalk pulses to reach full amplitude. Important factors are the mutual inductance and mutual capacitance of the lines. In general, crosstalk is not a major issue with TTL integrated circuit devices, where noise margins are some 400 mV.

Design of assemblies

Good practice to minimize crosstalk is to make spacings between signal lines as large as possible and signal line-to-ground spacing as small as possible. Where signal tracks are adjacent for, say, more than 250 mm, the receive ends of the signal lines should be terminated with a resistor termination of 330 Ω to Vcc, and 330 Ω to ground, say.

Main problems with crosstalk arise with backplane wiring of assemblies, where signal paths are long and current requirements high. Figure 4.12 shows a situation where long parallel signal lines are used. A noise pulse at the input to gate A reaches maximum amplitude when the coupled signal propagation time along length L is long compared with the rise time of the signal on the active line. For a delay of 6 ns m^{-1} and a fast rise time of 3 ns, noise pulses rise to a maximum for coupled lengths greater than about 250 mm.

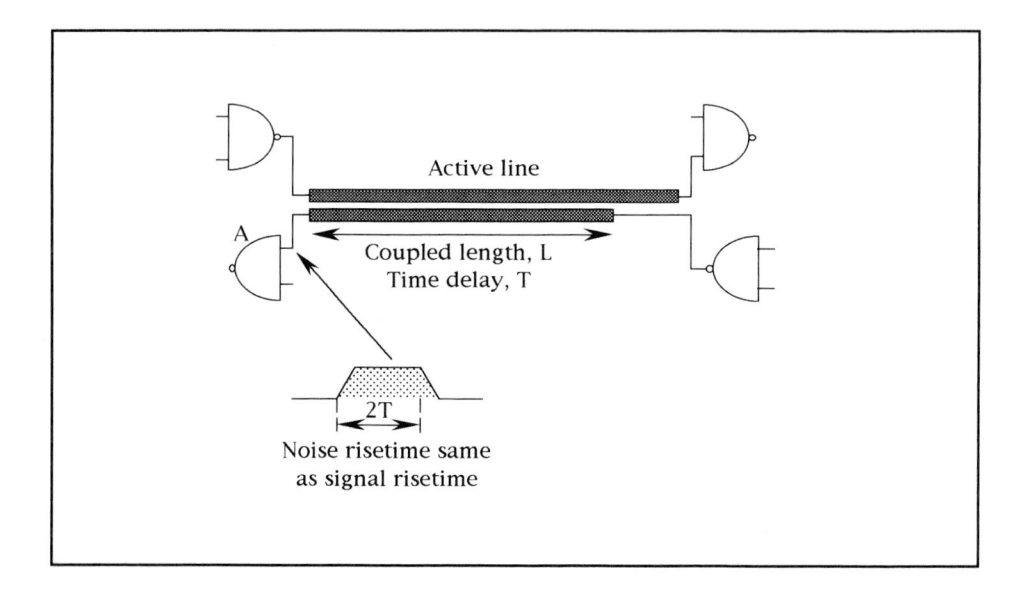

Figure 4.12 *Showing crosstalk occurring where two long lines run close and parallel*

A designer needs to decide the circuit implementation in terms of line drivers, buffers, Schmitt triggers and so on. Reflections can be avoided by terminating the bus with suitable resistor values, suggested in Figure 4.13.

Electromagnetic compatibility

A key issue in modern circuit design is **electromagnetic compatibility** (EMC). Many standards now specify electromagnetic emission limits, and these

Printed circuit board layout

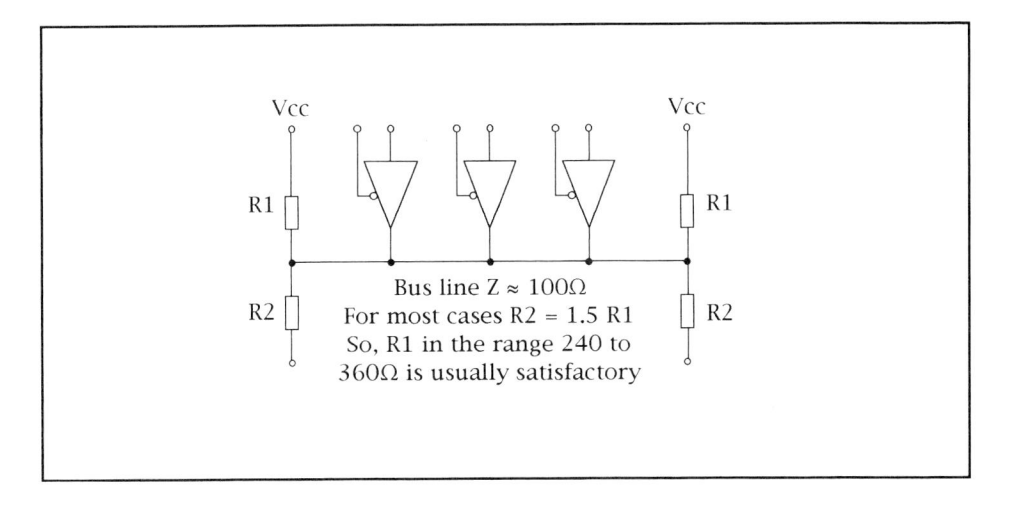

Figure 4.13 *Correct termination of bus lines is important*

Bus line Z ≈ 100Ω
For most cases R2 = 1.5 R1
So, R1 in the range 240 to 360Ω is usually satisfactory

may become increasingly more stringent with time. New designs must meet current limits.

However, one further consequence of electromagnetic compatibility standards is that manufacturers will have to demonstrate that any change to a circuit (layout, components and so on) arising in production still allows the product to meet emission regulations. Changes as simple as a change in supplier of an integrated circuit may be enough to degrade emission performance sufficiently to cause failure.

Radio-frequency emission phenomena are caused by current transients caused, in particular, by periodic clock signals above 500 kHz. These build up radio-frequency potentials in inductive ground return paths. Radiated emission is reduced by minimizing inductive loops as described earlier, as well as by following certain simple rules:

- integrated circuits which use or produce signals >500 kHz should be placed away from input/output drivers and connectors. Indeed, it is advisable to use a separate printed circuit board for input/output circuits
- integrated circuits generating signals >500 kHz require bypass capacitors as close to devices as possible (see Figure 4.14). Use capacitance of ground and power planes if possible
- choose clock designs with care
- dampen high frequency outputs with ferrite beads
- for densely populated printed circuit boards, consider use of multi-layered printed circuit boards
- lay out power supply lines in a grid pattern
- make high frequency periodic lines on printed circuit boards as short as possible

Design of assemblies

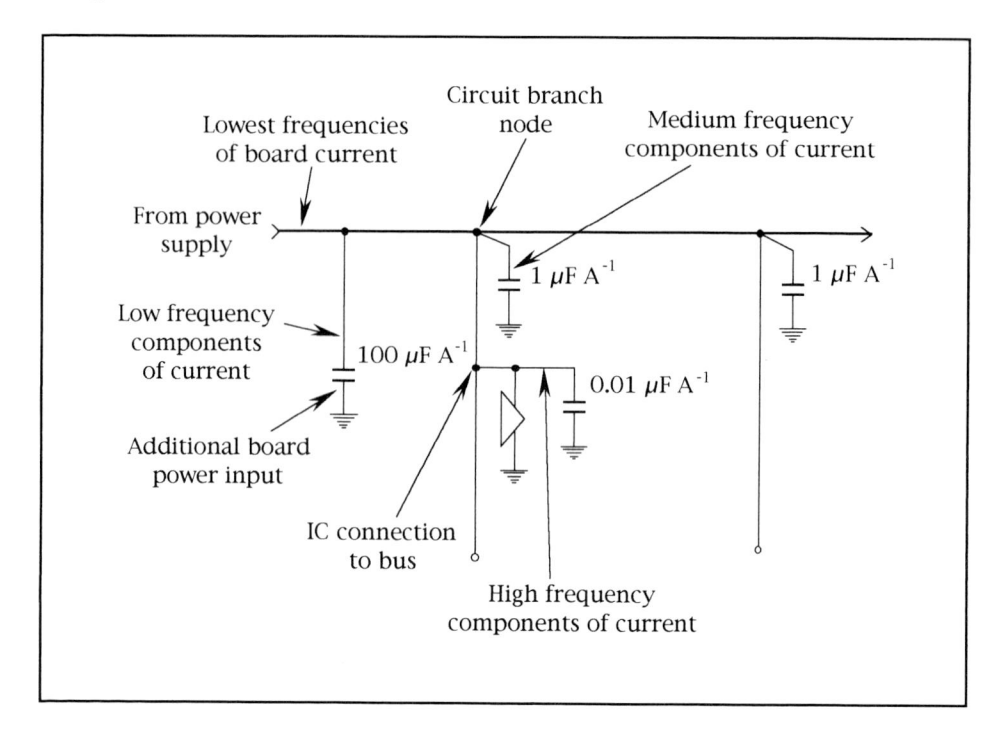

Figure 4.14 *Positions of capacitors relative to component parts and power supplies on an electronics assembly*

- choose logic families of integrated circuits with care and avoid types with inherent contention problems
- avoid bus contention.

Designing for assembly

Production of assemblies follows directly from design. Where computer-aided design is used there are a number of main outputs, which form the basic inputs of production and assembly of printed circuit boards. Typically, these outputs are as follows:

- parts lists and bills of materials
- tooling holes and fiducial markings
- component spacings
- printed circuit board drilling data and profiles
- clearances

Designing for assembly

- layout for automatic component insertion (ACI) or automatic component placement (ACP)
- coordinate data for automatic component insertion or automatic component placement
- pad diameters and dimensions
- legends and solder masks
- component polarities
- component rationalization
- test pads, test vectors and test jigs
- track pattern.

This list forms a simple design checklist which designers can use to ensure all required data is supplied. Relevant processes and concerns are now considered.

Components

We have seen in Chapter 3 how component technologies can directly affect a product's design. Whether leaded components or surface mounted components are used has relevance to how the printed circuit board is selected, designed, assembled and tested. Computer-aided design can help in correlating all the data to ease production tasks.

Parts lists and bills of materials

One of the first things to be dealt with in product assembly is purchase of components and materials. Parts lists and bills of materials are essential to make sure all parts and materials are supplied as and when required. Whether generated by computer-aided design system or manually, they cannot be avoided. Naturally, they must be correct, and up-to-date.

Component specifications

Not only do component values need to be specified in parts lists and so on, but their various other values need to be regarded. Clearance between components on densely-packed printed circuit boards is an issue which has to be considered, particularly when assembling automatically. Automatic assembly machines require room to position components in place. Some assemblers use small jaws to hold components, so there must be sufficient room around each component to ensure that jaws do not hit obstacles such as other components, or hardware.

Component polarities need to be taken into account where applicable, and automatic assembly machines programmed to deal with them.

Design of assemblies

Printed circuit boards

There are many important physical aspects of printed circuit boards which need to be considered in design stages. Often, how printed circuit boards are to be assembled and tested has a significant impact on how they must be designed.

Tooling holes and fiducial markings

Printed circuit boards need to be carefully aligned and positioned to allow automatic assembly machines to put components into place. Often accurately drilled **tooling holes** are used in printed circuit boards, so that as each board is positioned under the assembly machine head it fits onto a jig arrangement. Where such mechanical alignment and positioning is still insufficiently accurate (in, say, surface mounted assembly with large flat-pack and chip carrier integrated circuits), machines which use optical recognition are used. Such machines feature cameras which monitor printed circuit board position relative to the machine head, checking for alignment and position by means of optically recognizable location marks. These marks are known as **fiducials** and, once located by the machine's camera, allow extremely fine adjustments to be made to the printed circuit board under the machine's computer controller. Fiducials are considered further in Chapter 5, where a selection of typical fiducial marks is shown, in Figure 5.18.

Automatic component placement machines with vision systems incorporated are usually capable of placing components to within ±0.1 mm, although some machines are capable of accuracies as small as ±0.02 mm. Automatic component insertion and placement machines are considered further in Chapter 5.

Conductor dimensions

Any printed circuit board has restrictions on minimum track dimensions. Minimum sizes depend largely on the technology used to produce the printed circuit board and the soldering process used in assembly.

Main dimensions which must be considered are:

- minimum track width
- minimum spacing between adjacent tracks
- minimum pad size and shape
- minimum hole size (holes still exist in surface mounted printed circuit boards, for connection purposes between top and bottom tracks).

As a rule, all these are specified by standards set by each company, and are typically the minimum dimensions that allow quality products.

Minimum track widths and spacings between tracks depend totally on etching techniques used in printed circuit board fabrication. As most assembly manufacturers buy in ready-fabricated printed circuit boards, choice of which to use is largely a matter of cost. Basically there are three grades of etching technique, listed in Table 4.1 along with minimum track widths and spacings these grades can safely produce.

Pads of components are simply defined by components used on a printed circuit board. Generally, pad sizes and shapes are governed by whether components are of leaded types (for insertion *through* holes in the printed circuit board) or of leadless types (for surface mounting *on* the board). Each pad for a leaded component must be sufficiently large to allow a component lead to pass through its centre, and for solder to form a bond between the lead and the pad. Naturally, these pads are quite large. Pads for surface mounted components, on the other hand, are considerably smaller because no hole is required. Indeed, surface mounted component pads are more dependent on the soldering process than on anything else. British Standard BS 6221 defines common pad sizes and shapes, as well as track widths and spacings for printed circuit boards.

Test pads, test vectors and test jigs

Computer-aided design systems must take into account how an assembly is to be tested after manufacture. Tests to be undertaken depend on the type of assembly and what manufacturing philosophy is followed.

Assembly test is typically done with test probes, which allow an electrical contact between the test equipment and the assembly. To facilitate test probe access, many test points in the form of test pads are built in to a printed circuit board. For a full test of an assembly's functions, it is often necessary to have one test pad per circuit node. After the board is manufactured, it is then a reasonably simple job to access the test pads with the probes and perform the required electrical tests.

Test probes are usually sharp-pointed pins, mounted in spring-loaded connectors. They are located in a test jig, and as these jigs often hold many hundreds of probes they have the nickname of **bed-of-nails adaptors**.

Table 4.1 Minimum track widths and spacings recommended for standard etching techniques

Etching technique	Minimum track width (mm)	Minimum track spacing (mm)
Normal	0.6	0.6
Fine	0.3	0.3
Super-fine	0.2	0.15

Design of assemblies

Such large numbers of test pads and the physical aspects of bed-of-nails adaptors mean that assembly design must take into account many factors, including:

- minimum size of test pad — usually 0.9 mm in diameter
- test pad surface — bare copper is not a good surface as it readily oxidizes, creating an insulating barrier between test probe and circuit. Normally, test pads must be soldered to allow good electrical contact
- all test pads should be on one side of the printed circuit board (top or bottom), simply to prevent the need for two bed-of-nails adaptors
- test pads should be a minimum distance from components to allow test probe access. This minimum distance depends on component height so is difficult to stipulate exactly, although components of a height of 3 mm or less should be no closer than 2 mm to a test pad, components higher than this should be at least 4 mm away from any test pad.

While the physical aspects of testing assemblies are involved with reasonably simple problems of mechanical access to densely-populated printed circuit boards, what to do and what tests to perform once access has been obtained becomes a logical problem. It is possible, with techniques we consider in Chapter 7, to electrically isolate each component from its neighbours even while they are soldered in position on a printed circuit board. Thus, components may be tested individually as well as in the bounds of the whole circuit. It is the job of the test equipment to do these tests, but the choice of what tests to perform rests with the designer. Generally, tests are performed according to test equipment pulses and signals, which occur in a *test vector*. As a rule, the more complex an assembly, the more complex the test vector. Computer-aided design systems can help the designer decide which tests, how to perform them, and write the test vector which will carry them out.

Bed-of-nails adaptors, other test jigs and fixtures, test vectors and specific tests used in production test equipment are considered further in Chapter 7.

5 Assembly production

Production of assemblies commences with manufacture of the printed circuit board. Often this is made by an outside supplier, a specialist in printed circuit board fabrication techniques. Occasionally, however, boards are manufactured by assemblers as a process alongside other related manufacturing processes. Either way, a knowledge of how printed circuit boards are made, together with an understanding of relevant issues, is necessary.

Then, following printed circuit board manufacture, boards are assembled. Assembly is a matter of first loading boards with components (ie, putting components into their respective places on the printed circuit board), then soldering components into place. Processes involved in loading printed circuit boards are defined by the type of equipment used.

Printed circuit boards

Printed circuit boards (PCBs) serve two functions:

- to support components which make up a circuit, physically
- to allow connections between components within the circuit.

To do this, any printed circuit board comprises: (1) a **base**, which is a thin layer of insulating material to support components; (2) conducting **tracks**, usually copper (see later), on one or both sides of the base, making up all necessary electrical interconnections between components.

There are many variations of printed circuit boards, largely defined by the components used in a circuit, however they all follow basically three main formats:

- single-sided — in which an insulating layer has a conductive track on one side
- double-sided — in which a single insulating layer has a conductive track on both sides

Assembly production

- multi-layered — in which a number of insulating layers are bonded together with conductive tracks in between and on the two outer surfaces.

Examples of these are illustrated in Figure 5.1. A variety of materials can be used as insulating layers in printed circuit boards, and these are listed in Table 5.1. This lists base materials according to the standard IEC 249, which classifies materials as letter codes (also listed). An old — now superseded — standard known as NEMA LI1 is often still referred to and, where applicable, its classifications of base materials are cross-referred to correct IEC 249 classifications merely for information. Generally, glass fibre reinforced epoxide resin boards, and cellulose paper reinforced phenolic resin boards are used as printed circuit board bases, although specific applications often require alternatives. Base materials can be rigid or flexible, to suit the application.

Table 5.1 Common printed circuit board base materials, listed alphabetically according to standard IEC 249. Where applicable, outdated NEMA LI1 classifications are also given

Base material	Classification	NEMA LI1
Epoxide resin, woven glass fabric, bonding sheet for multi-layered printed circuit boards	EP-GC	
Epoxide resin, non-woven glass filaments in addition to woven glass fabric, copper conductor	EP-GCA-Cu	
Epoxide resin, woven glass fabric, copper conductor	EP-GC-Cu	G-10, G-11, FR-4, FR5, CEM-1, CEM-3
Phenolic resin, cellulose paper, copper conductor	PF-CP-Cu	X, XP, XPC, XX, XXP, XXPC, XXX, XXXP, XXXPC, FR-2
Polyethylene terephthalate (polyester) films, adhesive coated cover sheet for flexible printed circuit boards	PETP-F	
Polyethylene terephthalate (polyester), flexible, copper conductor	PETP-F-Cu	
Polyimide film, adhesive coated cover sheet for flexible printed circuit boards	PI-F	
Polyimide, flexible, copper conductor	PI-F-Cu	
Silicone resin, woven glass fabric, copper conductor	Si-GC-Cu	

Printed circuit boards

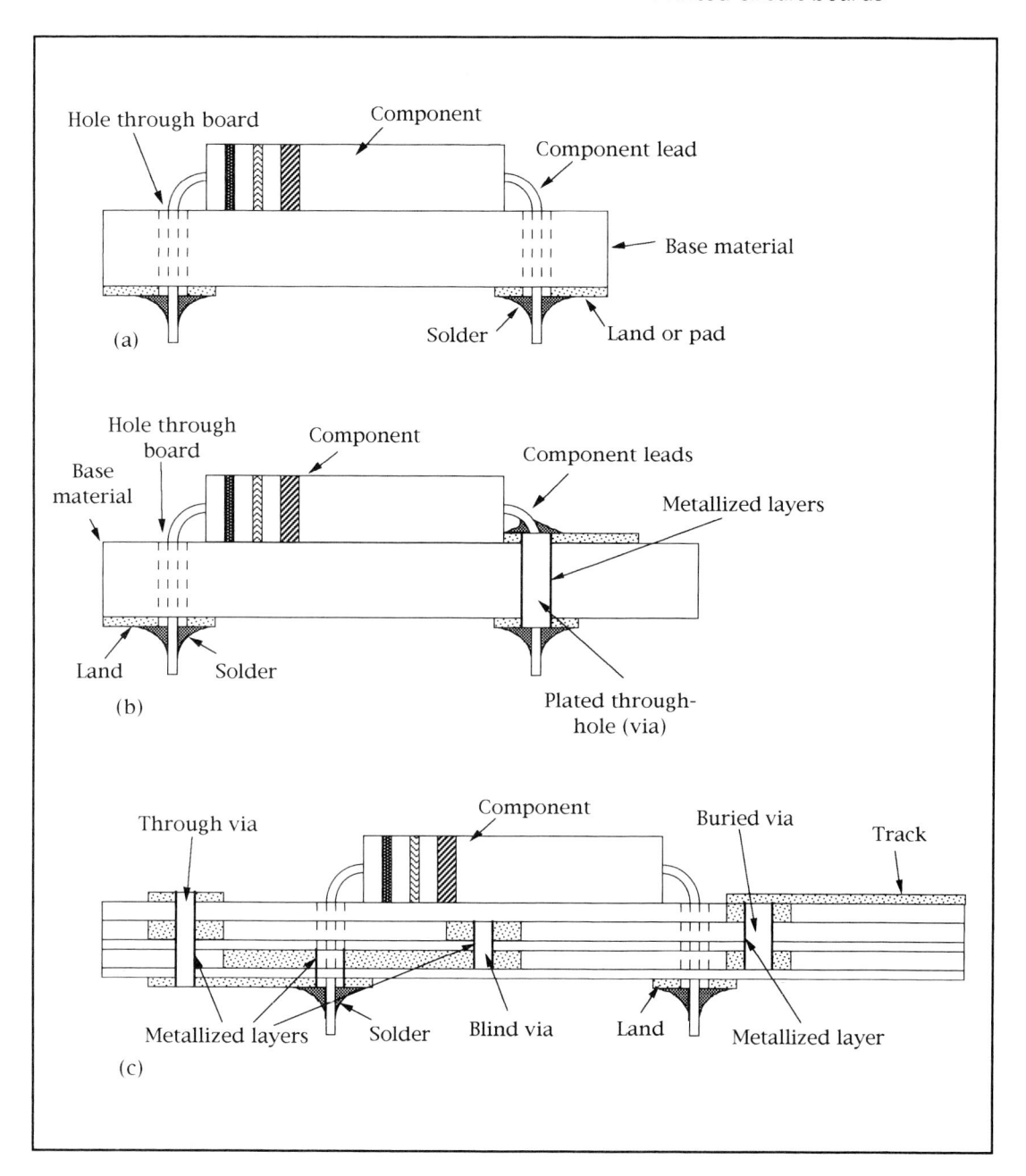

Figure 5.1 *Three main formats of printed circuit board assemblies (a) single-sided, with conductive track on one side (b) double-sided, with conductive track on top and bottom sides (c) multi-layered, with conductive track layers between and on the top and bottom sides*

Assembly production

Components are connected to a printed circuit board by soldering them to the conductive track. Component terminations are soldered to specific areas in the track, called **pads** or **lands**, shaped to suit the components to be fitted.

Lands may have holes drilled or punched through them and the base, to allow certain types of components to be fitted prior to soldering. In this case, the resultant board is known as a **through-hole printed circuit board**. Components to be fitted through these holes are sometimes called **through-hole components** but, as they must have leads as terminations, are more correctly known as **leaded components**. The examples already shown in Figure 5.1 are all of through-hole printed circuit boards. Where double-sided or multi-layered printed circuit board tracks are to be interconnected, holes between track layers are usually metallized, then plated to form an electrical connection. Such **plated-through holes** or **vias** can connect between outer track layers so are known as **through vias**, or may connect just internal layers so are **blind** or **buried vias**.

On the other hand, lands may not have holes, in which case components are mounted on the surface of the board prior to soldering. Here the board is said to be a **surface mounted board**, and components are known as **surface mounted components** (SMCs), **surface mounted devices** (SMDs), or simply **leadless components**. An example is shown in Figure 5.2. Leadless components have their terminations which are to be soldered to the printed circuit board as an integral feature of the component body shape.

While these two assembly variations, through-hole and surface mount, are often used alone, it is also common to see **mixed assemblies**, featuring both leaded and leadless components (Figure 5.3).

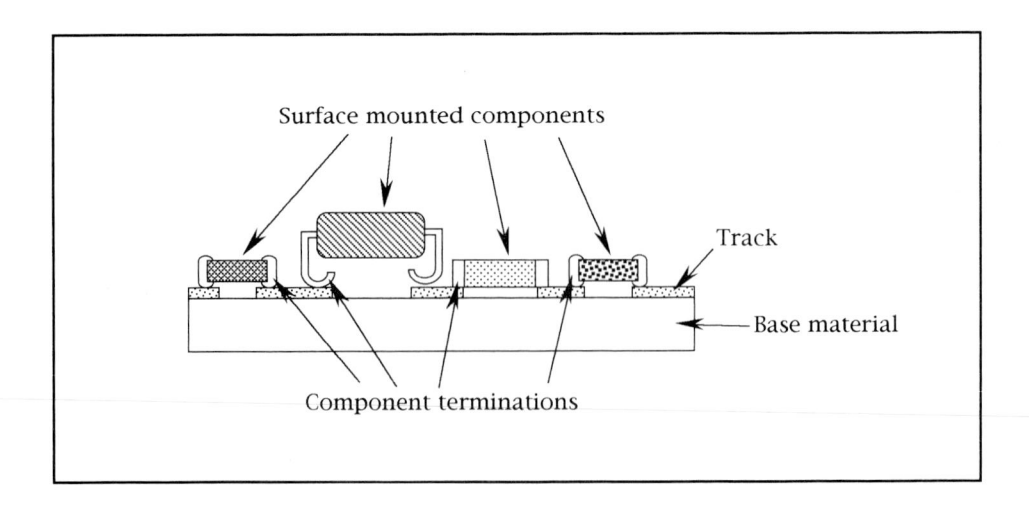

Figure 5.2 *A surface mounted printed circuit board assembly, featuring leadless components*

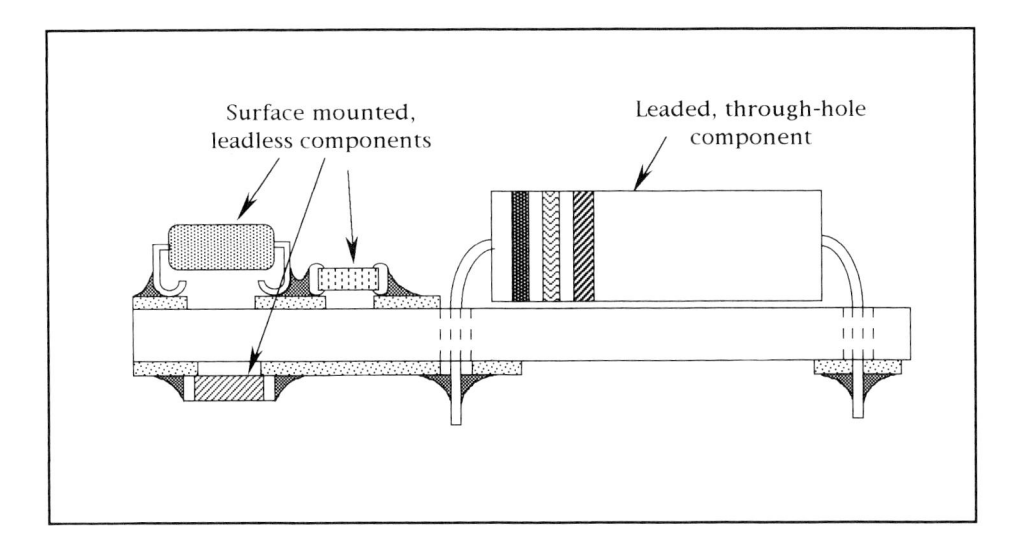

Figure 5.3 *A mixed assembly, featuring both leaded and leadless components mounted on a single printed circuit board*

Generally the conductive track layer is of plain copper but, as this readily oxidizes, it is common to coat the copper in some way to ensure a high level of solderability. Without this form of protection copper rapidly becomes unsolderable and may require considerable cleaning before it can be used. Often this coating is of solder itself, but organic resins are sometimes used, and precious metals are occasionally plated onto the copper.

Printed circuit board manufacture

Taken to their extremes, there are two basic manufacturing techniques for printed circuit boards. The first starts with a copper-clad base material (ie, the base material is laminated together with a copper sheet), and uses an etchant to dissolve away unwanted copper leaving behind the track on the base surface. This is **subtractive manufacture**, and is most common. Variations of this basic technique are known as **conventional** or **print and etch** techniques. The term *print and etch* refers to the two main stages in subtractive printed circuit board production:

- printing a pattern on the copper-clad board which is a replica of the required track pattern. Chemicals used must be etch resistant, to protect the copper underneath the pattern during the following stage
- etching away unwanted copper from the board surface, leaving behind the wanted track pattern.

Assembly production

Often, depending on the chemical used, the etch resist is then removed by solvent.

The second basic technique starts with bare base laminate, and adds copper to it to form the required track — **additive manufacture**. Although such techniques exist, they are rarely used, being time-consuming, complicated and therefore expensive.

In practice, a combination of subtractive and additive processes known as **semi-additive manufacture** is most commonly used. Here copper-clad base laminate is used and holes through the board are metallized and plated by additive techniques, prior to excess copper being etched away.

Photographic image transfer

Photoplotted image output is used in several stages of electronics assembly manufacture. All photoplotted images are based on photographic image transfer, using a photo-sensitive material on the board surface. Exposure to ultraviolet light hardens the photo-sensitive material, so areas of the photoplotted image which are dark shield the photo-sensitive material and prevent those parts from being hardened. Consequent washing with a solvent removes soft areas, leaving those hardened in the process.

This type of process is used, typically, to form a protective coating the shape of the track pattern on the surface of a copper-clad laminate. Excess copper is then etched away, leaving copper underneath the protective layer, the same shape as the photographic image. In such a process the protective coating is known as **photoresist**, and is shown in Figure 5.4.

A similar process may be used prior to soldering, to protect those areas of copper track which are not to be soldered. In this case the coating is known as a **solder resist**, a **solder stop-off**, or a **solder mask**. Layout of printed circuit boards is completed by the design function with master artworks comprising:

- track patterns (as many patterns as there are layers on or in the board)
- component position information in the forms of legends and hole positions
- solder masks
- solder paste print details
- component adhesive details
- board outline

and so on. There can be many artworks, depending on production technique. For example, a four-layered surface mounted technology printed circuit board could have as many as 28 drawings associated with it.

Manual design processes issue these drawings as conventional artwork. Computer-aided design processes, on the other hand, may output information as conventional drawings, or in data form (tape, disk and so on).

Artwork information in data form is often forwarded to a bureau, where data

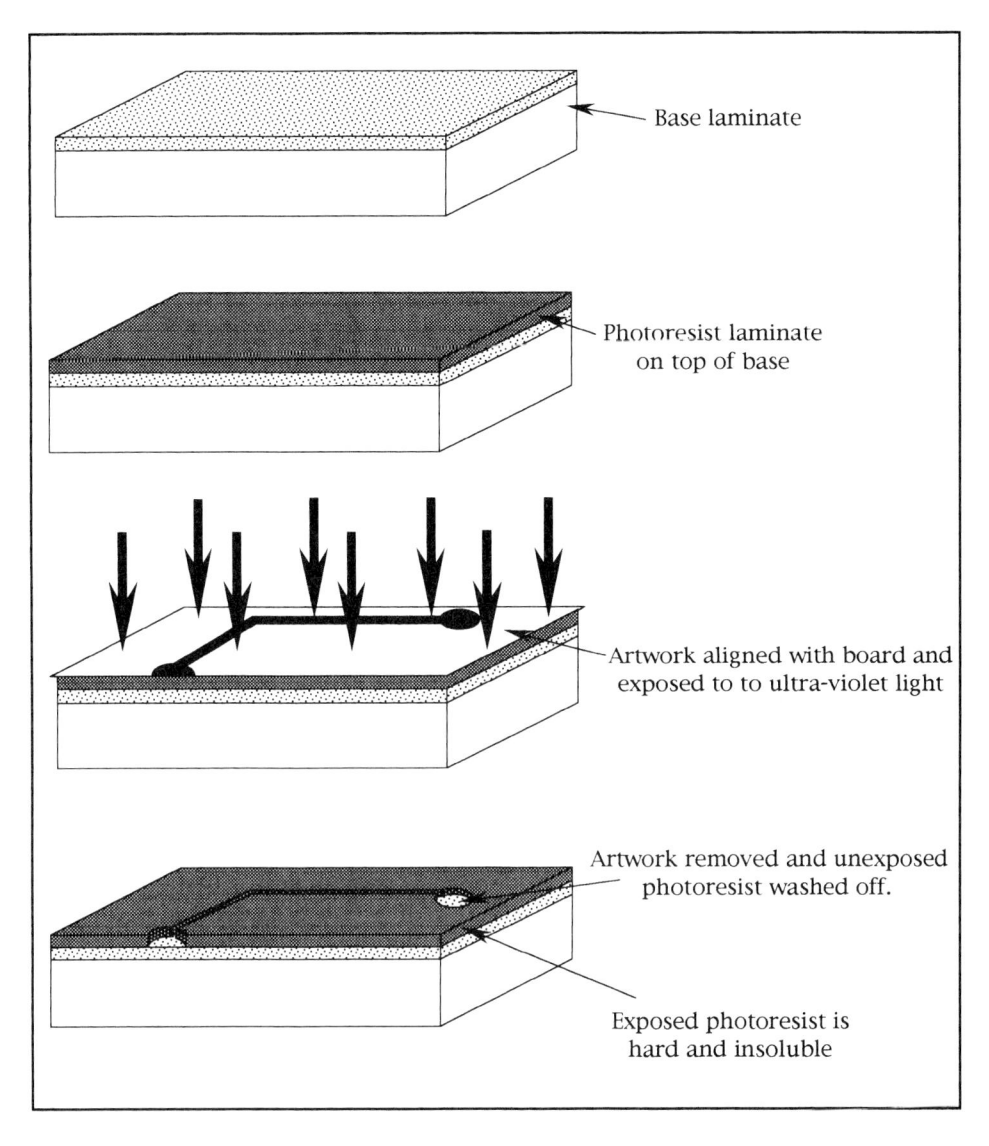

Figure 5.4 *Photographic image transfer of photoresist onto a copper-clad laminate board*

is photographically plotted into final artwork. Photoplotting is often a very expensive and time-consuming activity — occasionally a major bottleneck.

Photoplotting methods include:

- **vector plotting** — where a light source shines through an aperture, and is guided around the film in the shapes and patterns required. Layouts are drawn

Assembly production

track-by-track, pad-by-pad, onto silver halide film. Plotting time is dependent on size and complexity of a circuit, and can be several hours.

Systems can be of either flatbed or drum format. Drum systems are often smaller with claimed better dimensional stability. Accuracy of 25 μm and repeatability of 12 μm are claimed.

- **raster plotting** — where a computer controls a laser beam shutter as the beam is scanned across the film, building up the image as it goes. Plotting time is virtually independent of circuit complexity. Dimensionally stable films have been developed for laser plotting systems, and resolutions of 3 μm are possible, on positive or negative film. Plotting times of minutes are possible.

Apart from producing new output film artwork, laser beam scanning can be used to digitize *old* artwork into data form. This can then be input back to the computer-aided design system, to check for design rule infringements and so on, prior to outputting again on the plotter.

Plotters are either digital — where the next writing head position is specified by each control command — or incremental — where commands specify the distance and direction the head should move in relation to the current position.

Single-sided printed circuit boards

While not the most common type of printed circuit board these days, single-sided printed circuit board is still occasionally made for specific applications. A typical manufacturing process is illustrated in Figure 5.5, where copper-clad base material laminate is coated with etch resist, then etched. Resist is stripped from the board using a suitable solvent, holes are drilled and the board is trimmed to size.

Double-sided printed circuit boards

Steps in production of a double-sided plated-through hole printed circuit board by the plating process are shown in Figure 5.6. Copper-clad base laminate (clad on both sides) is the starting point. Computer-aided design data is used to control drilling machines to make required holes in the board. Holes are cleaned and deburred to provide necessary surfaces for plating. All board surfaces are prepared by removing grease and contaminants in a pickling process, dipping boards into acid.

In the next few stages, collectively known as **metallization**, the insides of hole barrels are plated to join top and bottom track layers. Metallization involves a number of stages. First, hole barrels are **seeded** with catalytic particles. Then, the board is placed in a bath of copper ions which deposits a thin copper layer in a non-electrolytic reaction. This process is known as **electroless copper plating**.

Printed circuit board manufacture

[base laminate block]	Base laminate, copper-clad
[block with resist patch]	Application of etch resist, in pattern of track
[etched block]	Etched
[block with track]	Resist stripped from track
[block with drilled hole]	Board drilled

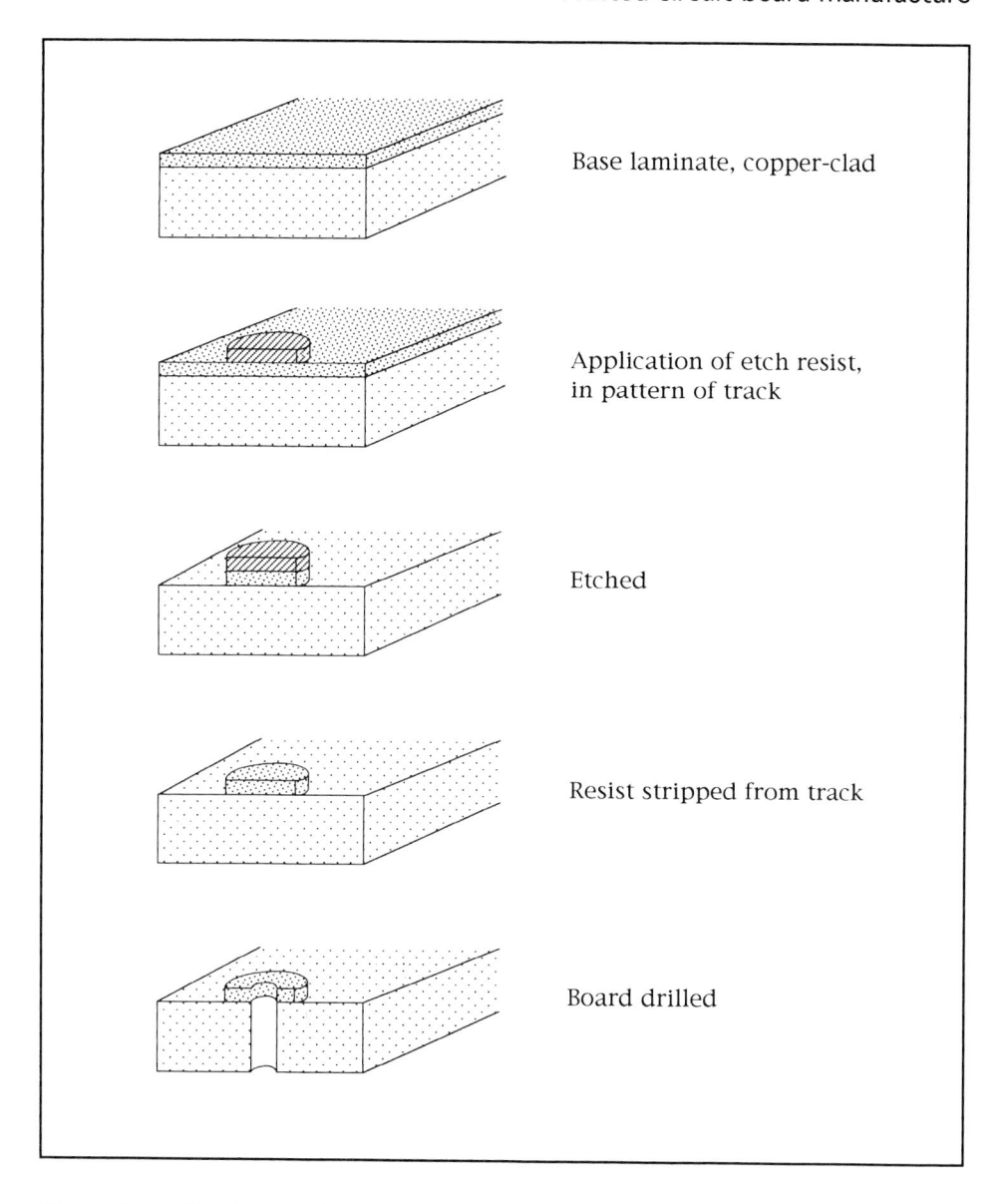

Figure 5.5 *Single-sided printed circuit board manufacture*

Ultra-violet-sensitive photo-resist is applied to both sides of the board, then the appropriate photoplotted artworks are accurately aligned with the drilled holes. This allows image transfer onto the resist, subsequent developing and washing, and exposure of required copper areas.

Assembly production

1 Base laminate, copper-clad

2 Hole drilling and cleaning

3 Activation, seeding and electroless copper plating

4 Photoresist application

5 Image transfer

6 Copper electroplating

7 Tin-lead electroplating

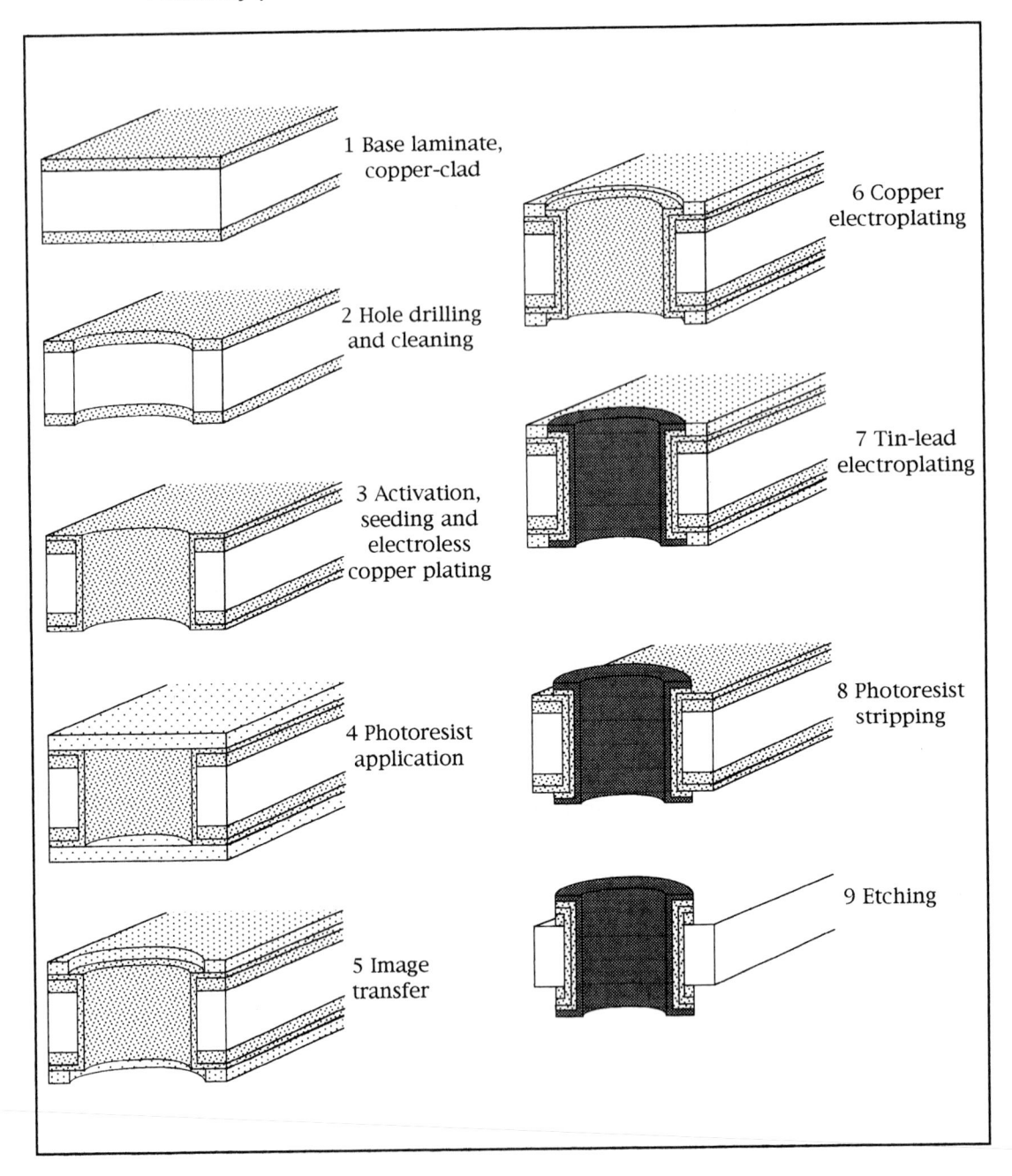

8 Photoresist stripping

9 Etching

Figure 5.6 Nine main steps in production of double-sided printed circuit board. This is a semi-additive process, which hinges on the metallization procedure made possible with electroless copper plating

The next stage is conventional copper electroplating. Following this the copper surfaces are electroplated with tin/lead. This serves two purposes:

- tin/lead is an etch resist, which protects copper underneath it from etchant in following etch stages
- tin/lead maintains solderability of the copper for relatively long periods.

Resist is no longer required, so is stripped from the board with a suitable solvent, exposing the original copper foil on the base material surface. Etching removes unwanted copper, while leaving copper underneath tin/lead electroplated areas.

The final stage is to apply a solder resist, using a photoplotted image transfer method similar to that described earlier.

Multi-layered printed circuit boards

Semi-additive processes are also used in manufacture of multi-layered printed circuit boards. The process for manufacture of a single layer is illustrated in Figure 5.7, while the overall process for complete multi-layered printed circuit boards is shown in Figure 5.8. Outer layers are of single-sided laminate and remain unetched until all layers have been bonded together.

Thin copper-clad laminate (0.2 to 0.8 mm) is used to make etched layers, which are then bonded together with thin (about 0.1 mm) glass fibre cloth sheets impregnated with epoxy resin. These glass fibre sheets are known as **prepreg**. A sandwich is made of all the layers, accurately aligned and bonded under pressure. Following curing under heat, the complete board is drilled, deburred and metallized in a process identical to that illustrated in Figure 5.6.

The main advantage of a multi-layered printed circuit board is the number of track layers available to the designer. Boards of up to 61 overall layers (ie, 30 track layers) have been manufactured, with more than 20 or 30 overall layers (ie, around 10 or 15 track layers) being common. These track layers can be used for interconnections between component terminals, ground planes for electromagnetic interference screening purposes, or power supply connections. An effective three-dimensional availability of tracks means that boards may be significantly smaller in terms of surface area than double-sided or single-sided counterparts.

Disadvantages, on the other hand, are complexity, long lead times and high cost.

A few pointers to assist printed circuit board production

Whatever type of printed circuit board is manufactured, many manufacturing functions remain the same. Very high levels of quality control are required — particularly where multi-layered printed circuit boards are manufactured. Accurate registration of artwork masks and layers is essential. Very accurate

Assembly production

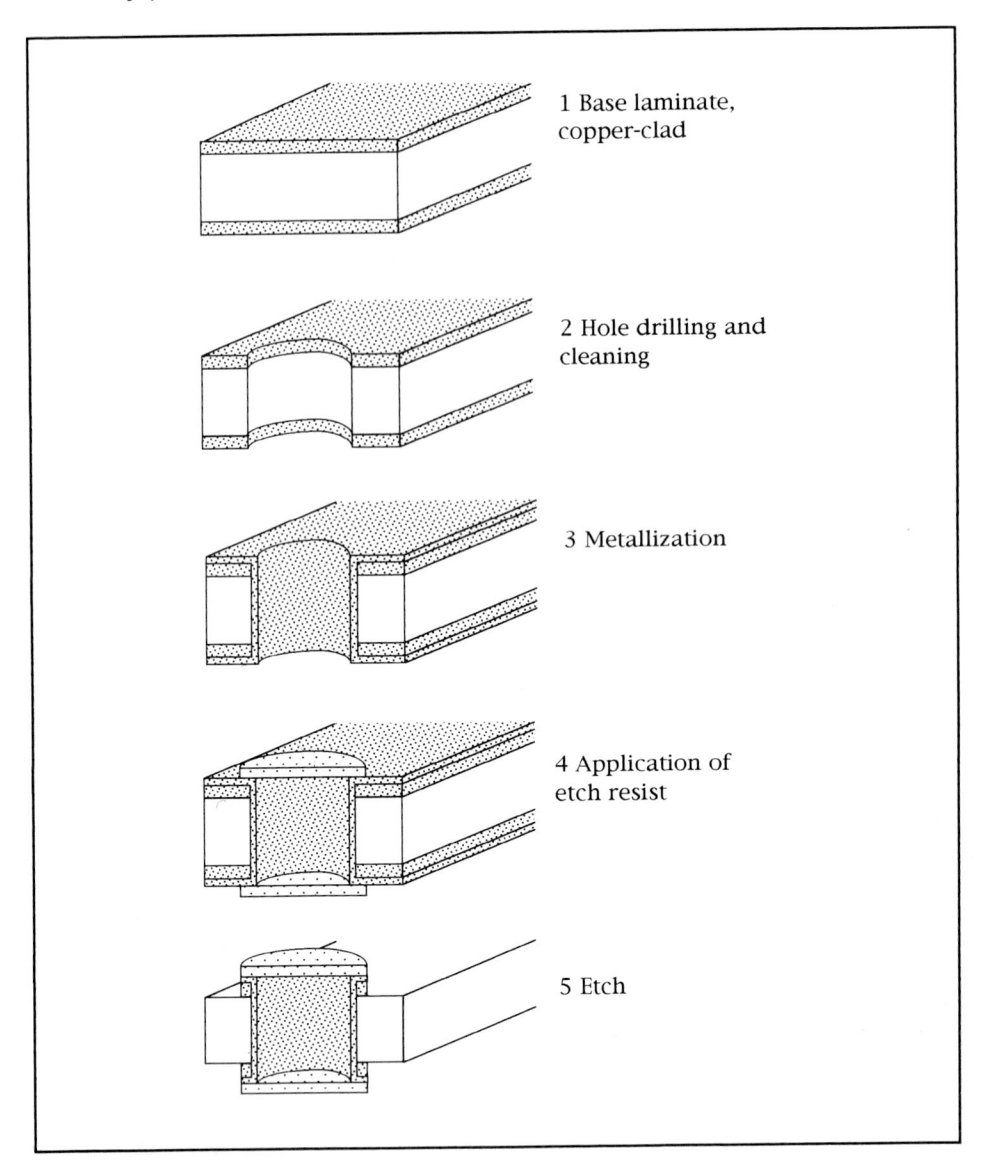

```
1 Base laminate, copper-clad

2 Hole drilling and cleaning

3 Metallization

4 Application of etch resist

5 Etch
```

Figure 5.7 *Manufacturing stages in a single layer of multi-layered printed circuit board*

drilling of through-holes and good hole metallization must be achievable. Holes must be well prepared for metallization; any swarf or chafing of the laminate may result in poor metallization and air entrapment, resulting in expansion of this air in soldering stages later. Such air expansion is known as **outgassing** and can literally blow solder away from the joint during the soldering process.

Printed circuit board manufacture

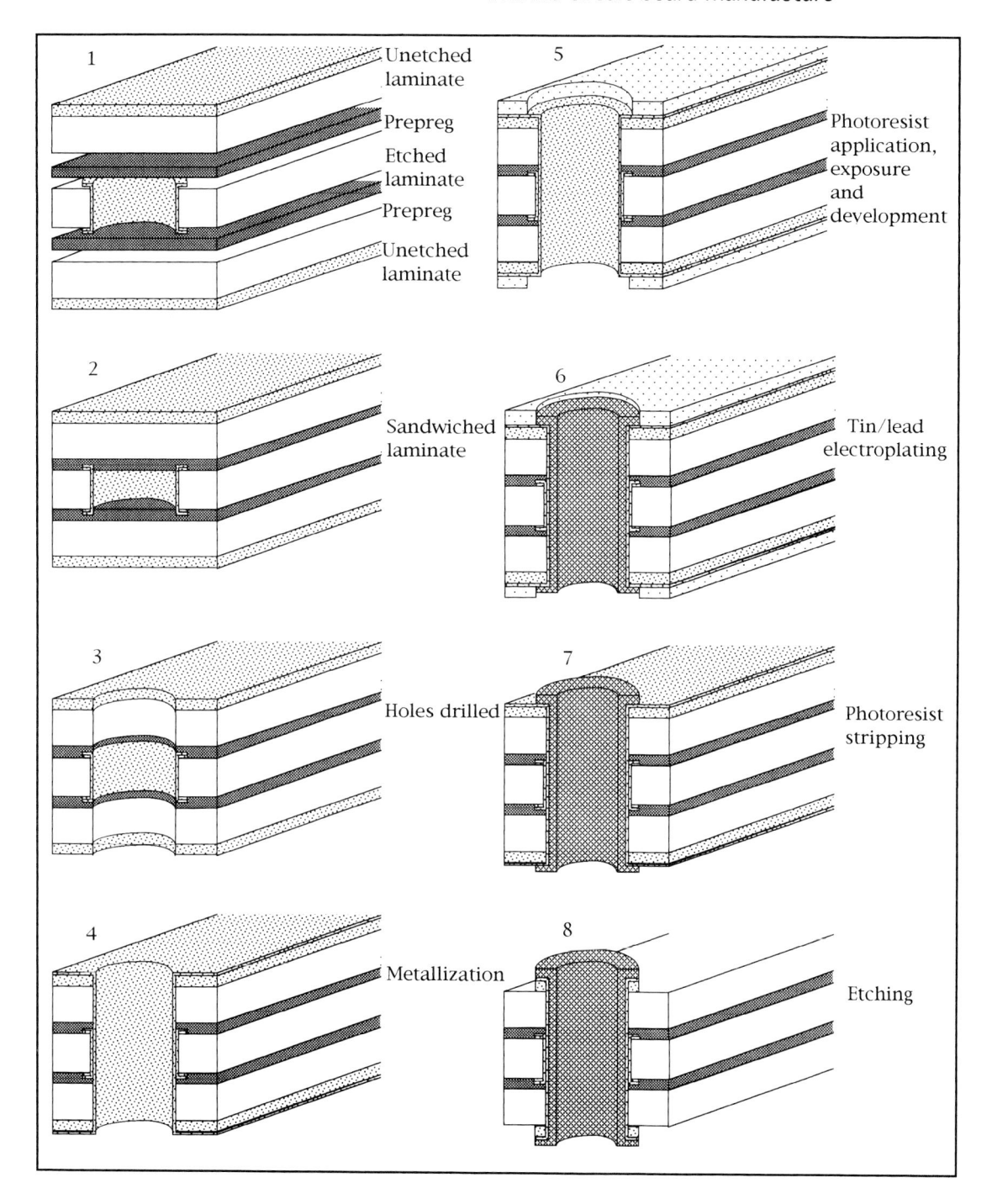

1. Unetched laminate / Prepreg / Etched laminate / Prepreg / Unetched laminate
2. Sandwiched laminate
3. Holes drilled
4. Metallization
5. Photoresist application, exposure and development
6. Tin/lead electroplating
7. Photoresist stripping
8. Etching

Figure 5.8 *Manufacture of multi-layered printed circuit board*

Assembly production

Poor metallization can result in breaks in through-hole plating. These arise from thermal expansion of the substrate thickness, of up to 250 ppm $°C^{-1}$, which can literally sever copper which is too thin. Copper thickness of at least 25 μm within through-holes is necessary to ensure severing doesn't occur.

Artwork must show well-defined tracks and pads. Layer-to-layer registration is all-important as is registration of solder resist, particularly on boards to carry surface mounted components. All layers should be clearly identified and numbered and, as an aid to later mechanical processes that position components on the board, should carry recognizable target marks — known as **fiducials** — outside the circuit area.

Drilling information generated by computer-aided design can be in the form of an ASCII text file, or sometimes as an Excellon file. Drilling data can also be extracted directly from Gerber photoplotting files. Whatever data format is used, it must be compatible with the computer-numerically-controlled drill, and should contain XY coordinate units used, data in incremental or absolute units, location of program origin, tool parameters, step and repeat functions and so on.

The following rules will aid printed circuit board manufacture:

- give as wide a tolerance as possible for hole diameters and positions
- use hole diameters between 0.8 mm and 6 mm for maximum economy
- don't plate inside datum and location holes
- don't position datum holes inside ground planes
- don't use buried vias — these increase costs
- don't use boards larger than 300 mm wide — these increase costs greatly.

MOS transistor fabrication

Processes involved in manufacturing transistors and other semiconductor devices can be very similar to processes used in printed circuit board manufacture. In Figure 5.9, stages in production of a metal-oxide semiconductor (MOS) transistor are shown.

Computer-aided design is used to generate information required to produce photomasks, in processes identical to those we've already seen in printed circuit board production. These masks enable resist methods to be used to create donor and acceptor regions in a silicon substrate.

An n-type silicon slice is oxidized and a photo-resist sequence used to form a window on the oxide. A new thin oxide layer is formed in the window, then a second resist process used to open windows for the transistor's drain and source diffusion.

Boron is diffused in and the thin oxide layer is stripped with acid. A new pure oxide layer is then grown over the device region and contact windows for source and drain are opened up with a further resist process.

Finally, aluminium is evaporated over the whole slice and removed from everywhere but in the source and drain contact windows, in yet another resist process.

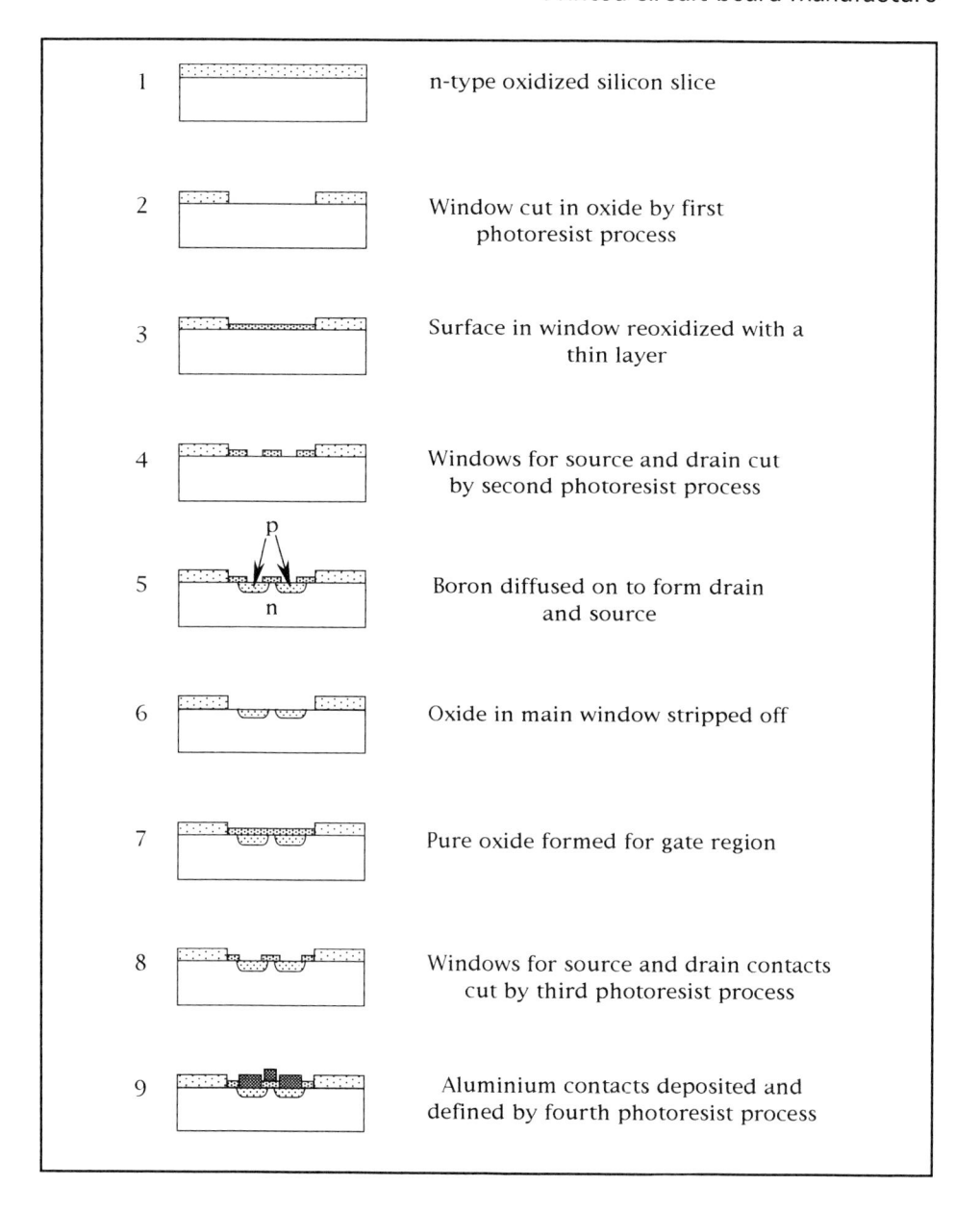

1		n-type oxidized silicon slice
2		Window cut in oxide by first photoresist process
3		Surface in window reoxidized with a thin layer
4		Windows for source and drain cut by second photoresist process
5	p / n	Boron diffused on to form drain and source
6		Oxide in main window stripped off
7		Pure oxide formed for gate region
8		Windows for source and drain contacts cut by third photoresist process
9		Aluminium contacts deposited and defined by fourth photoresist process

Figure 5.9 *Showing how processes in manufacture of a metal-oxide semiconductor transistor can be similar to processes in manufacture of printed circuit board*

Obviously, photographic image transfer and photo-resist techniques are central to both semiconductor device and printed circuit board manufacture.

Assembly production

Wafer patterning systems

Fabrication of semiconductor devices often requires mask definitions from 0.3 μm to 4 μm. Data to generate such masks is all extracted from computer-aided design systems and a range of techniques is illustrated in Figure 5.10, where resolutions obtained through techniques are shown.

Transfer of an image from a master pattern onto a photo-resist is called **lithography**. A computer-aided design system generates a digital image of each layer in a process known as **pattern generation**. This information is then projected onto a resist-coated glass substrate which is known as the **reticle**. This is normally generated at 10 times final size. The reticle is then either stepped down directly in a 10:1 direct step aligner, or is stepped down onto a chromium-coated master mask which, after developing, contains the 1:1 image of all dice to be patterned on the wafer.

Various photo-lithographic methods are shown in Figure 5.10. These involve many of the following processes:

- contact printing — wafer and mask are separated by just a few μm and brought into contact immediately prior to ultra-violet light exposure. Mask life is limited and the method is susceptible to dust particles
- proximity printing — mask and wafer are separate, and a collimated light source is used. Collimation minimizes diffraction
- scanning projection — projects a focused image of the photomask pattern directly onto the wafer in a scanned raster
- direct step — a 10 times image is focused directly onto the wafer, through a 10:1 lens system. After exposure of one die pattern the wafer is stepped to an adjacent die position and the process repeated
- E-beam lithography — a digital master image modulates an intense electron beam which scans the wafer in a raster
- X-ray lithography — similar to E-beam processes but without suffering from electron scattering, so offering better resolution.

Justification of surface mounted technology

It is not always easy to tell which manufacturing procedures to follow. It is particularly hard to determine whether to make electronics assemblies which use leaded components (through-hole assemblies) or use leadless components (surface mounted assemblies). Choice is usually made even more difficult by existence of so many variations of assembly types within each process.

Simply because there *are* so many variations in total, it's beneficial to restrict numbers to just a few types. Most assemblies which use surface mounted components fall into one of just three categories:

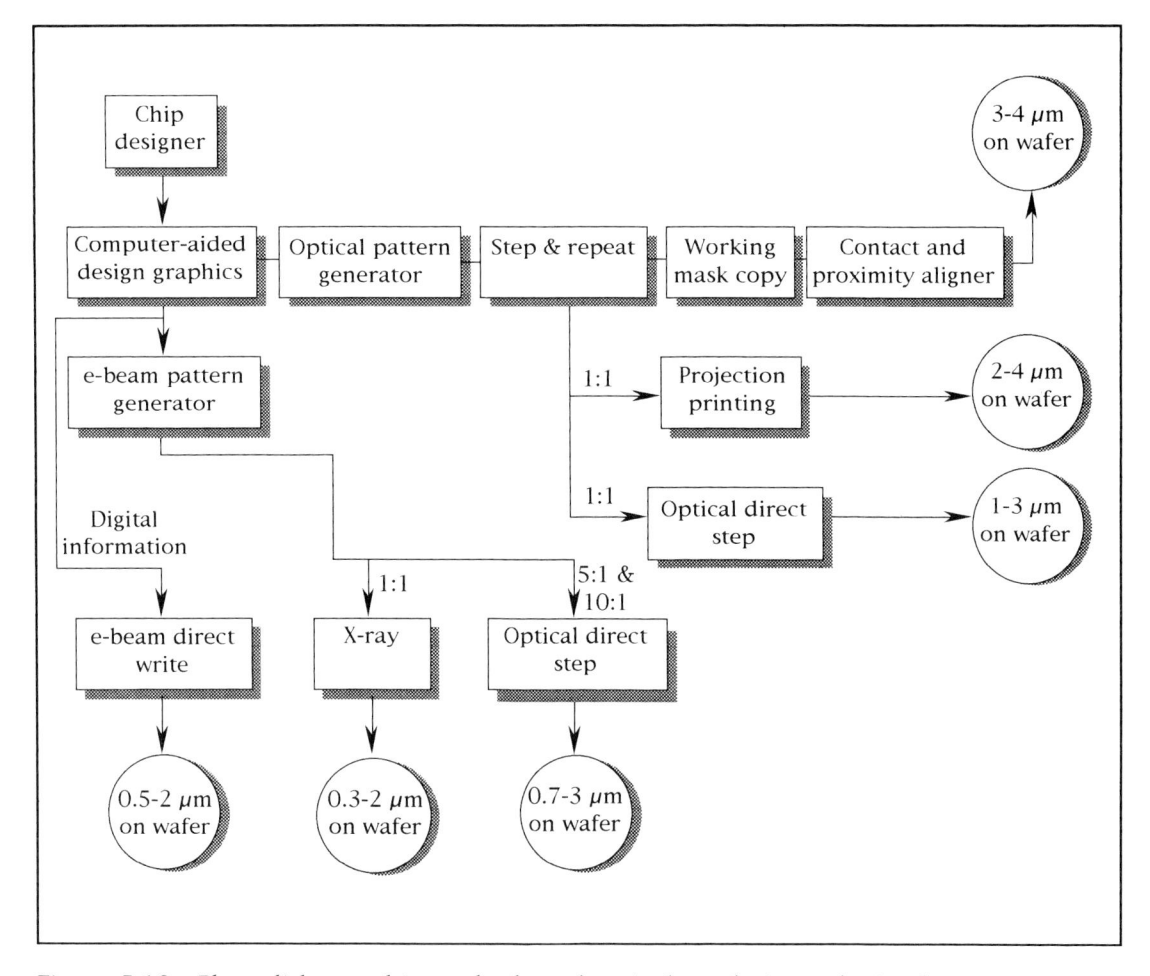

Figure 5.10 *Photo-lithographic methods and optical resolutions obtained*

- type I — surface mounted components only, on one or both sides of a printed circuit board
- type II — leaded components on one side of a printed circuit board, surface mounted components on the other
- type III — leaded components on one side of a printed circuit board, surface mounted components on both sides.

These are illustrated in Figure 5.11. There is also the category of assemblies comprising simply leaded components.

Note, however, these are just common, basic categories: there are many more, and many variations within each category.

A possible sequence for deciding whether or not to use surface mounted technology is shown in Figure 5.12.

Assembly production

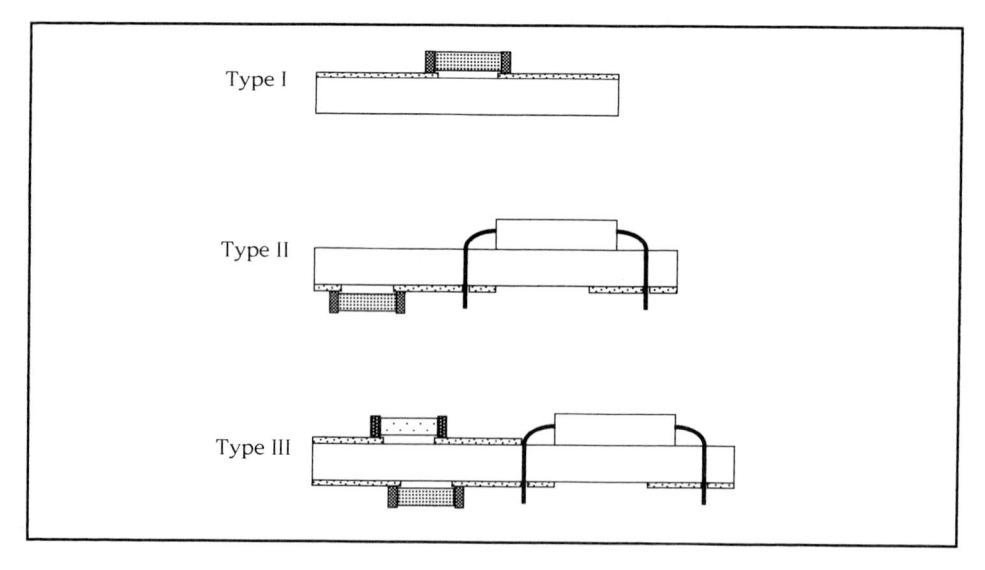

Figure 5.11 *Three main categories of printed circuit board assemblies*

Electronics assembly

In narrow terms electronics assembly is about soldering components to a printed circuit board. In wider terms, of course, considerably more than this is required in the manufacturing environment. Figure 5.13 shows some of the main areas involved in a total consideration of electronics assembly, giving some idea of how areas interact.

Shop-floor data capture

Keeping track of materials, work-in-progress, quality, trends, changes and modifications, and so on can be a major problem to the manufacturer. In particular, smaller batch production and the need to operate flexibly mean that system managers need fast and accurate feedback of information.

One way to help with this is to use a coding system which allows each assembly manufactured to carry all relevant information. An example of a bar-coding system which does this is shown in Figure 5.14.

Each assembly is labelled with a bar-code which carries information relating to the assembly's parts, jobs, test-routines and so on. As the assembly moves around the manufacturing plant, automatic bar-code readers maintain a link with a central computer to control the processes through which the assembly passes.

Typically, in the electronics industry, each character in the bar-code contains nine elements. As three of these elements are always wide, the code is commonly called the **3-of-9 code**. A wide element stands for logical 1, while a narrow element stands for logical 0.

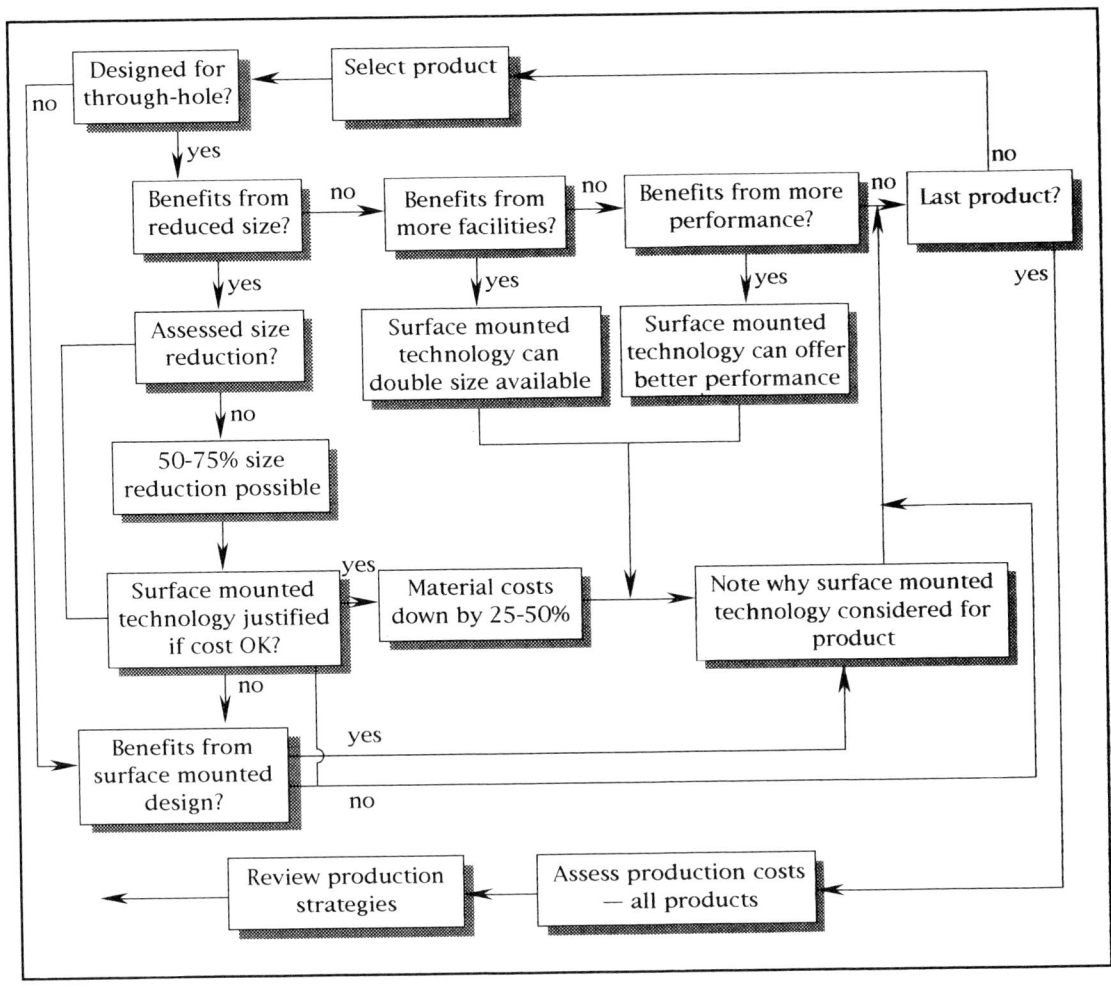

Figure 5.12 *Flow diagram which may be used to aid the decision whether or not to use surface mounted technology in electronics assembly production*

Design guidelines for leaded auto-insertion

Leaded components may be assembled onto printed circuit boards using manual, semi-automatic or fully automatic techniques. While manual and even semi-automatic processes may be sufficient for very low numbers of assemblies, they are neither fast enough nor accurate enough for most purposes. Assuming fully automatic component insertion (ACI) and fully automatic assembly is the goal, there are many factors which need to be considered.

In a fully automatic manufacturing system, for example, computer-aided design systems are used to co-ordinate assembly machines. It is the computer-

Assembly production

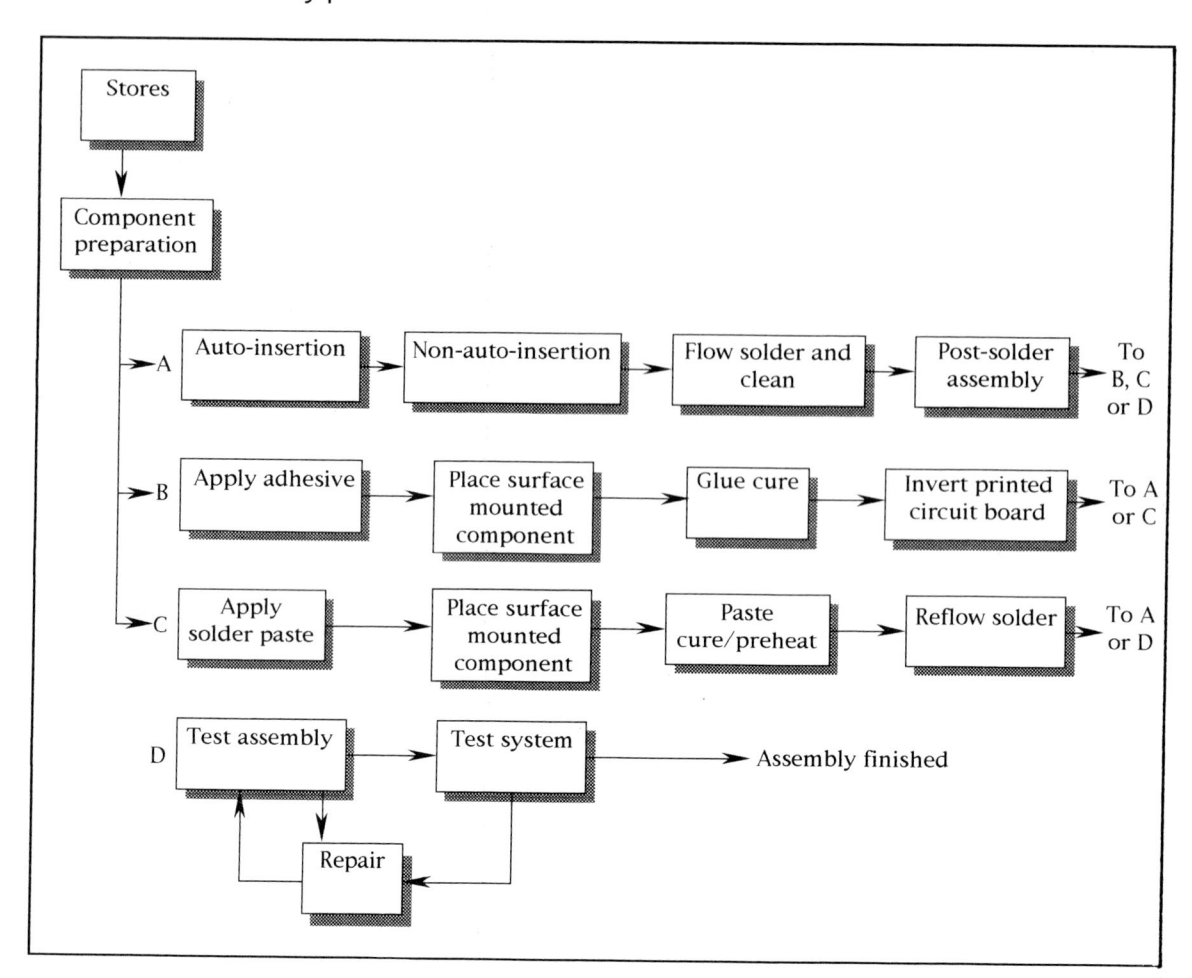

Figure 5.13 *Main areas of electronics assembly, showing interactions between areas*

aided design data which controls the assembly machine head, moving it to placement positions referenced to program and machine datum points. It is the job of the computer-aided design system, therefore, to define an appropriate component layout which assembly machines can follow. To do this, minimum spacings between components and component size tolerances must be defined by the designer at the outset.

Tolerances of hole positions

Any printed circuit board exhibits material movement due to temperature and humidity changes. However, it is essential that assembly machines can still insert components whether the temperature is hot or cold, whether humidity is

Design guidelines for leaded auto-insertion

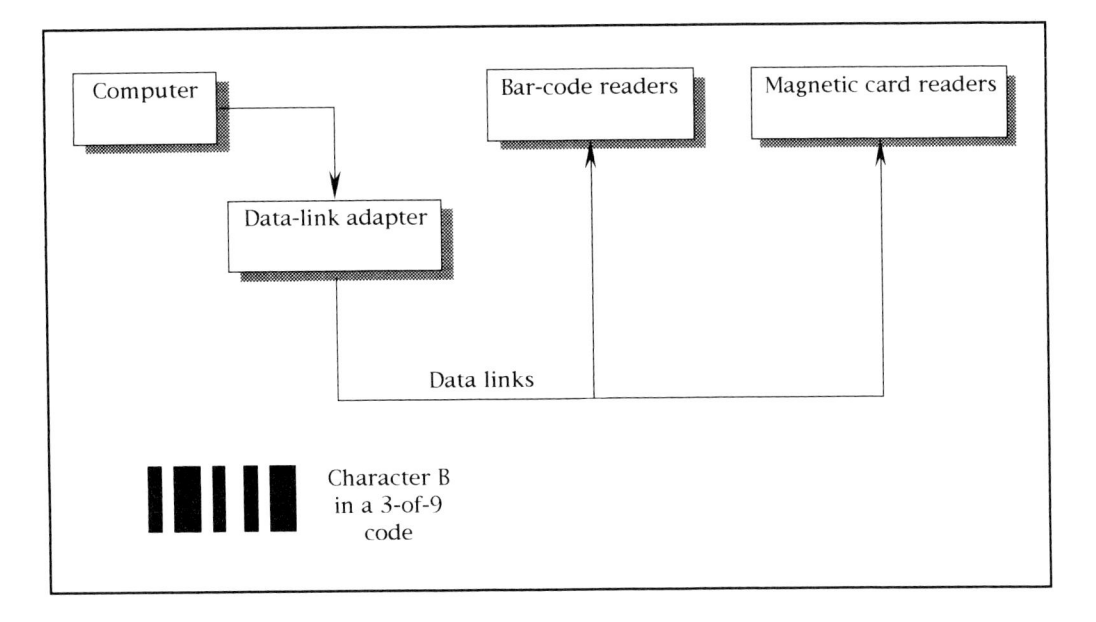

Figure 5.14 *A bar-coding system which allows each assembly to carry relevant information*

high or low. Additionally, errors can occur in drilling of a printed circuit board, due to minor variations in drilling table and drill spindle positions. Boards are usually drilled in stacks, for example, so drills can be deflected by the weave of the glass fibre cloth, so that the bottom board of a stack can have holes in positions up to 0.005 mm different from the top board. It is good practice to minimize numbers of different hole sizes in a printed circuit board, and further good practice to allow for drill deflection when drilling stacks. Also, keep holes on a well-defined grid.

To provide a reference datum, coupled as a means of fixing printed circuit boards on assembly machines and test equipment, tooling holes should be included. A reference datum hole and two tooling holes are commonly defined, in terms of position and dimension, on master artworks. Tooling hole sizes are typically 3.1 mm ± 0.05 mm, with a positioning tolerance of 0.025 mm.

Component insertion

It is tempting to compromise electrical factors slightly, to make automatic assembly of printed circuit boards more easy. For example, making tracks and pads bigger means holes may be drilled much larger, which makes placement of components a much easier task. While encouraging use of adequate tolerances in hole sizes, it is inadvisable to do much more than this, simply because

Assembly production

it makes assemblies generally larger. Indeed, there are reported cases where an increase in track density to the point where automatic assembly was easy has forced manufacturers to use a multi-layered board rather than a double-sided board. Obviously, this is false economy. Extra time and effort getting automatic assembly right in the first place is most economical in the long run.

Nevertheless, there are some simple guidelines to easier manufacture of automatically assembled printed circuit boards:

- as far as possible, keep components in rows or columns, uniformly pitched. This simplifies assembly *and* later inspection and test
- keep components of the same type and size grouped together
- mount axial components on the same centres, as far as possible. Most axial component insertion machines require axial-leaded components with differing mounting pitches to be mounted with component centres aligned
- decoupling capacitors on digital boards are more easily inserted if axial-leaded types are used, placed beside the integrated circuits
- mount polarized components in the same orientation
- make allowance for clearances between the head which carries the component down onto the board and adjacent components — otherwise collisions may result. The exact space required varies from machine to machine
- do not make hole sizes overlarge. On single-sided printed circuit boards, overlarge holes place stress on the pad itself. With printed circuit boards featuring plated-through holes, the barrel of the hole is stressed if holes are too big. For best capillary action on soldering, hole diameters should be around 0.15 mm larger than component lead diameters. Pads need only be large enough to cater for manufacturing tolerances.

Programming automatic component insertion systems

Efficiency of an automatic component insertion machine depends almost totally on its controlling program. Factors which must be taken into account when preparing an insertion machine program concern the mechanical capabilities of the machine. These include:

- how fast the table can be rotated
- speed of access to components
- possibilities of tool collisions with already inserted components.

Tool collisions often occur because the tool chosen to insert a run of different pin-numbered integrated circuit packages is that required to insert the largest package. For example, a 20-pin tool has to be used to insert 20, 18, 16, 14, 8 and 6-pin packages. As a consequence, tool overlap when inserting the smaller packages causes collisions with adjacent components, unless the component insertion sequence is carefully organized.

Figure 5.15 shows a possible scenario, where three integrated circuit packages are positioned closely. If packages are inserted in the order A, B, C, the tool

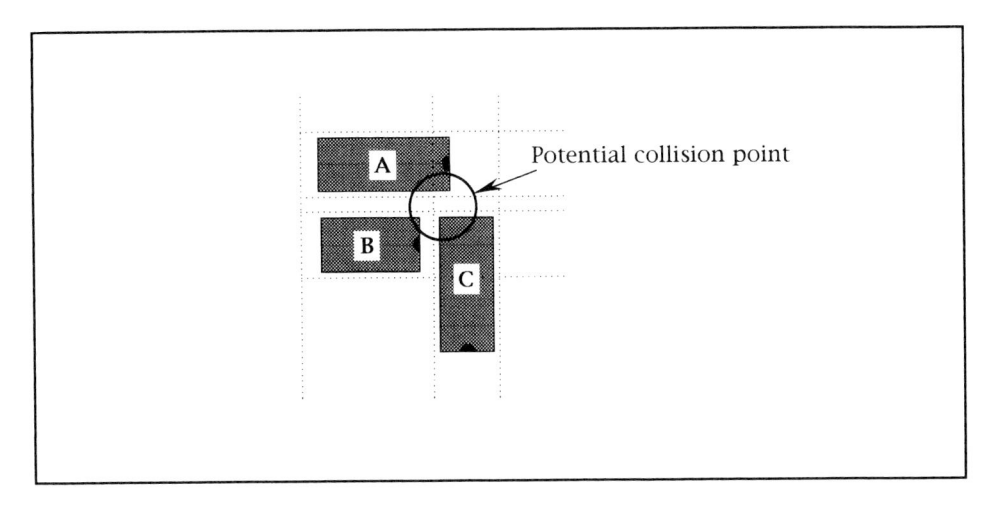

Figure 5.15 *Showing potential collision point in automatic insertion of components into a printed circuit board*

overlap when the machine inserts package A means a collision occurs. If packages are inserted in the order B, C, A, on the other hand, there will be no collision.

Software is available which aids optimization of insertion sequences, to reduce collisions as well as reducing programming times.

Elements of automatic leaded component insertion

Leaded components are most usually described in terms of their lead configurations. Most common are:

- dual-in-line (DIL) or dual-in-line package (DIP) — integrated circuits
- radial — round components with leads at radial points eg, transistors, some capacitors
- axial — rectangular or cylindrical components with leads emerging along the body axis eg, resistors, capacitors.

Whatever the body shape, leads must be bent or formed to shape (if not already done by the component manufacturer), then inserted through the holes in the printed circuit board, followed by cutting to length (if required) and bending or clinching into positions which hold the component in place. Actions required to automatically insert an axial component are shown in Figure 5.16.

Components are supplied in a taped form, in the correct order of assembly, by a machine called a **sequencer**, immediately preceding the insertion machine. Components of the same type and value are supplied on tapes called **bandoliers**. The sequencer selects components from a large number of

Assembly production

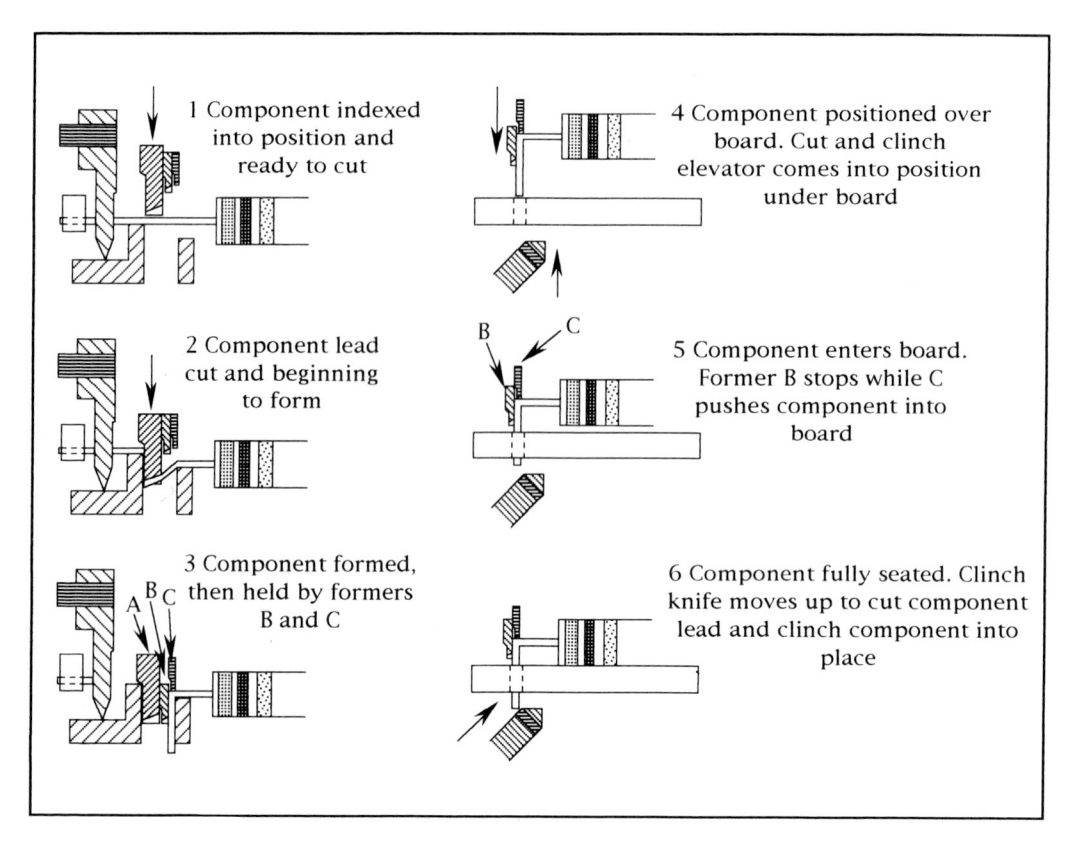

1 Component indexed into position and ready to cut

2 Component lead cut and beginning to form

3 Component formed, then held by formers B and C

4 Component positioned over board. Cut and clinch elevator comes into position under board

5 Component enters board. Former B stops while C pushes component into board

6 Component fully seated. Clinch knife moves up to cut component lead and clinch component into place

Figure 5.16 *Component insertion is a complex process, comprising a number of stages specifically to shape component leads prior to actually inserting the component in a printed circuit board*

individual component tapes and arranges them onto another tape in the required sequence for insertion. In doing so sequencers pre-check components for value and tolerance. This tape is then mounted onto the axial inserter.

Costs for such automatic component insertion systems are high. Sequencers alone can cost £300,000 or so. Axial and DIP inserters can cost over £75,000. To justify such expense a manufacturing system has to be capable of making over 500,000 assemblies a year. However, automatic component insertion has merits when compared with manual assembly.

For example, manual assembly rates of component insertion are around 500 components per hour, and error rates of 1 in 100 misplaced components are typical. On the other hand, automatic component inserters are capable of 32,000 components per hour for axial components — with zero errors.

Where full automatic component assembly cannot be justified, semi-automatic assembly can be used. Systems able to insert leaded components at rates up to about 1200 per hour, costing around £50,000, are available.

Surface mounted component placement machines

Any electronics assembly containing one or more surface mounted components needs to be considered in much the same way as leaded component assemblies: manual, semi-automatic and fully automatic assembly systems are available. Criteria determining choice are much the same, too.

Where leaded components are inserted through holes in a printed circuit board, leadless surface mounted components are merely placed on the board surface. For this simple reason, automatic placement machines used to place surface mounted components are nicknamed **onsertion machines**.

By way of comparison with insertion machine elements (Figure 5.16), elements of onsertion machines are shown in Figure 5.17. Here, surface mounted components are placed directly onto the surface of a printed circuit board and

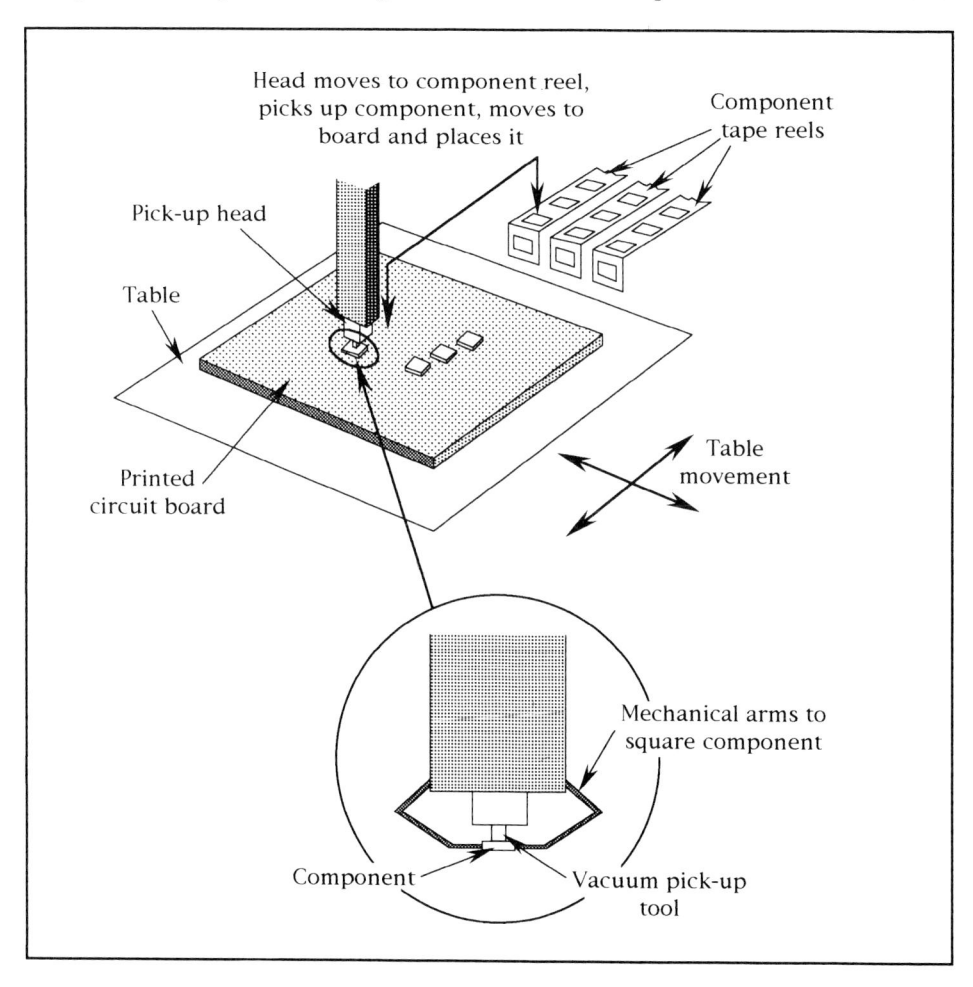

Figure 5.17 *Component onsertion is a simpler process than insertion*

Assembly production

there are no leads to be inserted through holes. As with an insertion machine, however, the machine head is programmed to move to a position over the printed circuit board, then to deposit the component onto the board. Unlike insertion machines, on the other hand, onsertion machine tables may also move underneath the machine head.

As surface mounted components are leadless, they can be significantly smaller than equivalent leaded components: so small, in fact — some surface mounted components have lead pitches of less than 0.5 mm — that mechanical tolerances of onsertion machines are too great for unaided positioning techniques. This can be further aggravated by variations in printed circuit board dimensions due to temperature and humidity variations, and board detail errors such as differences in track dimensions due to faulty manufacture. In effect, simple mechanical positioning techniques cannot place components accurately enough. Many onsertion machines therefore feature some form of pattern recognition system, whereby datum marks — known as **fiducials** — printed on the surface of the printed circuit board are detected by the machine, which can then compensate for tolerance to place components with a high degree of accuracy. Such pattern recognition systems commonly go by the name of **vision systems**. Typical fiducial marks are shown in Figure 5.18.

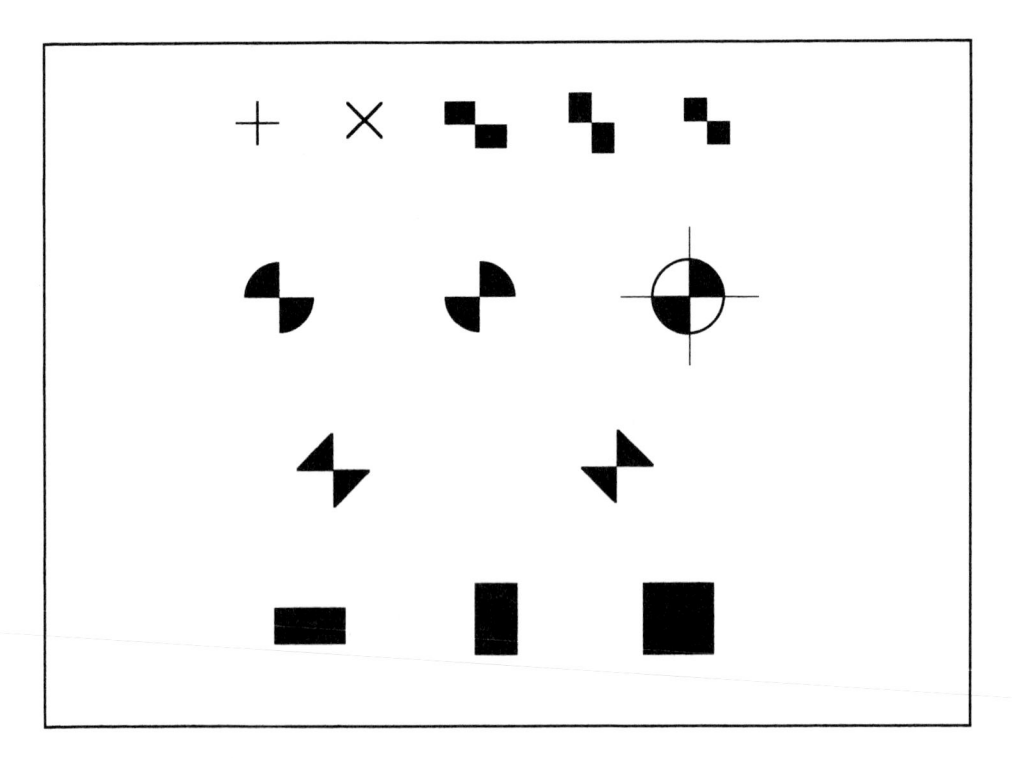

Figure 5.18 *Typical fiducials used as markings on printed circuit boards to aid component placement*

Surface mounted component placement machines

Surface mounted components are packaged in tape reels, tubes and trays. Tape sizes depend upon the component, but range between 8 mm and 56 mm. Packaging and component dimensions are standardized. Machine heads feature vacuum suction to literally suck a component from its external packaging. The component is then squared off ready for placement by mechanical arms situated on the head. The machine head moves the component to its position and lowers it onto the board, whereupon the vacuum is released and the machine head moves to pick up the next component. Fairly naturally, onsertion machines of this type are commonly called **pick-and-place machines.**

Onsertion systems capable of rates up to around 30,000 placements per hour are commonly available. A typical system capable of placing over 4500 components per hour, with a feeder capacity of 60 tape reels, costs around £50,000.

It should be noted that surface mounted components are significantly smaller than leaded components. Track lands onto which a surface mounted component is placed (commonly called a **footprint**) are similarly smaller than leaded component lands. A typical surface mounted component footprint is shown in Figure 5.19.

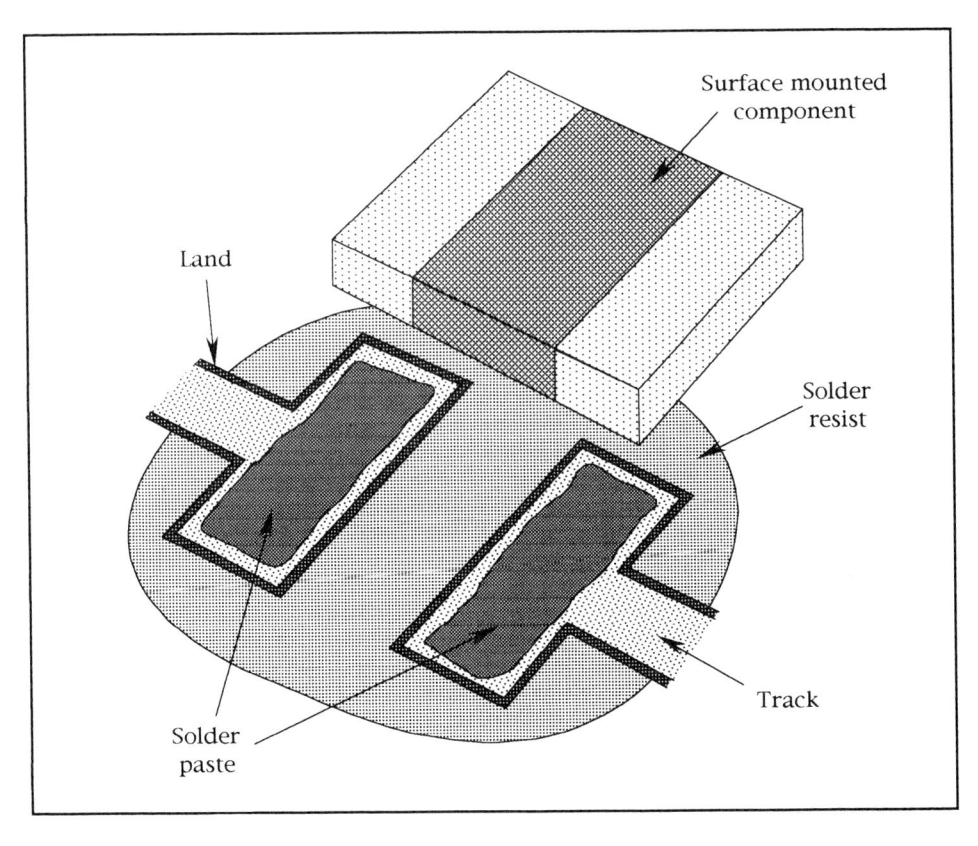

Figure 5.19 *A typical surface mounted component footprint*

Assembly production

Because of this small size, solder resists are commonly used. Where a leaded component is attached to a printed circuit board with its leads, a surface mounted component is simply placed on the board. Prior to placement of components, solder paste or adhesive (see Chapter 6) must be applied to the board. Consequently, printed circuit board details for surface mounted electronics assemblies must include:

- a pattern for the track
- a pattern for the solder resist
- a pattern for the solder paste or adhesive.

Because of all these features of surface mounted electronics assemblies, care must be taken in manufacture to ensure:

- minimum values between lands and tracks are maintained
- lands are at least a defined size larger than component terminations
- lands are free of solder resist
- components are placed uniformly, and on a defined grid. By using a uniform component placement system, in which components are placed on a uniform centre-to-centre spacing (Figure 5.20) of, say, 2.5 mm or 5 mm, placement machine programming is greatly simplified.

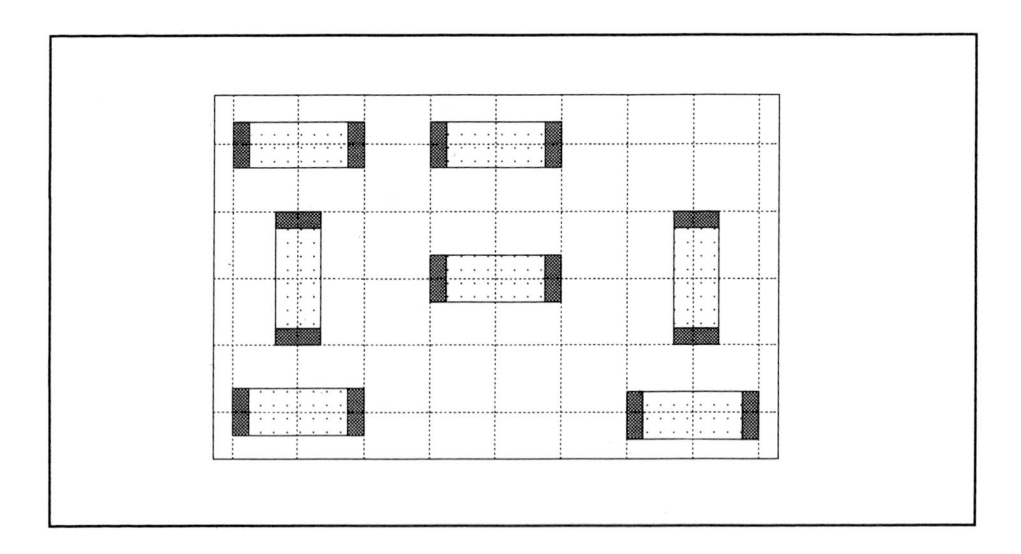

Figure 5.20 *Placement of components on a uniform grid eases the assembly process*

6 Soldering assemblies

While many leaded components are easily handled — they are quite large and may be manipulated by both hand and machine with ease — surface mounted leadless components are significantly smaller. Hand assembly and, particularly, hand soldering of surface mounted printed circuit boards, therefore, are not viable propositions for much other than prototype assembly.

Small components and consequent small joints require a mechanized soldering system in most applications. There are approximately five times more joints on a surface mounted printed circuit board than on a through-hole printed circuit board of the same area.

About 20% of the cost of assembling printed circuit boards with leaded components is currently spent on rework — physically unsoldering faulty or misplaced components by hand, then resoldering new, correct components back in. Smaller sized surface mounted components, and many more of them, make this cost even greater unless steps are taken to reduce (and hopefully, eliminate) faults.

Money can be saved by:

- designing printed circuit boards to make them easier to solder
- designing printed circuit boards with the specific soldering machine in mind
- ensuring that you maintain good process control on *all* assembly areas — component handling; printed circuit board handling; printed circuit board loading; application of solder paste or adhesive (see later); soldering itself; testing
- locating faults, categorizing them and tracking them back to their source
- removing causes of faults.

Note that the soldering process itself relies on preceding and subsequent processes to function correctly. If any other process within the electronics assembly line misfunctions — even slightly — the fault will first be seen as a

Soldering assemblies

soldering fault. This is particularly so in assembly of surface mounted printed circuit boards. It is important to remember, however, that in most instances the soldering process itself is not to blame!

Soldering basics

A soldered joint is a junction of two metals (normally copper in the electronics industry) which are held together with a thin layer of solder between them. A soldered joint is formed by heating the two metals, cleaning their surfaces, applying molten solder, allowing the joint to cool. These four steps *must* occur in any soldering process, although the order they follow and the method each takes may differ greatly from one soldering process to another.

Figure 6.1 shows the basic requirements of a hand soldering process. Here, a soldering iron at a temperature of about 320°C is first applied to the joint area, to heat both metals. A combination of solder and flux is applied, as a thin wire form of solder with cores of flux.

Flux flows from the solder cores onto the metal surfaces. Flux, at an elevated temperature (over 100°C or so), cleans the wire and base surfaces of contaminants — removing dirt, grease and oxides — then protects the surfaces from further contaminants.

Above 183°C solder melts, flowing by capillary action between the wire and base. A final temperature of around 215°C ensures that a good joint can be formed.

After the soldering iron tip is removed, temperature of the joint should be allowed to fall slowly.

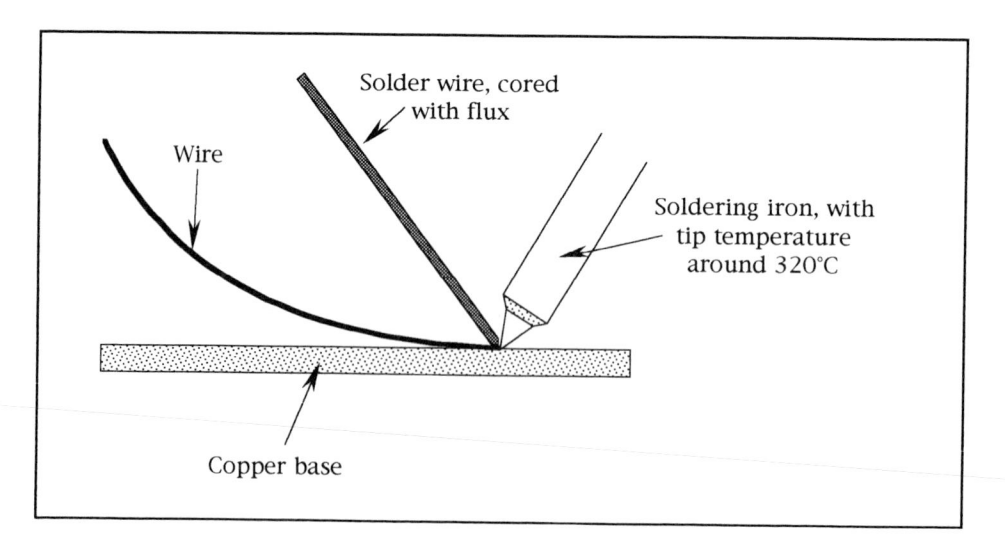

Figure 6.1 *A hand soldering process — basic requirements*

There are a few important points about a good soldered joint:

- the first soldering operation makes the strongest joint — subsequent reheating weakens a joint
- excessive dirt and grease on metal surfaces prior to soldering reduces flux cleaning action — too much dirt and grease prevents a good joint altogether
- thickness of solder between metals in a good joint need only be 1 μm. Too much solder actually weakens a joint, as joint strength then relies purely on the solder — which is quite a weak metal in itself.

Solder

Solder used in the electronics industry is an alloy of tin and lead, in the approximate proportions of 63% tin and 37% lead. These proportions result in an alloy which is eutectic: it melts and solidifies at a single temperature of 183°C — the **eutectic point** of a tin/lead alloy. A phase diagram of alloy proportions against temperature (Figure 6.2) shows this occurring for these proportions. Solder can be in one of three states at this range of temperatures: solid, plastic,

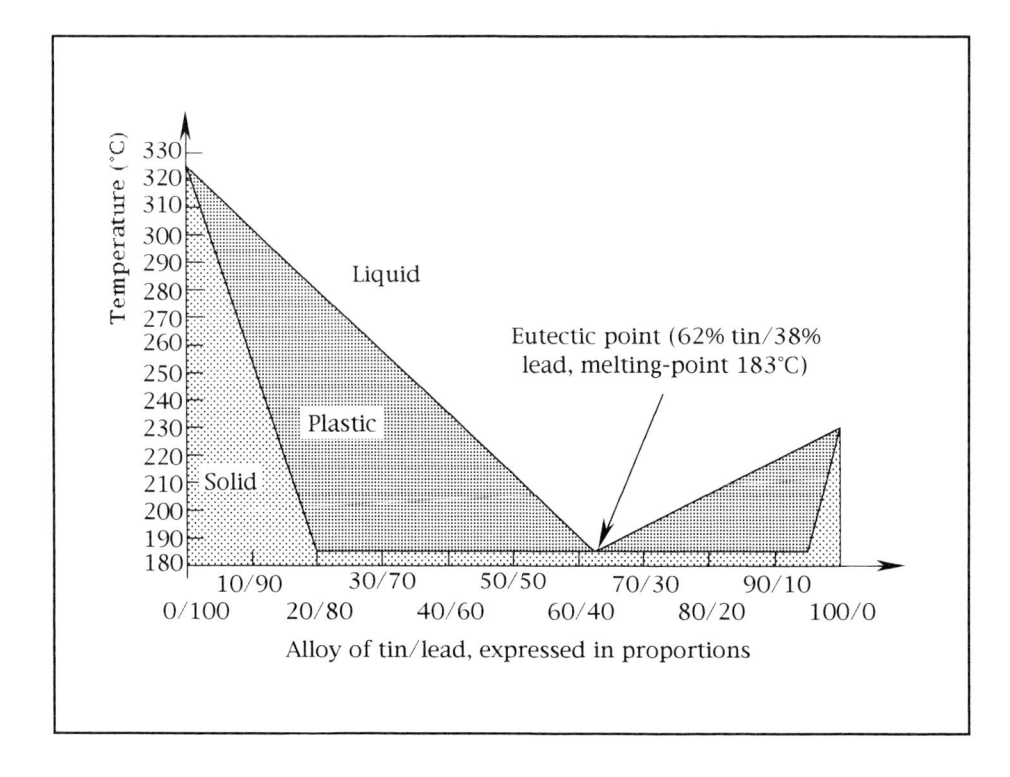

Figure 6.2 *Phase diagram of solder*

Soldering assemblies

or molten. Alloy proportions of solder define which of these states solder is in, at any particular temperature. Solder with 63% tin/37% lead proportions is commonly referred to as **eutectic solder.**

Occasionally, impurities may be added to solder, to vary characteristics within the soldering process in an attempt to improve performance. For example, addition of small quantities of antimony and copper can reduce the amount solder moves under stress when solid. For particular applications additions of impurities may be warranted but, in general, it is best to keep the solder used in a soldering process as pure as possible.

Flux

Flux is used to clean metals prior to soldering. It does this in an active reaction, generally after heat is applied. Fluxes vary in their level of activity: some flux only cleans general oxides off metal surfaces, while others clean off thick layers of dirt, grease and oxides.

The type of flux used in a soldering process depends primarily, therefore, on the cleanliness of the surfaces to be soldered. In view of this, a natural choice is to use a flux far more active than surface contamination requires. However, any flux leaves residues and, in general, a highly active flux leaves corrosive residues — which corrode solid solder itself. Corrosion of solder is not instant, but occurs after a period of time. In other words, if residues are left on an electronics assembly after manufacture, it may become faulty as the residues corrode the soldered joints on the printed circuit board.

There are only two alternatives, of course: (1) clean the joint surfaces prior to soldering and use a low-activity flux; (2) use a high-activity flux and clean the electronics assembly after soldering. While both are technically possible, it should be noted that cleaning electronics assemblies after soldering is an issue of worldwide environmental significance — as chlorofluorocarbons (CFCs) are sometimes used. Many companies within the industry have already stopped using chlorofluorocarbons, many companies are in the process of using less, and *all* companies must stop using chlorofluorocarbons very shortly, anyway. So, lower activity fluxes and pre-cleaned assemblies point the way forward.

Types of flux

There are typically thought to be two main types of flux used in soldering of electronics assemblies:

• organically soluble fluxes — historically, organically soluble fluxes are often based on the use of gum rosin, obtained from pine tree sap. The sap, after distillation, comes in a solid form, also often called **colophony.** However, rosin is only one of a group of flux types known as **resins** (technically, rosin is just one form of resin, where resins are any substance secreted by plants). Where rosin *is* the main agent of a flux, it is usually dissolved in an organic solvent. Rosin flux has two excellent properties which make it preferable to many others as an electronics flux. First, as a liquid at elevated temperatures, it is reasonably active — it is a mild organic acid — so cleans quite tarnished and dirty metals. Second, its residues are not particularly corrosive

- water soluble fluxes — water soluble fluxes are usually made to be highly active — to do the job when rosin-based fluxes can't cope. Water soluble flux residues are therefore usually very corrosive. However, as residues are water soluble, cleaning processes may be water-based and free of chlorofluorocarbons. It is important to note, though, that the term *water soluble* refers to the fact that residues left after soldering are soluble in water — and does not mean that fluxes themselves are soluble in water!

This simple categorization, unfortunately, belies the complexity of modern fluxes — there are many more types than we can cover here. International Standards Organization (ISO) has attempted to clarify the situation, distinguishing fluxes according to four main variables:

- flux type — whether resin, organic or inorganic
- flux basis — what the flux is based on
- flux activation — what type of activator in used
- flux form — liquid, solid, or paste.

The classification process is illustrated in Figure 6.3, showing how a number or a letter is given for each variable. Thus a resin-based resin flux, with a halide activator, in paste form, is classified as type 112C.

Table 6.1 lists common flux abbreviations and types prior to the ISO classification. These are still in use, so are included here for reference, in order of level of activity.

Activators

Flux activity can be increased by addition of **activators**. Indeed, water soluble fluxes are usually a simple combination of one or more activators and a suitable solvent. Rosin-based fluxes which have an added activator are typically called **activated fluxes**, while basic rosin fluxes are often called **non-activated fluxes**.

Typical activators are:

- halides
- ammonium chloride
- acids
- amines.

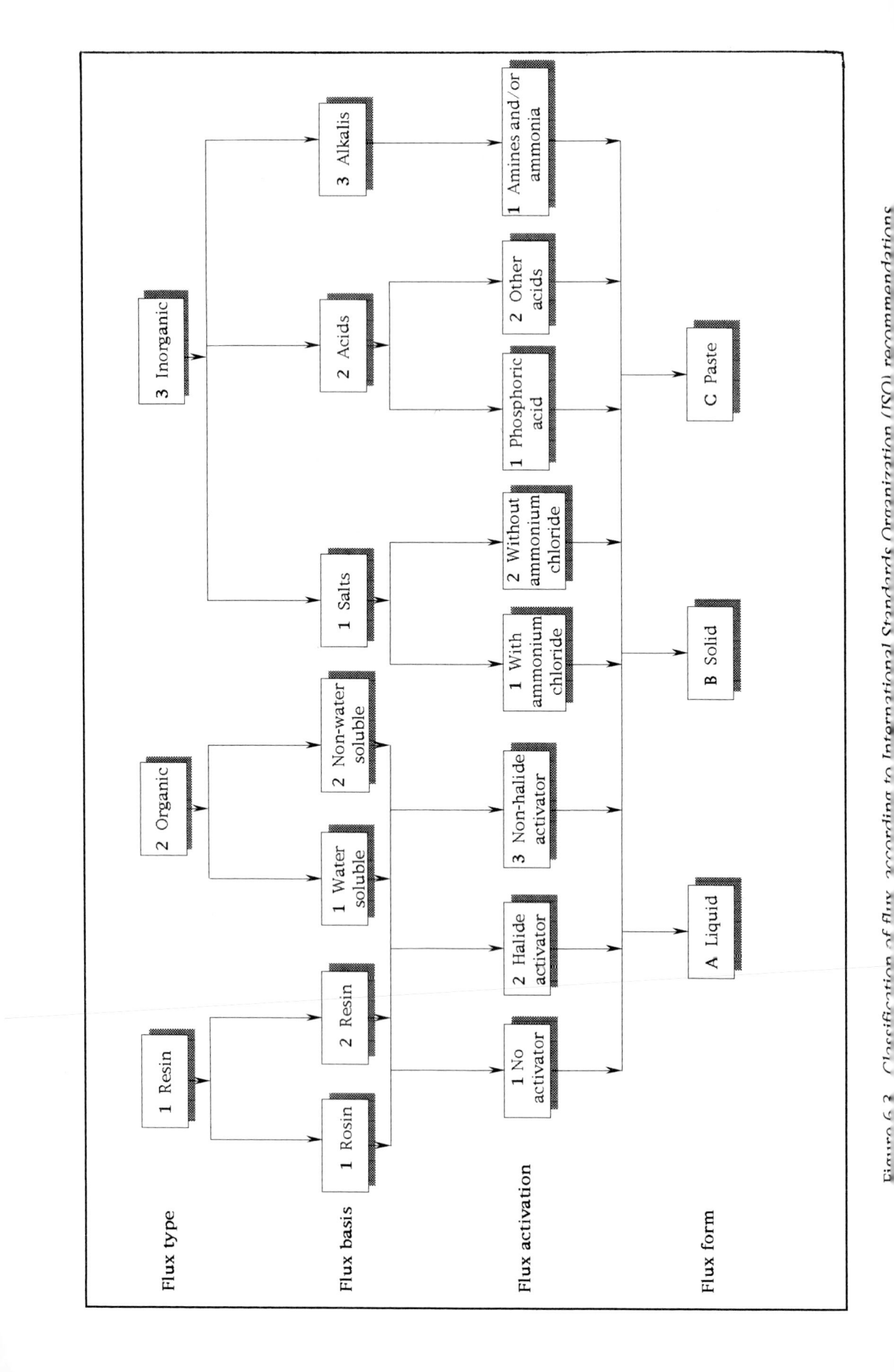

Figure 6.2 Classification of flux, according to International Standards Organization (ISO) recommendations

Soldering processes

Where leaded components alone are to be soldered into a printed circuit board, soldering is a straightforward process — following roughly the basic procedure discussed earlier. Machine soldering of through-hole printed circuit boards is very similar to hand soldering: component leads are inserted through holes in the printed circuit board, flux is applied, heat is applied, solder is applied.

Typical machine soldering processes follow this procedure closely. Indeed, it is easy to identify areas within an assembly line which fulfil these process parts.

Wave soldering

The most common form of soldering process used in through-hole electronics assembly is **wave soldering**, in which a wave of molten solder is maintained, while each electronics assembly is conveyed across the wave crest. The principle of wave soldering is illustrated in Figure 6.4. Various waveshapes are used by different machine manufacturers to adjust characteristics within the process, but any well-set-up wave soldering machine is able to solder through-hole electronics assemblies to a high performance.

The main waveshape used in wave soldering machines is the **extended wave**, shown in Figure 6.5, of which there are several variations.

Often, wave soldering machines feature two separate waves (Figure 6.6), the first of which is an agitating turbulent wave, to ensure solder reaches all parts — even where small components are closely fitted. The second wave in such **double-wave soldering machines** is a calm wave, to ensure the board leaves the soldering machine under ideal conditions. An extended wave, on the other hand, has a turbulent entrance to, and a calm exit from, the wave.

Some manufacturers use a **hot-air knife** immediately after the solder wave to help remove any excess solder which may bridge between closely positioned joints on a printed circuit board. This principle is illustrated in Figure 6.7.

Table 6.1 Common flux abbreviations, meanings, flux types and activities

Abbreviation	Meaning	Flux type	Level of activity
R	Rosin	Purest grade of rosin, no activator added	Very low
WW	Water white	Purest grade of rosin	Very low
RMA	Mildly activated rosin	Rosin, with addition of mild activators	Mildly active
OA	Organic acid	Organic acid activator	Strongly active
RA	Activated rosin	Rosin, with addition of strong activators	Strongly active
SA	Synthetic activated	Rosin, with synthetic activators	Strongly active
SRA	Superactivated rosin	Rosin, with very strong activators	Very strongly activ

Soldering assemblies

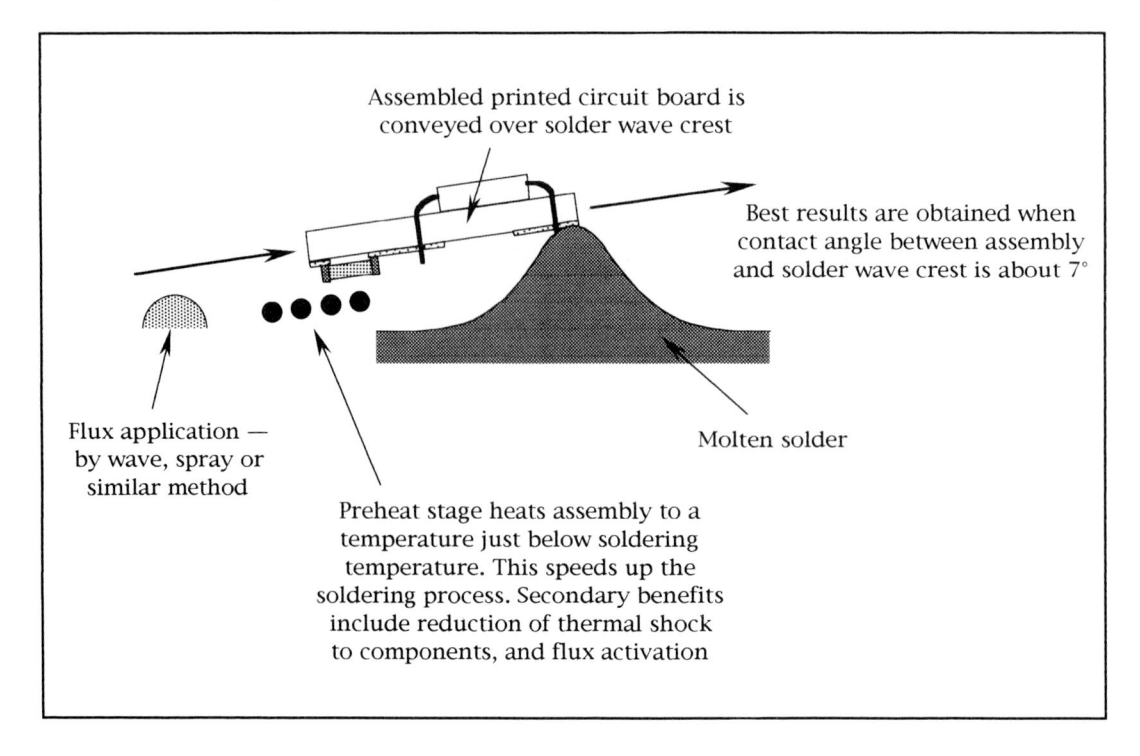

Figure 6.4 *Principle of wave soldering, in which a printed circuit board is conveyed over the crest of a wave of molten solder*

Reflow soldering

Any well-set-up wave soldering machine forms the basis of a process that is also suitable for soldering *some* surface mounted electronics assemblies. However, despite continuous refinements to the wave soldering process, no wave soldering machine is capable of soldering very small, high lead-count surface mounted components.

Typically, small surface mounted components are soldered to printed circuit boards using a second type of soldering process, in which solder and flux are applied first (before components, or heat) in a paste form. Components are then placed onto the board. Finally, the electronics assembly is heated to a temperature which melts the solder paste, forming a joint at each component termination.

This sort of process, commonly called **reflow**, is quite common wherever surface mounted components are to be soldered. In principle at least, leaded components can also be soldered this way, but to date no process has been developed to do so successfully. Thus, to solder an assembly which has both leaded *and* surface mounted components, a wave soldering process is necessary.

Soldering processes

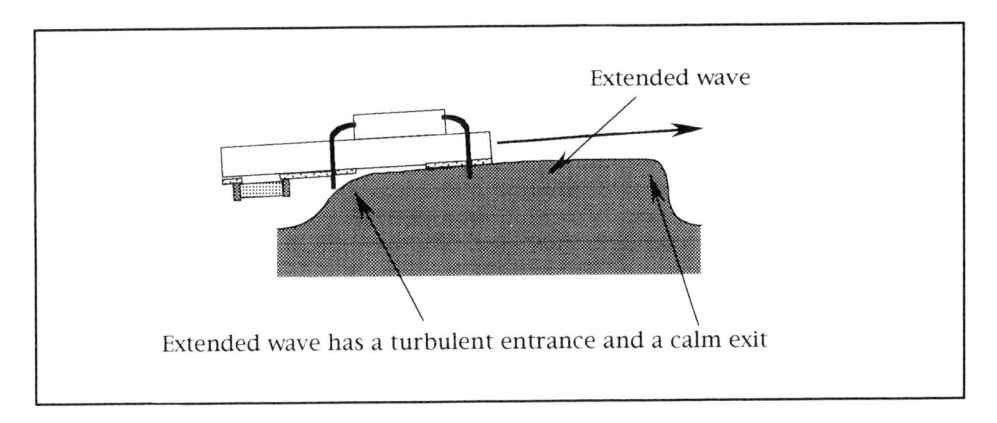

Figure 6.5 The extended wave

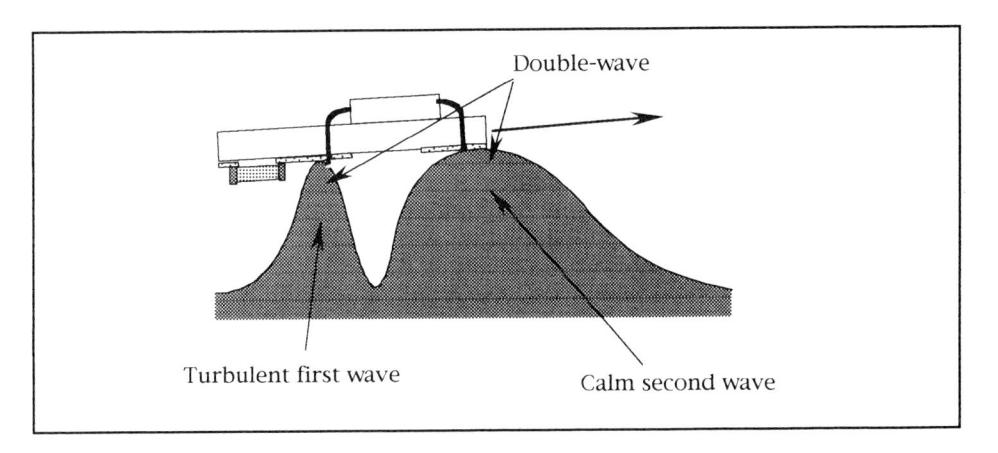

Figure 6.6 A double-wave

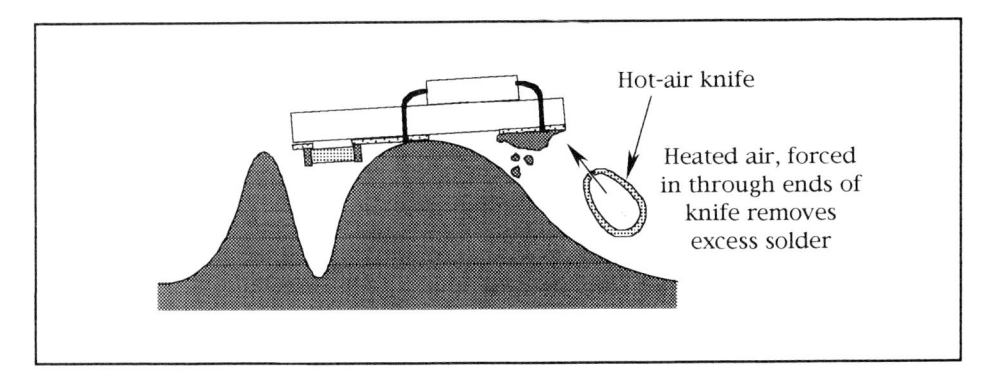

Figure 6.7 A hot-air knife positioned after a solder wave

Soldering assemblies

Where all components are on one side of the printed circuit board, and surface mounted components are not too small, wave soldering performs all soldering actions.

On the other hand, where surface mounted components are too small, or are on the other side of the printed circuit board from leaded components, both wave soldering *and* reflow processes are required.

Reflow soldering processes

There are two main reflow soldering processes:

- infra-red radiation soldering
- hot vapour soldering.

Basic infra-red soldering machines direct heat on to the assembled printed circuit board from above and below, as shown in Figure 6.8. Heat transferred, and so the temperatures of the joints being soldered, depends on many factors such as materials, sizes and shapes used in components and printed circuit board bases, and wavelength of the infra-red emissions. As a consequence, the soldering process must be carefully monitored to ensure that all joints on an electronics assembly reach the required temperature at the correct time. Assemblies should be carefully preheated (raised to a sub-soldering temperature in a gradual and controlled manner) prior to actual soldering to minimize any temperature differences on soldering.

More complex infra-red soldering machines use convected heat as well as infra-red radiant heat, to heat assemblies. Often these soldering machines are divided into zones, through which air is forced as shown in Figure 6.9, so that temperature in each zone is accurately maintained. Thus, an assembly passing through such a soldering machine is known to be at a pre-defined temperature in each zone.

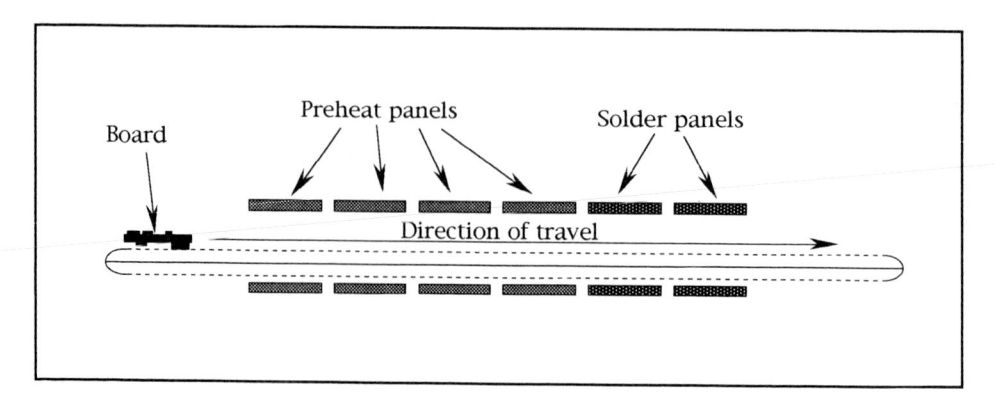

Figure 6.8 *Basic infra-red reflow soldering*

Soldering processes

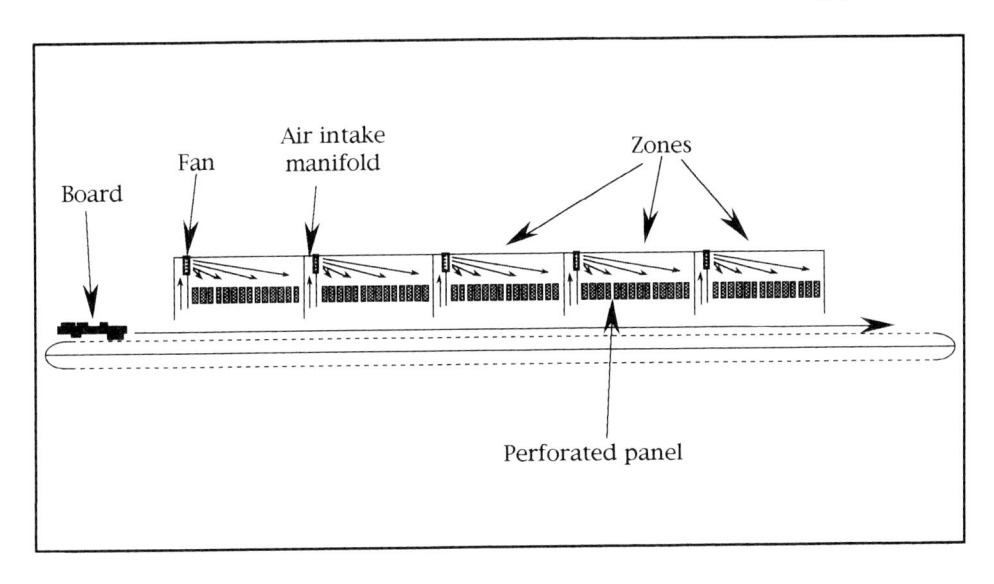

Figure 6.9 *Zoned, convection-aided infra-red reflow soldering*

Hot vapour soldering

Hot vapour soldering processes use the principle of heating printed circuit boards in a liquid which is in its saturated vapour phase. For this reason hot vapour soldering processes are often called **vapour phase soldering**, although this is something of a misnomer.

Heat transfer takes place when the saturated vapour of the liquid condenses on the electronics assembly, and is thus a product of the liquid's latent heat of evaporation. If a liquid is chosen that boils at the temperature required to convert solder paste into molten solder — around 215°C — then once the liquid's boiling point temperature is reached no further temperature rise can occur. This is useful, as it means assemblies cannot be overheated.

In principle, therefore, hot vapour soldering systems are quite simple. Figure 6.10 illustrates a basic machine, showing the boiling liquid, its hot vapour and an assembly conveyed through it. As in infra-red (and wave soldering) machines preheating of assemblies prior to entering the soldering stage is needed.

Temperature profiles

In all soldering processes, but particularly in reflow soldering processes, maintenance of each electronics assembly's temperature is of importance. Typically, this is portrayed in a soldering machine's **temperature profile**, such as that in Figure 6.11 which is a graph of time against temperature.

Soldering assemblies

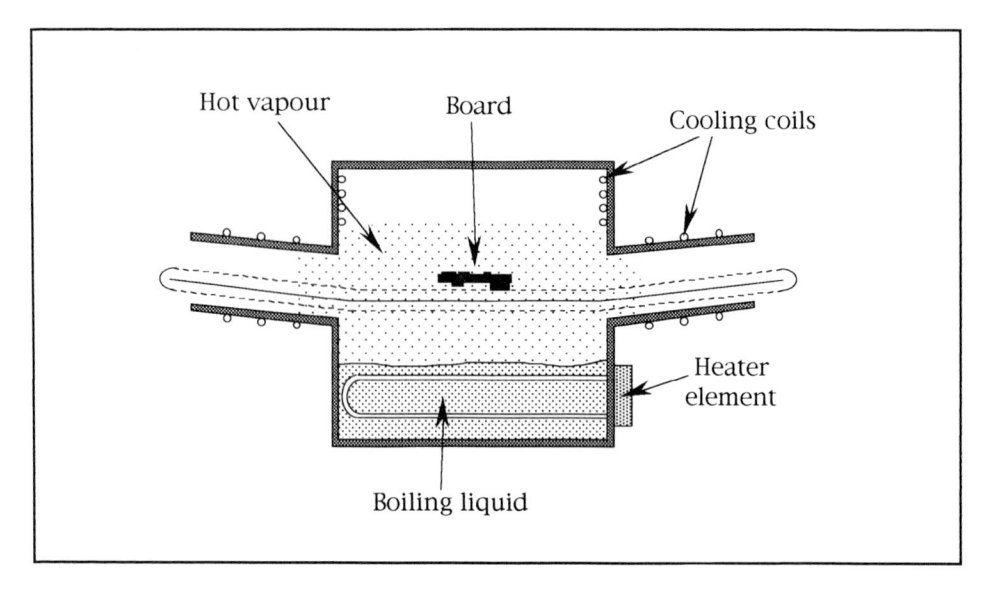

Figure 6.10 *Hot vapour (vapour phase) reflow soldering*

There are four important parts of a machine's temperature profile:

- preheat time — the length of time an assembly is subjected to preheat, raising the assembly's temperature to a maximum of just below soldering temperature
- dwell time — the length of time an assembly is subjected to this maximum preheat temperature. Aim of this is to soak the assembly for a sufficient time to

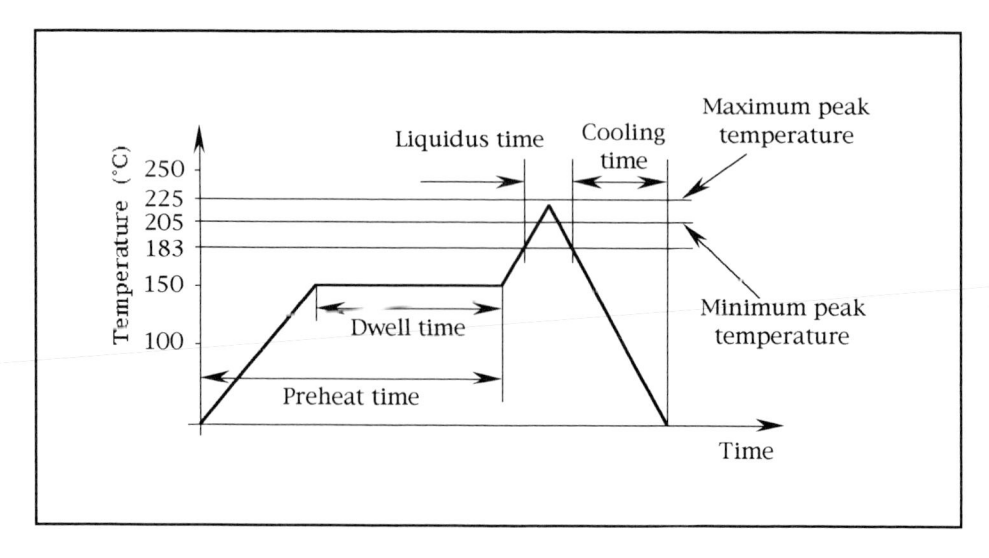

Figure 6.11 *Possible temperature profile of a reflow soldering process*

Solder paste or adhesive application

allow all parts to be at the same dwell temperature. Then, when final application of heat occurs, all parts rise to soldering temperature at more-or-less the same time
- liquidus time — the time during which solder on the assembly is molten
- cooling time — the time during which the assembly temperature cools.

Ideally, a soldering machine must be controllable, so that different temperature profiles can be set up for any particular type of electronics assembly.

Solder paste or adhesive application

Prior to placement of surface mounted components in a reflow soldering process, solder paste must be applied to the printed circuit board. Similarly, prior to surface mounted component placement in a wave soldering process, adhesive must be applied to a printed circuit board.

Solder paste and adhesive are each applied to printed circuit boards in one of three main ways which, in order of popularity, are:

- dispensing — shown in Figure 6.12, where syringe-type nozzles are used to apply solder paste or adhesive in small dots at required points. Nozzles are connected with tubing to a pump, which forces solder paste or adhesive from a reservoir out onto the board
- stencil transfer — shown in Figure 6.13, where a screen-printing process is used to print solder paste or adhesive onto a board. This is an adaptation of the standard screen-printing process used to print panels, cloth and so on. Two methods are used. (1) The stencil is a fabric screen, and holes between fibres of

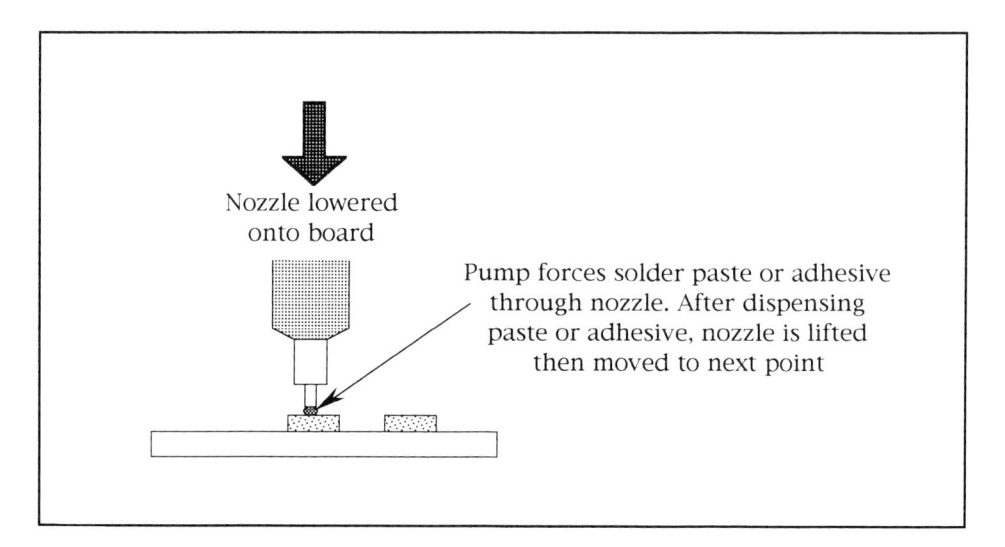

Figure 6.12 *Solder paste or adhesive dispensing through nozzles*

Soldering assemblies

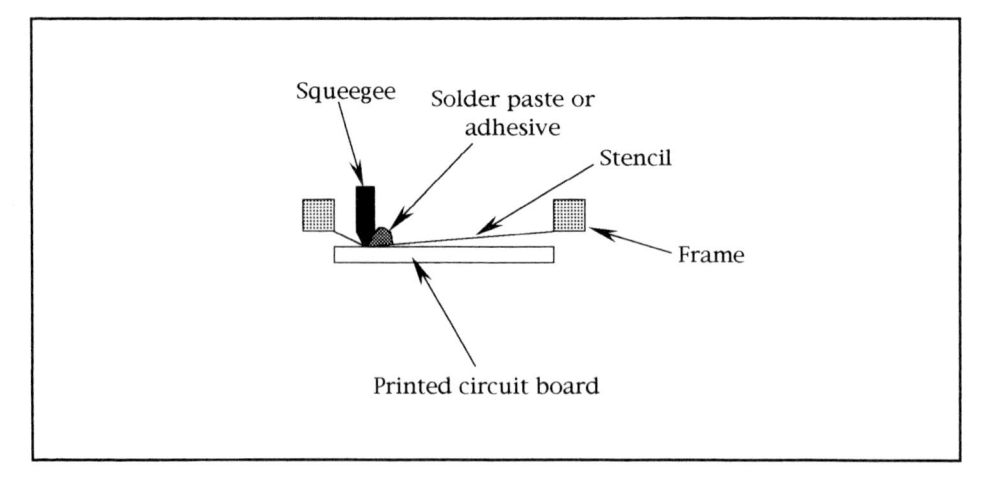

Figure 6.13 *Application of solder paste or adhesive by stencil transfer*

the screen are selectively filled with a lacquer or similar substance, corresponding to a negative image of the image required on the printed circuit board. Solder paste or adhesive is applied to the top of the screen and a squeegee is used to push the screen down and force the paste or adhesive through the screen onto the board. (2) A metal mask stencil is used, cut and formed to the required image

- pin matrix transfer — shown in Figure 6.14, where a matrix of pins is first dipped into a reservoir of solder paste or adhesive, then lowered onto the board.

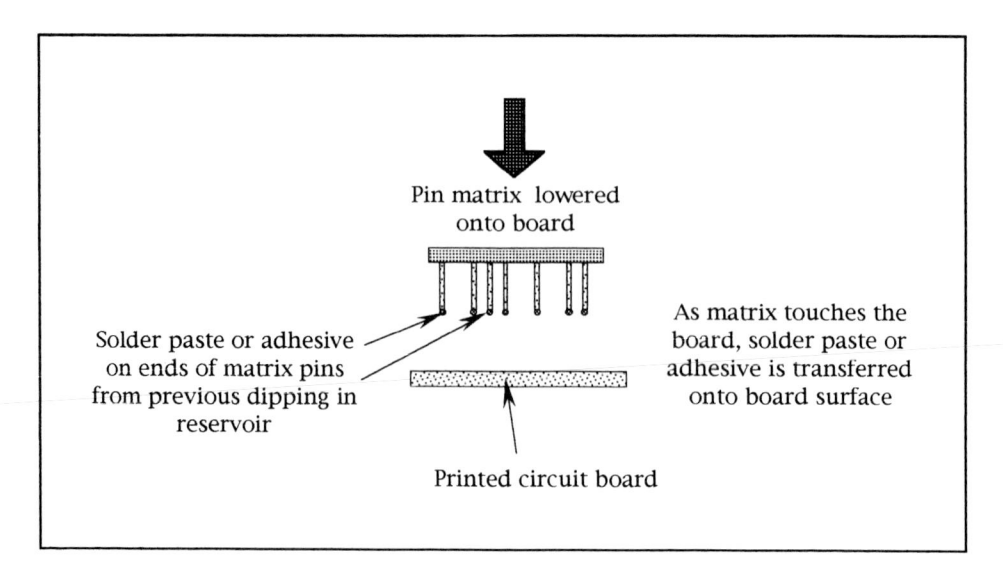

Figure 6.14 *Pin matrix transfer of solder paste or adhesive*

Cleaning of assemblies after soldering

All three methods are successful and regularly used, although high set-up costs of the last two mean that they are more useful for large batches of electronics assemblies. Dispensing machines, on the other hand, are usually microprocessor-controlled and easily adapted to dispense onto different printed circuit boards.

Cleaning of assemblies after soldering

Flux and activator residues left after soldering processes are a potential fault source. Residues can contain acid or other corrosive agents which may be active at ambient temperatures. If left on the printed circuit board these active agents can set up corrosive chemical reactions which, with time, create fault conditions in circuits. Other residues contain ionic carriers which provide the means for small leakage currents to flow, particularly if moisture is present — even just a small rise in humidity. Tiny leakage currents of the order of just nanoamps can trigger low-powered devices.

Small components — in particular, surface mounted components — introduce problems to printed circuit board cleaning simply because of their small stand-off heights. It becomes very difficult to clean beneath such components. High pressure spray cleaning processes (an example is given in Figure 6.15) are usually considered effective, using solvent or water systems. A major issue in printed circuit board cleaning is use of solvents that release chlorofluorocarbons. Environmental concern over chlorofluorocarbons has required manufacturers to consider alternatives.

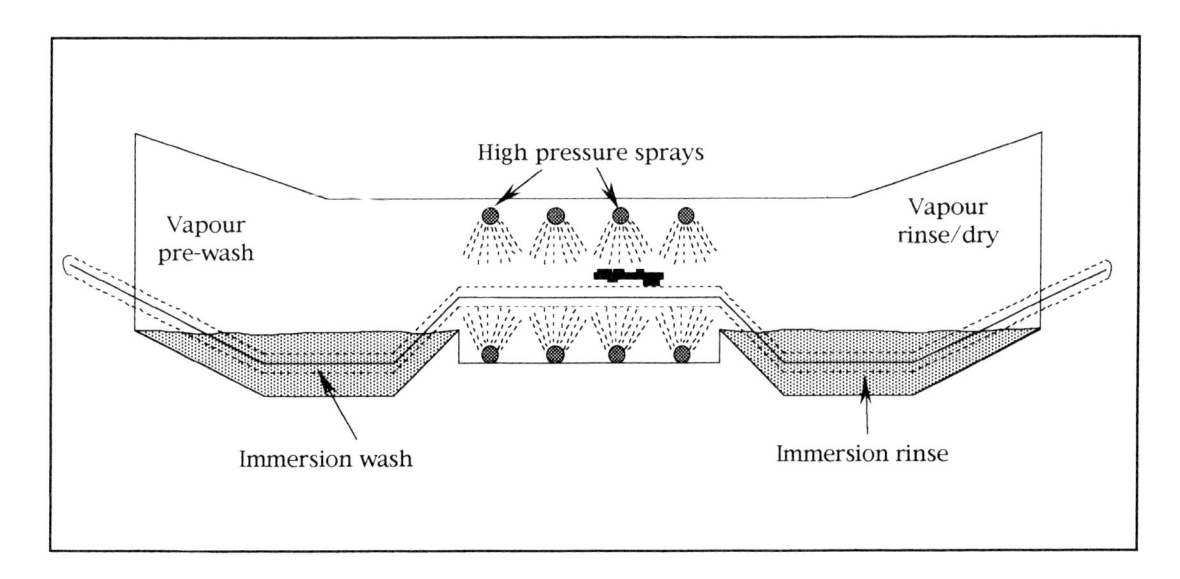

Figure 6.15 *Typical high pressure spray cleaning process*

Soldering assemblies

Testing of electronics assemblies

The quality of any product relies on being able to test it, to ensure that all potential faults are found and their causes eliminated. The more complex a product, the more tests have to be carried out to be certain all potential faults are located.

In electronics assembly, testing falls into three main categories:

- visual inspection
- in-circuit test
- functional test.

While aspects of in-circuit and functional tests are described in detail in Chapter 7, visual inspection of joints is described here.

Visual inspection

Where components are large and simple single-sided or double-sided printed circuit boards are assembled, a visual inspection by unaided eye may be sufficient to locate faults. But where densely-populated surface mounted components are mounted on double-sided or multi-layered printed circuit boards, which may feature tracks of only a few tens of micrometres width, unaided visual inspection is not practical. Often an optical aid can be used, preferably with switchable magnifications from around 5 times, to 250 times. Binocular devices, offering so-called stereo inspection, are available.

Visual inspection of electronics assemblies usually entails looking at each joint in turn, to inspect its contours and appearance. From this, a number of checks can be made, including:

- correct placement and orientation of components
- thermal damage to surrounding materials
- amount of solder
- solder bridges
- blow holes, cavities, inclusions or cracks
- concave shape to fillet
- solder surface itself.

Typically, a 45° viewing angle (Figure 6.16) gives an adequate view of most joints and components.

For this to be an effective method of assessing soldered joints, some form of reference must be closely adhered to. A complete pictorial reference manual may be formulated, showing in detail all joint types, possible faults, correct attributes and so on: this is the ideal. Posters around the test and inspection area may also be used to show main desired and undesired characteristics. Figure 6.17 shows examples of desired characteristics of three surface mounted component joint types, which could typically be found in such reference manuals or posters.

Testing of electronics assemblies

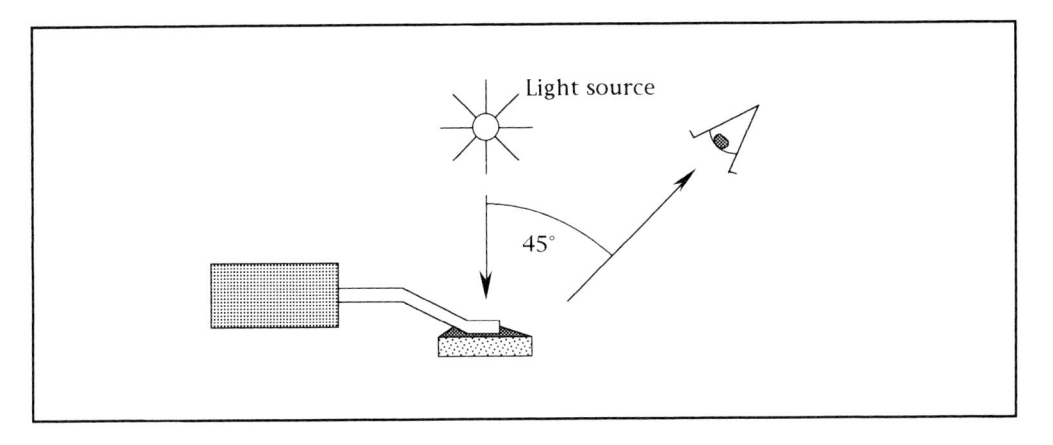

Figure 6.16 *Showing a suitable viewing angle for optical inspection of assembled and soldered printed circuit boards*

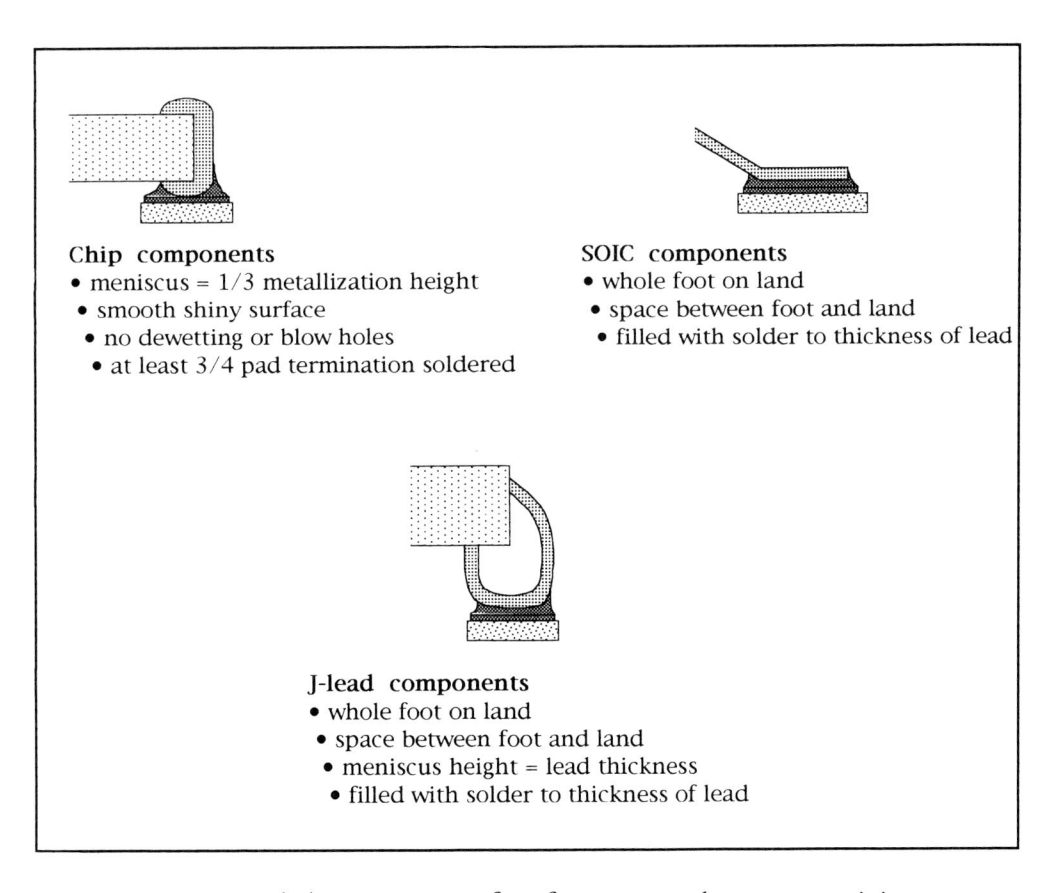

Chip components
- meniscus = 1/3 metallization height
- smooth shiny surface
- no dewetting or blow holes
- at least 3/4 pad termination soldered

SOIC components
- whole foot on land
- space between foot and land
- filled with solder to thickness of lead

J-lead components
- whole foot on land
- space between foot and land
- meniscus height = lead thickness
- filled with solder to thickness of lead

Figure 6.17 *Desired characteristics of surface mounted component joint types*

Soldering assemblies

Manual visual inspection is a time-expensive job — many man-hours are needed to fully inspect complex surface mounted electronics assemblies. Many **automated optical inspection** (AOI) systems are available which alleviate the task of checking for correctly situated and orientated components. Many systems are available, too, to check joint performance.

Infra-red signature analysis systems, for example, heat joints by laser beam, then observe their characteristics while cooling (Figure 6.18). Temperature rise and fall of a joint is compared with that of a known good joint, to see if it falls within tolerance limits. Each type of good joint has a more-or-less defined signature, which is stored in memory, so that each tested joint has a comparison match.

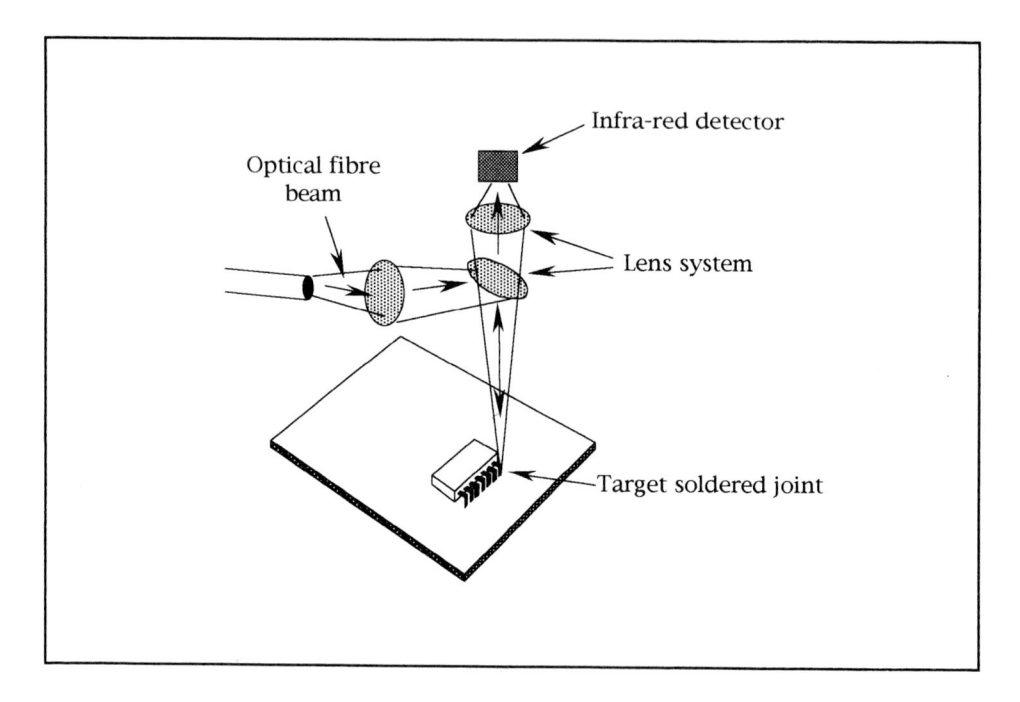

Figure 6.18 *Principle of infra-red signature analysis systems*

7 Test methods and strategies

Test is necessary, in the first instance, to identify faults and to confirm that a manufactured product meets its performance specification.

Yet, this is only half the story — testing does not *just* confirm that a product works properly or, if it doesn't work properly, show where any faults are. These are basic requirements of test equipment, true. But there is more to testing products than just these simple requirements.

Considered globally around a manufactured product, test is there essentially to confirm a product's good design. In this light, it's possible to view identification of faults and assurance of specification as really only *secondary* functions of test equipment.

In fact, so important is our new view of testing that we can redefine test as a process used by good designers to make sure products *are* of good quality. How are tests physically implemented? — what make of test equipment should be used? — and so on are practical questions, answered by the designer as a number of **test methods** which tackle each question individually. More important, though, is an overall **test strategy**, which ensures a required degree of quality is built in to a product. And we should not miss the point here: quality *is* built in — it doesn't happen without good design! Test, as a process, is simply a tool which helps a designer to build in quality to a product.

Test methods are those practical aspects of testing: things like the use of test probes to access test nodes within a circuit; the sort of test fixture required to interface the printed circuit board to the test equipment; electrical specifications of signals onto the printed circuit board *from* test equipment, and off the circuit board *to* test equipment.

Test strategies, on the other hand, are philosophies which concern themselves with a company's manufacturing priorities. Questions to be answered here include: do we want our customers to buy our products again? — how long can

Test methods and strategies

a customer expect our product to work? — does the customer consider our product to give value for money? Deciding a company's manufacturing priorities is not usually the province of a circuit designer — but the designer does need to know what is required of the product. Once assured of a company's priorities, the designer *can* implement the required test methods to meet the company's test strategy.

Faults

In a rough consideration, used by many observers, the cost of correcting a fault in an electronics product depends greatly on the stage in the product's life at which a manufacturer wishes to repair the fault. Cost effectively increases by a factor of 10 at each stage, so that a defect (say, a faulty resistor) which may cost 5p to correct at pre-assembly stage will cost 50p to correct at post-assembly stage (ie, once the printed circuit board is fully soldered), £5 once packaged, and £50 to correct in service (ie, when the customer is using it). Figure 7.1 shows this graphically. While this is only a rough guide, it is fairly true and the factor of 10 might even rise as products become more and more complex.

In essence, what we need to remember is that without attention to quality of products and how they are manufactured it is likely that a high defect rate will mean high rework costs, as much time and labour is spent repairing faults. In certain cases, more than 40% of total production cost has been known to be spent in test and resultant rework.

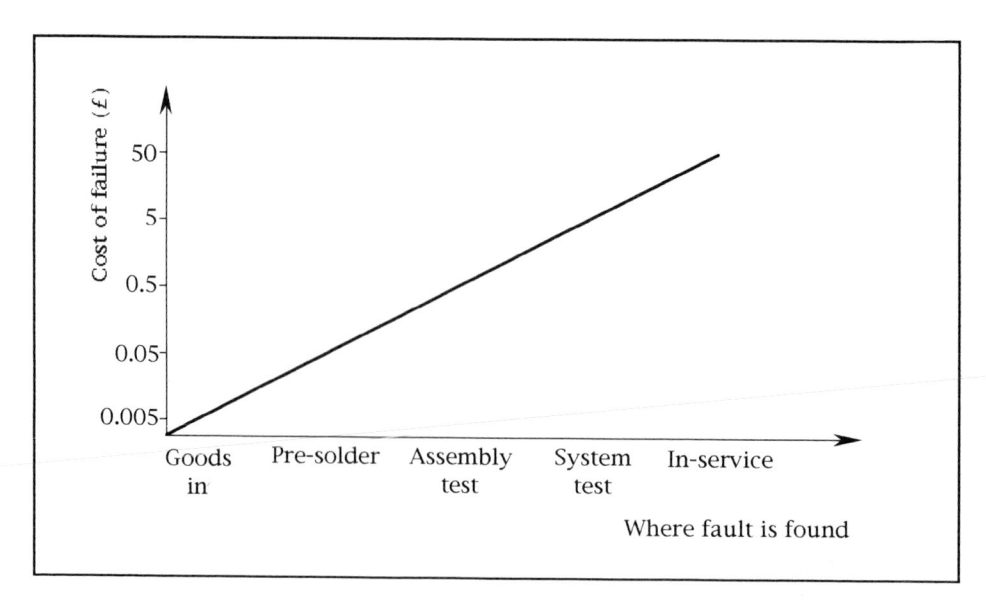

Figure 7.1 *Showing how cost or repair of faults increase tenfold at each manufacturing stage*

Faults

First-pass yield

We can consider faults in other ways, too. Figure 7.2, for example, looks at the number of faults on printed circuit boards related to the numbers of components on each board, while Figure 7.3 shows percentage of boards related to numbers of faults. While actual numbers of faults on any particular assembly

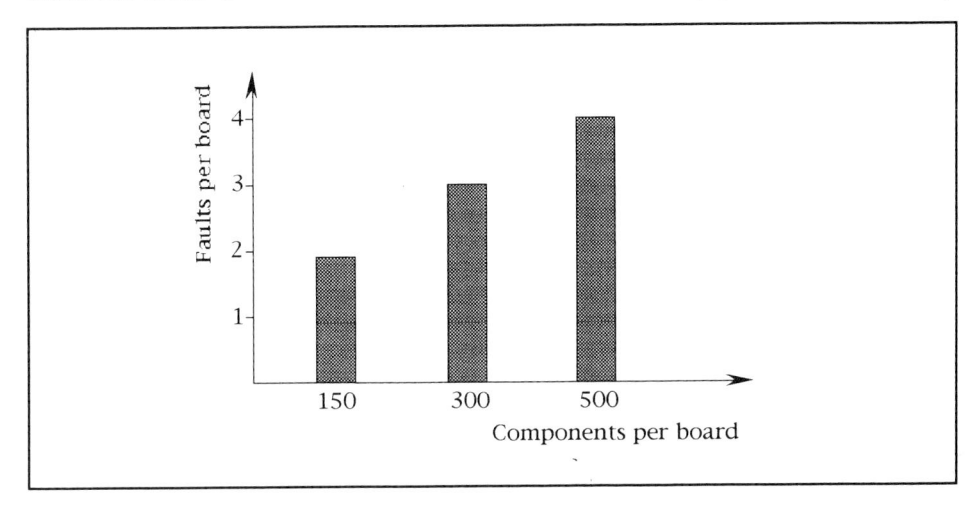

Figure 7.2 Faults on printed circuit boards, as a factor of numbers of components per board

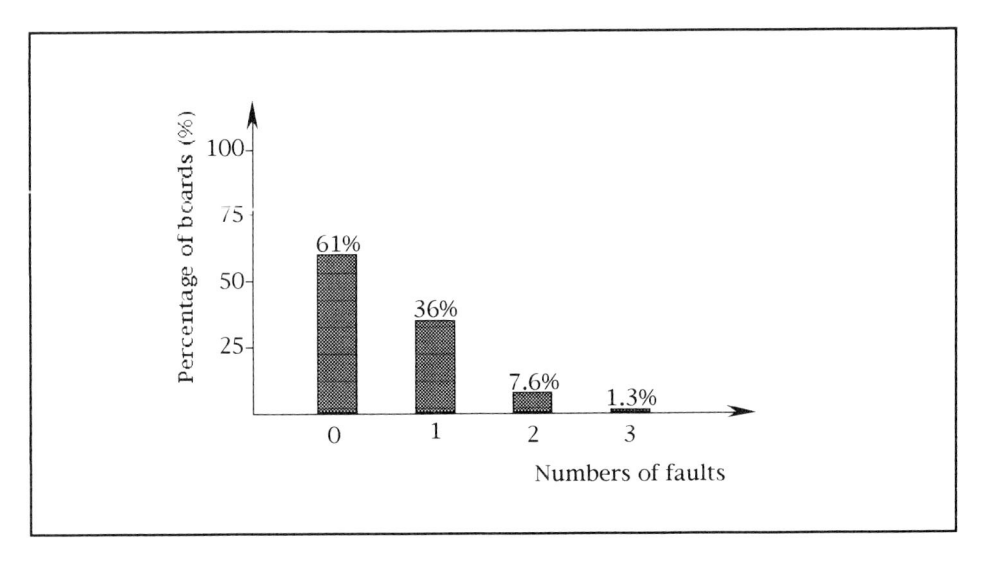

Figure 7.3 Percentages of printed circuit boards manufactured, related to numbers of faults

135

Test methods and strategies

depend largely on the production processes used, the approximations in Figures 7.2 and 7.3 allow us to consider what happens as assemblies become more and more complex. These are, hopefully, quite high levels of faults based on exaggerated data, but even where, say, failure rate of assemblies is measured in such small amounts as 100 parts per million (ppm), an assembly with 1000 components (not large by today's densely-populated standards) has a 1 in 10 chance of having a failure. Put the other way round, one in ten assemblies has a fault — 10%! Assemblies with, say, 10,000 components can be expected *each* to have a fault!

The percentage of assemblies which can be expected to work in any given organization, without need of repair, is generally called the **first-pass yield** for obvious reasons. High first-pass yields are those over about 80%, medium first-pass yields are between about 40% and 80%, while low first-pass yields are considered to be below about 40%.

Fault types

We can consider what types of faults are likely, by categorizing fault data obtained historically into groups. Figure 7.4 illustrates an example, showing how these groups give an idea of where faults can be expected. This leads us to assume that test equipment able to identify short circuits occurring on a soldered assembly will allow us to repair over 60% of faulty tested assemblies.

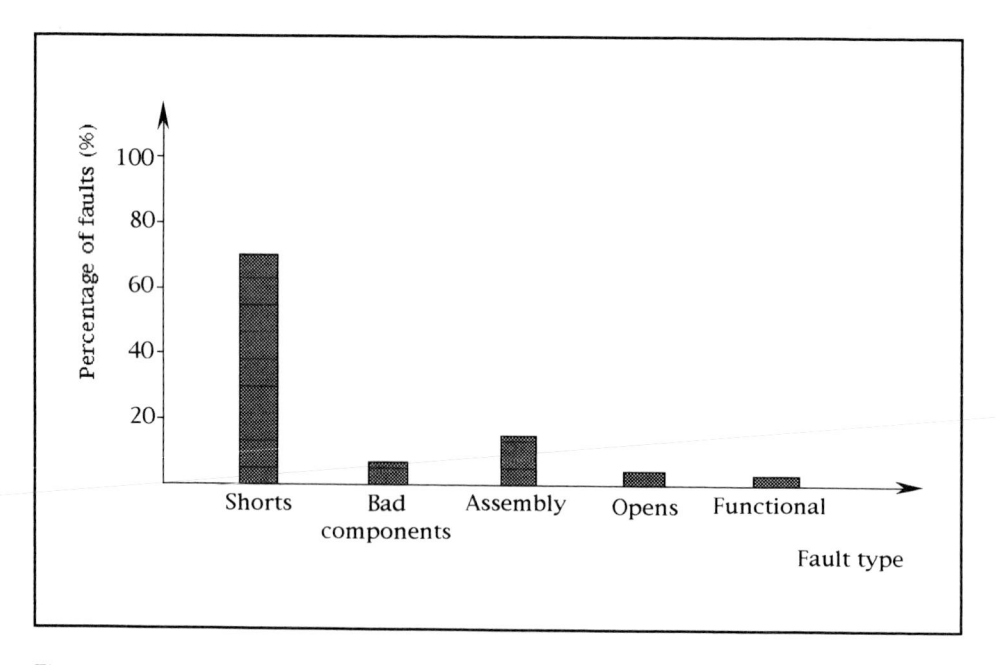

Figure 7.4 *Percentages of faults on assemblies, related to fault type*

A first-pass yield of, say, 60% allows us to produce 84% (60% + [60 x 40%]) of tested and working assemblies with only minor rework done to 24%. Possibly, yes — but not necessarily. If more than one fault exists on an assembly, and only one of these faults is a short circuit, the assembly remains faulty after identifying and repairing the short. So the final number is typically lower than the maximum potential of a system.

Nevertheless, considering faults by category means we can begin to formulate methods of identifying faults. Most faults are process-based. These include:

- short circuits
- open circuits
- faulty components
- incorrect components.

Such faults occur physically, they are results of something going wrong in the production process. Short circuits are often caused by incorrectly set up or maintained soldering machines, for example; likewise open circuits. Faulty components may be due to the supplier. Incorrect components are simple results of components being put into wrong positions on an assembly. Often these faults are easy to identify and, hopefully, easy to repair.

Functional faults, though relatively few in number, are usually more difficult to identify and may be impossible to repair. Functional faults are related to how well a product performs its designed job.

Test and inspection applications

There is a range of different approaches to test. These approaches define the test methods used and all the physical aspects which go with methods, such as test fixtures, test signals and results gathering. To start with, at least, test equipment can be classified according to the areas of a product's life in which it is used. So, there are four main groups of test equipment, used in the four stages of product life:

- design and development
- during production
- after production
- in service.

Often different test equipment can be used in more than one of these stages. It is even possible to have test equipment which can be used in all four stages.

From these product life stages, there appears a number of test equipment types. These test equipment types include:

- component testers — used to test each part prior to assembly, to make sure they are within specified tolerances
- unpackaged assembly testers — used to test assembled printed circuit boards

Test methods and strategies

- packaged assembly testers — used to test products immediately prior to shipment to customers
- service and maintenance testers — used to repair and overhaul products in their service environment at the customers' premises.

Often testers used in service and maintenance (meters, oscilloscopes and so on) are small-scale versions of testers of other types. We can rule them out of this consideration of test equipment, as they are not used in the production processes which form the area this book is concerned with.

Of the others, unpackaged assembly testers are given our main consideration here, but component testers and packaged assembly testers, too, must be looked at, however briefly.

Component testers

Testing of component parts is fairly simple. Often, all that is needed is a straightforward measurement of each component's main parameter (resistance of a resistor, capacitance of a capacitor, and so on). Sometimes, other parameters of each component are measured (dimensions, solderability, continuity and so on). Testing is performed merely to check the parts are of their specified quality.

Most parameters of passive components may be tested with simple meter or bridge circuits. Tests can be manual, or automatic with components picked, positioned, checked and output without interference from staff. More complex measurements may be carried out with test equipment which includes function generators, voltage supplies, analog and digital stimuli and so on.

Active components are usually tested for functionality. They are supplied with stimuli which simulate operating conditions, and resultant characteristics are measured and compared with ideal values. Again this may be manually or automatically done.

Apart from components, the only other product part sometimes tested by a manufacturer prior to assembly is the printed circuit board itself. Without components, printed circuit boards are generally known as **bare-boards**. Simple bare-boards may require nothing more than a visual check, perhaps with a magnifying aid of some description. More complex boards with many closely-spaced tracks cannot usually be visually checked by eye so test equipment is used. Typically, tests included here are for continuity of circuit and insulation between tracks. Automatic equipment is available, perhaps with a bed-of-nails fixture onto which the bare-board is positioned, or with moving probes (known as **fixtureless testing**) programmed to position at large numbers of test points around the board. Automatic optical inspection (AOI) using cameras, scanning lasers, infra-red emission, or sometimes X-rays is used to compare bare-boards with ideal images (often called a **golden image**). Internal track layers of multi-layered boards are often impossible to test fully, using any method.

Test and inspection applications

One way round having to test incoming parts prior to assembly of products is to use parts supplied to one of the national, regional, or international standard specification systems. Such specification systems monitor component suppliers, ensuring that suppliers themselves design and manufacture and test parts to a specified quality. The onus then lies with the suppliers rather than the users to ensure that components are reliable. This sort of self-assessment procedure is known as **vendor assessment**. In comparison, purchase of components outside such a procedure is known as **purchaser assessment** — the buyer has to test each part.

Approved components in standard specification procedures are listed in frequently-updated qualified products lists (QPLs). The UK system falls under British Standard BS 9000. In the UK and Europe, the Electronic Components Committee of CENELEC — the European Committee for Electrotechnical Standardization — operates the CECC system. Worldwide, the International Electrotechnical Committee Quality Assessment System (IECQ) operates. Any manufacturer attempting to make high-quality products is well-advised to follow such systems.

Unpackaged assembly testers

Test equipment in this group is used to test assemblies after they have been soldered but before they are housed in cases, housings, or packages. As, in all but a few cases, unpackaged assembly test equipment is programmable so that the tests they carry out depend on software, they are commonly grouped under the heading **automatic test equipment** (ATE).

Three main categories of automatic test equipment are used: in-circuit testers; functional testers; combinational testers.

In-circuit testers

In-circuit test (ICT) involves the physical requirement of electrically accessing circuit nodes within an assembly. Typically, bed-of-nails fixtures are therefore used for this purpose and often they have many hundreds, if not thousands, of test probes. Following measurements undertaken by the test equipment, a simple comparison of measured values with defined ideal values identifies faults. Typical faults which can be identified include short and open circuits, misplaced components, incorrect component values and inadequate soldered joints. These are all process-related faults, otherwise known as **manufacturing defects**, not operational (ie, functional) faults.

Where no power is applied to tested assemblies and all measurements are passive, in-circuit testers are known as **manufacturing defects analyzers**

Test methods and strategies

(MDAs). Manufacturing defects analyzers are therefore cheaper than true in-circuit testers, though they cannot check active components for correct function.

In-circuit tests on assemblies are performed sequentially, so complete tests may take some time if complex assemblies are being tested. However, as over 95% of all assembly faults are manufacturing defects, and as in-circuit testing can identify over 90% of these, in-circuit test can identify some 85% or so of *all* assembly faults. In-circuit test is therefore seen as a powerful test procedure. However, it is not capable of testing functionality of assemblies.

Functional testers

Functional test makes no initial attempt to identify isolated faults. There is no nodal access to the circuit, instead connections are generally made with edge connectors which the assembly uses in its service life, too. Functional testers are primarily concerned with a circuit's transfer function. Consequently, all a functional tester is interested in are the circuit's input, its output, and the job it is designed to do. This is true whether the functional tester is testing an analog or a digital circuit.

In this, basic functional test is quite simple; assemblies are plugged into the connectors on the test equipment, the test equipment provides power and stimuli simulating real-life operation, and the assembly itself either works or doesn't work depending on whether or not faults are present. Effectively the functional tester emulates a circuit's normal working electrical environment. By monitoring the circuit's outputs the functional tester can easily detect if the circuit works as designed. If something is not working properly, a basic functional tester merely notifies the operator.

This sort of pass or fail test (usually called **go/no go testing**) is a useful thing in high-volume production of assemblies where only the odd board is expected to fail.

However, the fact that an assembly has failed gives no indication of *why* it has failed. Consequently, further tests have to be carried out to identify faults. Sometimes these are carried out on the same functional tester, perhaps with the aid of probes placed manually onto the printed circuit board. Such tests are usually performed step by step, manually, under direction of the test equipment. The test equipment itself is programmed to instruct an operator where to place probes to test for faults. By isolating parts of the circuit in turn until a part is found which doesn't function correctly, the test equipment can isolate and identify most faults. Some functional testers have automatic guided probes, eliminating the requirement for an operator.

An alternative to this manual procedure if the fault is a manufacturing defect is to remove a failed assembly from the functional tester and put it, instead, on an in-circuit tester.

Naturally, these sorts of features are programmed into a functional tester, so depend totally on the program. Controlling programs are complex, and need to take into account all eventualities of faults.

Combinational testers

As we've seen, in-circuit testers can't identify functional faults. Similarly, functional testers can't identify all manufacturing defects. Sometimes it takes a combination of both test procedures to isolate some faults.

Combinational testers combine in-circuit and functional test methods in a way which neither in-circuit nor functional testers can do individually. They have the ability to isolate electrically parts of a circuit within the whole, in a process known as **partitioning.**

Partitioning of assemblies allows combinational testers to test these partitioned parts in total isolation from other parts. In-circuit and functional testers alone cannot do this. Some 99.5% of all possible faults have been reported to be identifiable with combinational testers.

Packaged assembly testers

Once assemblies are packaged, very few tests can be performed on assemblies. Instead, tests are carried out to determine how the whole product performs under stress conditions. These tests are designed to force failures to occur, prior to delivery to customers. This has two advantages. First, failures which would have occurred quite soon after delivery occur in the test area. Customers, therefore, don't have to suffer.

Second, regularly occurring faults quickly become known to the design department, which can then determine a procedure to reduce or eliminate them. Often, this entails as little as changing a component specification to a higher grade, if a particular component regularly fails. Sometimes, however, a design change may be called for.

Tests which stress a product for these purposes are called **screening tests**, and there are many. In order of effectiveness, these include:

- temperature cycling
- vibration
- high temperature
- electrical stress
- thermal shock
- low temperature
- mechanical shock
- humidity.

Test methods and strategies

A comparison of testers

Table 7.1 lists the various fault types which occur on electronic assemblies, relating them to the test equipment types we have looked at. The effectiveness of equipment types at identifying those faults is shown as a grading of 0 to 3, where 0 means the type is ineffective, while 3 means very effective.

Test methods

In all the tester types and test procedures used, there are only a few test methods, few enough that we can consider the main methods here.

Analog in-circuit testing

The principle of analog in-circuit test relies on the characteristics of the operational amplifier to measure unknown resistance, inductance or capacitance. Figure 7.5 illustrates the principle. Operational amplifiers have extremely high input impedances with low output impedances, coupled with very high gain. These factors ensure that the inverting input of an operational amplifier is always at earth potential, known as **virtual earth** or **virtual ground**.

Table 7.1 Test equipment types related to types of faults found on printed circuit assemblies

Assembly fault	Test equipment types				
	Component testers	Optical inspection	In-circuit testers	Functional testers	Stress screening testers
Component functionality	2	0	2	2	1
Component type	1	2	2	2	0
Component presence	0	3	2	2	0
Manufacturing defects	0	1	3	2	1
Circuit functionality	0	0	2	3	1
Latent defects	2	0	2	2	3

Test methods

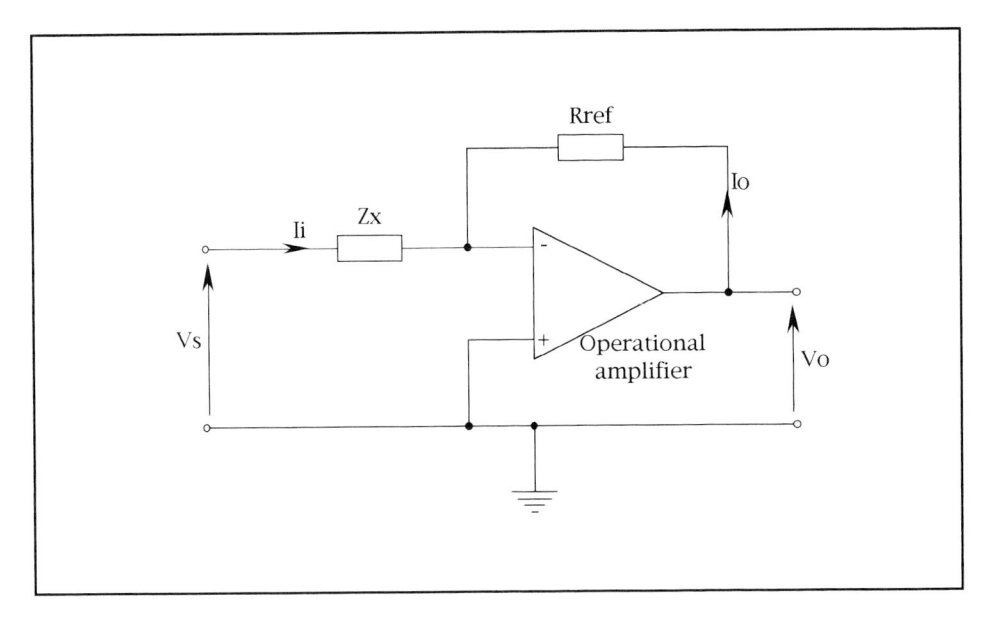

Figure 7.5 *Showing basic characteristics of an operational amplifier*

The signal from the operational amplifier's output in Figure 7.5 is the inverse of the signal at the - input, and is in phase with the + input. Output value is a function of the difference between - and + signals. In the inverting configuration shown:

$$V_s = I_i \times Z_x \times V_o = I_o \times R_{ref}$$

and so:

$$\frac{V_o}{V_s} = -\frac{I_i R_{ref}}{I_i Z_x}$$

and from this:

$$Z_x = -R_{ref} \frac{V_s}{V_o}$$

Guarding techniques

One of the main provisos of in-circuit automatic test equipment is that it must be able to look inside a circuit, electrically isolating parts of it from others. In analog in-circuit test this is done by nulling currents around a tested component, by connecting all surrounding nodes to the same potential. This allows the

Test methods and strategies

measurement circuit to make an accurate measurement of the component, or characteristic of the component. These isolating methods are performed by **guarding circuits**. There are many types, based on the same principle as that shown in Figure 7.6, where a tested resistor R_t is shown in parallel with two other resistors R_1 and R_2. Together they form a simple network with three test nodes.

Node A is the **force node**, sometimes called the **stimulus node**. Voltage from the automatic test equipment's internal measurement circuit is *forced* onto or *stimulates* that node.

Node B is the **sense node** or the **measurement node**, as current through the test resistor R_t is *sensed* or *measured* from that node.

Node C is the **guard node**, as the **guard** earth voltage is applied to it.

The inverting input of the test equipment's internal operational amplifier measuring circuit is connected to node B, so is at virtual earth potential. As node C is at earth anyway, no current flows through resistor R_1. Node A is connected to a test voltage V_t, so current through the resistor R_t is sensed by the operational amplifier. Output voltage of the operational amplifier is thus an indication of resistor R_t's value.

In practical in-circuit automatic test equipment systems connections to tested components entail quite long connecting leads and a bed-of-nails fixture. Inevitably, measurement errors due to system resistances, wiring crosstalk, switching relays and so on must be considered. Other methods, extending the basic guard technique shown here, are used to eliminate errors to give a high degree of accuracy.

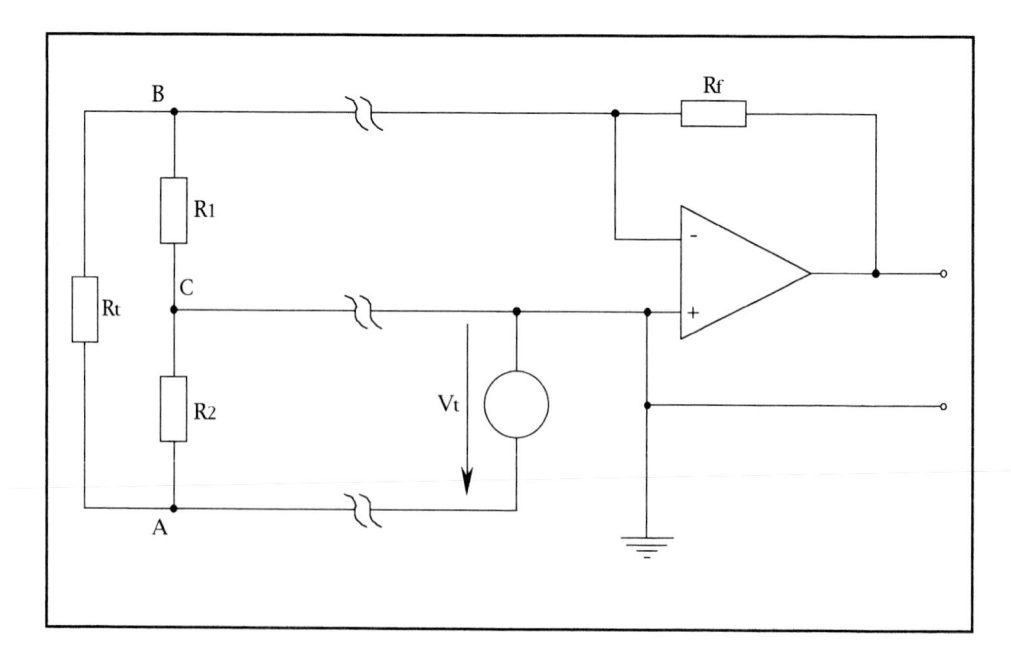

Figure 7.6 *Guarding circuit used in analog in-circuit test equipment*

Test methods

By using an alternating test voltage V_t, inductive, capacitive and active components can be isolated, guarded, tested and measured using this same technique.

Digital in-circuit testing

Testing of digital circuits requires that digital drivers and receivers interface with nodes on the circuit under test.

Figure 7.7 shows a basic digital in-circuit test system. The printed circuit board under test is connected to the test equipment with a bed-of-nails fixture. Some form of multiplexing arrangement is usual to connect the many hundreds or thousands of test points on the printed circuit board to the internal circuits of the test equipment. The **multiplexing ratio** of the test equipment defines how many internal drivers and receivers are connected to how many test points on the fixture. For example, a multiplexing ratio of 4:1 is common, so that if a printed circuit board has 1000 test points the test equipment must have at least 250 drivers and receivers.

In principle, operation of digital in-circuit test is straightforward. Logic devices on the tested printed circuit board are stimulated with patterns or sequences appropriate to each device. Then logic outputs of devices are compared with ideal values stored in the test equipment. If printed circuit

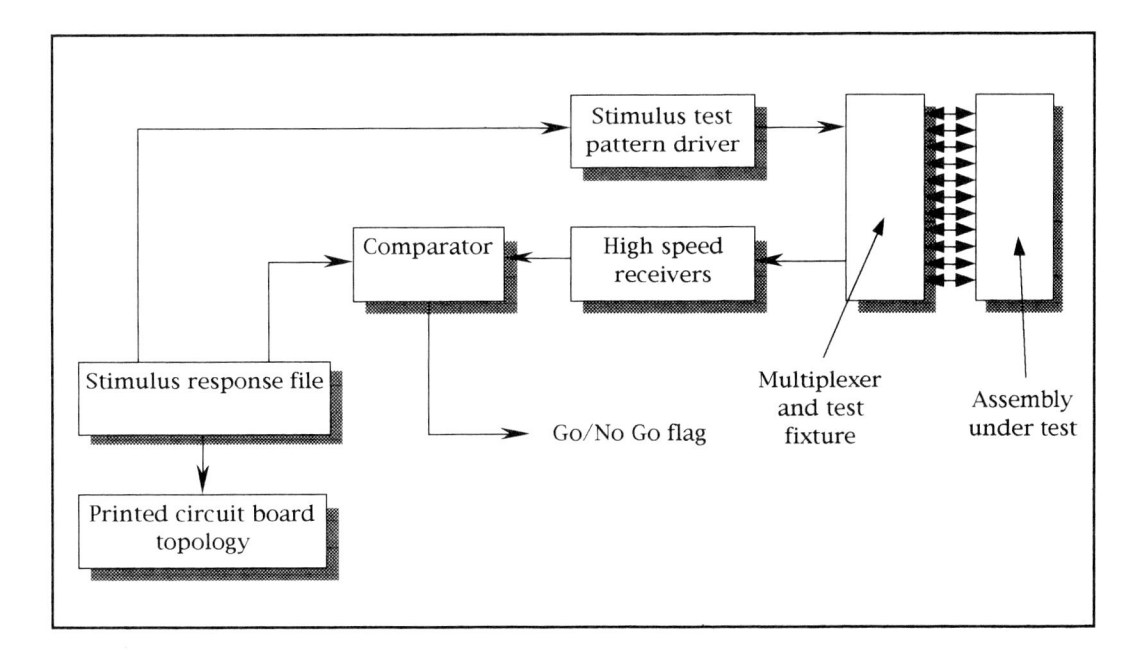

Figure 7.7 *Basic digital in-circuit test equipment*

Test methods and strategies

board outputs are identical with stored values, the circuit is defined as having no faults. If, on the other hand, circuit outputs differ from ideal values, a fault condition has been detected.

Digital drivers

Where analog in-circuit testers use operational amplifiers (the basic analog component), digital in-circuit test uses the basic logic component, the gate, as its drivers. Typically these are three-state gates which give high and low states, as well as a high-impedance undriven state. Such a gate is shown in Figure 7.8 with its truth table. Outputs from simple gates like this may be too simple. Often test equipment must impose timing stresses on the circuit under test, such as variable fall and rise times of pulses and specific **formatting** of outputs. Typical digital in-circuit test equipment is able to vary these features as required.

Timing stresses are useful in that they can test a circuit's function right to its timing limits. Also these limits are imposed at a much lower system speed than normal.

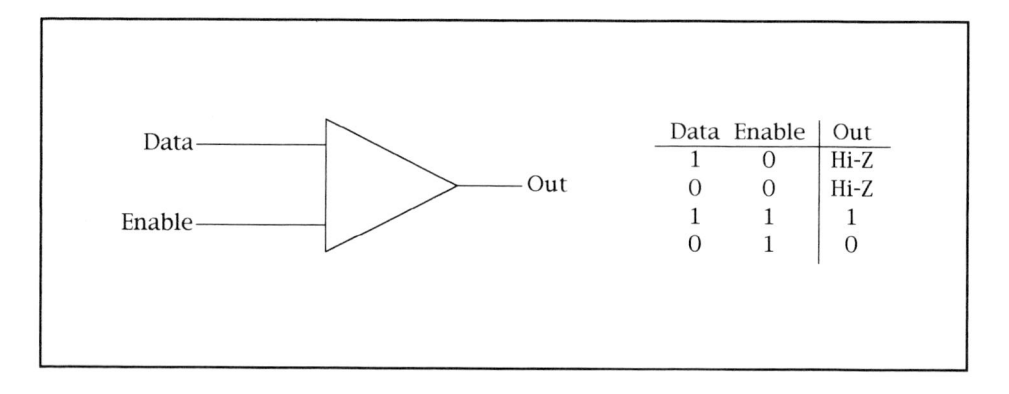

Data	Enable	Out
1	0	Hi-Z
0	0	Hi-Z
1	1	1
0	1	0

Figure 7.8 *Three-state gate used as a digital driver in in-circuit test equipment*

Digital receivers

Digital receivers in in-circuit test equipment are combinations of analog comparators and gates, as shown in Figure 7.9. Data from the circuit under test is compared with a voltage half of the logic difference, then the comparator output is combined with the reference expected data in an exclusive OR gate. Gate output is low when received data is the same as expected, but high if not as expected.

Test methods

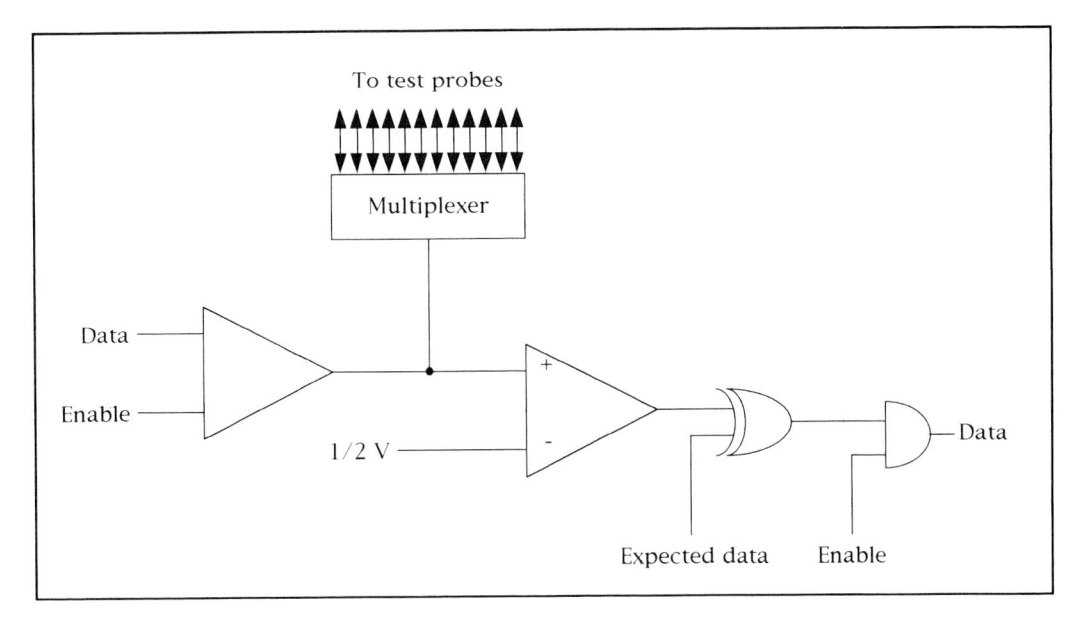

Figure 7.9 *Digital receiver of in-circuit test equipment, formed by combination of digital gates and analog comparator*

Digital isolation

Digital in-circuit test relies on being able to isolate parts or individual devices in a circuit, in a similar way to that in which analog guarding isolates parts or devices in an analog in-circuit test procedure. Basically, this is done in digital in-circuit testing by forcing outputs of a preceding device to defined logic states. While this may damage devices if maintained for a long period, for short periods of time at least it is most effective.

Such digital guarding is known as **overdriving** and there are two basic methods:

- **nodeforcing** — in which an output is high and forced low
- **backdriving** — in which an output is low and forced high.

These are illustrated in Figure 7.10, where two devices are overdriven by test equipment pulses. Loading of a previous component is considerably lower when nodeforcing than when backdriving.

Overdriving is the main principle behind the ability to isolate parts of a digital circuit from the remainder of the circuit. The principle is known as **partitioning** and those areas isolated are called **partitions** or, more usually, **clusters**. Often the whole process of digitally isolating these clusters is called **cluster testing**. Clusters can be quite large, or can be as small as individual devices of the circuit. It is the test equipment and its programmed pulses that define the cluster size.

Test methods and strategies

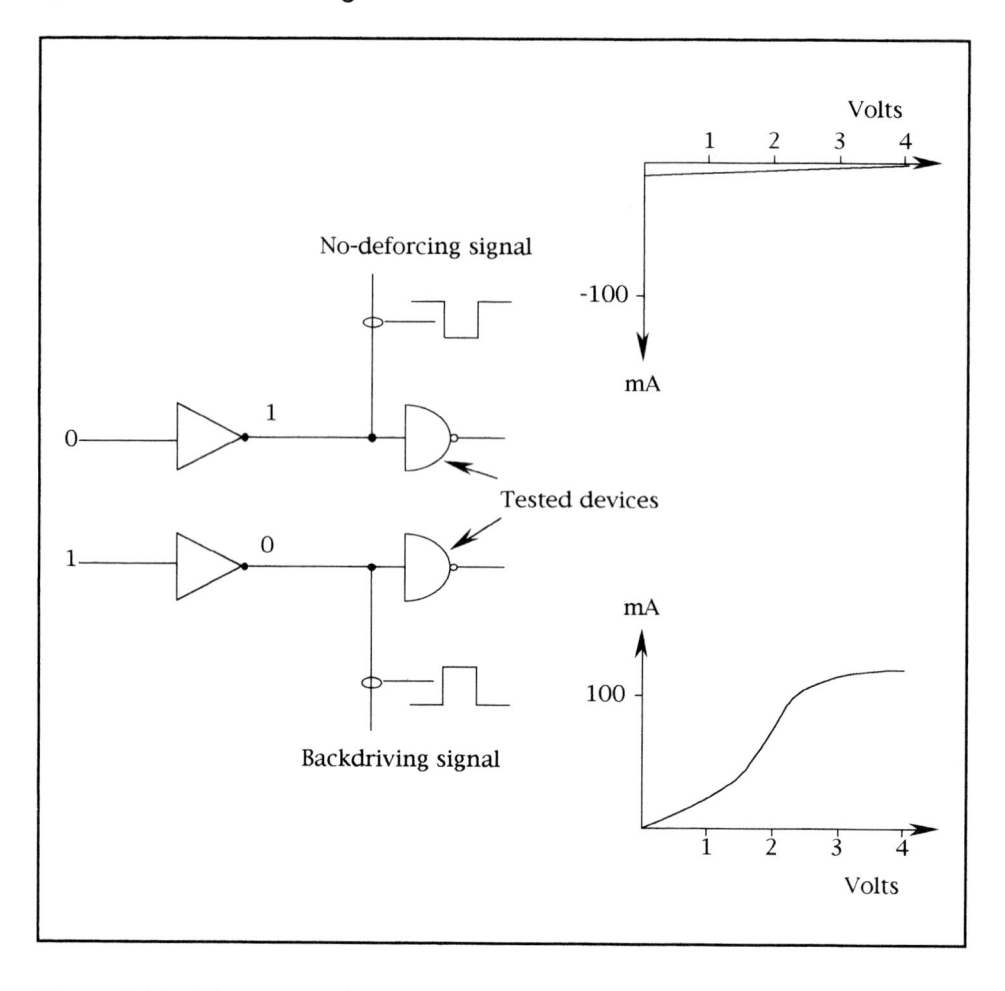

Figure 7.10 *Illustrating the principles of nodeforcing and backdriving, both digital guarding techniques of overdriving*

Scan testing

There is another method of isolating parts of digital circuits, more common in functional and combinational test procedures than in-circuit. It still can be used in in-circuit testing so is covered here. It is called **scan testing** and it allows specific sections of a circuit to be formed in a group whose operation can be stopped while inputs and outputs of the group can be checked, as well as specific test vectors being input into the circuit. Scan testing is a combination of hardware and software, because it relies on devices within the circuit having extra data paths in them to input and output information relating to test point logic states.

Test methods

Scan testing derives from a consortium of companies called the Joint Test Action Group (JTAG), which proposed that data paths be implemented within certain integrated circuits on manufacture. Such an integrated circuit is shown in Figure 7.11, where the device features scan test control and input/output latches as well as conventional functional circuits.

Any **scan design** device such as this has a four-wire bus, called the **four-wire testability bus**, which allows data to be entered and extracted under external control by the test equipment. All input/output latches of all scan design devices on an assembly may be connected together in serial manner, with the **test data out** (TDO) pin of one device joined to the **test data in** (TDI) pin of the next to form a long shift register known as the **scan path**.

The remaining two wires of the four-wire testability bus are for control purposes. Clocking of the data around the scan path is provided via the **test clock** (TCK) input, while **test-mode select** (TMS) switches the device into test mode. When in test mode a scan design device has all input/output latches connected together, while all normal inputs and outputs to and from it are suspended. This suspension of operation of devices in the midst of operation means that scan test allows real-time testing of a circuit's performance. This can be useful in in-circuit testing, but has more potential in functional testing (considered later), where test probe access to internal test nodes in a circuit is not usually possible. Here, scan paths can be routed to printed circuit board edge connectors, so functional testers can have internal circuit access they would not otherwise have.

By careful design, scan testing allows partitions to be built in to a circuit, so that the job of test equipment is made significantly easier. Partitions are decided by hardware considerations rather than by test equipment software, and they are fixed in size, so design is important to ensure that the right partitions are built in to circuits.

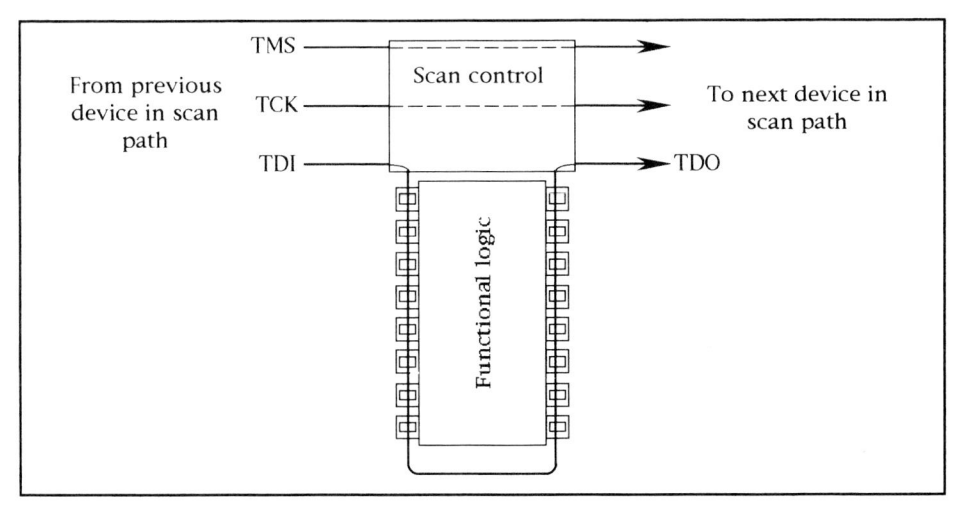

Figure 7.11 *Scan test integrated circuit, featuring scan control circuits*

Test methods and strategies

Digital in-circuit test methods

Test equipment for digital circuits depends on the type of assembly. Types of circuits found in assemblies are:

- combinational logic
- sequential logic
- bus-based logic.

Physical and mechanical parameters of automatic test equipment for digital in-circuit testing are similar for all three. Only the actual test methods vary.

Combinational logic test methods

Combinational logic (which features no memory of previous states) such as a NAND gate simply gives an output for a particular variation of inputs. Tests comprise a straightforward sequence of inputs to the circuit, with monitoring of the output. Ideal results, in the form of a truth table in memory, are known by the test equipment. Provided the output is correct for the complete sequence of inputs, the circuit is classed as working.

Ideally, all possible variations of inputs should be provided as a test stimulus, and all resultant output monitored. This is known as **exhaustive testing**, which is only really possible for circuits with only a small number of inputs. A circuit with, say, 20 inputs, has a total combination of 2^{20} possible input variations, and an exhaustive test with so many sequences might not be economic in terms of time and cost. It rapidly becomes impossible to test circuits exhaustively; usually a selection of input variations must be made.

Variations of inputs to combinational logic are known as **test vectors**, and form a type of **bit pattern measurement** common to most automatic test equipment. Often, outputs from a circuit are called **signatures**, and form just one number in a test process called **signature analysis**. This describes the required output as a collection of ideal test pattern outputs.

Signature analysis is used in most digital in-circuit testers, and the principle is illustrated in Figure 7.12. Stored test patterns are provided as test stimuli, and results are compared with stored responses. Its advantage is that dynamic testing is provided (typically using the circuit under test's system clock), so can be used for all types of logic circuit testing — combinational, sequential and bus-based logic.

Typically, the received response from a circuit is compressed into a signature, keeping memory requirements as low as possible.

There are two drawbacks to the signature analysis approach. First, an incorrect signature received from a circuit simply *indicates* a fault — with no identification of that fault or suggestion where it is. Second, all the response from the tested circuit has to be received before the complete signature can be compared with the ideal. In complex circuits, a complete signature analysis test can take quite some time.

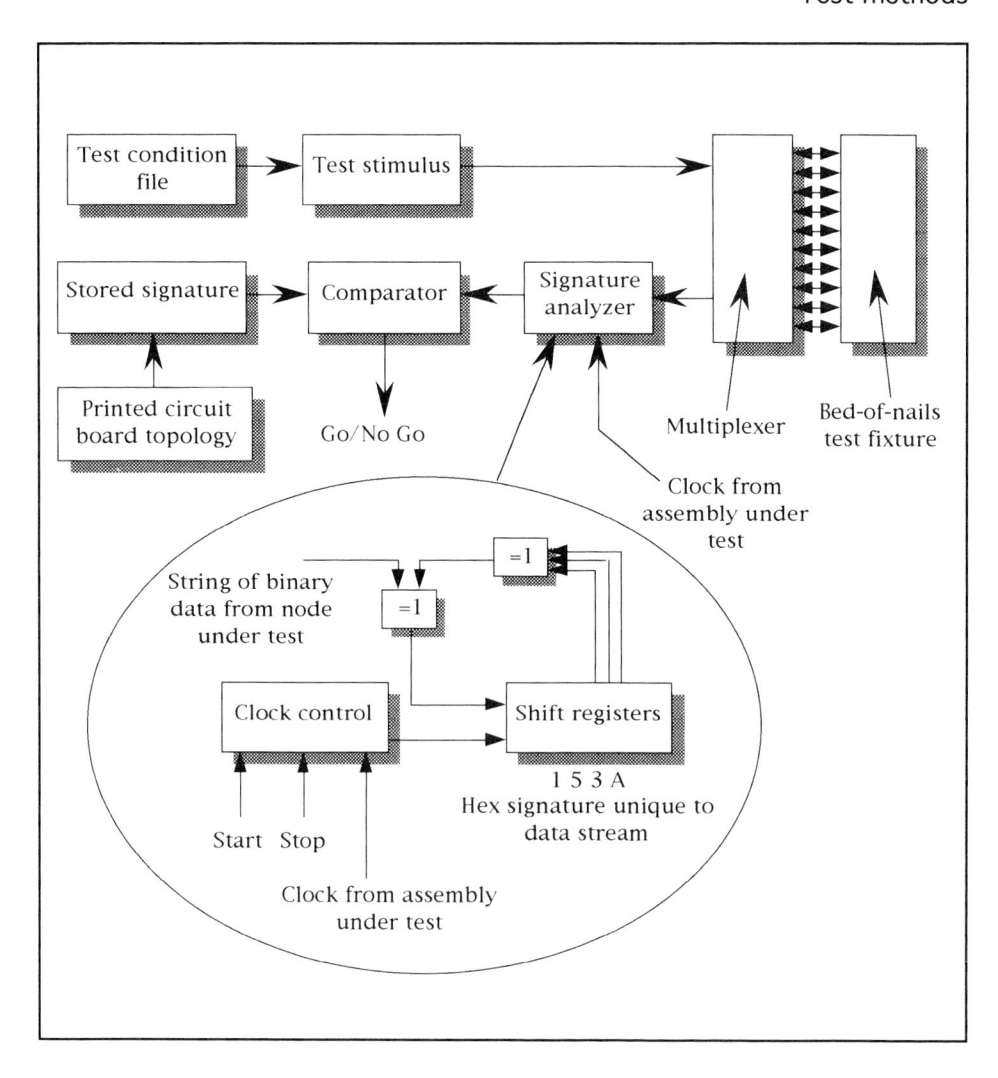

Figure 7.12 *Signature analysis, as a process used in digital in-circuit test equipment. Inset is shown the principle of a signature analyzer*

Sequential logic test methods

Sequential logic devices (which feature memory of previous states, and which depend on a previous state in determining the next state) such as bistables or microprocessors, are more difficult to test. This is because outputs are determined by inputs at a moment in time and the order or sequence in which inputs are applied. A state table, rather than a truth table, describes sequential logic.

Test methods and strategies

Sequential logic is tested by initializing the device, then driving its inputs according to the required pattern. Resultant patterns are compared with ideal patterns stored in the test equipment. As well as tests providing correct input sequences, it is usual for tests with known fault conditions to be used. Test equipment provides these fault conditions, then monitors test points in the circuit, watching the fault condition step through (known as **walking out**) to the outputs.

Sequences used in testing sequential logic are in two groups. Main sequences are of signature analysis form, usually. Initially, however, before sequential analysis can be used, circuits must be initialized to a known state. So **synchronizing sequences** of one form or another are used to reset the circuit. These are simply a set of test vectors applied after power-up, which are known to return the circuit to a state whereby further test should produce verifiable responses. Synchronizing sequences can be fixed (given to every similar circuit undergoing test) or variable according to condition of the circuit when they start — in which case they are known as **homing sequences**.

Bus-based logic test methods

Often, digital circuits are designed around a bus system and can be extremely complex. Testing has evolved with bus system complexity, and it is usual to see test equipment which features more than one test method. Three of the most important methods are:

- microprocessor emulation — in which a microprocessor in the tested circuit is forced into a hold state. Test equipment then takes over control of the circuit, emulating all the microprocessor's functions
- memory emulation — in which memory in the tested circuit is isolated, and replaced by memory within the test equipment. By masking the microprocessor's own on-board memory the test equipment memory effectively controls the microprocessor
- bus emulation — similar to microprocessor emulation in that the tested circuit's microprocessor is isolated and control is assumed by test equipment, but simply those commands and functions which perform communications tasks on the bus are emulated.

These methods are illustrated in Figure 7.13. Of the three approaches, bus emulation (sometimes called **bus timing emulation** or **bus-cycle emulation**) is the most popular and cost-effective. Both memory and microprocessor emulation require considerable knowledge of the particular microprocessor and its function, and consequent extensive diagnostic test routines to be written.

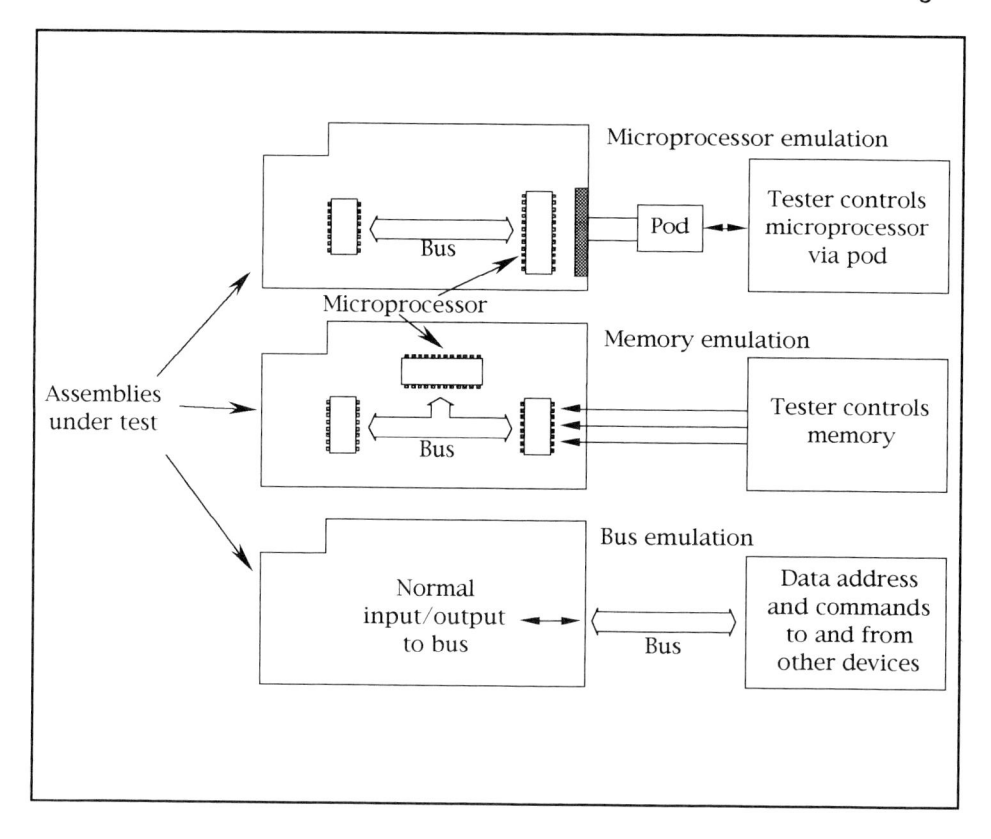

Figure 7.13 *Three of the most important bus-based logic test methods*

Test strategies

Basic test methods we've considered here are not alone sufficient to solve all test problems — particularly where products are complex or highly miniaturized. How the test methods are implemented, though, plays a large part in the process. Whether functional, in-circuit or combinational test equipment is used to test any particular product depends largely on the product itself and the manufacturer's requirements.

Multi-test methods

Rarely is it possible to test all products a manufacturer makes with a single tester. More often than not some combination of testers is needed, to iron out all possible faults likely to occur. For example, manufacturing defects can be

Test methods and strategies

identified by an in-circuit tester, used before assemblies pass on to a functional tester. Thus, manufacturing defects found by the in-circuit tester can be repaired before assemblies are functionally tested. Because of this, the functional tester is simply testing circuit functionality, and so may be far simpler (hence far cheaper) than a single functional tester to do both jobs. This set-up of an in-circuit tester in series with a functional tester is, incidentally, a common one in electronics manufacture and is called **screening** or sometimes **pre-screening**.

Where high volumes of products are manufactured it is sometimes necessary to have more than one tester performing identical tests. Typically a parallel combination is used — say two functional testers which test half of the assemblies each. The cost of two testers is often justified because a single functional tester powerful enough to test twice the throughput is usually much more than twice the price.

Obviously, multi-test combinations depend on what products, volumes and test requirements a manufacturer has.

Designing out faults

Obviously, the later in a product's life a manufacturer chooses to repair a fault, the more it costs the manufacturer. Looked at the other way, is it not surely better to try to correct faults in the earliest possible stages in a product's life? Thus, one of the basic test strategies is the idea of manufacturing a fault-free product. Such **zero defect** designs mean that the designer has to take into account all possible faults which can occur in any electronic product. We considered them earlier and re-group them here as:

- manufacturing defects — short circuits and open circuits, components in wrong positions
- faulty components
- functional faults.

If a circuit can be designed to take these factors into account, fault rates can be minimized. For example, with regard to manufacturing defects, the primary source of short circuits and open circuits in printed circuit board assemblies is the soldering stage. Often, problems like these occur because designers don't understand principles of soldering machines: what they are capable of, and what they are *not* capable of. Simple alterations to printed circuit board track layout or component positions can usually eliminate most soldering-related faults.

Incidence of faulty components can be minimized if not eliminated by buying components from the qualified products list of a vendor assessment approval scheme such as CECC, IECQ or BS 9000 standard specifications. The extra few pence spent on components might save hundreds of pounds in later rework.

Functional faults are usually the direct province of the designer. There is no cheap and easy way round them. The only method of reducing functional faults is to use a computer-aided design system to assist in initial circuit design. This is not merely a *circuit* design tool, however. A computer-aided design system is essentially a *product* design tool which, if used properly, can help to reduce all the other faults we've considered, too.

Designing for test

While the ideal is to produce a product which does not have faults, this rarely can be achieved in practice. Further, even if a product *can* be made with absolutely zero defects, we still have to test it as a quality-control procedure. So, having considered how to reduce faults by proper design, we come to the idea of designing a product to be easily tested.

The **design for test** principle is one of the most important factors helping to reduce test costs. By designing circuits with production processes and consequent tests in mind, assemblies can be manufactured which are both more easily made and more easily tested. Some of the basic rules for design include:

- provide test pads for test access
- enable automatic test equipment to initialize logic circuits
- provide means for automatic test equipment to inhibit timing circuits
- provide test access to address and data buses
- consider use of signature analysis for ROMs
- use scan test where possible.

Thus, design for test is not a single activity. It is a collection of test methods and ideas (all of which are considered in this chapter), not a unique function the designer carries out.

Managing test

We have considered how the design process can be used to aid manufacture and test, helping to make better, higher quality products. In the end, however, designers can only do this with management's backing. Production of testable, well-designed, functional products only happens if managers allow it to happen.

In conclusion, we have to understand that test is a process which maintains and can improve product quality. It is not a process done after an assembly is manufactured 'just to see if it works'.

8 Computer integrated manufacture

Throughout all other chapters one of the common themes has been the importance of information and how it is handled. Data needs to be held and controlled locally until it is ready for release in a controlled environment. At this point, control passes from the local to the global and so data becomes available for sharing.

A system to provide for this distribution of information must ensure security and integrity of data, control management of its distribution and allow change. One of the approaches to providing this type of system is shown in Figure 8.1. It provides distributed processing for the most intensive operations, allowing for cost effective systems while enabling sharing of commonly required data and invisible system management. Some larger multinational companies are developing and implementing such systems. However, there are problems — of incompatible hardware and software, and the need to define and agree common standards across the various equipment and software suppliers. These have all still to be solved fully although, as this chapter shows, there have been significant steps.

There are issues of information management, how to update information smoothly across operations that are at different stages in a process. In a simple example, customer services could be dealing with mark 1, production may be making mark 2 while designers might be at work on mark 3.

Consistency of the whole information set needs careful management, especially in the case of engineering changes to current or past production items. Such systems must be capable of evolution as computer-aided engineering and advanced manufacturing systems develop but the strategies for ensuring this are many.

Open systems interconnect

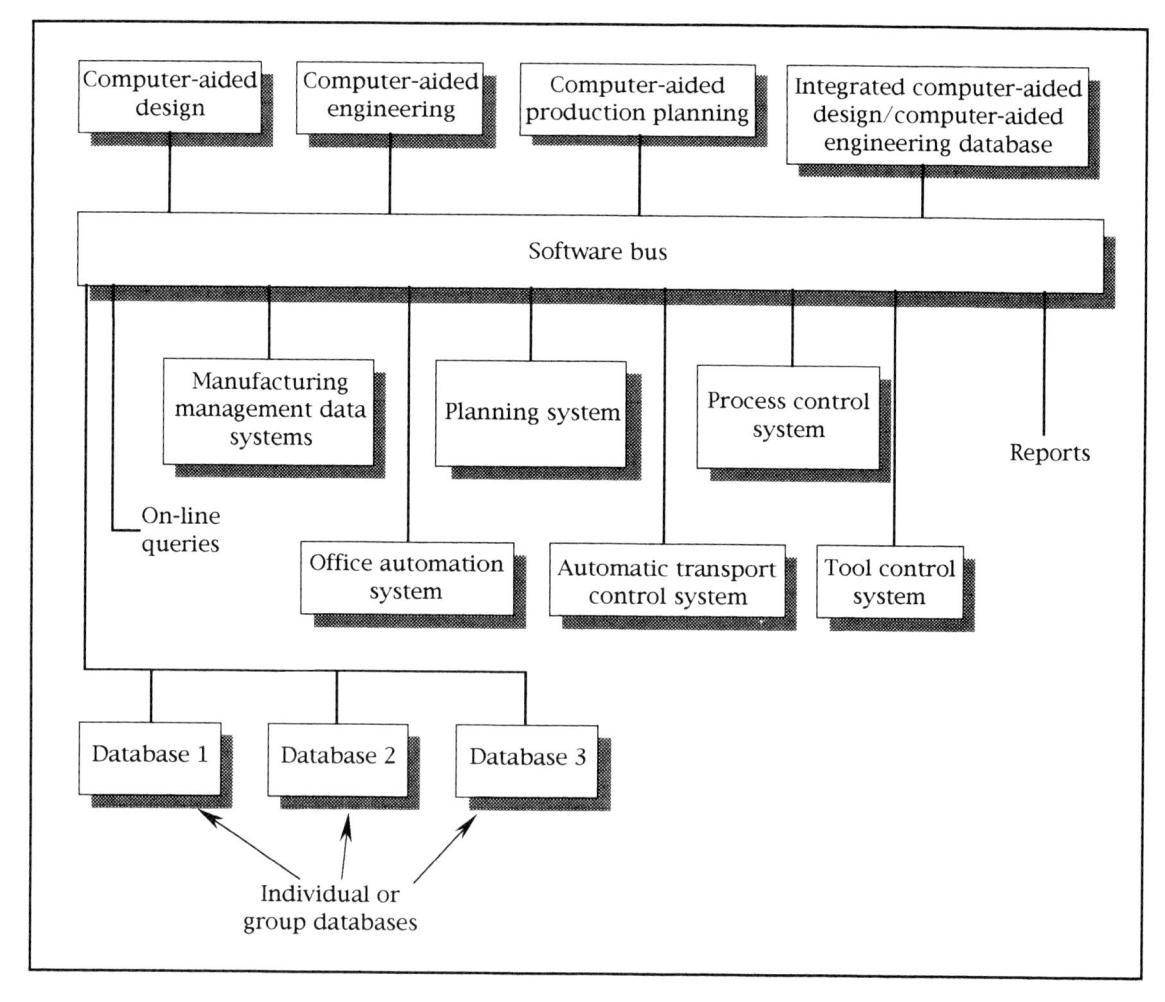

Figure 8.1 *Possible computer network to provide information distribution and maintenance*

Open systems interconnect

In recognition of the need for an integrated computing environment, the major manufacturers have been developing standards for interconnection based on a seven-layer model of program-to-program intercommunication.

The prospect is that instead of being tied to products of just one supplier to ensure inter-working, choice of supply will be greater. Products from any vendor will operate on the open systems interconnect network so choice of equipment can be made on grounds of, say, personal or price reasons. Data formats of this open systems interconnect (OSI) model are shown in Figure 8.2.

Computer integrated manufacture

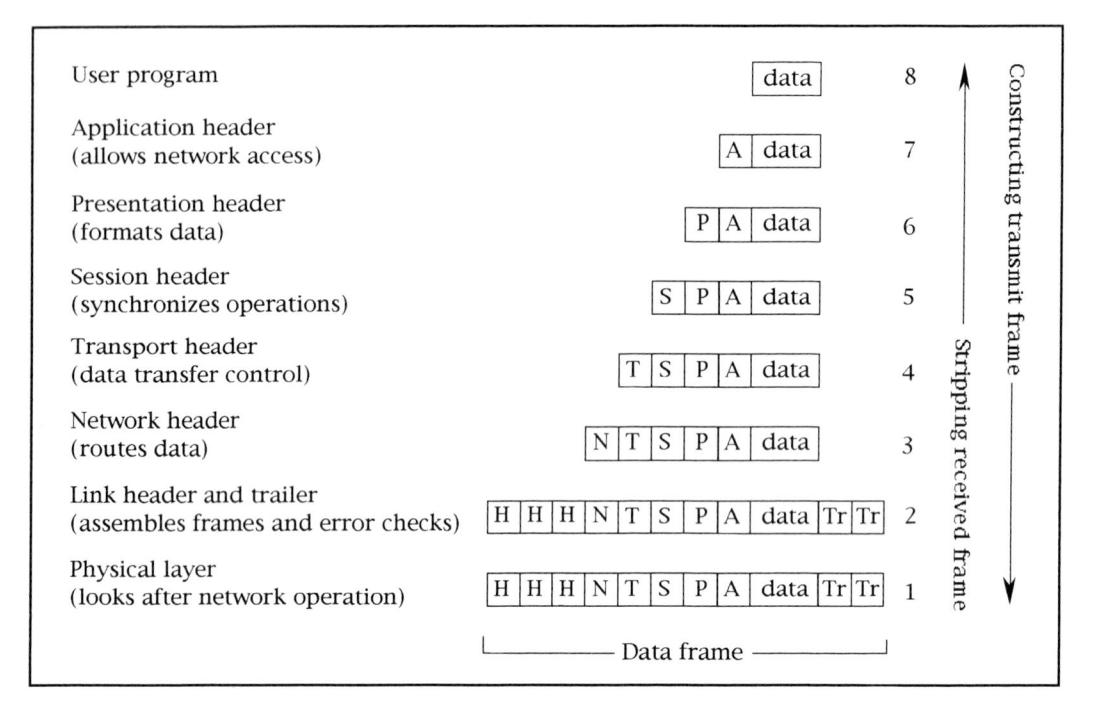

User program	data	8
Application header (allows network access)	A data	7
Presentation header (formats data)	P A data	6
Session header (synchronizes operations)	S P A data	5
Transport header (data transfer control)	T S P A data	4
Network header (routes data)	N T S P A data	3
Link header and trailer (assembles frames and error checks)	H H H N T S P A data Tr Tr	2
Physical layer (looks after network operation)	H H H N T S P A data Tr Tr	1

↑ Constructing transmit frame ── Stripping received frame ↓

└──── Data frame ────┘

Figure 8.2 *Data formats in the seven layers of an open systems interconnect network*

The seven layers of an open systems interconnect network are:

- the application layer (layer 7) — provides communication services to suit all types of computing application data. The application layer is the access point of programs to open systems interconnect systems. It sets up an open systems interconnect communications channel independent of the nature of the application
- the presentation layer (layer 6) — translates the data formats of the application layer to those required for data transfer and vice-versa
- the session layer (layer 5) — regulates the start, stop and resume states of the interconnecting applications (ie, it synchronizes data flow)
- the transport layer (layer 4) — provides communications link management. Includes error detection, correction, automatic re-routing and so on
- the network layer (layer 3) — sets up the required end-to-end link that may be over several different communication networks. Handles collection of layer 2 frames into packets
- the data link layer (layer 2) — manages transmission of data over physical links, assembles layer 1 data into frames, includes error detection
- the physical layer (layer 1) — enables the various data signals to be interfaced in a standard way. It covers subjects such as the voltage levels and pin assignments.

Manufacturing automation protocol

It can be understood from this, that communication builds up by layer. First the physical links, then protocols for the exchange of electrical signals across these links.

For all but the most basic situations, machines are part of a network (whether via public networks or private) and layer 3 is responsible for setting up the end-to-end connection.

Once set up, the link has to be managed to provide for error correction on the transmitted and received data.

It is only at the higher levels that the actual use of the data becomes significant. Layer 5, for example, is responsible for regulating flow of the information corresponding to the interaction of two similar applications, while layer 6 provides for applications using different data formats.

Layer 7 is the level at which application programs deal with the meaning and content of the data — the purpose of the interconnection.

Manufacturing automation protocol

The open systems interconnect model is most detailed at the simpler lowest levels: at higher levels the standards become more general. This has led to variety in the implementation of it. One such variation in the computer integrated manufacturing environment is the **manufacturing automation protocol (MAP)**. This was originally proposed by General Motors for linking robotics, numerically-controlled machines, testers and so on. It is designed to transfer large amounts of real-time data and uses a system of local area networks (LANs) called *token passing*, operating over co-axial or optical fibre cables. Manufacturing automated protocol is promoted in Europe by the European MAP User Group (EMUG) and the UK Department of Trade and Industry.

A schematic of a manufacturing automated protocol network is shown in Figure 8.3.

Work is in hand to integrate the manufacturing automated protocol with another open systems interconnect variant, **technical office protocol (TOP)**, devised to deal with office automation.

TOP was proposed by Boeing and a number of different companies currently use it. TOP uses the local area network known as Ethernet as its network. Although Ethernet is not capable of such high data rates as the manufacturing automated protocol network, this is of academic concern — as the data requirements of TOP are less onerous.

Data exchange standards

The problems of information interchange involving conversion between differing computer-aided design systems have been around for some time and there are now a few well supported standards. An idea of the complexity involved in the conversion process is shown in Figure 8.4.

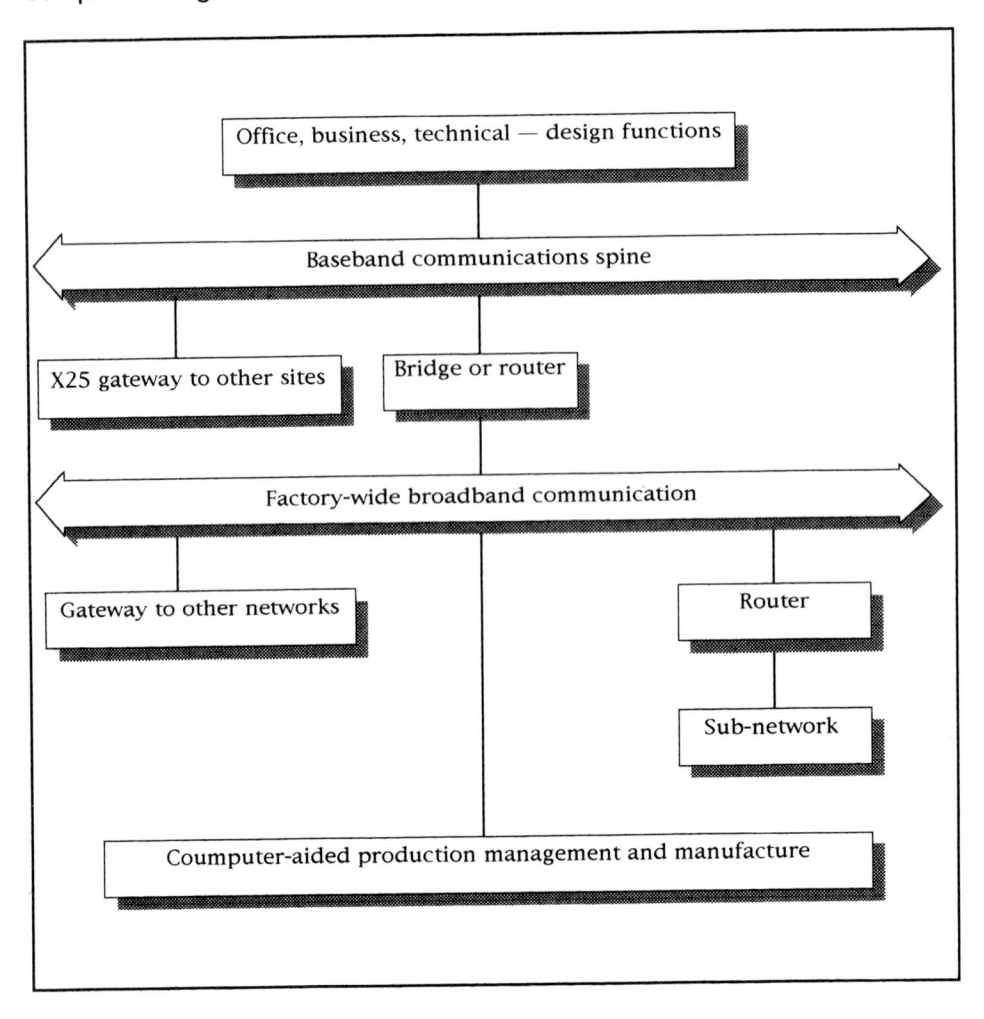

Figure 8.3 *A manufacturing automated protocol (MAP) network*

Initial graphics exchange specification

The initial graphics exchange specification (IGES) standard was developed for the interchange of mechanical design information between computer-aided design systems. The process works by adoption of a *neutral* data format — one system converts *to* it while the other converts *from* it. There has been a number of variations.

Version 3 includes rules for conversion of information about printed circuit boards such as schematics, connectivity, netlists, artwork and integrated circuit geometries.

A schematic representation of the process is shown in Figure 8.5.

Data exchange standards

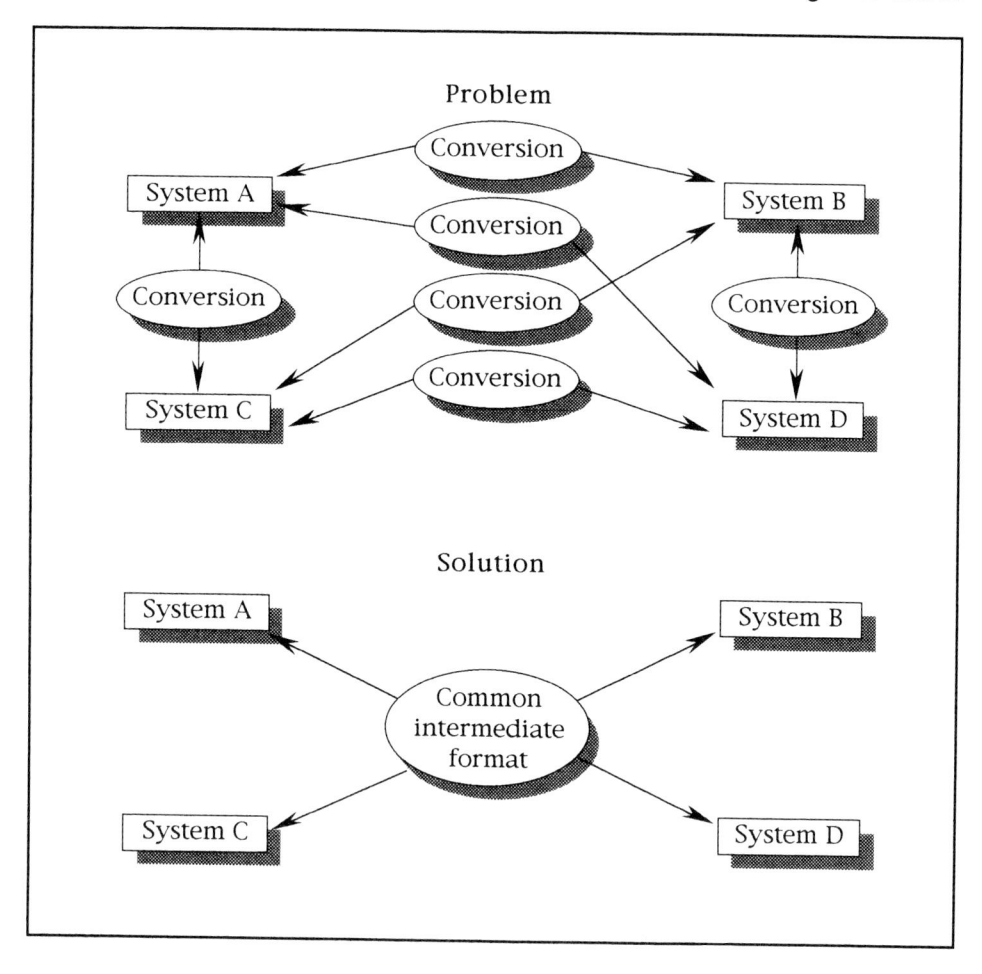

Figure 8.4 *Data conversion is made simpler if intermediate formats are standardized*

Electronic design information interchange format

The electronic design information interchange format (EDIF) standard was developed to aid transfer of data on the design of integrated circuits and, in particular, VLSI to silicon foundries.

Devices are described in a hierarchy of *cells*, descriptions of which are contained in *views*. These will describe the cell in terms of its functions, connectivity and physical layout. The input and output conditions of each cell are described in an *interface*.

Cells with the same implementation technology (eg, ECL, CMOS and so on) are grouped together in libraries. This is illustrated in Figure 8.6.

Computer integrated manufacture

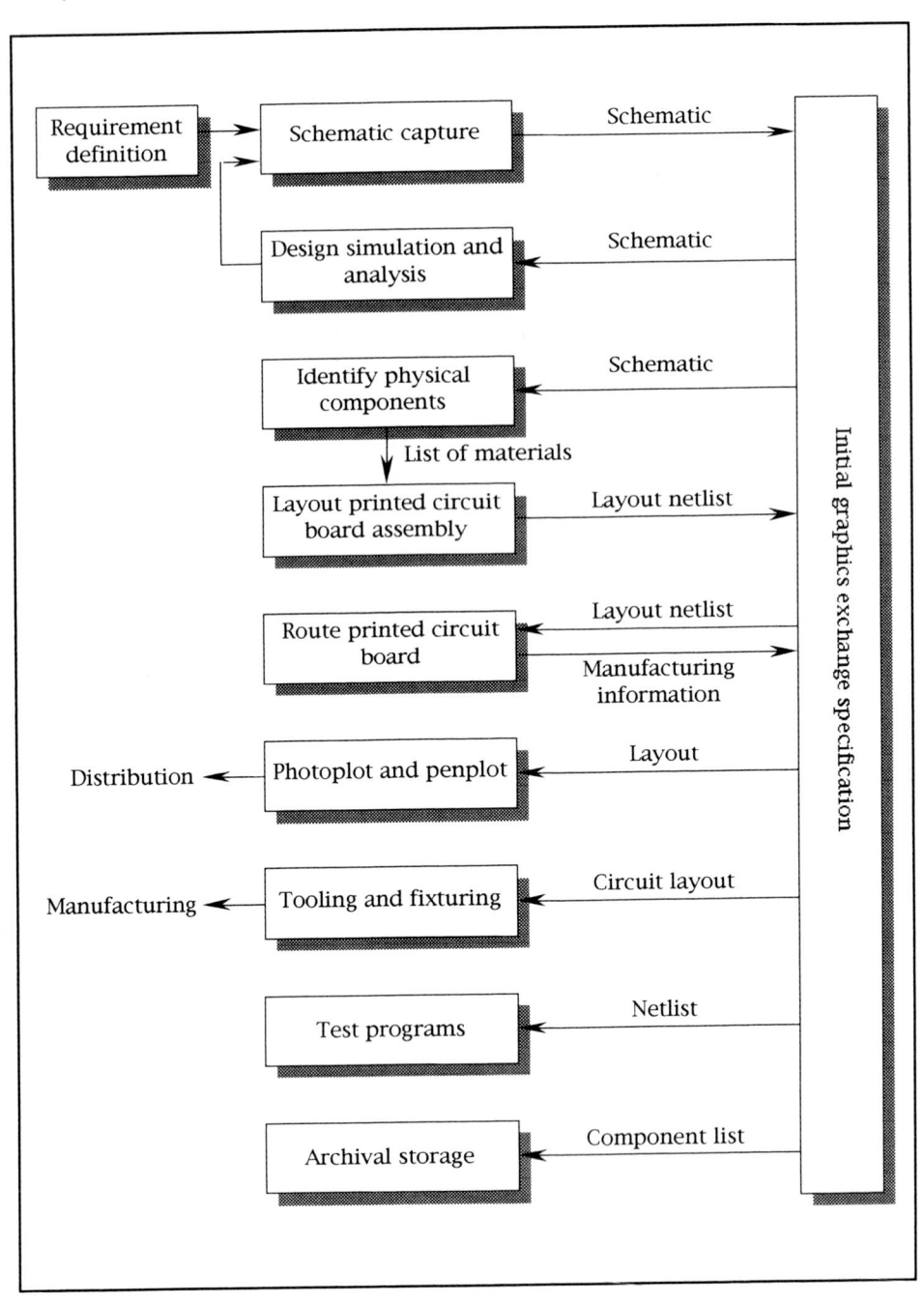

Figure 8.5 *The initial graphics exchange specification (IGES)*

Data exchange standards

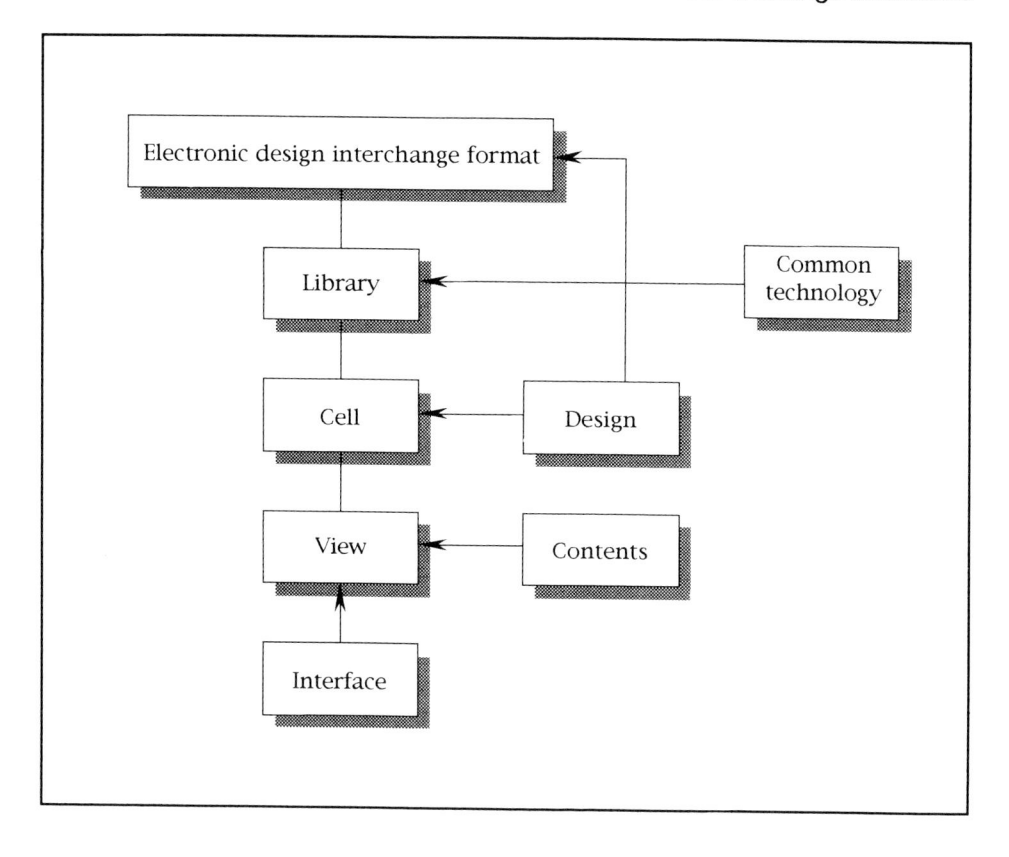

Figure 8.6 *The electronic design information interchange format (EDIF)*

Conversion programs translate the design into an ASCII text file for transfer. Recent versions and translators have been agreed to permit transfer of printed circuit board designs, too.

Efforts are continuing to embrace all neutral formats into a single set of standards, to cover the needs of *all* engineering disciplines. This is to be known as the **standard for exchange of product data** (STEP).

Glossary

Activated flux Rosin-based flux, with one or more activators added.
Additive Action of adding the track to a PCB base material.
Air levelling *Syn:* hot air levelling.
Alloy A combination of two or more metals. Alloys generally have significantly different properties than constituent elements. An example is solder, which is a mixture of tin and lead.
Aspect ratio Ratio of thickness of a printed circuit board to a hole's pre-printed diameter. If the aspect ratio is too high, say 3 or more, holes are susceptible to cracking.
Automated optical inspection (AOI) Text fixture method in which printed circuit boards are checked at bare-board, pre- or post-soldered stages of assembly by optical means.
Automatic component insertion (ACI) Insertion of components into a through-hole board by automatic means.
Bare-board testing Testing procedure in which printed circuit boards are tested prior to assembly of components.
Base (1) Insulating layer of a printed circuit board; (2) a substance dissolved in water which produces hydroxyl ions comprising an atom of oxygen and an atom of hydrogen.
Bed-of-nails fixture Arrangement of pin-type probes on a plate, which is pressed up against a printed circuit board, allowing electrical connections to be made for test purposes.
Blind via A via on a multi-layer PCB which does not go completely through the board. *Syn:* buried via.
Bonding wire Fine gold or aluminium wire between bonding pads on a semiconductor and base lands.
Bridging Where solder joins two or more conductive parts which are not meant to be connected.

Glossary

Bumps Inner terminations of a tape automated bond integrated circuit.

Buried via *See* blind via.

Butt joint A joint formed by a surface mount component lead which directly abuts the printed circuit board track. Butt joints are formed by J-lead and cropped-lead components.

Capability approval Component approval stage in BS9000/CECC/IECQ systems, for components designed and manufactured by the manufacturer.

Capability manual Documented manufacturing system required in the process of capability approval to BS9000/CECC/IECQ systems.

Capillary action Interaction between a liquid and a small diameter opening in a solid; whereby liquid is drawn into the opening by surface tension.

Carriers Holders for electronic parts which enable handling during production.

Chip (1) substrate on which semiconductor components are produced; (2) discrete surface mounted capacitors and resistors.

Chip carrier Holder for surface mounted integrated circuit devices.

Chip-on-board Technology using semiconductor die which are mounted directly onto printed circuit board terminations.

CFC Chlorinated fluorocarbon.

CLCC Ceramic leadless chip carrier.

Clinching Act of bending component leads underneath the board, on insertion, to hold the component in position.

Coefficient of thermal expansion (CTE) Ratio of dimensional change to a degree change in temperature.

Colophony *See* rosin.

Combinational test Test procedure using both in-circuit test and functional test methods.

Condensation soldering *Syn:* hot vapour soldering.

Conformal coating Encapsulation process, comprising a thin coating over an assembly.

Contact angle *See* wetting angle.

Contaminant An impurity or additive which affects characteristics of a material or surface.

Creep strength Resistance of a material to stretching and deformation.

CTE Coefficient of thermal expansion.

Device under test (DUT) Term used to describe a component, printed circuit board or assembly subjected to a test. *Syn:* unit under test (UUT), and loaded board.

Dewetting Occurrence during soldering, where an initial bond is formed, followed by a withdrawal of solder from the joint, leaving irregularly shaped mounds of solder separated by areas covered with a thin solder film. Base metal is not exposed.

DIL Dual-in-line. Refers to component shape with two parallel rows of connection leads. *Syn:* DIP.

DIP Dual in-line package. *See* DIL.

Glossary

Drawbridging Form of surface mount component mis-alignment occurring in some soldering processes, where chip components lift off their pads at one end to resemble a drawbridge. *See* mis-alignment, tombstoning.

Dross Solder oxides and impurities such as flux residues which float in or on a molten solder bath.

Dry-film photoresist Photoresist with thin surface layer of polyester, aiding handling.

Dual-in-line, dual in-line package Component type where leads are in two parallel rows. *See* DIL, DIP.

Dummy track Track underneath a surface mounted component, unused for electrical purposes, to aid component adhesion.

Electroless copper deposition Process in which base laminate is coated with a layer of copper due to electrolytic deposition.

Electromagnetic compatibility (EMC) Principle in which any electronic or electrical appliance should be able to operate without causing electromagnetic interference, and without being affected by electromagnetic interference.

Environmental stress screening (ESS) Manufacturing stage in which all assemblies are subjected to abnormal stresses, with the aim of forcing all early failures to occur. *Syn:* reliability screening.

Etchant Solution used to remove copper from non-circuit areas on printed circuit boards.

Etch resist Chemical applied to PCB track surface to prevent subsequent etch.

Eutectic point of solder Melting-point of solder with 62% tin and 38% lead alloy proportions. It has the lowest melting-point of any solder alloy proportions.

Failure Termination of a device or system's ability to perform its function.

Fiducials Optically recognizable location marks on a circuit board.

Fillet Solder between two metals in a joint.

Fine lines General term to suggest accurate PCB production with very narrow track widths.

Fine pitch Surface mount component shapes with lead pitches smaller than about 0.65 mm (0.025 inch).

Flatpack Integrated circuit type with semiconductor chip enclosed in a shallow rectangular or square package, having component terminations on two or four sides. Generally intended for surface mounted assemblies.

Fluorocarbon Compound of fluorine and carbon.

Flux Additive in the soldering process, which aids cleaning and wetting of the metal surfaces to be soldered.

Flux activity A measure of the cleaning ability of a flux in the soldering process.

Functional test Test procedure in which an assembly's overall operational characteristics are tested by simulating normal function. *Syn:* go/no-go test.

Golden image Term to describe the ideal properties of a printed circuit board.

Go/no-go test *See* functional test.

Glossary

Gull-wing lead Surface mount component lead configuration where end views of leads resemble a wing of a gull in flight. Gull-wing leads form simple lap joints when soldered.

Heated collet Method of soldering surface mounted components, where an electrically-heated collet is positioned over the component terminals so that solder under the terminals melts.

Heat management PCB design philosophy, ensuring adequate heat dissipation. *Syn:* thermal design.

Hot air levelling Process used to coat printed circuit boards with a thin and uniform solderable layer of solder. It involves immersion of the printed circuit board into molten solder then, on withdrawal, application of hot air from a hot air knife. This clears holes of solder, and removes excess solder from pads and track. *Syn:* air levelling.

Hot vapour soldering Soldering process using the latent heat of evaporation of a liquid, where the heat from the liquid's vapour heats the printed circuit board. *Syn:* vapour phase soldering.

Hybrid assembly Electronics assembly in which thin- or thick-film passive components, and leadless components, are mounted on a substrate.

Image *See* track.

Impregnation Encapsulation process, of protective material injected into all spaces or voids between components.

In-circuit test (ICT) Test procedure in which circuit nodes of an assembly are accessed by pin-type probes, to test individual components within the circuit. *Syn:* manufacturing defects analysis and pre-screening.

Infra-red fusing Use of infra-red radiation to melt solder in paste, cream, or electroplated form.

Infra-red radiation Band of electromagnetic wavelengths lying between the extreme of visible light and the shortest microwaves. Strong absorption of infra-red radiation by many substances makes it a useful means of applying heat energy.

Infra-red signature analysis Test procedure in which soldered joints are heated by laser then optically monitored during cooling.

Infra-red soldering Soldering process using infra-red radiating elements to create heat.

Intermetallic compound Compound of elements, having a fixed ratio of the elements in the compound.

J-lead Surface mount component lead configuration where leads bend underneath the component to resemble the letter *J*.

Joint Metallic bonds between two or more component metal terminals, using solder as the bonding material.

Kiss pressure Initial pressure applied to layers to be bonded into multi-layer PCB, whereby the prepreg layers soften and flow to fill voids within the layers.

Land Part of PCB track, allocated to the connection of a component lead. *Syn:* pad.

Lap joint Solder joint between two metal surfaces, where surfaces overlap.

Layout Overall shape of conductive track on a PCB. *Syn:* pattern, image.

LCCC Leadless ceramic chip carrier.

Glossary

Leaded component A component with wire terminations.

Leadless ceramic chip carrier (LCCC) Sealed, ceramic integrated circuit package.

Leadless component A component without wired terminations.

Lead pitch Distance between centres of adjacent leads of a component.

Levelling Process of removal of much of a thick tin/lead layer, to leave behind a thin, level, layer.

Liquidus Temperature at which an alloy is completely molten.

Loaded board *See* device under test.

Loading Supplying an automatic component insertion head with components.

Manufacturing defects analysis *See* in-circuit test.

Mask Metallic stencil-type structure, used to apply solder paste or cream.

Mass soldering Process which solders many components to a printed circuit board simultaneously.

MELF Metal electrode leadless face.

Metal electrode leadless face (MELF) Cylindrical surface mount component package, metallized at each end.

Metallization Processes involved in forming a conductive layer on a PCB base material, generally by electroless copper deposition, followed by subsequent copper and tin/lead plating.

Mixed assembly Electronics assembly in which leaded and leadless components are inserted and mounted. *Syn:* mixprint.

Moving probe Test fixture method, in which two or more probes are robotically controlled to move around points on a printed circuit board.

Multi-layered PCB A printed circuit board, comprising three or more layers of track, insulated and laminated together into one board.

Node Electrical junction between two or more components.

Non-activated flux Rosin-based flux without activator.

Non-wetting Condition where part or all of a surface does not wet during soldering. Non-wetting is evident because base metal is visible. It is usually due to presence of an interference layer such as organic contaminant, tarnish, dirt and so on, on the surface.

Onsertion Slang term for the placement of components on a PCB or surface mounting substrate.

Pad *See* land.

Panel plating Processes in metallization of PCB track, in which tin/lead is selectively plated.

Passivation Surface oxidation which acts as a barrier to further oxidation or corrosion.

Paste *See* solder paste.

Pattern *See* track.

Pattern plating Processes in metallization of PCB track, in which copper and tin/lead layers are plated selectively.

PCB Printed circuit board.

Glossary

Phase diagram Graphical representation of temperature phases in an alloy. A tin/lead (that is, solder) phase diagram shows solidus and liquidus temperatures for a range of tin/lead proportions.

Photo-printing Process of photographically applying a resist to the surface of a PCB.

Photoresist Layer, laminated onto the surface of a PCB, as part of a photo-printing process.

Pick and place Sequential placement of surface mounted components onto a circuit board.

Pickling Process in metallization, where the base laminate is prepared for subsequent electroless copper deposition.

Placement centre Area of an automatic component placement machine where the component is centred to an absolute position in the placement head.

Plastic leaded chip carrier (PLCC) Surface mount component rectangular package, with J-leads on all four sides.

Plated-through hole (PTH) Method of connecting between track layers on a PCB, where drilled or punched holes are metallized.

PLCC Plastic leaded chip carrier.

Potting Encapsulation process, of embedding the assembly inside a container.

Pre-screening *See* in-circuit test.

Preforming Act of shaping component leads prior to insertion into a PCB. *Syn:* prepping.

Prepping *See* preforming.

Prepreg Bonding layer of fibre glass impregnated with epoxy resin, used in multi-layer and similar PCB manufacture.

Print and etch *See* subtractive.

Printed circuit board (PCB) Assembly method using a base laminate of non-insulating material with selective tracks of conducting material to hold components and electrically connect between them. PCBs may be of through-hole or surface mount form. *Syn:* printed wiring board.

Protective coating Coating applied to a manufactured printed circuit board, prior to assembly with components.

PTH Plated-through hole.

PWB Printed wiring board.

Quadpack Surface mount component package with leads on all four sides, usually with gull-wing leads.

Qualification approval Component approval stage in BS9000/CECC/IECQ systems, for components simply manufactured (that is, not designed) by the manufacturer.

Qualified products list (QPL) List of components, whose manufacturers have been assessed as to their capability to manufacture.

Quality Achievement of a system to conform to its specified performance.

Reflow Soldering process in which solder is put onto the printed circuit board before components.

Registration Location of a circuit by means of fixed points.

Glossary

Reliability A system's ability to perform its required function.

Reliability screening *See* environmental stress screening.

Resin smear Prepreg between layers of a drilled multi-layered PCB which has softened and flowed to cover copper tracks within the structure.

Resist Chemical used to prevent part of a PCB from undergoing some action.

Resolution Measure of the thinness of a line a photoresist can successfully reproduce in a circuit.

Rosin Naturally occurring resin which is a mixture of several organic acids, of which abietic acid is the main component. Constituent of many organically soluble fluxes, distilled from pine tree sap. *Syn:* colophony.

Screen printing Process to coat boards with resist, using a stretched material suspended above the board. A squeegee is used to force the resist through holes in the material and to push the material down to touch the board. *Syn:* silk-screen printing.

Semi-additive PCB manufacturing technique which uses both subtractive and additive processes.

Sequential placement Placement of surface mounted components onto a circuit board one after the other.

Shadow effect Effect of different joint temperatures, in certain soldering processes, where component bodies prevent radiant heat from infra-red elements reaching joints. *See* shadowing.

Shadowing (1) Where radiant infra-red heat in certain soldering processes is prevented from reaching joints by local component bodies (2) where solder fails to wet joints of a wave soldered assembly because local component bodies block solder flow.

Silk-screen printing *See* screen printing.

Simultaneous placement Placement of more than one surface mounted component onto a circuit board at a time.

Small-outline integrated circuit (SOIC) Surface mount integrated circuit with two parallel rows of gull-wing leads.

Small-outline J-lead (SOJ) Surface mount integrated circuit with two parallel rows of J-leads.

Small-outline transistor (SOT) Surface mount component with two gull-wing leads on one side and one on the other.

SMC Surface mount component.

SMD Surface mount device.

SMOBC Solder mask over bare copper.

SMT Surface mount technology.

SOIC Small-outline integrated circuit.

SOJ Small-outline J-lead component.

Solder Alloy of tin and lead, used to form mechanical joints between electronic components and printed circuit board copper lands.

Solderability Ability of a metal to be wet by solder.

Solder balls Undesired small balls of solder remaining on a printed circuit board after soldering processes.

Glossary

Solder bridge Undesired connection between joints or tracks of a printed circuit board, in the form of excess solder.

Solder cream *See* solder paste.

Solder fillet *See* fillet.

Solder mask *See* solder resist.

Solder mask over bare copper (SMOBC) Assembly technique which uses a solder resist to protect part of a printed circuit board's copper track from oxidation while coating the remaining unprotected track with solder.

Solder paste Combination of solder, flux, solvent and suspension agent, used in certain soldering processes. *Syn:* solder cream.

Solder preform Solder moulded into predetermined shapes, for application around a joint area prior to application of heat.

Solder resist Selective coating on a printed circuit board, to prevent wetting of solder over covered areas. *Syn:* solder mask.

Solder skip Joint not properly soldered due to shadowing by one or more component bodies, as an assembly is wave soldered.

Solder thief Additional solder land, positioned to follow the last component mounting land of a surface mount assembly board through a mass process soldering machine, to prevent solder accumulation and bridging.

Solder wicking Where solder on the terminal of a surface mounted component soldered in a soldering process rises up from the printed circuit board land, leaving insufficient solder on the land to create a good joint.

Solidus Temperature at which a metal alloy begins to melt, although most of the alloy is solid.

SOT Small-outline transistor.

Substrate Base of a thick-film hybrid, or surface mounted, assembly.

Subtractive Action of defining track on a PCB and removing excess conductor. *Syn:* print and etch.

Surface insulation resistance Electrical resistance of insulating material, determined under specified environmental and electrical conditions, between a pair of contacts, conductors or grounding devices in various combinations. One of the most important parameters in determination of solder flux residues.

Surface mounted assembly (SMA) Electronics assembly in which leadless components are mounted directly on the board surface.

Surface tension Property of liquids created by molecular forces existing in the surface film. It tends to contract the volume into a form with the least surface area. Breakdown of surface tension can be accomplished by addition of certain chemical agents, resulting in the liquid flowing out and wetting surrounding material surfaces. One of the functions of flux in the soldering process is to break down surface tension of solder, thereby causing solder to wet metal surfaces to be jointed.

TAB Taped automated bonded.

Taped automated bonded (TAB) Semiconductor die assembly method, where the die is supplied in a tape-reel form, complete with terminating lead frame. Each die is mounted directly to a printed circuit board, so is a chip-on-board process. TAB devices are sometimes called *mikropacks*.

TCE Thermal coefficient of expansion.

Glossary

Termination   Leads or metallized surfaces of components.

Thermal coefficient of expansion (TCE)   Incremental change in dimension due to a 1°C temperature rise.

Thermal conductivity   Property of a material which describes its ability to conduct heat.

Thermal mis-match   Loose term describing problems of different thermal coefficients of expansion of surface mounted components and circuit board base materials.

Thermal plane   A heatsink, bonded to the surface of a PCB before component insertion, or laminated within a PCB, to aid heat dissipation, specifically in closely packed PCBs.

Thermal via   A via used specifically to aid heat dissipation from a component, thermally connecting the area around or underneath the component on a PCB to a thermally.

Through-hole assembly   Electronics assembly in which leaded component leads are inserted through holes in the board.

Tinning   Coating of a metal surface with tin or solder alloy to improve or maintain solderability, or to aid a later soldering process.

Unit under test (UUT)   *See* device under test.

Vapour phase soldering (VPS)   *See* hot vapour soldering.

Vendor assessment   Buying procedure in which the manufacturer of parts assesses the product, alleviating necessity for the purchaser to do so, prior to use.

Via   Plated-through hole connecting two or more conductor layers of a printed circuit board.

Vision   Inclusion of some form of camera on an automatic component insertion or placement machine, to enable high accuracy of component positioning.

Wave soldering   Mass soldering process in which assembled boards are conveyed across the surface of a wave (or waves) of molten solder.

Wetting   Action of initial flow of solder over a metal, under heat.

Wetting agent   Chemical material added to a liquid to reduce surface tension.

Wetting balance   Method of assessing solderability of metals.

Whiskers   *See* dendritic growth.

X-ray imaging   Optical test procedure, using the ability of x-rays to pass through certain substances more easily than others.

References and further reading

References

1 Deming, W Edwards. *Out of the crisis*. Cambridge University Press, Cambridge.

2 Juran, Joseph M. *On planning for quality*. Collier Macmillan.

3 Fisher, Sir Ronald. *The design of experiments*.

4 Taguchi, Genichi, and Yu-In Wu. *Introduction of off-line quality control*. Central Japan Quality Control Association.

5 Orlicky, J A. *Materials requirement planning*. McGraw-Hill, New York.

6 New, C C. *Requirements planning*. Gower Press.

7 Aggarwal, S C, and Aggarwal, S. *The management of manufacturing operations: an appraisal of recent developments*. International Journal of Operations and Production Management, volume 5, number 3.

Further reading

Following books are recommended for those readers who wish to broaden their knowledge of topics considered in this book.

Bolton, M J P. *Digital systems with programmable logic*. Addison-Wesley.

Brighthouse, B and Loveday, G. *Microprocessors in engineering systems*. Pitman Publishing.

References and further reading

Brindley, Keith. *Modern electronic test equipment* 2nd edition. Heinemann Newnes, Oxford.

Brindley, Keith. *Automatic test equipment*. Butterworth-Heinemann, Oxford.

British Standards Institution. *Quality electronics components*. British Standards Institution, Milton Keynes.

Cambridge University Press. *The art of electronics*. Cambridge University Press, Cambridge.

Department of Trade and Industry. *Printed circuit board assembly*. Department of Trade and Industry, Her Majesty's Government, England.

Klein Wassink, R J. *Soldering in electronics*. Electrochemical Publications Ltd, Scotland.

Lea, Colin. *A scientific guide to surface mount technology*. Electrochemical Publications Ltd, Scotland.

Leonida, G. *Handbook of printed circuit design, manufacture, components and assembly*. Electrochemical Publications Ltd, Scotland.

Manko, Howard H. *Solders and soldering*. McGraw-Hill, New York.

Prentice-Hall. *Integrated circuits: materials, devices and fabrication*. Prentice-Hall, Englewood Cliffs, NJ.

Sanson, Stewart. *Introduction to quality*. British Standards Institution, Milton Keynes.

Scarlett, J A. *An introduction to printed circuit board technology*. Electrochemical Publications Ltd, Scotland.

Scarlett, J A. *The multilayer printed circuit board handbook*. Electrochemical Publications Ltd, Scotland.

Siemens. *An introduction to surface mounting*. Siemens Aktiengesellschaft, Munich.

Sinnadurai, F N. *Handbook of microelectronics packaging and interconnection technologies*. Electrochemical Publications Ltd, Scotland.

Periodicals

Computer Design. Published fortnightly, by Penwell Publishing.

Electronic Design. Published fortnightly, by VNU Business Publications.

Index

A

Accounts 4
  balance sheet 5
  profit and loss account 4
  profitability 6
ACI 83, 105. *See* automatic component insertion
ACP 83. *See* automatic component placement
Adhesive 127
  application 127
AOI. *See* automated optical inspection
Application-specific integrated circuit 69
Application-specific integrated circuits 38
  ASIC 38
ASIC 38, 39. *See* application-specific integrated circuit
ATE. *See* automatic test equipment
Automated optical inspection 132
Automatic component insertion 83, 105
  elements 109
  programming 108
  sequencer 109
Automatic component placement 83, 84
  onsertion 111
  pick-and-place machines 113
  uniform grid 114
Automatic test equipment 139
  combinational testers 141
  functional testers 140
  in-circuit testers 139
  manufacturing defects analyzers 139

B

Back annotation 69
Backdriving 147
Balance sheet 5
  capital employed 5
  current assets 5
  fixed assets 5
Bar-code 104
Bed-of-nails adaptors 85
Behavioural simulation 63
Bill of materials 20
Bit pattern measurement 150
Bump. *See* taped automated bonded integrated circuits

Index

Bus emulation 152
Bus timing emulation 152
Bus-based logic test methods 152
Bus-cycle emulation 152
Business strategy 14

C

CAD 39, 58, 67. *See* computer-aided design
CFC. *See* chlorofluorocarbons
Chlorofluorocarbons 118
CIM. *See* computer integrated manufacture
Circuit simulation 63
Cleaning of assemblies 129
  high pressure spray 129
Cluster testing 147
Clusters 147
Combinational logic test methods 150
Combinational testers 141
Computer-aided design 58, 67, 82, 100, 105
  behavioural simulation 63
  circuit simulation 63
  environment 69
  logic simulation 63
  printed circuit board layout 75
  simulation 69
Computer-integrated manufacture 15
Control
  investments 2
  management's role 10
  working capital 2
Crosstalk 79
Current ratio 3

D

Data exchange standards 159
  electronic design information interchange format 161
  initial graphics exchange specification 160
  standard for exchange of product data 163
Decoupling capacitors 76

Deming 15
Design. *See* computer-aided design
  application-specific integrated circuit 69
  back annotation. 69
  behavioural simulation 63
Design for test 155
Designing for assembly 82
Designing for test 155
Double-wave 121. *See also* soldering

E

EDIF. *See* electronic design information interchange format
Electroless copper plating 94
Electromagnetic compatibility 80
Electronic design information interchange format 161
Electronics assemblies 130
  automated optical inspection 132
  infra-red signature analysis 132
  testing 130
  visual inspection 130
Electronics assembly 104
Electronics manufacturing 15
  quality 15
  total quality management 15
EMC 80. *See also* electromagnetic compatibility
Emulation 152
Eutectic solder. *See* phase diagram
Exhaustive testing 150
Extended wave 121

F

Fiducials 84, 100, 112
Fisher 33
Flux 116, 118
  activators 119
  type 118
Footprint 113
Functional testers 140
Funds flow 2
  current ratio 3
  lenders 3
  shareholders funds 4

Index

G
Gallium arsenide 41
Go/no go test 140
Guarding 143. *See also* in-circuit test

H
Hierarchical interconnect technology 56
HIT 56. *See also* hierarchical interconnect technology
Homing sequences 152
Hot vapour soldering 124. *See also* vapour phase soldering
Hot-air knife 121

I
ICT. *See* In-circuit test
IGES 160. *See also* initial graphics exchange specification
In-circuit test 139
   analog 142
      guarding 143
   digital 145
      guarding 147
Infra-red radiation soldering 124
Infra-red signature analysis 132
Initial graphics exchange specification 160
Investments 2

J
JEDEC 49. *See also* Joint Electronics Devices Engineering Council
JIT 21, 24. *See also* just-in-time
Joint Electronics Devices Engineering Council 49
Juran 15
Just-in-time 21
   kanban 23

K
Kanban 23. *See also* Just-in-time

L
Leaded components 39, 90. *See also* through-hole components
Leadless components 39
Leadless components. 90
Lenders 3
Liquidity 8
   asset turnover 9
   capital structure and gearing 8
Lithography 102
Local area networks 159
logic simulation 63

M
Management's role 10
Manufacturing automation protocol 159
Manufacturing defects analyzers 139. *See also* in-circuit test
MAP. *See* manufacturing automation protocol
Market share 14
Materials resource planning 18
Memory emulation 152
Metallization 94
Microprocessor development 38
Microprocessor emulation 152
Mixed assemblies 90
MRP 24, 26. *See also* materials resource planning
MRP II 19, 21, 22. *See also* materials resource planning

N
Nodeforcing 147

O
Onsertion 111
Open systems interconnect 157
OPT. *See* optimized production technology
Optical technology 43
Optimization 33
Optimized production technology 25

177

Index

OSI. *See* open systems interconnect
Outgassing 98
Overdriving 147

P

Partitioning 141, 147. *See also* in-circuit test
PCB. *See* printed circuit board
Phase diagram 117
Photo-resist 92, 95, 100, 102
Photographic image transfer 92
   raster plotting 94
   vector plotting 93
Photoplotted image output 92
   raster plotting 94
   vector plotting 93
Pick-and-place 113
Plated-through holes 90
Pre-screening 154
Preheat 126
Prepreg 97
Print and etch 91
Printed circuit
   board 39, 84, 87, 115
   additive manufacture 92, 94
     metallization 94
   base 87
   cost of assembling 115
   double-sided 87, 94
   metallization 94
   multi-layered 88, 97
   semi-additive manufacture 92
   single-sided 87, 94
   subtractive manufacture 91
   tracks 87
Printed circuit board layout 75
   bad layout practice 77
   crosstalk 79
   decoupling capacitors 76
   electromagnetic compatibility 80
   good layout practice 78
   legends 83
   switching effects 75
Process optimization
   Fisher 33
   statistical process control 33
   Taguchi 33
Profile 125

Q

Quality 15, 28
   quality systems 28
   reliability 31
   software 28
   total quality management 15
Quality systems 28

R

Reflow 122
Reflow soldering
   type 124
Reliability 31

S

Scan design device 149
Scan testing 148
   four-wire testability bus 149
Screening 154
Screening tests 141
Semiconductor 41
Sequencer 109
Sequential logic test methods 151
Signature 150
Signature analysis 150
Silicon 41
Silicon compilers 72
Silicon hybrids 48
Simulation 69
Single-point TAB. *See* taped automated bonded integrated circuits
SMC 40, 90. *See also* surface mounted components
SMD 40, 90. *See also* surface mounted devices
SMT 39. *See also* surface mount technology
Software quality 28
Solder 116, 117
   eutectic point 117
   phase diagram 117
Solder mask 83, 92
Solder paste 127
   application 127
Solder resist 92
Solder resists 114
Solder stop-off 92

Soldering   115
  basics   116
  processes   121
  reflow   122
  wave soldering   121
Standard for exchange of product data   163
Statistical process control   33
STEP. *See* standard for exchange of product data
Strategic statement   15
Structured software design   64
Surface mount component   49, 131
  failures in time standard   56
  lead terminations   50
  mismatch of coefficients of thermal expansion   51
  outlines   49
  reliability   56
Surface mount component joints characteristics   131
Surface mount components   40, 90
Surface mount devices   40, 90
Surface mount technology   39, 48, 102
  justification   102
  type   103
Synchronizing sequences   152

T

TAB   53. *See also* taped automated bonded integrated circuits
Taguchi   33
  process optimization   33
  statistical process control   33
Taped automated bonded integrated circuits   53
Technical office protocol   159
Temperature profile   125
Test   133
  fault types   136
Test fixture   133
Test methods   133, 142
  analog in-circuit   142
  bus-based logic   152
  digital in-circuit   145, 150
  digital isolation   147
  partitioning   141

scan testing   148
screening tests   141
Test strategies   133, 153, 154
  design for test   155
  pre-screening   154
  screening   154
Testing   130
Thick film circuits   47
Thin film circuits   46
Through-hole components   90
Through-hole printed circuit board   90
Through-hole technology   39
Tooling holes   84
TOP. *See* technical office protocol
Top-down design   59
  customer requirement   59
  hardware design   61
  system design   59
  system integration   61
Total quality management   15

V

Vapour phase soldering   125
Vendor assessment   139
Vision systems   112
Visual inspection   130

W

Walking out   152
Wave soldering   121
Working capital   2, 3

Z

Zero defect design   154